The Emotional Life of Nations

The Emotional Life of Nations

by

Lloyd deMause

KARNAC

New York

London

Production Editor: Robert D. Hack

This book was set in 11 point Berkley by Alpha Graphics of Pittsfield, NH.

10 9 8 7 6 5 4 3 2 1

Library of Congress Cataloging-in-Publication Data

DeMause, Lloyd.
    The emotional life of nations / by Lloyd deMause.
        p. cm.
    Includes index.
    ISBN 1-892746-98-0
    1. Children and violence. 2. Child abuse. 3. Aggressiveness.
4. Child rearing—History. 5. Psychohistory. 6. War—Psychological
aspects. I. Title.
HQ784.V55 D45 2002
303.6'083—dc21

                                                    2002066091

Contents

Preface

This book demonstrates how the source of most human violence and suffering has been a hidden children's holocaust throughout history, whereby billions of innocent human beings have been routinely murdered, bound, starved, raped, mutilated, battered, and tortured by their parents and other caregivers, so that they grow up as emotionally crippled adults and become vengeful time bombs who periodically restage their early traumas in sacrificial rites called wars.

Much of this book is upsetting and difficult to believe, despite the extensive historical, anthropological, clinical, and neurobiological evidence I will present. But the book demonstrates why history so far has been such a slaughterbench; why changes in child rearing precede social change; where we are today in the evolution of human nature; and what we can do now to improve the lives of children and bring about a more peaceful, trustful world.

This book accomplishes the following goals:

1. Provide a psychogenic theory of history that answers the question of *why* it happens—a theory of historical motivation—one that provides a psychohistorical alternative to the sociogenic theories of other social sciences.
2. Show that the evolution of child rearing is an independent cause of historical change, with the slow growth of love and trust in parent–child relations as the central sources of historical progress,

creating new modes of human nature—what I have termed new psychoclasses—which then change social institutions.

3. Demonstrate that historical progress depends less on political changes or military conquests and more on the daily living conditions and achievements of innovative mothers and their hopeful daughters.

4. Show how taking a psychohistorical view of political, religious, and social behaviors reveals that they are a restaging of early traumas, which are recorded in separate neuronal networks in the brain.

5. Show that social institutions are not simply utilitarian but are also shared ways of dealing with emotional problems caused by anxieties surrounding our personal search for love.

6. Explain how a new psychohistorical tool—fantasy analysis—can help in the difficult task of decoding our shared emotions, our historical group-fantasies.

7. Show that groups go to war both to revenge their childhood traumas and to rid themselves of feelings of sinfulness, hoping to cleanse their emotions and be reborn by sacrificing victims representing "bad" parts of themselves.

8. Show how wars and recessions are periodic manic-depressive group psychoses produced by feelings of growth panic.

9. Show why empathy for children is an uneven, late historical achievement, and how the world is now in a race between our slowly improving child rearing and our rapidly evolving destructive technology.

10. Describe a new hope for human history—a new way that society can help parents become more loving toward their children—that has been shown to eliminate child abuse and could eventually put an end to wars and social violence.

Part I of this book describes how shared early personal experiences determine political behavior. The three chapters describe historically recent political events—the shooting of two American presidents, the group-fantasies leading up to the Gulf War, and the childhood origins of terrorism—to demonstrate how shared emotions can cause political violence.

Part II details a psychohistorical theory of history, first as it applies to politics and second as it explains the causes of war.

Part III is a history of how child rearing has evolved and how more loving, trustful parenting has produced new kinds of human psyches, which in turn have resulted in new social and political institutions.

I have tried to include in this book most of what I have learned during the past four decades about childhood and the emotional life of nations. I welcome hearing what readers think about what I have to say, and I promise to respond to your email or letter.

Lloyd deMause
email: *psychhst@tiac.net*
Web site: *www.psychohistory.com*
140 Riverside Drive
New York, NY 10024-2605

I

Early Personal
Experiences Determine
Political Behavior

> *"We may expect that one day someone
> will venture to embark upon a
> pathology of cultural communities."*
> —Sigmund Freud

The Assassination of Leaders

"Peace is a helluva letdown."
—Field Marshall Bernard Montgomery

When Ronald Reagan became President in 1981, America was in a strange mood. The country had been experiencing a period of peace and prosperity. The Americans held hostage in Iran had been safely returned home without requiring military action. Our gross national product per person was the highest of any nation in history. Although America should have felt strong and happy, it instead felt weak and impoverished. The strongest nation on earth, with the highest personal income at any time in its history and the greatest human freedoms anywhere on earth, America during the Reagan election was filled with visions of imminent moral and economic collapse.[1]

Our new president voiced our fears: we were not strong at all, he said, but "weak and disintegrating," in a "ship about to go over the falls," and "in greater danger today than we were the day after Pearl Harbor." We had become so impotent, in fact, that we were in immediate danger of being overcome by "an evil force that would extinguish the light we've been tending for 6,000 years."[2]

During the early months of the Reagan presidency, I was teaching a course in psychohistory at the City University of New York. To show the class how to discover the shared moods of nations, I asked them to bring in current political cartoons, magazine covers, presidential speeches, and

---

1. See Lloyd deMause, *Reagan's America*. New York: Creative Roots, 1984, pp. 1–5.
2. All presidential speeches quoted in this book are taken from the *Weekly Transcript of Presidential Documents*.

Fig. 1–1. As Reagan became president, America felt it was sinking and besieged by evil forces

newspaper columns so that we could see what images and emotional words were being circulated in the body politic. When Reagan said in his inaugural address that we felt "terror" (of inflation), "doomed," "frightened," and "disintegrating" (as a nation), and full of "pent-up furies" (toward government), the class was asked to consider what the psychological sources might be for such apocalyptic language at this particular point in time in America's history.

The class had been studying earlier historical material on national moods to learn how to decode the fantasies that might affect the nation's political decisions. They learned that leaders are often expected to sense the irrational wishes and fears of their nations and do something to deflect or relieve their anxieties. In studying my book, *Jimmy Carter and American Fantasy*,[3] they saw how nations go through emotional cycles that are lawful and that affect political and economic decisions. They discovered, for instance, that American presidents were regularly seen as strong at the start of their first year, with high approval ratings in the polls, and then were depicted as weakening and eventually as collapsing as their polls declined, which they regularly did, regardless of how successful they actually were. Since leaders are imagined to be the only ones who can control the nation's emotional life, the nation's emotional life seems to be getting "out of control" as its leader is imagined to be growing more and more impotent. The

---

3. Lloyd deMause and Henry Ebel, Eds., *Jimmy Carter and American Fantasy: Psychohistorical Explorations*. New York: Two Continents, 1977.

class studied how major decisions by presidents over the past several decades were influenced by the four fantasized leadership stages: strong, cracking, collapse, and upheaval. Wars, for instance, have never begun in the first year of a president's term, when he was seen as strong and in control.[4]

Furthermore, the class saw the disappointment that had been felt when leaders *refuse* to take nations to war when they were emotionally ready, that is, when the leader seemed to be "collapsed" and impotent. The main case study the class examined to demonstrate this disappointment with the leader who was "too impotent to go to war" was the Cuban Missile Crisis.

When President John F. Kennedy announced in 1962 that the Russian missiles had to be removed from Cuba, the country was emotionally prepared for war. Kennedy massed a quarter of a million men and 180 ships at the tip of Florida, had 156 ICBMs ready to launch, and sent up bombers containing 1,300 nuclear weapons with Soviet cities as targets.[5] The nation was ready to go. Only 4 percent of Americans opposed Kennedy's actions, even though 60 percent thought they would lead to a nuclear World War III.[6]

When Khrushchev backed down and removed the missiles, so that the crisis suddenly ended without any war, Americans felt an enormous letdown.[7] The media reported on "The Strange Mood of America Today—Baffled and Uncertain of What to Believe."[8] It began to ask what were seen as frightening questions: "Will It Now Be a World Without Real War? Suddenly the World Seems Quiet . . . Why the Quiet? What Does It Mean?"[9] The prospect of peaceful quiet felt terribly frightening.

---

4. See Lloyd deMause, *Foundations of Psychohistory*. New York: Creative Roots, 1982, pp. 172–243; no American war began in the first year of any president except perhaps Abraham Lincoln, but in reality the first military actions of the Civil War and the secession of seven southern states occurred before he was inaugurated, so the war actually began during the final phase of President James Buchanan.

5. William L. O'Neill, *Coming Apart: An Informal History of America in the 1960's.* Chicago: Quadrangle Books, 1971, p. 69; Robert S. Thompson, *The Missiles of October: The Declassified Story of John F. Kennedy and the Cuban Missile Crisis.* New York: Simon and Schuster, 1992; C. David Heymann, *RFK: A Candid Biography of Robert F. Kennedy.* New York: Dutton, 1998.

6. Harris Wofford, *Of Kennedys and Kings: Making Sense of the Sixties.* New York: Farrar, Straus, Giroux, 1980, p. 292.

7. DeMause, *Foundations*, pp. 216–220.

8. *U.S. News & World Report*, February 25, 1963, p. 31.

9. *U.S. News & World Report*, December 17, 1962, p. 54.

Americans from all parties were furious with Kennedy under various pretexts. Many began calling for a new Cuban invasion, agreeing with Senator Barry Goldwater's demand that Kennedy "do anything that needs to be done to get rid of that cancer. If it means war, let it mean war."[10] Kennedy was accused of being soft on Communism for living up to his no-invasion pledge to the Soviets, and when he then proposed signing a limited nuclear test ban treaty with them, his popularity in the polls dropped even further.[11]

The nation's columnists expressed their fury toward the president, and political cartoonists pictured Kennedy with his head being chopped off by a guillotine (Fig. 1–2). Richard Nixon warned, "There'll be . . . blood spilled before [the election is] over,"[12] and a cartoon in *The Washington Post* portrayed Nixon digging a grave. Many editorialists were even more blunt. *The Delaware State News* editorialized: "Yes, Virginia, there is a Santa Claus. His name right now happens to be Kennedy—let's shoot him, literally, before Christmas."[13] Potential assassins all over the country—psychopaths who are always around looking for permission to kill—saw these media death wishes as signals, as delegations to carry out a necessary task, and began to pick up these fantasies as permission to kill Kennedy.[14] The developing group-fantasy was that if Kennedy wouldn't provide the war America wanted, he could be assassinated, and Vice President Lyndon Johnson would start the war.

Kennedy's aides warned him of an increase in the number of death threats against him. His trip to Dallas, known as the "hate capital of Dixie," was seen as particularly dangerous. His aides begged him to cancel his trip. Senator William Fulbright told him, "Dallas is a very dangerous place. . . . I wouldn't go there. Don't *you* go."[15] Vice President Johnson, writing the

---

10. Michael Beschloss, *The Crisis Years: Kennedy and Krushchev, 1960–1963*. New York: Edward Burlingame Books, 1991, p. 381.

11. Ibid., p. 641.

12. *Time*, November 22, 1963, p. 1.

13. *Delaware State News*, October 18, 1963, cited in William Manchester, *The Death of a President: November 20–November 25, 1963*. New York: Harper & Row, 1967, p. 46.

14. For the unconscious relationship between assassins and their victims, see Charles W. Socarides, "Why Sirhan Killed Kennedy: Psychoanalytic Speculations on an Assassination," *The Journal of Psychohistory* 6(1979): 447–460; and James W. Hamilton, "Some Observations on the Motivations of Lee Harvey Oswald," *The Journal of Psychohistory* 14(1986): 43–54.

15. William Manchester, *The Death of a President*, p. 39.

Fig. 1–2. America felt death wishes toward Kennedy for not starting a war with Cuba

opening lines of the speech he intended to make in Austin after the Dallas visit, planned to open with: "Mr. President, thank God you made it out of Dallas alive!"[16] Dallas judges and leading citizens warned the President he should not come to the city because of the danger of assassination. The day before the assassination, as handbills were passed out in Dallas with Kennedy's picture under the headline "Wanted For Treason," militants of the right-wing John Birch Society and other violent groups flooded into Dallas, and hundreds of reporters flew in from all over the country, alerted that something might happen to the president.[17]

Kennedy himself understood consciously he was in danger of being shot. Two months before the assassination, he made a home movie "just for fun" of himself being assassinated.[18] The morning of his assassination, an aide later recalled, Kennedy went to his hotel window, "looked down at the speaker's platform . . . and shook his head. 'Just look at that platform,' he said. 'With all those buildings around it, the Secret Service couldn't stop someone who really wanted to get you.'"[19] When First Lady Jacqueline Kennedy told him she was really afraid of an assassin on this trip, Kennedy agreed, saying, "We're heading into nut country today. . . . You know, last

---

16. Beschloss, *The Crisis Years*, p. 665.

17. Woffoard, *Of Kennedys and Kings*, p. 343.

18. Aaron Latham, "The Dark Side of the American Dream," *Rolling Stone*, August 5, 1982, p. 18.

19. Robert MacNeil, Ed., *The Way We Were: 1963—The Year Kennedy Was Shot*. New York: Carroll & Graf Publications, 1988, p. 185.

night would have been a hell of a night to assassinate a president. I mean it . . . suppose a man had a pistol in a briefcase." He pointed his index finger at the wall and jerked his thumb. "Then he could have dropped the gun and briefcase and melted away in the crowd."[20] The Dallas trip was looked upon as ripe for assassination attempts; Mrs. Kennedy told a member of the Secret Service, "We're nothing but sitting ducks in a shooting gallery."[21] And Kennedy himself told his wife the morning of the shooting, "Jackie, if somebody wants to shoot me from a window with a rifle, nobody can stop it."[22]

Despite the warnings, however, Kennedy unconsciously accepted the martyr's role. He was, after all, used to doing all his life what others wanted him to do,[23] and his parents had delegated him the role of risk-taker. So when the Secret Service told him the city was so dangerous that he had better put up the bulletproof plastic top on his limousine, he specifically told them *not* to do so.[24] In fact, the Secret Service was instructed *not* to be present ahead of time in Dallas and check out open windows along the route such as those in the book depository, as they normally did whenever a president traveled in public.[25] Only when the nation, the assassin, the Secret Service, and the president were all in unconscious collusion was the assassination successfully carried out.

By this point in our studies, my class began to see how assassinations might be delegated by nations to individuals for purely internal emotional reasons. We noted that six of the seven assassination attempts on American presidents took place either after unusually long peaceful periods, like the assassination of James Garfield on July 2, 1881, or after a peace treaty at the end of a war,[26] like the assassination of Abraham Lincoln six days

---

20. Manchester, *The Death of a President*, p. 121.

21. Gus Russo, *Live By the Sword: The Secret War Against Castro and the Death of JFK.* Baltimore: Bancroft Press, 1998, p. 291.

22. Ibid.

23. Doris Kearns Goodwin, *The Fitzgeralds and the Kennedys.* New York: Simon and Schuster, 1987; Thomas C. Reeves, *A Question of Character: A Life of John F. Kennedy.* New York: The Free Press, 1991; Nancy Clinch, *The Kennedy Neurosis: A Psychological Portrait of an American Dynasty.* New York: Grosset, 1973.

24. MacNeil, *The Way We Were*, p. 189.

25. "The Men Who Killed the President." *The History Channel*, June 19, 1996.

26. This period is termed an "introvert phase" of American history in Jack E. Holmes, *The Mood/Interest Theory of American Foreign Policy.* Lexington: The University Press of Kentucky, 1985, p. 32.

after the end of the Civil War.[27] It was as if peace was sometimes experienced by the nation as a betrayal, that nations expressed their rage at their leaders for bringing peace, and that assassins picked up the subliminal death wishes and tried to kill the leaders as an act of national regicide.

In studying the nation's anger that followed Kennedy's aborted war in Cuba, the class could not help but compare the nation's emotional mood in 1963 to the feelings at that moment in 1980 following the recently aborted war in Iran, just before Reagan was elected president. Furious with Iran over the long hostage crisis, America had been whipped into a war frenzy similar to the earlier one against Cuba by the media. "Kids Tell Jimmy to Start Shooting" the *New York Post* headlined, while a commentator summarized the bellicose mood by saying that "seldom has there been more talk of war, its certainty, its necessity, its desirability."[28] Polls showed most Americans favored invasion of Iran in 1980 even if it meant that all the hostages would be killed, since war, not saving lives, was what the country really wanted.[29] When the rescue attempt floundered because of a helicopter crash and President Jimmy Carter refused to send in the American troops, planes and ships that were massed for attack, the nation turned its fury against him, just as it had against Kennedy after the Cuban confrontation failed to produce war. Carter was buried in a landslide, rather than in a coffin like Kennedy, and Ronald Reagan was elected president.

The students wondered (as did their teacher) if the nation's fury had really subsided, or if its rage might continue toward the new president. Even though this made no rational sense—all the hostages, after all, had already been returned safely—it made sense emotionally.

That Reagan might be a target for our death wishes after the aborted Iranian invasion was hinted at by widespread speculation during his campaign regarding a "death jinx" that might strike him. Someone had figured out that no American president elected since 1840 in a year ending in zero had lived out his term. Bumper stickers had appeared joking "Re-elect Bush [Reagan's running mate] in 1984." Newspapers began running political cartoons and columns with subliminal messages similar to those that had

27. The other assassination attempts during peaceful periods besides Kennedy, Lincoln, and Jackson were Franklin D. Roosevelt, in 1933, and Gerald Ford, in 1975, both peaceful periods; only Harry S. Truman, in 1950, was shot at during a military action.

28. *New York Post*, January 8, 1980, p. 3; *Village Voice*, February 25, 1980, p. 16.

29. For press frenzy and polls on Iran invasion, see deMause, *Reagan's America*, pp. 28–35 and deMause, *Foundations of Psychohistory*, pp. 304–310.

Fig. 1–3. Guns were on our mind the week before the assassination

appeared before Kennedy's assassination, such as the cartoon of a guillotine being constructed on Reagan's inauguration platform and an Anthony Lewis column in *The New York Times* headlined "The King Must Die."

The climax for these shared fantasies that "the king must die" came in the final week of March 1981. That week, my students brought in numerous magazine covers, political cartoons, and newspaper articles that clearly showed these death wishes. *Time* and *Newsweek* ran scare stories about a "wildly out of control" crime wave that was supposed to be occurring— although they had paid little attention to crime in previous months and in fact the actual crime rate had been *decreasing* during those months[30]— illustrating the nation's death wishes with covers depicting menacing guns pointed at the reader.

The New Republic cover featured graves in Washington. One cartoonist showed Americans constructing a guillotine being built for Reagan (the same guillotine that had been shown chopping off the head of President Kennedy before his assassination). Another cartoonist showed Reagan next to targets and guns in the White House, with the odd suggestion that per-

---

30. See Frank Browning, "Nobody's Soft on Crime Anymore," *Mother Jones*, August, 1982, pp. 25–31; Christopher Jencks, "Is Violent Crime Increasing? *The American Prospect*, Winter, 1991, pp. 96–106.

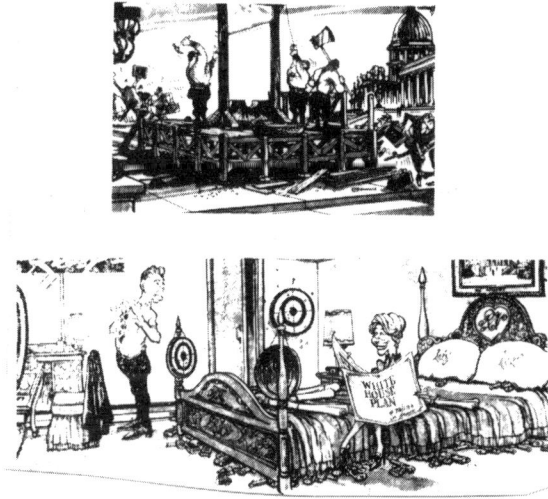

Fig. 1–4. Death wishes toward Reagan

haps his *wife* might want to shoot him with guns she has stored beneath their bed.

To see if our upsetting findings were just our own selection process creating a personal bias, we consulted with another psychohistory class that was also using the fantasy analysis technique to monitor the media. The class told us that it had independently been recently finding a predominance of these death wishes in cartoons and covers.[31]

The next day, one of the president's staff confirmed to the nation that assassination was "in the air." Secretary of State Alexander Haig, an excitable man, unexpectedly began to discuss in the media "who will be in charge of emergencies" should the president be shot. A great furor arose in the press and on TV talk shows as to just who would be "in charge" should the president be incapacitated. That the topic of succession seemed to come out of the blue was totally ignored by the media. Reagan's death just seemed to be an interesting political topic at that moment.

---

31. See Robert Finen and Jonathan Glass, "Two Student Views." *The Journal of Psychohistory* 11(1983):113, where they report that "classes had been picking up traces of a fantasy for Reagan's death in the media. . . .[When] the news came: a shooting in Washington! I was in shock. Here, in less than a week, was confirmation of a psychohistorical prediction!"

The class wondered if potential assassins might not also be sensing these subliminal messages, since there are always a large number of psychopathic personalities around the country waiting to be told when and whom to shoot, willing to be the delegate of the nation's death wishes. Some students wondered if we should phone the Secret Service and warn them about our fears, but thought they might consider a bunch of cartoons and magazine covers insufficient cause for concern.

The class was not wrong about a potential assassin picking up the death wishes and volunteering himself as our delegate. John Hinckley had been stalking President Carter, President-elect Reagan, and other political targets during the previous six months, but just couldn't "get myself into the right frame of mind to actually carry out the act," as he later put it. After all the media death wishes toward Reagan appeared, Hinckley finally got what he called "a signal from a newspaper" on March 30th and told himself, "This is it, this is for me," and, he said, decided at that moment to shoot the president.[32]

I was sitting in our classroom, waiting for the students to arrive, looking over some of the Reagan death wish material we had collected. I had been busy during the past few hours and hadn't listened to the radio before coming to class. Suddenly, I heard a group of students running down the hallway. They burst into the room. "Professor deMause!" they shouted, terribly upset. "They did it! They shot him! Just like we were afraid they would!"

---

32. Latham, "The Dark Side of the American Dream," p. 54.

2

The Gulf War as an Emotional Disorder

"He's going to get his ass kicked!"
—President George Bush

Not every American president has been able to resist his nation's call for war. Studies have shown the main determinant is the kind of childhood the president has experienced.[1] Jimmy Carter was unusual in being able to draw upon his having had fairly loving parents, in particular a mother who encouraged his individuality and independence, a very unusual quality for a parent in the 1920s.[2] It is no coincidence that when I once collected all the childhood photos I could find of American presidents, I noticed that only those of Jimmy Carter and Dwight Eisenhower (another president who resisted being drawn into war) showed their mothers smiling at them.

Ronald Reagan's childhood, in contrast, was more like that of most presidents: a nightmare of neglect and abuse, in his case dominated by an obsessively religious mother and a violent, alcoholic father who, he said, used to "kick me with his boot" and "clobber" him and his brother.[3] The

---

1. The best single study is Glenn David, *Childhood and History in America*. New York: Psychohistory Press, 1976. For bibliography of psychobiographical studies, see Henry Lawton, *The Psychohistorian's Handbook*. New York: Psychohistory Press, 1988, pp. 161–176.

2. See Paul H. Elovitz, "Three Days in Plains," and David Beisel, "Toward a Psychohistory of Jimmy Carter," in Lloyd deMause and Henry Ebel, Eds., *Jimmy Carter and American Fantasy: Psychohistorical Explorations*. New York: Two Continents, 1977, pp. 33–96.

3. Ronald Reagan, *Where's the Rest of Me?* New York: Karz Publishers, 1981, pp. 9 and 11.

result, as I have documented in my book, *Reagan's America*, was a child-hood of phobias and fears "to the point of hysteria," buried feelings of rage, and severe castration anxieties (the title of his autobiography was *Where's the Rest of Me?*). As an adult, Reagan took to carrying a loaded pistol, and once considered suicide, only to be saved by the defensive maneuver of taking up politics and becoming an anti-Communist warrior, crusading against imaginary "enemies" who were persecuted for the feelings he de-nied in himself.[4]

THE PRESIDENTIAL STYLE OF GEORGE H. BUSH

George H. Bush's childhood, though not as chaotic as Reagan's, was also full of fear and physical punishments. Psychohistorian Suzy Kane, inter-viewing George's brother, Prescott, Jr., discovered that Bush's father often beat him on the buttocks with a belt or a razor strap, the anticipation of which, Prescott, Jr. recalled, made them "quiver" with fear.[5] "He took us over his knee and whopped us with his belt," Prescott said. "He had a strong arm, and boy, did we feel it."[6] As he admitted to Kane, "We were all scared of him. We were scared to death of Dad when we were younger." Child-hood classmates of George described his father as "aloof and distant . . . formidable and stern . . . very austere and not a warm person." "Dad was really scary," George himself once admitted.[7] As a result, a desperate need to please was George's main trait as a child, and a depressive personality with an overwhelming need to placate became his trademark as president.

The mood of America as Bush ran for the presidency was also quite depressed, which favored his election over his less depressed opponent. During the 1980s, in what was often misnamed "a decade of indulgence," America had had an unprecedented period of peace and prosperity, the

4. See extensive psychobiography of Reagan in Lloyd deMause, *Reagan's America*. New York: Creative Roots, 1984, pp. 36–50.

5. Suzy T. Kane, "What the Gulf War Reveals About George Bush's Childhood." *The Journal of Psychohistory* 20(1992): 149–166.

6. Barbara T. Toessner, "Obedience, Diligence, and Fun: Bush's Extraordinary Family Life." Jacksonville, Florida, *Times Union*, January 15, 1989, p. A3. See also J. Hyams, *Flight of the Avenger: George Bush at War*. New York: Harcourt Brace Jovanovich, 1991.

7. Gail Sheehy, *Character: America's Search for Leadership*. New York: William Mor-row & Co., 1988, p. 160.

latter based mainly on manic spending binges on the military and on financial speculation, both financed by borrowing.[8] Manic periods such as these usually climax in wars. In 1989, however, America's traditional enemy, the Soviet Union, had collapsed, and a period of unprecedented world peace without any real enemies had "broken out all over," as *News week* put it.[9] Soon after the end of the Evil Empire, as the Soviet Union had been described, both America and Europe were plunged into economic recession. Psychohistorian David Beisel summarized the feeling:

> *The New York Times* speaks of "An Empty Feeling . . . Infecting Eastern Europe." An authority on Britain finds the British undergoing "self-doubt and self-humiliation . . . greater now than at any time . . . over the last thirty years." The cover of the *World Press Review* speaks of "Germany's Reunified Blues." Europe is depressed. Just three years ago, Germans were "delirious in the days before and after reunification," said *Current History*. "A couple of months later, their euphoria had turned to gloom."[10]

America, too, felt just terrible after the downfall of the Berlin Wall. "Democracy is winning," said *The New York Times* on March 3, 1990. "The arms race is over. Villains are friendly now . . . the jackpot so long desired was America's. So then why doesn't it feel better?"[11] Everywhere were predictions of doom, decline, and the death of the American dream. The media wondered why, despite the fact that world peace had been achieved and the American economy was expanding, "People are incredibly depressed" (*The New York Times*). "In the past month, there has been a distinct odor of collapse and doom around the city" (*New York Post*). "There is something catastrophic coming" (*Washington Post*).[12] With no foreign enemy into whom we could project our fears, America had only one choice to end its feelings of depression: have a sacrificial economic recession that would punish ourselves and our families for our peace and prosperity.

---

8. See deMause, *Foundations*, pp. 172–243.

9. "Is Peace Really Breaking Out All Over?" *Newsweek*, August 1, 1988.

10. David R. Beisel, "Europe's Feelings of Collapse 1990–1993." *The Journal of Psychohistory* 21(1993): 133.

11. *New York Times*, March 3, 1990, p. D1.

12. *The New York Times*, January 2, 1990, p. D11; *New York Post*, April 26, 1990, p. 4; *Washington Post*, October 2, 1990, p. A19.

One reason for Bush's election was his oft-repeated statement that "we must all sacrifice."[13] With the economy still expanding during 1989 and 1990, he unconsciously realized that he had to do something dramatic to stop this growth by making people feel even more depressed, so they would stop buying goods and making investments and thereby precipitate an economic downturn. His own mood had been affected by the guilty messages the media were repeating daily, as well as by his taking Halcion, a mind-altering drug that could make users so depressed they became suicidal.[14]

Bush's prescription for America was to make it feel depressed by raising taxes, cutting spending, and repeatedly vetoing all the legislation that was needed to keep the economy moving forward. Just as presidents did before previous recessions, Bush produced an economic downturn by raising taxes and reducing spending, costing jobs and destroying consumer demand. Although he knew that a big tax increase would make him unpopular[15] and would violate the promise he made in his "Read my lips: no new taxes" speech accepting his party's nomination in 1988, at a deeper level he was giving the nation the punishment it unconsciously wanted. As it turned out, the real revenue finally produced by the higher tax rates during the recession turned out to be much less than if rates had stayed the same.[16] Therefore, it was a recession—not additional tax revenue—that was the unconscious motive for the tax-increase package, a recession needed to cleanse the nation of its sinful prosperity, to "purge the rottenness out of the system," as one Bush official had put it.[17]

---

13. Lloyd deMause, "It's Time to Sacrifice . . . Our Children." *The Journal of Psychohistory* 18(1990): 135–144.

14. Benjamin J. Stein, "Our Man in Nirvana." *The New York Times*, January 22, 1992, p. A21.

15. *Washington Post*, October 5, 1992, p. A8.

16. The result of the $165–billion tax increase was to decrease tax receipts and push the deficit in 1991 to the highest level in American history, $385 billion, rather than the projected deficit of $63 billion, an error of $322 billion; see Lewis H. Lapham, "Notebook: Washington Phrase Book." *Harper's Magazine*, October 1993, p. 9; also see Dean Baker, "Depressing Our Way to Recovery." *The American Prospect*, Winter 1994, pp. 108–114.

17. The phrase is from the Federal Reserve in 1929, cited in William Greider, *Secrets of the Temple: How the Federal Reserve Runs the Country*. New York: Simon and Schuster, 1987, p. 300. The only economist who recognized the depressive intent of the 1991 budget deal was Robert Eisner, *The Misunderstood Economy: What Counts and How to Count It*. Boston: Harvard Business School Press, 1994, p. 83.

PEACE, PROSPERITY, AND POLLUTION

That personal achievement and prosperity often make individuals feel sinful and unworthy of their success is a commonplace observation of psychotherapy ever since Freud's first case studies of people "ruined by success."[18] Yet no one seems to have noticed that feelings of sinfulness are usually prominent in the shared emotional life of nations after long periods of peace, prosperity, and social progress, particularly if they are accompanied by more personal and sexual freedom.[19] As early as 1988, American political and business leaders had begun to wonder if the Reagan prosperity had not lasted too long, and some called for a cleansing recession. The Federal Reserve, pleased that their interest rate increase in the summer of 1987 had produced the sharpest one-day drop in the stock market in history, tightened rates again in the summer of 1988 in order to get the recession going, under the rationalization they had to "cool the economy down"—the usual code for "reduce the guilt for too much success." As one perceptive reporter described the plan in 1988, "After the election, the leadership of this country will say to the Fed, 'Go ahead and tighten [the money supply] boys.' The Federal Reserve tightens, interest rates rise, the economy slows. Then they will tell the next President and Congress to raise taxes. . . . It scares me."[20]

As my previous studies have documented,[21] the image of national sinfulness is usually pictured in political cartoons as pollution. Each time a nation feels too prosperous for its deprived childhood to tolerate, it imagines that it is sinful, and a national "pollution alert" is called, a purity crusade where the media suddenly notices such things as environmental pollution (acid rain), home pollution (dioxin), or blood pollution (AIDS)—all of which existed in reality before, but now suddenly became symbols in a fantasy of inner pollution (sin, guilt, hubris) that must be cleansed. What happens in these emotional purity crusades is that the media stops overlooking real dangers, raises

18. Sigmund Freud, "The Interpretation of Dreams," *The Standard Edition of The Complete Psychological Works of Sigmund Freud. Vol. IV*, p. 260.
19. See Lloyd deMause, "'Heads and Tails': Money As a Poison Container." *The Journal of Psychohistory* 16(1988): 1–18.
20. William Greider, "The Shadow Debate on the American Economy." *Rolling Stone*, July 14–28, p. 85.
21. See Chapter 7, "The Poison Builds Up: "There's a Virus in Our Bloodstream," in deMause, *Reagan's America*, pp. 114–135.

Fig. 2–1. America felt sinful after the peace and prosperity of the 1980s

hysterical alarms about how the world has suddenly become unsafe to live in, and then avoids really changing anything—since the pollution that is frightening the nation is actually internal, not external.

The banking community's role in 1988–89 in bringing about what the media began calling "the slump we need"[22] was to reduce the money supply, raise interest rates, and reduce lending. The Fed announced that it would like to push inflation "near zero," a goal that has never been achieved by any nation in history without a punishing depression. The central bank's usual role in killing prosperity was revealed earlier by Federal Reserve Chairman Paul Volcker, who, trying to make a joke, told a reporter that the secret of central bankers everywhere was that "we have a haunting fear that someone, someplace may be happy."[23]

---

22. Paul Blustein, "Squeeze Play: The Slump We Need Has Started," *Washington Post*, February 7, 1988, p. C1; Maxwell Newton, "Fed Must Move to Stem Growth in U.S. Economy," *New York Post*, January 26, 1988, p. 35; "The Inevitable Tax Hike," *U.S. News & World Report*, July 11, 1988, p. 17; Greider, "The Shadow Debate," *Rolling Stone*, p. 85.

23. Paul Volcker, cited in Greider, *Secrets of the Temple*, p. 70.

Fig. 2–2. America felt polluted in 1988

Many reporters recognized the depressive origins of the national mood and even the guilt that engendered it. The *Washington Post* said that, after eight years of optimism, "America is in . . . an ugly spasm of guilt, dread and nostalgia. Once more, America is depressed."[24] A columnist accurately diagnosed the mood of America in 1990:

> America is like a barroom drunk. One minute it brags about its money and muscle, and then for the next hour it bleats into its beer about failure and hopelessness. . . . America's depression is not brought on by plague, flood, famine or war. . . . We are guilty, guilty, guilty . . . depression, decline, depravity, dysphoria, deconstruction, desuetude, dog days, distrust, drugs, despair . . . "[25]

There was only one way that a lengthy economic recession need not be necessary to cure our national depression: an enemy abroad could be created who could be blamed for our "greediness" and then punished instead of punishing ourselves too much.

24. *Washington Post*, November 26, 1990, p. B1.
25. Henry Allen, "America, the Bummed." *Newsday*, December 4, 1990, p. 82.

At first blush, the idea of America starting a war for emotional reasons seems blasphemous. Although most people are familiar with the notion that homicidal acts of individuals stem from underlying emotional disorders, it is rare for anyone to inquire into whether wars—homicidal acts of entire nations—might stem from shared emotional disorders. Unless they are blamed on the psychological problems of a leader, like Hitler, wars are usually explained by economic motivations. But if nations went to war for utilitarian reasons, one should be able to find in the words and actions of leaders about to begin war discussions of the economic benefits of the proposed war. Yet this is precisely what is missing in the historical documents. Instead, wars regularly start with images of paranoia, homicide, and even suicide. For example, when the Japanese leadership was deciding whether to attack Pearl Harbor and begin their war with the United States, several ministers were asked by General Hideki Tojo to study what would happen if they attacked America. At a meeting, each minister around the table forecast defeat by the U.S., and by the time the last minister gave his assessment, it was obvious that an attack would be suicidal for Japan. Whereupon Tojo told those present: "There are times when we must have the courage to do extraordinary things—like jumping, with eyes closed, off the veranda of the Kiyomizu Temple! [This was the Tokyo temple where people regularly committed suicide.]"[26] Hitler, too, spoke in suicidal, not economic, imagery as he went to war,[27] promising Germans glorious death on the battlefield and calling himself a "sleepwalker" as he led the German people over the suicidal cliff.

All the historical evidence suggests that there were strong irrational reasons in America's decision to go to war in the Persian Gulf in 1991. To begin with, the president had earlier floated a trial balloon for the acceptability of a military solution to the nation's emotional problems by sending 25,000 U.S. troops to Panama, ostensibly to capture General Manuel Noriega for his role in the drug trade. Although the Panama invasion seemed to the military an embarrassment, calling it ridiculous because "the whole

---

26. John Toland, *The Rising Sun: The Decline and Fall of the Japanese Empire, 1936–1945.* New York: Random House, 1970, p. 112.

27. See David Beisel, *The Suicidal Embrace: Hitler, The Allies and The Origins of the Second World War*, forthcoming, a book that is the most thoroughly documented study of the emotional basis of nations going to war.

goddam operation depends on finding one guy in a bunker,"[28] the American people loved the show, Bush's polls went up, and permission was given for future military action.

Yet preparing for a new sacrificial war first requires avoiding the guilt for starting it; even Hitler thought it necessary to dress up some of his soldiers in Polish uniforms and have them pretend to attack Germans so he could present an excuse for his invasion of Poland. America, in its own mind, had never attacked another country at any time in its history; it had only defended itself or rescued others who were being attacked. So when the nation's depressed mood deepened in 1990, Bush's task was to find some country that was willing to start a war against a weaker country so that America could come to the rescue in a war that would make us feel better again.

THE SACRIFICE OF CHILDREN

Meanwhile, American magazine covers and political cartoons in the months before the Persian Gulf crisis began expressing subliminal death wishes toward America's youths, suggesting that they be sacrificed. Children were shown shot, stabbed, strangled, and led off cliffs as trial fantasies for the coming war. The images were identical in group-fantasy to the actual practice of ancient times of mass sacrifice of children to appease the gods for society's sinfulness.[29] *Money* magazine, writing a story on how easy it was to get into college, used as its cover illustration a wholly gratuitous drawing of a youth being stabbed by pennants with the headline "The Sacrifice of the Children," imagery exactly opposite to the main point of the story but accurately illustrating the main fantasy of the nation—child sacrifice. Children were increasingly shown on covers of magazines and newspapers as being killed in "War Zones," even though homicide had actually decreased in the previous decade.[30] A United Nations World Summit for

---

28. U.S. Army Chief of Staff Carl Vuono, cited in Rick Atkonson, *Crusade: The Untold Story of the Persian Gulf War*. Boston: Houghton Mifflin Co., 1993, p. 273.

29. Lawrence E. Stagher, "The Rite of Child Sacrifice at Carthage." In John Griffiths Pedley, Ed., *New Light on Ancient Carthage: Papers of a Symposium*. Ann Arbor: University of Michigan Press, 1980, pp. 4, 6.

30. Christopher Jencks, "Is Violent Crime Increasing?" *The American Prospect*, Winter, 1994, pp. 98–107; Richard Morin, "Crime Time: The Fear, The Facts." *Washington Post*, January 30, 1994, p. C1.

Fig. 2–3. Child sacrifice suggestion prior to the Persian Gulf crisis

Children conference was depicted in a cartoon with Bush saying that America's children deserved electrocution for being naughty.

That it was mainly the death of our own "bad selves" that was being suggested was made particularly clear early in 1990 by the sudden media focus on a physician who had long advocated assisted suicide and who had built a "suicide machine" to administer a lethal dose of poison. One cartoon even showed Bush himself as the "suicide doctor," suggesting that he was willing to help the nation commit suicide. The nation's mood had hit bottom. In two decades of collecting visual material, this was the first cartoon out of over 100,000 I had collected that showed a president about to kill the nation's citizens.

THE SPECTER OF THE TERRIFYING MOMMY

When a patient walks into a psychiatric clinic suffering from severe depression unrelated to life events and reports he has been having dreams of children being hurt and suicidal thoughts, the clinician begins to suspect a diagnosis of posttraumatic stress disorder (PTSD). This is particularly so

Fig. 2–4. Children were felt to be so naughty they deserved electrocution

Fig. 2–5. Bush was seen as a killing doctor

Fig. 2–6. Terrifying women were featured in the media

if—as with America in 1990—the patient has been experiencing extreme mood swings, frequent panic attacks, exaggerated fears for the future, manic episodes of frantic spending and borrowing, drug abuse, and feelings of unreality and detachment. As these are all symptoms of PTSD, one of the first questions the psychiatrist might ask about is whether the patient has been experiencing flashbacks to childhood traumas, in particular if he has had intrusive images of harmful parental figures, particularly of cruel or neglectful mothers. When these group-fantasies are widespread—as they are prior to most wars—it is an indication of a return to early traumas, evidence that the nation is going through a PTSD-type crisis, one that can only be defended against by inflicting its fears upon enemies.

The cartoon images and media preoccupations in America during these months show frightening female images in quantity. A bitchy, castrating Madonna dominated magazine covers. Ivanna Trump, wife of a real estate magnate, was depicted as having castrated her estranged husband. Dozens of *Fatal Attraction*–type movies were currently popular, featuring cruel women who were both seductive and murderous.[31] So prevalent were media

---

31. Miles Harvey, "Hollywood's mega-monster horror hits and misses." *In These Times*, March 20–26, 1991, pp. 22–25.

images of terrifying, castrating, and engulfing mommies and the subliminal suggestions of a child sacrifice that I published an article entitled "It's Time to Sacrifice . . . Our Children," detailing the evidence for America's wish to sacrifice its youth and forecasting that a new military venture might be started soon to accomplish this sacrifice.[32] The article, written four months *before* Iraq invaded Kuwait, said:

> Subliminal suggestions that children should be sacrificed have been exceptionally prevalent in American media during the past year. At our Institute for Psychohistory, we carefully analyze the kinds of images found in thousands of political cartoons and magazine covers in order to give us clues as to what our shared fantasies are about and what we are up to as a nation. What we have discovered is an upsurge in images of children being shot, stabbed, strangled, pushed off sacrificial cliffs and in general being punished for the sins of their elders.
>
> These media images, we find, are like trial balloons for actions the nation is about to undertake but that are split off and denied because they are so repugnant to our moral sense. In fact, we have found that these images in the media are an extremely important way for the nation to share its most powerful emotional fantasies. They resemble the repetitive dreams an individual may have—for instance, a series of dreams that their spouse might die—in that they represent wishes from deep in the unconscious.
>
> When media images of children being sacrificed proliferate, therefore, we are floating trial balloons on a subliminal level suggesting that it is time for our children to pay for our sinful excesses during our recent Decade of Indulgence.

What I couldn't figure out at the time was this: since the Evil Empire fantasy had collapsed, who would be our enemy in our next sacrificial war?

SEARCHING FOR AN ENEMY

President Bush soon began to sense that he was being sent unconscious messages that a new war had to be found soon. His masculinity began to

---

32. Lloyd deMause, "It's Time to Sacrifice . . . Our Children." *The Journal of Psychohistory* 18(1990): 142.

be questioned. He began to be pictured by cartoonists as wearing a dress and was referred to more often as a "wimp." Cartoons began showing him being attacked and devoured by monsters.[33] He sensed the nation's distress and rage, and decided he had better act soon. In such a peaceful post–Cold War world, where could he find an enemy crazy enough to be willing to fight the most powerful military force on earth, yet small enough for us to defeat easily?

Since it is the task of a leader to provide enemies when required, Bush was not about to be caught short when his nation asked him to find an enemy. Iraq's leader, Saddam Hussein, had long been a paid U.S. satrap. Bush, as vice president, had personally contacted Saddam in 1986 in a covert mission to get him to escalate the air war with Iran.[34] America had been secretly and illegally building up Iraq's military forces, including its nuclear weapons program, for over a decade, plus arranging billion-dollar "loan guarantees" that the U.S. would end up paying off.[35] Secret arms transfers to Iraq, money sent to Iraq via Italian banks, official approval of U.S. exports of military equipment, even shipment of weapons from our NATO stockpiles in Germany were all part of the clandestine buildup, all illegal, and all covered up by the Reagan administration.[36] Iraq, for its part, felt beholden to the U.S. As Kenneth Timmerman put it in his definitive book, *The Death Lobby: How the West Armed Iraq,* "The arming of Iraq was a 15-year love affair [for America]. Saddam Hussein was our creation, our monster. We built him up and then tried to take him down."[37]

---

33. Lloyd deMause, "The Gulf War as a Mental Disorder." *The Journal of Psychohistory* 19(1991): 1–22; also see the other articles in this Special Gulf War Issue (Fall 1990) of the *Journal.*

34. Murray Waas and Craig Unger, "In the Loop: Bush's Secret Mission." *New Yorker,* November 2, 1992, pp. 64–84; Kenneth Timmerman, *The Death Lobby: How the West Armed Iraq.* New York: Houghton Mifflin, 1992; Alan Friedman, *Spider's Web: The Secret History of How the White House Illegally Armed Iraq.* New York: Bantam Books, 1993.

35. "Iraqgate." *U.S. News & World Report,* May 18, 1992, pp. 42–51; "Did Bush Create This Monster?" *Time,* June 8, 1992, pp. 41–42; Stephen Pizzo, "Covert Plan." *Mother Jones,* July/August, 1992, pp. 20–22.

36. Alan Friedman, "The President Was Very, Very Mad." *The New York Times,* November 7, 1993, p. E15; Friedman, *Spider's Web.*

37. Ibid.

Saddam Hussein, like so many dictators, had an unbelievably traumatic childhood.[38] His mother tried to abort him by hitting her abdomen with her fists and cutting herself with a kitchen knife, yelling, "In
my belly I'm carrying a Satan!" She gave the infant Saddam away to his
uncle, a violent man who beat the boy regularly, calling him "a son of a
cur" and training him to use a gun and to steal sheep. Saddam committed his first homicide at age 11. His political career centered on the murder
of his fellow countrymen, and he particularly enjoyed watching the torture and execution of officers who had fought with him. Saddam would
obviously make an ideal enemy to whom America could delegate the task
of starting a new war.

In early 1990, before the Gulf crisis began, the U.S. military unexpectedly undertook four war games that rehearsed fighting Iraq, premised
on its invasion of Kuwait.[39] At the same time, Kuwait's rulers suddenly
adopted a provocative stance toward Iraq, refusing to discuss outstanding
issues over disputed lands and loans, an attitude that even Jordan's King
Hussein called "puzzling"[40] and regarding which one Middle East expert
stated that "if the Americans had not pushed, the royal family [of Kuwait]
would have never taken the steps that it did to provoke Saddam."[41] In
addition, the U.S. provided $3 billion in "agricultural loans" to Saddam,
which he promptly used for military equipment.

A special investigative report, based on leaked documents, published
by the London *Observer* and ignored by the rest of the world press, revealed
that early in 1990 "Bush sent a secret envoy to meet with one of Hussein's
top officials. According to a summary of this report,[42] "the envoy told the

---

38. Anna Aragno, "Master of His Universe." *The Journal of Psychohistory* 19(1991):
96–108; Peter Waldman, "A Tale Emerges of Saddam's Origins that Even He May Not Have
Known." *The Wall Street Journal*, February 7, 1991, p. A10; Gail Sheehy, "How Saddam
Survived." *Vanity Fair*, August 1991, pp. 31–53; J. Miller and L. Mylroie, *Saddam Hussein
and the Crisis in the Gulf*. New York: Times Books, Random House, 1990.

39. Ramsey Clark, *The Fire This Time: U.S. War Crimes in the Gulf*. New York:
Thunder's Mouth Press, 1992, pp. 12–16.

40. Ibid., p. 15.

41. Ibid.

42. Jonathan Vankin, *Conspiracies, Cover Ups, and Crimes: Political Manipulation and
Mind Control in America*. New York: Paragon House Publishers, 1991, p. 203.

dictator's confidant 'that Iraq should engineer higher oil prices to get it out of its dire economic fix.' . . . Hussein took the envoy's advice, and moved his troops to the border of Kuwait. 'The evidence suggests that U.S. complicity with Saddam went far beyond miscalculation of the Iraqi leader's intentions [and included] active U.S. support for the Iraqi President'" in his military threat toward Kuwait. So overwhelming was the evidence that the U.S. financed, provided equipment for, and encouraged Saddam's aggressive military venture that Senator Al Gore, when running for Vice President in 1992, said, "Bush wants the American people to see him as the hero who put out a raging fire. But new evidence now shows that he is the one who set the fire. He not only struck the match, he poured gasoline on the flames."[43]

Saddam reacted predictably to Bush's encouragement; he publicly threatened to use force against Kuwait and moved his troops to the border. To be certain he had U.S. backing for the invasion, he then summoned U.S. Ambassador April Glaspie to his office and asked her what Washington's position was on his dispute with Kuwait. Glaspie, acting on Bush's cable of the previous day, gave Saddam the barely disguised go-ahead by saying that "the President had instructed me to broaden and deepen our relations with Iraq" and to deliver America's warm sympathy with his problems. She then stated, "We have no opinion on Arab–Arab conflicts, like your border disagreement with Kuwait."[44] Senior Pentagon officials openly complained that Bush's cabled instructions would send a signal that it was all right with the U.S. if Iraq invaded Kuwait.[45] "This stinks," one said about the cable.

Just in case there was any question about the American signal to Hussein, on July 31, 1990, after Iraqi forces had moved fuel and ammunition to front-line Iraqi military units on Kuwait's border, Assistant Secretary of State John Kelly was asked at a public House subcommittee hearing, "If Iraq . . . charged across the border into Kuwait, for whatever reason, what would our position be with regard to the use of U.S. forces?" Kelly first replied, "I cannot get into the realm of 'what if' answers." Then, when the congressman asked, "Is it correct to say, however, that we do not have

---

43. Peter Mantius, "Iraqgate: Shell Game." *In These Times*, January 22, 1996, p. 28.

44. Ibid., p. 23; also see Clark's description of how Glaspie lied to Congress on what she said to Hussein, p. 24.

45. *The New York Times*, October 25, 1992, p. A1.

a treaty commitment which would obligate us to engage U.S. forces?" Kelly replied, "That is correct."[46] Yet General Norman Schwarzkopf had been planning and practicing through war games for nearly a year a massive attack by U.S. forces in case of Iraqi invasion of Kuwait.[47] Nevertheless, an implicit green light was given to Saddam that an attack on Kuwait would not be countered by the U.S. On August 2, 1990, Iraq invaded Kuwait.

THE GULF WAR AS A TRAUMATIC RESTAGING

Because it takes time for unconscious fantasies to become linked up with reality, Iraq's invasion of Kuwait went almost unnoticed at first. The day of the invasion, the *Washington Post* reported it in an unemotional article in a single column on the lower half of the page. Bush himself took a while to become conscious of his opportunity to go to war and initially saw no urgency to intervene, saying, "We're not discussing intervention. I'm not contemplating such action."[48] It was not until Bush met the next day with British Prime Minister Margaret Thatcher in Aspen, Colorado, that he recognized he was expected to turn the Iraqi invasion into an American war, Thatcher telling him that he was Churchill, Saddam was Hitler, and Kuwait was Czechoslovakia.[49] After Mrs. Thatcher told Bush that Saddam was "evil," he reversed his opinion; as one Thatcher adviser put it, "The Prime Minister performed a successful backbone transplant" on Bush.[50] Bush abruptly appeared on television and told Americans they had to "stand up to evil," proclaimed a policy of "absolutely no negotiations" with Iraq, and ordered American troops and planes into the Middle East.

America felt reinvigorated to once again have an enemy to lift it out of its depression. "We've felt bad for months," said one commentator. "Sud-

46. Ibid.; *The New York Times*, September 23, 1990, pp. L18 and L19; *Washington Post*, September 19, 1990, p. A19; Paul A. Gigot, "A Great American Screw-Up: The U.S. and Iraq, 1980–1990," *The National Interest*, Winter 1990/91, pp. 3–10.

47. Ramsey Clark, *War Crimes: A Report on United States War Crimes Against Iraq*. Washington, DC: Maisonneuve Press, 1992, p. 67.

48. Jean Edward Smith, *George Bush's War*. New York: Henry Holt and Co., 1992, p. 64.

49. Robert B. McFarland, "War Hysteria and Group-Fantasy in Colorado." *Journal of Psychohistory* 19(1991): 36; Smith, *George Bush's War*, pp. 7–8.

50. Smith, *George Bush's War*, p. 68.

Fig. 2–7. Saddam Hussein as Terrifying Mommy

denly we feel like we have a purpose. . . . Americans like action."[51] *The New Republic* agreed, saying, "Saddam Hussein did the world a favor by invading Kuwait," since it provided us relief from our depression.[52] "Thanks, Saddam. We Needed That" another reporter headlined his column on the Iraqi invasion.[53] Our shared emotions in a maelstrom, we would produce a "Desert Storm" to live out our fears and rage.

Bush's rationalizations about his reasons for going to war shifted with the desert sands, first saying it was about "our jobs," then "our way of life," and then "our freedom."[54] The real reason was a psychological one: we would cure ourselves of our depression and flashbacks of punitive mommies by inflicting the punishment we felt was deserved upon children.

Children were the real emotional focus of the Gulf War from the very start. While the images of terrifying American mommies completely disappeared from cartoons and magazine covers, we instead projected them into Saddam Hussein, and *he* was pictured as a terrifying mommy, a "child abuser" who liked to kill children. Was the war to be fantasied as an assault upon . . . a *mother*?

The "child killer" theme was soon spread by the media. Particularly convincing was a wholly invented story told by a 15-year-old girl, who

---

51. DeMause, "It's Time to Sacrifice," p. 143.

52. *The New Republic*, September 3, 1990, p. 9.

53. Ben Wattenberg, "Thanks Saddam. We Needed That." *New York Post*, January 17, 1991, p. 8.

54. Theodore Draper, "The True History of the Gulf War." *The New York Review of Books*, January 30, 1992, p. 41.

testified before the U.N. Security Council and the U.S. Congress that a surgeon in Kuwait had seen Iraqi soldiers taking hundreds of babies from incubators, "leaving them on the cold floor to die."[55] None of those hearing this testimony and none of the hundreds of reporters who swallowed the story thought to check out any of its details, since it confirmed the nation's unconscious fantasies. It wasn't until after the war ended that it was revealed that the "surgeon" and the girl had used false names and identities, that the girl was really the daughter of the Kuwaiti ambassador to the U.S.—a fact known to the organizers of the meeting—and that the story was completely fabricated, as were other stories of mass rape and torture by Iraqis.[56] But we needed stories of child abuse. We were about to restage our childhood traumas, just as posttraumatic stress patients often hurt their children or themselves to achieve temporary relief from their inner emotional distress. We therefore had to objectify our fantasies of terrifying mommies and hurt children to prepare ourselves for starting the war.

WAR AS RENEWAL THROUGH RITUAL COMBAT

The Gulf War was hardly the first to be started by creating an enemy and then engaging in combat with him. America has a long history of going to war with dictators it has previously armed.[57] The goal was national renewal through combat, as in early civilizations, where, when countries felt depressed, "polluted," they often openly arranged battles to "cleanse" themselves and "rebirth" their sinful people.[58] The Aztecs, for instance, would periodically decide that they had become polluted and would set up "Flower Wars," dividing their own armies into two sides and fighting a cosmic battle between them to revitalize their country. During this ritual combat, they not only slaughtered thousands to assuage their bloodthirsty female goddess—an early version of the Terrifying Mommy—but also took victori-

55. The entire deception is described in Clark, *The Fire This Time*, pp. 31–32, and in John R. MacArthur, "Remember Nayirah, Witness for Kuwait?" *The New York Times*, January 6, 1991, A17.

56. Ibid.

57. DeMause, "America's Search for a Fighting Leader," pp. 122–123.

58. DeMause, "Gulf War," pp. 12–14; Lloyd deMause, *Foundations of Psychohistory*, pp. 244–332.

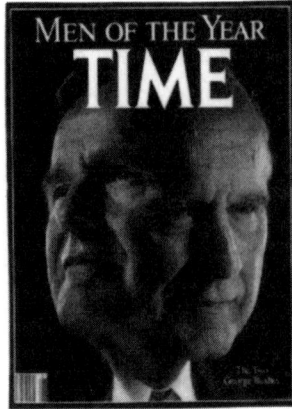

Fig. 2–8. George Bush as a "double," both a strong and a weak leader

ous warriors from the battle and ripped out their hearts in a ritual blood sacrifice to the goddess.[59]

War in early civilizations often began by making leaders undergo a ritual humiliation, the purpose of which was to symbolically restage the humiliation that they had experienced as children. The Babylonian king, for instance, would be slapped on the face, forced to kneel in abasement before a sacred image, and made to confess his sinfulness.[60] In America, in the months prior to the Gulf war, President Bush was forced to undergo a similar humiliation ritual by being called a "wimp" (the national cartoonist Pat Oliphant pictured Bush in cartoons carrying a woman's purse on his limp wrist) before he could regain his lost masculinity by going to war.

---

59. Burr C. Brundage, *The Fifth Sun: Aztec Gods, Aztec World*. Austin, Texas: University of Texas Press, 1979; Patricia R. Anawalt, "Understanding Aztec Human Sacrifice." *Archaeology* 35(1982): 38–45; Elizabeth P. Benson and Elizabeth H. Boone, Eds., *Ritual Human Sacrifice in MesoAmerica*. Washington, DC: Dumbarton Oaks Research Library, 1985; Burr C. Brundage, *The Jade Steps: A Ritual Life of the Aztecs*. Salt Lake City: University of Utah Press, 1985.

60. Details of the combat ritual are documented in Theodore H. Gaster, *Thespis: Ritual, Myth and Drama in the Ancient Near East*. New York: Harper and Row, n.d.; Valerio Valeri, *Kingship and Sacrifice: Ritual and Society and Ancient Hawaii*. Chicago: University of Chicago Press, 1985; Brundage, *The Jade Steps*; deMause, "Gulf War," pp. 12–14.

At the end of 1989, *Time* magazine even showed on their cover *two* George Bushes, one strong and one weak—a projection of the two halves of our own brain, one strong, one weak[61]—a device identical to that used by early societies that appointed a "double" of the king before wars to represent his weaker half and to depict his strong and weak selves.[62]

The sacrificial war ritual, then, had three main elements:

1. *A sinful, polluted world*, with a leader who is depicted as becoming more and more impotent in containing the nation's depressed, angry feelings.
2. *Terrifying mommy fantasies*, with images of angry goddesses threatening to devour the country unless a ritual sacrificial victim is provided.
3. *Sacrificial child victims*, whose blood will revitalize the country's emotional life and who ultimately represent the "guilty" child who was the victim of the original traumas.

Elements of the original childhood traumas can be seen in the Gulf War. Since George Bush had been beaten on his posterior during childhood, he threatened to "kick the ass" of Saddam Hussein. Many Americans, who had also had their posteriors beaten during childhood,[63] multiplied the image: "Kick Ass" T-shirts, flags, and belt buckles flooded the country; Americans told reporters they wanted to "whip that guy's butt" and "get him with his britches down"; cartoons even showed the U.N. building decorated with the words "KICK BUTT."[64]

Saddam Hussein, for his part, saw the coming war in terms of the typical childhood traumas he and his countrymen had experienced. For instance, most male Iraqis endured a bloody, terrifying circumcision at around the age of 6, and Saddam used metaphors that reflected fears of bloody castration, saying that it was Iraq's mission to "return the branch, Kuwait, to the root, Iraq" and vowing Americans would be made to "swim

---

61. For the dual-brain aspects of going to war, see Chapter 6.
62. Valeri, *Kingship and Sacrifice*, p. 165.
63. DeMause, *Foundations of Psychohistory*, pp. 1–83.
64. *New York Post*, June 11, 1991, p. 16; WABC-TV, February 28, 1991; *Washington Post*, February 24, 1991, p. A26.

in their own blood."[65] It was his mission, he said, to return to Iraq "the part that was cut off by English scissors."[66]

Both nations saw the war as a sacred combat between Good and Evil. Iraq said that Americans had "desecrated Mecca" and that the war would "purify our souls" in a "showdown . . . between Good and Evil."[67] U.S. Congressman Stephen Solarz, as he led the pro-war forces in the vote for invasion, said, "There is *Evil* in the world."[68] The conflict certainly wasn't about economics; the U.S. spends $50 billion a year to maintain its military in the Persian Gulf, while only importing $10 billion a year from the area.[69] Nor was it about politics; the U.S. had long refused to meet with the democratic Iraqi government in exile. The war and embargo were for purely internal emotional purposes. Like most modern nations, America had gone to war once every two decades, and it had been two decades since the Vietnam War. Since war was an addiction, an emotional disorder, America had to have a new war to clean out the guilt and anxiety from the progress and prosperity of the 1980s, and Saddam was a willing enemy who could give us the feeling of being cleansed, reborn.

Bush told the country it was fighting for a "new world order" that would produce a "new era of peace" everywhere in the world. Americans interviewed before the invasion told reporters, "The course of history has changed. . . . I don't know exactly what that means, but I know things are going to be different. . . . The country had crossed a threshold. . . . This [is] one of those events that marks the end of an old era and the start of a new one."[70] Like the ancient societies, America fantasized the world would be reborn through human sacrifice.

Since sacrificial rituals are scripted by God—unconscious emotional messages from the people—they have a compulsive quality that makes them feel like they are inevitable and out of the hands of those carrying them out. Although some Americans who had had better childhoods—including Jimmy

---

65. Rafael Patai, *The Arab Mind*. New York: Charles Scribners Sons, 1983; *The Wall Street Journal*, February 7, 1991, p. A1; *The New York Times*, January 7, 1991, p. A1.

66. *The New York Times*, October 11, 1994, p. A13.

67. *New York Post*, August 11, 1990, p. 3; *New York Newsday*, January 12, 1991, p. 10.

68. *New York Post*, January 17, 1991, p. 31.

69. Ramsey Clark, *The Children Are Dying*. Washington, DC: Maisonneuve Press, 1996, p. 113.

70. *The New York Times*, January 16, 1991, p. A1 and January 18, 1991, p. A1.

Carter and Chief of Staff General Colin Powell[71]—thought sanctions should be given a chance before starting the war, Bush rejected proposals from Soviet President Mikhail Gorbachev and Saddam in which Iraq agreed to remove its troops from Kuwait in exchange for a conference to resolve outstanding issues.[72] But what Bush was delegated to do was start a war, not just get Iraqi troops out of Kuwait, and when he heard about the Iraqi agreement to withdraw peacefully, he said, "Instead of feeling exhilarated, my heart sank."[73] He told his Secretary of State James Baker III, who said he could negotiate a peaceful Iraqi withdrawal, that there must not be peace, saying, "We have to have a war."[74] Even when Powell said he preferred to have a peaceful withdrawal by the Iraqi forces because this would save American lives, Bush refused to allow it.[75] The nation had delegated to him the task of providing a war, now. "There was always an inevitability about this," Bush proclaimed, as he unilaterally ordered half a million men and women to invade.

America began the war by dropping 88,000 tons of bombs on Iraq, 70 percent of them missing their targets and killing civilians.[76] TV provided the delusion that they were only "clean bombs." Illegal fuel air explosives— which before the war the press feared Saddam would use against Americans— were exclusively and widely used by American troops on both military and civilian areas, and illegal napalm was used to destroy civilian grain fields and cattle.[77] Americans watched as thousands of aerial sorties carpet bombed whole cities on TV, entranced—literally in a trance—devouring images of missiles going down air intakes, hospitals blown up, water reservoirs and filtration plants being destroyed, and schools being demolished.[78] Soldiers

---

71. David Roth, *Sacred Honor: The Biography of Colin Powell.* Zondervan Books, 1993; Howard Means, *Colin Powell: A Biography.* Ballantine Books, 1992.

72. Jean Edward Smith, *George Bush's War*, p. 8; Rick Atkinson, *Crusade: The Untold Story of the Persian Gulf War.* Boston: Houghton Mifflin Co., 1993, p. 347–348.

73. George Bush, *A World Transformed.* New York: Knopf, 1998, p. 201.

74. Bob Woodward, *Shadow: Five Presidents and the Legacy of Watergate.* New York: Simon & Schuster, 1999, p. 185.

75. Ibid., p. 187.

76. Ramsey Clark, *War Crimes: A Report on United States War Crimes Against Iraq.* Washington, DC: Maisonneuve Press, 1992, p. 15.

77. Ibid., p. 17.

78. U.S. bombs hit 28 civilian hospitals, 52 community health centers, 676 schools, and 56 mosques; see Clark, *The Fire This Time*, pp. 66. On the psychohistorical role of American TV, see Daniel Dervin, "From Oily War to Holy War: Vicissitudes of Group-Fantasy Surrounding the Persian Gulf Crisis." *The Journal of Psychohistory* 19(1991): 67–83.

SINGING IN THE RAIN.

Fig. 2–9. Americans felt reborn by war

said it was like "shooting fish in a barrel."[79] Despite efforts to deny the reality of the killing by calling the carpet bombings "surgical strikes" and tens of thousands of mangled Iraqi civilian bodies "collateral damage," the Pentagon later admitted it massively targeted civilian structures "to demoralize the populace."[80] In particular, attacks were targeted on sewage treatment plants, irrigation systems, and water purification plants, producing massive deaths of children from diarrhea, typhoid, and other contaminated-water–borne diseases.[81] The dissociation in our heads, however, was almost complete. We were killing people, but they weren't real. One TV reporter said, after the first 8,000 sorties had pulverized Iraqi civilian areas, "Soon we'll have to stop the air war and start killing human beings."[82] Riveted to our TV sets in our war trance, we found it had "an eerie, remote-control quality . . . it seemed that we were watching a war about technology."[83] or a scene out of the movie *Star Wars*, with Luke Skywalker blasting Darth Vader bunkers with high-tech laser bombs that only destroyed machines, not people.

---

79. Elizabeth Drew, "Letter from Washington." *New Yorker*, May 6, 1991, p. 101.
80. Ibid., p. 69.
81. David Barsamian, "Iraq: The Impact of Sanctions and U.S. Policy." *Z Magazine* July/August 1999, pp. 44–45.
82. WCBS-TV, January 21, 1991.
83. *The Nation*, December 14, 1998, p. 5.

The human carnage revived the American mood. Since Bush had fulfilled the central task of leadership—to cleanse the group of its sinful prosperity through sacrifice—his approval rating soared. Oliphant drew a cartoon of Bush's woman's handbag being "retired into the closet" in honor of his role as a now-potent war leader. Political cartoons were joyful, showing Americans holding hands and dancing while bombs fell on the enemy. Restaging of our childhood traumas with others as victims was once again extremely exciting.

The war was vicious, as promised. In 43 days of war plus the decade of embargo afterward, America achieved what the U.N. termed "the near apocalyptic destruction" of Iraq. Starting with 42 days of bombing, there were aerial sorties equivalent to seven Hiroshima bombs. Over one-half million children were killed[84]—most of whom died of malnutrition and epidemics caused by the targeting of irrigation canals and food-processing plants and of the continuing embargo, a genocidal violation of the Geneva Convention, which prohibits the starvation of civilians.[85]

After $100 billion wasted killing Iraqis, we of course hadn't killed the "evil" Saddam at all, merely reinstalled the Kuwaiti feudal monarchy. In fact, Bush elected to pull back from pursuing Saddam or taking any other actions that might depose him, sensing that the U.S. might need a reliable enemy in the future. We had mainly killed innocent women and children, representatives of Dangerous Mommies and Bad Children in our own unconscious minds. We had merged with the perpetrators of our childhood traumas, cleaned out the buried violence in our heads, and as a result of our ghastly human sacrifice of the innocent we felt much better about ourselves as a nation.[86]

---

84. Ramsey Clark, *The Children Are Dying.* Washington DC: Maisonneuve Press, 1996.

85. Out Now, "Weapons of Mass Destruction." *War Watch*, November-December 1991, pp. 1–10; Kane, "What the Gulf War Reveals About George Bush's Childhood," pp. 140–149; Robert Reno, "Heck, Let's Drop a Few More if the Allies Are Buying." *New York Newsday*, May 16, 1991, p. 50; William M. Arkin, "The Gulf 'Hyperwar'—An Interim Tally." *The New York Times*, June 22, 1991, p. 23; Nina Burleigh, "Watching Children Starve to Death." *Time*, June 10, 1991, p. 56; Ross B. Mirkarimi, "Disease, despair, destruction still plague Iraq." *In These Times*, June 10–23, 1992, p. 10; Clark, *The Fire This Time*, p. 43; Draper, "The True History of the Gulf War," pp. 36–45.

86. The U.S. government has used illegal blockade sanctions against the civilian populations in Cuba, Panama, Libya, Iran, Vietnam, Nicaragua, and Korea as well as Iraq.

Empathy for the innocent dead was totally absent. We barely noticed the genocide of children was happening. A decade later, water was polluted, garbage had to be dumped into the streets, and hospitals were nearly inoperative. Those children still alive despite our genocidal efforts were reported by War Watch as being "the most traumatized children of war ever described."[87] The war had accomplished our unconscious sacrificial goal. America held a massive victory parade, and the president told the American people that "the darker side of human nature" had been defeated—more accurately, the darker side of our own psyche had been restaged—assuring us that our nation had entered a new world order.

The sacrificial ritual had been carried out exactly as planned: by a genocide of women and children. The nation had been cleansed of its emotional pollution. The President's popularity rating rose to 91 percent, the highest of any American leader in history. The stock market soared. "Bush . . . restored America's can-do spirit. . . . It felt good to win."[88] The country had been united by slaughter as it had never been by any positive achievement. Our leader fulfilled his delegated task; after it was over, President Bush told a TV news anchor, "We did fulfill our aggression."[89] When Madeleine Albright, who later became President Bill Clinton's second-term secretary of state, was asked if the death of all those children from sanctions that were supposed to weaken Saddam was really necessary, she replied, "I think this is a very hard choice, but the price, we think the price is worth it."[90] Editorials across the country congratulated the president on his having "defeated evil," and speculated on what the new world order would look like and when it might begin. The victors no longer felt depressed. America's twenty-eighth war had once again seemed to have restored our potency. We felt cleansed, purified, as though we had been reborn.

---

87. Julia Devin, executive director of the International Commission on Medical Neutrality, November 13, 1991, cited in Draper, "True History of the Gulf War," p. 40.

88. Ann McFeatters, "The Good Guys Won, and America's Can-do Spirit Was Restored," *Chicago Tribune*, March 1, 1991.

89. Noam Chomsky, *Chomsky on MisEducation.* Lanham: Rowman & Littlefield Publishers, 2000, p. 33.

90. "60 Minutes." WCBS-TV, May 23, 1996.

3

The Childhood Origins of Terrorism

"He who washes my body around my genitals
should wear gloves so that I am not touched there."
—Will of Mohammed Atta

Because so much of the world outside the West has for historical reasons fallen behind in the evolution of their child-rearing modes, the
resulting vast differences between national personality types has recently
turned into a global battle of terrorism against liberal Western values. To
understand this new battle, it would be useful to know what makes a terrorist—what developmental life histories they share that can help us see
why they want to kill "American infidels" and themselves—so we can apply
our efforts to removing the sources of their violence and preventing terrorism in the future.

The roots of current terrorist attacks lie, I believe, not in this or that
American foreign policy error but in the extremely abusive families of
the terrorists. Children who grow up to be Islamic terrorists are products of a misogynist fundamentalist system that often segregates the family
into two separate areas: the men's area and the women's area. The children are brought up in the women's area, which the father rarely visits.[1]
Even in countries like Saudi Arabia today, women by law cannot mix with
unrelated men, and public places still have separate women's areas in res-
taurants and workplaces, because, as one Muslim sociologist put it
bluntly: "In our society there is no relationship of friendship between a

---

1. Soraya Altorki, *Women in Saudi Arabia: Ideology and Behavior Among the Elite.* New
York: Columbia University Press, 1986, p. 30; Mazharul Haq Khari, *Purdah and Polygamy:
A Study in the Social Pathology of the Muslim Society.* Peshawar Cantt., Nashiran-e-Ilm-o-
Taraqiyet, 1972, p. 91.

man and a woman."[2] Families that produce the most terrorists are the most violently misogynist; in Afghanistan, for instance, girls could not attend schools and women who tried to hold jobs or who seemed to "walk with pride" were shot.[3]

Young girls are treated abominably in most fundamentalist families. When a boy is born, the family rejoices; when a girl is born, the whole family mourns.[4] The girl's sexuality is so hated that when she is 5 or so the women grab her, pin her down, and chop off her clitoris and often her labia with a razor blade or piece of glass, ignoring her agony and screams for help, because, they say, her clitoris is "dirty," "ugly," "poisonous," "can cause a voracious appetite for promiscuous sex," and "might render men impotent."[5] The area is then often sewed up to prevent intercourse, leaving only a tiny hole for urination. The genital mutilation is excruciatingly painful. Up to a third die from infections, and mutilated women must "shuffle slowly and painfully" and usually are unable to orgasm.[6] Over 130 million genitally mutilated women are estimated to live today in Islamic nations, from Somali, Nigeria, and Sudan to Egypt, Ethiopia, and Pakistan. A recent survey of Egyptian girls and women, for instance, showed 97 percent of uneducated families and 66 percent of educated families still practicing female genital mutilation.[7] Although some areas have mostly given up the practice, in others—like Sudan and Uganda—it is increasing, with 90 percent of the women surveyed saying they planned to circumcise all of their daughters.[8]

---

2. Mona AlMunajjed, *Women in Saudi Arabia Today*. New York: St. Martin's Press, 1997, p. 45.

3. *The New York Times* October 19, 2001, p. A19.

4. Jan Goodwin, *Price of Honor: Muslim Women Lift the Veil of Silence on the Islamic World*. Boston: Little, Brown, 1994, p. 43.

5. Hanny Lightfoot-Klein, *Prisoners of Ritual: An Odyssey into Female Genital Circumcision in Africa*. New York: Harrington Park Press, 1989, pp. 9, 38, 39.

6. Ibid., p. 81.

7. Nawal El Saadawi, *The Hidden Face of Eve: Women in the Arab World*. Boston: Beacon Press, 1980, p. 34; for additional references, see Lloyd deMause, "The Universality of Incest." *The Journal of Psychohistory* 19(1991): 157–164.

8. Cathy Joseph, "Compassionate Accountability: An Embodied Consideration of Female Genital Mutilation." *The Journal of Psychohistory* 24(1996): 5; Lindy Williams and Teresa Sobieszczyk, "Attitudes Surrounding the Continuation of Female Circumcision in the Sudan: Passing the Tradition to the Next Generation." *Journal of Marriage and the Family* 59(1997): 996; Jean P. Sasson, *Princess: A True Story of Life Behind the Veil in Saudi Arabia*. New York: Morrow, 1992, p. 137; http://www.path.org/Files/FGM-The-Facts.htm.

The mutilation is *not* required by the Qu'an; Mohammad, in fact, said girls should be treated even better than boys.[9] Yet the women have inflicted upon their daughters for millennia the horrors done to them, reenacting the abuse men inflict on them as they mutilate their daughters while joyfully chanting songs such as this: "We used to be friends, but today I am the master, for I am a man. Look—I have the knife in my hand. . . . Your clitoris, I will cut it off and throw it away for today I am a man."[10]

As the girls grow up in these fundamentalist families, they are usually treated as though they were polluted beings, veiled, and sometimes gang-raped when men outside the family wish to settle scores with men in her family.[11] Studies such as a recent survey of Palestinian students show that the sexual abuse of girls is far higher in Islamic societies than elsewhere, with a large majority of all girls reporting that they had been sexually molested as children.[12] Even marriage can be considered rape, since the family often chooses the partner and the girl is as young as 8.[13] The girl is often blamed for her rape, since it is assumed that "those who don't ask to be raped will never be raped."[14] Wife beating is common and divorce by wives rare—in fact, women have been killed by their families simply because they asked for a divorce.[15] It is no wonder that Physicians for Human

---

9. Mona AlMunajjed, *Women in Saudi Arabia Today*, p. 14.

10. Ibid., p. 13.

11. Eleanor Abdella Doumato, *Getting God's Ear: Women, Islam and Healing in Saudi Arabia and the Gulf*. New York: Columbia University Press, 2000, pp. 23, 85; Peter Parkes, "Kalasha Domestic Society." In Hastings Donnan and Frits Selier, Eds., *Family and Gender in Pakistan: Domestic Organization in a Muslim Society*. New Delhi: Hindustan Publishing Corp., 1997, p. 46; Jan Goodwin, *Price of Honor*, p. 52.

12. Muhammad M. Haj-Yahia and Safa Tamish, "The Rates of Child Sexual Abuse and Its Psychological Consequences as Revealed by a Study Among Palestinian University Students." *Child Abuse and Neglect* 25(2001): 1303–1327, the results of which must be compared to comparable written responses for other areas, with allowance given for the extreme reluctance to reveal abuse that may put their lives in serious danger (p. 1305); for problems of interpretation of sexual abuse figures, see Lloyd deMause, "The Universality of Incest." *The Journal of Psychohistory* 19(1991): 123–165 (also on *www.psychohistory.com* in full).

13. Deborah Ellis, *Women of the Afghan War*. London: Praeger, 2000, p. 141.

14. S. Tamish, *Misconceptions About Sexuality and Sexual Behavior in Palestinian Society*. Ramallah: The Tamer Institute for Community Education, 1996.

15. "Women's Woes," *The Economist* August 14, 1999, p. 32.

Rights found, for instance, that "97 percent of Afghan women they surveyed suffered from severe depression."[16]

It is not surprising that these mutilated, battered women make less than ideal mothers, reinflicting their own miseries upon their children. Visitors to families throughout fundamentalist Muslim societies report on the "slapping, striking, whipping, and thrashing" of children, with constant shaming and humiliation, often being told by their mothers that they are "cowards" if they don't hit others.[17] Physical abuse of children is continuous; as the Pakistani Conference on Child Abuse reports, "A large number of children face some form of physical abuse, from infanticide and abandonment of babies, to beating, shaking, burning, cutting, poisoning, holding under water, or giving drugs or alcohol, or violent acts like punching, kicking, biting, choking, beating, shooting or stabbing."[18]

Islamic schools regularly practice corporal punishment—particularly the religious schools from which terrorist volunteers so often come—chaining up their students for days "in dark rooms with little food and hardly any sanitation."[19] Sexual abuse—described as including "fondling of genitals, coercing a child to fondle the abuser's genitals, masturbation with the child as either participant or observer, oral sex, anal or vaginal penetration by penis, finger, or any other object and [child] prostitution"—is extensive, though impossible to quantify.[20] Even mothers have been reported as often "rubbing the penis [of their boys] long and energetically to increase its size."[21] According to the recent survey of Palestinian students, boys report having been used sexually even more often than girls—men choosing to rape little boys anally to avoid what they consider the "voracious vaginas" of women.[22] In some areas, children are reported to have marks all over their bodies from being burned by their parents with red-hot irons or pins as punishment or to cure being pos-

---

16. MSNBC, October 4, 2001.

17. Mazharul Haq Khari, *Purdah and Polygamy*, p. 107.

18. Samra Fayyazuddin, Anees Jillani, Zarina Jillani, *The State of Pakistan's Children 1997*. Islamabad Pakistan: Sparc, 1998, p. 46.

19. Ibid., p. 47.

20. Samra Fayyazuddin et al., *The State of Pakistan's Children 1997*, p. 51.

21. Allen Edwardes, *The Cradle of Erotica*. New York: Julian Press, 1963, p. 40.

22. Muhammad M. Haj-Yahia and Safa Tamish, "The Rates of Child Sexual Abuse . . . ," p. 1320; Fatna A. Sabbah, *Woman in the Muslim Unconscious*. New York: Pergamon Press, 1984, p. 28.

sessed by demons.[23] Children are taught strict obedience to all parental commands, to stand when their parents enter the room, kiss their hands, don't laugh excessively, fear them immensely, and learn that giving in to any of their own needs or desires is horribly sinful.[24] All these child-rearing practices are very much like those that were routinely inflicted on children in the medieval West.[25]

The ascetic results of such punitive upbringings are predictable. When these abused children grow up, they feel that every time they try to self-activate, every time they do something independently for themselves, they will lose the approval of the parents in their heads—mainly their mothers and grandmothers in the women's quarters. When their cities were flooded with oil money and Western popular culture in recent decades, fundamentalist men were first attracted to the new freedoms and pleasures, but soon retreated, feeling they would lose their mommy's approval and be seen as "bad boys." Westerners came to represent their own "bad boy" self in projection, and had to be killed off, as they felt they themselves deserved, for such unforgivable sins as listening to music, flying kites, and enjoying sex.[26] As one put it, "America is Godless. Western influence here is not a good thing, our people can see CNN, MTV, [and] kissing."[27] Another described his motives thusly: "We will destroy American cities piece by piece because your life style is so objectionable to us, your pornographic movies and TV."[28] Many agree with the Iranian Ministry of Culture that all American television programs "are part of an extensive plot to wipe out our religious and sacred values,"[29] and for this reason feel they must kill Americans. Sayyid Qutb, the intellectual father of Islamic terrorism, describes how he turned against the West as he once watched a church dance while visiting America: "Every young man took the hand of a young woman. And these were the

23. Samuel M. Zwemer, *Childhood in the Moslem World*, p. 104; Hilma Natalia Granqvist, *Child Problems Among the Arabs: Studies in a Muhammadan Village in Palestine.* Helsingfors: Soderstrom, 1950, pp. 102–107.

24. Soraya Altorki, *Women in Saudi Arabia: Ideology and Behavior among the Elite.* New York: Columbia University Press, 1986, pp. 72–76.

25. Lloyd deMause, "The Evolution of Childrearing." *The Journal of Psychohistory* 28(2001): 362–451.

26. *Time*, October 22, 2001, p. 56.

27. Jan Goodwin, *Price of Honor*, p. 64.

28. MSNBC, October 1, 2001.

29. Benjamin R. Barber, *Jihad vx. McWorld.* New York: Ballantine Books, 1995, p. 207.

young men and women who had just been singing their hymns! The room became a confusion of feet and legs: arms twisted around hips; lips met lips; chests pressed together."[30]

Osama bin Laden himself "while in college frequented flashy night-clubs, casinos and bars [and] was a drinker and womanizer," but soon felt extreme guilt for his sins and began preaching killing Westerners for their freedoms and their sinful enticements of Muslims.[31] Most of the Taliban leaders, in fact, are wealthy, like bin Laden, have had contact with the West, and were shocked into their terrorist violence by "the personal freedoms and affluence of the average citizen, by the promiscuity, and by the alcohol and drug use of Western youth . . . only an absolute and unconditional return to the fold of conservative Islamism could protect the Muslim world from the inherent dangers and sins of the West."[32] Bin Laden left his life of pleasures, and has lived with his four wives and fifteen children in a small cave with no running water, waging a holy war against all those who enjoy sinful activities and freedoms that he cannot allow in himself.

From childhood, then, Islamist terrorists have been taught to kill the part of themselves—and, by projection, others—that is selfish and wants personal pleasures and freedoms. It is in the terror-filled homes—not just later in the terrorist training camps—that they first learn to be martyrs and to die for Allah. When the terrorist suicidal bombers who were prevented from carrying out their acts were interviewed on TV, they said they felt "ecstatic" as they pushed the button.[33] They denied being motivated by the virgins and other enticements supposedly awaiting them in Paradise. Instead, they said they wanted to die to join Allah—to get the love they never got. Mothers of martyrs are reported as happy that they die. One mother of a Palestinian suicide bomber who had blown himself to bits said "with a resolutely cheerful countenance," "I was very happy when I heard. To be a martyr, that's something. Very few people can do it. I prayed to thank God. I know my son is close to me."[34]

---

30. *The New York Times*, October 13, 2001, p. A15.

31. Yossef Bodansky, *Bin Laden: The Man Who Declared War on America*. Rocklin: Forum, 1999, p. 3.

32. Ibid., p. 4.

33. "60 Minutes," September 23, 2001.

34. Joseph Lelyveld, "All Suicide Bombers Are Not Alike." *New York Times Magazine*, October 28, 2001, p. 50.

Like serial killers—who are also sexually and physically abused as children—terrorists grow up filled with a rage that must be inflicted upon others. Many even preach violence against other Middle Eastern nations like Egypt and Saudi Arabia "for not being sufficiently fervent in the campaign against materialism and Western values."[35]

If prevention rather than revenge is our goal, rather than pursuing a lengthy military campaign against terrorists and killing many innocent people while increasing the number of future terrorists, it might be better for the U.S. to back a U.N.-sponsored Marshall Plan for them—one that could include community parenting centers run by local people who could teach more humane child-rearing practices[36]—in order to give them the chance to evolve beyond the abusive family system that has produced the terrorism, just as we provided a Marshall Plan for Germans after World War II for the families that had produced Nazism.[37]

35. *The New York Times*, October 22, 2001, p. B4.

36. Robert B. McFarland and John Fanton, "Moving Towards Utopia: Prevention of Child Abuse." *The Journal of Psychohistory* 24(1997): 320–331.

37. Lloyd deMause, "War as Righteous Rape and Purification." *The Journal of Psychohistory* 27(2000): 407–438.

II

Psychohistorical Theory

*"It is the theory that decides
what we can observe."*
                    —Albert Einstein

4

Restaging Early Traumas in War and Social Violence

> *"A just war for the true interests of the state*
> *advances its development within a few years*
> *by tens of years, stimulates all healthy elements*
> *and represses insidious poison."*
>
> —*Adolf Lasson*

When Adolf Hitler moved to Vienna in 1907 at the age of 18, he reported in *Mein Kampf* that he haunted the prostitutes' district, fuming at the "Jews and foreigners" who directed the "revolting vice traffic" that "defiled our inexperienced young blond girls" and injected "poison" into the bloodstream of Germany.[1]

Months before this blood poison delusion was formed, Hitler had the only romantic infatuation of his youth, with a young girl, Stefanie.[2] Hitler imagined that Stefanie was in love with him (although in reality she had never met him) and thought he could communicate with her via mental telepathy. He was so afraid of approaching her that he made plans to kidnap her and then murder her and commit suicide in order to join with her in death.

Hitler's childhood had been so abusive—his father regularly beat him "with a hippopotamus whip," once enduring 230 blows of his father's cane and another time nearly killed by his father's whipping[3]—that he was full

1. Adolf Hitler, *Mein Kampf*. Boston: Houghton Mifflin, 1971, p. 59.
2. Norbert Bromberg and Verna Volz Small, *Hitler's Psychopathology*. New York: International Universities Press, 1983.
3. Alice Miller, *For Your Own Good: Hidden Cruelty in Child-Rearing and the Roots of Violence*. New York: Farrar, Straus, Giroux, 1983, p. 152; George Victor, *Hitler: The Pathology of Evil*. Washington: Brassey's, 1998, p. 29.

of rage toward the world. When he grew up, his sexual feelings were so mixed up with his revenge fantasies that he believed his sperm were poisonous and might enter the woman's bloodstream during sexual intercourse and poison her.[4]

Hitler's rage against "Jewish blood-poisoners" was, therefore, a projection of his own fears that he might become a blood-poisoner. Faced with the temptation of the more permissive sexuality of Vienna, he wanted to have sex with women, but was afraid his sperm would poison their blood. He became obsessed with sexual perversions, and "talked by the hour" about "depraved sexual customs."[5] He then projected his own perverse sadomasochistic sexual desires into Jews—"The black-haired Jewboy lies in wait for hours, satanic joy in his face, for the unsuspecting girl"[6]—and ended up accusing Jews of being "world blood-poisoners" who "introduced foreign blood into our people's body."[7]

As is usually the case with delusional systems, Hitler's projection of his fears of his own poisonous sexuality into Jews helped him avoid a psychotic breakdown and allowed him to function during his later life. He recognized the moment he began projecting them in *Mein Kampf*, saying that when he "recognized the Jew as the cold-hearted, shameless, and calculating director of this revolting traffic in the scum of the big city, a cold shudder ran down my back . . . the scales dropped from my eyes. A long soul struggle had reached its conclusion."[8] From that moment on, Hitler became a professional antisemite, ordering Nazi doctors to find out how Jewish blood differed from Aryan blood, having his own blood regularly sucked by leeches to try to get rid of its "poison,"[9] giving speeches full of metaphors of blood poisoning and of Jews sucking people's blood out, and eventually ordering the extermination of all "world blood-poisoners" in the worst genocide and the most destructive war ever experienced by mankind.

The success of Hitler's ability to use antisemitism to save his sanity was dependent on there being millions of followers who shared his fantasies about poisonous enemies infecting the body of Europe. Much of Europe at that time shared Hitler's experience of a severely abusive child-

---

4. Bromberg and Small, *Hitler's Psychopathology*, pp. 137 and 280.
5. John Toland, *Adolf Hitler*. New York: Doubleday, 1976, p. 176.
6. Victor, *Hitler: The Pathology of Evil*, p. 128.
7. Hitler, *Mein Kampf*, p. 388.
8. Ibid., pp. 59-60.
9. Bromberg and Small, *Hitler's Psychopathology*, p. 281.

hood,[10] and many shared his fantasy that the ills of the modern world were caused by the poisonous nature of Jewish blood, claiming: "A single act of intercourse between a Jew and an Aryan woman is enough to poison her blood forever."[11] When Hitler used metaphors of blood in his speeches, saying the world was a constant warfare of one people against another, where "one creature drinks the blood of another," and that Jews were spiders that "sucked the people's blood out," he was cheered on by millions who shared his poison-blood fantasies.[12]

GROUP-FANTASIES OF POISON BLOOD

In studying the shared fantasies of nations connected with how it *feels* to be part of a group at a particular historical moment—what I have termed *historical group-fantasies*[13]—I have regularly found images of "poison blood" prior to outbreaks of war and violent revolution. In war, the enemy is imagined to be sucking out the blood of the nation; in revolution, the state is the blood-sucker, as in the fantasy before the French Revolution that the state was an "immense and infernal machine which seizes each citizen by the throat and pumps out his blood."[14] Images of poison blood return periodically in history. I have discovered they are usually found in conjunction with images of guilt for recent prosperity and progress that are felt to have "polluted the national blood-stream with sinful excess," making men "soft" and "feminine," a frightful condition that can only be cleansed by a blood-shedding purification.[15] This fantasy of periodic shedding of poisoned blood through war is

---

10. Lloyd deMause, *Foundations of Psychohistory*. New York: Creative Roots, 1982, pp. 48-59; Lloyd deMause, "Schreber and the History of Childhood," *Journal of Psychohistory* 15(1987): 426-427; Aurel Ende, "Battering and Neglect: Children in Germany, 1860–1978." *Journal of Psychohistory* 7(1980): 249-279; Aurel Ende, "Bibliography on Childhood and Youth in Germany from 1820–1978." *Journal of Psychohistory* 7(1980): 281-287; Aurel Ende, "Children in History: A Personal Review of the Past Decade's Published Research." *Journal of Psychohistory* 11(1983): 65–88.

11. Klaus Theweleit, *Male Fantasies. Vol. 2. Male Bodies: Psychoanalyzing the White Terror.*" Minneapolis: University of Minnesota Press, 1989, p. 12.

12. Bromberg and Small, *Hitler's Psychopathology*, p. 24.

13. Lloyd deMause, *Foundations of Psychohistory*, pp. 172–243.

14. Simon Schama, *Citizens: A Chronicle of the French Revolution.* New York: Alfred A. Knopf, 1989, p. 73.

15. Lloyd deMause, *Foundations of Psychohistory*, pp. 244–317.

based on the same presumed cleansing effects as the bloodletting therapies physicians prescribed through the nineteenth century to cure many diseases, which also were believed to be caused by "gluttony, luxury and lustful excesses."[16] As one military leader put it, war "is one of the great agencies by which human progress is effected. [It] purges a nation of its humors . . . and chastens it, as sickness or adversity . . . chastens an individual;" it cures people of their "worship of comfort, wealth, and general softness."[17] When John Adams asked Thomas Jefferson "how to prevent . . . luxury from producing effeminacy, intoxication, extravagance, vice and folly?" Jefferson's answer was that war was the only cure: "The tree of liberty must be refreshed from time to time with the blood of patriots."[18] As one author said in August 1914, rapid material progress had produced a feeling that "God's curse hung heavy over a degenerate world, for there was an awesome hush and a feeling of vague expectancy in the sultry and stagnant air . . . [but] a cleaner, better, stronger land will lie in the sunshine when the storm has cleared. . . . A bloody purging would be good for the country."[19]

Wars have often been thought of as purifying the nation's polluted blood by virtue of a sacrificial rite identical to the rites of human sacrifice so common in early historical periods, when the blood of those sacrificed was believed to renew all the people. War, said those preparing for the bloody Finnish Civil War, purges guilt-producing material prosperity through the blood of soldiers sacrificed on the battlefield: "The idea of sacrifice permeated the war. . . . Youth . . . have heard the nation's soul crying for its renewal, their heart's blood [because] nations drink renewal from the blood of the fallen soldiers."[20] Usually the blood of soldiers is thought of as being needed to feed a maternal figure, either Mother Earth or, like the Aztecs, a bloodthirsty mother-goddess.[21] By feeding blood to the goddess, the state was "reborn" by the soldier's blood, and war cleansed the polluted national bloodstream

---

16. K. Codell Carter, "On the Decline of Bloodletting in Nineteenth Century Medicine." *The Journal of Psychoanalytic Anthropology* 5(1982): 221.

17. Michael C. C. Adams, *The Great Adventure: Male Desire and the Coming of World War I.* Bloomington, IN: Indiana University Press, 1990, p. 57.

18. Ibid., p. 51.

19. Ibid., p. 61.

20. Juha Siltala, "Prenatal Fantasies During the Finnish Civil War." *The Journal of Psychohistory* 22(1995): 486.

21. Burr Cartwright Brundage, *The Fifth Sun: Aztec Gods, Aztec World.* Austin: University of Texas Press, 1979.

as if there was a "rebirth from the womb of history," a "bloody baptism" that removed all poisonous self-indulgence.[22] "A nation hath been born again,/ Regenerate by a second birth!" wrote W. W. Howe after the bloody American Civil War.[23] Another American, speaking of World War I, said, "It was like the pouring of new blood into old veins."[24]

The question immediately arises: How do such poisoned blood fears originate? And what is their connection with birth? The answers to these questions will become more convincing only after examining a prior question: Why is war so often depicted as a woman?

GROUP-FANTASIES OF DANGEROUS WOMEN

For the past two decades, I have been collecting historical material from sources such as magazine covers and political cartoons on images of war. One of the most unexpected findings was that war was so often shown as a dangerous, bloodthirsty woman.[25] Despite the fact that women don't play much part in either deciding on wars or in fighting them, war has so often been depicted as a dangerous woman that a visitor to our planet might wrongly conclude that females were our more bellicose sex. From Athena to Freyja, from Marianne to Brittania, terrifying women have been depicted as war goddesses,[26] devouring, raping, and ripping apart her children. The image has become so familiar we no longer think to question why women are so often shown as presiding over war rather than as its victims, as they are in reality.

Even in antiquity, when the god of war was usually male, his mother was imagined to have hovered above the battlefield, demanding blood to feed her voracious appetite.[27] And although it was almost always men who

---

22. Ibid., p. 487.

23. Michael C. C. Adams, *The Great Adventure*, p. 55.

24. Ibid., p. 53.

25. Lloyd deMause, "The Gulf War as a Mental Disorder." *The Journal of Psychohistory* 19(1991): 1–23.

26. Miriam Robbins Dexter, *Whence the Goddesses: A Source Book*. New York: Pergamon Press, 1990; Paul Friedrich, *The Meaning of Aphrodite*. Chicago: University of Chicago Press, 1978.

27. James A. Aho, *Religious Mythology and the Art of War: Comparative Religious Symbolisms of Military Violence*. Westport, CT: Greenwood Press, 1981; Wolfgang Lederer, *The Fear of Women*. New York: Grune & Stratton, 1968, p. 58.

Fig. 4–1. The Mother of all wars

fought the battles,[28] women in early societies were expected to come along to watch from the sidelines, rather like cheerleaders at a sports match, shrieking their own battle cries, heckling and insulting those warriors who held back, and demanding a plentiful show of blood on the battlefield.[29]

THE MARIE ANTOINETTE SYNDROME AND SOCIAL VIOLENCE

The French Revolution fully demonstrates the role of the dangerous woman fantasy in social violence, being preceded by a deluge of pamphlets and newspapers picturing Marie Antoinette—actually a rather sweet-natured young woman—as a sexually voracious, incestuous, lesbian, murderous "bloodsucker of the French."[30] The French Revolution, terror, and revolutionary wars were accompanied by increasingly violent Marie Antoinette fantasies, centering on grotesque images of her imagined sexual perversities, while the king was pictured as merely an impotent tool in her hands. Finally, the Tribunal, whipped up by the press, declared her a "ravening beast" and chopped off her head, after she had been accused of being a "tigress thirsty for the blood of the French," a "ferocious panther who devoured the French, the female monster whose pores sweated the purest blood of the sans-culottes," a "vampire who sucks the blood of the French," and a "monster who needed to slake her thirst on the blood of the French."[31]

---

28. Ilse Kirk, "Images of Amazons: Marriage and Matriarchy." In Sharon Macdonald, Pat Holden, and Shirley Ardener, Eds., *Images of Women in Peace and War*. Houndmills: Macmillan Education, 1987, pp. 27–39.

29. Burr Cartwright Brundage, *The Fifth Sun*, p. 201; Margaret Ehrenberg, *Women in Prehistory*. London: British Museum Publications, 1989, p. 163.

30. Joan Haslep, *Marie Antoinette*. New York: Weidenfeld & Nicolson, 1987; Lynn Hunt, "The Many Bodies of Marie Antoinette: Political Pornography and the Problem of the Feminine in the French Revolution" and Vivian Cameron, "Political Exposures: Sexuality and Caricature in the French Revolution." In Lynn Hunt, Ed., *Eroticism and the Body Politic*. Baltimore: Johns Hopkins University Press, 1991, pp. 109–130; Simon Schama, *Citizens: A Chronicle of the French Revolution*. New York: Alfred A. Knopf, 1989, pp. 203–227; Terry Castle, "Marie Antoinette Obsession." *Representations* 38(1992): 1–38; Madelyn Gutwirth, *The Twilight of the Goddesses*. New Brunswick: Rutgers University Press, 1992, pp. 136–200.

31. Lynn Hunt, "The Many Bodies of Marie Antoinette," pp. 122-123; Simon Schama, *Citizens*, p. 796.

I have found that group-fantasies of monstrous bloodthirsty women have preceded every war that I have analyzed. Even the most popular movies prior to wars reflect this dangerous woman fantasy. The biggest movie preceding World War II was *The Wizard of Oz*, which is about a wicked witch and how to kill her; the second biggest was *Gone with the Wind*, featuring a bitchy Scarlett; and the third biggest was *The Women*, which boasted that it featured 135 dangerous women. *All About Eve* before Korea and *Cleopatra* before Vietnam had similar dangerous women as leads, and the Persian Gulf War was preceded by a whole string of dangerous women movies, from *Fatal Attraction* to *Thelma and Louise*,[32] including a hit TV series entitled "Dangerous Women."

When war breaks out, these terrifying women images disappear from the nation's fantasy life. The dangerous woman image now is projected into the enemy, so that the war is experienced unconsciously as a battle with a mother figure. For example, when the United States attacked Libya, the *New York Post* reported the rumor that American intelligence had discovered that Moammar Khadafy was actually a "transvestite dressed in women's clothes and high heels,"[33] even touching up a photo to show how he "might look . . . dressed in drag." Even more often, the enemy is shown as a dangerous mommy, as in the Persian Gulf War when Saddam Hussein was depicted as a dangerous pregnant mother with a nuclear bomb in her womb or as the mother of a death-baby (see cartoons in Chapter 2).

Hallucinating dangerous female characteristics in one's enemies goes all the way back to antiquity, when the earliest battles were imagined to have been fought against female monsters, often the mother of the hero, whatever her name—Tiamat, Ishtar, Inanna, Isis, or Kali.[34] Typical is the Aztec mother-goddess Huitzilopochtli, who had "mouths all over her body" that cried out to be fed the blood of soldiers.[35] To attain full status, early Indo-European warriors had to pass through initiatory rituals in which they dressed up and attacked a monstrous dummy female poi-

---

32. Richard Grenier, "Killer Bimbos." *Commentary*, September 1991; "Kiss Kiss Slash Slash." *Newsweek*, March 23, 1992.

33. *New York Post*, June 16, 1986, p. 4.

34. James A. Aho, *Religious Mythology and the Art of War: Comparative Religious Symbolisms of Military Violence*. Westport, CT: Greenwood Press, 1981, pp. 21–23.

35. John Bierhorst, Ed., *The Hungry Woman: Myths and Legends of the Aztecs*. New York: William Morrow, 1984, p. 10.

sonous serpent, complete with three heads.[36] Although warriors fought against men, not women, they often castrated their enemies, turning them into symbolic women; from ancient Norse to ancient Egyptian societies, heaps of enemy penises on the battlefield are commonly portrayed.[37] Rape appears to be one of the most powerful motivations for war; according to the world's leading historian of war, "the opportunity to engage in wholesale rape was not just among the rewards of successful war but, from the soldier's point of view, one of the cardinal objectives for which he fought."[38] More women have been raped and killed in many wars than enemy soldiers. War is always *righteous rape*, inflicting revenge on the bad mommy, punching her around, beating her up, knocking her off her pedestal, teaching her a lesson. The hero is therefore simultaneously both a *self-killer*, punishing projected parts of himself, and a *mother-killer*, inflicting revenge for early traumas.[39]

Yet even though we understand that both the Motherland and the enemy in wars are ultimately the mother, the question remains: What could possibly be the infantile origin of fantasies of the enemy as a poisonous bloodsucking monster? Why did Americans before the Revolutionary War feel "poisoned by Mother England" and fight a bloody war over a minor tax? Why did Hitler fear "bloodsucking Jews and foreigners," and why did Aztec soldiers go to war to feed blood to a monstrous mother-goddess? Closer to today, why did Americans for so long fear their "national life-blood" was being poisoned by Communists? Why do so many today feel the government and welfare recipients are sucking their blood? Images of bloodsucking, engulfing enemies are ubiquitous throughout history. Surely our blood was never really poisoned or sucked out of us by a maternal monster in our past. Or was it?

---

36. Bruce Lincoln, *Death, War, and Sacrifice: Studies in Ideology and Practice*. Chicago: University of Chicago Press, 1991, p. 13.

37. Preben Meulengracht Sorensen, *The Unmanly Man: Concepts of Sexual Defamation in Early Northern Society*. Odense: Odense University Press, 1983, p. 82; Allen Edwardes, *Erotica Judaica: A Sexual History of the Jews*. New York: Julian Press, 1967, pp. 69–76.

38. Martin van Creveld, *The Transformation of War*. New York: The Free Press, 1991, p. 179.

39. Sidney Halpern, "The Mother-killer." *The Psychoanalytic Review* 52(1965): 73.

WAR AND THE FETAL DRAMA

As I described in my book, *Foundations of Psychohistory*,[40] when I first began collecting the emotional imagery surrounding the outbreak of war I was puzzled by recurring claims by aggressors that they were forced to go to war against their wishes because "a net had suddenly been thrown over their head" or a "ring of iron was closing about us more tightly every moment" or they had been "seized by the throat and strangled." I piled up hundreds of these images of nations prior to wars being choked and strangled, "unable to draw a breath," "smothered, walled-in," "unable to relieve the inexorable pressure" of a world "pregnant with events," followed by feelings of being "picked up bodily" in "an inexorable slide" toward war, starting with a "rupture of diplomatic relations" and a "descent into the abyss," being "unable to see the light at the end of the tunnel" as the nation takes its "final plunge over the brink," and even that wars were "aborted" if ended too soon. Given the concreteness of all this birth imagery, I concluded that war was a rebirth fantasy of enormous power shared by nations undergoing deep regression to fetal traumas.

War has long been described in images of pregnancy: "War develops in the womb of State politics; its principles are hidden there as the particular characteristics of the individual are hidden in the embryo" (Clausewitz); "Germany is never so happy as when she is pregnant with a war" (proverb).[41] Wars are felt to be life-and-death struggles for "breathing space" and "living room," *Lebensraum*, as though one of the traumas nations were reliving was the growing lack of space and oxygen common to all fetuses just prior to and during birth. Nations become paranoid prior to wars, and feel they have to resort to violence to get out of what feels like a choking womb and birth canal. Chancellor Theobald Bethmann-Hollweg, for example, told the Reichstag in announcing war in 1914 that Germany was surrounded by enemies, and "he who is menaced as we are and is fighting for his highest possession can only consider how he is to hack his way

---

40. Lloyd deMause, *Foundations of Psychohistory*, pp. 90–102, 244–332.

41. Nancy Huston, "The Matrix of War: Mothers and Heroes." In Susan Rubin Suleiman, *The Female Body in Western Culture: Contemporary Perspectives.* Cambridge: Harvard University Press, 1986, p. 133.

through."[42] As Hitler repeated over and over again, only a violent "rebirth" could avoid it being "asphyxiated and destroyed."[43]

Now, the notion that war might be fantasized as a battle against a dangerous mother is difficult enough to believe. That it also includes fantasies that you are hacking your way out of the asphyxiation of your own birth is infinitely harder to accept. But what followed then from my research into imagery prior to wars was a discovery that seemed to be a final step into the unbelievable, revealing a depth of regression prior to wars greater than anything yet contemplated in the psychological literature. Yet it was a discovery that for the first time seemed to explain the true origin of the poison blood imagery.

What I found was that the cartoons, past and present, of the enemy in war were dominated by an image that was even more widespread than that of the dangerous mommy: it was that of a *sea beast*, often with many heads or arms, a dragon or a hydra or a serpent or an octopus that threatened to poison the lifeblood of the nation. Most early cultures believed in this beast as a dragon that was associated with watery caves or lakes; modern wars show the beast as a bloodsucking, many-headed enemy. Indeed, the word *dragon* comes from the Greek stem for "womb," and the umbilical python-serpent sat on the Greek stone *omphalos*, the navel of the Earth.[44] This serpentine, poisonous dragon-monster I have termed the *Poisonous Placenta* (the capitals are in honor of it being the prototype for God and Nation), since it resembled what the actual placenta must have felt like to the growing fetus, particularly when the placenta fails in its tasks of cleansing the fetal blood of wastes and of replenishing its oxygen supply. When the blood coming to the fetus from the placenta is bright red and full of nutrients and oxygen, the fetus feels it is being fed by a *Nurturant Placenta*, but when the mother smokes, takes drugs, or is hurt or frightened, the placenta does not remove the wastes from the fetal blood, which therefore becomes polluted and depleted of oxygen. Under these stressful conditions, the helpless fetus experiences an

---

42. Ralph H. Lutz, *Fall of the German Empire 1914–1918: Documents of the German Revolution. Vol. I.* Stanford: Stanford University Press, 1932, p. 13.

43. Jeremy Noakes and Geoffrey Pridham, Eds., *Documents on Nazism, 1919–1945.* London: Jonathan Cape, 1974, p. 37; Robert Wistrich, *Hitler's Apocalypse: Jews and the Nazi Legacy.* New York: St. Martin's Press, 1985, p. 134.

44. Philip E. Slater, *The Glory of Hera: Greek Mythology and the Greek Family.* Princeton: Princeton University Press, 1968, p. 95.

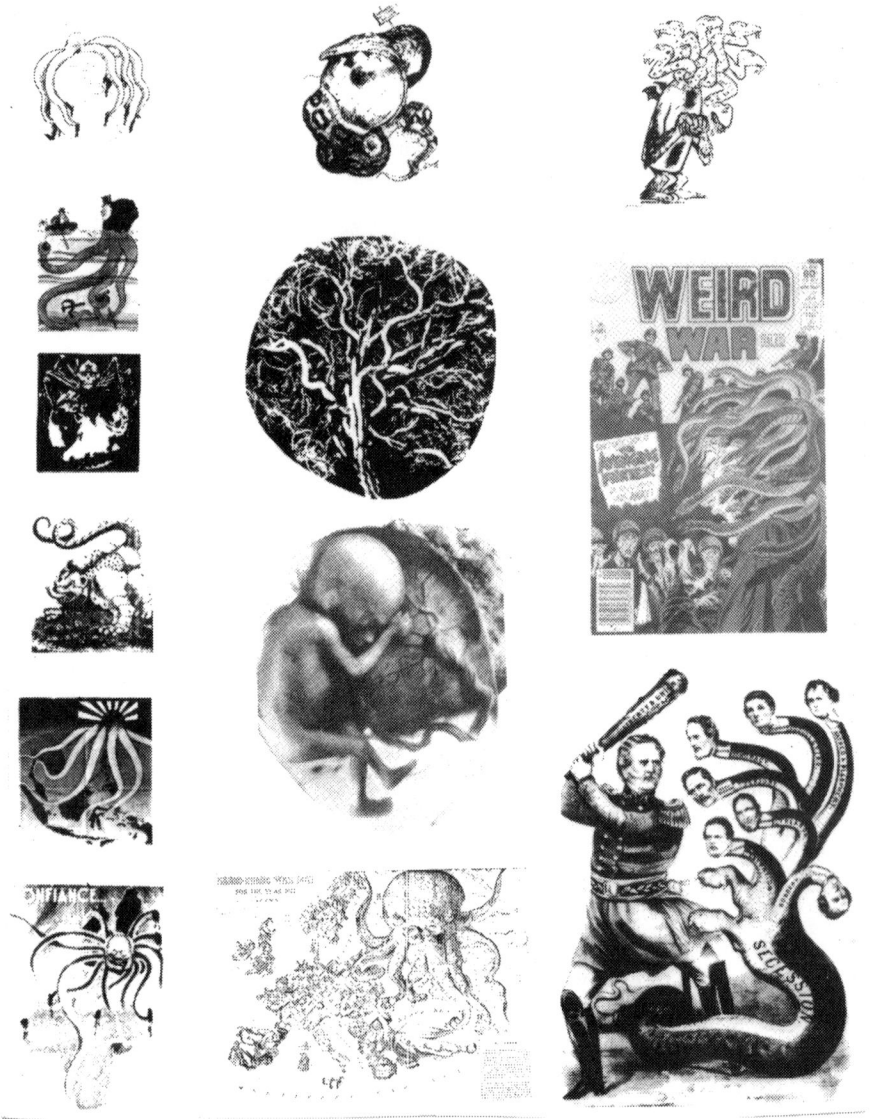

Fig. 4–2. War as a battle with the Poisonous Placenta

asphyxiating Poisonous Placenta, the prototype for all later hate relationships, including the murderous mother, the castrating father, and the dangerous enemy. It is even likely that the fetus, like Oedipus, feels it is actually battling with the dangerous beast (sphinx means "strangler" in Greek) to restore connections with the Nurturant Placenta. This battle, one that I have termed the *fetal drama*, is repeated in death-and-rebirth restagings of traumatic battles in wars and other social violence.

The cosmic battle with the Poisonous Placenta, where we repeat the fetal drama of a paradise lost, of being sucked into the whirlpool and crushing pressures of birth, and where we fight the placental dragon, is well depicted in a comic-book character, Conan the Barbarian, although I could just as easily have used pictures and texts from ancient myths of battles with sea beasts such as Tiamat, Rahab, Behemoth, Humbaba, Apophis, Hydra, Gorgon, or Typhon.[45] In this comic-book version, a baby is first shown abandoned, beginning his watery birth passage between head-crushing bones, going down the whirlpool of birth after the amniotic waters break, and then being choked by the Poisonous Placenta, a black sea-monster that tries to asphyxiate it. The hero, an imaginary powerful version of the fetus, battles with the Poisonous Placenta and frees the fetus, who reaches the safety of land. The final panel shows that the goal, however, is not birth, the arrival on land, but the reuniting with the placenta. That it is the Nurturant and not the Poisonous Placenta that holds the baby in its embrace is depicted by its being shown as a white rather than black sea beast.

In most cultures, the placenta is considered very much alive after delivery; it is felt to be so dangerous to the community that unless it is buried somewhere deep the whole tribe will fall sick.[46] Until modern times, the womb itself was believed to be beastlike, able to move about the woman's body, sometimes lodging in her throat and causing choking.[47] The Poisonous Placenta is usually shown in cartoons as a female

45. For further examples of the fetal drama, see Lloyd deMause, *Foundations of Psychohistory*, pp. 261–282.

46. J. R. Davidson, "The Shadow of Life: Psychosocial Explanations for Placenta Rituals." *Culture, Medicine and Psychiatry* 9(1985): 75–92.

47. Albertus Magnus, cited in Julia O'Faolain and Lauro Martines, Eds., *Not in God's Image*. New York: Harper & Row, 1973, p. 124.

The Fetal Drama
Birth and the Poisonous Placenta

The fetus, abandoned...   ...starts his birth between head-crushing bones.

The amniotic waters break and the whirlpool of birth begins.   The Poisonous Placenta...

...wants the fetus. The Hero must choke the Poisonous Placenta...

...to save the fetus from asphyxiation. But he might drown himself.

The battle with the Poisonous Placenta frees the fetus.

The fetus, at home in the water, is safely born on land.

The fetus is reunited with the Nurturant Placenta.

Fig. 4–3. The fetal drama

sea beast—what Jungians call the Dragon Mother[48]—who engulfs and devours innocent people. Many early cultures have versions of devouring dragons who "rebirth" initiates by regurgitating them.

Obviously, full understanding of the placental source of "poison blood" imagery and of the fetal origins of war and social violence is going to have to wait until we investigate more fully the psychology of dangerous wombs, Poisonous Placentas, and asphyxiating births—which is to say, until we understand more about both the psychology and neurobiology of fetal life.

THE ORIGINS OF FETAL PSYCHOLOGY

After Freud initially proposed that mental life began after birth, he later admitted that he had come to believe he was wrong, saying that "the act of birth is the first experience of anxiety."[49] Although most other psychoanalysts believed mental life began only with infancy, there were a number of exceptions, beginning with Otto Rank's *The Trauma of Birth* in 1923,[50] which began the investigation of birth anxiety derivatives in adult life and culture. After Rank, Donald Winnicott wrote in the early 1940s a paper on "Birth Memories, Birth Trauma, and Anxiety,"[51] which, however, was little noticed, since, as he said, "It is rare to find doctors who believe that the experience of birth is important to the baby, that it could have any significance in the emotional development of the individual, and that memory traces of the experience could persist and give rise to trouble even in the adult." While still a pediatrician, Winnicott saw that newborn babies varied enormously and that prolonged labor could be traumatic to the fetus, resulting in extreme anxiety—so much so that he thought "some babies are born paranoid, by which I mean in a state of expecting persecution."[52] He was even able to

---

48. A. Stevens, *Archetype: A Natural History of the Self*. London: Routledge and Kegan Paul, 1982, p. 129.

49. Sigmund Freud, "The Interpretation of Dreams," *Standard Edition*, Vol. 5. London: The Hogarth Press, 1959, p. 400.

50. Otto Rank, *The Trauma of Birth*. New York: Richard Brunner, 1952; Otto Rank, *The Myth of the Birth of the Hero and Other Writings*. New York: Random House, 1932.

51. In *Collected Papers: Through Paediatrics to Psycho-analysis*. New York: Basic Books, 1958, pp. 174–193.

52. Donald W. Winnicott, *Human Nature*. London: Free Association Books, 1988, p. 149.

conclude that "at full term, there is already a human being in the womb, one that is capable of having experiences and of accumulating body memories and even of organizing defensive measures to deal with traumata." He sometimes would allow his child patients to work through birth anxiety directly, having one child sit in his lap and "get inside my coat and turn upside down and slide down to the ground between my legs; this he repeated over and over again. . . . After this experience I was prepared to believe that memory traces of birth can persist."[53] He also encouraged some adult patients to relive the breathing changes, constrictions of the body, head pressures, convulsive movements, and fears of annihilation experienced during their births, with dramatic therapeutic results.[54]

After Winnicott, psychotherapists such as Fodor, Mott, Raskovsky, Janov, Grof, Verny, Fedor-Freybergh, Janus, and others published extensive work showing how their patients relived birth trauma in therapy and removed major blocks in their emotional lives.[55] These traumatic birth feelings—of being trapped, of crushing head pressures and cardiac distress, of being sucked into a whirlpool or swallowed by terrifying monsters, of explosive volcanoes and death-rebirth struggles—appear regularly in the 60 percent of our dreams that have been found to contain overt pre- and perinatal images.[56] Perhaps one of the most important results of clinical research by therapists sensitive to perinatal trauma—as described particu-

---

53. *Collected Papers*, pp. 177–178.

54. Ibid., pp. 249–250.

55. Nandor Fodor, *The Search for the Beloved: A Clinical Investigation of the Trauma of Birth and Prenatal Condition*. New Hyde Park, NY: University Books, 1949; Francis J. Mott, *The Universal Design of Creation*. Edenbridge: Mark Beech, 1964; Francis J. Mott, *Mythology of the Prenatal Life*. London: Integration Publishing Co., 1960; Arnaldo Rascovsky, *El Psiquismo Fetal*. Buenos Aires: Editorial Paidos, 1977; Stanislav Grof, *Realms of the Human Unconscious: Observations from LSD Research*. New York: Viking Press, 1975; Stanislav Grof, *Beyond the Brain: Birth, Death and Transcendence in Psychotherapy*. Albany: State University of New York, 1985; Arthur Janov, *The Primal Scream: Primal Therapy—The Cure for Neurosis*. New York: G. P. Putnam's Sons, 1970; Thomas R. Verny and John Kelley, *The Secret Life of the Unborn Child*. New York: Summit Books, 1981; Thomas R. Verny, Ed., *Pre- and Perinatal Psychology: An Introduction*. New York: Human Sciences Press, 1987; Peter Fedor-Freybergh and M. L. Vanessa Vogel, Eds., *Prenatal and Perinatal Psychology and Medicine: Encounter With the Unborn*. Carnforth: the Parthenon Publishing Group, 1988; Ludwig Janus, *Wie die Seele entsteht: unser psychisches Leben vor und nach der Geburt*. Hamburg: Hoffman und Campe, 1991.

56. Calvin S. Hall, "Prenatal and Birth Experiences in Dreams." *Psychoanalytic Study of the Child* 1(1967): 157–174.

larly in the work of Lynda Share[57]—is how regularly early trauma produces an overwhelming fear of all progress in life. It is as though the fetus concludes, "Going forward in life led to disaster; I must remain 'unborn' all my life to avoid a repetition of this horrible start." Fetuses that experience injuries in the womb, premature births, birth complications, and many other medical conditions as newborns have been shown to regularly live the rest of their lives in fear of all growth and individuation.[58]

RESEARCH INTO FETAL MEMORY

Much has changed in our knowledge of the fetus during the decades since the early pioneering excursions into perinatal psychology. Neurobiologists have made startling advances in the understanding of how the brain develops in the womb, experimental psychologists have discovered a great deal about fetal learning, pediatricians have linked all kinds of later problems to fetal distress, and one psychoanalyst has even begun to compare thousands of hours of ultrasound observations of individual fetuses with their emotional problems during infancy in therapy with her. There are now thousands of books and articles on the subject, as well as two international associations of pre- and perinatal psychology, each with its own journal.[59] I can only summarize some of the main trends of this extensive recent research.

57. Lynda Share, *If Someone Speaks, It Gets Lighter: Dreams and the Reconstruction of Infant Trauma.* Hillsdale, NJ: The Analytic Press, 1994.

58. K. Mark Sossin, "Pre- and Postnatal Repercussions of Handicapping Conditions Upon the Narcissistic Line of Development." *Pre- and Perinatal Psychology Journal* 7(1993): 197.

59. *The International Journal of Prenatal and Perinatal Psychology and Medicine* and *Pre- and Peri-Natal Psychology Journal.* For excellent recent bibliographies, see M. Maiwald and L. Janus, "Development, Behavior and Psychic Experience in the Prenatal Period and the Consequences for Life History: A Bibliographic Survey." *International Journal of Prenatal and Perinatal Psychology and Medicine* 5 (1993): 451-485; and M. Maiwald, "Development, Behavior and Psychic Experience in the Prenatal Period and the Consequences for Life History: A Bibliographic Survey." *International Journal of Prenatal and Perinatal Psychology and Medicine* 6(1994): Suppl. 1–48. More extensive bibliography of pioneering fetal psychologists can be found in Lloyd deMause, *Foundations of Psychohistory,* "The Fetal Origins of History," pp. 244–332.

Biologists used to think that because the fetus had incomplete myelination of neurons it couldn't have memories.[60] This notion has been disproved.[61] Indeed, far from being an unfeeling being, the fetus has been found to be exquisitely sensitive to its surroundings, and our earliest feelings have been found to be coded into our early *emotional memory system* centering in the amygdala, the central fear system, quite distinct from the *declarative memory system* centering in the hippocampus, the center of consciousness, that becomes fully functional only in later childhood.[62]

The fetal nervous system is so well developed by the end of the first trimester that it responds to the stroking of its palm by a light hair by grasping, of its lips by sucking, and of its eyelids by squinting.[63] It will jump if touched by the amniocentesis needle and turn away from the light when a doctor introduces a brightly lit fetoscope.[64] By the second trimester, the fetus is not only seeing and hearing, it is actively tasting, feeling, exploring, and learning from its environment, now floating peacefully, now kicking vigorously, turning somersaults, urinating, grabbing its umbilicus when frightened, stroking and even licking its placenta, conducting little boxing matches with its companion if it is a twin and responding to being touched or spoken to through the mother's abdomen.[65] Each fetus develops its own

---

60. Maggie Scarf, *Body, Mind, Behavior*. New York: Dell Publishing, 1976, pp. 23–40; Robert C. Goodlin, *Care of the Fetus*. New York: Masson Publishing, 1979, p. 192; Thomas R. Verny, *Pre- and Perinatal Psychology: An Introduction*. New York: Human Sciences Press, 1987, p. 25.

61. K. J. S. Anand and P. R. Hickey, "Pain and Its Effects in the Human Neonate and Fetus." *The New England Journal of Medicine*, 317 (1987): 1322.

62. Joseph E. LeDoux, "Emotion, Memory and the Brain." *Scientific American*, June 1994, pp. 50–57; John P. Aggleton, Ed. *The Amygdala: Neurobiological Aspects of Emotion, Memory, and Mental Dysfunction*. New York: John Wiley & Sons, 1992; Daniel Goleman, *Emotional Intelligence*. New York: Bantam Books, 1995. For how hippocampus-cortical loops lay down long-term memory, see Gerald Edelman, *The Remembered Present: A Biological Theory of Consciousness*. New York: Basic Books, 1989, p. 129.

63. Robert M. Bradley and Charlotte M. Mistretta, "Fetal Sensory Receptors." *Physiological Reviews* 55(1975): 358; Tryphena Humphrey, "Function of the Nervous System During Prenatal Life," in Uwe Stave, Ed., *Physiology of the Perinatal Period*. Vol. 2. New York: Appleton-Century-Crofts, 1970, pp. 754–789.

64. Robert Goodlin, *Care of the Fetus*, p. 1.

65. A. W. Liley, "The Foetus as Personality." *Australian and New Zealand Journal of Psychiatry* 6(1972): 99–105; Alessandra Piontelli, *From Fetus to Child: An Observational and Psychoanalytic Study*. London: Tavistock/Routledge, 1992; A. Ianniruberto and E. Tajani,

pattern of activity, so that ultrasound technicians quickly learn to recognize each fetus as a distinct personality.[66]

THE EMOTIONAL EFFECTS OF FETAL STRESS

In addition to what we know about the disastrous effects on the fetus of prenatal exposure to drugs and alcohol,[67] we now have considerable evidence on how maternal stress and other emotions are transmitted to the fetus. The fetus has been found to be sensitive to a wide range of maternal emotions in addition to any drugs the mother takes or physical traumas the mother endures.[68] When the mother feels anxiety, her increased heartbeat, frightened speech, and alterations in neurotransmitter levels are instantly communicated to the fetus, and her tachycardia is followed within seconds by the fetus's tachycardia; when she feels fear, within 50 seconds the fetus can be made hypoxic (low oxygen). Pregnant monkeys stressed by simulated threatening attack had such impaired blood circulation to their uteruses that their fetuses were severely asphyxiated.[69] Alterations in adrenaline, plasma epinephrine and norepinephrine levels, high levels of hydroxycorticosteroids, hyperventilation, and many other products of maternal anxiety are also known to directly affect the human fetus. Numerous other studies document sensory, hormonal, and biochemical mechanisms by which the fetus is in communication with the mother's feelings and with the outside

"Ultrasonographic Study of Fetal Movements." *Seminars in Perinatology* 5 (1981): 175–181; T. B. Brazelton and B. G. Cramer, *The Earliest Relationship.* New York: Addison-Wesley Publishing Co., 1990.

66. W. E. Rayburn, "Monitoring Fetal Body Movement." *Clinical Obstetrics and Gynecology* 3(1987): 889–911.

67. Jeanette M Soby, *Prenatal Exposure to Drugs/Alcohol: Characteristics and Educational Implications of Fetal Alcohol Syndrome and Cocaine/Polydrug Effects.* Springfield, IL: Charles C. Thomas, 1994.

68. Bibliographic references can be found in Christopher Norwood, *At Highest Risk: Environmental Hazards to Young and Unborn Children.* New York: McGraw-Hill, 1980, and *Child at Risk: A Report of the Standing Senate Committee on Health, Welfare and Science.* Quebec: Canadian Government Publishing Center, 1980.

69. R. E. Myers, "Production of Fetal Asphyxia by Maternal Psychological Stress." *Pavlovian Journal of Biological Science* 12(1977): 51–62.

world.[70] Even baby monkeys have been found to be hyperactive, with higher levels of the stress hormone cortisol after birth from a mother who was experimentally stressed during her pregnancy.[71]

Maternal distress has been shown to produce low birth weights, increased infant mortality, respiratory infections, asthma, and reduced cognitive development.[72] One study of 120 Swedish babies who were unwanted at conception found they were more aggressive, more rejected by peers, lower in academic achievement, more hyperactive, and had triple the criminal activity than a matched sample of babies who were wanted at conception.[73] Ultrasound studies record fetal distress clearly, as the fetus thrashes about and kicks in pain during hypoxia and other conditions. One mother whose husband had just threatened her verbally with violence came into the doctor's office with the fetus thrashing and kicking so violently as to be painful to her, with an elevated heart rate that continued for hours.[74] The same wild thrashing has been seen in fetuses of mothers whose spouses have died suddenly. Maternal fright can actually cause the death of the fetus.[75] Marital discord between spouses has been correlated "with almost 100 per cent certainty . . . with child morbidity in the form of ill-health, neurological dysfunction, developmental lags and behavior disturbance."[76]

Margaret Fries has conducted a 40-year longitudinal study predicting emotional patterns that remain quite constant throughout the lives of those studied, correlating the patterns to the mother's attitude toward the fetus

---

70. John T. Ham, Jr. and Jon Klimo, "Fetal Awareness of Maternal Emotional States During Pregnancy." *Journal of Prenatal and Perinatal Psychology and Health* 15(2000): 118–145.

71. *New York Newsday*, February 8, 1994, p. 69.

72. Thomas R. Verny, "Womb Ecology/World Ecology." Talk delivered at 2nd World Congress for Prenatal Education, Athens, Greece, May 14, 1994.

73. H. P. David et al., Eds., *Born Unwanted: Developmental Effects of Denied Abortion*. Avicenum: Prague, 1988.

74. Lester Sontag, "Implications of Fetal Behavior and Environment for Adult Personalities." *Annals of the New York Academy of Sciences* 134 (1965): 782–786.

75. Robert Goodlin, *Care of the Fetus*, p. 10; Dennis H. Stott, testimony, in Senate of Canada: Standing Senate Committee on Health, Welfare and Science. Third Session, Thirtieth Parliament, 1977, "Childhood Experiences of Criminal Behavior," Issue No. 1, Second Proceeding, Nov. 24, 1977.

76. *Child At Risk: A Report of the Standing Senate Committee on Health, Welfare and Science*. Hull: Canadian Government Publishing Center, 1980, p. 16.

during pregnancy.[77] Maternal emotional stress, hostility toward the fetus, and fetal distress have also been statistically correlated in various studies with more premature births, lower birth weights, more neonate neurotransmitter imbalances, more clinging infant patterns, more childhood psychopathology, more physical illness, higher rates of schizophrenia, lower IQ in early childhood, greater school failure, higher delinquency, and greater propensity as an adult to use drugs, commit violent crimes, and commit suicide.[78] This increase in social violence due to pre- and perinatal conditions has been confirmed by a major Danish study showing that boys of mothers who do not want to have them (25 percent of pregnant mothers admit they do not want their babies)[79] and who also experience birth complications are four

---

77. Margaret E. Fries, "Longitudinal Study: Prenatal Period to Parenthood." *Journal of the American Psychoanalytic Association* 25(1977): 115–140; Margaret E. Fries, Marie Coleman Nelson, and Paul J. Woolf, "Developmental and Etiological Factors in the Treatment of Character Disorders with Archaic Ego Function." *The Psychoanalytic Review* 67(1980): 337–352.

78. Lorraine Roth Herrenkohl, "The Anxiety-Prone Personality: Effects of Prenatal Stress on the Infant." In Roy J. Mathew, Ed., *The Biology of Anxiety*. New York: Brunner/ Mazel, 1982, pp. 51–86; Antonio J. Ferreira, "The Pregnant Woman's Emotional Attitude and Its Reflection on the Newborn." *American Journal of Orthopsychiatry* 30 (1960): 553– 556; *Child At Risk: A Report of the Standing Senate Committee on Health, Welfare and Science.* Hull: Canadian Government Publishing Center, 1980; John H. W. Barrett, "Prenatal Influences on Adaptation in the Newborn." In Peter Stratton, Ed., *Psychobiology of the Human Newborn.* New York: John Wiley & Sons, 1982, p. 270; *Psychology Today*, 4 (1971): 49; Abram Blau, et al., "The Psychogenic Etiology of Premature Births." *Psychosomatic Medicine* 25 (1963): 201–211; A. J. Ward, "Prenatal stress and childhood psychopathology." *Child Psychiatry and Human Development* 22 (1991): 97–110; Lars Billing, et al., "The Influence of Environmental Factors on Behavioral Problems in 8-Year-Old Children Exposed to Amphetamine During Fetal Life." *Child Abuse & Neglect* 18 (1994): 3–9; D. H. Stott, "Follow-up Study from Birth of the Effects of Prenatal Stress." *Developmental Medicine and Child Neurology* 15 (1973): 770–787; Norman L. Corah, et al., "Effects of Perinatal Anoxia After Seven Years." *Psychological Monographs* 79 (1965): 1–32; Sarnoff A. Mednick, "Birth Defects and Schizophrenia," *Psychology Today* 4 (1971): 48–50; Sarnoff A. Mednick et al., Eds., *Fetal Neural Development and Adult Schizophrenia.* New York: Cambridge University Press, 1991; "Delinquents Said to Have Perinatal Injuries," *Psychiatric News*, September 1, 1978, p. 26; David B. Chamberlain, "Prenatal Intelligence." In Thomas Blum, Ed., *Prenatal Perception, Learning and Bonding.* Berlin: Leonardo Publishers, 1993, pp. 14–21; A. J. Ward, "Prenatal Stress and Childhood Psychopathology." *Child Psychiatry and Human Development* 22(1991): 97–110; Adrian Raine, *The Psychopathology of Crime: Criminal Behavior as a Clinical Disorder.* San Diego: Academic Press, 1993.

79. Elaine Morgan, *The Descent of the Child: Human Evolution from a New Perspective.* New York: Oxford University Press, 1995, p. 78.

times more likely when they get to be teenagers to commit violent crimes than control groups.[80] American studies show similar higher violent crime rates correlated with maternal rejection during pregnancy.[81]

THE NEUROBIOLOGY OF EARLY TRAUMA

There are sound neurobiological reasons for this correlation between fetal trauma and social violence. Early brain development is determined both by genes and by cellular selection and self-organizational processes that are crucially dependent on the uterine environment.[82] Since fetal and early infantile traumas and abandonments occur while the brain is still being formed, while cell adhesion molecules are still determining the brain's initial mapping processes, and while synaptic connections are still undergoing major developmental changes, memories of early traumas cannot be handled as traumas are later in life and instead are coded in separate neuronal networks that retain their emotional power well into adulthood.[83]

Infants traumatized in utero and during birth are those Winnicott referred to as "born paranoid," and can remain hypersensitive to stress, overly fearful, withdrawn, and angry all of their lives. Fetal traumas and abandonments result in overstimulation of neurotransmitters, producing hypersensitivity and other imbalances in such important neurotransmitters as the catecholamines. The most important of these imbalances is low serotonin levels, which have been demonstrated to lead to persistent hyperarousal and compulsive reenactment in violent social behavior, including both homicide and suicide.[84] Because of this, reenactment in later life can be an even more

---

80. Adrian Raine, Patricia Brennan, Sarnoff A. Mednick, "Birth Complications Combined With Early Maternal Rejection at Age 1 Year Predispose to Violent Crime at Age 18 Years." *Archives of General Psychiatry* 51(1994): 984–988; Henry P. David, Zilenek Dybrich, Zilenek Matejcek, and Vratislav Schuller, *Born Unwanted: Developmental Effects of Denied Abortion.* New York: Springer Publications, 1988.

81. *The New York Times* October 3, 1995, pp. C1 and C10.

82. Michael S. Gazzaniga, *Nature's Mind: the Biological Roots of Thinking, Emotions, Sexuality, Language, and Intelligence.* New York: Basic Books, 1992.

83. Gerald M. Edelman, *The Remembered Present: A Biological Theory of Consciousness.* New York: Basic Books, 1989, p. 44; Joseph E. LeDoux, "Emotion, Memory and the Brain." *Scientific American*, June 1994, pp. 50–57.

84. Bessel A. van der Kolk and Jose Saporta, "The Biological Response to Psychic Trauma: Mechanisms and Treatment of Intrusion and Numbing." *Anxiety Research* 4(1991):

potent source of violent behavior in the case of fetal trauma than it has been found to be in the case of childhood or war trauma.[85]

The same neurobiological factors have been found to be responsible for the increase in violence against self. Suicide patterns are so strongly linked to birth that epidemiologists have found higher suicide rates in areas of the country that a few decades earlier had had higher birth injuries.[86] What happens is that birth traumas reset lifelong serotonin and noradrenaline levels to lower levels, since there is a strong statistical link between low serotonin and noradrenaline and violent suicides.[87] Other studies have shown that even the *types* of suicides were correlated with the kinds of perinatal traumas: asphyxia during birth leads to more suicides through strangulation, hanging, and drowning; mechanical trauma during birth correlates with mechanical suicide elements; drugs given during birth correlate to suicide by drugs; and so on.

Far from being the safe, cozy haven to which we all supposedly want to return, the womb is in fact often a dangerous and often painful abode,[88] where "more lives are lost during the nine gestational months than in the ensuing 50 years of postnatal life."[89] As the placenta stops growing during the final months of pregnancy, it regresses in efficiency, becoming tough and fibrous, as its cells and blood vessels degenerate and it becomes full of blood clots and calcifications, making the fetus even more susceptible to hypoxia (low oxygen) as it grows larger and making the late-term fetus "extremely hypoxic by adult standards."[90] Furthermore, the weight of the fetus pressing down

---

199–212; Herbert Hendin, *Suicide in America: New and Expanded Edition.* New York: W. W. Norton & Co., 1995, p. f16.

85. Jan Volavka, *Neurobiology of Violence.* Washington, DC: American Psychiatric Press, 1995; M. J. P. Kruesi, "Cruelty to Animals and CSF 5-HIAA." *Psychiatry Research* 28(1989): 115–116; Bessel A. van der Kolk, "The Trauma Spectrum: The Interaction of Biological and Social Events in the Genesis of the Trauma Response." *Journal of Traumatic Stress* 1(1988): 273–290.

86. Bertil Jacobson, "Perinatal Origin of Eventual Self-Destructive Behavior." *Pre- and Peri-Natal Psychology* 2(1988): 227–241.

87. Ronald Kotulak, *Inside the Brain: Revolutionary Discoveries of How the Mind Works.* Kansas City: Andrews and McMeel, 1996, p. 71.

88. Ernest M. Gruenberg, "On the Psychosomatics of the Not-So-Perfect Fetal Parasite." In Stephen A. Richardson and Alan F. Guttmacher, Eds., *Childbearing: Its Social and Psychological Aspects.* New York: Williams & Wilkins, 1967, p. 54.

89. Roger E. Stevenson, *The Fetus and Newly Born Infant: Influences of the Prenatal Environment.* 2nd Ed. St. Louis: C. V. Mosby, 1977, p. 3.

90. Heinz Bartels. *Prenatal Respiration.* New York: John Wiley and Sons, 1970, p. 47.

into the pelvis can compress blood vessels supplying the placenta, producing additional placental failure.[91] Practice contractions near birth give the fetus periodic "squeezes," decreasing oxygen level even further,[92] while birth itself is so stressful that "hypoxia of a certain degree and duration is a normal phenomenon in every delivery."[93] The effects on the fetus of this extreme hypoxia are dramatic: normal fetal breathing stops, fetal heart rate accelerates, then decelerates, and the fetus thrashes about frantically in a life-and-death struggle to liberate itself from its terrifying asphyxiation.[94]

THE REALITY OF FETAL MEMORY

That the fetal memory system is sufficiently mature not only to *learn* in the womb but also to *remember* prenatal and birth experiences is confirmed by a growing body of experimental, observational, and clinical data. Neonates can remember lullabies learned prenatally[95] and can pick out at birth their mothers' voices from among other female voices and respond differently (by the increased rate of sucking on a pacifier) to familiar melodies they had heard in utero.[96] As evidence of even more complex memories,

91. A. Briend, "Fetal Malnutrition: The Price of Upright Posture?" *British Medical Journal* 2(1979): 317–319.

92. Joseph Barcroft, *Researches in Pre-Natal Life*. Vol. 1. Springfield, IL: Charles C. Thomas, 1947, p. 209.

93. Lubor Jilek et al., "Characteristic Metabolic and Functional Responses to Oxygen Deficiency in the Central Nervous System." In Uwe Stave, Ed., *Physiology of the Perinatal Period*, p. 1043.

94. Peter Boylan and Peter J. Lewis, "Fetal Breathing in Labor." *Obstetrics and Gynecology* 56 (1980): 35–38; Peter Lewis, Peter Boylan, "Fetal Breathing: A Review." *American Journal of Obstetrics and Gynecology* 134 (1979): 270–275; Uwe Stave, Ed., *Physiology of the Perinatal Period*. Vol. 2. New York: Appleton-Century-Crofts, 1970, 987–992; Carl Wood, Adrian Walker, and Robert Yardley, "Acceleration of the Fetal Heart Rate." *American Journal of Obstetrics and Gynecology* 134 (1979): 523–527.

95. R. A. Polverini-Rey, *Intrauterine Musical Learning: The Soothing Effect on Newborns of a Lullaby Learned Prenatally*. Doctoral Thesis, Los Angeles: California School of Professional Psychology, 1992.

96. Anthony J. DeCasper and W. P. Fifer, "Of Human Bonding: Newborns Prefer Their Mother's Voices." *Science* 208 (1980): 1174–1176; P. G. Hepper and S. Shahidullah, "Newborn and Fetal Response to Maternal Voice." *Journal of Reproduction and Infant Psychology* 11(1993): 147–153; Thomas R. Verny, "The Scientific Basis of Pre- and Peri-Natal Psychology: Part 1." *Pre- and Peri-Natal Psychology* 3 (1989): 162–164; William P. Fifer, "Neonatal Preference for Mother's Voice." In Norman A. Krasnegor, et al., Eds., *Perinatal*

DeCasper had 16 pregnant women read either *The Cat in the Hat* or a second poem with a different meter to their fetuses twice a day for the last six weeks of their pregnancy.[97] When the babies were born, he hooked up their pacifiers to a mechanism that allowed them to chose one of two tape recordings by sucking slowly or quickly, choosing either the tape in which their mothers read the familiar poem or the tape where she read the unfamiliar poem. The babies soon were listening to the tape of the familiar poem, indicating their mastery of the task of remembering complex speech patterns learned in utero. Chamberlain sums up his extensive work on birth memories, which he found very reliable when comparing them with both the memories of the mother and hospital records: "They demonstrate the same clear awareness of violence, danger, and breech of trust which any of us adults might show in a similar situation. . . . Even three-year-olds sometimes have explicit and accurate birth recall."[98]

THE FINDINGS OF ULTRASOUND RESEARCH

Perhaps the most impressive observational work on the personality of the fetus is being done by the Italian psychoanalyst Alessandra Piontelli, by combining thousands of hours of ultrasound observations with clinical psychoanalytic work with young children. Her research into perinatal memories began after she encountered an 18-month-old child who was reported by sensitive parents as being incessantly restless and unable to sleep:

> I noted that he seemed to move about restlessly almost as if obsessed by a search for something in every possible corner of the limited space of my consulting room, looking for something which he never seemed able to find. His parents commented on this, saying that he acted like that all the time, day and night. Occasionally Jacob also tried to shake

Development: A Psychobiological Perspective. New York: Academic Press, 1987, pp. 111–115; Robert C. Goodlin, *Cry of the Fetus*. New York: Masson Publishing, 1979, p. 11.

97. Anthony DeCasper, "Studying Learning in the Womb." *Science*, 225 (1984): p. 384; "Human Fetuses Perceive Maternal Speech." *Behavior Today*, February 4, 1985, pp. 1–7.

98. David B. Chamberlain, "Prenatal Intelligence." In Thomas Blum, Ed., *Prenatal Perception*, pp. 20–21; David Chamberlain, *Babies Remember Birth*. Los Angeles: Jeremy P. Tarcher, 1988.

several of the objects inside my room, as if trying to bring them back to life. His parents then told me that any milestone in his development (such as sitting up, crawling, walking, or uttering his first words) all seemed to be accompanied by intense anxiety and pain as if he were afraid, as they put it, 'to leave something behind him.' When I said very simply to him that he seemed to be looking for something that he had lost and could not find anywhere, Jacob stopped and looked at me very intently. I then commented on his trying to shake all the objects to life as if he were afraid that their stillness meant death. His parents almost burst into tears and told me that Jacob was, in fact, a twin, but that his co-twin, Tino, as they had already decided to call him, had died two weeks before birth. Jacob, therefore, had spent almost two weeks in utero with his dead and consequently unresponsive co-twin.[99]

Verbalization of his fears that each step forward in his development might be accompanied by the death of a loved one for whom he felt himself to be responsible "brought about an incredible change in his behavior," says Piontelli.

THE POISONOUS PLACENTA

Until birth is complete, the fetus, of course, has never met a "mother," only a womb, a placenta, and an umbilicus. Piontelli's ultrasound observations reveal the complex relationship between the fetus and its placental/umbilical "first object." Fetuses stroke and explore the placenta in front of it all the time, and grab the umbilicus for comfort when distressed. Their behavior toward the placenta and umbilicus correlates with later behavior patterns in their infancy, so that, for instance, when Piontelli watches one fetus use the placenta as a pillow in the womb, observing it "sucking the cord [and] resting on the placenta as if it were a big pillow . . . burying himself in the placenta . . . as if it were a pillow," she then notices it has difficulty sucking the mother's breast after birth, preferring to use it as a pillow instead: "He is not sucking . . . he is leaning against it . . . it's not a pillow you know!"[100]

---

99. Alessandra Piontelli, *From Fetus to Child: An Observational and Psychoanalytic Study*. London: Tavistock/Routledge, 1992, p. 18.

100. Piontelli, *From Fetus to Child*, pp. 114, 120.

Overt placental images are often found by clinicians in deeply regressed patients, who often hallucinate bloodsucking monsters persecuting them. Most of these monster-phobias are extremely frightening, the patients fearing bloodsucking spiders or vampires or octopuses or Medusas or sphinxes.[101] It simply makes no sense to call these bloodsucking beasts and spiders "phallic mothers," as Freud and Abraham did,[102] particularly when they are accompanied by umbilical droplines.[103] The vampire as a blood-drinking woman is another widespread fantasy of patients.

THE FETAL DRAMA IN HISTORY

However disguised, the Poisonous Placenta and the Suffering Fetus are the most important images of the fetal drama, and the restaging of their violent encounter is a central religious and political task of society. I suggest that this battle with the persecuting placental beast constitutes the earliest source of war and social violence, traumas that must be restaged periodically because of the neurobiological imperatives of early brain development. The center of society is wherever the fetal drama is restaged—as at Delphi, it is often called the "navel of the world," and is associated with placental World Tree worship.[104] The evolution of society occurs as this fetal drama moves from tribe to kingdom to nation and is enacted with larger and larger numbers of people emotionally entrained through sacrificial rituals.

Group-fantasies of poisonous blood become particularly widespread after periods of progress and prosperity. They are particularly ubiquitous during apocalyptic millenarian periods. Traditional historians have blamed these apocalyptic fantasies, such as the periodic "Great Awakenings" in America[105] or the millenarian movements in England,[106] upon "collective

101. Ralph B. Little, "Spider Phobias." *Psychoanalytic Quarterly* 36(1967): 51–60.

102. Leonard Shengold, "The Effects of Overstimulation: Rat People." *International Journal of Psycho-Analysis* 48(1967): 409.

103. Ralph B. Little, "Umbilical Cord Symbolism of the Spider's Dropline." *Psychoanalytic Quarterly* 35(1966): 587–590.

104. E. A. S. Butterworth, *The Tree at the Navel of the Earth*. Berlin: Walter DeGruyter & Co., 1970.

105. Michael Barkun. *Disaster and the Millenium*. New Haven: Yale University Press, 1974.

106. J. F. C. Harrison, *The Second Coming: Popular Millenarianism 1780–1850*. London: Routledge & Kegan Paul, 1979.

stress."[107] The problem is that these movements always occur after periods of progress, peace, and prosperity. In fact, what is feared and what leads to the deepest regression is growth and new challenges, a growth that threatens a repetition of early traumas.

Ancient societies used to believe that because of growing pollution the universe periodically threatened to dissolve in primordial waters, and unless a war was fought between a hero and an asphyxiating sea monster, the world would disappear.[108] The purpose of war and all other sacrificial bloodletting, says Frazer, was "to reinforce by a river of human blood the tide of life which might grow stagnant and stale in the veins of the dieties."[109] We continue to believe the same right up into modern times—as Chapter 6 will document, most nations have repeated the cleansing war ritual four times a century for as far back as historical records have survived.[110]

THE NEUROBIOLOGY OF EARLY TRAUMA

The neurobiological effects of trauma and neglect—both prenatal and during childhood—and the compulsion to restage early traumatic violence and inflict it upon others and upon one's self are becoming fairly well understood through recent advances in neuroscience. Inescapable dangers and intolerable stresses subject the brain to massive secretions and subsequent depletions of a variety of neurotransmitters, including norephinephrine, dopamine, and serotonin, which lead to hypervigilance, explosive anger, and excessive sensitivity to similar events in the future that are ex-

107. Michael Barkun. *Crucible of the Millennium: The Burned-Over District of New York in the 1840s.* Syracuse: Syracuse University Press, 1986, p. 143.

108. Mircea Eliade, *The Myth of the Eternal Return; or, Cosmos and History.* Princeton: Princeton University Press, 1954; Mircea Eliade, *Rites and Symbols of Initiation: The Mysteries of Birth and Rebirth.* New York: Harper & Row, 1958; Norman Cohn, *Cosmos, Chaos and the World to Come.* New Haven: Yale University Press, 1993; Joseph L. Henderson and Maud Oakes, *The Wisdom of the Serpent: Myths of Death, Rebirth, and Resurrection.* Princeton: Princeton University Press, 1963.

109. James George Frazer, *The Golden Bough. Third Edition. Part VI. The Scapegoat.* New York: St. Martin's Press, 1913, p. vi.

110. Frank H. Denton and Warren Phillips, "Some Patterns in the History of Violence." *Conflict Resolution* 12(1968): 182–195.

perienced as though they were as dangerous as the earlier incident.[111] In addition, the hormones—especially cortisol—that flood the brain to mobilize it in the face of threats have been found to be toxic to cells in the hippocampus, the part of the brain that is the center of the neural system for consciousness, actually killing neurons and reducing the size of the hippocampus, making modification of early traumas nearly impossible.[112] Without the ability to remember and modify early traumas through new experiences, the brain continues to interpret ordinary stresses as recurrences of traumatic events long after the original trauma has ceased.

Paranoid results are particularly true of the earliest traumas of fetal and infantile life. This is so because the hippocampus is quite immature until the third or fourth year of life, and therefore the early trauma is encoded in the emotional memory system centering deep in the amygdala and extending particularly to the prefrontal cortex, the center of emotions[113]—memories that have been described as being nearly "impervious to extinction."[114] Early traumas record fearful memories that remain powerful for life, long after the memories of the traumatic event itself are forgotten.[115]

---

111. John P. Wilson, *Trauma, Transformation and Healing: An Integrative Approach to Theory, Research, and Post-Traumatic Therapy*. New York: Brunner/Mazel, 1989, pp. 27–33; Bessel A. van der Kolk and Jose Saporta, "The Biological Response to Psychic Trauma: Mechanisms and Treatment of Intrusion and Numbing." *Anxiety Research* 4(1991): 199–212; M. Michele Murburg, Ed. *Catecholamine Function in Posttraumatic Stress Disorder: Emerging Concepts*. Washington, DC: American Psychiatric Press, 1994.

112. J. Douglas Bremner, et al., "MRI-Based Measurement of Hippocampal Volume in Patients With Combat-Related Posttraumatic Stress Disorder." *American Journal of Psychiatry* 152(1995): 973–980; *The New York Times*, August 1, 1995, p. C3.

113. Anthony Demasio, *Decartes' Error: Emotion, Reason, and the Human Brain*. New York: Bantam, 1995.

114. Michael Davis, "The Role of the Amygdala in Conditioned Fear." In John P. Aggleton, Ed., *The Amygdala: Neurobiological Aspects of Emotion, Memory, and Mental Dysfunction*. New York: John Wiley & Sons, 1992, pp. 255–305; Joseph E. LeDoux, "Emotion and the Amygdala." In Ibid., p. 344.

115. Joseph E. LeDoux, "Emotion, Memory and the Brain." *Scientific American*, June, 1994, pp. 50–57. Van der Kolk and Saporta, "The Biological Response to Psychic Trauma," p. 204. LeDoux's two memory systems are divided somewhat differently into thalamocortical and limbic systems in Gerald M. Edelman, *The Remembered Present: A Biological Theory of Consciousness*. New York: Basic Books, 1989, p. 152. For multiple memory systems, see Daniel L. Schacter and Endel Tulving, *Memory Systems 1994*. Cambridge, MA: The MIT Press, 1994.

CULTURE AND HISTORY AS HOMEOSTATIC MECHANISMS

The social restaging of early trauma and neglect, predicated upon damaged neuronal and hormonal systems, is thus a homeostatic mechanism of the brain, achieved by groups through wars, economic domination, and social violence. Each of us constructs a separate neural system for these early traumas and their defenses—a dissociated, organized personality system that stores, defends against, and elaborates these early fetal, infantile, and childhood traumas as we grow up. Once this basic concept is realized, all the rationalizations of history become transparent. For instance, when Germans say they had to start World War II to get "revenge for the Day of Shame," one can ignore the ostensible reference (the Treaty of Versailles) and recognize instead the *real* source of "German shame"—the routine humiliations, beatings, sexual abuse, and betrayals of German children by their caregivers (see Chapter 6).

THE LEADER AS POISON CONTAINER

Because the fetus's umbilicus is like a pulsing fifth limb and because the placenta is the fetus's first love object, I believe we so deeply experience the loss of our umbilicus/placenta that we continue to feel we have still a "phantom placenta"—the same phenomenon as the phantom limb experienced by amputees[116]—and are constantly looking for a leader or a flag or a god to serve as its substitute. Just as gods are imagined as beings "from whom all blessings flow," leaders are seen as beings "from whom all power flows." In ancient Egypt, people saved the actual placenta of the Pharaoh and put it on a pole that they carried into battle; it was the first flag in history.[117] In America, we still ritually worship our placental flag—with its red arteries and blue veins at the end of an umbilical flagpole—in public gatherings, and the sacred flag is at the center of every sacrificial ritual called war that binds our

---

116. Amputees feel pain in the missing limb, a pain that disappears only when the physician provides a "mirror box" that allows the amputee to "see" his phantom limb restored; see *U.S. News & World Report*, October 2, 1995, p. 78. It is thus reasonable to assume that people join groups to restore their phantom placentas.

117. Lloyd deMause, *Foundations of Psychohistory*. New York: Creative Roots, 1982, p. 289.

nation together.[118] In Baganda, they put the king's placenta on a throne, prayed to it, and received messages from it through their priests.[119] We do the same when we look to the sky for UFOs—high-tech placental disks— that we hope might have messages for us.[120] Lawson has even experimentally correlated UFO abduction scenarios with the actual birth experiences of the abducted: those who had normal vaginal births imagined tunnel experiences during abduction, while those who had caesarean births experienced being yanked up by the UFO without the tunnel images.[121]

The yearning for a phantom placenta—a "poison container" for our dangerous emotions—to be our leader, and the search for a Poisonous Placenta to be our enemy with whom we can fight, are the central tasks of all social organizations, prior to any utility they may have. Leaders are not just mothers or fathers, and they are not always idealized. They are first and foremost poison containers for our feelings. Poison containers are objects into which we can dump our disowned feelings, just as we once pumped our polluted blood into the placenta, hoping for it to be cleansed.

People ascribe to their political and religious poison containers all kinds of magical placental significances, including the power to cleanse our emotions, which are felt to be like polluted blood. When the leader appears unable to handle these emotions, when he appears to be weakening and abandoning us, when our progress in life seems to involve too much independence and we reexperience our early abandonment by our placenta, we begin to look for enemies to inflict our traumas upon.[122]

WAR AS A SACRIFICIAL RITUAL

War, then, is a sacrificial ritual designed to defend against fears of individuation and abandonment by restaging our early traumas upon scapegoats. This theory is the exact opposite of the "social stress" theories of all

---

118. Carolyn Marvin and David W. Ingle, *Blood Sacrifice and the Nation: Totem Rituals and the American Flag*. Cambridge: Cambridge University Press, 1999.

119. John Roscoe, *The Baganda: An Account of Their Native Customs and Beliefs*. New York: Frank Cass & Co., 1965 (1911).

120. Alvin H. Lawson, "Perinatal Imagery in UFO Abduction Reports." *The Journal of Psychohistory* 12(1984): 211–239.

121. Ibid., p. 218.

122. Lloyd deMause, *Reagan's America*. New York: Creative Roots, 1984.

Fig. 4–4. The leader as a poison container

other social scientists, since it is usually successes—freedom and new challenges—that are experienced as triggers for wars, not economic or political distress. Wars sacrifice youth—symbols of our potency and hopefulness—because it is our striving, youthful, independent selves that we blame for getting us into trouble in the first place. Only if we can stop growing can we protect ourselves from our most horrible fear—the repetition of our earliest tragedies.

The imagery of war as a restaging of birth is ubiquitous. Consider just the birth imagery surrounding the nuclear bomb. When Ernest Lawrence cabled his fellow physicists that the bomb was ready to test, his said, "Congratulations to the new parents. Can hardly wait to see the new arrival."[123] When the bomb was exploded at Los Alamos, a journalist wrote, "One felt as though he had been privileged to witness the Birth of the World . . . the first cry of the newborn world."[124] When President Harry Truman met with world leaders at Postdam just before dropping the bomb on Japan, General Leslie Groves cabled him reporting that its test was successful: "Doctor has just returned most enthusiastic and confident that The Little Boy is as husky as his big brother. . . . I could have heard his screams from here."[125]

123. Herbert Childs, *An American Genius: The Life of Ernest Orlando Lawrence*. New York: Dutton, 1968, p. 340.

124. Ira Chernus, *Dr. Strangegod: On the Symbolic Meaning of Nuclear Weapons*. Columbia: University of South Carolina Press, 1986, p. 86.

125. Charles L. Mee, Jr. *Meeting at Postsdam*. New York: Evans and Co., 1975, p. 29.

When the Hiroshima bomb, named "Little Boy," was dropped from the belly of a plane—named after the pilot's mother—General Groves cabled Truman: "The baby was born." Even the survivors of the Hiroshima explosion usually referred to the bomb as "the original child."[126] Similarly, when the first hydrogen bomb was exploded, Edward Teller's telegram read, "It's a boy."[127] Obviously, nukes are felt to be powerful babies—avenging fetuses. With them, our revenge for our early traumas can now be infinite. One can see why Truman, hearing that the world's first nuclear bomb had just been dropped, exclaimed, "This is the greatest thing in history!"[128]

GROWTH PANICS AND INTERNAL SACRIFICES

Wars are sacrificial defenses that have proven to be effective in reducing fears of ego disintegration due to growth panic. But even more effective than sacrificing mothers and children in external wars is the *internal*, institutionalized wars against mothers and children that nations conduct periodically as social policy. Structural violence (excess deaths because of poverty alone) amount to 15 million persons a year worldwide, compared to an average 100,000 deaths per year from wars.[129] Economic downturns alone hurt or kill more mothers and children as sacrificial victims than most wars.[130] As in foreign wars (external sacrifices), economic wars against mothers and children (internal sacrifices) are regularly conducted even during periods of peace. These internal wars parallel the regressive images we have been discussing; for instance, as William Joseph found in studying the 1929 and 1987 stock market crashes, images of dangerous women proliferated in the media, indicating that the time for an internal sacrifice was near.[131]

---

126. Thomas Merton, *Original Child Bomb*. New York: New Directions, 1962.

127. Carol Cohn, "'Clean Bombs' and Clean Language." In Jean Bethke Elshtain and Sheila Tobias, Eds., *Women, Militarism, and War: Essays in History, Politics, and Social Theories*. Savage, MD: Rowman & Littlefield, 1990, p. 41.

128. Robert J. Lifton, *The Broken Connection*. New York: Simon & Schuster, 1979, p. 371.

129. James Gilligan, *Violence: Our Deadly Epidemic and Its Causes*. New York: G. P. Putnam's Sons, 1992, pp. 195–196.

130. Lloyd deMause, *Reagan's America*. New York: Creative Roots, 1984, p. 66.

131. William K. Joseph, "Prediction, Psychology and Economics." *The Journal of Psychohistory* 15(1987): 110–111.

That a prosperous America has arranged to have a third of its people live in poverty is a clue to why nations need poor people to punish for their prosperity. Since it is prosperity and the fear of intolerable growth that triggers the restaging of trauma, it makes sense that America today—the most prosperous and freest nation of any in history—has more women and children living in poverty than any other industrialized nation. American child poverty rates are four times those of most European nations, and are getting worse, rising 25 percent in recent years.[132] Childhood poverty in particular is a result of national policy; as one expert put it: "Children do not catch poverty but are made poor by state neglect."[133] All these deprived children are emotional scapegoats, poison containers for the wealth of the top rung of American society.

Economic success gives people increased opportunities for individuation; national prosperity and peace are therefore dangerous: "If I grow and enjoy myself, something terrrible will happen." Periods of extended prosperity without external "enemies" therefore produce *growth panics* that require sacrificial victims, whether in Hebrew or Aztec ritual sacrifice yesterday or in today's economic cycles. In good economic times, such as during the Clinton years, legislators in America, with the support of the majority of citizens, vigorously cut all kinds of aid to children. In New York City, 39 percent of the children are on welfare; in Chicago, 46 percent; in Detroit, 67 percent; and antiwelfare legislation has everywhere been put into effect.[134] In 1996, at the peak of our current prosperity, Americans of both parties, with the approval of the president, cut nutrition assistance for 14 million children and Social Security for 750,000 disabled children, along with cuts in school lunches, Head Start, child protection, education, child health care, and aid to homeless children—what the president of the Children's Defense Fund described as "an unbelievable budget massacre of the weakest."[135] Someone has to pay for our prosperity. That someone is our children. Scapegoating children in prosperous times isn't paradoxical; it's a historical regularity.

---

132. Duncan Lindsey, *The Welfare of Children*. New York: Oxford University Press, 1994, p. 224.

133. Ibid., p. 214.

134. Lars-Erik Nelson, "Welfare Plan Will Dump Children on the Streets." *Liberal Opinion Week*, September 18, 1995, p. 3.

135. *The New York Times*, October 23, 1995, p. A15; *The New York Times*, November 6, 1995, p. A17.

Fig. 4–5. Government as a devouring vampire

    That the group-fantasies behind cutting benefits for women and chil-
dren are similar to the bloodsucking fantasies discussed above could be
seen in any of the vampire movies that appeared at the same time or in the
fantasies of those in Congress and the media who claimed that welfare
recipients were "bleeding us dry" and "sucking the blood out of the citi-
zenry [like] a giant leech"—punishment for which was for the government
to "suck the blood" out of welfare recipients.[136] As presidential candidate
Senator Phil Gramm said, "If we continue to pay mothers who have illegitimate children, the country will soon have more illegitimate than legitimate
children," all feeding off of us. Historically, during every period of prosperity in American history (such as in the 1850s and the 1890s), there has been
legislation by the newly wealthy to stop welfare for what they called "the
undeserving poor." Antiwelfare legislation, now as then, had nothing to do
with saving money; in fact, the cuts would cost a hundred times more than
their savings through increases in drug addiction, theft, and murder. Each
time legislators condemn "moral decay" and "a breakdown in family values"—
code words for fear of freedom—they only mean that in fantasy social collapse can be avoided by "ending dependency"—code words for punishing
poor children, symbols of their own dependency needs.
    Although these conclusions about the relative permanence of early
trauma and its inevitable restaging in war, social violence, and economic

---

136. *The Washington Post*, February 26, 1995, p. C7.

injustice admittedly are discouraging, an awareness of the source of human violence can actually be enormously hopeful. For if early traumas rather than aggressive human nature are the cause of our violence, then efforts to radically reduce these traumas can be reasonably expected to reduce war and social domination. If, rather than continuing the millennia-old historical cycle of traumatized adults inflicting their inner terrors upon their children, we try kindness instead, effectively helping mothers and children as a society rather than burdening, abandoning, or punishing them, we will soon be able to end our need to reenact our traumatic memories on the social stage. Chapter 9 describes a new social outreach program consisting of parenting centers with home visiting programs, which can finally end the child abuse upon which wars and social violence are based. Only by investing in such a program, based on the real wealth of nations—its children—can the world eliminate its self-destructive violence and domination and live in peace and equality at last.

5

The Psychogenic Theory of History

"Trauma demands repetition."
—Selma Fraiberg

Social scientists have rarely been interested in psychology. Using the model of Newtonian physics, they have usually depicted individuals as opaque billiard balls bouncing off each other. That individuals might have their own complex internal motivations for the way they act in society—that they have emotions that affect their social behavior—has rarely been acknowledged. The social sciences reflect our routine habit of blaming the world outside ourselves rather than our inner decisions for our behavior. The most interesting question about any group—"Why are they doing that?"—is rarely asked. Durkheim, in fact, founded sociology with studies of suicide and incest that claimed these very private acts were wholly without individual psychological causes, claiming that understanding individual motivations is irrelevant to understanding society.[1] By eliminating psychology from the social sciences, Durkheim laid down the principle followed by most social theorists today: "The determining cause of a social fact should be sought among the social facts preceding it and not among the states of individual consciousness."[2]

THE DENIAL OF PSYCHOLOGY IN THE STUDY OF SOCIETY

Sociologists still echo Durkheim's bias against psychology. Most agree with the sociologist C. Wright Mills, who advised me when I was his research

---

1. Emile Durkheim, *Suicide: A Study in Sociology.* Glencoe, IL: Free Press, 1951; *Incest: The Nature and Origin of the Taboo.* New York: L. Stuart, 1963.
2. Emile Durkheim, *The Rules of the Sociological Method.* Glencoe, IL: Free Press, 1962 (1895), p. 110.

assistant at Columbia University, "Study enough psychoanalysis to make sure you can answer the bastards when they attack you." Most sociologists agree: "There is a strong tradition in modern scholarship in the human sciences of ignoring emotions as causes."[3] Political scientists follow the same assumptions: "Political attitudes are generally assumed to be the result of a rational, reflective process."[4] Most anthropologists concur: "The science of culture is independent of the laws of biology and psychology."[5] Those anthropologists who have studied the effects of childhood on culture have been grossly ignored by other anthropologists who maintain that anthropology has no concern with the inner states of its subjects.[6] Most historians, too, have assiduously avoided psychology, either saying that history "consists in saying what happened," no more,[7] or trying to explain history by "impersonal structural forces," as though such a passionate human enterprise as history could be "impersonal."

This denial of the importance of individual emotional life on societies has been at the center of the social science theory since its beginnings. The actions of individuals in society have a priori been assumed by social philosophers from Hobbes to Marx to be determined by pure self-interest, "a war of every man against every man," based on an assumed utilitarian nature of humanity.[8] The same is true of economics. As one economist puts it, "Economic man must be both rational and greedy."[9] Humans acting in society might be shortsighted or uninformed, but they can never be unreasonable, self-destructive, or vicious—that is, not human.

---

3. Thomas J. Scheff, *Bloody Revenge: Emotions, Nationalism, and War*. Boulder: Westview Press, 1994, p. 63. Scheff's work is an exception to this tradition. Two earlier theories of social change that contained psychological dimensions have been ignored by academics: Everett Hagen, *On the Theory of Social Change*. Homewood, IL: Dorsey Press, 1962, and David McClelland, *The Achieving Society*. New York: Van Nostrand, 1961.

4. Michael A. Milburn and S. D. Conrad, "The Politics of Denial." *The Journal of Psychohistory* 23(1996): 238.

5. G. P. Murdock, "The Science of Culture." *American Anthropologist*, 34(1932): 200.

6. Raymond Firth, *Elements of Social Organization*. New York: Philosophical Library, 1956, p. 224.

7. Paul Veyne, *Writing History*. Middletown: Wesleyan University Press, 1984, p. 183.

8. Thomas Hobbes, *Leviathan*. Baltimore: Penguin Books, 1968, p. 186. To see how little the psychology of social action has changed for most social theorists, see John Sinisi, "The Shadow of Hobbes." *Rethinking Marxism* 7(1994): 87–99.

9. George P. Brockway, *The End of Economic Man: Principles of Any Future Economics*. New York: HarperCollins, 1986, p. 16.

The exclusion of the most powerful human feelings other than greed from social theory and the elimination of irrationality and self-destructiveness from models of society explain why the social sciences have such a dismal record in providing any historical theories worth studying. As long as social structure and culture are deemed to lie solely outside human psyches, personal motivations are bound to be considered secondary, reactive to outside conditions rather than themselves being determinative for social behavior.

THE NEUROBIOLOGY OF HISTORY

Although history is obviously not reducible to human biology, a historian cannot avoid contending with the hard facts of neurobiology, since the mind—and therefore the brain—is a highly complex, flawed end result of an extremely imperfect evolutionary process. Society is the way it is because the brain is constructed the way it is, and this depends on the specific way the brain has evolved. Societies are not constructed in the most logical or even most adaptive forms possible. Given the hominid brain we started with, even the most bizarre forms of society revealed by the historical record can be understood as the flawed products of evolving psyches and evolving brains. It is therefore essential that one understands the latest concepts in what has been called the "social neurosciences"[10] that are beginning to be able to determine the effects of early interpersonal experiences between parents and children on the neurobiological development of the brain.

Since, as the neurobiologist Gerald Edelman has put it, "The likelihood of guessing how the brain works without looking at its structure seems slim,"[11] we will begin with a brief overview of brain structure. The brain is composed of over 100 billion neurons, with trillions of connections, dendrites, which are branching extensions from the body of the neuron that pass stimuli received by axons on to other neurons through synapses, the specialized connections between neurons. Since this synaptic activity is either excitatory or

---

10. B. Hopkins and G. Butterworth, "Concepts of Causality in Explanations of Development." In G. Butterworth and P. Bryant, *Causes of Development.* Hillsdale, NJ: Lawrence Erlbaum Assoc., 1990, p. 3.

11. Gerald M. Edelman, *Bright Air, Brilliant Fire: On the Matter of the Mind.* New York: Basic Books, 1992, p. 68.

inhibitory, much of mental life and therefore of social life is either manic or depressive, and the main task of a leader is therefore to adjust through manic and depressive political projects the level of excitation of the brain to achieve a homeostasis of brain activity through social action.

Memorization is thought to occur through repeated stimulation of synapses, making them grow bigger and stronger, as neurotransmitters are released across synaptic gaps.[12] Specific memories are stored all over the brain, in a much more fractured way than a computer stores memory in many files. Early emotional memories are indexed in a network centering in the amygdala, while the conscious self system is indexed more in the hippocampus and orbital prefrontal cortex,[13] giving the brain the ability to retrieve information stored elsewhere and providing a working memory system that receives feelings from the amygdalan emotional network.[14]

The amygdalan network is predominantly excitatory, stimulating externally oriented behavior, and the hippocampus network is predominantly inhibitory, comparing current information with existing knowledge. In current situations of danger, the amygdalan system is the first to make your muscles tense and heart beat faster, while the hippocampal-prefrontal cortical circuit will remember whom you were with and what you were doing during the danger, so as to be able to avoid it in the future.[15] It is the growth of the hippocampus, prefrontal cortex, and related areas that represents the main evolutionary development of self-consciousness (beyond simple growth of cortical storage areas), allowing *Homo sapiens sapiens* to delay responses while comparing them to past experience and self-concepts. When one dreams, one's amygdala lights up in the brain scanner like a pinball machine, as powerful early emotional memories are accessed and incorporated by the hippocampus and prefrontal cortex with current daily events into long-term personality modules. The hippocampal and amygdalan memory systems act like two brains that dissociate more rational conscious self systems from unconscious emotional memories.

---

12. Christof Koch, "Computation and the Single Neuron." *Nature* 385(1997): 207–210.

13. Allan N. Schore, *Affect Regulation and the Origin of the Self: The Neurobiology of Emotional Development*. Hillsdale, NJ: Lawrence Erlbaum, 1994.

14. Neal J. Cohen and Howard Eichenbaum, *Memory, Amnesia, and the Hippocampal System*. Cambridge, MA: MIT Press, 1994.

15. Joseph LeDoux, *The Emotional Brain: The Mysterious Underpinnings of Emotional Life*. New York: Simon & Schuster, 1996, p. 202.

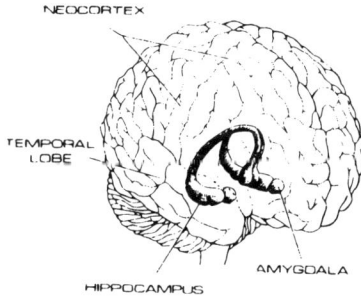

Fig. 5–1. The human brain

When emotional memories are traumatic—either because the trauma was so early that the hippocampus was not yet functional or because it was so powerful that the hippocampal-prefrontal cortical circuit couldn't fully register it—they become permanent, dissociated fears of anything that might resemble the traumatic situation. Traumas that are inescapable because of helplessness can actually severely damage the hippocampus, killing neurons. Survivors of severe childhood abuse and veterans with posttraumatic stress disorder are found to have smaller hippocampal volumes than other patients.[16] This damage is caused by the release during traumatization of a cascade of cortisol, adrenaline, and other stress hormones that not only damage brain cells and impair memory but also set in motion a long-lasting disregulation of the brain's biochemistry. Animals that are traumatized when they are young grow up to be bullies, with less vasopressin, which regulates aggression, and serotonin, the calming neurotransmitter that has been shown to be low in delinquents and in children who have been regularly beaten by their parents.[17] Low serotonin is the most important marker for violence in animals and humans, and has been correlated with high rates of homicide, suicide, arson, antisocial disorders, self-mutilation, and other disorders of

16. J. Douglas Bremner, et al., "MRI-Based Measurement of Hippocampal Volume in Patients with Combat-Related Posttraumatic Stress Disorder." *American Journal of Psychiatry* 152 (1995): 973–980; Katy Butler, "The Biology of Fear." *Family Therapy Networker*, July/August 1996, p. 42.

17. Daniel Goleman, "Early Violence Leaves Its Mark on the Brain." *The New York Times*, October 3, 1995, p. C10; Daviel S. Pine, et al., "Platelet Serotonin 2A (5–HT2A) Receptor Characteristics and Parenting Factors for Boys at Risk for Delinquency." *American Journal of Psychiatry* 153(1996): 538–544.

aggression.[18] Early emotional abandonment by the mother or significant family members regularly lowers the serotonin level of children.

THE PSYCHODYNAMICS OF RESTAGING

The massive secretion of norepinephrine, dopamine, serotonin, and peptides that follows inescapable trauma is followed by a subsequent depletion of hormones, presumably because utilization exceeds synthesis. Eventually receptors of emotion become hypersensitive, leading to excessive responsiveness to even the possibility of trauma in later life.[19] It is this massive "false-alarm system" that leads to reenactments and then to *restagings of trauma*—reenactments with new anxiety-reducing elements—that are at the heart of social behavior in humans.

Depletion of neurotransmitters after traumatic flooding results in hyperalertness to any situations that seem to indicate they may lead to reexperiencing the trauma. This, of course, is true of all animals, and they later simply avoid the dangers in the future. But humans are unique in possessing a developed hippocampal-prefrontal cortical-centered consciousness whose task it is to change action so as to avoid potentially traumatic situations. When trauma occurs, humans are unique in believing they are responsible for the trauma. It is astonishing how early and consistently this is seen in clinical practice. Lenore Terr tells of a girl playing with dolls and repeating her sexual molestation by pornographers that happened when she was 15 months old.[20] She was dissociated from any conscious memories of the events, but accurately repeated being penetrated by an erect penis the same way she had been in the pornographic films, which had been retrieved by the police. What

---

18. Jan Volavka, *Neurobiology of Violence*. Washington, DC: American Psychiatric Press, 1995; P. T. Mehlman, et al., "Low CSF 5-HIAA Concentrations and Severe Aggression and Impaired Impulse Control in Nonhuman Primates." *American Journal of Psychiatry* 151(1994):1483–1492; Herbert Hendin, *Suicide in America: New and Expanded Edition*. New York: W. W. Norton & Co., 1995, p. 17; Ronald M. Winchel, "Self-Mutilation and Aloneness." *Academy Forum*. New York: American Academy of Psychoanalysis, 1991, p. 10.

19. Bessel A. van der Kolk, "The Trauma Spectrum: The Interaction of Biological and Social Events in the Genesis of the Trauma Response." *Journal of Traumatic Stress* 1(1988): 276.

20. Lenore Terr, *Too Scared to Cry: Psychic Trauma in Childhood*. New York: Harper & Row, 1990, p. 30.

was even more astonishing was what she said as she restaged the raping scene: "Who is this? My doll. She's laying on the bed naked. I cover her up. . . . I'm yelling at the doll. She was bad! I yell at my doll, 'You! You bad thing! Get to bed, you!'" She felt guilty about her own rape!

Children almost always feel guilty about being traumatized. "I must have been too noisy, because Mommy left me" was my sincere belief when my mother left my father. I also believed I deserved my father's beatings because I wasn't obedient enough. This is why children set up a separate, internal self (called an *alter*) as a protector to try to stop themselves from ever being noisy, pushy, dirty, sexual, demanding—in fact, to stop themselves from growing and thus having to reexperience trauma. At first, these internal protectors are friendly; sometimes they are represented as imaginary playmates or even as protective alters if the traumas are severe or repetitive.[21] Later, particularly when adolescence brings on opportunities for greater exploration, these protective alters become *persecutory alters* that "have had it" with the host self and actually try to harm it.[22] The persecutory self says, "It's not happening to me, it's happening to her, and she deserves it!" Rather than take a chance that the early trauma will once again catch one unaware and helpless, one might restage the trauma upon oneself or others, at least controlling the timing and intensity of the trauma itself.[23]

Revictimization is actually the central cause of antisocial behavior, and addiction to trauma is at its core.[24] It is not surprising that prison psychiatrists find violent criminals invariably repeat in their crime the emotional traumas, abuse, and humiliation of their childhood,[25] or that women who have been sexually abused in childhood are more than twice as likely as others to be raped when they become adults.[26] As one prostitute who had

---

21. Lisa Goodman and Jay Peters, "Persecutory Alters and Ego States: Protectors, Friends, and Allies." *Dissociation* 8(1995): 92.

22. Ibid., p. 93–94.

23. Spencer Eth and Robert S. Pynoos, *Post-Traumatic Stress Disorder in Children*. Washington, DC: American Psychiatric Press, 1985, p. 142.

24. Bessel A. van der Kolk, "The Compulsion to Repeat the Trauma: Re-enactment, Revictimization, and Masochism." *Psychiatric Clinics of North America* 12(1989): 389–411.

25. James Gilligan, *Violence: Our Deadly Epidemic and Its Causes*. New York: G. P. Putnam's Sons, 1996.

26. David Sandber, et al., "Sexual Abuse and Revictimization: Mastery, Dysfunctional Learning, and Dissociation." In Steven Jay Lynn and Judith W. Rhue, Eds., *Dissociation: Clinical and Theoretical Perspectives*. New York: Guilford Press, 1994, p. 244.

been sexually victimized as a child said, "When I do it, I'm in control. I can control them through sex."[27] *Restaging as a defense against dissociated trauma is the crucial flaw in the evolution of the human mind*—understandable from the viewpoint of the individual as a way of maintaining sanity, but tragic in its effects upon society, since it means that early traumas will be magnified on the historical stage into war, domination, and self-destructive social behavior. History is therefore a social mechanism expected to help keep us personally sane—for controlling maladaptive brain states by restaging early traumas upon others. And because we also restage by inflicting our childhood terrors upon our children, generation after generation, our addiction to the slaughterbench of history has been relentless.

FEARS OF INDIVIDUATION AND GROWTH PANIC

The crowning achievement of the human species—our self-consciousness, the awareness of oneself and others as unique selves with a past history and future goals—has taken so long to evolve and has been so uneven that humanity is a species with extremely fragile selves. Chimpanzees barely have enough self-awareness to recognize themselves in a mirror,[28] and early humans began to evolve self-consciousness through slowly improving parenting, resulting mainly from the mother's growing empathy toward her child (see Chapter 8). Eigen observes from the disintegrating selves of psychotics: "The way individuals are ripped apart by psychotic processes brings home the realization that the emergence of a viable sense of self and other must be counted as one of the most creative achievements of humankind"[29]—an achievement it has taken millennia to accomplish. As Modell points out,[30] the emergent private self grows as the child explores its environment with the regular help of its caregivers. Therefore, children whose immature parents use them for their own emotional needs, and who reject them when the children's needs do not reflect their own, develop what Winnicott calls a "false self," or even multiple selves, which may conform to society but cannot improve upon it. It is because of this that social evolution depends on the

---

27. Ibid.

28. Sue Taylor Parker, et al., Eds., *Self-Awareness in Animals and Humans: Developmental Perspectives*. New York: Cambridge University Press, 1994.

29. Michael Eigen, *The Psychotic Core*. Northvale, NJ: Jason Aronson, 1986, p. 29.

30. Arnold H. Modell, *The Private Self*. Cambridge, MA: Harvard University Press, 1993.

slow evolution of the viable self, which in turn is achieved solely through the slow and uneven evolution of child rearing.

Traumas are defined as injuries to the private self, rather than just painful experiences, since nonpainful injuries such as being told by parents that they wished the child would die are more traumatic to the self than, say, painful accidents.[31] Without a well-developed, enduring private self, people feel threatened by all progress, all freedom, all new challenges, and experience annihilation anxiety, fears that the fragile self is disintegrating. As adults we keep searching for the parental love we missed as children. Masterson calls this by the umbrella term *abandonment depression*, beneath which, he says, "ride the Six Horsemen of the Psychic Apocalypse: Depression, Panic, Rage, Guilt, Helplessness, and Emptiness [that] wreak havoc across the psychic landscape."[32]

As Socarides has observed,[33] fears of growth, individuation, and self-assertion that carry threatening feelings of disintegration lead to desires to merge with the omnipotent mother—literally to crawl back into the womb—desires that immediately turn into fears of maternal engulfment, since the merging would involve total loss of the self. When Socarides' patients make moves to individuate—such as moving into their own apartment or getting a new job—they have dreams of being swallowed by whirlpools or devoured by monsters. The only salvation from these maternal engulfment wishes/fears is a "flight to external reality from internal reality,"[34] a flight in which social institutions play a central role. Patients who have been in psychotherapy often become conscious of this individuation panic when they begin to grow and break free of old emotional patterns. These fears can be characterized as an all-pervasive growth panic that traumatized individuals—nearly everyone—carry around during their daily lives. "If we grow, we will never be what Mommy or Daddy wants us to be, and we will never get their love." Masterson quotes one of his patients:

31. Lenore Terr, *Too Scared to Cry: Psychic Trauma in Childhood.* New York: Harper & Row, 1990; Bessel A. van der Kolk et al., Eds., *Traumatic Stress: The Effects of Overwhelming Experience on Mind, Body, and Society.* New York: Guilford Press, 1996; Spencer Eth and Robert S. Pynoos, *Post-Traumatic Stress Disorder in Children.* Washington, DC: American Psychiatric Press, 1985.

32. James F. Masterson, *The Search for the Real Self: Unmasking the Personality Disorders of Our Age.* New York: The Free Press, 1988, p. 61.

33. Charles W. Socarides, *The Preoedipal Origin and Psychoanalytic Therapy of Sexual Perversions.* Madison, CT: International Universities Press, 1988.

34. Ibid., p. 159.

I was walking down the street and suddenly I was engulfed in a feeling of absolute freedom. I could taste it. I knew I was capable of doing whatever *I* wanted. . . . I was just being myself and thought that I had uncovered the secret of life: being in touch with your own feelings and expressing them openly with others, not worrying so much about how others felt about you.

Then just as suddenly as it came, it disappeared. I panicked and started thinking about the million things I had to do at the studio, of errands I needed to run after work. I began to feel nauseous and started sweating. I headed for my apartment, running most of the way. When I got in, I felt that I had been pursued. By what? Freedom, I guess.[35]

It is this manic flight to action—a flight that is a defense against growth panic— that is the emotional source of much of social behavior. Historical behavior acts as a homeostatic mechanism that attempts to correct brain imbalances, with the leader as a sort of psychiatrist who is expected to heal our shared mood disorders. Manic acting-out in political activity—mainly involving delusional domination fantasies—is therefore a universal human addiction, similar in its effects to the dopaminergic effects of cocaine. That's why leaders so often take mania-producing drugs, like John F. Kennedy during the Cuban Missile Crisis (amphetamines) and George Bush during the Gulf War (Halcion). Like drugs, grandiose manic social activities such as war and political domination can produce a temporary elation and a dopamine surge, but not the lasting joy of self-discovery and love.

HOW TRAUMATIC IS CHILDHOOD?

The incidence of trauma in childhood, past and present, is a central focus of this book. My overall conclusions have not changed after three decades of additional research from what I wrote in *The History of Childhood*: "The history of childhood is a nightmare from which we have only recently begun to awaken. The further back in history one goes, the lower the level of child care, and the more likely children are to be killed, abandoned, beaten, terrorized, and sexually abused."[36] Indeed, my conclu-

---

35. Masterson, *The Search for the Real Self*, p. 10.

36. Lloyd deMause, "The Evolution of Childhood." In Lloyd deMause, Ed., *The History of Childhood*. New York: Psychohistory Press, 1974, p. 1.

sion from a lifetime of study of the history of childhood is that society is founded upon the abuse of children. Just as family therapists today find that child abuse often functions to hold families together as a way of solving their emotional problems, so, too, the routine assault, torture, and domination of children has been society's most effective instrument of collective emotional homeostasis. Most historical families once practiced infanticide, incest, and beating and mutilation of their children to relieve anxieties. We continue today to arrange the killing, maiming, molestation, and starvation of our children through our military, social, and economic institutions.

This is why domination and violence in history has such continuity: betrayal and abuse of children has been a consistent human trait since our species began. Each generation begins anew with fresh, eager, trusting faces of babies, ready to love and create a new world. And each generation of parents tortures, abuses, neglects, and dominates its children until they become emotionally crippled adults who repeat in nearly exact detail the social violence and domination that existed in previous decades. Should a minority of parents decrease the amount of abuse and neglect of its children a bit and begin to provide somewhat more secure, loving early years that allow a bit more freedom and independence, history soon begins to move in surprising new directions and society changes in innovative ways. History needn't repeat itself; only the traumas demand repetition.

THE PSYCHOGENIC THEORY OF HISTORY

The psychogenic theory of history is a scientific, empirical, falsifiable theory based on a model that involves shared restagings of dissociated memories of early traumas, the content of which changes through the evolution of childhood. It is based on the conclusion of clinical psychology that psychic content is organized by early emotional relationships, so that psychic structure must be passed from generation to generation through the narrow funnel of childhood. Thus a society's child-rearing practices are not just one item in a list of cultural traits but are the very condition for the transmission and development of all cultural elements. Child rearing, therefore, is crucial because it organizes the emotional structure that determines the transmission of all culture and places definite limits on what can be achieved by society. Specific childhoods sustain specific cultural traits, and once these early experiences no longer occur, the trait disappears or is modified. It is the first social theory that posits love as the central mechanism for historical change, because the clinical sciences have shown that love produces the individuation needed for human innovation—that is, for cultural evolution.

The theory is termed "psychogenic" rather than "economic" or "political" because it views humans more as *Homo relatens* than *Homo economicus* or *Homo politicus*—that is, as searching for relation, for love, more than just for money or power. The theory considers evolving *psychoclasses*—shared child-rearing modes—as more central than economic classes or social classes for understanding history, since political history is fought out mainly along the lines of child-rearing modes, with more punitive child rearing producing more punitive political behaviors.[37]

This psychogenic theory is contrasted with the sociogenic theory of other social sciences, which see individual change as merely a reflection of social change. It instead views adults as having developed new kinds of personalities due to new child-rearing modes, and then as projecting onto the historical stage earlier traumas and feelings in such a manner that events appear to be happening to the group rather than being internal, creating shared dreams, group-fantasies, that are so intense and compelling that they take on a life of their own.

Consider a typical example of a traumatized child growing up and joining others in fashioning a historical group-fantasy. Timothy McVeigh, one of the bombers of the federal building in Oklahoma City, in which 168 people were killed, experienced continuous maternal abandonment as a child, according to neighbors and relatives, as his restless mother, who regularly cheated on her husband, kept leaving the family for weeks at a time.[38] Timothy kept asking friends, "Is it something I did?" when trying to understand why his mother wasn't there. When he was 10, he became interested in guns and became a survivalist, collecting rifles in case Communists took over the country. When he was 16 and his mother left him for good, he began to refer to her as "a bitch" and as "that no-good whore." Neighbors reported he was often like two people, "angry and screaming one minute, then switch-

---

37. Michael A. Milburn and S. D. Conrad, "The Politics of Denial." *The Journal of Psychohistory* 23(1996): 238–251.

38. *The Washington Post National Weekly*, July 24–30, 1995, p. 8; WNBC-TV, "Rage and Betrayal," April 11, 1996; WABC News Special, April 11, 1996; *The New York Times*, December 31, 1995, p. 24; Brandon M. Stickney, *"All-American Monster": The Unauthorized Biography of Timothy McVeigh*. Amherst: Prometheus Books, 1996; *The New York Times*, May 13, 1997, p. A14.

```
┌─────────────────────────────────┐
│        Physical Reality         │
└─────────────────────────────────┘
     ↑   ↓            ↑   ↓
  ┌─────────┐      ┌─────────┐
  │ Group-  │      │ Group-  │
  │ Fantasy │      │ Fantasy │
  └─────────┘      └─────────┘
  ┌─────────┐      ┌─────────┐
  │  Adult  │      │  Adult  │
  └─────────┘      └─────────┘
       ↑      ↘        ↑
  ┌─────────┐      ┌─────────┐
  │  Child  │      │  Child  │
  └─────────┘      └─────────┘
  Generation 1     Generation 2
```

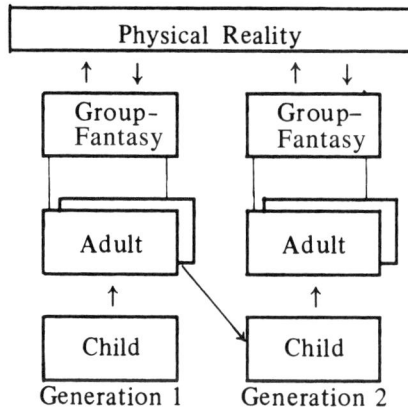

Fig. 5–2. The psychogenic theory of history

ing to quite normal" for no apparent reason, obvious traits of dissociation of personalities. In the army, when he failed the Green Beret test—another rejection—he quit in disgust and began hanging out with right-wing militarists. After going to Waco, Texas, to watch how the government had abandoned the children during the siege, he went to Oklahoma City to act out a scene in a rightist novel where a group packed a truck with a homemade bomb and set it off at FBI headquarters. The clue to the restaging occurred four months before he acted out this rage. McVeigh visited the day-care center in the same building, pretending he had children he wanted to enroll.[39] Thus he picked out a site where *children who had been left by their mothers* would be blown up too, *thus punishing abandoned children*—representatives of himself—restaging through the death of 168 innocent people both his own abandonment and the carrying out the punishment he thought he deserved for his rage at his mother.

The raging part of Timothy McVeigh was undoubtedly an actual alter, or alternate personality, similar to those in people who have multiple personality disorder, a diagnosis recently renamed dissociated identity disorder (DID). Severe, repeated child abuse and neglect almost always lie behind DID. Alters often have different names, handwriting, voices, vocabularies, expressions, even EEG alpha rhythms, and are sometimes am-

---

39. Danielle Hunt, head of the day-care center, said on "Rivera Live," CNBC-TV, June 10, 1997, that she was "absolutely certain the visitor was McVeigh."

nesic of one another's activities. In addition to the host personality, who is often depressed, masochistic, compulsively good, and suffers from time losses, there are alters such as *fearful children* who recall the traumas, *inner persecutors*, containers of forbidden impulses, *avengers*, *apologists* for the abusers, *idealized figures* who deny dangers, and so on. The formation of such alters is lifesaving, allowing the host personality to defend against unbearable trauma and continue living. Their tragedy is that these alters restage their traumas in adult life, in what Kluft calls "revictimization behaviors" or "the sitting-duck syndrome," during which they feel they are taking control of the abuse and ending the intolerable agony of waiting for it to happen by restaging it.[40]

SOCIAL ALTERS AND THE SOCIAL TRANCE

Child psychologists have suggested that perhaps "all children have dissociative-like states" and that abuse and neglect lead to the "establishment of centers of experience external to the core self during transient hypnotic-like states" that act as early alters.[41] As they grow up, these dissociated parts of their psyche are organized into persecutory social scenarios that are shared with others, which could be termed *social alters*. McVeigh switched into and out of his angry, militarist self, his social alter, each time he reexperienced further evidence of abandonment by mother figures. It is a process we all share to some extent with McVeigh. Rather than living our lives wholly in our private selves, we choose to live partly in our social alters, where ghosts of our past—"the family inside"[42]—are disguised as social roles in the present. Social alters of individuals collude to produce the social trance and have five characteristics:

1. They are separate neural networks that are repositories for feelings, images, and scenarios connected with traumatic abuse and neglect, including the defensive fantasies that go with them.

---

40. Richard P. Kluft, "Basic Principles in Conducting the Psychotherapy of Multiple Personality Disorder." In Richard P. Kluft and Catherine G. Fine, Eds., *Clinical Perspectives on Multiple Personality Disorder*. Washington, DC: American Psychiatric Press, 1993, p. 39.

41. Theresa K. Albini and Terri E. Pease, "Normal and Pathological Dissociations of Early Childhood." *Dissociation* 2(1989): 144.

42. Doris Bryant, Judy Kessler, and Lynda Shirar, *The Family Inside: Working With the Multiple*. New York: W. W. Norton & Co., 1974.

2. They are organized into dynamic structures containing an alternate set of goals, values, and defenses from those of the main self, to help prevent the traumas from overwhelming one's life and to defend against remembering the humiliations and persecutions of childhood.

3. They have the central task of organizing and carrying out in society the main actors in childhood: the sadistic, persecutory persons (perpetrator alters), the hurt children (victim alters), angry children (protector alters), idealized adults (caring alters), and others.[43]

4. They are co-conscious[44] with the host personality, yet they are split off by a seamless wall of denial, depersonalization, discontinuity of affect, and disownership of responsibility that is maintained by collusion with others pretending the alters are normal.

5. They are shared and restaged in historical group-fantasies that are elaborated into political, religious and social institutions.

Social alters contain memories of severe traumas and rejections and have their own repertoire of defensive behaviors. Experiments have shown that adults who were traumatized as children are more susceptible to hypnosis, to group suggestions, to hysterical religious behavior, and to paranormal experiences.[45] Dissociative disorders are what Winnicott called "the psychosis hidden behind the neurosis."[46] More organized and dissociated than just "false selves,"[47] social alters differ from alters of multiple personalities in that they replace the usual denial by amnesia with denial by dissociation of emotional connections, maintained through group collusion. Even though one may be more or less conscious of the activities of one's social, the emotional connections between the two selves are missing. Thus, people can imagine they go to war or conduct a genocide because of the

---

43. Doris Bryant, Judy Kessler, and Lynda Shirar, *The Family Inside: Working with the Multiple*. New York: W. W. Norton & Co., 1992, pp. 80–99.

44. J. O. Beahrs, "Co-Consciousness: A Common Denominator in Hypnosis, Multiple Personality, and Normalcy." *American Journal of Clinical Hypnosis* 26(1983): 100.

45. John F. Schumaker, *The Corruption of Reality: A Unified Theory of Religion, Hypnosis, and Psychopathology*. Amherst, NY: Prometheus Books, 1995, pp. 82–83, 163.

46. D. W. Winnicott, "The Use of an Object and Relating Through Identifications. *International Journal of Psycho-analysis* 48(1967): 87.

47. D. W. Winnicott, *The Maturational Processes and the Facilitating Environment*. New York: International Universities Press, 1965.

chance appearance of a suitable enemy, never because of anything emotional happening in their own heads.

It is important to remember that a person's social alter depends on the early amygdalan memory system, repository for our dissociated traumas. Social alters do not include the more mature areas of the brain, those containing the developed self-consciousness necessary for empathy.[48] It is this missing capacity for empathy that allows violent acting-out in the social sphere—people become so filled with their alter projections that it becomes impossible for them to feel their feelings.

Social alters are like suitcases into which we stuff our most traumatic split-off fears and rages, containing our continuing lives as traumatized children, abuser apologists, inner persecutors, parental avengers, and other consciously intolerable parts of ourselves, all organized into social postures. Perhaps a more accurate metaphor would be time bombs rather than suitcases, since social alters can eventually explode and produce genocides. The social alter is based on fantasies that are defenses against early traumas—not upon present-day reality—even when it participates in present-day political or religious group activities. The defensive fantasies are unreal even when the entire society may agree upon their reality. When a group of men collects human heads, believing that this will increase their genital potency, or a group of women chop off their little girls' clitorises, believing that otherwise they might grow to be a foot long, these beliefs are obviously derived from defensive group-fantasies, not from experience. The same people can have an excellent knowledge of reality in their host personalities, with extensive hunting or agricultural skills based on the real-life experiences of their group, but in their social alters they are nevertheless convinced of the efficacy of chopping off heads and clitorises.

Except for a few psychopaths and psychotics, most of us keep these suitcases for our social alters in the closet with the door locked, seemingly away from our daily lives—but then we lend the keys to *emotional delegates* whom we depend on to act out their contents for us so we can deny ownership of the actions. Periodically, when the group and its leader are imagined to be collapsing—when our despair becomes too great, our social alters seem too distant so that we feel depleted of vital parts of ourselves, and our hypervigilance is at an unbearable peak—the contents of these suitcases seem

---

48. Richard M. Restak, "Possible Neurophysiological Correlates of Empathy." In Joseph Lichtenberg et al., Eds., *Empathy I*. Hillsdale, NJ: The Analytic Press, 1984, p. 70.

to break loose, we enter a panic state, and our early fears and other emotional memories are restaged in wars or other forms of social violence.

All the accomplishments of our more mature personalities—self-awareness, the ability to imagine the consequences of actions and learning from experience, the capability of feeling empathy for others, the awareness of the passage of time, the ability to construct a realistic future, responsibility for one's actions—are missing in our social alters, and are not part of the group-fantasies we act out in history. Depersonalization is experienced whenever we are in our social alters, and we enter into a trance-like state—what happens in society has a feeling of unreality or strangeness of self, a loss of affective response. Even though, as with other dissociative disorders, some reality testing remains intact, an absence of normal feelings and a disconnection from one's usual range of emotions are regularly felt when in one's social alter. Empathy with others especially disappears. When you listen to the tapes of President John F. Kennedy and his advisors sitting in the Oval Office discussing whether to start World War III and incinerate 100 million people because they felt insulted by a Russian leader, what you are witnessing is actually a séance where everyone is in a deep trance, revisiting their childhood humiliations.

Even the language of group-fantasies is special, since social alters must communicate in elliptical form so that their unacceptable true contents may remain hidden to their main selves. Therefore, group-fantasies are often conveyed by subliminal embedded messages rather than clear, overt language. We will shortly see how to decode these embedded messages through fantasy analysis, the *via regia* for understanding shared emotional life. Groups speak this embedded language when they are in a social trance,[49] when they reexperience the same trance-like dissociation they felt during early traumas. Leaders of groups, therefore, must be adept at trance induction techniques to accomplish their delegated tasks. Leaders must contain our angry alters successfully, mainly by finding "enemies" to punish. When a group temporarily lacks a leader to contain its projected alters, it feels like it is going crazy, because the angry-child victim

---

49. Lloyd deMause, *Foundations of Psychohistory*. New York: Creative Roots, 1982, p. 188; Joe Berghold, "The Social Trance: Psychological Obstacles to Progress in History." *The Journal of Psychohistory* 19(1991): 221–243; Jerrold Atlas, "Understanding the Correlation between Childhood Punishment and Adult Hypnotizability as It Impacts on the Command Power of Modern 'Charismatic' Political Leaders." *The Journal of Psychohistory* 17(1990): 309–318.

alters return to the host psyches and drive the perpetrator alters into a fury. All political group-fantasies are conducted in this dissociative trance atmosphere, whose features are identical to the eight cognitive distortions of dissociation that Fine found in her dissociated patients: catastrophizing, overgeneralization, selective abstraction, dichotomous thinking, time distortion, misassessing causality, irresponsibility or excessive responsibility, and circular thinking.[50]

The social alter is the inheritor of earlier dissociated persecutory feelings and has as one of its roles the setting up of group punishments that are object lessons to us all. The usual formula for restaging early traumas is (1) fuse with your perpetrator alter ("terrifying mommy"); (2) find an alter container, a leader alter, whom you can follow to (3) kill the victim alter ("bad child") as an object lesson. When an American senator, voting for more nuclear weapons, said that even if a nuclear holocaust was unleashed it wouldn't be too bad because we would win it ("If we have to start over with another Adam and Eve, I want them to be Americans"), the weird trance logic can only be understood if nuclear war is seen as an object lesson, enabling us to start afresh with a clean slate.

THE SOCIAL ALTER IN SMALL GROUPS

All groups, even small face-to-face groups, organize group-fantasies out of the pooled social alters of its members. Because even in small groups we feel vulnerable to the shame and humiliation that reminds us of our earlier helplessness, we defend ourselves by switching into our social alters and preparing ourselves for expected attacks. Although groups can also be used for utilitarian purposes, they more often form so that people can act out their persecutory social alters. When people construct a group-fantasy, they give up their idiosyncratic defensive fantasies and become entrained in the social trance. Group analysts have found that even small groups collude in delusional notions: that the group is like a disapproving mother, that the group is different from and superior to all other groups, that it has imaginary boundaries that can protect it, that it can provide endless sustenance

50. Catherine G. Fine, "The Cognitive Sequelae of Incest." In Richard F. Kluft, Ed., *Incest-Related Syndromes of Adult Psychopathology.* Washington, DC: American Psychiatric Press, 1990, pp. 169–171.

to its members without their individual efforts, that its leader should be deified and should be in constant control of its members, that scapegoating is useful and sacrifice necessary for cleansing the group's emotions, that it is periodically besieged by monstrous enemies from without and stealthy enemies from within, that no individual is ever responsible for any of the group's actions, and so on—all defensive structures organizing and restaging shared traumatic content.[51] Recruiters for cults, for instance, make use of the propensity for people to need groups to control them and act out their group-fantasies; in fact, over 20 million Americans belong to cults and cult-like groups that enable them to collude with idealizing and persecutory parts of other people's social alters.[52]

It is not hard to see face-to-face group members become entrained and switch into their social alters, forming group-fantasies. As the group first gathers, people chat, laugh, argue, and interact with other individuals from their host selves. At a certain moment, however, when the time comes for the group to form, individuals switch into their social alters, a social trance forms,[53] and the group-fantasy takes over. Language and demeanor change, and people feel somehow detached, estranged from their usual range of feelings and deskilled of critical faculties. A leader is imagined to be in control even if he isn't actually present, group boundaries are imagined, work is thought able to be accomplished effortlessly, magical thinking spreads, enemies arise, factions form to act out splits, and empathy diminishes, since others are now so full of the group's projections.

All this usually takes only a few minutes. It becomes acceptable to exploit and abuse others, as members were themselves once exploited and abused. Scapegoats volunteer for sacrifice, a group bible and group his-

---

51. W. R. Bion, *Experiences in Groups*. London: Tavistock, 1961; W. R. Bion, *Learning from Experience*. London: Heinemann, 1962; Richard D. Mann with Graham S. Gibbard and John J. Hartman, *Interpersonal Styles and Group Development: An Analysis of the Member-Leader Relationship*. New York: John Wiley & Sons, 1967; Graham S. Gibbard, John J. Hartman, Richard D. Mann, Eds., *Analysis of Groups*. San Francisco: Jossey-Bass Publishers, 1974; Didier Anzieu, *The Group and the Unconscious*. London: Routledge & Kegan Paul, 1984; Howard Stein, "Organizational Psychohistory." *The Journal of Psychohistory* 21(1993): 97–114; C. Fred Alford, *Group Psychology and Political Theory*. New Haven: Yale University Press, 1995.

52. Margaret Thaler Singer, *Cults in Our Midst: The Hidden Menace in Our Everyday Lives*. San Francisco: Jossey-Bass, 1995, p. 5.

53. Lloyd deMause, *Foundations of Psychohistory*. New York: Creative Roots, 1982, p. 192.

tory and group spirit and other delusional group-fantasies form, and group life begins, seemingly a more emotionally vital life than everyday life, despite an omnipresent sleepiness common in groups that is a result of the social trance. When the group ends, often with a trance-breaking clap of hands termed "applause," people wake up, break the entrainment, switch back to their central personalities, and experience a tremendous emotional letdown as vital parts of themselves are lost, disoriented for a moment, and the group begins to mourn its own ending—in the same manner as multiple personalities often feel more connected to their real feelings when they have switched into their alters. Aristotle intuited the emotional importance of the social alter when he said man was a *zoon politikon* and was incomplete without his "political self," his social alter.

OBEDIENCE TO AUTHORITY IN A SOCIAL TRANCE

It is only when one realizes that we all carry around with us social alters that become manifest in groups that such unexplained experiments as those described in Stanley Milgram's classic study *Obedience to Authority*[54] become understandable. In this experiment, people were asked to be "teachers" and, whenever their "learners" made mistakes, to give them massive electric shocks. The learners, who were only acting the part, were trained to give out pained cries even though the electric shocks were nonexistent. Of the 40 teachers, 65 percent delivered the maximum amount of shock even as they watched the learners scream out in pain and plead to be released, despite their having been told they didn't *have* to step up the shock level. The teachers often trembled, groaned, and were extremely upset at having to inflict the painful shocks, but continued to do so nonetheless. That the teachers believed the shocks were real is confirmed by another version of the experiment in which real shocks were inflicted on a little puppy, who howled in protest; the obedience statistics were similar.[55]

Social scientists have been puzzled by Milgram's experiments, wondering why people were so easily talked into inflicting pain so gratuitously. The real explanation is that, by joining a group—the university experiment—they switched into their social alters and merged with their own sadistic internalized persecutor, which was quite willing to take responsi-

54. Stanley Milgram, *Obedience to Authority*. New York: Harper & Row, 1974.
55. Ibid., 152.

bility for ordering pain inflicted on others. Their struggle with themselves over whether to obey was really a struggle between their social alters and their host selves.

Although many subsequent experiments varied the conditions for obedience,[56] what Milgram did *not* do is try the experiment without the social trance. If he had not framed it as a *group* experience, if he had simply on his own authority walked up to each individual, alone, and, without alluding to a university or any other group, asked him or her to come to his home and give massive amounts of electric shock to punish someone, he would not have been obeyed, because they would not have switched into their social alters. The crucial element of the experiments was the existence of the group-as-terrifying-parent, the all-powerful university, which became the alter container. Not surprisingly, when the experiment was repeated using children—who go into trance and switch into traumatized content more easily than adults—they were even more obedient in inflicting the maximum shock.[57] Subjects were even obedient when they themselves were the victims: 54 percent turned a dial upon command to the maximum limit when they had been told it was inflicting damage on their ears that could lead to their own deafness, and 74 percent ate food they thought could harm them, thus confirming that they were truly in a dissociated state, not just obeying authority or trying to hurt others, and that it was actually an alternate self doing the hurting of the host self.[58] The only time they refused to obey was when experimenters pretended to act out a group rebellion, since the social trance was broken.[59]

Milgram could also have tested whether it was simple obedience that was really being tested by asking his subjects to reach into their pockets and contribute some of it to needy children. They would have refused to do so, because they weren't obeying just any old command, they were using the experimental situation to hurt scapegoats. Nazis wouldn't have obeyed Hitler either if he had asked them to be nice to Jews. It is the internal content of the social alter and not obedience to authority that is effective in producing destructive obedience. Milgram's subjects, like all of us who participate in wars and social violence, lost their capacity for empathy with

---

56. Arthur G. Miller, *The Obedience Experiments: A Case Study of Controversy in Social Science.* New York: Praeger Scientific, 1986.

57. Ibid., p. 76.

58. Ibid., p. 78–79, 148.

59. Ibid., p. 60.

victims only when in a social trance. Those who continue to replicate Milgram's experiments and who are still puzzled as to why "the most banal and superficial of rationales . . . is enough to produce destructive behavior in human beings"[60] simply underestimate the amount of trauma most people have experienced and the effectiveness of the social trance in allowing them to restage these hurts.

THE GROUP-FANTASIES OF NATIONS

Even though no group is too small to synchronize and act out the group-fantasies of its members, the larger the group the more deeply it can enter into the social trance and the more irrational the group-fantasies it can circulate and act out. The dissociated shame that is operative in small groups is equally there in nations, whether it is President Kennedy nearly triggering a nuclear apocalypse in Cuba to revenge his nose being rubbed in it by Premier Khrushchev or Germany starting World War II to revenge the shame of Versailles. (*die Sham* is a term often used in German for the genital area.)[61]

That nations have a central persecutory task is a widely denied truth. In fact, most members of most nations participate in one way or another in the torture and killing of others and/or in economic and political domination. We only deny it by colluding in such delusions as that leaders are to blame, that suffering is deserved, that punishment reforms, that killing is moral, that some people are not human, that sacrifice brings renewal, and that violence is liberating. Indeed, most of what is in history books is stark, raving mad—the maddest of all being the historian's belief that it is sane.

It is only when we begin to recognize the ubiquity of these delusional historical group-fantasies that our personal responsibility begins to return to us—reading the newspaper, watching the nightly news, and much of daily life becomes both more painful and more meaningful as empathy returns to our social lives. For some time now, for instance, I often cry when I watch the evening news, read newspapers, or study history books, a reaction I was trained to suppress in every school I attended for 25 years.

---

60. Irving I. Janus, *Victims of Groupthink*. Boston: Houghton Mifflin, 1982, p. 70.

61. On the origin of personal and social violence in shame, see James Gilligan, *Violence: Our Deadly Epidemic and Its Causes*. New York: G. P. Putnam's Sons, 1996.

In fact, it is because we so often switch into our social alters when we try to study history that we cannot understand it—our real emotions are dissociated and therefore unavailable to us.

The concept of the social alter explains why guilt does not prevent people from killing others nor leaders from ordering men to their death. Getting soldiers to kill others is not easy; studies have shown that 80 percent of the soldiers in the wars of the twentieth century refused to shoot at the enemy, even when it meant they themselves might have died because of their refusal.[62] The task of the military is to condition the process of switching into the soldier's persecutory social alter so that he can be cut off from his normal empathic personality. Only when switched into his persecutory social alter can a soldier kill without overwhelming guilt; rarely will he later then connect enough to this killing to admit, as one veteran did, "It didn't hit me all that much then, but when I think of it now—I slaughtered those people. I murdered them."[63] Because soldiers in early wars fought up close so that they could more easily experience personal guilt, rarely more than a few hundred men were usually killed during a battle,[64] while modern wars, specializing in distancing, denial, and trance induction training,[65] have in the twentieth century killed over 100 million people.

CHILD REARING AND THE SOCIAL TRANCE

Experimental evidence has shown that there is a direct correlation between traumatic childhood and the ability to go into trance.[66] The depersonalization made necessary by childhood trauma as a form of hypnotic evasion to avoid the painful impact of early trauma gets called into use as an

---

62. Dave Grossman, *On Killing: The Psychological Cost of Learning to Kill in War and Society*. Boston: Little, Brown and Co., 1995, p. 3.

63. Ibid., p. 88.

64. Ibid., p. 13.

65. Ibid., pp. 99–113.

66. Josephine Hilgard, *Personality and Hypnosis: A Study of Imaginative Involvement*. Chicago: University of Chicago Press, 1970; Jerrold Atlas, "Understanding the Correlation between Childhood Punishment and Adult Hypnotizability as It Impacts on the Command Power of Modern 'Charismatic' Political Leaders." *The Journal of Psychohistory* 17(1990): 309–318.

adult. Thus, it is not surprising to find that a survey of political attitudes finds that there is a clear correlation between harsh child rearing and authoritarian political beliefs, the use of military force, belief in the death penalty, and other punitive political actions.[67]

Those who are able to remain outside the social trance are the rare individuals whose child rearing is less traumatic than that of the rest of their society—or whose personal insights, through psychotherapy or other means, are beyond those of their neighbors. For instance, extensive interviews of people who were rescuers of Jews during the Holocaust in comparison to a control group of people who were either persecutors or just stood by and allowed the killing of Jews shows startling differences in child rearing.[68] While all other dimensions of the lives of the rescuers were similar to the control group—religion, education, even political opinions—what distinguished the rescuers from others was their childhood; their parents used reasoning in bringing them up, rather than the customary use by European parents early in the century of beating and kicking children to force obedience. The rescuers' parents were found to have invariably showed an unusual concern for equity, more love and respect for their children, more tolerance for their activities, and less emphasis on obedience, all allowing rescuers to remain in their empathic central personalities and not enter into social alters and dissociate their feelings for Jews as human beings. The rescuers risked their lives to save Jews not because they had some connection with Judaism or were politically radical, but because they remained in their compassionate personal selves rather than switching into the social trance constructed by the rest of their society.

THE DREAM WORLD OF THE SOCIAL TRANCE

Relatively few people are clinically diagnosed as having clinically dissociated personalities.[69] Virtually all of those who are have experienced extreme early trauma: 85 percent were sexually abused, 75 percent were

---

67. Michael A. Milburn and S. D. Conrad, "The Politics of Denial." *The Journal of Psychohistory* 23(1996): 238–250.

68. Samuel P. Oliner and Pearl M. Oliner, *The Altruistic Personality: Rescuers of Jews in Nazi Europe*. New York: The Free Press, 1988.

69. See Frank W. Putnam, *Diagnosis and Treatment of Multiple Personality Disorder*. New York: Guilford, 1989, p. 55, for bibliography of studies on incidence.

severely physically abused, 60 percent had been subject to extreme neglect, 40 percent had witnessed violent death, and a large number of them had been victims of extreme sadism, including torture, childhood prostitution, near-death experiences, being locked in cellars and trunks, and so on.[70] Dissociation scores in a randomized sample of the general population have shown that dissociative experiences of various sorts are quite common— tens of millions of Americans have experienced dissociation during religious and other rituals—and that dissociation is a continuum ranging from minor to major forms.[71] Yet most of us only massively dissociate when we are in our social alters, when we participate in the dream world of the group trance.

Social alters have a developmental history for each of us. They begin their independent existence in our earliest hours as protectors, then as persecutors, and finally develop into the organized persecutory group-fantasies of adulthood, while retaining elements that betray their early origins. Thus the traumatic material of our earliest years, full of hellish wombs, hurt and abandoned children, terrifying mommies and violent daddies, is organized by fairy tales, movies, TV programs, and schools, first into dragons and knights and eventually into Evil Empires and American presidents fighting Star Wars. However disguised from their infantile origins, these adult political fantasies are organized into persecutory social alters, then made real by shared delusional visions of the world and trillion-dollar weapon systems—our group-fantasies made concrete.

MERGING WITH THE PERPETRATOR

Ultimately our social alters merge with the perpetrator of early traumas. In group-fantasy, we merge with the aggressor to avoid feeling helpless and then inflict damage upon child scapegoats, often under the guise of saving children. We see this merging with the perpetrator in every scapegoating group-fantasy. When people persecute Jews, they are merged with the abusing parent and punishing the abused child. Jews must be persecuted, says St. John Chrysostom, for their "lewd grossness and extremes of glut-

70. Ibid., pp. 47–49.

71. John E. Mack, *Abduction: Human Encounters With Aliens*. New York: Scribner's, 1994; Frank W. Putnam, "Dissociative Phenomena." In David Spiegel, Ed., *Dissociative Disorders: A Clinical Review*. Lutherville, MD: The Sidran Press, 1993, pp. 2–4.

tony"—betraying the sexual seduction and hunger experienced by children of his time. Jews are "murderers of the Lord" and must be punished for the murderous rage children felt toward their abusers, their Lords, their caregivers.[72] The idea that "all Jews must be killed or they will destroy the German people" is simply the social alter's version of "all angry children must be punished or they will kill their parents." Adult historical events, political or economic, provide only proximate causes of scapegoating group-fantasies—their ultimate cause lies in earlier traumatic events.

FUNCTIONS OF SOCIAL ALTERS

Social alters are a product of the evolution of the human brain, which began with dissociated modules and only slowly evolved into a more integrated self. Our species began with little more private selves than chimpanzees, controlled mainly by our unconscious amygdalan memory systems and living with little self-consciousness or empathy. Humans only began being able to form more fully conscious selves as the acquisition of language and the evolution of child rearing produced a major epigenetic (additional to genetic) evolution of our psyche. By splitting off and then sharing the feelings in our social alters, we have become able to remain sane some of the time and get about the daily business of living our lives, while walling off in a separate part of our psyches our most painful traumas and deepest feelings.

Our social alters contain early levels of our unbearable hurts ("Why didn't Mommy want me?" "Why did Daddy hit me?"), restaged as fairy tales ("Are there witches?" "Will the monster kill me?") and then as social questions ("Shall we take children away from teenage mothers?" "Is Saddam Hussein a new Hitler who will blow up the world?"). The adaptive function of social alters is that they allow people to go about their daily business without being overwhelmed by traumatic memories and resulting despair—as crazy people are overwhelmed. By dissociating early persecutors into our social alters and then identifying with these persecutors in our social lives, human beings manage to live somewhat more sane daily lives, while warding off unseen but felt dangers by "feeding" victims of society to terrifying religious, political, and economic divinities.

---

72. Ervin Staub, *The Roots of Evil: The Origins of Genocide and Other Group Violence.* Cambridge: Cambridge University Press, 1989, p. 101.

INDUCING THE SOCIAL TRANCE

Earlier societies were so deep into the social trance that although they often had excellent intellectual knowledge about the world, based on experience, they nevertheless shared the most bizarre magical beliefs imaginable while in their social alters. Adaptationist evolutionary theories flounder on the ubiquity of these bizarre and patently nonadaptive cultural traits. There is nothing adaptive in maintaining a belief that if you put a stick into a cowrie shell and it falls to the side, someone will soon die,[73] or the belief that wars restore the potency of men and societies. Most of culture consists of behaviors like these, which become explainable by developmental psychology, not by theories of adaptation to environments. Because early societies had so little development of private self in childhood, they lived most of their lives in their social alters—in a dream world of malevolent witches, ghosts, and other persecutory spirits. Both devouring witches and the helpful animal familiars of shamans, for instance, have been shown to be actual alters that are first constructed in childhood as imaginary companions[74]—that is, they are created by the child to "hold" the trauma. Whether you are a New Guinea cannibal, an ancient Greek mother, a Balinese trancer or a Nazi antisemite, you first form an alter in your head of a devouring, bloodthirsty demon—using traumatic memories going all the way back to the Poisonous Placenta—and then you collude with others to project this image onto that of a horrible witch, a devouring Striga, a bloodthirsty leyak spirit or a poisonous Jew to relieve intrapsychic stress.

Our political beliefs today are often no less magical than the religious beliefs of earlier times. The belief that killing and burning Jews can cleanse German blood is based on the same kind of trance logic as earlier beliefs that killing and burning children in sacrifices to gods will assure better crops. Both depend on social alters to keep their real selves sane. Only after switching into their social alters can normally peaceful people become persecutors, don frightful masks or swastika uniforms, and chop enemies'

---

73. Michele Stephen, *A'aisa's Gifts: A Study of Magic and the Self*. Berkeley: University of California Press, 1995, p. 83; the tribe is the Mekeo of New Guinea, and the fallen stick in the cowrie shell an obvious symbol of impotence.

74. Gilbert Herdt, "Spirit Familiars in the Religious Imagination of Sambia Shamans." In Gilbert Herdt and Michele Stephen, Eds., *The Religious Imagination in New Guinea*. New Brunswick: Rutgers University Press, 1989, pp. 99–121.

heads off or gas Jews. Then, their traumas restaged, they can go home, remove their masks and alters, and have dinner with their families.

Every known society has trance rituals designed to help switch members into their social alters, entrain their group-fantasies, and prepare them for social action designed to relieve emotional distress. Bourguignon counts 437 societies out of 488 studied that have formal trance rituals,[75] but she uses a very narrow definition of what constitutes a trance. In fact, no society lacks its trance rituals. Apparently being dissociated from your social alters for any length of time leaves you feeling that you have lost important parts of your self. As the !Kung bushman said when asked why he had to join a trance dance ritual every week, "I can really become myself again."[76]

The anthropology and neurobiology of ritual trances has been extensively studied.[77] The time-honored techniques of formal trance induction are well known: fasting, rapid breathing, inhalation of smoke and ingestion of drugs, infliction of pain, and the use of drumming, pulsing music and dancing—all "driving behaviors" designed to reproduce the pain, hypoxia, and shock of early trauma and entrain the biological rhythms of the group. Neurobiologically, the amygdaloid-hippocampal balance plays a pivotal role in trance states, with an increase in theta-wave rhythm in the hippocampus, indicating increased attentional activity to early amygdalan-centered memories, allowing access to dissociated traumatic experience.[78] The motivations for going into the group trance, however, have remained unstudied.

The leader of any group is an emotional delegate for the group's trance induction needs. Freud, following LeBon, noticed the resemblance of group

---

75. Erika Bourguignon, "Dreams and Altered States of Consciousness in Anthropological Research, " in F. K. L Hsu, Ed., *Psychological Anthropology*, 2nd ed. Homewood, IL: The Dorsey Press, 1972, p. 418.

76. Robert Katz, "Education for Transcendence: !Kia-Healing with the Kalahari !Kung." In Richard B. Lee and I. DeVore, Eds., *Kalahari Hunter-Gatherers*. Cambridge: Harvard University Press, 1976, p. 76.

77. Erika Bourguignon, "Dreams and Altered States of Consciousness in Anthropological Research"; Eugene G. d'Aquili et al., *The Spectrum of Ritual: A Biogenetic Structural Analysis*. New York: Columbia University Press, 1979; Ronald C. Simmons et al., "The Psychobiology of Trance," *Transcultural Psychiatric Research Review* (1988): 249–288; Ede Frecska and Zsuzsanna Kulcsar, "Social Bonding in the Modulation of the Physiology of Ritual Trance," *Ethos* 17(1989): 70–94.

78. Peter Brown, *The Hypnotic Brain: Hypnotherapy and Social Communication*. New Haven: Yale University Press, 1991, pp. 115–118.

Fig. 5–3. A man in his social alter

fascination to a hypnotic trance. Hitler confirmed his insight: "I have been reproached for making the masses fanatic. . . . But what you tell the people in the mass, in a receptive state of fanatic devotion, will remain like words received under an hypnotic influence, ineradicable, and impervious to every reasonable explanation."[79]

That recapturing and restaging early traumas are the goals of the so-cial trances is suggested by the discovery by Hilgard of the correlation between the severity of childhood punishment and ability to go into a hypnotic trance.[80] Although many small groups admit that the goal of their trance rituals is an attempt to heal trauma through exorcism rituals, we tend to deny this today. Yet when the rationalizations of our trance rituals are stripped away and their hidden rhythms and embedded messages are revealed to analysis, their traumatic bases and the modern forms of ritual exorcism of alters/devils are made convincingly evident.

---

79. Quoted by Morris Berman, *Coming to Our Senses: Body and Spirit in the Hidden History of the West*. New York: Simon & Schuster, 1989, p. 286.

80. Josephine Hilgard, *Personality and Hypnosis: A Study of Imaginative Involvement*. Chicago: University of Chicago Press, 1970; see also Jerrold Atlas, "Understanding the Correlation Between Childhood Punishment and Adult Hypnotizability as It Impacts on the Command Power of Modern 'Charismatic' Political Leaders." *The Journal of Psychohistory* 17(1990): 309–318, and Joe Berghold, "The Social Trance: Psychological Obstacles to Progress in History." *The Journal of Psychohistory* 19(1991): 221–243.

FANTASY ANALYSIS

I have developed and tested over the past two decades a technique I call fantasy analysis, which reveals the hidden emotional messages embedded within seemingly bland and boring speeches and press conferences of leaders as well as other verbal and nonverbal political material.[81] The purpose of fantasy analysis is to capture how it feels to be part of a nation's shared emotional life. Others have confirmed that doing a fantasy analysis of political material can be a Rosetta Stone that can uncover new dimensions to our group-fantasies and can even be used to try to forecast future political behavior.[82] Just as experimental psychologists have shown that visual stimuli subliminally presented tachistoscopically for a hundredth of a second register in the unconscious and in dreams while bypassing consciousness,[83] so too subliminal messages are embedded in speeches and in the media by their choice of certain metaphors, similes, and emotional images rather than others. A fantasy analysis of a speech or other historical document will remove the defensive posturing and locate the emotionally powerful fantasy words that contain the embedded real message, decoding the hidden content through the relationships of the imagery. The rules for fantasy analysis are simple:

1. Record all strong feeling words, even when they occur in innocuous contexts, such as "*kill* the bill in Congress or "*cut* the budget." Be abstemious; recording mild anxiety words simply clutters the analysis, although it rarely changes the emotional content of the hidden message.
2. Record all metaphors, similes, and gratuitously repeated words.
3. Record all family terms, such as mother, father, children.

---

81. Lloyd deMause, *Foundations of Psychohistory*. New York: Creative Roots, 1982, pp. 194–217.

82. Casper Schmidt, "The Abnormally Popular George Bush." *The Journal of Psychohistory* 18(1990): 123–134; Howard Stein, "Organizational Psychohistory." *The Journal of Psychohistory* 21(1993): 97–114; David Beisel, "Thoughts Concerning Some Objections to Group-Fantasy Analysis." *The Journal of Psychohistory* 9(1982): 237–240; Paul H. Elovitz et al., "On Doing Fantasy Analysis." *The Journal of Psychohistory* 13(1985): 207–228.

83. C. Fisher, "Subliminal (Preconscious) Perception: The Microgenesis of Unconscious Fantasy." In H. Blum et al., Eds., *Fantasy, Myth and Reality*. Madison, CT: International Universities Press, 1988, pp. 93–108.

4. Eliminate negatives, since "we don't want *war*" still is about war and could have been phrased "we want *peace*."
5. Rewrite the fantasy words in sentences to reveal the hidden messages.

My books and articles over the past two decades have contained extensive fantasy analyses of presidential speeches and press conferences, and can be consulted as examples of how the process reveals the group-fantasies of the nation at specific historical moments.[84] The following analysis of President Ronald Reagan's acceptance speech for reelection in 1984 is an example of the fantasy analysis technique and illustrates the process of trance induction, the search for traumatic content and the leader's unconscious pact with the nation on what should be done.

Most political meetings are usually held not to make decisions but to deepen the social trance, to switch into social alters, and to entrain the group's unconscious emotional strategies for handling the inner emotional problems of its hidden world. The following speech was given by Ronald Reagan at the 1984 Republican convention. Even before political speeches begin, important trance induction conditions are established. The audience is usually immobilized in crowded seats, recapturing the helplessness of infancy. At the 1984 Republican convention, a special film was shown to the delegates on a huge television screen above the podium before Reagan began speaking. It was so boring—mainly his giant face, as though he were a huge mother and the delegates were infants—that the audience already began to regress in age and dissociate. As hypnotherapist Milton Erickson writes, being very boring is one of the most powerful trance induction techniques, since the conscious mind soon loses reality anchors.[85] The only persons the audience could focus on were cadres of young Republicans pumping their arms in the air and shouting rhythmically, "U.S.A.! U.S.A!"[86]

---

84. Lloyd deMause, *Foundations of Psychohistory; Reagan's America;* "'Heads and Tails': Money As a Poison Container." *The Journal of Psychohistory* 16(1988): 1–18; "America's Search for a Fighting Leader." *The Journal of Psychohistory* 20(1992): 121–134.

85. For trance induction techniques, see Milton Erickson, *The Nature of Hypnosis and Suggestion.* New York: Irvington Publishers, 1980; Milton Erickson and Ernest Rossi, *Hypnotherapy: An Exploratory Casebook.* New York: Irvington Publishers, 1987 and Stephen Lankton and Carol Lankton, *The Answer Within: A Clinical Framework of Ericksonian Hypnotherapy.* New York: Brunner/Mazel, 1983.

86. Jack Germond and Jules Witcover, *Wake Us When It's Over: Presidential Politics of 1984.* New York: Macmillan, 1985, p. 430.

FEELING GOOD...YOU ARE BETTER OFF..., YOU ARE GETTING SLEEPY...."

Fig. 5–4. Ronald Reagan shown as trance inducer

Reagan began the trance induction part of his speech at heartbeat speed—that is, with a rhythm of about seventy beats per minute, although normal speaking rates are usually above 120 beats per minute. Almost all politicians speak at this abnormally slow rate of seventy beats per minute, even when microphones make their words quite clear to a large audience. This is because this is the rate of the mother's heart beat that one first heard in the womb. Other trance inducers—priests and hypnotists—also instinctively slow down to seventy beats per minute, entraining their audiences to a mother's heartbeat. To emphasize this regression to the warmth of the womb, Reagan's first fantasy words (put in **bold** type) to his audience and to the nation watching on TV are (read this to yourself very slowly to feel its dissociative effect):

> Thank you very much. Mr. Chairman, Mr. Vice President, delegates to this convention, and fellow citizens. In 75 days, I hope we enjoy a victory that is the size of the **heart** of Texas. Nancy and I extend our deep thanks to the Lone Star State and the "Big D," the city of Dallas, for all their **warmth** and hospitality.

After these womb-like words, Reagan begins to speak baby language, as though he were talking to an audience of 3-year-olds—a technique also used by the hypnotherapist Milton Erickson to induce trances through age regression. Erickson usually tells parables, in baby language, often about animals; Reagan does the same (again, read very slowly and watch your eyelids begin to feel heavy):

> Four years ago I didn't know precisely every duty of this office, and not too long ago, I learned about some new ones from the first graders of Corpus Christi School in Chambersburg, Pennsylvania. Little Leah Kline was asked by her teacher to describe my duties. She said: "The president goes to meetings. He **helps** the animals. The president gets frustrated. He talks to other presidents."

What is astonishing isn't just that the leader of the most powerful nation on earth—faced with soaring deficits because of his huge military buildup and threatening a war with Nicaragua—should begin his explanation of his plans for the nation for the next four years with baby talk. What is more surprising is that no one noticed anything strange! The speech seemed like normal politics, and Reagan was called a master speaker. We are all quite used to leaders speaking boring baby language to us at an exaggeratedly slow pace. We periodically ask our leaders to put us into a trance so we can switch into our social alters and coordinate our fantasies. Reality is quite beside the point.

Reagan repeats more "heart" words (which I will skip to save space) and then begins to further dissociate the conscious mind from the unconscious with repeated splitting words, in much the same way that a hypnotist splits your attention by telling you to watch one of your arms rise while the other one falls:

> The choices this year are not just between **two different** personalities or between **two different** visions of the future, two fundamentally **different** ways of governing—**their** government of pessimism, **fear**, and limits, or **ours** of **hope**, confidence, and growth. Their government—**their** government sees people only as members of groups. **Ours** serves all the people of America as individuals. **Theirs** lives in the past, seeking to apply the old and failed policies to an era that has passed them by. **Ours** learns from the past and strives to change by boldly charting a new course for the future. **Theirs** lives by promises, the bigger, the better. We offer proven, workable answers.

The final induction technique is age regression:

> Our opponents began this campaign hoping that America has a poor **memory**. Well, let's take them on a little stroll down **memory** lane . . .

The social trance is now becoming effective, and the group has switched into its social alters. The audience members have become biologically entrained with the speaker and with one another; they are moving subtly together, though no one has thought it important to measure this in political meetings other than such obvious entrainments as synchronized flag movements or mass Nazi salutes. This entrainment itself evokes early memories, since it recalls how babies entrain to the voices of the adults around them within minutes of birth (and possibly even in utero),[87] swaying and moving their head, arms, body, and fingers to the sounds of adults.

After the trance induction, Reagan then begins what Erickson terms the *unconscious search*, attempting to locate what feelings are bothering the audience and nation at this particular historical moment. (I will from here on only reproduce sentences with fantasy words to save space.) Here is what Reagan says is bothering the nation at the end of 1984:

> Inflation was not some **plague** borne on the wind. . . . They were **devastated** by a wrong-headed grain embargo. . . . Farmers have to **fight** insects, weather, and the marketplace—they shouldn't have to **fight** their own government. . . . Under their policies tax rates have gone up three times as much for families with **children** as they have for everyone else. . . . Some who spoke so **loudly** in San Francisco of fairness were among those who brought about the biggest single individual tax increase in our history. . . . Well, they received some relief in 1983 when our across-the-board tax **cut** was fully in place. . . . Would that really **hurt** the rich?

That the first fantasy word of the unconscious search for shared feelings should be **plague** warns us of serious emotional disturbance, since this has been the code word for paranoid fantasies of group pollution from the delusional apocalyptic plagues of antiquity to "the Jewish plague" of modern antisemitism. What could be the source of the feelings of a **plague** and

---

87. William S. Condon, "Neonatal entrainment and enculturation." In Margaret Bullowa, Ed., *Before Speech: The Beginnings of Interpersonal Communication*. New York: Cambridge University Press, 1979, pp. 131–169.

of a **devastated** society? Perhaps something to do with **fight** and **children** who are **loudly cut** and **hurt**? Maybe **hurt children** are too **loud**? The search continues (I now only record the fantasy words to save space):

> pushed . . . creep . . . out of control . . . control . . . control. . . . control
> . . . tightening . . . strangling . . . misery . . . misery . . . misery . . . drop-
> ping . . . births . . . relief . . . shrinking . . . shrink . . . fell . . . fallen . . .
> children . . . controlling . . . children . . . grandchildren . . . immoral . . .

Feelings of **strangling**, being **pushed** and general **misery** seem to be the problem. All this **misery** is blamed on **out-of-control, immoral children**. As usual, we blame our own out-of-control growing childhood selves for our troubles. (The immorality of children is confirmed later in the convention by the Christian right attack on teenage sex.)

What can be done to stop these immoral children? In the main section of his speech, Reagan now tells what should be done, thus giving a posthypnotic command to the nation and concluding a "trance pact" between the leader and his people:

> sell out . . . betray . . . fear . . . wars . . . strong . . . warlike . . . students
> . . . crushing . . . genocide . . . young men lost their lives . . . sacrifice
> . . . murderous . . . students . . . war . . . cut . . . cut . . . violence . . . burial
> . . . children . . . buried . . . drunken . . . war . . . war . . . children . . .
> ridding the earth . . . threat . . .

Rewriting Reagan's fantasy words in complete sentences, we find that the audience, the nation, and Reagan have made the following trance pact:

> We will **sell out** and **betray** to **fear** in **wars strong warlike students**. In a **crushing genocide young men** will have **lost their lives** in a **sacrifice** that will be **murderous**. **Students** in the **war** will be **cut, cut** with such **violence** we will have a **burial** of **children**. They will be **buried** in a **drunken war**. The **war** on **children** will accomplish **ridding** the earth of the **threat** in our heads.

The central project of Reagan's second term of office—going to war against Nicaragua—is now a posthypnotic command, a pact with that part of the nation that has become entranced with him (entered the social trance). Only those Americans who were not in the social trance—more recent psychoclasses whose childhoods were better than the majority—ended up opposing Reagan's push in the next three years toward a Central American war, which was then only narrowly avoided.

The speech ends with the audience switching out of their social alters back to their main personalities, accomplished by images of peace, warmth, and, again, "heart":

> peace . . . cradle . . . peace . . . torch . . . torch . . . torch . . . torch . . .
> torch . . . bloodlines . . . torch . . . torch . . . torch . . . torch . . . lamp
> . . . children . . . heart

The people in the audience then hit their hands together to awaken themselves from the deep social trance—for ten full minutes. The nation, watching, now knows what it should be trying to do for the next four years: sacrificing young men to end the plague of out-of-control, immoral children. Reagan went on to be reelected by an overwhelming majority of the nation.

Confirmation of the group-fantasy in the leader's message can be obtained by watching the political cartoons appearing at the same time showing the nation's hidden feelings in visual, preverbal form. At the end of 1984, for the first time in Reagan's presidency, cartoons appeared of children being sacrificed, supposedly to deficits or abortions or antiabortion terrorism or Mother Russia, but really to our needs for child sacrifice.

GROWTH PANIC AND MATERNAL ENGULFMENT

One of the most thoroughly documented results of the past three decades of study of group-fantasies is that they are inexorably tied into the person of the leader. Since political feelings are so much a defense against growth panic and resulting fears of abandonment by early love objects, groups organize and entrain their fantasies about how it feels to be part of the group at any particular historical time more around feelings about the leader than any actual historical events.

The central fantasy function of the leader of any group, small or large, is to defend against repetitions of early trauma and abandonment, along with handling wishes for merging with the terrifying mother. Leaders are usually imagined as male protectors against maternal engulfment fears. Group analyst Didier Anzieu describes the small groups he studies as follows: "The group is a mouth . . . essentially female and maternal. . . . One of the most active, or rather paralyzing, unconscious group representations

Fig. 5–5. Fantasies of child sacrifice in Reagan's America

is that of a Hydra: the group is felt to be a single body with a dozen arms at the ends of which are heads and mouths . . . ready to devour one another if they are not satisfied."[88]

When the leader is imagined to be strong, he can successfully defend against the group's engulfment fears; when the leader appears to weaken, all growth is dangerous, and desires for merging and fears of maternal engulfment increase, so the leader must somehow act to defend against the growth panic. Extensive studies by Gibbard and Hartman of fantasies of small groups have found that

> groups center on the largely unconscious fantasy that the group-as-a-whole is a maternal entity, or some facet of a maternal entity. . . . The fantasy offers some assurance that the more frightening, enveloping or destructive aspects of the group-as-mother will be held in check. . . . A

---

88. Didier Anzieu, *The Group and the Unconscious*. London: Routledge & Kegan Paul, 1984, pp. 160–161.

major function of the group leader is to ward off envelopment by the group-as-mother. . . . The group leader is imagined to have mastered the group-as-mother and thus to have gained some of her *mana* for himself. This makes him a threat as well as a protector.[89]

Thus all groups—from bands to nations—experience growth, progress, and social development with fears of maternal engulfment and abandonment. The worse the child rearing, the more growth panic is triggered by individuation and self-assertion. The course of cultural evolution is determined by the reduction of this growth panic through the evolution of more supportive child rearing. Since this childhood evolution is very uneven, more advanced psychoclasses cause too much social progress for the majority of society. Old defenses become unavailable and people cannot dominate and punish various traditional scapegoats—wives, slaves, servants, minorities—the same way as before. These less advanced psychoclasses—the majority of society—begin to experience tremendous growth panic, and new ways to handle their anxiety must be invented. For them, change is everywhere; things seem to be getting out of control. This is why growth and self-assertion, whatever it is called—*hubris, chutzpah*, original sin, human desire itself—are proscribed by the religious and political systems of most societies. Societies whose institutions progress beyond their average child-rearing mode become the most fearful and most violent, since their growth panic depends on both the amount of early trauma and the amount of social progress.

The violence resulting from the fear of maternal engulfment has, in fact, been empirically found to be related to the mother's actual engulfing behavior. For instance, Ember and Ember[90] found in their cross-cultural studies that where the mother sleeps closer to the baby than to the father, and therefore tends to use the baby as a substitute spouse, there is more homicide and assault, and there is also a higher frequency of war, both correlations as predicted by the psychogenic theory.

Maternal engulfment fears can also be handled by merging with the engulfing mother in fantasy and then sacrificing oneself or a substitute for oneself to the engulfing mother. Many early religions feature a female beast

---

89. Graham S. Gibbard and John J. Hartman, "The Significance of Utopian Fantasies in Small Groups." *The International Journal of Group Psychotherapy* 23(1973): 125–147.

90. Carol R. Ember and Melvin Ember, "Issues in Cross-Cultural Studies of Interpersonal Violence." In R. Barry Rubach and Neil Alan Weiner, Eds., *Interpersonal Violent Behaviors: Social and Cultural Aspects.* New York: Springer Publishing Co., 1995, pp. 32–33.

that is worshiped and to whom human sacrifices are made. The Mayans, for instance, sacrificed human hearts torn out of a living victim's chest to jaguar gods and even handed over their children to living jaguars to be eaten, while in one section of India sharks were until recently worshiped and "both men and women went into a state of ecstasy and offered themselves to the sharks [by entering] the sea up to their breasts and are very soon seized and devoured [by the sharks.]"[91] Maternal engulfment fantasies are very often acted out in concrete form in social rituals—whether religious or military. Initiation ceremonies usually feature men in animal masks who "devour" initiates, and battlefields are often pictured as "devouring mouths" engulfing soldiers "sent into their maw" to sacrifice themselves "for their motherland."

LEADERSHIP AND DEFENSES AGAINST GROWTH PANIC

Political leaders are intuitively aware that their main function is to provide grandiose manic antidotes to growth panic. Every society acknowledges somehow its function as a defense against maternal engulfment. Most Melanesian societies openly admit that the main function of their rituals is to counter the disastrous effects of polluted menstrual blood.[92] Ancient Egyptian and Mesopotamian societies were constructed around rituals that countered their panic about succumbing to chaos, constantly fearing female "chaos-monsters [who] drank people's blood and devoured their flesh."[93] Many Western political theorists, such as Machiavelli, have also seen political authority as necessary to combat "feminine chaos." My psychogenic theory only differs in ascribing this fear of maternal abandonment to fantasy, not reality—to childhood family life, not adult social life.

The more primitive the dominant child-rearing mode of a society, the more growth panic must be defended against. New Guinea fathers are often so certain their boys are going to be engulfed by poisonous menstrual blood and eaten up by witches that they cut themselves to get their own "strong"

91. Barbara Ehrenreich, *Blood Rites: Origins and History of the Passions of War.* New York: Henry Holt and Co., 1997, pp. 74–75.

92. Gilbert H. Herdt, Ed., *Ritualized Homosexuality in Melanesia.* Berkeley: University of California Press, 1984.

93. Norman Cohn, *Cosmos, Chaos and the World to Come: The Ancient Roots of Apocalyptic Faith.* New Haven: Yale University Press, 1993, pp. 22 and 54.

male blood and feed it to the boys to strengthen them.[94] Most sacrificial rites are performed to ward off dangerous "blood pollution."[95] Political leaders regularly go to war over fears of the enemy's polluting dangers, such as Hitler's fears of "foreign blood introduced into our people's body."[96] Wars are said to be particularly useful in "scrubbing clean national arteries clogged with wealth and ease."[97] Indeed, *poison-cleansing is a central purpose of all social rituals*, whether the cleansing is accomplished by wars, religious sacrifices, or depressions, all of which have been said to cleanse the body politic of sinful pleasures and freedoms.[98]

The fears of abandonment that are triggered by social progress are felt by nations to be dramatized in their relationship with their leader, who is felt to be growing more and more distant and less and less able to provide grandiose manic projects to defend against their growing growth panic. The increasing impotence and weakness of the leader can be seen in the much-watched ratings he gets in his public opinion polls, which, after starting at a peak, usually decline during his term, unless revived by some particularly effective defensive manic action that the leader engages in.[99] This is just the opposite of what one would rationally expect, which is that as a nation gets more and more evidence of what the leader can accomplish, it should become more confident in his capacities. But leaders instead usually are imagined to weaken in office, because growing growth panic makes them seem more distant and less potent.

Ancient societies knew this feeling of weakening of leadership very well, and regularly set up some of their most important rituals to revitalize the powers of their kings. The earliest of these rituals were held annually, climaxing in rituals of purgation, whereby the community rids itself of

---

94. Fitz John Porter Poole, "Coming into Social Being: Cultural Images of Infants in Binim-Kuskusmin Folk Psychology." In Geoffrey M. White and John Kirkpatrick, Eds., *Person, Self, and Experience: Exploring Pacific Ethnopsychologies.* Berkeley: University of California Press, 1985, p. 194.

95. J. H. M. Beattie, "On Understanding Sacrifice." In M. F. C. Bourdillon and Meyer Fortes, *Sacrifice.* New York: Academic Press, 1980, p. 42.

96. Adolf Hitler, *Mein Kampf.* Boston: Houghton Mifflin, 1971, p. 388.

97. Michael C. C. Adams, *The Great Adventure: Male Desire and the Coming of World War I.* Bloomington, IN: Indiana University Press, 1990, p. 51.

98. Lloyd deMause, "'Heads and Tails': Money As a Poison Container." *The Journal of Psychohistory* 16(1988): 1–18.

99. Casper G. Schmidt, "The Use of the Gallup Poll as a Psychohistorical Tool." *Journal of Psychohistory* 10(1982): 141–162.

pollution; rituals of mortification and sacrifice, whereby fasts and other punishments were undergone to purge people of their dreaded desires; and rituals of combat, whereby battles were fought with projected forces of evil.[100] Later, divine kings provided defenses against maternal pollution, and were held to be intimately connected with the health of the crops, animals, and people. Early Greek kings reigned for eight years, and were thought to have weakened so badly during this time that they either were killed themselves, found a substitute (sometimes the eldest son) to kill, or else they had to go through regeneration rituals to cleanse their pollutions. To be regenerated, the king would go first through a humiliation ritual— be slapped on the face to repeat the people's childhood humiliations—and might even go through the ritual process of dying and being born again.[101] Thus the phrase: "The King is dead; long live the King!" Or, as Robespierre declared in 1792, "Louis must die because the *patrie* must live."[102]

In modern democratic nations, we usually don't actually kill our leaders; we periodically throw them out of office and replace them with revitalized substitutes. But the decline in potency of the leader—his inexorable abandonment of us as we grow—still is felt today. This is because the leader is less a figure of authority than he is an emotional delegate, someone who tells us to do what we tell him we want done, someone who "takes the blame" for us. As poison container for our dissociated social alter, the leader is expected to absorb our violent feelings without collapsing. Many societies actually designate "filth men" to help the leader with this task, relatives who exchange blood with him so they can intercept the poisonous feelings of the people directed at him. In modern nations, cabinet members are our filth men, and are regularly sacrificed when the leader is under attack.

This leadership task of being the emotional delegate of irrational desires of the people makes leaders experts in masochism, rather than sadisim, as traditional power theory requires. This explains why Janus found in his study of Washington, D.C. prostitutes that powerful politicians got their sexual thrills by playing masochistic, not sadistic, sexual roles, finding that "by far the most common service politicians demand from call girls is to

---

100. Theodore H. Gaster, *Thespis: Ritual, Myth and Drama in the Ancient Near East.* New York: Henry Schuman, 1950, pp. 4–10.

101. James George Frazer, *The Golden Bough: The Dying God.* New York: St. Martin's Press, 1911.

102. Susan Dunn, *The Deaths of Louis XVI: Regicide and the French Political Imagination.* Princeton: Princeton University Press, 1994, p. 15.

be beaten," hiring women to pretend to inflict upon them "torture and mortification of the flesh . . . and mutilation of their genitals."[103]

Only by being our emotional delegates—by carefully following our unconscious commands—are leaders followed. We might follow them into war and lay down our lives to combat an enemy they alone designated, but the moment they try to ignore the group-fantasy and avoid our hidden commands, people simply do not hear them. The notion that leaders lead us against our will is as much a group-fantasy as the leader's charismatic power to command the sun's rise and fall.[104] A leader is a single individual sitting at a desk in one corner of one city. The power we conditionally delegate to him resides in our group-fantasy, since the leader's central function is to act as a poison container for our group-fantasies. If he should unexpectedly die, the container disappears and our fears return to us in a rush. Small-scale societies often erupt into a fury of witch fears following the death of a leader,[105] and early societies often accompanied the death of the king with the slaughter of hundreds of victims.[106] The leader is seen as omnipotent only because he must appear strong enough to contain our projections. But this strength is pure fantasy and has nothing to do with real accomplishments. The Maoris often renew their vigor by crawling through their leader's legs and touching his powerful penis, and rich Americans have paid hundreds of thousands of dollars to touch the president in the White House.[107] Since the charisma of leaders is purely a defensive grandiosity of our own, compensating for our feelings of childhood helplessness, a leader's strength inevitably decays with time.

THE FOUR PHASES OF LEADERSHIP

Politics is not simply a way to accomplish utilitarian social tasks, as is usually thought. It is first of all a place to put disowned emotions and uncon-

103. Sam Janus et al., *A Sexual Profile of Men in Power*. Englewood Cliffs, NJ: Prentice Hall, 1977, pp. 101 and 170.

104. Rudolph Binion, *Hitler among the Germans*. New York: Elsevier, 1976.

105. Michele Stephen, "Contrasting Images of Power." In Michele Stephen, Ed., *Sorcerer and Witch in Melanesia*. New Brunswick: Rutgers University Press, 1987, p. 280.

106. Eli Sagan, *At the Dawn of Tyranny: The Origins of Individualism, Political Oppression, and the State*. Santa Fe: FishDrum Magazine Press, 1993, p. 122.

107. Bradd Shore, "*Mana* and *Tapu*." In Allan Howard and Robert Borofsky, Eds., *Developments in Polynesian Ethnology*. Honolulu: University of Hawaii Press, 1989, p. 142.

scious parts of individual selves, in an attempt to overcome feelings of fragmentation and internal despair. It is the primary task of a political leader to embody and try to resolve the shared internal emotional problems of his people.

Fantasy analyses I have done of magazine covers and political cartoons over the past two decades[108] reveal that for leaders who are in office for a period of years there are four phases of group-fantasies about leaders, as they become less and less able to provide grandiose manic solutions to the nation's growing growth panic. Casper Schmidt has shown that the Gallup poll approval of American presidents steadily declines as his term of office progresses, unless he provides a military or other sacrificial project that drains him of his "poison."[109]

Since group anxieties are embedded in a fetal matrix, these four leadership phases of group-fantasy parallel the four phases of birth.[110] The four leadership phases are (1) strong, (2) cracking, (3) collapse, and (4) upheaval.

In the first year or so of his term of office, the leader is portrayed as grandiose, phallic, and invincible, able to hold all forces of evil at bay and able to contain the unconscious anxieties of the nation. Photos of the leader appearing on magazine covers and in newspapers are mainly taken from the level of a small child, making him seem like a strong parent. International political crises occurring in this strong phase are rarely seen as dangerous or as requiring an active response; wars are rarely started in the first year of leadership.[111] The strong phase is actually as unrealistic as later phases, since people imagine that their private emotional lives will be magically much better simply because yet another savior sits in an office somewhere, not because they plan to devote themselves to real change.

---

108. Lloyd deMause, *Foundations of Psychohistory* and *Reagan's America*; Casper Schmidt, "The Use of the Gallup Poll as a Psychohistorical Tool." *The Journal of Psychohistory* 10(1982): 141–162; Casper Schmidt, "A Differential Poison Index from the Gallup Poll." *The Journal of Psychohistory* 10(1983): 523–532; Daniel Dervin, *Enactments: American Modes and Psychohistorical Models*. Madison: Fairleigh Dickinson University Press, 1996; Lloyd deMause, "Shooting at Clinton, Prosecuting O.J., and Other Sacrificial Rituals." *The Journal of Psychohistory* 22(1995): 378–393. These have all been done for American leadership phases, and have yet to be tested for the group-fantasies of other nations and groups.

109. Casper Schmidt, "The Use of The Gallup Poll as a Psychohistorical Tool." *The Journal of Psychohistory* 10(1982): 141–151.

110. Lloyd deMause, *Foundations of Psychohistory*, pp. 245–332.

111. Ibid., pp. 153–155.

Fig. 5–6. Strong phase

In the next year or so, the leader's deification begins to fail, and he is shown as weakening, often appearing in cartoons with actual cracks in him as he is seen as increasingly impotent and unable to handle the emotional burdens of the nation. The media spend an inordinate amount of time analyzing whether this or that minor event might make the leader weaker. While the nation responds to solid economic growth through more and more manic overinvestment and overproduction, fears of growth are increasingly expressed, as "things seem to be about to get out of control"— that is, the nation's real progress begins to stir up abandonment fears. The nation engages in an increasing number of economic and political manic projects to ward off its abandonment depression and it searches for external poison containers to hold its split-off early traumas. Evil monsters are depicted in cartoons as starting to pursue the leader, and the group's boundaries are felt to be cracking, with images of leaking water and crumbling walls predominating, as though the nation's womb-surround is cracking. Complaints of being crowded, hungry, and breathless begin, and enemies start to proliferate and become more threatening.

The third group-fantasy phase of leadership, the collapse phase, also lasts one year or more and expresses the nation's extreme anxieties about its dangerous progress. Pressures are shown as inexorably building up inside a collapsed, poisonous world, as memories of childhood humiliations and

Fig. 5–7. Cracking phase

fears flood back into consciousness as floating anxieties awaiting external poison containers. Images of devouring mouths and dangerous, engulfing women proliferate. As the growth panic reaches its peak, manic economic and political projects and troop movements begin to anticipate attack from external poison containers, while the leader seems powerless to end the nation's feelings of pollution, shame, and sinfulness, as shown by images of choking, falling, abandonment, disintegration, poisoning, death, and rebirth. People begin to search for some sort of punishment to cleanse away the feelings of being bad. They feel alone, helpless, and humiliated, and become hypervigilant to attack.

The leader and various delegate groups are expected to voice and take some grandiose manic action to relieve those feelings, restaging the imagined threat rather than remaining hypervigilant and paranoid forever. Risky manic overinvestment and overproduction of goods prepare for depressive collapse of markets—similar to the rock musician who reacts to his success by manic sex, drug, and spending binges. Nations regularly respond to foreign policy crises more belligerently in their collapse phases than in their strong phases.[112] Even before an enemy is chosen, the government

---

112. Lloyd deMause, *Foundations of Psychohistory*, pp. 154–158.

Fig. 5–8. Collapse phase

often takes irrational economic measures to stop things from getting out of control, making more and more mistakes in economic policy that are unconsciously designed to slow progress, such as deflationary monetary policies. The nation also begins to conduct "purity crusades" to put an end to the sexual and other liberties supposedly responsible for the nation's moral collapse.[113] Troops are often scurried around the world to meet minor emergencies or to prepare for action. Free-floating paranoid fantasies of poisonous enemies multiply, and the enemies are often pictured as envious of the nation's progress and about to strike, so that preemptive action against them seems necessary.

The collapse phase ends with a hypervigilant paranoid search for a humiliating other—an enemy who, in a moment of group-psychotic insight, can be identified as the concrete source of the nation's distress.

The leader begins the upheaval phase pictured in the media and in cartoons as a wimp, overwhelmed by poisonous forces, impotent to ward off disaster, which is often depicted as a dangerous water-beast (poisonous placenta) or a Terrifying Woman, along with images of floods, whirlpools, and devouring mouths—imagery similar to medieval depictions of hell as a devouring demon.[114] Purity crusades intensify to cleanse dangerous sexual and other wishes. Antichildren crusades multiply, attacking people's projected inner child for being spoiled, shameful, greedy, out of control, and

---

113. Lloyd deMause, "American Purity Crusades." *The Journal of Psychohistory* 14(1987): 345–348.

114. Lloyd deMause, *Foundations of Psychohistory*, pp. 86–88.

Fig. 5–9. Upheaval phase

needing punishment. When the growth panic is at a peak, "poison alerts" are declared and fears of maternal abandonment and wishes for maternal engulfment and rebirth proliferate. Political cartoons and popular movies contain more and more apocalyptic upheaval birth fantasies, full of vaginal tunnels and exploding pressures. The world seems full of humiliating enemies. Manic, risky financial activities proliferate. Rational progress seems to be unimportant, group delusions are at a peak, and action becomes irresistible as the nation searches for some sacrificial victim to effect a magical restoration of potency and cleansing of sinful wishes.[115] The leader switches from being a container of the nation's irrational emotions to a punisher of bad children, scapegoats for the vital, growing parts of ourselves as we are now seen as having too much hubris. The purification, restoration, rebirth, or revitalization wishes can then be acted out in a cleansing ritual, a purity crusade that can move toward one or more of three solutions:

1. *Regicidal solution*—If the leader fails to find an appropriate enemy to punish, he himself can be designated as the enemy of the nation, full of poisonous sex and aggression, and a ritual slaying is enacted, either by actual regicide or by throwing him out of office. Should he be reelected at the end of his first term, a symbolic death and rebirth ritual is enacted during the election, and the revitalized reelected leader has time to respond to the growth panic.

---

115. Charles W. Socarides, *The Preoedipal Origin and Psychoanalytic Therapy of Sexual Perversions*. Madison, CT: International Universities Press, 1988, p. 17.

2. *Martial Solution*—If an external enemy can be found who will co-
operate by humiliating the nation as it felt humiliated by its parents during childhood, this enemy can now be seen as the source
of all the nation's fears, and military action can be taken by the
now-heroic leader to cleanse the pollution and produce a rebirth
of national strength and purpose. Wars are often preceded by
apocalyptic growth panic movements, Great Awakenings, and other
end-of-the-world group-fantasies.[116] The leader is split into two
parts, representing the two emotional sides of the brain, and the
poisonous traumatized part is projected into the enemy leader, who
agrees to engage in a mutual humiliation ritual and then fight the
cosmic battle between good and evil and purge the nation's fears.
Wars, therefore, are cleansing rituals, purity crusades, and national
purification solutions to growth panic crises. People go to war both
to punish the imaginary engulfing mommy (righteous rape) and
to eliminate their own bad, selfish, childhood alters, projected into
the enemy (purification), so they can finally be loved for the first
time by their parents.

The nation often feels enormous relief by the designation of the
enemy, rather than being rationally fearful of war's destructiveness.
The finding of an external enemy as a poison container produces
a burst of dopamine-filled euphoria. As Winston Churchill wrote
his wife in 1914, as England prepared for war, "Everything tends
toward catastrophe and collapse. I am interested, geared up, and
happy." Similarly, on the day President Harry Truman decided to
send U.S. troops to Korea, one American wrote from Washington,
D.C., "Never before . . . have I felt such a sense of relief and unity
pass through this city. . . . When the President's statement was read
in the House, the entire chamber rose to cheer."[117] The sending
off of the nation's youth to be killed in wars becomes a scapegoating
of one's own bad self, the blood shed is felt to be a purging of the
polluted blood infecting the nation's arteries, and the identification with the nation's grandiose military leaders is felt to be a
magical restoration of potency. Genocidal wars are the most ex-

---

116. Charles B. Strozier, *Apocalypse: On the Psychology of Fundamentalism in America.*
Boston: Beacon Press, 1994.
117. Lloyd deMause, *Foundations of Psychohistory*, p. 160.

treme example of cleansing group-fantasies. They are most often engaged in recently by nations with especially poor child rearing compared to their neighbors, at times when they are attempting to make a leap into modernity, so that the unaccustomed freedom creates an intense growth panic that can only be cleansed by a sacrifice of millions of helpless scapegoats, containers for the nation's polluted self-image.

3. *Internal sacrifice solution*—If the leader cannot find an external enemy with whom to engage in a sacrificial war, he often turns to an internal sacrifice, either a violent revolution or a purifying economic purge. At the end of the 1920s, for instance, as economic and social progress seemed to have gotten out of control, world bankers—chief sacrificial priests of modern nations—pursued deflationary economic policies, raising interest rates and trade barriers, and making other purifying mistakes, producing the Great Depression that sacrificed so much of the wealth of the world. The goal is purification; as Treasury Secretary Andrew Mellon said in 1929 as the Federal Reserve helped push the world into the Great Depression, "It will purge the rottenness out of the system."[118] Business cycles are driven by alternating manic and purifying stages of group-fantasy,[119] as manic defenses against growth panic are followed by purifying collapses into puritanical economic policies, emotional despair, and inaction. As might be expected, most death rates—car crashes, homicides, cancer, pneumonia, heart and liver diseases—rise during prosperous, manic times and are lower during depressions and recessions.[120] Only suicide rates rise during economic declines, reflecting the need for internal sacrifice.

Depressions and recessions are thus not due to the "invisible hand" of economics but are motivated cleansings, periodic sacrifices that often kill more people than wars do, halting dangerous prosperity and social progress that seem to be getting out of control. That growing wealth often produces anxieties rather than

---

118. William Greider, *Secrets of the Temple: How the Federal Reserve Runs the Country*. New York: Simon and Schuster, 1987, p. 300.

119. William K. Joseph, "Prediction, Psychology and Economics." *The Journal of Psychohistory* 15(1987): 101–112; William K. Joseph, "Will Peace Panic the Market?" *The Journal of Psychohistory* 16(1989): 405–409. See also Lloyd deMause, *Reagan's America*.

120. *Business Week*, July 1, 1996, p. 22.

happiness can be shown empirically. From 1957 to 1995, Americans doubled their income in real dollars, but the proportion of those telling pollsters that they are "very happy" *declined* from 35 to 29 percent[121]—because their prosperity and individuation increased faster than their child rearing. Periodic economic downturns are puritanical antidotes administered by sacrificial priests for the disease of greed. Cartoons prior to economic downturns often portray greedy people being sacrificed on altars or children being pushed off cliffs,[122] scapegoats for greedy childhood selves felt to be responsible for the trauma once experienced. Like Aztec human sacrifices,[123] recessions and depressions are accompanied by national sermons, cautionary tales about how sacrificial cleansings are necessary to purge the world of human sinfulness.

The choice between these different solutions to growth panic follows cyclical patterns, wars and depressions alternating in group-fantasy cycles of varying lengths. These long cycles of group-fantasy are examined in the next chapter.

---

121. David G. Myers and Ed Diener, "The Pursuit of Happiness." *Scientific American*, May 1996, p. 70.

122. Lloyd deMause, *Reagan's America*, pp. 56–57.

123. Ptolemy Tompkins, *This Tree Grows Out of Hell: Mesoamerica and the Search for the Magical Body*. San Francisco: Harper, 1990, p. 120.

6

War as Righteous Rape and Purification

*"War! It meant a purification, a liberation
. . . and an extraordinary sense of hope."*
—Thomas Mann

Happy people don't start wars. They don't need purifying or liberation, and their everyday lives are already full of hope and meaning, so they don't need a war to save them from anything.

What sort of strange emotional disorder is it from which war cleanses and liberates people? And how can killing, raping, and torturing people be acts that purify and restore hope in life? Obviously war is a serious psychopathological condition, a recurring human behavior pattern whose motives and causes have yet to be examined on any but the most superficial levels of analysis.

STANDARD THEORIES OF CAUSATION OF WAR

Standard theories of war deny that it is an emotional disorder at all.[1] Unlike individual violence, war is usually seen solely as a response to events outside the individual. Nations that start wars are not considered emotionally disturbed—they are either seen as rational or they are evil, a religious category. Although homicide and suicide are now studied as clinical disorders,[2] war, unfortunately, is not.

---

1. Seyom Brown, *The Causes and Prevention of War*, 2nd ed. New York: St. Martin's Press, 1994.

2. Adrian Raine, *The Psychopathology of Crime: Criminal Behavior as a Clinical Disorder*. New York: Academic Press, 1993.

Most historians of war have given up any attempt to understand its causes, claiming "it is simply not the historian's business to give explanations."[3] Genocide, in particular, appears outside the universe of research into motivations, and if one tries to understand the Holocaust's perpetrators, one is said to be "giving up one's right to blame them." At best, historians avoid the psychodynamics of the perpetrators of wars entirely, saying, "Leave motivation to the psychologists."[4]

Social scientists ascribe the causes of war to three general categories:

1. *Instincts and other tautologies*: The most cited cause of war is that it is a result of a human instinct for destruction. From Clausewitz's "instinctive hostility"[5] and Freud's "instinct for hatred and aggression"[6] down to biologists' statements that war is "macho male sexual selection" that "accelerates cultural evolution,"[7] none of them notices that simply assuming an instinct for war without any genetic evidence at all is wholly tautological, saying no more than "the group's desire for war is caused by the individual's desire for war." Since tribes and states spend more of their time at peace than at war, one must also then posit an "instinct for peace," which, through group cooperation, should favor survival even more. One can proliferate tautological instincts at will, but only evidence counts. Unfortunately, all tests for the heritability of violence have failed completely.[8] The best study of instinct theories concludes: "Human warfare, and indeed killing, are too rare to be the product of a drive that needs to be satisfied. There is no drive or in-

3. Hidemi Suganami, *On the Causes of War*. Oxford: Clarendon Press, 1996, p. 115.

4. Michael Berenbaum and Abraham J. Peck, Eds., *The Holocaust and History: The Known, the Unknown, the Disputed and the Re-examined*. Bloomington, IN: Indiana University Press, 1998, p. 4.

5. Michael P. Ghiglieri, *The Dark Side of Man: Tracing the Origins of Male Violence*. Reading, MA: Helix Books, 1999, p. 211.

6. Sigmund Freud, "Why War?" In *The Complete Psychological Works of Sigmund Freud*. Vol. XXII. London: Hogarth Press, 1964, p. 209.

7. Michael P. Ghiglieri, *The Dark Side of Man*, p. 10; Irenaus Eibl-Eibesfeldt, *The Biology of Peace and War: Men, Animals and Aggression*. London: Thames & Hudson, 1979, p. 123.

8. Adrian Raine, *The Psychopathology of Crime: Criminal Behavior as a Clinical Disorder*. San Diego: Academic Press, 1993, p. 63.

stinct that builds up, gives rise to aggression, is satiated upon release, and then builds up again."[9]

Tautological explanations proliferate in the field of war studies.
Historians are particularly prone to claiming that the reason a lot of
people do something is because they all are just following each other,
a perfect tautology. War is often said, for instance, to be caused by
ideology or by "the culture of militarism" of this or that state,[10] or
by "a marked tendency for the military to prepare offensive military
plans."[11] But saying war is caused by an arms race is about as useful
as saying homicide is caused by someone buying a gun. What one
expects when asking for the motivation for violence is not how the
perpetrator got the weapon, but the internal development of his
psyche plus the events leading up to the violent act. One must not
reify groups; only individuals have motives.

2. *Greed as a motive for war*: War is usually claimed to be purely plun-
der by social scientists: "War is defined as stealing en masse what
other men own."[12] Yet we would never accept greed as a real motive from a man who murders his family after taking out life insurance on them, nor would we accept the greed as the motive of a
man who raped and murdered women and then took some of their
jewelry. As James Gilligan, a prison psychiatrist who has spent his
life analyzing the lives of criminals, puts it: "Some people think
armed robbers commit their crimes in order to get money. But when
you sit down and talk with people who repeatedly commit such
crimes, what you hear is, 'I never got so much respect before in
my life as I did when I first pointed a gun at somebody.'"[13]

That anyone should imagine that hundreds of millions of people
can enthusiastically engage in mutual mass butchery over minor
pieces of territory for utilitarian purposes is so patently ludicrous
that it is a wonder anyone could ever have taken it seriously. Yet
this is what historians and political scientists still ask us to believe.

---

9. John A. Vasquez, *The War Puzzle*. Cambridge: Cambridge University Press, 1993,
p. 140.

10. Niall Ferguson, *The Pity of War*. New York: Basic Books, 1999, p. 1.

11. Hidemi Suganami, *On the Causes of War*, p. 168.

12. Michael P. Ghiglieri, *The Dark Side of Man*, p. 16.

13. James Gilligan, *Violence: Reflections on a National Epidemic*. New York: Vintage
Books, 1996, p. 109.

The entire rational-decisions school of war theorists, all of whom claim utility as the ultimate motive for war, run up against the extensive empirical research done on hundreds of wars in recent years that consistently shows that wars are destructive, not utilitarian; that wars usually cost even winners more than they gain; that those who begin wars usually lose them; and that leaders who start wars never bother to calculate whether the gains will exceed the costs.[14] Otterbein demonstrates that cross-culturally there is "no influence on war of economic or ecological factors"; even tribal warfare destroys far more than it gains, and tribes rarely say they are going to war to gain territory.[15] Rummel concurs, finding from his huge historical database that a country's propensity to go to war is unrelated to its economic development, its technological abilities, or even its military capabilities.[16]

The costs of wars have repeatedly been demonstrated to be far in excess of any gains that could be hoped for.[17] In Vietnam, it cost America hundreds of thousands of dollars to kill each enemy soldier; the world even today spends trillions of dollars every year to fight wars and maintain military forces, far in excess of anything that could be gained by war. Wars are so self-destructive that when a nation goes to war, leaders usually use explicit suicidal imagery. Leaders promise nations that a war is needed not to achieve riches, but to *destroy riches*, which are ruining them by making them soft. My decades-long search of speeches of leaders addressing nations about to go to war has failed to turn up one who promised material advantages by the action. Leaders promise "sacrifice," not gain. As John Adams asked Thomas Jefferson before the American Revolution: "Will you tell me how to pre-

14. William R. Thompson, *On Global War: Historical-Structural Approaches to World Politics*. Columbia: University of South Carolina Press, 1988, p. 257.

15. Keith F. Otterbein, *The Evolution of War: A Cross-Cultural Study*. Chicago: HRAF Press, 1970.

16. R. J. Rummel, "The Relationship Between National Attributes and Foreign Conflict Behavior." In J. D. Singer, Ed., *Quantitative International Politics: Insights and Evidence*. New York: Free Press, 1968, pp. 187–214.

17. R. Hobbs, *The Myth of Victory*. Boulder: Westview, 1979; John V. Denson, Ed., *The Costs of War: America's Pyrrhic Victories*. New Brunswick: Transaction Publishers, 1997; Michael Cranna, Ed., *The True Cost of Conflict*. London: Earthscan Publications, 1994.

vent luxury from producing effeminacy intoxication, extravagance, vice and folly?"[18] The answer: only "hard, masculine war" brought rejuvenation.

3. *Stress theories of war*: Even those theories of war that allow that it is irrational often end up blaming economic distress as the cause of the irrationality. "Hard times make people feel threatened and frustrated," they say, so people go to war from the emotional stress of economic downturns. As Sumner Hull put it: "By eliminating the economic dissatisfaction that breeds war we might have a chance for lasting peace."[19] Marxist theorists in particular believe wars break out because of capitalist economic downturns. Most people, for instance, believe World War II was caused by stresses of the economic Depression.

The problem with these stress theories is that empirically wars have usually occurred during economic upswings, not during depressions. Goldstein has found that large wars have occurred toward the end of the economic upturn phase of the Kondratieff cycle.[20] Wars not only occurred far more frequently after prosperous periods, but were longer and bigger after prosperity, "six to twenty times bigger as indicated by battle fatalities."[21] Macfie finds "the outbreak of wars has avoided years of heaviest unemployment. . . . Excessive expansions are required to germinate the seeds of war."[22] In Europe since 1815, no great-power wars have been started during a depression.[23] World War I broke out after 40 years of growth of real incomes for workers, and even World War II broke

---

18. Michael C. C. Adams, *The Great Adventure*. Bloomington, IL: Indiana University Press, 1990, p. 51.

19. Kalevi J. Holsti, *Peace and War: Armed Conflicts and International Order 1648–1989*. NY: Cambridge University Press, 1991, p. 246.

20. Joshua S. Goldstein, *Long Cycles: Prosperity and War in the Modern Age*. New Haven: Yale University Press, 1988.

21. Joshua S. Goldstein, "Kondratieff Waves as War Cycles." *International Studies Quarterly* 29(1985): 425.

22. A. L. Macfie, "The Outbreak of War and the Trade Cycle." *Economic History* 4(1938): 90, 96.

23. Raimo Vayrynen, "Economic Fluctuations, Military Expenditures, and Warfare in International Relations." In Robert K. Schaeffer, Ed., *War in the World-System*. New York: Greenwood Press, 1989, p. 121.

out several years *after* Germany had regained and surpassed pre-Depression levels of production—the supposed cause, economic distress, having disappeared by 1939. Wars are in fact prosperity-*reducing* rituals. They are responses to what we have earlier termed *growth panic*—responses to progress and prosperity, not to depletion. What is depleted when nations decide to go to war is their emotional, not their economic, resources.

By examining only the sociogenic and not the psychogenic sources of war, major theorists to date have been disappointed by the total lack of results of their research. Singer concludes that the study of war has failed to "achieve any significant theoretical breakthrough" and is saddened by the fact that no one has found any "compelling explanation" for war.[24] Bueno de Mesquita admits "we know little more about the general sources of international conflict today than was known to Thucydides. . . . [Perhaps] scientific explanations of such conflicts are not possible."[25] But the failure to find valid motives for wars only applies to sociogenic theories, ones that carefully avoid the psychological study of human violence that has proved so fruitful in finding the causes of homicide and suicide. We will first turn to the results of recent clinical studies of individual violence before we propose a psychogenic theory of war.

THE CLINICAL STUDY OF HUMAN VIOLENCE

Because those societies that have the harshest child-rearing practices have been shown to produce low-esteem adults who have the highest incidence of murder, suicide and war,[26] the study of human violence can most fruitfully begin with examining the findings of clinicians who have closely interviewed murderers and determined their motives.

---

24. J. David Singer, *Explaining War*. Beverly Hills: Sage, 1979, p. 14.

25. Bruce Bueno de Mesquita, "Theories of International Conflict: An Analysis and and Appraisal." In Ted Robert Gurr, Ed., *Handbook of Political Conflict: Theory and Research*. New York: The Free Press, 1980, p. 361.

26. Richard G. Sipes, "War, Combative Sports and Aggression: A Preliminary Causal Model of Cultural Patterning." In Martin A. Nettleship et al., Eds., *War, Its Causes and Correlates*. Paris: Mouton Publishers, 1975, p. 758; Michael A. Milburn and S. D. Conrad, "The Politics of Denial." *The Journal of Psychohistory* 23(1996): 238–259.

Both statistically and clinically, researchers have found violent adults have only one thing in common: poor child rearing.[27] Studies of homicidal youths, for instance, found 90 percent could be documented as coming from families with severe emotional, physical, or sexually abusive histories.[28] James Gilligan summarizes his decades of interviewing murderers.

> In the course of my work with the most violent men in maximum-security settings, not a day goes by that I do not hear reports—often confirmed by independent sources—of how these men were victimized during childhood. Physical violence, neglect, abandonment, rejection, sexual exploitation, and violation occurred on a scale so extreme, so bizarre, and so frequent that one cannot fail to see that the men who occupy the extreme end of the continuum of violent behavior in adulthood occupied an extreme end of the continuum of violent child abuse earlier in life. . . . As children, these men were shot, axed, scalded, beaten, strangled, tortured, drugged, starved, suffocated, set on fire, thrown out of windows, raped, or prostituted by mothers who were their "pimps."[29]

The cause of adult violence, says Gilligan, is a "collapse of self-esteem" triggered by an incident in which the murderer imagines himself or herself to be humiliated and shamed, resorting to what he calls a "logic of shame, a form of magical thinking that says, 'If I kill this person in this way, I will kill shame—I will be able to protect myself from being exposed and vulnerable to and potentially overwhelmed by the feeling of shame.'"[30] Gilligan points out that shame is at the root of mass violence, too, pointing out that "Hitler came to power on the campaign promise to undo 'the shame of Versailles'—and clearly that promise, and the sensitivity to shame from which it derived its power, struck a responsive chord in the German people as a whole."[31] Though criminologists report that in homicides "the most common altercation was of relatively trivial origin: insult, curse, jostling, etc.,"[32] these shaming events turn childhood traumas into current rage, what

27. Richard M. Yarvis, *Homicide: Causative Factors and Roots*. Lexington, MA: D.C. Heath & Co., 1991.

28. Robin Karr-Morse and Meredith S. Wiley, *Ghosts From the Nursery: Tracing the Roots of Violence*. New York: Atlantic Monthly Press, 1998, p. 119.

29. James Gilligan, *Violence: Reflections on a National Epidemic*, p. 45.

30. Ibid., p. 64.

31. Ibid., p. 67.

32. Michael P. Ghiglieri, *The Dark Side of Man*, p. 138.

Katz terms "righteously enraged slaughter,"[33] producing a "tremendous rush [that is] almost orgasmic" for the murderers[34] as they avenge all their past hurts and humiliations. "All violence," says Gilligan, "is an attempt to achieve justice."[35] As we shall shortly see, this includes mass violence as well, which also involves imagining that one achieves justice through violent, righteous vengeance for earlier wrongs—attacking enemies "out there" to revenge the continuing humiliations by the parental alters inside ourselves.

People start wars when something changes in their brains—neurotransmitters, hormones, and cellular neuropeptide systems.[36] This "something" is the end result of a developmental process that begins before birth and is turned into a capacity for violence during childhood. Children are actually quite empathic toward others from birth. Neonates cry in response to the crying of another baby: "Even 6-month-olds . . . responded to distressed peers with actions such as leaning toward, gesturing toward, touching, or otherwise contacting the peer."[37] Babies can be quite generous with their love, gently touching and patting other babies and even their mothers when they notice they look sad.

But the majority of children throughout history—particularly boys, who are physically and emotionally abused more than girls—feel so helpless and afraid because of their traumatic child rearing that they grow up in what has been called a "culture of cruelty,"[38] where they graduate from violent families to form gangs that dominate and hurt others in order to be perpetrators rather than victims, thereby preparing themselves for cooperating in the violence of war. Studies report "a significantly greater proportion of very violent children demonstrated . . . paranoid symptomology [and] believed that someone was going to hurt them . . . constantly feeling the need to carry weapons such as guns and metal pipes for their own

---

33. Jack Katz, *Seductions of Crime: Moral and Sensual Attractions in Doing Evil.* New York: Basic Books, 1988, p. 18.

34. Ibid., p. 71.

35. James Gilligan, *Violence*, p. 11.

36. Candace B. Pert, *Molecules of Emotion: Why You Feel the Way You Feel.* New York: Simon & Schuster, 1997.

37. Nancy Eisenberg, *The Caring Child.* Cambridge: Harvard University Press, 1992, p. 8.

38. Dan Kindlon and Michael Thompson, *Raising Cain: Protecting the Emotional Life of Boys.* New York: Ballatine Books, 1999, p. 72.

protection."[39] The more violent children "had been physically abused by mothers, fathers, stepparents, other relatives and 'friends' of the family. The degree of abuse to which they were subjected was often extraordinary. One parent broke her son's legs with a broom; another broke his fingers and his sister's arm; another chained and burned his son; and yet another threw his son downstairs."[40] Severe neglect and emotional abuse have been shown to be equivalent to and often worse than physical abuse in producing lasting traumatic effects upon children.[41]

The effects of abuse upon children have been extensively studied. As we have discussed earlier, serotonin levels are reduced by trauma, and are found in reduced levels in adult antisocial personalities, because the lower level of their inhibiting ability allows less control over impulsivity and therefore higher rates of violence.[42] External stress also increases corticosterone production, decreasing the effectiveness of the hippocampal system, which evaluates the emotional meaning of incoming stimuli.[43] Very early maternal neglect in particular produces an undersized orbitofrontal cortex, resulting in such a diminished self and such a low capacity for empathy that the child grows up unable to feel guilt about hurting others.[44] Thus swaddled babies abandoned to cribs in dark rooms—as most children were in history—who totally miss the mother's gaze and loving interaction in their early years are programmed for later impulse disorders, psychopathic personalities, and the need for killing in war simply because they have never developed what today we consider normal-sized orbitofrontal cortexes through sustained eye contact and mutual play with the mother. As Allan Schore puts it:

---

39. Richard Rhodes, *Why They Kill: The Discoveries of a Maverick Criminologist.* New York: Alfred A. Knopf, 1999, p. 206.

40. Ibid.

41. Adrian Raine, *The Psychopathology of Crime*, pp. 85, 263; Brett Kahr, "Ancient Infanticide and Modern Schizophrenia: The Clinical Uses of Psychohistorical Research." *The Journal of Psychohistory* 20(1993): 267–273.

42. Adrian Raine, *The Psychopathology of Crime*, pp. 85, 260; David M. Stoff and Robert B. Cairns, Eds., *Aggression and Violence: Genetic, Neurobiological and Biosocial Perspectives.* Mahwah, NJ: Lawrence Erlbaum, 1996.

43. Bessel A. van der Kolk and Jose Saporta, "The Biological Response to Psychic Trauma: Mechanisms and Treatment of Intrusion and Numbing." *Anxiety Research*, 4(1991): 205.

44. Allan N. Schore, *Affect Regulation and the Origin of the Self: The Neurobiology of Emotional Development.* Hillsdale, NJ: Lawrence Erlbaum, 1994.

> The orbitofrontal cortex functionally mediates the capacity to empathize
> with the feelings of others and to reflect on internal emotional states,
> one's own and others'. . . . The socioaffective stimulation produced by
> the mother's face facilitates the experience-dependent growth. . . . Chil-
> dren deprived of early visual sensory stimulation . . . frequently show
> impairments in representational and affective functions that are respon-
> sible for severe emotional problems.[45]

Lesions of the orbitofrontal cortex produce unregulated aggression and
dramatic mood state alterations in both humans and other animals because
"unmodulated rage represents a hyperactivation of the . . . dopaminergic
system [and] impulsive acting out episodes [of] narcissistic rage."[46] Children neglected and abused in early months "manifest pathological self-
importance, or narcissism, displayed as . . . grandiosity, recklessness . . .
insecurity and emotional shallowness [plus] the inability to feel ordinary
human empathy and affection for others and the perpetrating of repeated
antisocial acts."[47]

DISSOCIATION OF THE TWO BRAINS

One of the most important findings of Lonnie Athens from his lifetime of
interviewing violent criminals is that before they kill, they consult "phantom communities" in their heads who approve of their violent acts as re-
venges for past humiliations.[48] These phantom communities are identical
to the social alters discussed previously, where dissociated violent selves
and internalized harmful caregivers are stored. Athens determined that
violence didn't just follow trauma; it required a further "belligerency stage
of violentization" during which the brutalized subject resolves in consul-
tation with his inner phantoms, his alters, that he or she has had enough,

---

45. Allan N. Schore, "A Century After Freud's Project: Is a Rapprochement Between
Psychoanalysis and Neurobiology at Hand?" *Journal of the American Psychoanalytic Association* 45(1997): 831; Allan N. Schore, *Affect Regulation*, p. 174.

46. Ibid., p. 339.

47. Robert I. Simon, *Bad Men Do What Good Men Dream: A Forensic Psychiatrist Illuminates the Darker Side of Human Behavior*. Washington, DC: American Psychiatric Press,
1996, p. 28.

48. Richard Rhodes, *Why They Kill*, p. 95; Lonnie Athens, *The Creation of Violent
Criminals*. Urbana: University of Illinois Press, 1992.

that violence is sometimes necessary if one isn't to remain a victim one's whole life, and that he or she will now use physical violence for those who unduly provoke or humiliate him or her.

These dissociated violent alters, it turns out, are concentrated in only one hemisphere of the brain, but not the same one in each of us. Fredric Schiffer explains how his studies of dual-brain psychology led him to ask his psychiatric patients to look through special glasses, one pair of which had only the left side of the left eye uncovered (reaching only the right hemisphere), the other only the right side of the right eye (reaching only the left hemisphere), so that the patient would transmit information only to one half of the brain at a time.[49] He found that in the majority of patients one hemisphere looked at the world with extreme anxiety and the other saw things more maturely:

> One patient, a Vietnam veteran, whom I had diagnosed with a severe posttraumatic stress disorder, looked out of one side and developed an expression of intense apprehension as he looked at a large plant in my office. "It looks like the jungle," he said with some alarm. I asked him to look out the other side, and he said, "No, it's a nice-looking plant."[50]

Schiffer finds he can help patients by having them analyze the emotional attitudes of the traumatized hemisphere, since "the troubled side is often like a traumatized person who hasn't been able to move beyond the trauma, even when removed from it, because he continues to expect retraumatization."

These alters, which still live in the past, seeing the world as threatening and abusive, constitute two separate minds, one frightened and angry, the other denying the concerns of its partner. When the more grown-up hemisphere moves into new freedom and new behavior, the traumatized hemisphere reexperiences the helplessness, fears, and humiliations it stores from early childhood. This struggle between the hemispheres is usually dissociated, with one hemisphere being unaware of the feelings with which the other hemisphere is filled. When Rudolf Hess, SS Kommandant at Auschwitz, wrote, "I have never personally mistreated a prisoner, or even killed one. I have also never tolerated mistreatment on the part of my sub-

---

49. Fredric Schiffer, *Of Two Minds: The Revolutionary Science of Dual-Brain Psychology*. New York: The Free Press, 1998.
50. Ibid., p. 12.

ordinates,"[51] he was not being disingenuous. The nontraumatized half of his brain sincerely believed he and his subordinates never mistreated a Jew as they were beating and torturing and murdering them by the hundreds of thousands. His social alter in his traumatized hemisphere was fully in control and cut off all meaning of what he was doing, which to his nontraumatized hemisphere appeared as normal. He simply had two brain modules that he kept separate.

Without the laterality of the brain, neither politics nor religion can exist, as they do not in other animals that do not have divided selves. It is only because humans have radically lateralized hemispheres that they are able to go to war with one hemisphere and build the League of Nations with the other.

The lower the child-rearing mode, the more divided are the hemispheres. New Guinea natives can be warm and friendly while in their more mature hemisphere and suddenly switch into their social alters in the other hemisphere and kill you because they think you are bewitching them. The lower the child-rearing mode, the more traumatic the early experiences and the more divided the hemispheres. In tribal societies, switching into warrior alters is a simple process: "The man or boy leaves his former self behind and becomes something entirely different, perhaps even taking a new name. . . . The change [is] usually accomplished through ritual drumming, dancing, fasting and sexual abstinence . . . into a new, warriorlike mode of being, denoted by special body paint, masks, and headdresses."[52] In modern societies, with a wide range of more healthy child-rearing modes, switching is more difficult, because "only 2 percent of recruits kill easily, so the rest must be brought to do so by careful military training."[53]

The split mind begins to form with early trauma, even perinatally.[54] The two halves of the brain are even sometimes recognized in political imagery. Hitler, for instance, often spoke of a strange "kinship" between the Aryan and Jew (the two sides of his brain): "Has it not struck you how

51. Rudolf Hess, *Death Dealer: The Memoirs of the SS Kommandant at Auschwitz*. New York: Da Capo Press, 1996, p. 183.

52. Barbara Ehrenreich, *Blood Rites: Origins and History of the Passions of War*. New York: Henry Holt and Co., 1997, p. 10.

53. David Grossman, *On Killing: The Psychological Cost of Learning to Kill in War and Society*. New York: Little, Brown & Co., 1995, p. 13.

54. Frederick Leboyer, *Birth Without Violence*. London: Inner Traditions International, 1995.

the Jew is the exact opposite of the German in every single respect, and yet is as closely akin to him as a blood brother?"[55] The split mind is responsible for what is termed "the banality of evil"; one side is banal and responsible for denial (Winnicott's "false self"), the other side evil and responsible for humiliation (the perpetrator alter). Only the dual brain explains, for instance, how ordinary Germans could have, during the Holocaust, "humiliated, beat, and tortured defenseless people and then shot them in the back of the neck without the slightest hesitation [and then dissociate and] pose before their living or dead victims, laughing into the camera [and] write home that these snapshots and extermination anecdotes would someday be 'extremely interesting to our children.'"[56]

EARLY MOTHER–CHILD INTERACTIONS AS THE SOURCE OF HUMAN VIOLENCE

The primary sources of violent political behaviors are the concrete mother–child interactions of one generation earlier—how mainly the mother responded to, cared for, and conveyed her feelings and fears to her fetus, infant, and young child. We have already described in Chapter 4 how going to war is preceded by flashbacks to intrauterine, perinatal traumas and group-fantasies of the need for national rebirth. Here we will begin to examine the sources of human violence in early mother–child interactions.

Videotape recordings of children's relationships with their mothers in the preverbal period "have been shown to remain essentially the same over time and to be duplicated with other 'substitute' mother figures. A child who has a warm, affectionate relationship with the mother will relate to others in a warm, affectionate manner, whereas a child with a guarded, distant relationship will relate to others in a guarded, distant manner."[57] This maternal relationship is eventually restaged in international relations in a concrete manner, being acted out in "the sandbox of history,"

55. George Victor, *Hitler: The Pathology of Evil*. Washington: Brassey's, 1998, p. 144.

56. Götz Aly, "The Universe of Death and Torment." In Robert R. Shandley, Ed., *Unwilling Germans? The Goldhagen Debate*. Minneapolis: University of Minnesota Press, 1998, p. 169.

57. Ronald Katz, "Mothers and Daughters—The Tie that Binds: Early Identification and the Psychotherapy of Women." In Gerd H. Fenchel, Ed., *The Mother-Daughter Relationship: Echoes Through Time*. Northvale, NJ: Jason Aronson, 1998, p. 248.

with nations playing the emotional roles of the mothers and children from early life.

Mothers who, because of their own life experiences, see their children as harmful and aggressive have historically treated them mainly in ways that have made them grow up as violent adults, by routinely inflicting upon them murder, abandonment, neglect, binding, enemas, domination, beatings, sexual assaults, and emotional abuses[58] that are later restaged in wars and political behavior. Necessity was not the main source of these cruelties toward children—wealthy parents were historically even more overtly rejecting, giving their children to others at birth for years for what they expected would be abusive caregiving. Fathers have until recently usually only worsened this early traumatic upbringing, since historically the father has almost always been mostly absent from the child's early life—most fathers in history spending their days in the fields or factories and their nights in the taverns (see Chapter 8). When home, fathers have lent little support to mothers in caregiving and emotional nurturance, requiring that their wives "mother" them rather than their children.

Growing up, Mahler found, is built upon basic maternal care, since "differentiation is from the mother, not from the father."[59] Psychotherapists have during the past century built up a convincing body of data showing that the traumas of the earliest years are the hardest to overcome. Therefore, women, not men, have until recently, for better or worse, been the main sources of care, neglect, and abuse throughout history. As St. Augustine put it, "Give me other mothers and I will give you another world." What Erikson said about girls has been found to be true of all children: "By the time a girl developmentally turns to the father, she has normally learned the nature of an object relationship once and for all from her mother."[60] In short, *mothers are major actors in childhood history*; they are perpetrators[61] and not just victims. This does not mean that mothers are to be blamed for everything that happens in history. Psychohistorians, like psychotherapists, are not moralists who blame people; they only look for causes and trace psychodynamics.

---

58. See Chapter 8.

59. Margaret Mahler, "Aggression in the Service of Separation-Individuation." *Psychoanalytic Quarterly* 50(1981): 631.

60. Ronald Katz, "Mothers and Daughters," p. 245.

61. Joseph C. Rheingold, *The Fear of Being a Woman: A Theory of Maternal Destructiveness*. New York: Grune & Stratton, 1964.

Most of the extremely abusive historical child-rearing practices that are detailed in the next two chapters are routine reactions to the child's daily needs and growth process, wherein immature mothers and fathers expect their child to give them the love they missed when they were children, and therefore experience the child's independence as rejection. Mothers in particular have had extremely traumatic developmental histories throughout history; one cannot severely neglect and abuse little girls and expect them to magically turn into good mothers when they grow up. As one battering mother said, "I have never felt really loved all my life. When the baby was born, I thought he would love me, but when he cried all the time, it meant he didn't love me, so I hit him."[62] Childbirth often triggers postpartum depression and feelings of emptiness[63] because it means the mother must give up her own hopes to receive the care she missed from her own mother.[64] The moment the infant needs something or turns away from her to explore the world, it triggers her own memories of maternal rejection. When the infant cries, the immature mother hears her mother, her father, her siblings, and her spouse screaming at her. She then "accuses the infant of being unaffectionate, unrewarding and selfish . . . as not interested in me."[65] All growth and individuation by the child is therefore experienced as rejection. "When the mother cannot tolerate the child's being a separate person with her own personality and needs, and demands instead that the child mirror her, separation becomes heavily tinged with basic terror for the child."[66] Children first experience growth panic anxieties because their mother rejects, humiliates, or punishes them for their needs and for their individuation. As adults, they then turn to paranoid and violent political behavior during periods of growth and individuation because society threatens to reproduce this intolerable early maternal rejection, shame, and punishment. Because these maternal interactions are so early, they are primarily nonverbal, which means that politics has a dominantly nonverbal quality that can only be studied by research into media illustra-

---

62. Brandt F. Steele, "Parental Abuse of Infants and Small Children." In E. James Anthony and Therese Benedek, Eds., *Parenthood: Its Psychology and Psychopathology.* Boston: Little, Brown, 1970, p. 32.

63. Ibid., p. 170.

64. T. Berry Brazelton and Bertrand G. Cramer, *The Earliest Relationship: Parents, Infants and the Drama of Early Attachment.* Reading, MA: Perseus Books, 1990, p. 11.

65. Ibid., p. 145.

66. Ibid., p. 255.

tions rather than words—group-fantasies shown in cartoons, magazine covers, and TV images.

It is likely that the centrality of mothers in bringing up children is even responsible for the fact that men are more violent than women and universally fight wars. Testosterone is not the cause, as is usually imagined, since (1) testosterone levels are actually *lower* in the most aggressive boys;[67] (2) testosterone is present in boys and girls in roughly the same amounts before the age of 10; and (3) although "all normal boys experience a huge surge of testosterone in early adolescence, [they] do not all display increased aggression . . . [so] testosterone does not cause aggression."[68] Evidence is beginning to accumulate that it is differential treatment of boys, especially by mothers, that is responsible for their higher rates of violence by men. Boys are physically punished more often and with greater severity than girls;[69] boys are more often used sexually by their mothers in their early years;[70] boys are given less nurturance, are ignored more often, are spoken to less, and are coached to be more violent;[71] boys are subject to overcontrol by humiliation and shame;[72] and boys are more harshly disciplined for the same actions by both parents and teachers.[73]

Although the battlegrounds may change, wars are inevitably about the basic feelings of infancy: trust, security, approval, domination, envy, rage, threats, shame, and independence.[74] Since having a child revives in mothers

---

67. Stephen S. Hall, "The Bully in the Mirror." *The New York Times Magazine*, Feb. 6, 2000, p. 34.

68. Dan Kindlon and Michael Thompson, *Raising Cain: Protecting the Emotional Life of Boys*. New York: Ballantine Books, 1999, p. 13.

69. Ibid., p. 55; Michael P. Ghiglieri, *The Dark Side of Man: Tracing the Origins of Male Violence*. Reading, MA: Perseus Books, 1999, p. 5; Janet Ann DiPietro, "Rough and Tumble Play: A Function of Gender." In Juanita H. Williams, Ed., *Psychology of Women: Selected Readings*. 2nd ed. New York: W. W. Norton & Co., 1985, p. 156; Murray A. Straus, "Spanking by Parents and Subsequent Antisocial Behavior of Children." *Archives of Pediatric and Adolescent Medicine* 151(1997): 762.

70. G. Fritz et al., "A Comparison of Males and Females Who Were Sexually Molested as Children." *Journal of Sex and Marital Therapy* 7(1981): 55.

71. Jeffrey Z. Rubin et al., "The Eye of the Beholder: Parents' Views on Sex of Newborns." In Juanita H. Williams, Ed., *Psychology of Women: Selected Readings*. 2nd ed. New York: W. W. Norton & Co., 1985, pp. 147–152; Dan Kindlon and Michael Thompson, *Raising Cain*, p. 41.

72. Dan Kindlon and Michael Thompson, *Raising Cain*, p. 11.

73. Ibid., p. 53.

74. Ibid., p. 46.

long-dormant wishes for the closeness that they missed from their own mothers, mothers often envy the child each of the needs they are asked to satisfy, thinking, "I never got that; why should my child?" But before the nineteenth century, mothers thought their infants were so full of violence that they would "scratch their eyes out, tear their ears off, or break their legs" if they didn't tie them up in endless bandages, "so as to resemble billets of wood."[75] Therefore, during most of history, early mother–child interactions that most good-enough mothers today are capable of—with mutual gazing, babbling, and smiling[76]—were missing, because mothers tightly bound their babies up at birth and stuck them in another room, severely neglecting them the first years of their lives.[77] International affairs have not usually been negotiated in a secure and peaceful manner because infantile life has been neither secure nor peaceful.

Sociologists and historians have avoided looking for the family sources of wars and social violence. Whenever a group produces murderers, the early parental relationship must have been abusive and neglectful. Yet this elementary truth has not even begun to be considered in historical research; just stating that poor mothering lies behind wars seems blasphemous. Instead, the grossest sorts of idealizations of historical mothering proliferate. When, for instance, studies of the extreme violence of the Mafia turn to depictions of Sicilian family relations, they inevitably resemble the happy families straight out of *The Godfather*. Yet Italian psychoanalyst Silvia di Lorenzo's book, *La Grande Madre Mafia*, describes actual Sicilian mother–child interactions and gives us an accurate picture of the maternal origins of Mafia violence:

> If a boy of theirs commits a slight fault, [mothers] do not resort to simple blows, but they pursue him on a public street and bite him on the face, the ears, and the arms until they draw blood. In those moments even a beautiful woman is transformed in physiognomy, she becomes purplish-red, with blood-shot eyes, with gnashing teeth, and trembling convulsions, and only the hastening of others, who with difficulty tear away the victim, put an end to such savage scenes.[78]

75. Lloyd deMause, *Foundations of Psychohistory*. New York: Creative Roots, 1982, p. 41.

76. Allan N. Schore, *Affect Regulation and the Origin of the Self*, p. 102.

77. Lloyd deMause, *Foundations of Psychohistory*, p. 41.

78. Silvia di Lorenzo, *La Grande Madre Mafia: Psicoanalisi del Potere Mafioso*. Milano: Pratiche Editrice, 1996, p. 44.

Thus the conditions of early mothering have had profound effects on adult human violence. Every child-rearing practice in history is restaged in adult political behavior. Children whose mothers swaddled them and were "not there" emotionally could not as adults maintain object consistency, and they became paranoid, imagining enemies everywhere. Children whose mothers regularly did not feed them in a timely fashion experienced the world as malevolently withholding. Children whose mothers rejected them with depressive silence experienced peaceful international periods as threatening. Children whose mothers dominated them and who were engulfing chose totalitarian political leaders. Children whose mothers were so needy they described their children as "born selfish and demanding" or who saw them as "angry since birth" experienced other nations as demanding too much or as angry "bad boys." Children whose mothers used them as antidepressants sacrifice themselves to overcome their mothers' depression; as one soldier said about sacrificing oneself in wars, "We have laid ourselves over the body of the motherland in order to revive her."[79] And children whose mothers ridiculed and humiliated them experienced the international sphere as a container for intolerable ridicule and shame. It is not surprising that violent, authoritarian political behavior has been statistically correlated with rejecting, punitive parenting.[80] As Godwin put it, society is an "exopsychic structure" where adults restage the "parental purification system" of childhood by "cleansing bad, frustrating, and abusive aspects of the parent–child relationship" in the political arena.[81]

THE PSYCHOGENIC THEORY OF WAR

War, then, is a ritual that restages early traumas for the purpose of revenge and self-purification. Wars are clinical emotional disorders, periodic shared psychotic episodes of delusional organized butchery intended to turn a severe collapse of self-esteem into a rage to achieve justice. Wars are both

---

79. Adam Zamoyski, *Holy Madness: Romantics, Patriots and Revolutionaries 1776–1871.* New York: Viking Penguin, 2000, p. 23.
80. Michael A. Milburn and S. D. Conrad, "The Politics of Denial." *The Journal of Psychohistory* 23(1996): 238–251.
81. Robert Godwin, "The Exopsychic Structure of Politics." *The Journal of Psychohistory* 23(1996): 252–253.

homicidal and suicidal; the Germans who cheered Hitler on as he promised to start an unwinnable world war against the overwhelming power of
opposing nations knew deep down they were committing suicide. Like all
homicides and suicides, wars are results of our failed search for love, magical
gestures designed to ensure love through projection into enemies, by knock
ing the terrifying mommy off her pedestal and by killing the bad-child self:

1. *War as righteous rape—revenge against the terrifying mommy*: Enemy
   nations in wars are often pictured as women, witches, even placental beasts. Enemies experienced as mommies are there to be
   pushed around and even raped, but not eliminated, since even
   when raging against a bad mommy the hurt child knows he needs
   her desperately. Unloved children continue to hope they will be
   accepted by their mothers, however much they are angry with
   them. This is why Hitler kept hoping to manipulate Mother England into being friendly. And it is why he didn't destroy Paris when
   he marched into La Belle France. Nations to the west of Germany
   were mainly seen as mommies, to be knocked off their pedestals
   but not to be eliminated. "France . . . was not marked for subjuga-
   tion but rather for a secondary role in the Nazi scheme [and] Hitler
   was always keen on reaching some settlement with the British. . . .
   [Therefore] the German army fighting in the west was given strict
   orders to conduct itself according to the rules of war."[82] The same
   group-fantasy of war as righteous rape was voiced by Germans in
   1914, when they imagined that "only if we are able to hurt England badly will she really leave us unmolested, perhaps even
   become a 'friend.'"[83]
2. *War as purification—killing off the bad-child self*: Enemy nations are
   also imagined as bad children, disobedient, disgusting, violent,
   sexual—everything one was accused of as a child by one's caregivers. If the bad-child self can be killed off entirely, "finally
   mommy will love me." This is why Hitler vowed to wipe out the
   "evil" nations to the east and settle "good Germans" in their place.
   Poles, Russians, Slavs, Jews—every nationality east of Germany was

82. Omer Bartov, "Savage War." In Michael Burleigh, Ed., *Confronting the Nazi Past:
New Debates on Modern German History*. New York: St. Martin's Press, 1996, p. 126.
83. Gustav Krupp, cited in *The Nation*, August 9/16, 1999, p. 36.

projected with bad-child imagery: "Slavs were considered sub-humans, to be either murdered . . . or starved to death."[84] Moscow, Hitler promised, would be leveled and turned into a reservoir, and Jews would be totally eliminated. In addition, World War II would be a suicidal mission for millions of Germans, thus sacrificing the bad-child part of themselves—their most vital, growing, independent self. Then the good-German self that remained would be purified and would finally be loved by the Motherland.

It is not surprising that in early societies bloodthirsty war goddesses ruled over battlefields—from "blood-thirsty Innana" and "the lady of battles Ishtar" to "crazed Athena"—since wars are all about how terrifying mommies sacrifice bad children in sacrificial slaughters termed "Inanna's dance."[85] Even the French Revolution was shown in drawings as a violent triumph of Marianne or a liberty-goddess over bad-boy Frenchmen.[86] Leaders are delegated the task of being priests in the cleansing sacrifice, modern shamans who must organize the battle against projected maternal and devil-self alters. Even simple societies go to war to win the love of mommy. In the Yanomamo war ritual myth, for instance, the culture hero-spirit Child of Water goes to war and slays enemies to "end chaos" and "do what his mother desires and thereby win her approval."[87] The role of the father in war is quite different: it is to provide the violence needed to rape and revenge the terrifying mommy and to punish and sacrifice the bad baby. Hitler carried a dog whip everywhere he went, the same whip he and many other German children were beaten with by their fathers.[88] Oddly enough, nations don't go to war as revenge against bad fathers—the crucial drama is based earlier than that. Even though children are terribly frightened by their father's violence in the family, the goal in starting wars isn't finally to take revenge against the father, but to kill the shame, to purify the self and to

84. Ibid.

85. David Kinsley, *The Goddesses' Mirror: Visions of the Divine from East and West.* Albany: State University of New York Press, 1989, pp. 133–151.

86. Madelyn Gutwirth, *The Twilight of the Goddesses: Women and Representation in the French Revolutionary Era.* New Brunswick: Rutgers University Press, pp. 263–268.

87. Sue Mansfield, *The Gestalts of War: An Inquiry into Its Origins and Meanings as a Social Institution.* New York: The Dial Press, 1982, p. 62.

88. Martin Broszat, *Hitler and the Collapse of Weimar Germany.* Oxford: Berg, 1987, p. 4.

force mother to love you—to organize men into Fatherlands so they can conquer Motherlands.

Nations switch into their dissociated traumatized hemispheres after periods of peace and prosperity because the individuation challenges of historical progress means separating from mommy, a dangerous act in adulthood if it was not allowed during childhood. Increases in freedom and prosperity for people who have been abused as children lead first to fears of separation and then to a clinging to the early abusive mommy, even to merging with her. But to merge with a mommy means losing one's masculinity—it means becoming a woman. Therefore, long periods of peace mean castration. Thus Kant's statement that wars are necessary because "prolonged peace favors . . . effeminacy" parallels Machiavelli's claim that war exists to purge nations of *effeminato*, the "daily accretion of poisonous matter [caused by women's] conspiracy to 'poison' . . . manhood."[89] In fact, in groups where they do not have effective war rituals available when people experience severe ego disintegration, people often go amok—a dissociative state where people suddenly kill people in wild, uncontrolled sprees, as often occurs in the otherwise placid Balinese.[90] Even chimpanzees go amok when given food supplies by humans and "engage in episodes of apparently unprovoked explosive . . . behavior . . . as though they had entered an ASC [alternate state of consciousness] . . . to discharge an inner state of tension . . . similar to human dissociative behaviours."[91]

Prosperity leads to starting wars most often in societies where the economic advances of a minority, a more advanced psychoclass, outrun the child-rearing evolution of the majority, producing in the less advanced psychoclasses extreme anxieties about changes that require individuation. Thus some of the most destructive wars have occurred in recent centuries when there was a "leap into modernity"[92] by nations whose average child-rearing lagged badly behind their social and economic progress, so that

---

89. Ralph Greenson, "Why Men Like War." In R. Nemiroff et al., Eds., *On Loving, Hating and Living Well*. New York: International Universities Press, 1992, p. 127; Hanna Fenichel Pitkin, *Fortune Is a Woman: Gender and Politics in the Thought of Niccolo Machiavelli*. Berkeley: University of California Press, 1984, pp. 25, 274.

90. Luh Ketut Suryani and Godon D. Jensen, *Trance and Possession in Bali: A Window on Western Multiple Personality, Possession Disorder and Suicide*. Oxford: Oxford University Press, 1993, p. 44.

91. Ibid., p. 32.

92. Jack Snyder, *From Voting to Violence: Democratization and Nationalist Conflict*. New York: W. W. Norton & Co., 2000.

they tried to run modern capitalist systems with crippled human capital. The most peaceful periods, on the other hand—for instance, Europe's century of peace from 1815 to 1914[93]—occurred while the child rearing of most Western European nations was most rapidly evolving and could keep up with the individuation challenges of modernity.[94]

WAR AND GROUP-FANTASY CYCLES

In the previous chapter, evidence was presented that wars most often occur after leaders have been in office for some time and are seen as weakening in their ability to be in control of national group-fantasies. Thus, the longer the leader is in office, the more likely he will be to take the nation to war. This is confirmed in the case of the United States, where no president has gone to war during his first year, his "strong" phase; where smaller wars sometimes begin in the second and third year in office, as the president weakens; and where its three most destructive wars began at 45, 48, and 103 months into the presidencies of Buchanan, Wilson, and Franklin Roosevelt, after their group-fantasy strength had collapsed.

Much empirical work has been done on the historical study of war cycles.[95] A cycle of about 25 years in the level of violence for most nations in recent centuries has been documented[96]—as though each new generation must be thrown into the mouth of Moloch as a purification sacrifice to the war goddess. There has also been considerable work done on economic cycles and their close relationship to war cycles,[97] with the finding

---

93. Kalevi J. Holsti, *Peace and War: Armed Conflicts and International Order 1648–1989*. Cambridge: Cambridge University Press, 1991, p. 59.

94. See Chapters 7–9.

95. J. David Singer and Melvin Small, *The Wages of War 1816–1965: A Statistical Handbook*. New York: John Wiley & Sons, 1972; Quincy Wright, *A Study of War*, 2nd ed. Chicago: University of Chicago Press, 1962; Francis A. Beer, *Peace Against War: The Ecology of International Violence*. San Francisco: W. H. Freeman and Co., 1981; George Modelski, *Long Cycles in World Politics*. Seattle: University of Washington Press, 1987.

96. Frank H. Denton and Warren Phillips, "Some Patterns in the History of Violence." *Conflict Resolution* 12(1968): 193; William R. Thompson, *On Global War: Historical-Structural Approaches to World Politics*. Columbia: University of South Carolina Press, 1988, p. 94.

97. Brian J. L. Berry, *Long-Wave Rhythms in Economic Development and Political Behavior*. Baltimore: Johns Hopkins University Press, 1991.

that "wars between great powers occur during periods of economic expansion, while stagnation hinders their outbreak."[98] Thus, although wars have been confirmed to be correlated with prosperity, it is because no psychological analysis has ever been attempted that scholars have had to admit: "We do not understand the causal dynamics of the long wave . . . encompassing political and economic elements."[99] The remainder of this chapter presents a psychogenic theory of group-fantasy cycles that explains this periodic alternation between economic depressions and wars.

In the chart below, four American group-fantasy cycles have been drawn for the past two centuries of American history, each consisting of four phases: (1) innovative, (2) depressed, (3) manic, and (4) war. At the bottom of the chart are listed the major depressions and wars, which coincide with the second and fourth phases of group-fantasy. In the middle of the chart is drawn Klingberg's extrovert-introvert foreign policy mood curve, which he compiled by counting such foreign policy indices as the proportion of presidential speeches given over to positive action needed in world affairs.[100] As can be seen, there is a close correlation between Klingberg's mood index stages and my independently derived group-fantasy phases.

Here is an outline of the four group-fantasy phases, stressing American and other national emotions and their resulting political and economic behavior:

1. *Innovative phase*: A new psychoclass comes of age after the previous war, a minority of the cohort born two to three decades earlier and raised with more evolved child-rearing modes. This new psychoclass introduces new inventions, new social and economic arrangements, and new freedoms for women and minorities, producing an Era of Good Feelings or a Gilded Age that for a few years is tolerated even by the earlier psychoclasses. By the end of the innovative phase, however, the challenges produced by progress

98. Christopher Chase-Dunn and Kenneth O'Reilly, "Core Wars of the Future." In Robert K. Schaeffer, Ed., *War in the World-System*. New York: Greenwood Press, 1989, p. 121.

99. Ibid., p. 434.

100 Frank Klingberg, "The Historical Alteration of Moods in American Foreign Policy." *World Politics* 4(1952): 239–273. See also Jack E. Holmes, *The Mood/Interest Theory of American Foreign Policy*. Lexington: University Press of Kentucky, 1985.

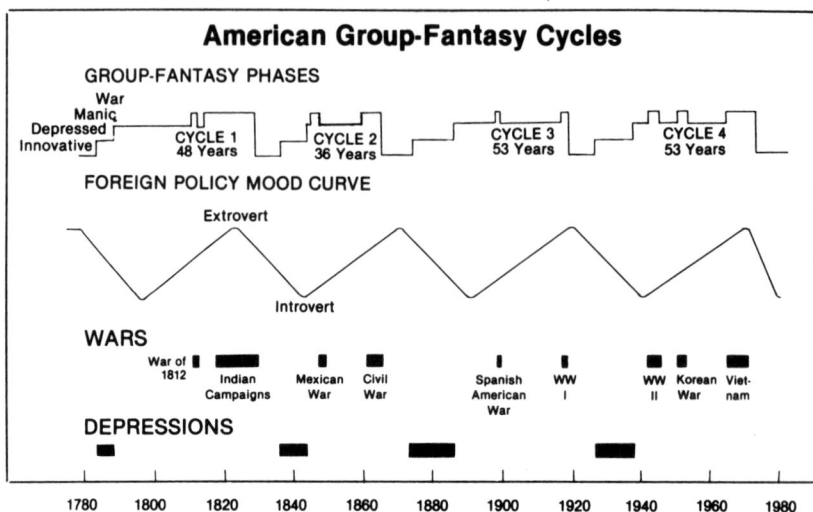

Fig. 6–1. American group-fantasy cycles

and individuation begin to make everything seem to be getting out of control, as wishes surface that threaten to revive early maternal rejection and punishment. In addition, as women, children, and minorities get new freedoms, older psychoclasses find they cannot be used as much as they previously had been as poison containers that can be punished for one's sins. Purity crusades begin, antimodernity movements demanding that new sexual and other freedoms be ended to reduce the anxieties of the nation's growth panic and turn back the clock to more controlled times and social arrangements.

2. *Depressed phase*: The older psychoclasses become depressed because of their new individuation challenges, expecting punishment for them, and produce an economic depression by withdrawing money from circulation, by raising interest rates, by reducing consumption, by limiting trade, and by making all the other surplus-reducing motivated mistakes in fiscal policies that are so familiar in economic history. Economic depressions are motivated internal sacrifices that often kill as many people as wars do.[101] Cartoons

---

101. Lloyd deMause, *Reagan's America*. New York: Creative Roots, 1984.

prior to and during depressions often show sinful, greedy people being sacrificed on altars,[102] and the depressed nation becomes paralyzed politically, unable to take action to reverse the economic downturn. Just as depressed individuals experience little conscious anger—feeling they deserve to be punished—so, too, nations in depressions are characterized by introverted foreign policy moods, start fewer military expeditions, and are less concerned with foreign affairs. The feeling during depressions is "I should be killed" for my wishes rather than "I want to kill others." The nation begins to look for a phallic leader with whom they can merge and regain their failed potency, and who can protect them against their growing delusional fears of a persecutory mommy.

3. *Manic phase*: As eventual economic recovery threatens fresh anxiety, manic economic, social, and military activity builds up as a defense against depressive anxieties. The nation engages in speculative investment, credit explosions, foreign belligerence, military buildups, and other grandiose attempts to demonstrate omnipotent control of symbolic love supplies. Usually the mood is one of fearless risk taking, sometimes punctuated by brief financial panics. Apocalyptic group-fantasies of a world full of evil and a God who is furious and about to end it all proliferate, producing severe growth panics such as the American Great Awakenings. Continued prosperity leads to a search for enemies, both internal (minorities, criminals, children) and external (foreigners), who can be punished in national purity crusades as bad children who embody the nation's sinful greed. Maternal engulfment fears increase as grandiose defenses and memories of being a helpless baby return; people imagine their nations as "pitiful, helpless giants," with gigantic needs, but helpless to satisfy them. As paranoid delusional enemies seem to surround the nation, sacrificial rebirth group-fantasies appear, complete with devouring placental sea monsters, picturing violence as the only antidote to growing fears of disintegration of self.[103]

4. *War phase*: When another nation is found that agrees to provide the humiliation episode needed as a *casus belli*, a tremendous re-

---

102. Ibid., pp. 56–57.

103. For an attempt to quantify group-fantasy cartoon images, see Winfried Kurth, "The Psychological Background of Germany's Participation in the Kosovo War." *The Journal of Psychohistory* 27(1999): 101–102.

lief is felt: "Aha! I *knew* the enemy was real and not just in my head." The group psychotic insight that diabolical enemies are strangling and poisoning one's nation forces a final switch into the social trance wherein group-fantasy becomes reality and violent action becomes irresistible.[104] The neurotransmitters, hormones, and neuropeptides of the nation change dramatically, in the same manner as the neurochemistry of individuals changes as they move toward violence.[105] War provides the opportunity for both righteous rape and purification. The righteous rape can be described as both maternal (raping Mother England) and homosexual (penetrating soldiers). The purification accomplishes the sacrifice of the bad-child self, both through the suicidal part (killing the nation's youth) and the homicidal part (killing the enemy).

Thus wars and depressions can be seen as occurring in cycles similar to individual manic-depressive cycles of violence, only stretched out into periods of approximately one full generation in length. Each of the first three American group-fantasy cycles in the chart above is approximately 50 years long and ends with two wars, first usually a "nice little war" as a sort of trial balloon and then a full-fledged war that produces the rebirth of national virility. This pattern has been modified after World War II, when improving child rearing reduced the size of both economic downturns and wars. Although most Western nations in the past three centuries have had the same four-wars-a-century pattern as the United States, whether they also have followed the same four-stage group-fantasy cycle has yet to be investigated.[106]

THE INNOVATIVE PHASE: PROGRESS AND PURITY CRUSADES

The central force for change in economic life is the result of changes in child rearing among a minority of the society. The usual causal chain of modernization theory—that more prosperity means more money for im-

---

104. Lloyd deMause, *Foundations of Psychohistory*, pp. 189–192.

105. Candace B. Pert, *Molecules of Emotion: The Science Behind Mind-Body Medicine.* New York: Simon & Schuster, 1997.

106. See the "public moods" cycles described for Western Europe since 1876 in Keith L. Nelson and Spencer C. Olin, Jr., *Why War? Ideology, Theory and History.* Berkeley: University of California Press, 1979.

proving child rearing—is simply backward, both because empirically child-rearing change always precedes economic change[107] and because the wealthy families have not usually given better care to their children— they have sent them out at birth to abusive caregivers. Those children whose parents actually bring them up themselves and try to surpass tra ditional child-care practices grow up as a new, innovative psychoclass that tries new social and economic ventures, which appear dangerous to the earlier psychoclasses.

The innovative phases in the chart of American group-fantasies above are familiar to every student of American history as periods of unparalleled growth and technological invention. They contain the early growth of steamboats, railroads, and telegraphs; the two phases of the nineteenth-century Industrial Revolution with its rapid industrialization; the second Industrial Revolution after World War I; and even the computer revolution produced by the Benjamin Spock generation.[108] In each period, emotional investment in children paid off as an increase in productivity.

During these innovative phases, governments manage to work out various formal and informal rules to settle international disagreements. Since peace is not just an absence of war and involves establishing intergovernmental organizations and conferences to resolve disputes, nations that are not in an emotional state of collapsed self-esteem have regularly found ways to break stalemates and settle their disagreements without violence.[109] Whether by bilateral agreement or through the restraints of peace conferences, innovative psychoclasses have demonstrated that there are many ways whereby issues can be resolved outside of power politics, which leads to wars.

Each of these peaceful innovative phases also were periods of women's rights, the best known of which in America were the early nineteenth-century groups pressing for women's education, jobs, new divorce laws, and property rights; the post–Civil War woman's sufferage movement; the post–World War I women's rights movement; and the post–Vietnam War

---

107. See Chapters 8 and 9.

108. Sean Dennis Cashman, *America in the Gilded Age: From the Death of Lincoln to the Rise of Theodore Roosevelt*, 3rd ed. New York: New York University Press, 1993; William E. Leuchtenburg, *The Perils of Prosperity 1914–1932*, 2nd ed. Chicago: University of Chicago Press, 1958.

109. John A. Vasquez, *The War Puzzle*. Cambridge: Cambridge University Press, 1993, pp. 263–280.

feminist movement. The lagging psychoclasses—both men and women—reacted to each of these periods of freedom for the "new women" with extreme horror.[110] Just as the economic advances of early modern Europe resulted in a million women killed as witches, the progress of the modern innovative periods engendered fears of the *femme fatale*[111] who was "strongly passionate and . . . endowed with strong animal natures,"[112] and who produced "sexual anarchy" where "men became women [and] women became men."[113] Ever since Cato wailed in 195 B.C., after a few Roman women sought to repeal a law that forbade them from wearing multicolored dresses, that "women have become so powerful that our independence has been lost in our own homes and is now being trampled and stamped underfoot in public,"[114] innovative periods in history have produced misogynous purity crusades designed to reverse social progress and return to more familiar repressive times.[115]

Purity crusades have centered on sexual morality, whether they combated Noyes's "free love" debates before the Civil War or Margaret Sanger's birth control ideas in the 1920s.[116] They include moral-reform crusades against prostitution, against pornography, against alcohol—against everything that represented unfulfilled wishes, including even bicycle seats, that "might cause women's moral downfall."[117] Even the reduction of the workweek—the Saturday Half-Holiday Act of 1887—was opposed as likely to cause the masses to turn to "dancing, carousing, low behavior, rioting, shooting, and murder."[118] Children's rights were opposed because

---

110. Susan Faludi, *Backlash: The Undeclared War Against American Women*. New York: Crown Publishers, 1991.

111. Debora Silverman, "The 'New Woman,' Feminism, and the Decorative Arts in Fin-de-Siecle France." In Lynn Hunt, Ed., *Eroticism and the Body Politic*. Baltimore: Johns Hopkins University Press, 1991, p. 144.

112. Kenneth Alan Adams, "Arachnophobia: Love American Style." *The Journal of Psychoanalytic Anthropology* 4(1981): 193.

113. Elaine Showalter, *Sexual Anarchy: Gender and Culture at the Fin de Siècle*. New York: Penguin Books, 1990.

114. Susan Faludi, *Backlash*, p. 62.

115. Lloyd deMause, "American Purity Crusades." *The Journal of Psychohistory* 14(1987): 345–350.

116. David J. Pivar, *Purity Crusade, Sexual Morality and Social Control, 1968–1900*. Westport, CT: Greenwood Press, 1973.

117. Ibid., p. 176.

118. Ibid., p. 233.

any relaxation of punitive child rearing would inevitably lead to "running wild, blatant disobedience . . . masturbation, and insanity."[119] Cars for women were opposed because they could be turned into "houses of prostitution on wheels."[120] And after the purity crusade began, it usually continued right into the next war, which borrowed its language and moral fervor, so that it seemed the war itself was a purification of the morals of the nation. Thus purity reformers of the 1850s, reacting to the feminism of the time, began a crusade against sex between southern white men and black women, objecting to slavery not so much on behalf of the rights of the slaves but in order "to protect the sexual purity of America." In the words of purity crusaders: "The Southern states are one Great Sodom . . . a vast brothel" which only a war between the North and the South could clean up.[121] Thus, too, World War I was said to have been needed to be fought "to save men from moral decay [from homosexuality],"[122] and the Vietnam War was preceded by a fantasy that, according to *Time*'s special issue on "Sex in the U.S.," found a dangerous demise of puritanism in America due to Freudian psychology that had made "America one big Orgone Box [of] pornography."[123]

THE DEPRESSED PHASE: THE DRAGON MOTHER AND THE PHALLIC LEADER

The task of controlling growth panic by depressions is given during the modern period mainly to central banks, which first flood the nation with low-interest liquidity to encourage overinvestment, excess borrowing, inflation, and stock market bubbles, and then, when the expansion becomes too sinful for the national psyche, reverse the monetary expansion by in-

---

119. Jayme A. Sokolow, *Eros and Modernization: Sylvester Graham, Health Reform, and the Origins of Victorian Sexuality in America*. Rutherford: Fairleigh Dickinson University Press, 1983, p. 80.

120. Edward Chancellor, *Devil Take the Hindmost: A History of Financial Speculation*. New York: Farrar Straus Giroux, 1999, p. 204.

121. Ronald G. Walters, "The Erotic South: Civilization and Sexuality in American Abolitionism." *American Quarterly* 25(1973): 183.

122. George L. Mosse, *Nationalism and Sexuality: Respectability and Abnormal Sexuality in Modern Europe*. New York: Howard Fertig, 1985, p. 33.

123. *Time*, January 24, 1964, p. 54.

creasing interest rates and reducing liquidity ("Taking away the punch bowl when the party gets going").[124] Depressions occur because people actually become depressed, reducing their spending and investment, and feel hopeless. Depressions are, as Keynes said, "a crisis of sentiment . . . a collapse of confidence."[125] The task of government, he said, was to recognize that demand (desire) is subject to irrational contractions that had to be offset through fiscal and monetary manipulations—rather like a psychiatrist prescribing medications to restore depleted serotonin levels. Yet neither Keynes nor any other economist asked why people periodically become depressed and reduce their economic activities.

In fact, nations enter into depressions because they feel persecuted for their prosperity and individuation by what Jungians have termed the "dragon mother"—the needy, "devouring mother of infancy . . . who cannot let her children go because she needs them for her own psychic survival."[126] Weston has found anorexics in particular are dominated by fantasies of persecution by the terrifying dragon mother who "gives her child the impossible task of filling her 'limitless void'" so the child fears being "eaten alive."[127] To prevent this, when these children grow up and try to individuate, they refuse to eat so they won't have any flesh on them for the dragon mother to devour. Economic depressions evidence similar group-fantasies of devouring mommies; they are "economic anorexias" where nations inflict economic wounds upon themselves and limit consumption," become "all bones" so as not to tempt the devouring dragon mother. Banks, in particular, are often pictured as greedy dragons. For instance, President Andrew Jackson imagined the Bank of the United States was what he called the "Mother Bank," which by issuing paper money he said was a "bad mother dominating her children" who had to be stopped before the nation was eaten up, and so conducted a "kill the Great Monster" campaign that would "strangle the many-headed hydra" and kill it.[128] Needless to say, his success in "crushing the Mother Bank dragon" led to a severe depression.

124. Lloyd deMause, "'Heads and Tails': Money as a Poison Container." *The Journal of Psychohistory* 16(1988): 12.

125. James A. Estey, *Business Cycles: Their Nature, Cause, and Control*, 3rd ed. Englewood Cliffs, NJ: Prentice-Hall, 1956, p. 95.

126. Marisa Dillon Weston, "Anorexia as a Symbol of an Empty Matrix Dominated by the Dragon Mother." *Group Analysis* 32(1999): 71–85.

127. Ibid., p. 74.

128. Michael Paul Rogin, *Fathers and Children*, p. 291.

That depressions purposefully punish families is rarely acknowledged. In the depression beginning in 1873, for instance, produced by "a decade of speculative excess and overinvestment,"[129] "20 percent [were] unemployed, 40 percent worked for only six or seven months a year, and only 20 percent worked regularly."[130] Depressions have quietly killed hundreds of thousands of women and children, a sacrifice of "bad children" greater than many wars. Yet depressions are still seen as beneficial purges of the economic bloodstream; as the treasury secretary said in 1929 as the Federal Reserve helped push the world into the Depression: "It will purge the rottenness out of the system."[131] Depressions are indeed blood purges, only sacrificial, similar to the practice of the Aztecs sacrificing humans and regularly drawing blood from their thighs and genitals to feed the goddess to prevent her from becoming angry with them for their sinful prosperity.[132] Thus William K. Joseph's study of political cartoons and magazine advertisements during 1929 found they were "full of strong, wealthy women, but the men were pictured as puny, neurotic, and insignificant."[133]

That depressions—like all blood sacrifices—are self-inflicted wounds and not just the results of "mysteriously wrongheaded monetary policies"[134] is still not admitted by most economists. The end of prosperity comes "with a sense of relief."[135] Even the mistakes by authorities that lead to a downturn are unconsciously motivated. For instance, the mistake of the Federal Reserve in 1925 in lowering interest rates and igniting the stock market bubble, followed by the mistake of their overly restrictive monetary policy after 1929 that reduced the stock of money by a third and turned the downturn into the Depression, plus the mistake of passing higher tariffs of the

129. Edward Chancellor, *Devil Take the Hindmost: A History of Financial Speculation*. New York: Farrar Straus Giroux, 1999, p. 186.

130. Sean Dennis Cashman, *America in the Gilded Age: From the Death of Lincoln to the Rise of Theodore Roosevelt*, 3rd ed. New York: New York University Press, 1993, p. 107.

131. William Greider, *Secrets of the Temple: How the Federal Reserve Runs the Country*. New York: Simon and Schuster, 1987, p. 300.

132. Lloyd deMause, *Reagan's America*. New York: Creative Roots, 1984, p. 55.

133. William K. Joseph, "Prediction, Psychology and Economics." *The Journal of Psychohistory* 15(1987): 111.

134. Paul Krugman, "Financial Crises in the International Economy." In Martin Feldstein, Ed., *The Risk of Economic Crisis*. Chicago: The University of Chicago Press, 1991, p. 108.

135. William E. Leuchtenburg, *The Perils of Prosperity 1914–1932*, 2nd ed. Chicago: University of Chicago Press, 1958, p. 265.

Hoover administration and the doubling of the income tax, all were *motivated* mistakes.[136]

One of the best defenses against fears of maternal engulfment is merging with a phallic leader to restore potency. Anzieu found small groups regularly searched for a narcissistic, aggressive leader when they were being devoured by the group mother and felt that "everything is crumbling" in the group.[137] Parin found that the Anyi tribe, where the mothering was neglectful and incestuous, produced men who feared being "poisoned, devoured, and castrated by women" and who therefore chose exceptionally violent leaders because they felt that merging with a "strong and severe father" saved them from feeling castrated.[138] And Blum found that when nations choose "hypnotic-like surrender to the leader," they overcome "infantile helplessness and weakness, childhood traumata, child abuse and neglect, and feelings of being unloved [through] an escalation to war [whereby] the sacrifice of the sons in battle by their oedipal fathers and a 'macho' defense against femininity are powerful dynamics."[139]

The initial task of the phallic leader is to make real the growing paranoia of the nation by finding an enemy:

> It is as if a therapist said to the paranoid-schizoid patient, "You really are being persecuted. Let me help you by naming your persecutors. . . . You and your true friends can fight the persecutors and praise each other's righteousness, which will help you realize that the source of aggression and evil is out there, in the real world. And you thought it was all in your head!"[140]

The most effective phallic leaders have been found to be "narcissistic personalities who are characterized by intense self-involvement [whose] interpersonal relations are frequently marked by a lack of empathy, [who] oscillate between feelings of grandiosity and omnipotence . . . and feelings

136. Edward Chancellor, *Devil Take the Hindmost*, pp. 198–223.

137. Didier Anzieu, *Le Groupe et l'inconscient*. Paris: Dunod, 1975, p. 319.

138. Paul Parin et al., *Fear Thy Neighbor as Thyself: Psychoanalysis and Society among the Anyi of West Africa*. Chicago: University of Chicago Press, 1980, p. 282.

139. Harold P. Blum, "Sanctified Aggression, Hate, and the Alternation of Standards and Values." In Salman Akhtar, et al., Eds., *The Birth of Hatred: Developmental, Clinical, and Technical Aspects of Intense Aggression*. Northvale, NJ: Jason Aronson, 1995, p. 19.

140. Robert S. Robins and Jerrold M. Post, *Political Paranoia: The Psychopolitics of Hatred*. New Haven: Yale University Press, 1997, p. 98.

of inferiority and low self-esteem [and who] are particularly susceptible to feelings of shame and humiliation."[141] Only narcissistic leaders who from early childhood have felt shamed and humiliated could, like Richard Nixon, lead wars that had no other purpose than to avoid accepting "a national humiliation [that would] destroy our country's confidence in itself."[142] The deep well of loneliness created in them by the emotional distancing of their mothers is usually worsened by the absence of their fathers, which has been found by Broude to result in phallic hypermasculinity and violence.[143] Conquering women and conquering nations are the same task for many phallic leaders.[144] It is no coincidence that so many of America's wartime presidents were adulterers or compulsive womanizers.[145] Conquest is the central political function of the phallic leader. Alternatively, messianic heroes who rescue groups from severe growth panic can sometimes be personally ascetic—only conquering nations, not real women.[146] As Hitler put it, "The crowd is a woman. . . . After a speech I feel as if I had a sexual release."[147] Dominance and violence restores and purifies the self. As Hitler said after the Röhm massacre: "So! Now I have taken a bath, and feel clean as a new-born babe again."[148]

A phallic leader wards off the humiliations of maternal abuse and neglect by political violence. Lyndon Johnson, for instance, remembers his engulfing mother's withdrawal of affection whenever he failed to do as she wished, "walking around the house pretending I was dead [and] refusing to speak or even look at [me]."[149] He had a recurring dream that a stampede of cattle—a symbol of maternal engulfment[150]—was coming toward

141. Blema S. Steinberg, *Shame and Humiliation: Presidential Decision Making on Vietnam*. Pittsburgh: University of Pittsburgh Press, 1996, p. 2.

142. *The Wall Street Journal*, April 27, 1994, p. A12.

143. Gwen J. Broude, "Protest Masculinity: A Further Look at the Causes and the Concept." *Ethos* 18(1990): 103–121.

144. Lloyd deMause, "The Phallic Presidency." *The Journal of Psychohistory* 25(1998): 354–357.

145. Ibid.

146. John J. Hartman and Graham S. Gibbard, "Bisexual Fantasy and Group Process." *Contemporary Psychoanalysis* 9(1973): 316.

147. George Victor, *Hitler: The Pathology of Evil*. Washington: Brassey's, 1998, p. 105.

148. Ibid., p. 78.

149. Blema S. Steinberg, *Shame and Humiliation*, p. 31.

150. Charles W. Socarides, *The Preoedipal Origin and Psychoanalytic Therapy of Sexual Perversions*. Madison, CT: International Universities Press, 1988, p. 47.

him while he was paralyzed in a chair; in the dream, he cried out for his mother, but no one came.[151] His fear of helplessness and humiliation returned just before Vietnam, when, he said, "I felt that I was being chased on all sides by a giant stampede coming at me. . . . The American people were stampeding me to do something about Vietnam. . . . I deserved something more than being left alone in the middle of the plain, chased by stampedes on every side."[152] According to his biographer, he "avoided at all costs the threat to his self-esteem that . . . public humiliation might entail"[153] and started the war. The war restored his and the nation's masculinity: "Unzipping his fly, [Johnson] pulled out his penis and asked the reporters (according to one who was there): 'Has Ho Chi Minh got anything to match that?'"[154] The war castrated the enemy: "I didn't just screw Ho Chi Minh. I cut his pecker off."[155] One is reminded of the fact that until recently warriors actually castrated their enemies on the battlefield after defeating them.[156] Those who opposed the war, Johnson said, were women: "[They have] to squat to piss."[157] Going to war meant not being a woman, not being overwhelmed by and merged with mommy.

Because nations continue to live in both hemispheres as they go to war, they must both prepare for war by maneuvering an enemy into a pose where they can be righteously attacked and at the same time provide deniability that their nation is really responsible for the war. Leaders might recognize that, as Theodore Roosevelt wrote to a friend in 1897, "In strict confidence . . . I should welcome almost any war, for I think this country needs one."[158] But phallic leaders usually find ways to invent unprovoked attacks, from Wilson's lies about the sinking of the *Lusitania* and Lyndon Johnson's lies about the attack in the Gulf of Tonkin, to Hitler's lies about

---

151. Doris Kearns Goodwin, *Lyndon Johnson and the American Dream.* New York: St. Martin's Press, p. 191.

152. Ibid., p. 200.

153. Blema S. Steinberg, *Shame and Humiliation*, p. 79.

154. Michael Hutchison, *The Anatomy of Sex and Power: An Investigation of Mind-Body Politics.* New York: William Morrow and Co., 1990, p. 44.

155. David Halberstam, *The Best and the Brightest.* New York: Random House, 1972, p. 414.

156. Walter Burkert, *Homo Necans: The Anthropology of Ancient Greek Sacrificial Ritual and Myth.* Berkeley: University of California Press, 1983, p. 68.

157. Blema S. Steinberg, *Shame and Humiliation*, p. 99.

158. Howard Zinn, *The Zinn Reader: Writings on Disobedience and Democracy.* New York: Seven Stories Press, 1997, p. 230.

an attack by Polish forces. One of the most complex lies that carefully provoked an attack that was then passed off as a surprise was that of President Franklin Roosevelt's year-long actions to get Japan to attack the United States. Stinnett's voluminously documented book, *Day of Deceit*, demonstrates that in October 1940 Roosevelt secretly began to carry out a series of eight actions that forced the hawks in the Japanese government to go to war with the U.S.—embargoing trade, "tightening the noose" on their economy, and deploying American warships on "pop-up" cruises within the territorial waters of Japan, then leaving the U.S. fleet unprotected at Hawaii and hiding the fact that Japanese codes had been broken so that the attack would appear as a "surprise."[159]

Another case of provoking an enemy can be shown in the actions of John F. Kennedy in the Cuban Missile Crisis. Kennedy's childhood was typically abusive, dominated by his mother's emotional distancing of him— "She was never there when we really needed her. . . . [She] never really held me and hugged me. Never."—and her brutality, battering him with "hairbrushes, coat hangers, belts, and shoes, [and] once slapping young Bobby's face so viciously that she punctured his eardrum and split his lip."[160] The result, for John Kennedy, was a phallic-narcissistic personality focused on conquering women in "daily assignations and a lifetime of venereal disease [plus] a steady diet of mood-altering drugs."[161] Claiming a mythical "missile gap" with the Russians, John Kennedy was elected president to "get America moving again" after the too-peaceful Eisenhower era, and soon authorized the Bay of Pigs invasion of Cuba over the objections of most experts, who said it would fail, telling his aides he "wasn't going to be 'chicken.'"[162] The resulting failure was taken by him as a personal humiliation, for which he needed revenge. He authorized various assassination attempts against Castro, but success evaded him.[163]

By 1962, Kennedy decided to try to regain his potency by preparing an invasion of Cuba by U.S. forces. He asked his staff to formulate a pre-

159. Robert B. Stinnett, *Day of Deceit: The Truth About FDR and Pearl Harbor*. New York: The Free Press, 2000.

160. C. David Heymann, *RFK: A Candid Biography of Robert F. Kennedy*. New York: Dutton, 1998, p. 17.

161. Ibid., pp. 238 and 387.

162. Gus Russo, *Live By the Sword: The Secret War Against Castro and the Death of JFK*. Baltimore: Bancroft Press, 1998, p. 18.

163. Ibid., p. 64.

text that would give an appearance of a Cuban attack on a U.S. airline that would justify his invasion.[164] But war with a small neighbor would not be enough—Kennedy actually tried to make certain the Russians would be involved in the war. On January 31, 1962, he asked Khrushchev's son-in-law, Aleksei Adzhubei, to meet with him and, in order to humiliate the Russians as he felt humiliated, told him he was preparing to attack Cuba like Russia attacked Hungary: "If I run for reelection and the Cuban question remains as it is," he said, "we will have to do something" about Cuba. Kennedy told a startled Adzhubei: "I called [Central Intelligence Agency director] Allen Dulles into my office [after the Bay of Pigs] and dressed him down. I told him: 'You should learn a lesson from the Russians. When they had difficulties in Hungary, they liquidated the conflict in three days [by sending in troops.]'" Adzhubei repeated this invasion threat to Khrushchev, who told Soviet diplomats: "An attack on Cuba is being prepared. And the only way to save Cuba is to put missiles there."

In April 1962, 40,000 American troops began practicing to invade Cuba in North Carolina.[165] By October 6, 1962, thousands of American troops were positioned for invasion, along with plans and equipment, and prepared to invade on October 20, 1962, using the Bahamas as an invasion base camp. But on October 16, 1962, the CIA took clear U-2 photos that told them Russian nuclear missiles were in Cuba. Kennedy told no one of his own bellicose actions and threats, instead declaring the Russian move wholly unprovoked. Despite the fact that 100 million Americans lived in the range of the Russian missiles—and despite the opinion of his staff that they made no military difference at all because nuclear missiles on Russian submarines had long been stationed a few miles off Cuba—Kennedy instituted a naval embargo and prepared for a full-scale attack on Cuba, risking a nuclear World War III. Saying "if Khrushchev wants to rub my nose in the dirt, it's all over,"[166] and "we must not look to the world as if we were backing down,"[167] Kennedy fully expected war. When his staff told him there were diplomatic means that could be used to remove the missiles, he replied: "The object is not to stop offensive weapons, because the offensive weapons are already there, as much as it is to have a

164. Ibid., p. 77.
165. Ibid., p. 164.
166. Richard J. Barnet, *Roots of War*. New York: Atheneum, 1972, p. 82.
167. James N. Giglio, *The Presidency of John F. Kennedy*. Lawrence, KS: University Press of Kansas, 1991, p. 150.

showdown with the Russians of one kind or another."[168] He bragged to his associates that he would "cut off the balls" of Khrushchev.[169] Since Kennedy had already publicly declared the U.S. was "prepared to use nuclear weapons at the start" of any war,[170] Kennedy's embargo would have meant nuclear war if the Russians didn't accept the humiliation and back down. As American demonstrators marched with signs saying, "Invade Red Cuba," Kennedy admitted "there may be 200 million dead" in America if Khrushchev didn't remove the missiles.[171] It was "one hell of a gamble," as he put it.[172] Not one person in Kennedy's cabinet—outside of Adlai Stevenson, his ambassador to the U.N.—suggested he hold negotiations with Khrushchev.[173] Expecting the Russians to reject his demands, Kennedy put American nuclear bombers on Defcon 2 status (ready for war) and moved staff into the White House bomb shelter as the bombers, armed with nuclear bombs, went into the air, ready to begin their flight to Russia.[174] Luckily for mankind, Khrushchev backed down, removed the Cuban missiles in exchange for a Kennedy promise not to invade, and a nuclear World War III was avoided.

THE MANIC PHASE: EGO DISINTEGRATION AND PARANOIA

Nations engage in manic economic and political projects for the same reasons newly successful rock stars go to all-night parties and take drugs—to get a dopamine "rush" that counters the depression and guilt produced by their success. Political paranoia and ego disintegration are seen in conspiratorial group-fantasies, fears of femininity, and imagined humiliations by

168. Ernest R. May and Philip D. Zelikow, Eds., *The Kennedy Tapes: Inside the White House During the Cuban Missile Crisis.* Cambridge: Harvard University Press, 1997, p. 424.

169. Michael R. Beschloss, *The Crisis Years: Kennedy and Khrushchev, 1960–1963.* New York: HarperCollins, 1991, p. 375.

170. Gus Russo, *Live By the Sword*, p. 177.

171. Bruce J. Allyn, James G. Blight and David A. Welch, *Back to the Brink: Proceedings of the Moscow Conference on the Cuban Missile Crisis, 1989.* Cambridge: Harvard University Press, 1992, p. 76.

172. Aleksandr Fursenko and Timothy Naftali, *"One Hell of a Gamble": Khrushchev, Castro, and Kennedy, 1958–1964.* New York: W. W. Norton & Co., 1997, p. 245.

173. Michael R. Beschloss, *The Crisis Years: Kennedy and Khrushchev, 1960–1963*, p. 148.

174. *The New York Times*, January 5, 2001, p. A17.

other nations. These are paralleled in the economic sphere by manic overinvestment, risky ventures, excess money supply growth, soaring debt, and stock market speculations, and in the political sphere by jingoistic nationalism, expansionist ventures, military buildups, and belligerent foreign affair provocations. As in drug addiction, each dopamine rush leaves a dopamine hangover that requires an even larger manic activity to overcome the resulting depression. A search for external enemies results from the growing ego disintegration as grandiosity fails and poison alerts and sacrificial group-fantasies proliferate. As patients in therapy who are trying to change sometimes say: "Going beyond what my mother wanted me to be makes me feel like I'm falling apart, disintegrating, and sets off a minefield of attack, destruction, and killing."[175]

In America, these paranoid fears of apocalyptic punishment for success have taken the form of revivalist Great Awakenings, which occurred at the end of a long period of peace: the first after 24 years of peace (1714–38) under King George I and II, the second after 30 years of peace (1815–45) under Madison and Monroe, and the third after 31 years of peace (1866–97) following the Civil War. These apocalyptic fantasies merge into the wars that follow. The American Revolution has been said to have been "caused by a pandemic of persecutory delusions" featuring "a fear of effeminacy"[176] and a fantasy of "Mother England persecuting her children."[177] Similarly, beginning with the *Annus Mirabilis* of 1858, daily gatherings of thousands of people in spontaneous prayer meetings took place, where people fell down, saw visions, and went out and destroyed their goods in preparation for the end of the world.[178] This apocalyptic mood merged with the "cleansing in the fires of war" that would "purge the virus" of the nation in Civil War bloodshed that was "sacramental, erotic, mystical, and strangely gratifying."[179]

---

175. JoAnn Culbert-Koehn, "Birth, Violence and the Millennium." *International Journal of Prenatal and Perinatal Psychology and Medicine* 11(1999): 430–431.

176. Gordon S. Wood, "Conspiracy and the Paranoid Style: Causality and Deceit in the Eighteenth Century." *William & Mary Quarterly* 39(1982): 410.

177. James H. Hutson, "The American Revolution: The Triumph of a Delusion?" In Erich Angermann, Ed., *New Wine in Old Skins*. Stuttgart: Klett, 1976, p. 179; Lloyd deMause, *Foundations of Psychohistory*. New York: Creative Roots, 1982, p. 113.

178. Timothy L. Smith, *Revivalism and Social Reform In Mid-Nineteenth Century America*. New York: Abingdon Press, 1962, pp. 63–79.

179. Charles Strozier, *Apocalypse: On the Psychology of Fundamentalism in America*. Boston: Beacon Press, 1994, pp. 172–173.

Perhaps the classic era of paranoid fears leading to apocalyptic group-fantasies as punishment for prosperity is the period before World War I, when the world growth rate jumped to over 5 percent, and when Europe appeared to be going clinically paranoid from what was termed "the decadence of the times [when] no more rank, titles, or race [meant] all is mixed, confused, and blurred [and] the end of the world seemed nigh."[180] Prosperity and liberal reforms produced a growth panic that decried "the decline of religiosity, the disintegration of the patriarchal family, and the decline of respect for authority."[181] Fears of becoming "feminine" proliferated, along with campaigns against homosexuals. Books like *The World's End Soon* pictured the degeneration and apocalyptic demise of Europe, and feminine blood-sucking vampires derived from representations of the New Woman as an "oversexed wife who threatened her husband's life with her insatiable erotic demands"[182] flooded the popular literature. Artists featured vampires devouring helpless men,[183] and invented modern art as "a pervasive vision of Fragmentation" showing that "everything disintegrated into parts . . . whirlpools [that] led into the void."[184] Journalists wondered if "Europe was about to become a gigantic madhouse."[185] Nations felt they had to defend themselves against their growing paranoid delusions. "That the English are merely waiting for a chance to fall upon us is clear," declared the German chancellor.[186] Only starting a "preventive war" could save the nation.[187] "I believe a war to be unavoidable and the sooner the better," said the German chief of staff.[188] Europe was swept up in "a ter-

180. Eugen Weber, *France: Fin de Siècle*. Cambridge: Harvard University Press, 1986, p. 10.

181. Edward Ross Dickinson, *The Politics of German Child Welfare from the Empire to the Federal Republic*. Cambridge: Harvard University Press, 1996, p. 39.

182. Elaine Showalter, *Sexual Anarchy: Gender and Culture at the Fin de Siècle*. London: Penguin Books, 1991, p. 180.

183. Bram Dijkstra, *Idols of Perversity: Fantasies of Feminine Evil in Fin-de-Siècle Culture*. New York: Oxford University Press, 1986, p. 347.

184. Louis A. Sass, *Madness and Modernism: Insanity in the Light of Modern Art, Literature, and Thought*. New York: Basic Books, 1992, p. 57.

185. *The Nation*, January 10/17, 2000, p. 11.

186. Gordon A. Craig, *Germany 1866–1945*. New York: Oxford University Press, 1978, p. 312.

187. Keith Wilson, Ed., *Decisions for War 1914*. New York: St. Martin's Press, 1995.

188. Donald Kagan, *On the Origins of War and the Preservation of Peace*. New York: Doubleday, 1995, p. 185.

rible readiness, indeed a thirst, for what Yeats was to call the 'blood-dimmed tide' . . . fascinated by the prospect of a purging fire."[189] Going to war would prevent engulfment by the terrifying mommy, would avenge humiliations, would avoid effeminacy and restore potency, and would purge the national arteries with a good bloodletting that would cleanse the polluting prosperity[190] and sacrifice the sinful bad child.

WAR PHASE: RIGHTEOUS RAPE OF MOTHER SUBSTITUTES

Even though wars are supposed to be fought between men, they have equally affected women and children. In most wars, more civilians are killed than soldiers, and, according to UNICEF, "in the wars fought since World War II 90 percent of all victims are found in the civilian population, a large share of them women and children."[191] In our imaginations, wars are mainly about women and children. Divine wars were always fought for a goddess of war, from Ishtar to Teshub, almost always mothers of the war heroes,[192] "crying to be fed . . . human blood."[193] The prototypical war is in the Mesopotamian myth of the war fought by Marduk against the poisonous, devouring dragon-goddess, Tiamat.[194] Every tribe and nation intimately combines war and rape, in order to "teach her a lesson." Socarides describes the function of rape as follows:

> [It] forces and extracts love; destroys the threatening body of the mother rather than be destroyed by her, discharges aggressive impulses that threaten annihilation of the self even to the point of sexual murder;

---

189. George Steiner, *In Bluebeard's Castle: Some Notes Towards the Re-Definition of Culture*. London: Faber & Faber, 1971, p. 27.

190. Michael C. C. Adams, *The Great Adventure: Male Desire and the Coming of World War I*. Bloomington, IN: Indiana University Press, 1990, p. 51.

191. Ruth Seifert, "War and Rape: A Preliminary Analysis." In Alexandra Stiglmayer, Ed., *The War Against Women in Bosnia-Herzegovina*. Lincoln: University of Nebraska Press, 1993, p. 63.

192. Sa-Moon Kang, *Divine War in the Old Testament and in the Ancient Near East*. New York: Walter de Gruyter, 1989, p. 10.

193. John Bierhorst, *The Hungry Woman: Myths and Legends of the Aztecs*. New York: William Morrow, 1984, p. 10.

194. Norman Cohn, *Cosmos, Chaos and the World to Come: The Ancient Roots of Apocalyptic Faith*. New Haven: Yale University Press, 1993, p. 46.

Fig. 6–2. A man escapes engulfment by women by going to war

achieves temporary freedom from fear of the engulfing mother . . . re-assures against and lessens castration fear.[195]

Clinical studies of rapists find their crime a result of extreme child-hood neglect and abuse, continuous shaming and humiliation—and often even of actual sexual abuse as a child.[196] The rapist's fantasies center around control and dominance, and the actual rape is often triggered by flashbacks to earlier humiliations that had to be restaged in sexual violence, where "my life would flash in front of my mind . . . so I went out looking for a victim."[197] Rape is a pseudosexual act, first done for violence and revenge, then sexualized. Often the rapist cannot even achieve orgasm, but this doesn't matter because he has defiled, degraded, and humiliated the woman. Sex may be the weapon, but revenge is the motive.

Rape fantasies are extremely widespread. In America, a third of all men regularly fantasize about raping women during masturbation or inter-

---

195. Charles W. Socarides, *The Preodipal Origin and Psychoanalytic Therapy of Sexual Perversion.* Madison, CT: International Universities Press, 1988, p. 67.

196. Robert K. Ressler et al., *Sexual Homicide: Patterns and Motives.* New York: Lexington Books, 1988.

197. A. Nicholas Groth, *Men Who Rape: The Psychology of the Offender.* New York: Plenum Press, 1979, p. 27.

course,[198] while in a country like Yugoslavia—where earlier historical child-rearing practices were still prevalent into the twentieth century so that the rape of children was routine—rape was a common, everyday part of life even in peacetime.[199] Before wars, humiliation group-fantasies proliferate, as nations spend more and more time trading gratuitous insults and complaining about being humiliated and pushed around by others.[200] The child's unrequited love for the mother is reexperienced in rejected overtures with other nations. Hitler, for instance, clearly explained his reasons for starting World War II as arising out of rejected maternal love: "I have repeatedly offered England our friendship, and if necessary closest cooperation. Love, however, is not a one-sided affair, but must be responded to by the other side. . . . I do not want to conquer her. I want to come to terms with her. I want to force her to accept my friendship."[201] The war that began as conquering to win love ended as rape to win love. When the war was nearly over, Hitler, sitting in his bunker, justified his righteous rape of Europe as necessary because, he said, "It could not be conquered by charm and persuasiveness. I had to rape it in order to have it."[202]

In a world full of humiliating, rejecting, provocative motherlands, neighboring countries seem to be "just asking to be raped." Group-fantasies of wanting to "explode into her," to "penetrate her life," and to avenge her for "turning down our overtures" in order to "knock her off her throne" and "teach her a lesson she won't forget" begin to be expressed in diplomacy, political cartoons, and in the media.[203] Hypermasculinity begins to infect the nation's mood with the need for "standing tall" and "displaying our firmness" with a "stiffening of the national will." Newspapers headline rape fantasies to goad leaders into war—as the British tabloids screamed out before the Falkland invasion: "STICK IT UP YOUR JUNTA." Cartoons begin showing barbarian men in neighboring nations about to rape men's

---

198. Robert I. Simon, *Bad Men Do What Good Men Dream: A Forensic Psychiatrist Illuminates the Darker Side of Human Behavior*. Washington, DC: American Psychiatric Press, 1996, p. 78.

199. Alenka Puhar, "On Childhood Origins of Violence in Yugoslavia: II. The Zadruga." *The Journal of Psychohistory* 21(1993): 181.

200. John A. Vasquez, *The War Puzzle*. New York: Cambridge University Press, 1993, p. 115.

201. John Toland, *Adolf Hitler*. New York: Doubleday Anchor, 1992, pp. 569.

202. Ibid., p. 620.

203. Klaus Theweleit, *Male Fantasies. Vol. 1: Women, Floods, Bodies, History*. Minneapolis: University of Minnesota Press, 1987, p. 205.

Fig. 6–3. Fears of rape were overt in Slovenia before the 1991 Yugoslav war

wives.[204] Leaders begin to express projections of rape in meetings, as when Lyndon Johnson excitedly asked before expanding the war in Vietnam: "How many times do I let a fiend rape my wife?"[205] Finally, when the group-fantasies peak and action to "get some respect" is irresistible, war begins as righteous rape against any enemy that can be imagined to be a convenient humiliating mommy. War, gang-rape fantasies, and the degradation of women merge into one.

WAR PHASE: PURIFICATION OF THE BAD-CHILD SELF

While war is seen as a way to avenge maternal mistreatment, it is also a merging with the terrifying mommy to wipe out the bad-child self whose fault it must be that mommy wasn't loving. Therefore, war is a sacrificial solution to our search for love. Every nation elects leaders who are expected to arrange the supply of bad-child "enemies" somehow so as to be able to provide a war when emotionally needed.

---

204. Sam Keen, *Faces of the Enemy: Reflections of the Hostile Imagination.* San Francisco: Harper & Row, 1986, p. 76.

205. Henry F. Graff, *The Tuesday Cabinet: Deliberation and Decision on Peace and War Under Lyndon B. Johnson.* Englewood Cliffs, NJ: Prentice-Hall, 1990, p. 106.

The purification of mankind through the sacrifice of children to an avenging goddess was the practice of ancient societies like Carthage, where tens of thousands of jars have been found with charred bones of sacrificed children along with inscriptions saying they had been killed by their parents to cleanse their sinfulness.[206] In every war, young men march off to commit suicide as heroic acts of sacrifice, "losing ourselves [in] ecstasy because we are conscious of a power outside us with which we can merge."[207] As one soldier wrote during World War I, "Sacrificing oneself is a joy, the greatest joy. . . . Never before has such a powerful desire for death and passion for sacrifice seized mankind."[208] It is no coincidence that the word *infantry* comes from the Latin word *infans*, "infant." The bad-child self must die for the good-child self to be loved. Men must suffer and blood must flow to renew/rebirth the sinful nation: "The souls of nations are drinking renewal from the blood of fallen soldiers."[209] Soldiers may be sent back to their mothers dead, but they are wrapped in "living flags," maternal symbols, as though they had been reborn into new swaddling clothes with a new chance to be loved.[210] A soldier "dies peacefully. He who has a Motherland dies in comfort . . . in her, like a baby falling asleep."[211]

The ecstatic relief once war begins is felt because it is the *revanche suprême* for early abuse and because it promises to cleanse the self of sinfulness. However convinced people are as they begin wars that the enemy is outside themselves, they are in fact fighting *alters inside themselves*. War is "the highest happiness that ordinary men can find,"[212] a "purifying thun-

---

206. Lloyd deMause, "The History of Child Assault." *The Journal of Psychohistory* 18(1990): 16–18; Michael Newton, "Written in Blood: A History of Human Sacrifice." *The Journal of Psychohistory* 24(1996): 104–131.

207. Sue Mansfield, *The Gestalts of War: An Inquiry Into Its Origins and Meanings as a Social Institution.* New York: The Dial Press, 1982, p. 161.

208. Maria Tatar, *Lustmord: Sexual Murder in Weimar Germany.* Princeton: Princeton University Press, 1995, p. 182.

209. Juha Siltala, "Prenatal Fantasies During the Finnish Civil War." *The Journal of Psychohistory* 22(1995): 484.

210. Carolyn Marvin and David W. Ingle, *Blood Sacrifice and the Nation: Totem Rituals and the American Flag.* Cambridge: Cambridge University Press, 1999, p. 53.

211. Daniel Rancour-Laferriere, *The Slave Soul of Russia: Moral Masochism and the Cult of Suffering.* New York: New York University Press, 1995, p. 226.

212. Elwin H. Powell, *The Design of Discord: Studies of Anomie.* Oxford: Oxford University Press, 1970, p. 169.

BRITTANNIA ROUSED, OR THE COALITION MONSTERS DESTROYED

Fig. 6–4. Mother England destroying bad children

derstorm"[213] that provides a chance to be "born again,"[214] a "triumph of righteousness,"[215] and a "magical restoration of potency."[216] "It is a joy to be alive," rejoiced a German paper in 1914.[217] "The heather is on fire. I never before knew what a popular excitement can be," wrote an American as the Civil War began, describing jubilant crowds "with flushed faces, wild eyes, screaming mouths."[218] At last, one could simultaneously take revenge against the terrifying mommy alter, kill the bad-child alter, be reborn, and become pure and lovable, all in one splendid act of mass butchery.

---

213. Martin Broszat, *Hitler and the Collapse of Weimar Germany*. Oxford: Berg, 1987, p. 40.

214. Michael C. C. Adams, *The Great Adventure: Male Desire and the Coming of World War I*. Bloomington, IN: Indiana University Press, 1990, p. 55.

215. Herbert Rosinski, *The German Army*. New York: Praeger, 1966, p. 132.

216. Charles Socarides, *The Preoedipal Origin and Psychoanalytic Treatment of Perversions*, p. 7.

217. Barbara Tuchman, *The Guns of August*. New York: Macmillan, 1962, p. 121.

218. Bruce Catton, *The Coming Fury*. Garden City, NY: Doubleday & Co., 1961, p. 325.

THE CAUSES OF WORLD WAR II AND THE HOLOCAUST

Historians and political scientists have proposed any number of causes for World War II and the Holocaust.[219] Unfortunately, detailed research has disproved every one of them. Goldhagen's claim that ordinary Germans had long held "exterminationist" antisemitic views[220] has been disproved by careful historical studies that showed Germany was "a safe haven in late-nineteenth-century Europe [where] when German Jews looked toward France, they saw the startling antisemitism unleashed by the Dreyfus Affair and when they looked eastward, they saw pogroms and thousands of Jews fleeing toward Germany's safer political climate."[221] The reason "why so many Jews failed to leave Germany [was] they really couldn't believe that this Germany, which they loved [and] felt gratitude toward" would ever harm them.[222] In fact, earlier antisemitic movements in Germany were small, and "most historians believe that the Nazis had no deep roots in German history and that antisemitism in Germany was not essentially different from that of some other nations."[223] Careful studies of Nazi party members have even found that most were not antisemitic when they joined: "Most people were drawn to antisemitism because they were drawn to Nazism, not the other way around."[224] Kershaw's careful studies confirm that antisemitism was not a major factor in attracting support for Hitler.[225] As we shall shortly detail, what made Germans antisemitic was the anxieties of the manic period after the Great Depression had ended, later in the 1930s after Hitler gained power, and were not due to some mysterious German antisemitic gene.

---

219. P. M. H. Bell, *The Origins of the Second World War in Europe*, 2nd ed. New York: Longman, 1997.

220. Daniel Goldhagen, *Hitler's Willing Executioners: Ordinary Germans and the Holocaust*. New York: Alfred A. Knopf, 1996.

221. Marion A. Kaplan, *Between Dignity and Despair: Jewish Life in Nazi Germany*. New York: Oxford University Press, 1998, p. 13.

222. Ron Rosenbaum, *Explaining Hitler: The Search for the Origins of His Evil*. New York: Random House, 1998, p. 335.

223. John Weiss, *Ideology of Death: Why the Holocaust Happened in Germany*. Chicago: Ivan R. Dee, 1991, p. vii.

224. Christopher R. Browning, *Ordinary Men: Reserve Police Battalion 101 and the Final Solution in Poland*. New York: HarperCollins, 1998, p. 199.

225. Ian Kershaw, *The Nazi Dictatorship: Problems and Perspectives of Interpretation*. London: E. Arnold, 1993.

All the other explanations for World War II and the Holocaust have been similarly disproved by recent historical research. Klaus Fischer's "no Hitler, no Holocaust,"[226] along with all the other studies blaming German violence on obedience to Hitler's "hypnotic eyes,"[227] have been thrown out by the dozens of studies of the spontaneous, gratuitous violence engaged in by average Germans even when they could have easily opted out. "Only following orders" is simply no longer considered a serious motivation for the war and genocide. What is, however, most widely accepted is that Germans were under stress, voted Nazi, and then turned to violence because of the Great Depression.

Numerous detailed studies of Nazi membership all disprove this economic stress argument. The model Nazi party member joined before the Depression: "His economic status was secure, for not once did he have to change his occupation, job, or residence, nor was he ever unemployed."[228] "The only group affected [by the Depression] were the workers. . . . Yet paradoxically the workers remained steadfast in support of the [democratic] status quo while the middle class, only marginally hurt by the economic constriction, turned to revolution."[229] Most workers did not vote for the Nazis and of those who did, who "believed in Hitler the magician," most soon felt disappointed.[230] Hitler admitted "economics was not very important to him [and] very few Germans had any information about what his economic program actually was."[231] Germans who became violent Nazis came primarily from authoritarian middle-class backgrounds, not from poverty. Indeed, "those who grew up in poverty showed the least prejudice" in Merkl's study of Nazi stormtroopers.[232] The stress that triggered the war and genocide was

---

226. Klaus P. Fischer, *The History of an Obsession: German Judeophobia and the Holocaust*. New York: Continuum, 1998, p. 5.

227. George M. Kren and Leon Rappoport, *The Holocaust and the Crisis of Human Behavior*, rev. ed. New York: Holmes & Meier, 1980, p. 40.

228. Theodore Abel, *Why Hitler Came Into Power*. Cambridge: Harvard University Press, 1938, p. 6.

229. William Sheridan Allen, *The Nazi Seizure of Power: The Experience of a Single German Town, 1922–1945*. New York: F. Watts, 1984, pp. 24, 69.

230. Ian Kershaw, *Popular Opinion and Political Dissent in the Third Reich: Bavaria 1933–1945*. Oxford: Clarendon Press, 1983, p. 47.

231. Paul Bookbinder, *Weimar Germany: The Republic of the Reasonable*. Manchester: Manchester Universtiy Press, 1996, p. 219.

232. Peter H. Merkl, *The Making of a Stormtrooper*. Princeton: Princeton University Press, 1980, p. 228.

related to economics, but it in fact came from renewed prosperity in the late 1930s, not from the economic collapse of 1929.

THE SOURCES OF WORLD WAR II AND THE HOLOCAUST IN GERMAN CHILD REARING

If German child-rearing practices are not considered as the cause of German mass violence, there is no way to avoid Goldhagen's conclusion that the war and the Holocaust must be due to "something monstrously Germanic . . . at bottom unexplainable [and not] a product of human decisions."[233] But if German childhood around 1900 is recognized as a nightmare of murder, neglect, battering, and torture of innocent, helpless human beings, then the restaging of this nightmare four decades later in the Holocaust and World War II can at last be understood.

Historians have avoided researching German child rearing at the end of the nineteenth century. The few that have begun to do the research have found German childhood uniformly more brutal than French and British childhood. A comparison by Maynes of ninety German and French autobiographies of late nineteenth-century working-class childhoods found the German ones far more brutal and unloving, with the typical memory of home being that "no bright moment, no sunbeam, no hint of a comfortable home where motherly love and care could shape my childhood was ever known to me."[234] In contrast, "French workers' autobiographies tell somewhat different childhood tales. To be sure, there are a few French accounts of childhoods marked by cruelty, neglect, and exploitation."[235] Yet "much more common are stories of surprisingly sentimental home loves and warm relationships with mothers (and often fathers), even in the face of material deprivation."[236] Maynes found unrelenting child labor, sexual molestation, and beatings at home and at school were consistently worse in the German accounts.

233. Mitchell G. Ash, "American and German Perspectives on the Goldhagen Debate." *Holocaust and Genocide Studies* 7(1997): 402.

234. Mary Jo Maynes, *Taking the Hard Road*. Chapel Hill: University of North Carolina Press, 1995, p. 63.

235. Ibid., pp. 66–67.

236. M. J. Maynes, "Childhood Memories, Political Visions, and Working-Class Formation in Imperial Germany: Some Comparative Observations." In Geoff Eley, Ed., *Society, Culture, and the State in Germany, 1870–1930*. Ann Arbor: University of Michigan Press, 1997, p. 157.

Most of the research into primary sources on the history of German child rearing has been done by psychohistorians connected with the *Deutsche Gesellschaft für psychohistorische Forschung*, the German branch of the Institute for Psychohistory.[237] The two main studies covering nineteenth-century German child rearing were those published in *The Journal of Psychohistory* by Aurel Ende and Raffael Scheck. Both found uniform cruelty and neglect in their detailed review of 154 German autobiographies studied. Child battering was so common in German families that Scheck concludes: "There is virtually no autobiography which doesn't tell something about violence against children and almost no author who has not been beaten as a child."[238] Ende's massive study confirms that "nowhere in Western Europe are the needs of children so fatally neglected as in Germany," where "infant mortality, corporal punishment, cruelties against children, the exploitation of working children and the teacher-pupil relationship" were so brutal that he feels he has to apologize "for not dealing with the 'brighter side' of German childhood because it turns out that there is no 'bright side.'"[239]

Visitors to German homes at the end of the nineteenth century found that, in general, "one feels sorry for these little German children; they must work so hard and seem to lack that exuberance of life, spirits, and childish glee that make American children harder to train but leave them the memory of a happy childhood."[240] In particular, visitors noted the German preference for boys and their maltreatment of girls. Whereas in France and England, there was "an increasing appreciation of girl children," beginning

---

237. Lloyd deMause, Hg., *Hört ihr die Kinder weinen: Eine psychogenetische Geschichte der Kindheit.* Frankfurt am Main, 1977; Friedhelm Nyssen, *Die Geschichte der Kindheit bei L. deMause: Quellendiskussion.* Frankfurt/M.: Peter Lange, 1987; Ute Schuster-Keim u. Alexander Keim, *Zur Geschichte der Kindheit bei Lloyd deMause: Psychoanalytische Reflexion.* Frankfurt/M: Peter Lange, 1988; Aurel Ende, "Battering and Neglect: Children in Germany, 1860–1978." *The Journal of Psychohistory* 7(1979): 249–279; Aurel Ende, "Bibliography on Childhood and Youth in Germany from 1820–1978: A Selection." *The Journal of Psychohistory* 7(1979): 281–288; Raffael Scheck, "Childhood in German Autobiographical Writings, 1740–1820." *The Journal of Psychohistory* 15(1987): 397–422; Friedhelm Nyssen, Ludwig Janus, Hg., *Psychogenetische Geschichte der Kindheit: Beiträge zur Psychohistorie der Eltern-Kind-Beziehung.* Giessen: Psychosozial-Verlag, 1997; Ralph Frenken, *Kindheit und Autobiographie vom 14. bis 17. Jahrhundert: Psychohistorische Rekonstruktionen.* 2 Bände. Kiel: Oetker-Voges-Verlag, 1999.

238. Raffael Scheck, "Childhood in German Autobiographical Writings," p. 409.

239. Aurel Ende, "Battering and Neglect," pp. 249–250.

240. Emma Louise Parry, *Life Among the Germans.* Boston: Lothrop Publishing Co., 1887, p. 20.

in the eighteenth century, with parents often openly expressing their preference of having a girl,[241] in Germany even at the end of the nineteenth century girls were resented and uniformly neglected. When a girl was born, Germans usually felt sad:

> At last the child was born. . . . "Is it a boy?" shouted the farmer. "No, a girl." He could not believe me, and almost wrenched the child out of my hands. Then, in a fury, he flung it on to the bed by the mother so violently that he might have broken its spine. "The devil take the pair of you!" he shouted, and rushed off.[242]

"From childhood on, the lives [German] women led were exceedingly harsh . . . dominated by memories of paternal brutality or negligence. . . . Drunkenness and violence was a routine part of life [including] a father's incestuous advances . . . [and] abuse with sexual overtones at the hands of her mother . . . beatings and other forms of violent punishment."[243] Germany was far behind the rest of Western Europe in the education of girls and in women's rights, so that innovative mothers and hopeful daughters were found far less than in other countries.[244]

German family maxims described the lack of love of mothers toward their children, saying tenderness was "generally not part of the mother's character. . . . Just as she kept her children . . . short on food and clothing, she also was short on fondling and tenderness . . . [feeling] the children should . . . regard themselves as useless weeds and be grateful that they were tolerated."[245] Children were expected to give love to their parents, not the parents to their children: "We always appeared trembling before our parents, hoping that our official kiss of their hands would be accepted."[246] One boy

---

241. Judith Schneid Lewis, *In the Family Way: Childbearing in the British Aristocracy, 1760–1860.* New Brunswick, NJ: Rutgers University Press, 1986, p. 65.

242. Lisbeth Burger, *Memoirs of a Midwife.* New York: The Vanguard Press, 1934, p. 29.

243. Mary Jo Maynes, "Gender and Class in Working-Class Women's Autobiographies." In Ruth-Ellen B. Joeres and Mary Jo Maynes, Eds., *German Women in the Eighteenth and Nineteenth Centuries: a Social and Literary History.* Bloomington, IN: Indiana University Press, 1986, pp. 238–239.

244. Ute Frevert, *Women in German History: From Bourgeois Emancipation to Sexual Liberation.* Oxford: Berg, 1989.

245. Katharina Rutschky, *Deutsche Kinder-Chronik: Wunsch- und Schreckensbilder aus vier Jahrhunderten.* Köln: Kiepenheuer & Witsch, 1983, p. 189.

246. Ibid., p. 200.

reported his mother once dropped a word of praise, saying to someone that "He is good and well-liked," so that the boy remembered it all his life "because the words were totally new sounds to my ear."[247] But kind words were rare in German homes, so most Germans remembered "no tender word, no caresses, only fear"[248] and childhood was "joyless," "so immeasurably sad that you could not fathom it."[249]

GERMAN INFANTICIDE, WET-NURSING, AND SWADDLING

Since German fathers at the end of the nineteenth century spent little time at home, child rearing was overwhelmingly the job of the mother: "The care and training of the children are almost entirely in her hands for the first five years."[250] The mother especially ruled the nursery and kitchen, where the children spent their time, and "she may actually exclude men from these restricted areas"[251] when they were at home. Thus, although most studies of the treatment of infants and young children in Germany stress the admitted brutality and authoritarianism of fathers, the real lives of young German children in the past centered more on their murder, rejection, neglect, tying up, and beating by their mothers and other women.

Infanticide and infant mortality rates at the end of the nineteenth century were much higher in Germany and Austria than in England, France, Italy, and Scandinavia.[252] Newborns were not considered as fully human since they were not thought to have a soul until they were 6 weeks old, and so

---

247. Ibid., p. 186.

248. Adelheid Popp, *Jugend einer Arbeiterin*. Berlin: Verlag Dietz Nachf, 1977, p. 1f.

249. Fritz Stern, *The Politics of Cultural Despair: A Study in the Rise of the Germanic Ideology*. Berkeley: University of California Press, 1961, p. 5.

250. Bertram Schaffner, *Father Land: A Study of Authoritarianism in the German Family*. New York: Columbia University Press, 1948, p. 35.

251. Ibid., p. 34.

252. Robert Woods, "Infant Mortality in Britain." In Alain Bideau, et al., Eds., *Infant and Child Mortality in the Past*. Oxford: Clarendon Press, 1997, p. 76; Pier Paolo Viazzo, "Alpine Patterns of Infant Mortality." In Bideau; Lorenzo Del Panta, "Infant and Child Mortality in Italy," In Bideau; Jörg Vögele, "Urbanization, Infant Mortality and Public Health in Imperial Germany." In Carlo A. Corsini and Pier Paolo Viazzo, Eds., *The Decline of Infant and Child Mortality: The European Experience: 1750–1990*. The Hague: Martinus Nijhoff Publishers, 1997, pp. 6, 110–111, 194; Jeffrey S. Richter, "Infanticide, Child Abandonment, and Abortion in Imperial Germany." *Journal of Interdisciplinary History* 28(1998): 511–551.

could be "killed in a kind of late abortion."[253] Women giving birth in Germany often "had their babies in the privy, and treated the birth as an evacuation."[254] Births that were "experienced as a bowel movement made it possible for the women [to] kill their children in a very crude way, by smashing their heads [like] poultry and small animals."[255] Mothers who killed their newborn babies were observed by others as being without remorse, "full of indifference, coldness, and callousness [and gave] the impression of a general impoverishment of feeling" toward their children.[256] Even if the infant was allowed to live, it could easily be neglected and not fed enough, and it would be made to "go straight to heaven." Infant mortality rates in Germany ranged from 21 percent in Prussia to an astonishing 58 percent in Bavaria during the latter part of the nineteenth century,[257] the figures in the south being partly due to the practice of not breast-feeding,[258] since hand-fed babies died at a rate three times that of breast-fed babies.[259] The best figures for overall German infanticide at the end of the century were over 20 percent, half again higher than France and England.[260] Even when the newborn were allowed to live, they were quite likely to be abandoned. Vienna, in particular, had one of the highest abandonment rates in Europe, with half the newborns still being abandoned by their mothers in the nineteenth century.[261]

Nineteenth-century doctors condemned the practice of German mothers refusing to breast-feed their babies, saying the pap made of flour and water or milk was "usually so thick that it has to be forced into the child and only becomes digestible when mixed with saliva and stomach fluids.

253. Regina Schulte, "Infanticide in Rural Bavaria in the Nineteenth Century." In Hans Medick and David Warren Sabean, Eds., *Interest and Emotion: Essays on the Study of Family and Kinship.* Cambridge: Cambridge University Press, 1984, pp. 91, 101.

254. Ibid., p. 87.

255. Ibid., p. 89.

256. Mary Jo Maynes and Thomas Taylor, "Germany." In Joseph M. Hawes and N. Ray Hiner, Eds., *Children in Historical and Comparative Perspective.* New York: Greenwood Press, 1991, p. 309.

257. Aurel Ende, "Battering and Neglect," p. 252.

258. John E. Knodel, *Demographic Behavior in the Past: A Study of Fourteen German Village Populations in the Eighteenth and Nineteenth Centuries.* Cambridge: Cambridge University Press, 1988, p. 543.

259. Ann Taylor Allen, *Feminism and Motherhood in Germany.* New Brunswick, NJ: Rutgers University Press, 1991, p. 178.

260. Ibid., p. 177.

261. David I. Kertzer, *Sacrificed for Honor: Italian Infant Abandonment and the Politics of Reproductive Control.* Boston: Beacon Press, 1993, p. 10.

At its worst it is curdled and sour."[262] Infants were so commonly hungry that "those poor worms get their mouths stuffed with a dirty rag containing chewed bread so that they cannot scream."[263] Ende reports that for centuries "one rarely encounters a German infant who is fully breast-fed. . . . Everywhere they got their mouths stuffed with *Zulp*, a small linen bag filled with bread. . . . Swaddled babies could hardly get rid of these often dirty rags."[264] Mothers who could afford it sent their newborn to wet nurses—commonly called *Engelmacherin*, "angelmakers," because they were so negligent toward the children. The mothers complained, "Do you think I am a farmer's daughter, that I should bother myself with little children? That a woman of my age and standing should allow her very strength to be sucked dry by children?"[265] While English gentry began to nurse their infants themselves during the seventeenth century, the mothering revolution had not yet really reached Germany by the end of the nineteenth century.[266] Visitors who wrote books on German home life reported: "It is extremely rare for a German lady to nourish her own child,"[267] and "It would have been very astonishing indeed if a well-to-do mother had suggested suckling her own baby."[268] Almost all mothers who refused to breast-feed could have done so "if they seriously wanted to," according to a 1905 German medical conference.[269] Those who did not gave "completely trivial reasons," such as "because it is messy," because they "didn't want to ruin their figures," or because breast-feeding was "inconvenient."[270] Even after

262. Mary Jo Maynes and Thomas Taylor, "Germany," p. 308.

263. Aurel Ende, "Battering and Neglect," p. 260.

264. Aurel Ende, "The Psychohistorian's Childhood and the History of Childhood." *The Journal of Psychohistory* 9(1981): 174.

265. Ute Frevert, *Women in German History: From Bourgeois Emancipation to Sexual Liberation*. Oxford: Berg, 1989, p. 28.

266. Valerie A. Fildes, *Breasts, Bottles, and Babies: A History of Infant Feeding*. Edinburgh: Edinburgh University Press, 1986, pp. 98–122, 152–163.

267. Marie van Bothmer, *German Home Life*, 2nd ed. New York: Appleton & Co., 1876, p. 15.

268. Clara Asch Boyle, *German Days: Personal Experiences and Impressions of Life, Manners, and Customs in Germany*. London: John Murray, 1919, p. 228.

269. Edward Ross Dickinson, *The Politics of German Child Welfare from the Empire to the Federal Republic*. Cambridge: Harvard University Press, 1996, p. 62.

270. Karin Norman, *A Sound Family Makes a Sound State: Ideology and Upbringing in a German Village*. Stockholm: Stockholm Studies in Social Anthropology, 1991, p. 97; Heide Wunder, *He Is the Sun, She Is the Moon: Women in Early Modern Germany*. Cambridge: Harvard University Press, 1998, p. 20.

their children returned from the wet nurse, "noble ladies showed not the slightest interest in their offspring"[271] and turned them over to nursemaids, governesses, and tutors. The result was that parents were often strangers to their children. When one German father asked his child whom he loved the most and the child replied, "Hanne [his nurse]," the father objected, "No! You must love your parents more." "But it is not true!" the child replied. The father promptly beat him.[272]

Mothers and other caregivers of newborn German babies were so frightened of them that they tied them up tightly for from six to nine months and strapped them into a crib in a room with curtains drawn to keep out the lurking evils.[273] Two centuries after swaddling had begun to disappear in England and America, two British visitors described it as routine throughout Germany:

> A German baby is a piteous object; it is pinioned and bound up like a mummy in yards of bandages. . . . It is never bathed. . . . Its head is never touched with soap and water until it is eight or ten months old, when the fine skull cap of encrusted dirt which it has by that time obtained is removed.[274]

"In Germany, babies are loathsome, foetid things . . . offensive to the last degree with the excreta that are kept bound up within their swaddling clothes. . . . The heads of the poor things are never washed, and are like the rind of Stilton cheese.[275] When the children were finally removed from their swaddling bands after six to twelve months, other restraint devices such as corsets with steel stays and backboards continued their tied-up condition to assure the parents they were still in complete control.[276] The result of all this early restraint was the same production of later violence in children as that obtained by experimenters physically

---

271. Ibid., p. 27.

272. Katharina Rutschky, *Deutsche Kinder-Chronik*, p. 161.

273. Peter Petschauer, "Growing Up Female in Eighteenth-Century Germany." *The Journal of Psychohistory* 11(1983): 172.

274. Anon., *Cornhill Magazine* 1867: 356.

275. Henry Mayhew, *German Life and Manners as Seen in Saxony at the Present Day*. London: William H. Allen, 1864, p. 490.

276. Lloyd deMause, "Schreber and the History of Childhood." *The Journal of Psychohistory* 15(1987): 427.

restraining rats and monkeys—marked by depletions of serotonin and massive increases in terror, rage, and eventually actual violence toward others.[277]

The fear of one's own children was so widespread in German families that for centuries autobiographies told of a tradition of abandonment of children by their parents to anyone who would take them, using the most flimsy of excuses.[278] Children were given away and even sometimes sold[279] to relatives, neighbors, courts, priests, foundling homes, schools, friends, strangers, "traveling scholars" (to be used as beggars)—anyone who would take them—so that for much of history only a minority of German children lived their entire childhoods under their family roof. Children were reported to be sent away to others as servants or as apprentices, "for disciplinary reasons," "to be drilled for hard work," "to keep them from idleness," because of a "domestic quarrel," "because it cried as a baby," "because his uncle was childless," etc.[280] Scheck notes in his study of autobiographies, "When their parents came to take them home, their children usually didn't recognize them any more."[281] Peasants gave away their children so regularly that the only ones who were guaranteed to be kept were the first-born boys—to get the inheritance—and one of the daughters, who was sometimes crippled in order to prevent her from marrying and force her to stay permanently as a cheap helper in the parental household.[282] After two children, it was said that "the parental attitude to later offspring noticeably deteriorated [so that] a farmer would rather lose a young child than a calf."[283]

---

277. F. Lamprecht et al., "Rat Fighting Behavior." *Brain Research* 525(1990): 285–293.

278. Ralph Frenken, *Kindheit und Autobiographie.*

279. Aurel Ende, "Battering and Neglect," p. 252.

280. Raffael Scheck, "Childhood in German Autobiographical Writings," p. 401; Heide Wunder, *He Is the Sun*, p. 23.

281. Raffael Scheck, "Childhood in German Autobiographical Writings," Ibid.

282. Michael Mitterauer, "Servants and Youth." *Continuity and Change* 56(1990):21; Albert Ilien, *Jeggle, Utz, Leben auf dem Dorf: zur Sozialgeschichte des Dorfes und zur Sozialpsychologie seiner Bewohner.* Opladen: Westdeutscher Verlag, 1976, p. 76.

283. Robert Lee, "Family and 'Modernization.'" The Peasant Family and Social Change in Nineteenth-Century Bavaria." In Richard J. Evans and W. R. Lee, Eds., *The German Family: Essays on the Social History of the Family in 19th- and 20th-Century Germany.* London: Croom Helm, 1981, p. 96.

Those children who were kept by their parents were considered, in Luther's words, "obnoxious with their crapping, eating, and screaming,"[284] beings who "don't know anything, they aren't capable of doing anything, they don't perform anything . . . [and are] inferior to adults"[285] and are therefore only "useless eaters"[286] until they began to work. "When little children die, it's not often that you have a lot of grief [but] if an older child dies, who would soon be able to go off to work . . . everybody is upset—it's already cost so much work and trouble, now it's all been for nothing."[287] As "useless eaters" children were mainly resented: "Rarely could we eat a piece of bread without hearing father's comment that we did not merit it."[288] The children grew up feeling that "my mother was fond of society and did not trouble much about me" (Otto Bismarck) or "[my mother] did not conduce to evolve that tender sweetness and solicitude which are usually associated with motherhood. I hardly ever recollect her having fondled me. Indeed, demonstrations of affection were not common in our family" (Richard Wagner).[289] It is not surprising, therefore, with such a drastic lack of maternal love, that historically outsiders complained that German mothers routinely abandoned their children, "paid less attention to their children than cows."[290]

BEATING, TERRORIZING, AND SEXUALLY MOLESTING GERMAN CHILDREN

Although little children can be made less threatening by being given away, tied up, or ignored, as they grow older they must be forced to conform to parental images of them as poison containers by being beaten and terror

---

284. Carl Haffter, "The Changeling: History and Psychodynamics of Attitudes to Handicapped Children in European Folklore." *Journal of the History of the Behavioral Sciences* 4(1968): 58.

285. Katharina Rutschky, *Deutsche Kinder-Chronik*, p. 189.

286. Raffael Scheck, "Childhood in German Autobiographical Writings," p. 402.

287. Regina Schulte, "Infanticide in Rural Bavaria in the Nineteenth Century." In Hans Medick and David Warren Sabean, Eds., *Interest and Emotion: Essays on the Study of Family and Kinship.* Cambridge: Cambridge University Press, 1984, p. 90.

288. Raffael Scheck, "Childhood in German Autobiographical Writings," p. 403.

289. Charlotte Sempell, "Bismarck's Childhood: A Psychohistorical Study." *The Journal of Psychohistory* 2(1974): 115; Melvin Kalfus, Richard Wagner As Cult Hero: The Tannhäuser Who Would Be Siegfried." *The Journal of Psychohistory* 11(1984): 325.

290. J. F. G. Goeters, *Die Evangelischen Kirchenordnungen des XVI Jahrhunderts, Vol. XIV.* Tübingen: Kurpfalz, 1969, p. 294.

ized. German parents throughout history have been known as the most violent batterers in Europe,[291] particularly toward their boys,[292] seconding Luther's opinion that "I would rather have a dead son than a disobedient one."[293] The mother was far more often the main beater than the father.[294] Scheck and Ende found brutal beating in virtually all autobiographies at the end of the nineteenth century; Hävernick found that 89 percent were beaten at the beginning of the twentieth century, over half of these with canes, whips, or sticks.[295] More recent surveys report 75 percent of German adults say they had suffered from violence from their parents during their childhood, although hitting with instruments was decreasing compared to earlier periods.[296]

Battering of babies sometimes begins in the womb. Violence against pregnant women has always been prevalent throughout human history, and since even today around 30 percent of pregnant women are assaulted by their partners,[297] this suggests that many fetuses were probably physically abused at the end of the nineteenth century. The physical assaults resumed as soon as the little child was out of swaddling bands, whenever he or she cried for anything. The widely followed Dr. Schreber said the earlier one begins beatings the better: "One must look at the moods of the little ones which are announced by screaming without reason and crying . . . [inflicting] bodily admonishments consistently repeated until the child calms down or falls asleep. Such a procedure is necessary only once or at most twice and—one is *master* of the child *forever*. From now on a glance, a word, a single threatening gesture, is sufficient to rule the child."[298]

---

291. Priscilla Robertson, "Home As a Nest: Middle Class Childhood in Nineteenth-Century Europe." In Lloyd deMause, Ed., *The History of Childhood*. New York: Psychohistory Press, 1974, p. 419.

292. Walter Hävernick, *"Schläge" als Strafe: Ein Bestandteil der heutigen Familiensitte in volkskundlicher Sicht*. Hamburg: Museum für Hamburgische Geschichte, 1964, p. 53.

293. Ewarld M. Plass, comp., *What Luther Says: An Anthology*. St. Louis: Concordia Publishing House, 1959, p. 145.

294. Walter Hävernick, *"Schläge" als Strafe*, p. 102.

295. Ibid.

296. *Der Spiegel*, September 19, 1978, p. 66; Detlev Frehsee, *Einige Daten zur endlosen Geschichte des Züchtigungsrechts*. Bielefeld, privately printed, 1997.

297. Amy L. Gilliland and Thomas R. Verny, "The Effects of Domestic Abuse on the Unborn Child." *Journal of Prenatal and Perinatal Psychology and Health* 13(1999): 236.

298. Morton Schatzman, "Paranoia or Persecution: The Case of Schreber." *History of Childhood Quarterly: The Journal of Psychohistory* 1(1973): 75.

Schreber was overly optimistic and, like other German parents, continued to be threatened by imagined disobedience from his children, and so the beatings continued throughout their childhood. Every independent move of children was seen as done, says Krüger, "with the intent of defying you"; it is "a declaration of war against you" for which you must "whip him well till he cries so: Oh no, Papa, oh no!"[299] These are not just spankings; they are whippings, like Hitler's daily whippings, which sometimes put him into a coma.[300] Parents were often described as being in a "righteous rage" during the beatings,[301] and the children often lost consciousness.[302] "At school we were beaten until our skin smoked. At home, the instrument for punishment was a dog-whip. . . . My father, while beating, more and more worked himself into a rage. I lost consciousness from his beatings several times."[303]

Klöden writes that the motto of German parents at the end of the nineteenth century was simple: "Children can never get enough beatings."[304] Although few German parents from the past would today escape being thrown in jail for their batterings, children at the end of the nineteenth century found little protection from society, since their own word and even physical evidence of severe abuse counted for nothing. Ende's survey describes typical court cases where a neighbor would alert police to "a three-year-old girl [whose] body was covered with welts. Lips, nose, and gums were open wounds. The body showed numerous festering sores. The child had been placed on a red-hot, iron stove—two wounds on the buttocks were festering," but the court let the parent go free.[305] Ende describes routine beating, kicking, strangling, and making children eat excrement, saying: "The cases I have presented are not the most extreme; they are typical

299. Cited in Alice Miller, *For Your Own Good: Hidden Cruelty in Child-Rearing and the Roots of Violence.* New York: Farrar Straus Giroux, 1990, p. 15.

300. Ibid., p. 152; Robert G. L. Waite, *Kaiser and Führer: A Comparative Study of Personality and Politics.* Toronto: University of Toronto Press, 1998, p. 329; George Victor, *Hitler: The Pathology of Evil.* Washington, DC: Brassey's, 1998, p. 29.

301. Bertram Schaffner, *Father Land: A Study of Authoritarianism in the German Family.* New York: Columbia University Press, 1948, p. 21.

302. Raffael Scheck, "Childhood in German Autobiographical Writings," p. 411.

303. Katharina Rutschky, *Deutsche Kinder-Chronik,* p. 167.

304. Cited in Raffael Scheck, "Childhood in German Autobiographical Writings," p. 411.

305. Aurel Ende, "Battering and Neglect," p. 259.

of the vast literature on German families."[306] The result was that German childhood suicides were three to five times higher than in other Western European countries at the end of the nineteenth century,[307] fear of beatings by parents being the reason most often cited by the children for their suicide attempts.[308] Few people cared about the reason for the suicides, since "suicidal children were thought to be spineless creatures, spoiled by indulgent parents. . . . Newspapers wrote: 'A boy who commits suicide because of a box on the ears has earned his fate; he deserved to be ruined.'"[309] There simply was no one around to sympathize with battered children in Germany. Even the small feminist movement in Germany failed to speak out for the rights of children, declaring motherhood "oppressive."[310]

Although these constant beatings quickly produced compliant, obedient children, parental projections into them made continuous overcontrol appear necessary. German children were "often locked in a dark room or a closet or fastened to a table leg,"[311] were "hardened" by washing them with ice-cold water before breakfast,[312] and were tightly tied up in various corsets, steel collars, and torturous back-support devices with steel stays and tight laces to hold them in controlled positions all day long.[313] Children were not only controlled by being frightened by endless ghost stories where they were threatened with being carried away by horrible figures.[314] In addition, the parents "dressed up in terrifying costumes [as] the so-called *Knecht Ruprecht*, made their faces black, and pretended to be a messenger

---

306. Ibid., p. 260.

307. Ibid., p. 258.

308. Herman Baartman, "Child Suicide and Harsh Punishment in Germany at the Turn of the Last Century." *Paedagogica Historica: International Journal of the History of Education* 30(1994): 851.

309. Ibid., pp. 852, 857.

310. Ann Taylor Allen, *Feminism and Motherhood in Germany, 1800–1914.* New Brunswick: Rutgers University Press, 1991, pp. 139, 150.

311. Raffael Scheck, "Childhood in German Autobiographical Writings," p. 404.

312. Katharina Rutschky, *Deutsche Kinder-Chronik*, p. 93.

313. Raffael Scheck, "Childhood in German Autobiographical Writings," p. 403; Lloyd deMause, "Schreber and the History of Childhood." *The Journal of Psychohistory* 159(1987): 427; Morton Schatzman, "Paranoia or Persecution: The Case of Schreber." *History of Childhood Quarterly: The Journal of Psychohistory* 1(1973): 66–70; Katharina Rutschky, *Deutsche Kinder-Chronik*, pp. 17, 59.

314. Raffael Scheck, "Childhood in German Autobiographical Writings," p. 405.

of God who would punish children for their sins."[315] At Christmas adults dressed as *Pelznickel*, "armed with a rod and a large chain. . . . If they have been bad children, he will use his rod; if good, he will bring them nuts."[316] Petschauer remembers being threatened by a "hairy monster [that] chased me under the living room table, chains clanking, hoofs stomping, appearing it wanted to drag me off in its carrying basket, the *Korb*."[317] Scheck sums up the effects of these terrifying devices: "Most children had been so deeply frightened that their 'demons of childhood' persecuted them at night and in feverish dreams for their whole lives."[318]

Toilet training was an early, violent battleground for parental control over the infant. Since "babies and young children won't obey, don't want to do what grownups want them to do but instead test them, resist them, and tyrannize them, [and since] they are impure, unclean and messy,"[319] toilet training begins at around 6 months of age, long before the infant has sphincter control. The training is done by regular use of enemas and by hitting the infant: "The baby cannot walk yet [Nana] spanks the baby. Hard. 'He is a dirty, dirty Hansi-baby,' she says, as she spanks. 'He made pooh-pooh last night! Dirty Hansi!' Nana slaps the little red buttocks." Traditional German obsession with children's feces is well known; both Dundes and von Zglinicki have written entire books on the subject.[320] The enema in particular was used as a frightening domination device, a fetish object often wielded by the mother or nurse in daily rituals that resembled sexual assaults on the anus, sometimes including tying the child up in leather straps as though the mother were a dominatrix, inserting the two-foot-long enema tube over and over again as punishment for "accidents."[321] There

---

315. Raffael Scheck, "Childhood in German Autobiographical Writings," p. 405.

316. William Howett, *The Rural and Domestic Life of Germany*. Frankfurt: Jugel, 1843, p. 236.

317. Peter Petschauer, "Children of Afers, or 'Evolution of Childhood' Revisited." *The Journal of Psychohistory* 13(1985): 138.

318. Raffael Scheck, "Childhood in German Autobiographical Writings," p. 406.

319. Arno Gruen, "The Need to Punish: The Political Consequences of Identifying with the Aggressor." *The Journal of Psychohistory* 27(1999): 142.

320. Alan Dundes, *Life Is Like a Chicken Coop Ladder: A Portrait of German Culture Through Folklore*. New York: Columbia University Press, 1984; Friedrich von Zglinicki, *Geschichte des Klistiers: Das Klistier in der Geschichte der Medizin, Kunst und Literatur*. Frankfurt: Viola Press, n.d.

321. Gerhart S. Schwarz, Personal Interview, manuscript with author, February 10, 1974.

Fig. 6–5. German baby being assaulted with an enema

were special enema stores that German children would be taken to in order to be "fitted" for their proper size of enemas. The ritual "stab in the back" was a central fear of German children well into the twentieth century, and they learned "never to speak of it, but always to think about it."[322]

The punitive atmosphere of the German home was so total that one can convincingly say that totalitarianism in the family led directly to totalitarianism in politics. Children were personal slaves of their parents, catering to their every need, waiting on them, trying to fulfill their every whim, even if only to be poison containers for their moods. Many accounts of the time describe a similar tense home atmosphere:

> When the father came in from work, the children were expected to be at home. Neighbours . . . would warn . . . "[Your father's] coming! We ran like a flash, opened up and were inside in time!" The children would bring him his slippers, help him off with his coat, lay the table or just retreat in silence to a corner of the room. . . . Right away we got punished, whack, a clip round the ear or something. . . . "You take off my shoes; you go and get water; you fill my pipe for me and you fetch my

---

322. Ibid.

books!" And we had to jump to it, he wouldn't have stood for it if we hadn't all done just as we were told . . . we had to kneel, one by the one window, another by the other . . . we would kneel with our heads against the wall . . . we had to stay there for two hours."[323]

German children were also used by parents and servants as sexual objects from an early age.[324] German doctors often said "nursemaids and other servants carry out all sorts of sexual acts on the children entrusted to their care, sometimes merely in order to quiet the children, sometimes 'for fun.'"[325] Even Freud said he was seduced by his nurse, and said "nursemaids, governesses, and domestic servants [were often] guilty of [grave sexual] abuses" and that "nurses put crying children to sleep by stroking their genitals."[326] Children were used like a comfort blanket: "If the father goes away on a journey, the little son can come to sleep in mother's bed. As soon as father returns, the boy is banished to his cot" next to the parents' bed, where he will continue to observe their intercourse.[327] These incestuous assaults were regular enough to be remembered rather than repressed in the autobiographies of the period.[328] In poorer families, "it was unheard of for children to have their own beds,"[329] but even in wealthy families parents brought their children to bed with them. After using them sexually, they then would threaten to punish the child for their sexuality. "Little Hans," for instance, reported he regularly was masturbated by his mother, "coaxed [Freud's footnote: 'caressed'] with his Mummy [Freud's footnote: 'meaning his penis']," but then told she

323. Reinhard Sieder, "'Vata, derf i aufstehn?': Childhood Experiences in Viennese Working Class Families Around 1900." *Continuity and Change* 1(1986):62–64.

324. Florence Rush, *The Best Kept Secret: Sexual Abuse of Children.* Englewood Cliffs, NJ: Prentice-Hall, 1980, pp. 85–93.

325. Albert Moll, *The Sexual Life of Children.* New York: 1913, p. 219.

326. Sigmund Freud, *Standard Edition of the Complete Psychological Works of Sigmund Freud.* Vol. III, p. 164, Vol. VII, p. 180.

327. Fritz Wittels, *Set the Children Free!* New York: W. W. Norton & Co., 1933, p. 124.

328. Mary Jo Maynes, "Gender and Class in Working-Class Women's Autobiographies." In Ruth-Ellen Joeres and Mary Jo Maynes, Eds., *German Women in the Eighteenth and Nineteenth Centuries*, Bloomington, IN: Indiana University Press, 1986, pp. 238–239.

329. David Clay Large, *Where Ghosts Walked: Munich's Road to the Third Reich.* New York: W. W. Norton, 1997, p. xix.

would "send for Dr. A. to cut off your widdler" if he touched his penis.[330] It is no wonder that Freud reported that his patients "regularly charge their mothers with seducing them,"[331] but not because "they had been cleansed by their mothers" as he claimed but because they had in fact been used sexually by them. They then imposed various punishments and anti-masturbation devices such as penis rings, metal cages with spikes, and plaster casts to prevent erections while sleeping, in order to punish the child for the incestuous acts of the parent.[332]

As children left their families in pedophile-prone nineteenth-century Germany, they were again raped at school, as servants, on the streets, and at work. The majority of prostitutes were minors, often starting their careers as young as age 7, with parents often living off the prostitution of their daughters.[333] Virgins were particularly valuable, since "a superstition prevails . . . that venereal diseases may be cured by means of sexual intercourse with a virgin."[334] Bloch thought seducing children was "very widespread" because "timidity and impotence on the part of adult men, rendering intercourse with adult women difficult" led to their commonly raping children.[335] Rape by employers of servants was widespread, but since no one wanted illegitimate children, the servant girl was expected to kill any offspring.[336] Girls leaving school at 13 regularly told tales of sexual assault at the hands of factory employers and managers, or by bosses in the office.[337] And both boys and girls were open to rape in schools, by teachers as well as older students; there were even "free schools" known for pederastic use of young boys that espoused "pedagogical Eros" concepts that were popular in the

---

330. Sigmund Freud, *Standard Edition*, Vol. X, p. 8.

331. Ibid., Vol. XXI, p. 234.

332. Lloyd deMause, "The Evolution of Childhood," pp. 57–58; Gerhart S. Schwarz, "Devices to Prevent Masturbation." *Medical Aspects of Human Sexuality* May 1973, pp. 150–151.

333. Sander L. Gilman, *Difference and Pathology: Race, Stereotypes of Sexuality, Race and Madness*. Ithaca: Cornell University Press, 1985, pp. 41–45; Florence Rush, *The Best Kept Secret: Sexual Abuse of Children*. Blue Ridge Summit, PA: Tab Books, 1980, p. 63.

334. Albert Moll, *The Sexual Life of the Child*, p. 219; Iwan Bloch, *The Sexual Life of Our Time*. New York: Rebman, 1980, p. 631.

335. Ibid., 633.

336. Regina Schulte, "Infanticide in Rural Bavaria in the Nineteenth Century." In Hans Medick and David Warren Sabean, Eds., *Interest and Emotion*, p. 85.

337. Mary Jo Maynes, "Adolescent Sexuality and Social Identity in French and German Lower-Class Autobiography." *Journal of Family History* 17(1992): 407.

Fig. 6–6. A day in a nineteenth-century German school

period.[338] Even the daily beatings so commonly reported at schools had overtones of sexual assault—after all, the German schoolmaster who boasted he had given "911,527 strokes with the stick, 124,000 lashes with the whip, 136,715 slaps with the hand, and 1,115,800 boxes on the ear"[339] was engaged in a severe sexual compulsion, not a disciplinary act. One can easily sense the sexual excitement behind the claim that teachers must "know how to love with the cane,"[340] in schools that were

> real torture-chambers for children and young people. All day long the hazel-rod, the ruler . . . and the cowhide reign, or they fly around in the class-room to warn the sluggish ones and the chatter-boxes or to

338. Klaus Theweleit, *Male Fantasies: Vol. 2 Male Bodies: Psychoanalyzing the White Terror*. Minneapolis: University of Minnesota Press, 1989, p. 320; Katharina Rutschky, *Deutsche* Kinder-Chronik, 1983, p. 811; Thijs Maasen, "Man-Boy Friendships on Trial: On the Shift in the Discourse on Boy Love in the Early Twentieth Century." In Theo Sandfort et al., *Male Intergenerational Intimacy: Historical, Socio-Psychological, and Legal Perspectives*. New York: Harrington Park Press, 1991, pp. 47–53.

339. Preserved Smith, *A History of Modern Culture* Vol. 2. New York: Henry Holt & Co., 1934, p. 423.

340. Aurel Ende, "Battering and Neglect," p. 255.

call them to step out. Then, they were given a sound thrashing. How inventive were some school tyrants concerning their punishments. . . . There is rarely a morning on which we do not see servants or even parents in the streets, dragging violently to school boys who cry at the top of their voices.[341]

THE INNOVATIVE PHASE: WEIMAR GERMANY AND THE LEAP INTO MODERNITY

A small minority of Germans at the turn of the century, however, had more modern, less brutal child rearing, and it was these who in every economic class managed to provide the new psychoclass that supported the democratic and economic reforms of the Weimar Republic. These Germans were able to borrow more advanced social and economic models from other nations nearby, creating an even larger gap between the majority of Germans brought up in medieval child-rearing ways and the needs of modern capitalism and democratic forms of government. The advanced minority did not mainly come from the wealthier economic classes. Wealthy mothers regularly sent their newborns out to peasants who had reputations for being totally without feeling for the infants for whom they were supposed to care. The new psychoclass of German parents can be found in the historical record in exceptional autobiographies and diaries, more in the north than the south (where as we have seen the mothers didn't even breast-feed), more in the middle classes than in the wealthy, more in urban areas than rural, and more in certain ethnic groups, particularly the Jews.

That German Jewish families "constituted one of the most spectacular social leaps in European history [and] produced some of the most fiercely independent minds" in Germany[342] is a little-understood cause of their persecution during the Holocaust, since a nation afraid of independence naturally chooses the most independent people in their population as scapegoats for their fear of freedom. Jews in Germany were far more literate (even the females) than others since medieval times, when most populations were nearly totally illiterate. Jewish families, smaller and more urban than other

---

341. Raffael Scheck, "Childhood in German Autobiographical Writings," p. 412.

342. Fritz Stern, *Dreams and Delusions: The Drama of German History*. New Haven: Yale University Press, 1987, pp. 105, 110.

German families and far less authoritarian,[343] for centuries almost always nursed their own children,[344] so that in 1907, for instance, in the south "44 percent of the children of Christian families died, but only 8 percent of the Jewish children."[345] Jewish immigrants who lived in poverty in various European cities had lower infant mortality rates than their neighbors.[346] Even poor Jewish families further east took much better care of their children and had much lower infant death rates than the families around them.[347] Two major studies of German Jewish family life confirm that it was quite different from most of the other families around them, so much more loving and compassionate that even after the end of World War II, after experiencing during the Holocaust the most "severe abuse and unimaginable stress, there were no suicides [in survivors]. . . . The people are neither living a greedy, me-first style of life, nor are they seeking gain at the expense of others. . . . Most of their lives are marked by an active compassion for others."[348] As was stressed earlier, what produces violent restaging of early trauma isn't merely the severity of the trauma, but whether or not the child blames himself. [349]

Two similar studies—one by Dicks of Nazis and another by the Oliners of rescuers of Jews—clearly reveal the different family backgrounds of the more advanced psychoclass represented by rescuers. Just as Dicks found brutal, domineering parents of Nazis who had "particularly destructive mother images,"[350] the Oliners interviewed over 406 rescuers of Jews, compared them with 126 nonrescuers, and found that their economic class, their religion, their education, jobs, and other social characteristics were

---

343. Marion A. Kaplan, *Between Dignity and Despair: Jewish Life in Nazi Germany.* New York: Oxford University Press, 1998, p. 55; Ute Frevert, *Women in German History: From Bourgeois Emancipation to Sexual Liberation.* Oxford: Berg, 1989, p. 111.

344. Marvin Lowenthal, Trans., *The Memoirs of Glückel of Hamlen.* New York: Schocken Books, 1977, p. 36.

345. Aurel Ende, "Battering and Neglect," p. 262.

346. Lara V. Marks, *Model Mothers: Jewish Mothers and Maternity Provision in East London, 1870–1939.* New York: Oxford University Press, 1994.

347. David L. Ransel, *Village Mothers*, p. 33.

348. Sarah Moskovitz, *Love Despite Hate: Child Survivors of the Holocaust and Their Adult Lives.* New York: Shocken, 1983, p. 23; Martin Gilbert, *The Boys: The Untold Story of 732 Young Concentration Camp Survivors.* New York: Henry Holt & Co., 1997.

349. Jeanne Hill, "Believing Rachel." *The Journal of Psychohistory* 24(1996): 132–146.

350. Henry V. Dicks, *Licensed Mass Murder: A Sociopsychological Study of Some SS Killers.* New York: Basic Books, 1972, p. 205.

all similar, only their child rearing was different.[351] Altruistic personalities, they found, had families that showed them more respect, more concern for fairness, more love, and had less emphasis on obedience and more on individuality. They were almost never sent out to others to be cared for, and if they were sometimes hit by their parents, the parents often apologized.[352] The result was that Jews were the most liberal group in Weimar Germany.[353] A new child-rearing mode had penetrated to a minority of Germans at the beginning of the twentieth century, in time to produce a new innovative phase and an attempted leap to modernity during the Weimar Republic.

During this decade of prosperity, "many Germans enjoyed a temporary triumph of *eros* over *thanatos*, experiencing a sense of liberation hitherto unknown in a land where strong discipline and public conformity had held sway for generations."[354] Universal suffrage allowed women to vote, a minority of parties were even fairly democratic in intent, economic freedoms multiplied and produced unaccustomed prosperity, women's rights over their children were promoted, and sexual material and even contraception became widely available, reducing for the first time the number of children per family to two.[355] But all this political, economic, and social liberation produced terror in the average German— a fear of freedom that threatened loss of maternal approval and that led to fantasies of merging with the punitive, controlling mother. Democracy was seen as "a beast of a thousand heads [that] crushes anything it cannot swallow or engulf."[356] Weimar purity crusades began to call for "emancipation from emancipation" and "a restoration of authoritarian rule."[357] Antipornography laws "to protect youth against literary rubbish

---

351. Samuel P. Oliner and Pearl M. Oliner, *The Altruistic Personality: Rescuers of Jews in Nazi Europe*. New York: The Free Press, 1988.

352. Ibid., p. 181.

353. Donald L. Niewyk, *The Jews in Weimar Germany*. Piscataway, NJ: Transaction Publishers, 2000.

354. Klaus P. Fischer, *The History of an Obsession: German Judeophobia and the Holocaust*. New York: Continuum, 1998, p. 158.

355. Ute Frevert, *Women in German History: From Bourgeois Emancipation to Sexual Liberation*. New York: Berg, 1989, p. 188.

356. Klaus Theweleit, *Male Fantasies: Vol. 2: Male Bodies: Psychoanalyzing the White Terror*. Minneapolis: University of Minnesota Press, 1989, p. 45.

357. Claudia Koonz, *Mothers in the Fatherland: Women, The Family, and Nazi Politics*. New York: St. Martin's Press, 1981, pp. 12–13.

and dirt" began to be passed as early as 1926.[358] Even women delegates in the Reichstag opposed "the masculinization of women" that they said was the result of women's rights, which were deemed "un-German."[359] Like other groups and other nations that felt their traditional authoritarian way of life was being lost,[360] Germany felt it needed a messianic hero, a phallic leader who would punish those who wanted freedom, who would give them "a national enema," a purging, a purifying of foreign liberalism to "unify and cleanse"[361] the body politic as their mothers or wet nurses had forcefully purged them of feces and cleansed them of their desires for independence. The myth about "the stab in the back"—the enema—being the underlying cause of Germany's problems had deeper meaning than the political. It was agreed that "the stab in the back [is] a crime . . . the cause of our general paralysis and joylessness . . . "[362] What was needed, it was said, was something to "remove the *Verstopfung* [constipation]" that was obstructing German culture.[363] Germans complained throughout the Weimar period about "the stab in the back" they had received at the end of World War I, and said about the Versailles Treaty, "Always think about it, never speak of it," both phrases originally used in referring to childhood enema assaults. The more prosperous Weimar became, the more growth panic Germans experienced—as reflected in the sharp increase in manslaughter rates during the later Weimar years.[364] Thus it was that Germany—the nation that during the 1920s enjoyed higher standards of living than any other in Europe[365]—began its search

358. E. J. Feuchtwanger, *From Weimar to Hitler: Germany, 1918–33*. New York: St. Martin's Press, 1995, p. 182.

359. Ibid., pp. 32, 98.

360. John J. Hartman and Graham S. Gibbard, "Bisexual Fantasy and Group Process." *Contemporary Psychoanalysis* 9(1973): 314–319.

361. Fritz Stern, *The Politics of Cultural Despair: A Study in the Rise of the Germanic Ideology*. Berkeley: University of California Press, 1961, pp. xi–xix.

362. Anton Kaes et al., Eds., *The Weimar Republic Sourcebook*. Berkeley: University of California Press, 1994, p. 17.

363. Peter S. Fisher, *Fantasy and Politics: Visions of the Future in the Weimar Republic*. Madison: University of Wisconsin Press, 1991, p. 95.

364. Eric A. Johnson, "The Crime Rate: Longitudinal and Periodic Trends in Nineteenth- and Twentieth-Century German Criminality, from *Vormärz* to Late Weimar." In Richard J. Evans, Ed., *The German Underworld: Deviants and Outcasts in German History*. London: Routledge, 1988, p. 172.

365. Claudia Koonz, *Mothers in the Fatherland*, p. 41.

for a violent, purging dictator long before the Depression began—the supposed cause of the dictatorship.

THE DEPRESSIVE PHASE: CHOOSING THE PHALLIC LEADER

Careful studies of the rise of Nazism conclude that the Depression came after, not before, the death of Weimar democracy and that "the decay of parliamentary government preceded the Nazi rise."[366] Nor did the economic burden of the Versailles Treaty and Allied demands for reparations cause it, since "German borrowing from abroad always far exceeded her reparation payments."[367] Nor, as we have documented, was antisemitism the cause of the rise of the Nazis. Most Germans were "relatively indifferent towards the Jewish Question,"[368] and "the vast majority of the general population did not clamor or press for antisemitic measures [even by] the *Kristallnacht* pogrom of November 1938."[369]

The call for a dictatorship, in fact, came before it began to center on Hitler, first in films and other cultural material (Kracauer calls Weimar culture "a procession of tyrants"[370]) and then in the Reichstag. The middle classes ("hardly touched by the Depression"[371]) and the wealthy ("the richer the precinct the higher the Nazi vote"[372]) were the main sources of the more than two-thirds of delegates who voted Hitler dictator. Women, in fact, voted for Hitler in even greater proportions than men.[373] The ecstatic enthusiasm of the jubilant masses of people who celebrated their phallic leader

---

366. E. J. Feuchtwanger, *From Weimar to Hitler*, p. 200; Ian Kershaw, *Weimar: Why Did German Democracy Fail?* New York: St. Martin's Press, 1990, p. 22.

367. P. M. H. Bell, *The Origins of the Second World War in Europe*, 2nd ed. London: Longman, 1997, p. 41.

368. Ian Kershaw, *Popular Opinion and Political Dissent in the Third Reich. Bavaria 1933–1945*. Oxford: Clarendon Press, 1983, p. 231.

369. Christopher R. Browning, *Ordinary Men: Reserve Police Battalion 101 and the Final Solution in Poland*. New York: HarperCollins, 1998, p. 200.

370. Siegfried Kracauer, *From Caligari to Hitler: A Psychological History of the German Film*. Princeton: Princeton University Press, 1947, p. 55.

371. Peter Fritzsche, *Germans into Nazis*. Cambridge: Harvard University Press, 1998, p. 159.

372. Ibid., p. 206.

373. Renate Bridenthal et al., Eds., *When Biology Became Destiny: Women in Weimar and Nazi Germany*. New York: Monthly Review Press, 1984, p. 34.

came directly from his promises of a violent purity crusade that would end what Hitler called the "poisoning hothouse of sexual conceptions and stimulants [and the] suffocating perfume of our modern eroticism [that is] the personification of incest"[374]—all three images suggesting flashbacks to the sexually engulfing mommy of the German family bed. Even during the Depression, Germans said: "We are somebody again!"[375] because of their delusional merger with their phallic leader. Economics, political forms, antisemitism—all played second fiddle in the Nazi propaganda to Hitler's "ranting about prostitution and moral decadence."[376] What made Germans say about Hitler's dictatorship "the joy inside me was impossible to describe"[377] was his violent purity crusade, a dopamine rush that warded off engulfment by the terrifying mother—using his hatred of his own mother that can be glimpsed in his saying about a frightening painting of Medusa he kept on his walls: "Those eyes! They are the eyes of my mother!"[378]

THE MANIC PHASE: BEGINNING THE KILLING OF "USELESS EATERS"

The Depression was relatively short in Germany. Since economic downturns are caused by motivated mistakes in restricting liquidity, Hitler performed what was called an economic miracle simply by reversing the supposed mistakes of late Weimar economic policies, so that by the end of 1936 Germany surpassed the highest levels of gross national product (GNP) achieved during the 1920s.[379] It was only as the manic phase was well under way that Germans really felt their growth panic and completed their merger with the Fatherland and the promised violence of the phallic leader. Protected against growing body disintegration anxieties by

---

374. Adolf Hitler, *Mein Kampf*. New York: Reynal & Hitchcock, 1940, pp. 346, 160.

375. Willy Schumann, *Being Present: Growing Up in Hitler's Germany*. Kent, OH: Kent State University Press, 1991, p. 145.

376. Ian Kershaw, *Hitler: 1889–1936: Hubris*. New York: W. W. Norton & Co., 1998, p. 46.

377. Claudia Koonz, *Mothers in the Fatherland*, p. 62.

378. Robert G. L. Waite, *The Psychopathic God: Adolf Hitler*. New York: Da Capo Press, 1977, pp. 6–7, 157; Waite reproduces the Medusa picture next to a photo of Hitler's mother, showing their similarity.

379. Detlev J. K. Peukert, *Inside Nazi Germany: Conformity, Opposition, and Racism in Everyday Life*. New Haven: Yale University Press, 1982, pp. 69, 200.

fetishistic Nazi leather boots and uniforms, Nazis could accomplish the purification of their nation by "stopping the creeping poison" exuded by terrifying mommies and bad-child selves, at home and abroad. Germans said "Halt" to freedom in order to be acceptable to mommy; after all, the "Heil Hitler!" salute, with arm stiffly outstretched and palm out, is a universal symbol of "Halt." Germans who as children were made to kneel silently against the wall for hours encountered American swing music as adults and wanted to dance, but still were under their internal parents' injunction to "Halt." So Nazi soldiers halted all swing dancing in Germany and sent those who swing danced to concentration camps.[380] Only if Germans could stop being individuals living in freedom could they go back and live as one family in the "joyful rapture" of one *Volk*, cleansed of sinful freedoms. Only if they were slaves to totalitarian Nazi whims could they restage their slavery to their parents in the totalitarian family of their childhoods. Thus, even the chains of swaddling bands were embedded in the Nazi dicta: "He who can do what he wants is not free . . . . He who feels himself without chains is not free."[381] Only those who could worship the Motherland (the swastika is an ancient symbol of mother goddess worship) could feel reborn and be accepted by mommy, as they felt they deserved to be. Since group-fantasies of merging with mommy proliferated, men feared they would become feminine, so homosexuals too began to be persecuted with a vengeance.

Indeed, all of post-Depression Europe, America and even Asia were in their manic phase in the late 1930s and felt the need for a cleansing world war and sacrifice of scapegoats. American antisemitism, for instance, was on the rise, with a steady minority feeling that Jews were a menace to America[382] and two-thirds indicating Jewish refugees should be kept out of the country.[383] In the summer of 1939 when over a thousand German Jews arrived in the New World, they were sent back.[384] The bill to accept 20,000 Jewish children into the United States was received with massive opposition because "20,000 children will soon turn into 20,000 ugly

---

380. Detlev J. K. Peukert, *Inside Nazi Germany*, p. 167.
381. George L. Mosse, *The Fascist Revolution: Toward a General Theory of Fascism*. New York: Howard Fertig, 1999, p. 34.
382. David S. Wyman, *The Abandonment of the Jews*. New York: Pantheon Books, 1984.
383. Klaus P. Fischer, *The History of an Obsession*, p. 277.
384. Ibid., p. 288.

adults."[385] Thirty-two nations assembled at a conference on Jewish emigration and voted they "regretted" they could not take in more Jews.[386] When the British were approached to save Jews in exchange for goods, they replied, "What on earth are you thinking of? . . . What shall I do with those million Jews? Where shall I put them?"[387] Nor was Hitler without his admirers in other countries before the invasion. Churchill called him "an indomitable champion [who could] restore our courage."[388] Anthony Eden said of him "without doubt the man has charm. . . . I rather liked him."[389] Indeed, Beisel's research into the group-fantasies of Western nations before the war concludes that Germany was the "bad boy" of Europe who was delegated the starting of the war by others in the family of nations, just as many bad boys are delegated the acting out of violence felt by others in individual families.[390]

Before the war broke out, however, the killing of "bad children" had begun in earnest. The earliest death camps, in fact, were set up to kill children who were "useless eaters," the same term applied to the Germans themselves by their parents when they were children at the turn of the century. Long before the Holocaust of Jews began, medical officers sent questionnaires to parents and guardians of children in mental hospitals and homes for delinquent children, asking them if they would give their consent to killing them. So powerful was the unconscious group-fantasy at that time that "bad" children were polluting the German nation that most parents and guardians agreed to the killing of what they called their "useless children."[391] The doctors, including pediatricians, spontaneously set up a Reich committee "to exterminate 'undesirable' children," which drew up standards that read exactly like the child care manuals at the end of the nineteenth century, asking whether the child had been "late in being toilet

385. "The American Experience," WNYC-TV, April 7, 1994.

386. Marion A. Kaplan, *Between Dignity and Despair*, p. 70.

387. George M. Kren and Leon Rappoport, *The Holocaust and the Crisis of Human Behavior*, rev. ed. New York: Holmes & Meier, 1980, p. 104.

388. Anthony P. Adamthwaite, *The Making of the Second World War*. New York: Routledge, 1977, p. 43.

389. Richard Lamb, *The Drift to War: 1922–1939*. New York: St. Martin's Press, 1989, p. 85.

390. David Beisel, *The Suicidal Embrace: Hitler, the Allies and the Origins of World War II*, forthcoming.

391. Götz Aly et al., *Cleansing the Fatherland: Nazi Medicine and Racial Hygiene*. Baltimore: Johns Hopkins University Press, 1994, pp. 29–55.

trained" or had used "dirty words" or were "slow learners." If they were, they were exterminated in gas chambers and crematorium ovens.[392] Over 70,000 of these "useless eaters" were murdered by doctors to "cleanse the German national body"[393] before the war began.[394] So proud were these doctors of their murder of "bad children" that they actually made a popular film of the killings, which was shown in theaters.[395] At the same time, throughout Germany, "midwives and nurses were instructed to report births of defective infants . . . including 'racially undesirable' ones. . . . Thousands were killed by injection or deliberate starvation."[396] The wiping out of bad-child alters "out there" in Germany to remove them from "inside here," in the traumatized hemisphere of the brain, had begun. Killing millions more "bad children" in the Holocaust and World War II soon followed.

THE WAR PHASE: RAPING MOMMIES AND KILLING BAD CHILD ALTERS

Killing mommies and children were the two tasks of Germans in starting World War II. Hitler made this clear in the speech he gave before his generals ordering the invasion of Poland. Note the exact words he used: "Genghis Khan has sent millions of women and children into death knowingly and with a light heart . . . I have put my death's head formations in place with the command relentlessly and without compassion to send into death many women and children of Polish origin."[397] After quoting these sentences, Fischer says "Hitler had exclaimed that he would kill without pity all men, women, and children."[398] But men were not in fact mentioned in his quote. Hitler said "women and children" must die—women as sym-

---

392. Ibid., pp. 55, 188–189; Henry Friedlander, *The Origins of Nazi Genocide: From Euthanasia to the Final Solution*. Chapel Hill: University of North Carolina Press, 1995, pp. 39–61.

393. Götz Aly, *"Final Solution": Nazi Population Policy and the Murder of the European Jews*. London: Arnold, 1999, p. 30.

394. Götz Aly et al., *Cleansing the Fatherland*, p. 46.

395. Ibid., p. 27.

396. George Victor, *Hitler: The Pathology of Evil*. Washington: Brassey's, 1998, p. 171.

397. Klaus P. Fischer, *Nazi Germany: A New History*. New York: Continuum, 1998, p. 439.

398. Ibid.

bolic terrifying mothers, and children as symbolic bad children. Even all the soldiers who must die—including the German soldiers who must die—were "youth," victim alters, vital, growing inner childhood selves sacrificed to Moloch.

The path to war, however, did not begin with the killing of bad-child "useless eaters" to the East. Indeed, Hitler temporarily made a nonaggression pact with Russia and attempted to extend it to Poland. Germany's first task was *righteous rape*, the knocking of Mother England and Marianne off their pedestals and, while still wooing them, teaching them a lesson of how they must stop humiliating Germans by rejecting their courtship. Nazi diplomatic language dripped with maternal imagery for France and England, as when Goering asked, "Why should France continue to tie herself to a decayed old nation like England—a rouged old maid trying to pretend that she is still young and vigorous?"[399] Hitler believed that war would teach England a lesson and make her respect Germany, predicting that "the end of the war will mark the beginning of a durable friendship with England. But first we must give her the K.O.—for only so can we live at peace with her, and the Englishman can only respect someone who has first knocked him out."[400] Mother England, in particular, was a "purely Germanic nation" who, like a good German mother, ruled over her children (colonies) with an iron fist.[401] Germany had to rape her to dominate and really have her, but, Hitler said, "This doesn't prevent me from admiring [the English]. They have a lot to teach us."[402]

Historians agree that during the 1936–38 period "Hitler assumed that Britain could be wooed or forced into an alliance."[403] When England finally said they would defend Poland, Hitler responded by "abandoning his courtship of England, which had rejected him,"[404] and proceeded with what was called "the rape of Austria," what Hitler called "the return of German-Austria to the great German motherland."[405] All Germans had long blamed England

---

399. Orville H. Bullitt, Ed., *For the President: Personal and Secret: Correspondence Between Franklin D. Roosevelt and William C. Bullitt*. London: Andre Deutsch, 1973, p. 308.

400. H. R. Trevor-Roper, *Hitler's Secret Conversations 1941–1944*. New York: Farrar, Straus and Young, 1953, p. 11.

401. Ibid., p. xviii.

402. Ibid., p. 22.

403. Anthony P. Adamthwaite, *The Making of the Second World War*. New York: Routledge, 1977, p. 72.

404. Joachim C. Fest, *Hitler*. San Diego: Harcourt Brace & Co., 1973, p. 578.

405. Adolf Hitler, *Mein Kampf*. New York: Reynal & Hitchcock, 1939, p. 3.

and France for the ineffective "Treaty of Shame" (Versailles) and promised to fight the West to "restore to each individual German his *self-respect.* . . . We are not *inferior*; on the contrary, we are the complete equals of every other nation."[406] Even those Germans who were turned over to nurses by their mothers knew what Hitler meant when he declared that "Germany would not suffer under the tutelage of governesses,"[407] i.e., England.

Nazi *Blitzkreig* and dive-bomber tactics were particularly loaded with righteous rape fantasies featuring powerful thrusts and penetration of enemy bodies, wreaking vengeance for earlier wrongs. The war began in the East, restaging German childhood traumas in Poland, and it involved from the start suicidal intent and the killing off of sinful Germans. Historians admit that fighting "an unlimited war of conquest [against] a worldwide coalition of states . . . was in itself an insane undertaking"[408] that was suicidal and sacrificial from the beginning. As Hitler promised nothing but death to what he called the "thousands and thousands of young Germans who have come forward with the self-sacrificial resolve freely and joyfully to make a sacrifice of their young lives,"[409] German mothers marched through the streets chanting, "We have donated a child to the Führer." Nazi soldiers felt "politically reborn [when] filled with a pure joy I realized that what my mother had once said was true after all—that it was a hallowed act to give up one's life for Germany," and Hitler Youth sang: "We are born to die for Germany."[410] At no point was mere conquest of land the goal of Germany's invasions. Hitler hated British Prime Minister Neville Chamberlain for making concessions and avoiding war at Munich, telling his soldiers later, "We want war. I am only afraid that some *Schweinehund* will make a proposal for mediation" like at Munich.[411] "I did not organize the armed forces in order not to strike. . . . The idea of getting out cheaply is

406. Thomas J. Scheff, *Bloody Revenge: Emotions, Nationalism, and War.* Boulder: Westview Press, 1994, p. 116.

407. Andrew J. Crozier, *The Causes of the Second World War.* Oxford: Blackwell Publishers, 1997, p. 147.

408. Jost Dülffer, *Nazi Germany 1933–1945: Faith and Annihilation.* London: Arnold, 1996, p. 61.

409. Peter Fritzsche, *Germans into Nazis.* Cambridge: Harvard University Press, 1998, p. 7.

410. Richard Grunberger, *The 12–Year Reich: A Social History of Nazi Germany 1933–1945.* New York: Da Capo Press, 1995, p. 236; Theodore Abel, *Why Hitler Came into Power.* Cambridge: Harvard University Press, 1938, pp. 212, 236.

411. William L. Shirer, *The Rise and Fall of the Third Reich*, p. 708.

dangerous. . . . We must burn our boats."[412] He instructed his diplomats always to demand "so much that we can never be satisfied."[413] When asked about Poland, "What is it that you want? Danzig? The Corridor?" the answer was, "We want war."[414] The goal was to "Act brutally! Be harsh and remorseless!"[415] While Germans marched west with visions of raping French women and climbing the Eiffel Tower, they marched east with visions of smashing Jewish babies' heads against walls[416] and turning Moscow into "an artificial lake."[417] All bad-child alters to the east must be eliminated. The orders were: "Complete destruction of Poland. . . . Pursue until complete annihilation"[418] and "Moscow must be destroyed and completely wiped from the earth."[419]

Jewish annihilation plans only came later, actually during the summer months of 1941 when, "convinced that the military campaign was nearly over and victory was at hand, an elated Hitler gave the signal to carry out [the] racial 'cleansing' [of the Jews]."[420] Initially, for many years, Jews were to be resettled, part of Hitler's "grandiose program of population transfers"[421]—90 percent of whom were ethnic Germans and others, and only 10 percent of whom were Jews. This was a "massive upheaval of humanity"[422] that restaged upon five million people[423] the experiences of having to leave home that were endured during childhood by most Germans as their parents endlessly moved them around to wet nurses, relatives, schools, and work sites. In 1940 Hitler and Himmler had rejected the "physical

---

412. Gordon A. Craig, *Germany 1866–1945.* New York: Oxford University Press, 1978, p. 713.

413. Anthony P. Adamthwaite, *The Making of the Second World War,* p. 77.

414. Klaus P. Fischer, *Nazi Germany,* p. 439.

415. William L. Shirer, *The Rise and Fall of the Third Reich,* p. 709.

416. Heinz Höhne, *The Order of the Death's Head: The Story of Hitler's SS.* New York: Ballantine, 1971, p. 409.

417. John Toland, *Adolf Hitler,* p. 680.

418. John G. Stoessinger, *Why Nations Go to War,* 7th ed. New York: St. Martin's Press, 1998, p. 29.

419. John Toland, *Adolf Hitler,* p. 685.

420. Christopher R. Browning, *The Path to Genocide: Essays on Launching the Final Solution.* New York: Cambridge University Press, 1992, p. 111.

421. Ibid., p. 9.

422. Ibid., p. 20.

423. Götz Aly, *'Final Solution': Nazi Population Policy and the Murder of the European Jews.* London: Arnold, 1999, p. 7.

extermination of a people out of inner conviction as un-German and impossible."[424] It was only by the summer of 1941, in victory and afraid of running out of "bad children" to kill in the east, that Hitler would approve of "the mass murder of all European Jews . . . in the form of deportation to death camps equipped with poison gas facilities"[425] like those used for murdering the 70,000 German children killed earlier. Christopher Browning correctly points to mania and success as the source of the Holocaust when he concludes: "Hitler [only] opted for the Final Solution in the 'euphoria of victory' of midsummer 1941."[426] Jews were the ultimate "bad children," symbols of liberalism, freedom, and prosperity in the stock market, and so finally must be totally eliminated for Germans to return to the "pure" authoritarian family atmosphere of 1900 where only "good boys" survived.

Even the notion that Germany had to kill Poles and Jews for the acquisition of *Lebensraum*, or living space, completely misses the motive for the Holocaust. *Lebensraum* was a completely phony concept. It was actually a code word for the desire to break free, to have room to live and grow, to throw off swaddling bands and corsets, to get up from crouching against the wall as children. Conquering foreign lands or annihilating Jews to expand the actual amount of soil Germany could farm made no sense at all, because Germany already had so much unused land that they had to import a steady stream of foreign workers to farm it.[427] Germans ate well under Hitler. The only reality behind the popular *Lebensraum* notion that the "Germanic mother could not feed her children adequately"[428] was the inability of German mothers and wet nurses four decades earlier to empathize with and adequately feed their infants and children.

Jews, then, were the main poison containers for the restaging of traumatic German child-rearing practices four decades earlier. Jews represented every German child's independence, crippled children their helplessness, Communists their rebelliousness, homosexuals their sexual freedom, gyp-

---

424. Christopher R. Browning, *The Path to Genocide*, p. 25.

425. Ibid.

426. Eberhard Jäckel, "The Holocaust: Where We Are, Where We Need to Go." In Michael Berenbaum and Abraham J. Peck, Eds., *The Holocaust and History: The Known, the Unknown, the Disputed, and the Reexamined.* Bloomington, IN: Indiana University Press, 1998, p. 25.

427. Ian Kershaw, *Popular Opinion and Political Dissent in the Third Reich*, p. 58.

428. Rudolph Binion, *Hitler Among the Germans*. New York: Elsevier, 1976, p. 58.

sies their "carefree" lives—every type of Nazi victim was a bad-child trait that must be wiped out. Each of the specific things done to Jews and others in the Holocaust can be found to have been perpetrated by parents and others on German children at the turn of the century. The precise details of the earlier events that were later inflicted on victims of the Holocaust are astonishingly literal. To begin with, Jews were murdered by the millions, just as German children had watched their siblings murdered by the millions in infanticidal acts earlier, regularly using the exact same phrase for the genocide of Jews—"elimination of useless eaters"—as parents had used earlier for their infants as they murdered them at birth.[429] Because infanticide rates were so high, the majority of German children would have been around during the murder of newborn siblings by their mothers, would have heard the baby being called a "useless eater," and would themselves have been called a "useless eater" and wondered if they too might be murdered. Children were at the center of the Holocaust: one can hardly read a single Holocaust book without having to wade through endless accounts of children buried alive by Nazis, "children having their heads beaten in like poultry and thrown into a smoking pit," "babies thrown from the fourth floor and crushed on the pavements," "children's bodies lay around, torn in half with the heads smashed in," and "'little Jews' caught on bayonets after being thrown from upper story windows."[430] Even the specific methods German mothers had used for killing their newborn—especially smashing the baby against a wall or throwing it into a latrine—were "a regular occurrence"[431] against Jews in concentration camps:

> When mothers succeeded in keeping their babies with them . . . a German guard took the baby by its legs and smashed it against the wall of the barracks until only a bloody mass remained in his hands. The unfortunate mother had to take this mass with her to the "bath." Only those who saw these things with their own eyes will believe with what delight the Germans performed these operations. [Also] SS men used to amuse themselves by swinging Jewish children by their legs and then flinging them to their deaths. He who threw a Jewish child farthest won.[432]

---

429. Götz Aly, 'Final Solution,' p. 215.

430. Martin Gilbert, *The Holocaust*, pp. 155, 320, 330, 442, 687.

431. Richard C. Lukas, *Did the Children Cry? Hitler's War Against Jewish and Polish Children, 1939–1945.* New York: Hippocrene Books, 1994, p. 75.

432. Martin Gilbert, *The Holocaust: A History of the Jews of Europe During the Second World War.* New York: Holt, Rinehart and Winston, 1985, pp. 457, 546.

Jews were also regularly tied up and made to live in their own filth, exactly as swaddled German infants were earlier. Rarely washed, Germans had spent their early lives covered with their own excreta, addressed by their parents simply as "little shitter."[433] In the concentration camps, Jews were subject to what Des Pres calls a constant "excremental assault," in which they were forced to defecate and urinate upon each other, were often thrown into the cesspool if they were too slow, lived in barracks "awash with urine and feces," walked about "knee-deep in excrement," were forced to eat their own feces, and finally died in gas chambers "covered all over with excrement."[434] In one camp, 30,000 women not only had to use a single latrine, but in addition, "we were permitted to use it only at certain hours of the day. We stood in line to get into this tiny building, knee-deep in human excrement."[435] Holocaust scholars, missing the childhood origins of all these gratuitous excremental cruelties, have been puzzled by how much of the concentration camp routine was devoted to the endless humiliations. "Why, if they were going to kill them anyway, what was the point of all the humiliation, why the cruelty?" Gitta Sereny asked of Franz Stangl.[436] But of course the humiliation was the point, restaging early German childhood exactly. Hitler—himself swaddled and left alone in his feces by his mother—had told Germans in *Mein Kampf*: "If the Jews were alone in this world, they would suffocate in dirt and filth."[437] In the Holocaust the Jews would suffocate in dirt and filth, as all little, helpless German babies did all day long at the hands of their mothers. And since the "little shitter" German babies were also covered with lice, vermin, and rodents as they lay swaddled in their cradles, unable to move, Jews too were called "lice, vermin, and rats" as they were locked into the concentration camps, told: "This is a death camp. . . . You'll be eaten by lice; you'll rot in your own shit, you filthy shitface."[438] Some guards even restaged the ro-

---

433. Stanley Rosenman, "The Fundament of German Character." *The Journal of Psychohistory* 14(1986): 67.

434. Terrence Des Pres, *The Survivor: An Anatomy of Life in the Death Camps*. New York: Pocket Books, 1977, p. 58; Klaus P. Fischer, *Nazi Germany*, pp. 53, 55, 338.

435. Terrence Des Pres, *The Survivor*, p. 58.

436. Gitta Sereny, *Into That Darkness: An Examination of Conscience*. New York: Random House, 1974, p. 101.

437. Adolf Hitler, *Mein Kampf*, p. 416.

438. David R. Beisel, "Europe's Killing Frenzy." *The Journal of Psychohistory* 25(1997): 207.

dent attacks "by inserting a tube into the victim's anus, or into a woman's vagina, then letting a rat into the tube. The rodent would try to get out by gnawing at the victim's internal organs."[439] The toilet training of German children was also restaged, often in precise detail, as by having the ghetto latrine supervised by a "guard with a big clock, whom the Germans dressed comically as a rabbi and called the 'shit-master.'"[440]

Every extermination camp reproduced elements of a typical German home. Jews were not said to be there to be murdered, they were there to be "housecleaned."[441] Mommy hated her children's "dirtiness," wanted them "clean," so "dirty Jews" were killed so only "clean Germans" would be left. Jews were *Untermenschen* (a phrase with overtones of "little people") who were forced to crawl on the floor naked like babies,[442] and who were tied up, starved, made to kneel for hours, doused with ice water, terrorized, and beaten just like most German children.[443] The battering of Jews in camps followed the hallowed German child-beating pattern of the child being expected to "be strong" (not making the perpetrator feel guilty by crying out):

> I dropped to my knees without uttering a sound. I knew what was expected of me. I looked at the commandant from my knees as he smiled back at me with approval. He swung the chair at me again, striking me on the shoulder. I sprawled on the ground, bruised and dizzy, but I still made no sound. He raised the chair and brought it down on my head, shattering it. . . . I bit my tongue to stop myself making a sound. . . . I knew that if I made another sound, nothing could save me. "Very good, for being strong. You shall be rewarded. Get some food. Tell them I sent you."[444]

---

439. Ervin Staub, *The Roots of Evil: The Origins of Genocide and Other Group Violence.* Cambridge: Cambridge University Press, 1989, p. 223.

440. Gitta Sereny, *Into That Darkness*, p. 166.

441. R. J. Rummel, *Democide: Nazi Genocide and Mass Murder.* New Brunswick, NJ: Transaction Publishers, 1992, p. 70.

442. Christopher R. Browning, *Ordinary Men*, p. 83.

443. Henryk Grynberg, *Children of Zion*. Evanston, IL: Northwestern University Press, 1997, pp. 21, 23; Terrence Des Pres, *The Survivor*, p. 53; Nili Keren, "The Family Camp." In Israel Gutman and Michael Berenbaum, Eds., *Anatomy of the Auschwitz Death Camp.* Bloomington, IN: Indiana University Press, 1994, p. 432.

444. Martin Gilbert, *The Boys: The Untold Story of 732 Young Concentration Camp Survivors.* New York: Henry Holt and Co., 1996, p. 206.

The beatings and tortures were, as is so often the case with sadism, often sexualized:

> The SS camp commander stood close to the whipping post throughout the flogging. . . . His whole face was already red with lascivious excitement. His hands were plunged deep in his trouser pockets, and it was quite clear that he was masturbating throughout. . . . On more than thirty occasions, I myself have witnessed SS camp commanders masturbating during floggings.[445]

Sexual tortures of prisoners were legion, including pushing sticks up into boys' penises and breaking them off, brutally massaging prostates with pieces of wood inserted into the rectum, castrating men and removing the ovaries of women, training dogs to attack their genitals, etc.[446] Victims were all "bad boys" and "bad girls," needing to be punished for their sexuality, as the German guards' parents had punished them. Jews *must* have been "bad boys": why else would their parents have castrated (circumcised) them? The Holocaust was, in fact, one gigantic, bizarre cautionary tale, teaching everyone the same lessons taught to children as they were assaulted, so when civilians during the Holocaust saw Jews being clubbed to death in the street, they *cheered*, "with mothers holding up their children to enjoy the spectacle and soldiers milling around to watch the fun like a football match."[447]

THE HISTORICAL EVOLUTION OF CHILD REARING AND THE DECREASE IN HUMAN VIOLENCE

As the next three chapters will document, child rearing has steadily improved historically, even if very unevenly, so if the psychogenic theory is correct, then human violence should have decreased steadily over the past

---

445. Klaus Theweleit, *Male Fantasies*, p. 301.

446. Binjamin Wilkomirski, *Fragments: Memories of a Wartime Childhood*. New York: Schocken Books, 1995, p. 60; Robert Jay Lifton, *The Nazi Doctors: Medical Killing and the Psychology of Genocide*. New York: Basic Books, 1986, p. 282; Israel Gutman and Michael Berenbaum, Eds., *Anatomy of the Auschwitz Death Camp*, p. 308, Gitta Sereny, *Into That Darkness*, p. 202.

447. Klaus P. Fischer, *The History of an Obsession: German Judeophobia and the Holocaust*. New York: Continuum, 1998, p. 346.

millennia. Yet the twentieth century has been widely reported as the most violent in history. How can childhood be the source of human violence if violence has vastly increased while child rearing has improved?

That twentieth century wars have been more violent seems to be an obvious fact. Technology alone allows us to be far more lethal than in earlier centuries, when wars causing 250,000 or more deaths were rare,[448] while World War II alone killed 15 million people in battle, and total battlefield deaths for the twentieth century have exceeded 100 million.[449] What's more, if one expands the definition of war deaths to what Rummel terms "democide"—so that the 40 million Russian deaths ordered by Stalin, for instance, are included—the number of "deaths by government" in the twentieth century jumps past 170 million.[450] Surely Nordstrom is right in saying, "This past century was the bloodiest century in human existence,"[451] thus disproving the psychogenic theory of decreasing violence resulting from improving child rearing.

Yet Nordstrom's pessimistic conclusion is reversed if one measures the rate of violence by the likelihood of one's dying by war and democide. With several billion people on earth during the twentieth century, the rate of death by wars is in fact less than 2 percent of the population.[452] Although individual wars in the past have killed fewer in numbers, they could easily wipe out many times this percentage of the population, particularly if—as is rarely done—the battlefield deaths are increased to include the democides of the past, when massacring civilians in entire cities was a common practice.[453] Further, what is more relevant to the child-rearing comparison is that lumping all nations in the twentieth century together regardless of their

448. Evan Luard, *War in International Society: A Study in International Sociology.* London: I. B. Tauris, & Co., 1986, p. 394.

449. R. J. Rummel, *Death By Government.* New Brunswick: Transaction Publishers, 1997, p. 25.

450. Ibid., p. 9.

451. Cited in Kim A. McDonald, "Anthropologists Debate Whether, and How, War Can be Wiped Out." *The Chronicle of Higher Education*, December 3, 1999, p. A21.

452. L. F. Richardson, *Statistics of Deadly Quarrels.* Pittsburgh: Boxwood, 1960.

453. Frank Chalk and Kurt Jonassohn, *The History and Sociology of Genocide: Analyses and Case Studies.* New Haven: Yale University Press, 1990, p. 33; William J. Brandt, *The Shape of Medieval History: Studies in Modes of Perception.* New Haven: Yale University Press, 1966, p. 133; Kalevi J. Holsti, *Peace and War: Armed Conflicts and International Order 1648–1989.* New York: Cambridge University Press, 1991, p. 28; R. J. Rummel, *Death By Government*, p. 69.

childhood evolution masks the fact that advanced democratic nations like the United States, England, and France have lost only a fraction of 1 percent of their populations in wars during the century. The United States, for instance, lost 120,000 soldiers in World War I, only 0.12 percent of the population, and 400,000 soldiers in World War II, only 0.34 percent of the population.[454] The Korean War only lost 0.04 percent, the Vietnam War only 0.03 percent, and the Gulf War 0.0003 percent of Americans. The facts are that the more advanced the child rearing, the more democratic the society and the less percentage lost in wars.

Anthropologists have promulgated the myth of the peaceful savage so effectively that when actual deaths by war are tabulated for prestate simple societies, one is astonished by how such a notion can continue to be taught to students.[455] Keeley documents 22 prestate tribes with war deaths five to ten times that of contemporary democratic nations, concluding that "what transpired before the evolution of civilized states was often unpleasantly bellicose."[456] Death rates in areas like New Guinea and South America, where there has been less Western policing of war than in Africa and Asia, range from 25 to 35 percent of all adult deaths.[457] The most warlike society ever described is the Waorani of the Amazon, which produced 60 percent of all adult deaths from war raids.[458] It is likely that prestate societies 10,000 years ago had similar astronomical death rates

---

454. Carolyn Marvin and David W. Ingle, *Blood Sacrifice and the Nation: Totem Rituals and the American Flag.* New York: Cambridge University Press, 199, p. 88.

455. Lawrence H. Keeley, *War Before Civilization.* New York: Oxford University Press, 1996.

456. Ibid., pp. 89, 183.

457. M. J. Meggitt, *Blood is Their Argument: Warfare Among the Mae Enga Tribesmen of the New Guinea Highlands.* Palo Alto: Mayfield, 1977, p. 110; Bruce M. Knauft, "Melanesian Warfare: A Theoretical History." *Oceania* 60(1990): 286, 274; Bruce M. Knauft, "Reconsidering Violence in Simple Human Societies." *Current Anthropology* 28(1987): 457–499; F. Barth, "Tribes and Intertribal Relations in the Fly Headwaters." *Oceania* 41(1970–71): 175; D. K. Feil, *The Evolution of Highland Papua New Guinea Societies.* New York: Cambridge University Press, 1987, p. 71; N. A. Chagnon, *Yanomamo: the Fierce People.* 3rd ed. New York: Holt, Rinehard and Winston, p. 171; Richard Wrangham and Dale Peterson, *Demonic Males: Apes and the Origins of Human Violence.* Boston: Houghton Mifflin Co., 1996, p. 77.

458. J. A. Yost and P. M. Kelley, "Shotguns, Blowguns, and Spears: the Analysis of Technological Efficiency." In R. B. Hames and W. Vickers, Eds., *Adaptive Responses of Native Amazonia.* New York: Academic Press, 1983.

from wars, if the number of human bones with stone axes and arrowheads embedded in them are counted.[459] Indeed, archeologists now think early stone hand axes were useless for hunting or butchering, and were used solely in battles.[460] The overall historical decline from 30 percent of adult population to under 1 percent for war/democide adult deaths for democratic nations has therefore been plotted in the graph below as a clear downward trend through history, as child rearing improves through the ages and gradually reduces the inner need to kill others.

Besides war and democide, the graph also shows the decline of the two other outlets for human violence: infanticide and homicide/suicide. Infanticide is usually not counted as murder by demographers, since they usually do not consider newborns as humans. But most human murders in history were in fact committed by mothers killing their newborns. The rates of infanticide in contemporary prestate tribes are enormous: Australian Aborigine mothers, for instance, killed about 50 percent of all newborns, and the first missionaries in Polynesia estimated that two-thirds of the children were murdered by their parents.[461] Birdsell hypothesized infanticide rates as high as 50 percent for prehistoric tribal societies, based on high fertility rates and slow growth of populations.[462] My own cross-historical study, "On the Demography of Filicide,"[463] is based on a large number of boy/girl ratios in census figures that ran as high as 135 to 100, which showed that girls until modern times were killed in sufficiently higher numbers than boys to have affected boy/girl ratios. Tribal societies often kill enough of their newborn girls at a higher rate than boys to produce childhood sex ratios of from 140

459. Lawrence H. Keeley, *War Before Civilization*, p. 38; Marilyn Keys Roper, "A Survey of the Evidence for Intrahuman Killing in the Pleistocene." *Current Anthropology* 10(1969): 427–459; Irenäus Eibl-Eibesfeldt, *The Biology of Peace and War: Men, Animals and Aggression*. London: Thames and Hudson, 1979, p. 127; Harvey Hornstein, *Cruelty and Kindness: A New Look at Aggression and Altruism*. Englewood Cliffs: Prentice-Hall, 1976, p. 64.

460. Chris Knight, *Blood Relations: Menstruation and the Origins of Culture*. New Haven: Yale University Press, 1991, p. 262.

461. Joseph B. Birdsell, *An Introduction to the New Physical Anthropology*. New York: Rand McNally, 1965, p. 97; W. Ellis, *Polynesian Researches, Vol. 1*. Rutland: Charles E. Tuttle Co., 1969, p. 251.

462. Joseph B. Birdsell, "Some Predictions for the Pleistocene Based on Equilibrium Systems Among Recent Hunter-Gatherers." In Richard B. Lee and Irv DeVore, Eds., *Man the Hunter*. Chicago: Aldine, 1968, pp. 229–249.

463. Lloyd deMause, *Foundations of Psychohistory*, pp. 117–123.

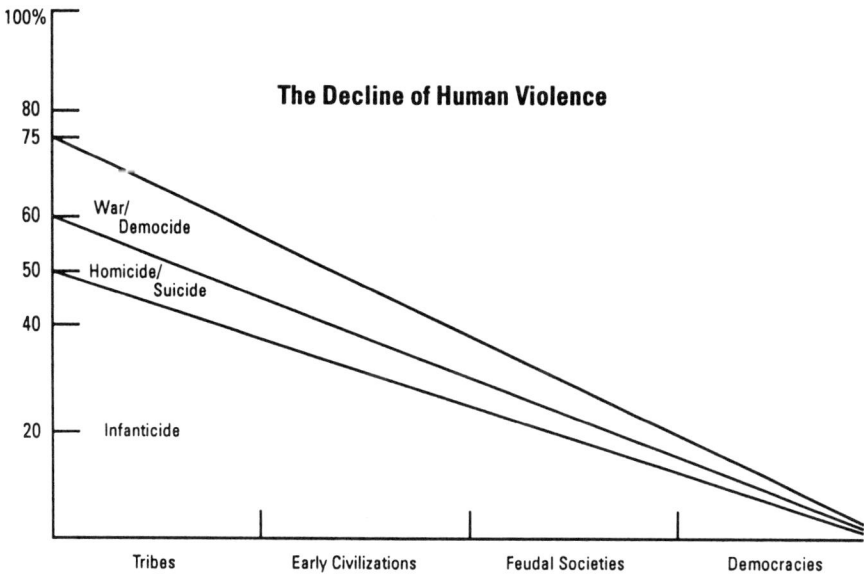

Fig. 6–7. The decline of human violence

to 100 (Yanomamö) to 159 to 100 (Polynesian),[464] meaning that virtually all families killed at least one child and most killed several, averaging perhaps half of all children born, especially if "late infanticide" (such as letting an infant starve to death) is counted. Since 50 percent infanticide rates seems to be the norm around which all these studies of simple tribes center, it is what is shown at the left of the chart.

The third outlet for human violence is homicide/suicide. Many simple tribes had homicide rates of up to 50 or 60 percent, causing one anthro-

---

464. Napoleon A. Chagnon and William Irons, *Evolutionary Biology and Human Social Behavior: An Anthropological Perspective*. North Scituate, Mass.: Duxbury Press, 1979, p. 140; Wulf Schiefenhövel, "Melanesian Ritualized Male Adult/Adolescent Sexual Behavior." In Jay R. Feierman, Ed., *Pedophilia: Biosocial Dimensions*. New York: Springer-Verlag, 1990, p. 417; William Tulio Divale and Marvin Harris, "Population, Warfare, and the Male Supremacist Complex." *American Anthropologist* 78(1976): 521–538; Laila Williamson, "Infanticide: An Anthropological Analysis," in Marvin Kohl, Ed., *Infanticide and the Value of Life*. Buffalo: Prometheus Books, 1978.

pologist to conclude about one group: "There was not a single grown man who had not been involved in a killing in some way or another."[465] Even so-called peaceful tribes like the famous !Kung of Africa actually have twenty to fifty times the current modern homicide rates.[466] Knauft's careful study found the Gebusi homicide rate to be sixty times the current U.S. rate,[467] with 60 percent of all males admitting to having committed one or more homicides;[468] while Steadman found the Hewa—who specialize in killing witches—had a homicide rate of one percent of the population per year, a thousand times the current U.S. rate.[469] Most tribal homicide rates run at least 10 percent of the adult population over a lifetime. Suicide in small societies is usually higher among the women, since they live lives of despair, often reaching 10 to 25 percent of adult women's deaths, staying high in antiquity but declining under Christianity.[470] Homicide rates in medieval times, when almost everyone carried a knife or sword and often used them, ran 50 times higher than today's rate of about a quarter of 1 percent,[471] while suicide rates today run about a half of 1 percent of adult population over a lifetime.[472] Thus homicide/suicide rates, like those of war and infanticide, have decreased steadily, to less than 1 percent in most democratic nations today. Added together, then, the rate of human vio-

465. Brude M. Knauft, *Good Company and Violence: Sorcery and Social Action in a Lowland New Guinea Society*. Berkeley: University of California Press, 1985, p. 379; Bruce M. Knauft, "Reconsidering Violence in Simple Human Societies." *Current Anthropology* 28(1987): 458.

466. Robert Wright, *Nonzero: The Logic of Human Destiny*. New York: Pantheon Books, 2000, p. 55.

467. Bruce M. Knauft, *Good Company and Violence*, p. 55.

468. John Craig, "Kindness and Killing." *Emory Magazine*, October 1988, p. 26.

469. Lyle B. Steadman, "The Killing of Witches." *Oceania* 62(1991): 110.

470. Michel Tousignant, "Suicide in Small-Scale Societies." *Transcultural Psychiatry* 35(1998): 291–306; Dan Jorgenson, "The Clear and the Hidden: Person, Self and Suicide Among the Telefomen of Papua New Guinea." *Omega* 14(1983): 113–125; Georges Minois, *History of Suicide: Voluntary Death in the Western World*. Baltimore: Johns Hopkins University Press, 1999.

471. T. R. Gurr, "Historical Trends in Violent Crime: A Critical Review of the Evidence." *Crime and Justice: An Annual Review of Research* 3(1981): 313.

472. Fox Butterfield, "A History of Homicide Surprises the Experts." *The New York Times*, October 23, 1994, p. 16; James Buchanan Given, *Society and Homicide in Thirteenth-Century England*. Stanford: Stanford University Press, 1977; Richard Rhodes, *Why They Kill: The Discoveries of a Maverick Criminologist*. New York: Alfred A. Knopf, 1999, p. 216; David Lester, *Patterns of Suicide and Homicide in the World*. New York: Nova Science Publishers, 1996.

lence has dropped from around a 75 percent chance of being murdered by your fellow human beings to around 2 percent for advanced democratic nations today, as a result of the slow and steady improvement in child rearing over the centuries.

WHAT WILL WARS BE LIKE DURING THE NEXT CENTURY?

Even just 2 percent of six billion people is 120 million people. Should we still expect violence to kill this many people each generation during the next century? What's more, only a part of the world today is democratic. Most of the world is still leaping into modernity, just becoming more free, democratic, and prosperous, but with their child rearing not yet modern—thus going through the same severe growth panic process that Germany went through in the middle of the twentieth century. We can therefore expect higher rates of deaths by war and democide in the coming decades in the developing countries. Yugoslavia, as an example, became democratic only recently, and only then began expressing its panic over democratization through mass murdering and raping its neighbors—much like the Nazis did—since its child rearing was still medieval.[473] With the earth's population nearly doubling in the next 50 years, virtually all of the increase being in the poorest regions with the worst child rearing, the coming leap to modernity in developing nations could be extraordinarily explosive.[474] Especially with nuclear and biological weapons proliferating, might we expect major wars in the next century to again kill many hundreds of millions of people, despite slowly improving child rearing?

Mature democracies today have sufficient proportions of good parents to be satisfied with working off their growth panics by small wars and recessions rather than world wars and depressions.[475] Since the end of World War II, wars have been far smaller in fatalities—at least for the democracies, if not for their opponents. Military spending in democratic nations has dropped from around 75 percent of government spending in

---

473. Alenka Puhar, "Childhood Nightmares and Dreams of Revenge." *The Journal of Psychohistory* 22(1994): 131–170.

474. Robert D. Kaplan, *The Coming Anarchy: Shattering the Dreams of the Post Cold War.* New York: Random House, 2000, p.22.

475. See Chapter 6; also see Glenn Davis, *Childhood and History in America.* New York: Psychohistory Press, 1976.

the late eighteenth century to around 10 percent today.[476] These smaller wars have been more frequent and have alternated more frequently with small recessions, so the classic 50-year manic/depressive cycle of the previous centuries that we graphed earlier has been drastically shortened, and recessions and small wars seem to substitute for each other as sacrificial rituals rather than alternating as in past centuries.

But all this has happened mainly in developed, democratic nations with better child rearing, so the answer to the question about war in the next century has to be ambivalent. I am confident that I can wholly trust my children and their wonderful friends on the West Side of Manhattan—who have loving, helping-mode parents who come from every ethnic and economic strata—to make a nonviolent world in the next century. But the average Chinese or African or Russian child has still so often been brought up in an atmosphere of infanticide, battering, sexual molestation, and severe domination that they can be predicted to need to repeat their parental holocausts on the historical stage in the future as they experience their new freedoms, repeating the democides of the twentieth century but with even greater destructive weapons. For that matter, the average American today was hit and in many ways abused as a child,[477] and as a result American military expenditures never went down after the end of the Cold War and "Fortress America" continues to prepare for a World War III.[478] Just allowing the usual slow historical evolution of child rearing may not be enough to outweigh the escalating destructiveness of our weapons as more and more nations become able to trigger global nuclear annihilation. *Therefore, the more advanced psychoclasses will have to actually intervene in the world's families to help change parenting and thus childhood for nearly everyone on earth.* Unless this can be done during the twenty-first century, it seems likely that the proliferating power of our weaponry could outrun the evolution of our child rearing and make the coming decades even more devastating in numbers than the twentieth century has been.

---

476. Stephen K. Sanderson, *Social Transformations: A General Theory of Historical Development: Expanded Edition.* Lanham: Rowman & Littlefield Publishers, 1999, p. 292.

477. Murray A. Strauss, *Beating the Devil Out of Them: Corporal Punishment in American Families.* New York: Lexington Books, 1994; Lloyd deMause, "The Universality of Incest." *The Journal of Psychohistory* 19(1991): 123–164.

478. William Greider, *Fortress America: The American Military and the Consequences of Peace.* New York: Public Affairs, 1999.

A new way to change parenting, community parenting centers, has in fact begun to be developed in a few American cities, and their surprising success provides hope that they can effectively decrease human violence around the world at affordable costs. Parenting centers not only have free classes and other help at the center for parents; they also have a staff that visits the homes of every child born in the community weekly during their first two years of life for free and helps the parents parent, teaching them what no school has ever thought it worthwhile to teach—that you need not be afraid of your children, that you need not hit them or use them for your needs, that you can love and trust them to grow up and turn out better than you did by not repeating on them the abuse you once endured. Exactly how these parenting centers work will be described in detail in Chapter 9. They promise to be able to eliminate child abuse and thereby drastically reduce human violence around the globe, with costs only a tiny fraction of the $8 trillion the world has spent on warfare since World War II.[479]

Removing the causes of violence only takes empathy, foresight, and will, not huge resources. We are today like a group of people standing on the banks of a river trying desperately to save people we see drowning, but refusing to go upstream and stop them from being thrown in. The reduction of human violence involves prevention first of all—the removal of the source of the pathology—just like the prevention of any other human clinical disorder. That enough of us can summon the empathy and understanding needed to actually go out and change what has long been called our violent human nature is our main hope for the future of our precious world.

---

479. Ruth Leger Sivard, *World Military and Social Expenditures.* Washington, DC: World Priorities, 1998.

III

Psychohistorical Evolution

> *"One may say anything about the history of the world—anything that might enter the most disordered imagination. The only thing one can't say is that it's rational. The very word sticks in one's throat."*
>
> —Fyodor Dostoyevsky

7

Childhood and Cultural Evolution

"The child feels the drive of the Life Force. . . .
You cannot feel it for him."
                              —George Bernard Shaw

Since nearly all of the cultural evolution of *Homo sapiens sapiens* has taken place during the past 100,000 years—only about 5,000 generations—and since this time span is too short to allow the human gene pool to mutate very much, *epigenetic* evolution of the psyche—the evolution of the architecture of the brain occurring during development in the womb and during early childhood—must be the central source of cultural change, rather than genetic evolution. After decades of sociobiologists' claims that "social structures and culture are but more elaborate vessels or survivor machines for ensuring that genes can maximize their fitness,"[1] there still is not a shred of evidence that any cultural change has been due to neo-Darwinian natural selection mechanisms. The short stature of Pygmies may have been selected by genetic evolution over millions of years as an adaptation to the environment of the tropics,[2] but even the most ardent sociobiologists have not claimed to show that belief in witches or divine leaders—found in every environment—have been selected for by any environmental condition.[3] One recent study of 100 major genetic human traits

---

1. Alexandra Maryanski and Jonathan H. Turner, *The Social Cage: Human Nature and the Evolution of Society.* Stanford: Stanford University Press, 1992, p. 2.

2. Part of the short stature of African Pygmies is genetic, part nutritional; see Barry Bogin, "The Tall and the Short of It." *Discover*, February 1998, p. 43.

3. Luigi Luca Cavalli-Sforza and Francesco Cavalli-Sforza, *The Great Human Diasporas: The History of Diversity and Evolution.* Reading, MA: Addison-Wesley Publishing Co., 1995, p. 97.

concluded that "no absolute differences between populations of primitive and civilized humans are known."[4] Unfortunately, this means that the causes of cultural evolution of our species remain a total mystery.

Since neo-Darwinian theory of differential genetic replication requires massive extinctions for the selection of random mutations, the lack of evidence of many mass extinctions during the past 100,000 years means differential reproductive rates have little value in explaining the relatively rapid evolution of the psyche and culture of *Homo sapiens sapiens*. In addition, the trillions of neuronal connections in the brain are simply far too numerous to be determined by the limited number of genes in the gamete. As Mayr puts it: "The brain of 100,000 years ago is the same brain that is now able to design computers. . . . All the achievements of the human intellect were reached with brains not specifically selected for these tasks by the neo-Darwinian process."[5] Since environmental selection of random genetic variations is not the central mechanism for evolution in modern human neuronal networks, the question is what *non-Darwinian* processes have been responsible for the enormous evolution of brain networks and cultures in modern humans?

THE FAILURE OF ENVIRONMENTAL DETERMINISM OF CULTURAL EVOLUTION

That so many social scientists remain environmental determinists is puzzling. It certainly is not because the method has any empirical verification—environment is simply assumed to be causal in culture change because historical progress in human nature is so often a priori assumed to be impossible. As Leslie White once put it, since it is assumed in advance that human nature cannot change, "We see no reason why cultural systems of 50,000 B.C. . . . could not have been capable of originating agriculture as well as systems in 8,000 B.C. . . . We must look, then, to environmental [factors] for the answers to these questions."[6] For instance, most social scientists believe that

---

4. James V. Neel, "Some Base Lines for Human Evolution and the Genetic Implications of Recent Cultural Development." In Donald J. Ortner, Ed., *How Humans Adapt: A Biocultural Odyssey*. Washington, DC: Smithsonian Institution Press, 1983, p. 82.

5. Ernst Mayr, *This Is Biology: The Science of the Living World*. Cambridge: Harvard University Press, 1997, p. 75.

6. Leslie White, *The Evolution of Culture: The Development of Civilization to the Fall of Rome*. New York: McGraw-Hill, 1959, pp. 283–286.

"the primary motor for cultural evolution is population growth" determined by environmental conditions,[7] overlooking the fact that population growth relies on the reduction of infanticide and the growth of the ability to devise new ways to produce more food—both psychological traits. In fact, empirical studies have rejected simple population growth as the mainspring of evolution, pointing out, for instance, that many advanced chiefdoms have in fact formed in areas of quite low population density.[8] As Hallpike put it, "There are many societies with sufficient population density but which have nevertheless not developed the state. . . . Population density is merely an index of the abundance of a vital raw material—people—and has by itself no power to determine how that raw material will be used."[9] Hayden summarized recent empirical studies testing environmental factors in evolution by saying "neither population pressure nor circumscription appears to have played a significant role in creating inequality or complexity."[10] Environments are opportunities, not just straightjackets.

The psychogenic theory sees environments as presenting both the constraints and the opportunities for cultural evolution, while the evolution of psychological development, of "human nature," determines how these challenges are met.

This of course does not mean that environment counts for nothing. Jared Diamond has convincingly shown how environmental differences have raised and lowered the steepness of the ladder of cultural evolution, demonstrating that the availability of a few good plant and animal domesticates crucially determines the rates of evolution of cultures in different parts of the world, with those areas that have domesticable grains and cattle being able to evolve faster than those that did not.[11] But the evolutionary problem isn't only about the availability of environmental resources. Ob-

7. Allen W. Johnson and Timothy Earle, *The Evolution of Human Societies: From Foraging Group to Agrarian State.* Stanford, CA: Stanford University Press, 1987, p. 15.

8. Timothy Earle, "The Evolution of Chiefdoms." In Timothy Earle, Ed., *Chiefdoms: Power, Economy, and Ideology.* Cambridge: Cambridge University Press, 1991, p. 4.

9. C. R. Hallpike, *The Principles of Social Evolution.* Oxford: Clarendon Press, 1988, pp. 237–238.

10. Brian Hayden, "Pathways to Power: Principles for Creating Socioeconomic Inequalities." In F. Douglas Price and Gary M. Feinman, Eds., *Foundations of Social Inequality.* New York: Plenum Press, 1995, p. 74; Hayden stresses the central role of "non-utilitarian 'ritual' and feasting activities [in] cultural evolution."

11. Jared Diamond, *Guns, Germs, and Steel: The Fates of Human Societies.* New York: W. W. Norton & Co., 1997.

viously one cannot develop much agriculture in the Arctic, and obviously tropical regions have too many parasites and too severe droughts that hinder development.[12] But environment is only part of the answer to evolutionary differences. Environmental change cannot explain cultural evolution since culture has often *evolved* while the ecology has *devolved* because of soil exhaustion and other factors. The central question of evolution is how effectively any environment is developed by evolving humans. The secret as to why England and not France, Germany, or Poland was the first modern society[13] and spawned the Industrial Revolution first goes back to England's advanced child rearing in its more nuclear medieval households, not to any ecological advantage.[14] English political freedom, religious tolerance, industry, and innovation were all psychoclass achievements, dependent on child-rearing evolution. The most important unsolved question in cultural evolution is therefore to explain the rate of innovation and adoption of new techniques of exploiting what resources exist—factors that depend crucially on the local rate of evolution of child rearing.

Despite their advocacy of unicausal environmental determinism, anthropologists have regularly demonstrated that similar environments have produced quite different psyches and cultures. Even though most follow Whiting's paradigm that environment determines childhood, personality, and culture,[15] others describe quite different personalities and cultures coming out of identical environments—one tribe that is gentle, loving, and peaceful and the other composed of fierce headhunting cannibals—but then leave the cause of their stark differences as unexplained as if the two groups were dropped down on earth from two different planets.[16] Others describe

---

12. David S. Landes, *The Wealth and Poverty of Nations: Why Some Are So Rich and Some So Poor.* New York: W. W. Norton & Co., 1998, pp. 6–14.

13. A. L. Beier, David Cannadine, and James M. Rosenheim, Eds., *The First Modern Society: Essays in English History in Honour of Lawrence Stone.* Cambridge: Cambridge University Press, 1990.

14. Ibid., pp. 213–230; Vivian C. Fox, "Poor Children's Rights in Early Modern England." *The Journal of Psychohistory* 23(1996): 286–306.

15. John W. M. Whiting and Irving L. Child, *Child Training and Personality.* New Haven: Yale University Press, 1953, p. 310; Eleanor Hallenberg Chasdi, Ed., *Culture and Human Development: The Selected Papers of John Whiting.* Cambridge: Cambridge University Press, 1994, p. 90; Robert A. LeVine, *Culture, Behavior, and Personality: An Introduction to the Comparative Study of Psychosocial Adaptation.* New York: Aldine Publishing Co., 1982, p. 57.

16. Margaret Mead, *Sex and Temperament in Three Primitive Societies.* New York: William Morrow, 1935.

quite similar cultures developing in wholly different environments. Lacking any evidence for their theories of environmental determinism, anthropologists admit that the sources of cultural evolution are simply inexplicable.

Archaeologists often speak of "new kinds of people" who emerge in prehistory and engage in competitive feasts that require more food production, leading to the evolution of agriculture.[17] They talk about "a new attitude toward change" that sometimes appears in history, "though the reason for it remains obscure."[18] Discovering what causes these new kinds of people and new attitudes toward change to mysteriously emerge throughout history is therefore the central task of the psychogenic theory of evolution.

DIFFERENCES BETWEEN HISTORICAL AND NEO-DARWINIAN EVOLUTION

Problems of explaining evolution are central to all sciences, including the social sciences. Just as nothing in biology makes complete sense except in the light of genetic evolution, nothing in human history makes complete sense except in the light of epigenetic (psychogenic) evolution. Neo-Darwinian theory of biological evolution explains all behavioral change in animals as resulting from the accretion of random variations produced by mutation, recombination, and genetic drift selected as better adaptations to changing environments. But what is usually overlooked is that genetic evolution only provides the capacity for adult behavioral variations *assuming a specific developmental environment*.[19] The road from genotype to phenotype is a long one. What trait actually appears in the mature individual depends on the actual course of epigenetic development, beginning in the womb and continuing throughout childhood—an extraordinarily complex and variable journey for each individual. The most important environments are the mother's body and behavior, and the most important competition for survival is not in the sperm or ovum

---

17. Ibid., p. 145.

18. Allen W. Johnson and Timothy Earle, *The Evolution of Human Societies: From Foraging Group to Agrarian State*. Stanford: Stanford University Press, 1987, p. 254.

19. Gilbert Gottlieb, *Individual Development and Evolution: The Genesis of Novel Behavior*. New York: Oxford University Press, 1992.

but at the neuronal level, in the brain, with the mother acting as the "agent of natural selection."[20]

What is little recognized is that recent revolutionary discoveries in molecular biology by Gottlieb, Lipton, and others have begun to show that early environments actually change genetic expression.[21] Gottlieb speaks of how a recent "virtual revolution has taken place in our knowledge of environmental influences on gene expression that has not yet seeped into the social sciences in general and the behavioral sciences in particular."[22] The genes do not activate themselves—a substantial body of evidence now shows that external environmental influences are normally occurring events in gene activation. Genes are now seen to "operate at the lowest level of organismic organization and they do not, in and of themselves, produce finished traits or features of the organism."[23] Even traits that can be shown to be inherited must be turned on in order to be effective.[24] They are less a blueprint and more "an organic *promise*, utterly reliant on environmental direction to select, control, and regulate gene expression. . . . From the earliest stages of development, the outside world reaches in to select and activate relevant genes, to shape and weave the tapestry of a unique nervous system."[25] Maternal prenatal environment and early parental care can

---

20. Gerald M. Edelman, *Bright Air, Brilliant Fire: On the Matter of the Mind*. New York: Basic Books, 1992; Allan N. Schore, *Affect Regulation and the Origin of the Self: The Neurobiology of Emotional Development*. Hillsdale, NJ: Lawrence Erlbaum Associates, 1994, p. 253.

21. Gilbert Gottlieb, *Individual Development & Evolution: The Genesis of Novel Behavior*. New York: Oxford University Press, 1992; Gilbert Gottlieb, *Synthesizing Nature-Nurture: Prenatal Roots of Instinctive Behavior*. Mahwah, NJ: Lawrence Erlbaum Associates, 1997; Bruce H. Lipton, "Adaptive Mutation: A New Look At Biology: The Impact of Maternal Emotions on Genetic Development." *Touch the Future*, Spring 1997, pp. 4–6; Richard C. Strohman, "Epigenesis and Complexity: The Coming Kuhnian Revolution in Biology." *Nature Biotechnology* 15(1997): 194–200; Eva Jablonka and Marion J. Lamb, *Epigenetic Inheritance and Evolution: The Lamarckian Dimension*. Oxford: Oxford University Press, 1995; Mae-Wan Ho and Peter T. Saunders, Eds., *Beyond Neo-Darwinism: An Introduction to the New Evolutionary Paradigm*. New York: Academic Press, 1984; Richard Milton, *The Facts of Life: Shattering the Myth of Darwinism*. London: Fourth Estate, 1992.

22. Gilbert Gottlieb, "Normally Occurring Environmental and Behavioral Influences on Gene Activity: From Central Dogma to Probabilistic Epigenesis." *Psychological Review* 105(1998): 792.

23. Ibid., p. 794.

24. Gilbert Gottlieb, *Individual Development and Evolution*. New York: Oxford University Press, 1987, p. 254.

25. Debra Niehoff, *The Biology of Violence: How Understanding the Brain, Behavior, and Environment Can Break the Vicious Circle of Aggression*. New York: The Free Press, 1999, p. 51.

actually be passed down to succeeding generations by changing genetic expression and the accessing of genes, quite contrary to traditional biological dogma. Since genes cannot independently turn themselves on or off, they need signals from their environment. Genetic structure is wide open to environmental changes, rather than being wholly immune from environmental input as has been thought to date. This isn't Lamarckianism; Lamarck didn't know anything about gene behavior. What has changed is the discovery that cells contain receptors that respond and adapt to environmental signals—the mother being the main controller of genetic accessing.[26] In addition, it has been discovered that only 3 percent of nuclear genes are used to code human expression, while the remaining 97 percent—previously thought of as useless baggage and referred to as "junk DNA"—contains extra DNA that can create new gene expression and new behavior.[27] Even maternal emotions can be passed to the next generation. Studies have shown how stressed children "change from being victims to being victimizers" because of imbalanced noradrenaline and serotonin levels, which, he believes, can then be passed down through both genetic and epigenetic changes.[28]

The laws of historical evolution are therefore quite different from the laws of neo-Darwinism. The central hypothesis of the psychogenic theory of historical evolution is that *epigenetic neuronal variations originating in changing interpersonal relationships with caregivers are the primary source of the evolution of the psyche and society.* "The more evolved the species is . . . the greater the role of epigenetic mechanisms in the structure of the nervous system."[29] The fundamental evolutionary direction in *Homo sapiens sapiens* is toward better interpersonal relationships, not just the satisfaction of instincts. While adaptation to the natural environment is the key to genetic evolution, relationship to the *human* environment is the key to psychological evolution, to the evolution of "human nature." Every generation—every new relationship between a parent and a child—provides an epigenetic chance to rewire the psyche, to improve child rearing, and

26. Richard B. Carter, *Nurturing Evolution: The Family As a Social Womb.* Lanham: University Press of America, 1993, p. xxxvii.

27. Bruce H. Lipton, "The Biology of Consciousness." Lecture presented at the University of British Columbia, May 7, 1995.

28. Ronald Kotulak, *Inside the Brain: Revolutionary Discoveries of How the Mind Works.* Kansas City: Andrews and McMeel, 1996, pp. 82–85.

29. Alain Prochiantz, *How the Brain Evolved.* New York: McGraw-Hill, 1992, p. 41.

thereby expand on the self, the core of consciousness.[30] Psychogenesis is also the key to cultural evolution, since the range of evolution of child rearing in every society puts inevitable limits upon what it can accomplish—politically, economically, and socially.

It isn't, of course, that "genes don't count." It's that history changes rapidly, whereas gene pools remain much the same. During the past 100,000 years, developmental changes in the three-pound, trillion-celled human brain have completely overwhelmed purely genetic changes as causes of psychological and cultural evolution. The causal mechanisms for the evolution of human psyche and culture have more and more decoupled from the neo-Darwinian causal mechanisms that depend solely on breeding success.[31] The psychogenic theory of evolution is therefore based not on Spencer and Darwin's "survival of the fittest"—children of the most ruthless parents—but upon the "survival of the most innovative and cooperative"—children of the most loving parents. The processes of psychogenic evolution through the slow growth of love and cooperation are therefore the exact opposite of those of natural selection, based on conflict and competition. They include the following:

1. The *production of variations* through psychogenesis occurs through innovative mothers creating different early epigenetic environments by providing more love and more advanced fetal and early childhood developmental paths.
2. The *vehicles of transmission* include neuronal groups in the brains of individual parents and children, not solely genes in the sexual organs of parents.
3. The *selection of variations* is accomplished mainly through changes in a very narrow part of the human environment—the *family*, the main organizer of emotional symbols, rather than only through changes in ecology.
4. The *preservation of emergent variations* in some individuals is often prevented from being swamped by the less developed child-rearing practices of the rest of the culture via the *psychogenic pump* effects of migration.

---

30. Antonio R. Damasio, *The Felling of What Happens: Body and Emotion in the Making of Consciousness*. New York: Harcourt Brace & Co., 1999, p. 7.

31. Henry Plotkin, *Evolution in Mind: An Introduction to Evolutionary Psychology*. Cambridge: Harvard University Press, 1998, p. 231.

5. The *limitations to emergent variations* occur because of conditions adverse to child rearing, such as wars, plagues, and droughts.
6. The *main locus of epigenetic variations* is the slow evolution of the integrated conscious self that looks forward to its future and creates its own extended present.
7. The *rate of innovation in cultural evolution* is determined by the conditions for parental love and therefore increase in individual self-assertion in each society, so that all cultural evolutions are preceded by child-rearing evolutions.
8. The *rate of psychogenic evolution* has historically been affected more by maternal than paternal influence, rather than males and females each contributing half of the genetic information as in neo-Darwinian evolution.

This last point will become fully evident in the next chapter, where it will be documented that the task of fathering—of playing a real role in forming a child's psyche—is in fact a very late historical invention. Most fathers among our closest ape relatives don't have much to do with their children,[32] and a nurturing role during early childhood for the human father turns out to be a far more recent historical innovation than has heretofore been assumed. The major advances in the structures of the brain, therefore, have mainly been evolved by females, not males, so to discover the laws of cultural evolution one must "follow the mothers" through history. This is why only the psychogenic theory posits that for most of history women are the primary source of all historical change.

THE "HOPEFUL DAUGHTER" AND
THE PSYCHOGENIC CUL-DE-SAC

Since for most of history mothers raise boys who then go off and hunt, farm, build things, and fight wars rather than directly contributing much new to the psyche of the next generation, the course of evolution of the

---

32. Jane Beckman Lancaster, *Primate Behavior and the Emergence of Human Culture.* New York: Holt, Rinehart and Winston, 1975, p. 23. For a limited role of macaque males in child care, see David Taub, "Female Choice and Mating Strategies Among Wild Barbary Macaques (*Macaca sylvanus* L.)." In D. Lundburg, Ed., *The Macaques: Studies in Ecology, Behavior and Evolution.* New York: Van Nostrand-Reinhold, 1980, p. 335.

psyche has overwhelmingly been dependent on the way mothers have treated their daughters, who become the next generation of mothers. Since early emotional relationships organize the entire range of human behavior, all cultural traits do not equally affect the evolution of the psyche—those that affect the daughter's psyche represent the main narrow bottleneck through which all other cultural traits must pass.

The evolution of the psyche and culture has been crucially dependent on turning the weak bonds between mother and daughter of apes and early humans[33] into genuine love. This means that historical societies that create optimal conditions for improving the crucial mother–daughter relationship by surrounding the mother with support and love soon begin to show psychological innovation and cultural advances in the next generations. In contrast, societies that cripple the mother–daughter emotional relationship experience psychogenic arrest and even psychogenic devolution.

Paralleling the term *hopeful monster* that biologists use to indicate speciating biological variations,[34] the idea that the mother–daughter emotional relationship is the focal point of epigenetic evolution and the main source of novelty in the psyche can be called the "hopeful daughter" principle. When innovative mothers love and support their daughters, a series of generations can develop new child-rearing practices that grow completely new neuronal networks and behavioral traits. If daughters are instead emotionally crippled by a society, a psychogenic cul-de-sac is created, so that generations of mothers cannot innovate and cultural evolution stagnates.[35]

For instance, in China before the tenth century A.D. men began to bind little girls' feet as a sexual perversion, making them into sexual fetishes, penis substitutes that the men would suck on and masturbate against during sex play.[36] Chinese literature reports the screaming cries of the 5-year-

---

33. Alexandra Maryanski, "African Ape Social Networks." In James Steele and Stephen Shennan, Eds., *The Archaeology of Human Ancestry: Power, Sex and Tradition.* London: Routledge, 1996, pp. 77–79.

34. Richard Goldschmidt, "Some Aspects of Evolution." *Science* 78(1933): 539–547.

35. Lloyd deMause, "The Role of Adaptation and Selection in Psychohistorical Evolution." *The Journal of Psychohistory* 16(1989): 355–372.

36. Howard S. Levy, *Chinese Footbinding: The History of a Curious Erotic Custom.* London: Neville Spearman, 1978; Jicai Feng, *The Three-Inch Golden Lotus.* Honolulu: University of Hawaii Press, 1994, p. 52; Lloyd deMause, "The Universality of Incest." *The Journal of Psychohistory* 19(1991): 151.

old girl as she hobbles about the house for years to do her tasks while her feet are bound, because in order to make her foot tiny, her foot bones are broken and the flesh deteriorates. She loses several toes as they are bent under her foot, to emphasize the big toe as a kind of female penis. This practice was added to the many brutal practices of what was perhaps the world's most anti-daughter culture, where over half the little girls were killed at birth without remorse and special girl-drowning pools were legion, where beating little girls until bloody was a common parental practice, and where girl rape and sex slavery were rampant.[37] This vicious anti-daughter emotional atmosphere—extreme even for a time that was generally cruel and unfeeling toward females—was obviously not conducive to little girls producing innovations in child rearing when they grew up to be mothers. Therefore China, which was culturally ahead of the West in many ways at the time of the introduction of foot binding, became culturally and politically "frozen" until the twentieth century, when foot binding was stopped. The result was that whereas for much of its history China punished novelty,[38] during the twentieth century rapid cultural, political, and economic evolution could resume. Japan, which shared much of Chinese culture but did not adopt foot binding of daughters, avoided the psychogenic arrest of China and could therefore share in the industrial revolution as it occurred in the West. The same kind of psychogenic arrest can be seen in the damage caused by genital mutilation of girls among circum-Mediterranean peoples that began thousands of years ago and continues today. Since "hopeful daughters" do not thrive on the chopping off of their clitorises and labias, the present cultural and political problems of those groups who still mutilate their daughters' genitals are very much a result of this psychogenic cul-de-sac.[39]

---

37. Arthur P. Wolf and Chieh-shan Huang, *Marriage and Adoption in China, 1845–1945.* Stanford: Stanford University Press, 1980, p. 8; Margery Wolf and Roxane Witke, Eds., *Women in Chinese Society.* Stanford: Stanford University Press, 1975; Ching-li How, *Journey in Tears: Memory of a Girlhood in China.* New York: McGraw-Hill Book Co., 1978; Margery Wolf, *Women and the Family in Rural Taiwan.* Stanford: Stanford University Press, 1972, p. 69.

38. David S. Landes, *The Wealth and Poverty of Nations: Why Some Are So Rich and Some So Poor.* New York: W. W. Norton & Co., 1998, p. 342.

39. Lloyd deMause, "The Universality of Incest." *The Journal of Psychohistory* 19(1991): 160–163; Cathy Joseph, "Compassionate Accountability: An Embodied Consideration of Female Genital Mutilation." *The Journal of Psychohistory* 24(1996): 2–17.

The historical evolution of the psyche is a process that mainly involves removing developmental distortions, so that each psyche can develop optimally in its own way. The evolution of childhood mainly consists of parents slowly giving up killing, abandoning, mutilating, battering, terrorizing, sexually abusing, and using their children for their own emotional needs, and instead creating loving conditions for growth of the self. The evolution of the psyche, as the next chapter will document, is mainly accomplished by removing the terrible historical abuses of children and their resulting developmental distortions, allowing the psyche to produce historical novelty and achieve its inherent human growth path. "Human nature" is a historical achievement. Civilization is not, as everyone including Freud has assumed, a "taming of the instincts." Nor does "the evolution of mankind proceed from bad to worse," as Roheim thought,[40] with early societies being indulgent toward their children and modern societies more often abusive. The evidence is that just the reverse is true—that culture evolves through the increase of love and freedom for children, so that when they grow up they can expand their self-consciousness and invent more adaptive and more loving ways of living.

EMPATHY, TRUST, AND FREEDOM—NOT COMPLEXITY— THE MEASURES OF EVOLUTIONARY PROGRESS

The measure of the evolution of psyche and culture is actually quite different from that assumed by most social theories. Social evolution is usually defined simply as the degree of complexity—as measured by population or social hierarchy or technology[41]—with such elements as the increasing amounts of knowledge supposedly causing cultures to grow more complex.[42] But there is no evidence that modern brains contain more items of information than those of foragers of 100,000 years ago. What has evolved

40. Géza Róheim, "The Evolution of Culture." In Bruce Mazlish, Ed., *Psychoanalysis and History*. Englewood Cliffs, NJ: Prentice-Hall, 1963, p. 84.

41. C. R. Hallpike, *The Principles of Social Evolution*. Oxford: Clarendon Press, 1988, p. 277.

42. A. Terry Rambo, "The Study of Cultural Evolution." In A. Terry Rambo and Kathleen Gillogly, Eds., *Profiles in Cultural Evolution: Papers from a Conference in Honor of Elman R. Service*. Ann Arbor: Anthropological Papers, Museum of Anthropology, University of Michigan, no. 85, 1991, p. 43.

is the integrated self.[43] Contemporary foragers, for instance, know an enormous amount of ecological information; the forager who can name hundreds of species of plants and animals and their characteristics probably has as many neurons in his cortex as most Westerners. Similarly, their cultural system cannot be said to be less complex, since it usually contains some of the most complicated kinship, belief systems, and languages extant. What is less evolved is their childhoods and the personality systems dependent on this child rearing. Societies with poor child rearing produce historical personalities—psychoclasses—that have too much anxiety and conflict to maintain good object relations, so they tend to deny their real needs—for love, for freedom, for achievement—and their cultures therefore oppose change and have not evolved.

The psychogenic theory defines progress in evolution as increases in self-integration, freedom, empathy, love, trust, and a preponderance of conscious decisions, rather than as an increase in social complexity. This means that some cultures on low technological levels[44] could actually be further evolved in human terms than others that are more complex technologically and politically. Because the psychogenic theory makes the individual psyche both the source of variation and the unit of selection, it posits that childhood is the central focal point of social evolution. The amount of time and resources any society devotes to its children's needs is far more likely to be an accurate index of its level of civilization than any of the anthropological indices of complexity or energy utilization.

The central direction of evolutionary progress, therefore, is from personal neediness to personal independence, from family enmeshment to family caregiving, from social dependency and violence to social dependability and empathy. Each step in the evolutionary process represents major changes in brain structure—a different historical personality results, a new psychoclass. Although this progress is extraordinarily uneven, the general progressive direction is evident. The evolution of childhood has been from incest to love and from abuse to empathy, and progress in child rearing has regularly preceded social, political, and technological progress. The main thrust of the psychogenic theory of cultural evolution is simple: The

---

43. Richard M. Restak, "Possible Neurophysiological Correlates of Empathy." In Joseph Lichtenberg, Melvin Bornstein, and Donald Silver, Eds., *Empathy I*. Hillsdale, NJ: The Analytic Press, 1984, p. 70.

44. See Jean Briggs, *Never in Anger: Portrait of an Eskimo Family*. Cambridge: Harvard University Press, 1970.

evolution of culture is ultimately determined by the amount of love, understanding, and freedom experienced by its children, because only love produces the self-integration and individuation needed for cultural innovation. Every abandonment, every betrayal, every hateful act toward children returns tenfold a few decades later upon the historical stage, while every empathic act that helps a child become what he or she wants to become, every expression of love toward children, heals society and moves it in unexpected, wondrous new directions.

PSYCHOGENESIS—THE SOURCE OF EPIGENETIC VARIATION

Psychogenesis is the process of forming historically new brain networks that develop the self and produce psychic innovation. It is a "bootstrapping" evolutionary process[45] that occurs in the interpersonal relationships between generations. Babies begin with the need to form intensely personal relationships with their caregivers, and provide a fresh start every generation for human development—eager faces ready to respond to the challenges of growth in ways their parents never envisioned. The parents, in turn, respond with ambivalent needs to (a) use the baby as a poison container for their own projections, or (b) go beyond their own child rearing and give the child what it needs rather than just responding to whatever they project into it. The ability of successive generations of parents to work through their own childhood anxieties the second time around is a process very much like that of psychotherapy, which also involves a return to childhood anxieties and, if successful, a reworking of them with support of the therapist into new ways of looking at others and at oneself. It is in this sense of the psychogenic process that history can be said to be a psychotherapy of generations, producing new developmental variation and then cultural evolution.

Psychogenesis is not a very robust process in caregivers. Most of the time, parents simply reinflict upon their children what had been done to them in their own childhood. It has taken literally millennia, for instance, for mothers to learn they need not be afraid of their own newborn infants. The production of developmental variations can occur only in the quiet, mostly unrecorded decisions by parents to go beyond the traumas they them-

---

45. Gerald M. Edelman, *Bright Air, Brilliant Fire: On the Matter of the Mind.* New York: Basic Books, 1992.

selves endured. It happens each time a mother decides not to use her child as an erotic object, not to tie it up so long in swaddling bands, not to hit it when it cries. It happens each time parents encourage their child's explorations and independence, each time they overcome their own despair and neediness and give their child a bit more love and empathy. These private moments are rarely recorded for historians, and social scientists have completely overlooked their role in the production of cultural variation, yet they are nonetheless the ultimate sources of the evolution of the psyche and culture. Every time a caregiver and a child can allow growth without anxiety, society can later grow without destructive consequences. Indeed, the ultimate source of all advances in human civilization—political, social, economic, individual—can be found in the day-to-day innovations in child rearing invented by each caregiver and child in their developing relationship.

The generational pressure for epigenetic, developmental evolution does not occur in a vacuum, of course. Many conditions impinge on the parent–child relationship, and these all affect psychogenesis. The crucial study of precisely what conditions are responsible for the evolution, arrest, or devolution of child rearing has barely begun. One cannot simply conclude that the more complex or more technologically or economically advanced societies become, the better the conditions for parenting. Particularly crucial are the conditions favoring the survival of nascent variations in parent–child relationship across generations without being swamped, paralleling the problem in neo-Darwinian theory of the swamping of mutations by a large gene pool. Indeed, the crucial problem in human evolution is not the learning of new child-rearing patterns—it is the forgetting of old ones, those deeply embedded in the psyche of parents.

The effects of other conditions upon child rearing are not all that obvious, which is why so few historians have studied the subject. Material conditions are not the most important of these; more crucial is the attitude of the society toward women and help in the overcoming of maternal despair. Particularly harmful are such abandonment practices as child sale in antiquity, child oblation in early medieval times, child prostitution until modern times, the routine breaking up of slave families in the American South, and all the other rarely considered horrors of childhood.

Because child-rearing evolution determines the evolution of the psyche and society, the causal arrows of all other social theories are reversed by the psychogenic theory. Rather than personal and family life being seen as dragged along in the wake of social, cultural, technological, and economic change, society is instead viewed as the outcome of evolutionary changes that first occur in the psyche. Because the structure of the psyche changes from generation to generation within the narrow funnel of childhood, child-rearing practices are not just one item in a list of cultural traits—they are the very condition for the transmission and further development of all other cultural elements, placing limits on what can be achieved in all other social areas.

THE EVOLUTION OF PARENTING

Most parents through most of history relate to their children most of the time as though the children were poison containers, receptacles into which they project disowned parts of their psyches. In good parenting, the child uses the caregiver as a poison container—as he or she earlier used the mother's placenta to cleanse its poisonous blood—the good mother reacting with calming behavior to the cries of her baby, helping the baby "detoxify" his or her anxieties. But the child historically has usually either been experienced as a persecutory parent—"When he screams he sounds just like my mother"—or as a guilty self—"He keeps wanting things all the time." Either way, the child must either be strictly controlled, hit, or rejected, usually in ways that restage the child-rearing methods of the grandparent. Since the grandmother has historically so often been present in the home, strictly controlling the child rearing, it is doubly difficult to break old patterns.

Psychogenesis isn't inevitable, so the psychogenic theory isn't teleological. As it is a very uneven process, there are in all modern nations many parents whose families have not historically evolved very much and who are therefore still extremely abusive. In fact, there are whole cultures that did not evolve much in parenting, for reasons that we will examine. But the generational pressure of psychogenesis—the ability of human parents to innovate better ways of child rearing and for children to strive for relationship and growth—is everywhere present, and is an independent source of change in historical personality, allowing humans to develop new neuronal networks that are more integrated than those of our ancestors.

Because psychogenesis is such a private process, it is rarely recorded in historical documents. Most of the documentation of what it feels like to go beyond one's own child rearing is found in such material as mothers' letters and diaries and doctors' reports beginning in the early modern period. Until then, it had been the habit of most mothers who could afford it to send their children to a wet nurse,[46] where they were left for several years. It was in England and America that middle-class mothers began to try nursing and relating to their children, being well aware that most children died at the wet nurse because of lack of care. These mothers wrote letters to each other about the surprising joys of doing the nursing themselves, how babies during breast-feeding "kisseth [the mother], strokes her haire, nose, and eares [causing] an affection" to grow between mother and infant.[47] If the husband objects, they report—saying his wife's breast belongs to *him*—he should be asked to hold the baby, and he'll be delighted by the baby, too. In France, by contrast, most newborn were sent out to wet nurses, termed "professional feeders and professional killers."[48] As early as the seventeenth century, a Frenchman observed: "They have an extraordinary regard in England for young children, always flattering, always caressing, always applauding what they do; at least it seems so to us French folks."[49] Since England led the rest of Europe in ending swaddling and wet nursing, it is no accident that soon after it also led the world in science, political democracy, and industrialization.

THE SIX CHILD-REARING MODES

In *The History of Childhood*,[50] I proposed six modes of child rearing that societies evolve. The chart's time line is for Western Europe, showing the first indications of each mode I found in my historical research. Child-rearing progress is not, however, inevitable, since many societies around the world remain stranded in earlier modes of child rearing, and since all six modes are found in today's most advanced societies. As the graph below indicates, most modern nations today contain all six stages in varying pro-

---

46. Valerie Fildes, *Breasts, Bottles and Babies*. Edinburgh: Edinburgh University Press, 1986.

47. Thomas Muffett, *Healths Improvement*. London: T. Newcomb, 1655, p. 119.

48. Maria Piers, *Infanticide*. New York: Norton, 1978, p. 52.

49. F. M. Mission, *Memoirs and Observations in His Travels Over England*. London: 1719, p. 33.

50. Lloyd deMause, Ed., *The History of Childhood*. New York: Psychohistory Press, 1974, pp. 51–53.

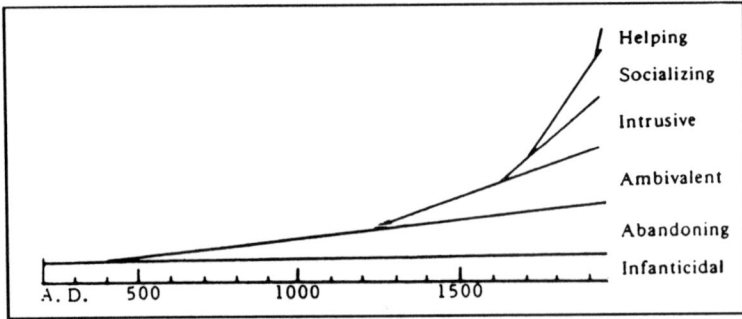

Fig. 7–1. The evolution of child-rearing modes in the West

portions. The child-rearing modes have been tested and generally confirmed by five book-length historical studies,[51] in addition to over 100 scholarly articles on the history of childhood during the past three decades in *The Journal of Psychohistory*.[52] The time periods in the chart represent the earliest evidence for the mode and are only true for a minority of the population during the period indicated.

1a. *Early infanticidal mode (bands to tribes):* This mode is characterized by very high infanticide rates, incest, body mutilation, child rape, tortures, and emotional abandonment by parents. The father is still too immature to act as a real caregiver and is emotionally absent in the early years. Prepubertal marriage of little girls is common. The dissociative personality structure of the infanticidal mode is permanently fragmented and dominated by alters, into which adults regularly switch and spend much of their

---

51. Ralph Frenken, *Studien zur Eltern-Kind-Beziehung anhand deutscher Autobiographien des 14.bis 17. Jahrhunderts: Ein Beitrag zur psychogenetischen Geschichte der Kindheit,* forthcoming; Ute Schuster-Keim and Alexander Keim, *Zur Geschichte der Kindheit bei Lloyd deMause*; Frankfurt am Main: Peter Lang, 1988; Friedhelm Nyssen, *Die Geschichte der Kindheit bei L. deMause.* Frankfurt am Main: Peter Lang, 1984; Friedhelm Nyssen and Ludwig Janus (Hg.), *Psychogenetische Geschichte der Kindheit: Beiträge zur Psychohistorie der Eltern-Kind-Beziehung.* Giessen: Psychosozial-Verlag, 1998; and Glenn Davis, *Childhood and History in America.* New York: Psychohistory Press, 1976.

52. See Lloyd deMause, "On Writing Childhood History." *The Journal of Psychohistory* 16(1988): 135–170; and Lloyd deMause, "25-Year Subject Index to *The Journal of Psychohistory.*" *The Journal of Psychohistory* 25(1998): 401–406.

time in ritual and magical projects, so they are not able to evolve beyond foraging and early horticultural levels.

1b. *Late infanticidal mode* (*chiefdom to early states*): Though Medea rules antiquity—infanticide rates remaining very high and child rape is still routine—the young child is not overtly rejected as much by the mother, and the father begins to be more involved with the instruction of the older child. Child sacrifice as a guilt-reducing device for social progress is found in early states, as the use of children as poison containers becomes more socially organized. Infant restriction devices such as swaddling and cradle boards spread and sibling caregivers replace child gangs. Various institutionalized schemes for care by others become popular, such as adoption, wet nursing, fosterage, and the use of the children of others as slaves and servants. Child battering is now less impulsive and used more as discipline, and because the child is somewhat closer emotionally and used more for farming chores, discipline becomes more controlling, leading to more complex societies whose innovations are offset by genocidal slaughter and the routine enslavement of women and children.

2. *Abandoning mode* (*beginning in the first century*): Once the child is thought of as having a soul of its own at birth, routine infanticide becomes emotionally difficult. Early Christians were considered odd in antiquity: "They marry like everybody else, they have children, but they do not practice the exposure of new-born babes."[53] These Christians began Europe's two-millennia-long struggle against infanticide, replacing it with abandonment—in the oblation of young children to monasteries, in a more widespread use of wet nurses if one could afford them, in the practices of fosterage and sending children out to be servants and apprentices. Child sacrifice was replaced by joining in the group-fantasy of the sacrifice of Christ, who was sent by his father as a poison container to be killed for the sins of others. Routine pederasty of boys continued, including in monasteries, and the rape of girls continued to be widespread. The child was thought to be born full of evil—the parents' alter projections—and so was beaten early and severely. Abusive child care was not mainly due

---

53. *Epistle to Diognetus.* In Arnold Toynbee, *The Crucible of Christianity.* New York: World Publishing Co., p. 296.

to economics, since the rich as well as the poor during the middle ages had high infanticide, abandonment, sexual molestation, and physical abuse rates. The masochistic personality structure of Christianity expects maternal forgiveness in return for the demonstration of self-inflicted wounds and stresses clinging to authority figures as defense against emotional abandonment.

3. *Ambivalent mode (beginning in the twelfth century)*: The ability to sustain ambivalence—both love and hate—toward children is a big step forward beyond simple fear and abandonment. The twelfth century began reducing the oblation of children to monasteries, began child instruction manuals, began to consider child rape illegal, expanded schooling, expanded pediatrics, saw the first child-protection laws, and began to tolerate ambivalence—both love and hate—for the child, marking the first movement toward a child's independent rights. Although most mothers still emotionally rejected their infants—so that wet nursing and pap feeding were still widespread—the child was nevertheless experienced less as a sinful-at-birth poison container and more as soft wax that could be beaten into whatever shape the parent wished so that it could be forgiven for sinning. This improvement in child rearing produced a further reduction of dissociation in the later medieval borderline personality structure, which in turn allowed the discovery of the individual, the advances in technology, and the rise of cities, eventually including the beginning of the rise of the early modern state.

4. *Intrusive mode (beginning in the sixteenth century)*: The intrusive parent in the early modern period began to unswaddle the child and even the wealthy began to bring up the infant themselves rather than sending it elsewhere (or at least have the wet nurse come into the home), thus allowing closer emotional bonds with parents to form. The sixteenth century, particularly in England, represents a watershed in reduction of parental projections, when parents shifted from trying to stop children's growth to trying to control them and make them "obedient." The freedom of being allowed to crawl around rather than being swaddled and hung on a peg plus the individuation of separate child beds and separate child regimens meant parents approached closer to their children and could give them attention—as long as they controlled their minds, their insides, their anger, their lives. The child

raised by intrusive parents was nursed by his or her mother, not swaddled, not given regular enemas but toilet trained early, prayed with but not played with, hit but not battered, punished for masturbation but not raped, taught and made to obey promptly with threats and guilt as often as physical means of punishment. Intrusive overcontrol of children was particularly made necessary as outright abandonment ended, and mothers began to feel they were being "driven crazy" by their children's freedom. Empathy began with intrusive mode parents, producing a general improvement in the level of care and reduced child mortality, leading to fewer births and more investment in each child. As a result of better child rearing, arranged marriages declined, spousal battering was reduced, and real married love and companionship began, contributing to the child's ability to identify with loving parents and allowing them to be a model so they could begin to achieve more advanced personal growth. The resulting healing of dissociation and increase in individuation of the depressive personality of early modern times produced the religious, scientific, political, and economic revolutions of the period.

5. *Socializing mode (beginning in the eighteenth century)*: Something new entered the world when society could claim for the first time that "God planted this deep, this unquenchable love for her offspring in the mother's heart."[54] During this period the number of children most women gave birth to dropped from seven or eight to three or four, long before any medical discoveries were made in limiting reproduction, because parents now wanted to be able to give more care to each child. Their aim, of course, remained instilling their own goals in the child rather than producing individuation; as one mother put it, "Is there not a strange fullness of joy in watching the reproduction of your traits, physical, mental, and moral, in your child?"[55] The socializing mode use of psychological manipulation, along with spanking of little children,

54. Jan Lewis, "Mother's Love: The Construction of an Emotion in Nineteenth-Century America." In Peter N. Stearns and Jan Lewis, Eds., *An Emotional History of the United States*. New York: New York University Press, 1998, p. 52.

55. Jan Lewis, "Mother's Love: The Construction of an Emotion in Nineteenth-Century America." In Rima D. Apple and Janet Golden, Eds., *Mothers & Motherhood: Readings in American History*. Columbus, OH: Ohio State University Press, 1997, p. 58.

remains the most popular model of parenting in Western European nations and the Americas today, training children to assume their role in the parents' society.[56] The socialized child was allowed far more freedom and respect than any previous mode—even young women were beginning to be allowed to have their own education, careers, and sexual lives.[57] Mothers began to actually enjoy child care—mother's love went from being thought of as dangerous to being a duty[58]—and even fathers began to play with and teach their young children. The socializing mode built the modern industrialized world, and its new values of nationalism and democracy represent the social models of most people today as the end of childhood battering allows the socializing psychoclass to reduce its need to cling to an authoritarian leader.

6. *Helping mode (beginning mid–twentieth century)*: The helping mode involves acknowledging that the parents' main role is to help the child reach his or her own goals at each stage of life, rather than being socialized into adult goals. For the first time, parents consider raising children not a chore but a joy. Both mother and father are equally involved with the child from infancy, helping him or her become an autonomous, self-directed person. Children grow up bathed in unconditional love, are not hit, are trusted to develop their own life goals and are apologized to if yelled at under stress. The result is that children grow up expecting to be loved because they are trying to become the best individuals they can be, not because they are obedient. The helping mode involves a great deal of time and energy by parents and others during the child's early years, caregivers taking their cues from the child as he or she tries to achieve individuation. The result is that the helping psychoclass is far more empathic toward others in society than earlier generations. Though Benjamin Spock's child care book was actually of the late socializing mode, some of the "Spock

56. See Glenn Davis, *Childhood and History in America*. New York: Psychohistory Press, 1976 for a breakdown of the socializing mode into four submodes.

57. John C. Spurlock and Cynthia A. Magistro, *New and Improved: The Transformation of American Women's Emotional Culture*. New York: New York University Press, 1998.

58. Jan Lewis, "Mother's Love: The Construction of an Emotion in Nineteenth-Century America. " In Rima D. Apple and Janet Golden, Eds., *Mothers & Motherhood: Readings in American History*. Columbus: Ohio State University Press, 1998, p. 53.

generation" adolescents after the mid–twentieth century were products of helping mode parents and have felt empowered to explore their own unique social roles and go beyond nationalism, war, and economic inequality.

Parents from each of the six child-rearing modes coexist in modern nations today. Political parties divide by psychoclasses (adults with similar child-rearing modes) more than by economic classes. Indeed, much of political conflict occurs because of the vastly different value systems and tolerance for freedom of the six psychoclasses. Cyclical swings between liberal and reactionary periods are an outcome of a process whereby more evolved psychoclasses introduce more innovation into the world than less evolved psychoclasses can tolerate. The latter try then to turn the clock back and reinstate less anxious social conditions to reduce their growth anxiety, and when this fails, as the previous chapter has shown, the nation attempts to cleanse the world of its "sinfulness" through a war or depression.

THE PSYCHOGENIC PUMP

The psychogenic pump effect is a way evolving parents can avoid the swamping of variety in child rearing. Parents are continually having their child-rearing practices dictated to them by their kin and neighbors, so they are unable to innovate new ways of relating to their children. Those parents who migrate therefore have more of a chance to work out for themselves new child-rearing modes and encourage more innovative mothers and hopeful daughters. This is what I have termed the "psychogenic pump" effect, an important mechanism of psychospeciation.[59] It is similar to the finding by evolutionary biologists that migrating species that move to isolated geographical areas are far more likely to preserve new genetic variations because they are not swamped by the gene pool of the area from which they emigrated. Thus psychospeciation closely parallels genetic speciation in the way it preserves emergent variety in child rearing.

For instance, a mother who wants to try to leave her child unswaddled after only a few months rather than a full year finds that her own mother

---

59. Lloyd deMause, "The Formation of the American Personality through Psychospeciation." In deMause, *Foundations of Psychohistory*, pp. 105–131.

and every other mother around her are vigorously opposed to her innovation. If she moves to America, she can swaddle for a shorter time without getting into trouble. Sometimes this community opposition to new child-rearing modes can actually be lethal. I once asked Arthur Hippler, the editor of the *Journal of Psychological Anthropology*, if he had ever met a more evolved Athabascan mother than the generally infanticidal mothers he had been studying in Alaska. He said he had—she was far more empathic than the other mothers. He said the other mothers shunned her and shut her out of activities, which would in precontact times have been tantamount to death in such a severe environment. But, according to Hippler's ethnographic studies, most more evolved Athabascans actually migrated south, with the result that those who settled along the northeast coast of America had better child rearing and more advanced cultures than those that remained behind in Alaska.[60]

The same principle is present in societies where extended, stem, or joint families allow the grandmothers and other kin to continue to live with the new mothers and dominate them mercilessly. Puhar has provided much evidence that child rearing was severely arrested in a brutal, neglectful medieval mode in Yugoslavia by the *zadruga* joint family arrangement.[61] Those daughters who manage to move north out of the extended family and innovate in their own child-rearing practices inevitably evolved less neglectful modes.[62]

The effects of the psychogenic pump in preserving emerging variety can be seen in a variety of similar historical migration patterns of parents practicing more advanced child-rearing modes:

1. The migration of colonists into New England involved more advanced parents and more numerous hopeful daughters than those in families that stayed behind, since the most advanced child rearing—the intrusive mode—was being practiced by the Puritans who were chased out of England or who emigrated to escape "unrea-

60. Lloyd deMause, "The Role of Adaptation and Selection in Psychohistorical Evolution." *The Journal of Psychohistory* 16(1989): 365.

61. Alenka Puhar, "On Childhood Origins of Violence in Yugoslavia: II. The Zadruga." *The Journal of Psychohistory* 21(1993): 171–197.

62. See also Peter Petschauer, "Intrusive to Socializing Modes: Transitions in Eighteenth-Century Germany and Twentieth-Century Italy." *The Journal of Psychohistory* 14(1987): 257–270.

sonable authority."[63] The result was, as Condorcet put it, Americans seemed to have "stepped out of history," because they had less infanticide, less wet nursing, shorter swaddling, and better parent–child relations than European parents at the time, as can be seen when European visitors complained about the spoiling and indulgence that made American children "domestic tyrants."[64] The psychogenic pump, however, applied more to New England parents; those who migrated to the South usually did not do so as intact families and comprised far more bachelor latter-born sons, servants, indentured children, and others who were not members of intact, advanced families escaping from religious persecution.[65] Therefore, the South lagged behind the North in its average level of child rearing, a condition that eventually led to the American Civil War— a typical internal war involving psychoclass differences.

2. The migration of more advanced parents in Europe took place from east to west, as migrating farmer populations moved from Asia to Western Europe,[66] displaced foragers, and tried innovative living arrangements compared to those that stayed behind. This is the ultimate reason why Eastern Europe even today remains far behind Western Europe and the United States in child rearing and in democracy and industrialization.

3. More advanced mothers have generally tended to move more to the big cities, leaving the domination of their own mothers; thus, cities are almost always more politically liberal than rural areas.

4. Jews who had emigrated into Europe were more advanced in child rearing, as we have seen. Jews since antiquity didn't just "disperse" (*diaspora*); they differentially migrated, with those with more ad-

---

63. Lloyd deMause, "The Formation of the American Personality Through Psychospeciation." In Lloyd deMause, *Foundations of Psychohistory*. New York: Creative Roots, 1982, pp. 105–128; Gert Raeithel, "Philobatism and American Culture." *The Journal of Psychohistory* 6(1979): 447–460.

64. Charles Sherrill, *French Memories of Eighteenth-Century America*. New York: C. Scribner's Sons, 1915, p. 71.

65. Lloyd deMause, "The Role of Adaptation and Selection in Psychohistorical Evolution." *The Journal of Psychohistory* 16(1989): 365; LeRoy Ashby, *Endangered Children: Dependency, Neglect, and Abuse in American History*. New York: Twayne Publishers, 1997, p. 8.

66. L. L. Cavalli-Sforza, "The Transition to Agriculture and Some of Its Consequences." In Donald J. Ortner, Ed., *How Humans Adapt: A Biocultural Odyssey*. Washington, DC: Smithsonian Institution Press, 1983, p. 112.

vanced parenting modes striking out to new homes, where their success made them poison containers for the growth fears of others.

5. The psychogenic pump favors extremities, peripherally isolated areas that capture late arrivals—the most innovative parents and the most hopeful daughters. The most advanced child rearing in Asia was in Japan, like England a large island at the extreme end of the Eurasian land mass. Japan, in fact, developed agriculture very late, only 2,000 years ago,[67] when the psychogenically most advanced families in Asia migrated there from Korea. Those that stayed behind in China were swamped by less evolved child-rearing modes and were therefore more subject to psychogenic arrest and even devolution.

PSYCHOGENIC DEVOLUTION

One of the hardest things to understand in studying childhood history is how parenting can stay the same for millennia or sometimes even get worse. How can a Balkan peasant mother in the twentieth century, as in antiquity, kill her newborn without remorse or tightly bind her baby to a cradle and keep it isolated in a dark room for a year or more, oblivious to his or her screams?[68] How can so many fathers today still batter their little kids? Is empathy for children so fragile? Why does psychogenic evolution in many areas not take place, or even devolve? Why have a portion of parents in every society remained at the infanticidal and abandoning modes? What happened in previous generations that arrested or extinguished the evolution of parental love so thoroughly?

People throughout history defend against their despair and shame by finding poison containers to restage their early traumas and remove the cause of their inner agony. Men do so mainly by going to war and torturing, enslaving, and killing sacrificial victims. But women only have their

---

67. Luigi Luca and Francesco Cavalli-Sforza, *The Great Human Diasporas: The History of Diversity and Evolution*. Reading, MA: Addison-Wesley Publishing Co., 1995, p. 163.

68. Lotte Danzinger and Liselotte Frankl, "Zum Problem der Funktionsreifung." *Zeitschrift für Kinderforschung* 43(1934): 219–254; Alenka Puhar, "On Childhood Origins of Violence in Yugoslavia: II. The Zadruga." *The Journal of Psychohistory* 21(1993): 171–198; Ernestine Friedl, *Vasilika: A Village in Modern Greece*. New York: Holt, Rinehart and Winston, 1962.

children to torture, enslave, and kill. One thing is clear: the cause is not merely economic since the rich abandoned, tortured, and killed their children just as often as the poor did. Only rarely can this "war on children" resulting from too much change be documented in more specific detail.

One of these periods is when serfdom ended in Hungary in the 1840s, as women in rural areas responded to the prospect that at last they were to be free. But women cannot be free if they have many children, so "there was a panic reaction and a brutal, drastic reduction of family size was put speedily into practice, first by simple infanticide and crude abortion techniques and later by the one-child system."[69] Although poverty was not a problem in the area, for a full century "one-child families" were the cultural norm for the area, and most mothers increased the killing of their babies. As a result, "families shrank into nonexistence, leaving house and farm vacant" in order to adhere to a norm that "became irrational and, indeed, suicidal for entire families, villages, and ethnic groups."[70] In what has been called a period of "terrible matriarchy," killing mothers established a "dark belt of one-child-system villages"[71] by crude abortion techniques using sharp objects and winding ropes tightly around the mothers' body and soaking them in water, by strangling or freezing newborn babies, even by mothers-in-law "sleeping with the young couple to ensure they did not have intercourse."[72]

Growth panic from too-fast progress being turned against children is an everyday phenomenon, only no one recognizes it because children are rarely seen as poison containers for adult anxieties. Times of prosperity and progress are often times when poor children are used as poison containers and are punished for the prosperity of adults. For instance, while the average income of the wealthiest 1 percent of Americans rose 72 percent between 1977 and 1994, and while the average income of the highest-earning 20 percent rose 25 percent, that of the poorest 25 percent shrank 16 percent, throwing millions more children under the poverty line while both the federal government and states were busy throwing children off of welfare.[73]

69. Ildiko Vasary, "'The Sin of Transdanubia': The One-Child System in Rural Hungary." *Continuity and Change* 4(1989): 447.

70. Ibid., p. 448.

71. Ibid., p. 435.

72. Ibid., p. 452.

73. *The Washington Post National Weekly Edition*, April 13, 1998, p. 18; Greg J. Duncan and Jeanne Brooks-Gunn, Eds., *Consequences of Growing Up Poor*. New York: Russell Sage Foundation, 1998.

Yet the central evolutionary question remains: Why are some societies so far behind in child rearing? To begin to answer this crucial question, we will first analyze what childhood is really like in simpler societies.

THE IDEALIZATION OF CHILDHOOD IN SIMPLE SOCIETIES

Unfortunately for the psychogenic theory, nearly all social scientists currently agree that there is an inverse relationship between child rearing and social evolution, with parents becoming less loving and more abusive as cultures move from simple to complex societies.[74] Agreeing with Rousseau and Freud, most anthropologists today see civilization as being achieved at the expense of childhood freedom and nurturance, with the quality of child care going straight downhill and becoming more punitive and less nurturing as societies become more complex. Rohner, for instance, concludes from his cross-cultural review of parenting from the Human Relations Area Files that virtually all mothers in simpler societies are "warm and nurturant toward their children,"[75] so that "the more complex a sociocultural system is, the less warm parents in general tend to be."[76] Whiting summarizes the results anthropological studies of childhood as follows: "Children in simple cultures are high on nurturance and low on egoism, whereas children brought up in complex cultures are egoistic and not very nurturant."[77] Stephens summarizes the current state of anthropological opinion: "When one reads an ethnographic account of child rearing in a primitive society, one will usually find some statement to the effect that the people 'love their babies' . . . the ethnographer seems amazed at the amount of affection, care, attention, indulgence, and general 'fuss' lavished upon infants and young children."[78]

---

74. Marc Howard Ross, "Socioeconomic Complexity, Socialization, and Political Differentiation: A Cross-Cultural Study." *Ethos* 9(1981): 217–245.

75. Ronald P. Rohner, *They Love Me, They Love Me Not: A Worldwide Study of the Effects of Parental Acceptance and Rejection*. New Haven, CT: HRAF Press, 1975, p. 157.

76. Ronald P. Rohner, *The Warmth Dimension: Foundations of Parental Acceptance-Rejection Theory*. Beverly Hills: Sage Publications, 1986, p. 64.

77. Eleanor Hollenberg Chasdi, Ed., *Culture and Human Development: The Selected Papers of John Whiting*. Cambridge: Cambridge University Press, 1994, p. 100.

78. William N. Stephens, *The Family in Cross-Cultural Perspective*. New York: Holt, Rinehart and Winston, 1963, p. 357.

When I first discovered in the anthropology course I took with Margaret Mead at Columbia University over four decades ago that anthropologists were unanimous in thinking that child rearing had evolved from nurturant and loving to neglectful and abusive as the level of civilization increased, I was puzzled as to how anyone could at the same time think that childhood had any effect on adult personality, since this meant that the extremely violent cannibals, headhunters, and warriors I was studying had supposedly had loving, nurturant childhoods. I soon began to wonder about the accuracy of all these cross-cultural studies of child rearing, and began researching whether those who classified techniques of parenting[79] could have been actually coding the degrees of distortion and denial of the ethnographers rather than what was really happening to children.

When I found the same unanimity regarding loving child rearing in past times among historians—equally unsupported by historical evidence— I set out on my decades-long task of combing primary sources to find out the truth about what it must have felt like to have been a child, both in the past and in other cultures. With ethnological accounts, I was dependent on the reports of the ethnographer, since I could not myself observe at first hand the child-rearing practices of hundreds of cultures. So rather than relying on selective Human Relations Area File cards, I constructed my own more extensive files over the next four decades from reports of all ethnographers who had said anything about child rearing—being careful to separate their glowing adjectives from their descriptions of events they actually saw happen.

When I began publishing the results of my research into both historical and cross-cultural childhoods, documenting how childhood both in the past and in other cultures had been massively idealized, both historians and anthropologists concluded that I surely must have been mad. As Melvin Konner put it in his book *Childhood*:

> Lloyd deMause, then editor of the *History of Childhood Quarterly*, claimed that all past societies treated children brutally, and that all historical change in their treatment has been a fairly steady improvement toward the kind and gentle standards we now set and more or less meet. . . .
> Now anthropologists—and many historians as well—were slack-jawed and nearly speechless. Studies of parents, children, and the fam-

---

79. Herbert L. Barry, III, E. Lauer and C. Marshall, "Agents and Techniques of Child Training: Cross-Cultural Codes." *Ethnology* 16(1977): 191–230.

ily in cultures on every inhabited continent had turned up not a single case—with one or two possible exceptions—of extant patterns of child care that corresponded to the brutal neglectful approach these historians were assigning to all the parents of the past.

On the contrary, serious students of the anthropology of childhood beginning with Margaret Mead have called attention to the pervasive love and care lavished on children in many traditional cultures. They even found much Westerners could admire and possibly emulate.[80]

The only way to disprove this widespread opinion about parenting in traditional cultures is to examine what anthropologists have written and see whether their evidence actually shows something other than "pervasive love and care lavished on children." In order that the effects of culture contact with the West may be kept to a minimum, I will concentrate here on child rearing in New Guinea, with a few forays into nearby areas, because Western contact was in these areas both late and minimal as compared with Africa and other areas.

THE INFANTICIDAL MODE OF CHILD REARING IN NEW GUINEA

As in most simple cultures, New Guinea mothers can be considered infanticidal mode because they kill a third or more of their newborn, and most mothers have killed one or more of their children. Though the practice is common, it is usually downplayed by anthropologists. Margaret Mead, for instance, kept infanticide out of her published reports, but wrote in her letters home such observations as "we've had one corpse float by, a newborn infant; they are always throwing away infants here."[81] Some sense of its dimensions can be seen in the imbalance of males over females at birth, ratios that run from 120:100 to 160:100.[82] Since both male and female

---

80. Melvin Konner, *Childhood*. Boston: Little, Brown and Co., 1991, p. 193.

81. Margaret Mead, *Letters From the Field, 1925–1975*. New York: Harper and Row, p. 132.

82. William Tulio Divale and Marvin Harris, "Population, Warfare, and the Male Supremacist Complex." *American Anthropologist* 78(1976): 521–538; Laila Williamson, "Infanticide: An Anthropological Analysis." In Marvin Kohl, Ed., *Infanticide and the Value of Life*. Buffalo: Prometheus Books, 1978; L. A. Malcolm, "Growth, Malnutrition and Mortality of the Infant and Toddler in the Asai Valley of the New Guinea Highlands." *American*

newborn are killed, this ratio only reflects the amount of excess female infanticide, so the combined rate of infanticide is even higher. These high rates are common to the culture area. As I mentioned earlier, the Australian Aborigines destroyed as many as 50 percent of all infants,[83] and the first missionaries in Polynesia estimated that two-thirds of the children were murdered by their parents.[84] Anthropologists commonly pass over these statistics quickly, since high infanticide rates do not reflect well upon their "pervasive love" claim. For instance, Herdt says that, since "Sambia love children, it is hard to imagine that infanticide was done except in desperate circumstances."[85] He then says that "throughout New Guinea, males outnumber females at birth, often in high ratios." It is of course biologically impossible that so many more males were naturally born than female.

Although anthropologists commonly excuse infanticide as required by necessity—and of course never count it as part of the homicide rate—their informants report otherwise. When asked why they kill their infants, they routinely state that they killed them because "children are too much trouble,"[86] because "the mothers were angry at their husbands,"[87] because they are "demon children,"[88] because the baby "might turn out to be a sorcerer,"[89] "because her husband would go to another woman" for sex if

Journal of Clinical Nutrition 23(1970): 1090–1095; Wulf Schiefenhövel, "Preferential Female Infanticide and Other Mechanisms Regulating Population Size Among the Eipo." In N. Keyfitz, Ed., *Population and Biology.* Liege: Ordina, 1984, p. 171.

83. Joseph B. Birdsell, *An Introduction to the New Physical Anthropology.* New York: Rand McNally, 1965, p. 97.

84. W. Ellis, *Polynesian Researches, Vol 1.* Rutland, VT: Charles E. Tuttle Co., 1969, p. 251.

85. Gilbert Herdt, *The Sambia: Ritual and Gender in New Guinea.* New York: Holt, Rinehart and Winston, 1987, p. 85.

86. Maria Lepowsky, *Fruit of the Motherland: Gender in an Egalitarian Society.* New York: Columbia University Press, 1993, p. 84.

87. Marilyn Strathern, *Women in Between: Female Roles in a Male World: Mount Hagen, New Guinea.* London: Seminar Press, 1972, p. 44; Aloys Kasprus, *The Tribes of the Middle Ramu and the Upper Keran Rivers (North-East New Guinea): Studia Instituti Anthropos, Vol. 17.* St. Augustin bei Bonn: Verlag des Anthropos-Instituts, 1973, 52.

88. Shirley Lindenbaum, "Variations on a Sociosexual Theme in Melanesia." In Gilbert H. Herdt, Ed., *Ritualized Homosexuality in Melanesia.* Berkeley: University of California Press, 1984, p. 352.

89. Bruce M. Knauft, *Good Company and Violence: Sorcery and Social Action in a Lowland New Guinea Society.* Berkeley: University of California Press, 1985, pp. 118, 407.

she had to nurse the infant,[90] because they didn't want babies to tie them down in their sexual liaisons,[91] because it was a female and must be killed, because "they leave you in a little while,"[92] or because "they don't stay to look after us in our old age."[93] Necessity is almost never cited as a reason for killing a child. Indeed, infanticide by mothers in simpler societies can be thought of as a part of what more evolved mothers experience as postpartum depression. Children commonly watch their mothers kill their siblings and are sometimes forced to take part in the murder. In many tribes, the newborn is "tossed to the sows, who promptly devour it. The woman then takes one of the farrows belonging to the sow who first attacked her baby's corpse and nurses it at her breast."[94] The children often witness the infanticidal act: "The mother . . . buries it alive in a shallow hole [so] that the baby's movements may be seen in the hole as it is suffocating and panting for breath; schoolchildren saw the movements of such a dying baby and wanted to take it out to save it. However, the mother stamped it deep in the ground and kept her foot on it."[95]

In some parts of New Guinea and Australia, mothers are both child murderers and cannibals, who commonly kill both their own and others' children and eat them, as well as feed them to their siblings.[96] The most complete description of the practice comes from Róheim:

> It had been the custom for every second child to be eaten by the preceding child. . . . When the Yumu, Pindupi, Ngali, or Nambutji were hungry, they ate small children with neither ceremonial nor animistic motives. Among the southern tribes, the Matuntara, Mularatara, or

90. Aloys Kasprus, *The Tribes of the Middle Ramu* . . . St. Augustin bei Bonn: Verlag des Anthropos-Instituts, 1973, p. 61.

91. Arthur E. Hippler, "Culture and Personality Perspective of the Yolngu of Northeastern Arnhem Land: Part I—Early Socialization." *Journal of Psychological Anthropology* 1(1978): 230.

92. Gillian Gillison, *Between Culture and Fantasy: A New Guinea Highlands Mythology.* Chicago: University of Chicago Press, 1993, p. 234.

93. L. L. Langness, "Sexual Antagonism in the New Guinea Highlands." *Oceania* 37(1967): 166.

94. Wolfgang Lederer, *The Fear of Women.* New York: Grune & Stratton, 1968, p. 65.

95. Aloys Kasprus, *The Tribes of the Middle Ramu,* p. 58.

96. J. Van Baal, *Dema: Description and Analysis of Marind-Anim Culture (South New Guinea).* The Hague: Martinus Nieshoff, 1966, p. 746; Géza Róheim, "The Western Tribes of Central Australia: Childhood." In Warner Muensterberger and Sidney Axelrad, Eds., *The Psychoanalytic Study of Society: Vol. II.* New York: International Universities Press, 1962, pp. 199–200.

Pitjentara, every second child was eaten in the belief that the strength of the first child would be doubled. . . . [My informants] had, each of them, eaten one of their brothers. . . . They eat the head first, then the arms, feet, and finally the body. Jankitji, Uluru, and Aldinga have all eaten their siblings. . . . Daisy Bates writes: "Baby cannibalism was rife among these central-western people. . . . In one group . . . every woman who had a baby had killed and eaten it, dividing it with her sisters, who in turn killed their children at birth and returned the gift of food, so that the group had not preserved a single living child for some years. When the frightful hunger for baby meat overcame the mother before or at the birth of the baby, it was killed and cooked regardless of sex."[97]

Róheim states with great conviction, though providing no evidence, that the children who were forced to eat their siblings "are the favored ones who started life with no oral trauma,"[98] that eating one's siblings "doesn't seem to have affected the personality development" of these children,[99] and that "these are good mothers who eat their own children."[100] When I suggested in *Foundations of Psychohistory* that it was doubtful that children remained unaffected by their joining in their mother's killing and eating of their siblings,[101] Robert Paul, editor of the journal *Ethos*, was adamant that I must not question the rosy conclusions of Róheim: "Remember that the anthropologist in question here is Róheim himself, who can hardly be accused of being psychoanalytically unsophisticated, or of denying or resisting. Indeed, deMause readily accepts his reportage about the facts. Why does he question his conclusion? Róheim was nobody's fool."[102]

Most ethnologists scrupulously avoid describing how these children feel about participating in the killing or eating of their siblings. Lindenbaum simply says of the Fore tribe that "cannibalism was largely limited to adult women [and] to children of both sexes,"[103] but doesn't mention that the

---

97. Géza Róheim, *Psychoanalysis and Anthropology: Culture, Personality and the Unconscious.* New York: International Universities Press, 1950, pp. 60–62.

98. Ibid., p. 150.

99. Ibid., p. 63.

100. Ibid., p. 60.

101. Lloyd deMause, *Foundations of Psychohistory.* New York: Creative Roots, 1982, p. 274.

102. Robert A. Paul, "Review of Lloyd deMause's Foundations of Psychohistory." *The Journal of Psychoanalytic Anthropology* 5(1982): 469.

103. Shirley Lindenbaum, *Kuru Sorcery: Disease and Danger in the New Guinea Highlands.* Palo Alto: Mayfield Publishing Co., 1979, p. 20.

mothers force the children to eat human flesh and doesn't say how they reacted to this. Only Poole actually reported the reaction of some New Guinea children to their seeing their parents eat their children:

> Having witnessed their parents' mortuary anthropophagy, many of these children suddenly avoided their parents, shrieked in their presence, or expressed unusual fear of them. After such experiences, several children recounted dreams or constructed fantasies about animal-man beings with the faces or other features of particular parents who were smeared with blood and organs.[104]

Individuals or groups who kill and eat babies are in fact severely schizoid personalities[105] who handle their own rage, engulfment fears, and devouring emotional demands upon them by either murdering children to wipe out the demands they project into them, or by eating them in order to act out their identification with devouring internal parental alters.

INCEST AND THE SEXUAL ABUSE OF CHILDREN IN NEW GUINEA

As with infanticide, the sexual abuse of children is widely reported by anthropologists, but in positive terms. Maternal incest is seen as indulging the infant's sexual needs, oral and anal rape of boys is described as both desirable and as desired by the boys, and rape of both girls and boys is presented as an unmotivated cultural artifact.

Anthropologists often maintain that "the incest taboo is the very foundation of culture"[106] and that "the taboo on incest within the immediate family is one of the few known cultural universals."[107] The culturally approved sexual use of children, therefore, must be renamed wherever it is found as some-

---

104. Fitz John Porter Poole, "Cannibals, Tricksters, and Witches: Anthropophagic Images Among Binim-Kuskusmin." In Paula Brown and Donald Tuzin, Eds., *The Ethnography of Cannibalism*. Washington, DC: Society for Psychological Anthropology, 1983, p. 13.

105. Harry Guntrip, *Schizoid Phenomena, Object-Relations and the Self*. Madison, CT: International Universities Press, 1968.

106. Claude Lévi-Strauss, *The Elementary Structures of Kinship*. Boston: Beacon Press, 1969, p. 41.

107. James L. Peacock and A. Thomas Kirsch, *The Human Direction: An Evolutionary Approach to Social and Cultural Anthropology*. New York: Appleton-Century-Crofts, 1970, p. 100.

thing other than incest. Ford and Beach's widely cited *Patterns of Sexual Behavior* makes this false distinction clear. Incest, they say, "excludes instances in which mothers or fathers are permitted to masturbate or in some other sexual manner to stimulate their very young children."[108] They then go on to call incest "rare." The authoritative *Growing Up: A Cross-Cultural Encyclopedia* covers eighty-seven cultures in which it says there is no incest—just adults playing with, stroking, masturbating, and sucking their baby's genitals: "Truk adults play with an infant's genitals. . . . In China, Manchu mothers tickle the genitals of their little daughters and suck the penis of a small son. . . . In Thailand, a Banoi mother habitually strokes her son's genitals."[109] But they maintain, this isn't incest. Davenport's cross-cultural study similarly concludes that "mother–son incest is so rare that it is insignificant and irrelevant [since] genital stimulation as a means of pacifying a child may be regarded as nonsexual."[110] Konker reviews cross-cultural adult–child sexual relations and finds that "the ethnographic record contains many . . . examples of normative adult/child sexual contact" but says this isn't a problem since experts have found there is "no reason to believe that sexual contact between an adult and child is inherently wrong or harmful."[111] Korbin likewise finds that mothers masturbating children are widespread in her large sample, but she says it is not incest since the society itself doesn't call it incest: "In some societies, children's genitals are fondled to amuse and please them, calm them, or lull them to sleep. . . . This would not constitute 'abuse' if in that society the behavior was not proscribed."[112]

Since the use of infants and children as erotic objects is so common cross-culturally,[113] it is not surprising that New Guinea adults other than

108. Clelland S. Ford and Frank A. Beach, *Patterns of Sexual Behavior.* New York: Harper & Row, 1951, p. 119.

109. Given J. Broude, *Growing Up: A Cross-Cultural Encyclopedia.* Santa Barbara: ABC-CLIO, 1995, p. 303.

110. William H. Davenport, "Adult-Child Sexual Relations in Cross-Cultural Perspective." In William O'Donohue and James H. Geer, Eds., *The Sexual Abuse of Children: Theory and Research. Vol. I.* Hillsdale, NJ: Lawrence Erlbaum Associates, 1992, p. 75.

111. Claudia Konker, "Rethinking Child Sexual Abuse: An Anthropological Perspective." *American Journal of Orthopsychiatry* 62(1992): 148.

112. Jill E. Korbin, "Child Sexual Abuse: Implications from the Cross-Cultural Record." In Nancy Sheper-Hughes, *Child Survival: Anthropological Perspectives on the Treatment and Maltreatment of Children.* Boston: D. Reidel Publishing Co., 1987, p. 251.

113. Lloyd deMause, "The Universality of Incest." *The Journal of Psychohistory* 19(1991): 123–164.

parents also commonly use children sexually. Babies in particular are treated as if they were breasts, to be sucked and masturbated all day long. Whenever ethnologists mention childhood in any detail, they often begin with such comments as this: "My strongest impression among women was created by their incessant fondling of infants,"[114] or "As babies and small children their genitalia are fondled."[115] Gillison describes the process of masturbating infants among the Gimi:

> The mother insists upon continued contact, interrupting her toddler's play repeatedly to offer the breast. Masturbation . . . with a baby girl [occurs when] the mother or *amau* holds her hand over the vulva and shakes it vigorously. She may kiss the vagina, working her way up the middle of the body to the lips and then inserting her nipple (often when the child has given no sign of discontent). With a boy, she kisses the penis, pulls at it with her fingers and takes it into her mouth to induce an erection. Several women may pass a baby boy back and forth, each one holding him over her head as she takes a turn sucking or holding the penis in her mouth.[116]

Maternal incest, like other sexual perversions, often reveals the sadism of the mother as she uses the child as an erotic object to overcome her depression and despair, rooted in her own loveless childhood. As Poole reports, "It should be noted that these erotic acts are often somewhat rough. Mothers' stimulation of the penis may involve pulling, pinching, and twisting in a manner that produces struggling and crying in infant boys."[117] Róheim reports that mothers will sometimes "lie on their sons in the [female on top] position and freely masturbate them" at night.[118] That all this

---

114. Gillian Gillison, *Between Culture and Fantasy: A New Guinea Highlands Mythology.* Chicago: University of Chicago Press, 1993, p. 176.

115. Ronald M. Berndt, *Excess and Restraint: Social Control Among a New Guinea Mountain People.* Chicago: University of Chicago Press, 1962, p. 91.

116. Gillian Gillison, *Between Culture and Fantasy,* p. 176.

117. Fitz John Porter Poole, "Coming into Social Being: Cultural Images of Infants in Bimin-Kuskusmin Folk Psychology." In Geoffrey M. White and John Kirkpatrick, Eds., *Person, Self, and Experience: Exploring Pacific Ethnopsychologies.* Berkeley: University of California Press, 1985, p. 232.

118. Géza Róheim, *Psychoanalysis and Anthropology: Culture, Personality and the Unconscious.* New York: International University Press, 1950; Géza Róheim, "The Western Tribes of Central Australia: The Alknarintja." In Warner Muensterberger and Sidney Axelrad, Eds., *The Psychoanalytic Study of Society,* Vol. III. New York: International Universities Press, 1964, pp. 194, 231.

masturbation of children by parents is socially acceptable is shown by how often the mothers do it in front of the anthropologist.[119]

The incestuous use of children in New Guinea and Australia extends to the other Melanesian and Polynesian islands, although as the societies become more complex the sexual practices become more ritualized. For instance, in the Marquesas Islands, besides simple masturbation of infants,[120] "the *mons Veneris* is massaged during infancy and girlhood . . . accompanied by stretching of the labia to elongate them. This was done by the mother during the daily bath. The child was seized by the ankles and its legs held apart while the mother manipulated the labia with her lips."[121] In Hawaii, a "blower" is designated for each male infant, ostensibly to prepare him for subincision of the foreskin, and "the penis was blown into daily starting from birth. The blowing was said to loosen and balloon the foreskin [and] continued daily . . . until the young male was 6 or 7."[122] For infant females in Hawaii, "milk was squirted into her vagina, and the labia were pressed together. The mons was rubbed with candlenut oil and pressed with the palm of the hand to flatten it. . . . The molding continued until the labia did not separate. This chore usually was done by the mother."[123] The Ponapé islanders "pulled and tugged at the labia of the little girls to lengthen them, while men pulled on the clitoris, rubbing it and licking it with their tongues and stimulating it by the sting of a big ant."[124] This oral manipulation of the labia and clitoris extends to many of the other Pacific islands.[125] Indeed, so widespread was the use of little children as sexual objects in traditional Polynesia that early Europeans could

---

119. Géza Róheim, "The Western Tribes of Central Australia," p. 236.

120. Lia Leibowitz, *Females, Males, Families: A Biosocial Approach.* North Scituate, MA: Duxbury Press, 1978, p. 135.

121. Robert C. Suggs, *Marquesan Sexual Behavior.* New York: Harcourt, Brace & World, 1966, p. 42.

122. Milton Diamond, "Selected Cross-Generational Sexual Behavior in Traditional Hawaii: A Sexological Ethnography." In Jay R. Feierman, Ed., *Pedophilia: Biosocial Dimensions.* New York: Springer-Verlag, 1990, p. 430.

123. Ibid., p. 431.

124. Herman Heinrich Ploss, *Das Weib in der Natur- und Völkerkunde: Anthropologische Studien. II. Band 1.* Leipzig: Th. Grieben's Verlag, 1887, p. 144.

125. Herman Heinrich Ploss, Max Bartels and Paul Bartels. *Femina Libido Sexualis: Compendium of the Psychology, Anthropology and Anatomy of the Sexual Characteristics of the Woman.* New York: The Medical Press, 1965, p. 140; Robert C. Suggs, *Marquesan Sexual Behavior.* New York: Harcourt, Brace & World, 1966, p. 177.

report: "Little children hardly ever live to the age of seven ere they are deflowered."[126]

Although fathers in New Guinea are often reported avoiding their infants during the nursing years because they say they get sexually aroused when they watch them nurse,[127] when they do handle their infants, they too are reported as using them erotically. Langness reports: "There was a great deal of fondling of the boys' penes by males. Women fondled infants but not older boys. Individuals of both sexes would pick up infants and mouth their genitals."[128] Like all other anthropologists who report the regular masturbating and sucking of children's genitals, he calls this "love."[129] Róheim, too, describes similarly widespread oral-genital contact by fathers: "The father . . . stimulates [his children] sexually at a very early period while they are still being carried. He playfully smells the vagina or touches it with his mouth; with the boys he playfully bites the penis."[130] It is this common use of the child as a breast by the father that is mistaken by so many anthropologists as "close, loving fathering" in New Guinea and elsewhere.

Since Poole was the only New Guinea ethnologist who interviewed both mothers and children, he obtained the most complete reports of maternal incest.[131] Like infanticidal psychoclass mothers everywhere, Bimin-Kuskusmin mothers consider their babies to be part of their own

---

126. Niko Besnier, "Polynesian Gender Liminality Through Time and Space." In Gilbert Herdt, Ed., *Third Sex, Third Gender: Beyond Sexual Dimorphism in Culture and History*. New York: Zone Books, 1996, p. 290.

127. Gilbert Herdt and Robert J. Stoller, *Intimate Communications: Erotics and the Study of Culture*. New York: Columbia University Press, 1990, pp. 139, 274.

128. L. L. Langness, "Oedipus in the New Guinea Highlands?" *Ethos* 18(1990): 395.

129. Ibid., p. 399.

130. Géza Róheim, *Psychoanalysis and Anthropology*, p. 160.

131. Fitz John Porter Poole, "Folk Models of Eroticism in Mothers and Sons: Aspects of Sexuality Among Bimin-Kuskusmin." Presented at the Annual Meeting of the American Anthropological Association, 1983; "Cultural Images of Women as Mothers: Motherhood Among the Bimin-Kuskusmin of Papua New Guinea." *Social Analysis* 15(1984): 73–93; "Coming Into Social Being: Cultural Images of Infants in Bimin-Kuskusmin Folk Psychology." In G. M. White and J. Kirkpatrick, Eds., *Person, Self, and Experience: Exploring Pacific Ethnopsychologies*. Berkeley: University of California Press, 1985, pp. 183–242; "The Ritual Forging of Identity: Aspects of Person and Self in Bimin-Kuskusmin Male Initiation." In Gilbert H. Herdt, Ed., *Rituals of Manhood: Male Initiation in Papua New Guinea*. Berkeley: University of California Press, 1982, pp. 99–154; "Personal Experience and Cultural Representation in Children's 'Personal Symbols' Among Bimin-Kuskusmin." *Ethos* 15(1987): 104–132; "Images of an Unborn Sibling: The Psychocultural Shaping of a Child's

bodies, "never permitting the infant to be detached from contact with her body" and breast-feeding the baby "not only on demand, but also sometimes by force," whenever the mother feels depressed.[132] Mothers, Poole says, constantly masturbate the penes of their baby boys, while trying not to let their incest get out of hand: "She is expected to masturbate him periodically to ensure the growth of his genitalia, but she must carefully avoid the excessive development of erotic 'infant lust' which may injure his *finiik* [spirit]. . . . When mothers rub the penes of their infant sons, the little boys wriggle on their mothers' laps and have erections."[133] Most of the incest occurs at night, however, when mothers can rub against their children's entire bodies because they sleep naked with them, "together in each other's arms," and when they also can "regularly rub" the boy's penis to erection.[134]

That these infants and children who are used as erotic objects function as poison containers for the mothers' split-off and denied anxieties and anger is quite clear. Poole interviewed one young boy, Buuktiin, who described how when his mother was depressed or angry she often "pulled, pinched, rubbed, or flicked a fingernail against his penis"[135] until he cried, afraid it might break off. "When he struggled to escape, she held him tightly and rubbed his penis even harder."[136]

> [His mother] had masturbated him earlier as mothers often do. . . . [But] now she increased the tempo and roughness of the episodes . . . and he often jerked at her touch and struggled to get away, hitting her and complaining of throbbing pain in his penis. "It hurts inside. It goes 'koong, koong, koong' inside. I think it bleeds in there. I don't like to touch it anymore. It hurts when I pee."[137]

Like so many victims of maternal incest, Buuktiin constantly cut himself, both to get the "bad maternal blood" out of himself, since he feels polluted

Fantasy Among the Bimin-Kuskusmin of Papua New Guinea." In L. Bryce Boyer and Simon A. Grolnick, Eds., *The Psychoanalytic Study of Society*, Vol. 15. Hillsdale, NJ: The Analytic Press, 1990, pp. 105–175.
    132. Poole, "Cultural Images," p. 87.
    133. Poole, "Images of an Unborn Sibling," pp. 127, 106.
    134. Poole, "Personal Experience," p. 115.
    135. Ibid., p. 118.
    136. Poole, "Images of an Unborn Sibling," p. 159.
    137. Ibid., p. 137.

by the constant incest, and to punish himself, since children regularly blame themselves for the mother's sexual abuse:

> Sometimes after such [incestuous] encounters, he wounded himself slightly in the thigh and the abdomen with a sharp stick and with slow deliberation, drawing blood and watching his penis. "Now it hurts here, outside, not in penis. Look, blood. Feels good. . . . Good to be a girl, no penis. . . . Mother twist penis, tight, tight. . . . Hurt, hurt, inside. Cry, she not listen. Why? She cut off father's penis? She cut off mine? Father tell her, cut off Buuktiin's penis? Mother angry, hurt Buuktiin's penis. Mother sad, hurt Buuktiin's penis. . . . Mother not like Buuktiin's penis, want to cut off.[138]

MATERNAL REJECTION IN NEW GUINEA

The "love" of the infanticidal mode parent is mainly evident when the child is useful as an erotic object. When children are off the breast or otherwise not useful, they are rejected as emotionally meaningless. The infanticidal parents' emotional bond does not really acknowledge the separate existence of the child, whose main function is to provide "bodily stimulation [that] helps the mother to come alive, and she seeks this from the child . . . countering her feelings of lethargy, depression, and deadness."[139] As with all pedophiles, the child is a "sexual object . . . that must show a readiness to comply, lend itself to be manipulated, used, abused [and] discarded."[140] There is never just incest—it is always incest/rejection.

There are many ways New Guinea parents demonstrate that when the child cannot be used erotically, it is useless. One is that as soon as infants are not being nursed, they are paid no attention, and even when in danger are ignored. Anthropologists regularly notice that little children in their tribes play with knives or fire and adults ignore them. Edgerton comments on the practice: "Parents allowed their small children to play with very sharp knives, sometimes cutting themselves, and they permitted them to sleep unattended next to the fire. As a result, a number of children burned themselves seri-

---

138. Ibid., pp. 137, 159.

139. Stanley J. Coen, "Sexualization as a Predominant Mode of Defense." *Journal of the American Psychoanalytic Association* 29(1981): 909.

140. Charles W. Socarides, *The Preoedipal Origin and Psychoanalytic Therapy of Sexual Perversions*. Madison, CT: International Universities Press, 1988, p. 93.

ously. . . . It was not uncommon to see children who had lost a toe to burns, and some were crippled by even more severe burns."[141] Langness says that in the Bena Bena "it was not at all unusual to see even very small toddlers playing with sharp bush knives with no intervention on the part of caretakers."[142] But this is good for children, say the anthropologists, since when "children as young as two or three are permitted to play with objects that Westerners consider dangerous, such as sharp knives or burning brands from the fire, [it] tends to produce assertive, confident, and competent children."[143] As Whiting says, when he once saw a Kwoma baby "with the blade of a twelve-inch bush knife in his mouth and the adults present paid no attention to him," this was good for the infant, since in this way "the child learns to discriminate between the edible and inedible."[144]

Children are experienced by mothers as extensions of their bodies, and any separation or independence is seen as rejection of the mother, as reminders of the severe rejection of the mothers' own childhood. Mothers do not allow others to nurse their children, saying their milk is "poison," and even do not allow their 1- to 2-year-olds to visit their relatives for fear they would "poison" them.[145] When a mother dies, often the "infant would be buried with her even if perfectly healthy."[146] When infants begin to show any sign of independence, they are either wholly rejected or forced to stay still. Typical is the Wogeo child, who Hogbin describes as often being "put in a basket, which is then hung on a convenient rafter . . . or tree" and "discouraged from walking and not allowed to crawl . . . [forced to] sit still for hours at a time [and only] make queer noises" as he or she is immobilized to avoid even the slightest movement of independence from the mother.[147] Anthropologists regularly see these ubiquitous New Guinea baskets and net bags in which the infants are trapped and in which they are often hung on a tree as "com-

---

141. Robert B. Edgerton, *Sick Societies: Challenging the Myth of Primitive Harmony*. New York: The Free Press, 1992, p. 56.

142. L. L. Langness, "Oedipus in the New Guinea Highlands?" *Ethos* 18(1990): 390.

143. Maria Lepowsky, *Fruit of the Motherland: Gender in an Egalitarian Society*. New York: Columbia University Press, 1993, p. 90.

144. John W. M. Whiting, *Becoming a Kwoma: Teaching and Learning in a New Guinea Tribe*. New Haven: Yale University Press, 1941, p. 25.

145. H. Ian Hogbin, "A New Guinea Infancy: From Conception to Weaning in Wogeo." *Oceana* 13(1943): 295.

146. Ibid.

147. Ibid., pp. 298–301.

forting," even though it means that the infants often live in their own feces and urine and can neither crawl nor interact with others.

Parental rejection in preliterate cultures is often overt—it is what Boyer found was called "throwing the child away." Boyer discovered that "a great many mothers abandon or give children away babies they have been nursing lovingly only hours before" when he and his wife were offered babies, a practice he ascribed to the mothers' "shallow object relations."[148] Few anthropologists have seen the high adoption and fosterage rates in the New Guinea area—some as high as 75 percent[149]—as rejection, but of course that is what they are.

Since to the infanticidal mother, as Hippler puts it, "the child is an unconscious representative of [her own] mother, his autonomous actions are seen by the mother as abandonment. The response on the part of the mother to this 'abandonment' by her infant . . . is anger" and rejection.[150] Mothers throughout the South Pacific are said to "hold their small infants facing away from them and toward other people while the mother speaks *for* them rather than *to* them."[151] Obviously the infant is an extension of the mother's body, not an independent human being at all. "No one says very much to babies,"[152] and when they begin to walk, they are felt to be abandoning the parent and are emotionally rejected.

MALNUTRITION AND THE WEANING CRISIS IN NEW GUINEA

So difficult is it for New Guinea mothers to relate to their children as independent human beings that they are unable to feed them regularly once they are off the breast. Like contemporary pedophiles, they do not

148. L. Bryce Boyer, "On Man's Need to Have Enemies: A Psychoanalytic Perspective." *The Journal of Psychoanalytic Anthropology* 9(1986): 109.

149. Thomas S. Weisner, "Socialization for Parenthood in Sibling Caretaking Societies." In Jane B. Lancaster, et al., Eds., *Parenting Across the Life Span: Biosocial Dimensions.* New York: Aldine De Gruyter, 1987, p. 248.

150. Arthur E. Hippler, "Culture and Personality Perspective of the Yolngu of Northeastern Arnhem Land: Part I—Early Socialization." *Journal of Psychoanalytic Anthropology* 1(1978): 234.

151. Michael Cole, *Cultural Psychology: A Once and Future Discipline.* Cambridge: Belknap Press, 1996, p. 205.

152. Annette Hamilton, *Nature and Nurture: Aboriginal Child-Rearing in North-Central Arnhem Land.* Canberra: Australian Institute of Aboriginal Studies, 1981, p. 40.

so much love their children as need them as erotic objects. When still on the breast, New Guinea children are constantly being force-fed, so that nursing "becomes a battle in which the mother clutches the child, shaking it up and down with the nipple forced into its mouth until it must either suck or choke."[153] As soon as they are off the breast, the mothers have difficulty understanding that their children need three meals a day. Although there is almost always plenty of food to eat for both adults and children, "several authors have stressed what appears to be a nonchalant attitude toward infant and child feeding on the part of Papua New Guinea mothers,"[154] so that "over 90 percent of children under five have been measured as having mild to moderate undernutrition."[155] In one careful statistical study, almost all children remained underweight for years, because "none were fed three times daily as clinic sisters encourage."[156] In the New Guinea–Australian culture area, meat, in particular, is rarely given to children, being eaten up by the adults first.[157] Hippler reports that "parents eat all the substantial food . . . before the child can get any. Adults . . . do not believe that deaths result from anything but sorcery, they make no connection between these practices and childhood illness and attendant death."[158] In a careful study of Kwanga child malnutrition, 2-year-olds who had been weaned were found to average only two meals a day, so that child mortality was extremely high.[159] Nurses in the clinic kept telling the mothers: "Why don't you tell me the truth? You do not

---

153. Annette Hamilton, *Nature and Nurture*, p. 32.

154. Carol L. Jenkins, Alison K. Orr-Ewing, and Peter F. Heywood, "Cultural Aspects of Early Childhood Growth and Nutrition Among the Amele of Lowland Papua New Guinea." In Leslie B. Marshall, Ed., *Infant Care and Feeding in the South Pacific*. New York: Gordon and Breach, 1985, p. 29.

155. Paula Brown, *Highland Peoples of New Guinea*. Cambridge: Cambridge University Press, 1978, p. 64; Katherine A. Dettwyler, "Styles of Infant Feeding: Parental-Caretaker Control of Food Consumption in Young Children." *American Anthropologist* 91(1989): 700.

156. Carol L. Jenkins et al., "Cultural Aspects of Early Childhood Growth," pp. 34–35, 47.

157. Maria A. Lepowsky, "Food Taboos, Malaria and Dietary Change: Infant Feeding and Cultural Adaptation on a Papua New Guinea Island." In Leslie B. Marshall, Ed., *Infant Care and Feeding in the South Pacific*. New York: Gordon and Breach, 1985, p. 70.

158. Arthur Hippler, "Culture and Personality," p. 236.

159. Brigit Obrist van Eeuwijk, *Small But Strong: Cultural Contexts of (Mal-) Nutrition Among the Northern Kwanga (East Sepik Province, Papua New Guinea)*. Basel: Wepf & Co., 1992, p. 200.

feed your child properly!" But the mothers didn't seem to comprehend why it was necessary to feed their children regularly each day, and so the weaned children kept losing weight and even dying from starvation while the mother watched them die.[160]

In her book on child malnourishment in New Guinea, Patricia Townsend cites all the studies showing the majority of children are underweight between age 1 and 4, emphasizing that toddlers after weaning are most malnourished, since their mothers do not feed them regularly.[161] Little children are constantly being described as throwing tantrums "for hours" trying to get food, "standing in the middle of the house floor and shrieking monotonously until someone stops work to cook for them."[162]

Parents also seem unable to empathize with the feelings of the children as they subject them to all kinds of tortures, which anthropologists dismiss as merely "cultural practices" and therefore dismiss as unmotivated. For instance, babies in many areas have their skulls deformed, highly elongated with painfully tight bindings that are renewed every day for months.[163] Making infants crawl over dead bodies and terrorizing little children with frightening masks and threats of devouring witches are also quite common.[164] Although children are regularly described as "shouted at, jerked roughly, slapped, shaken," bitten and hit with sticks,[165] the standard study on child abuse in New Guinea claims they are "rarely abused" because although "it is not uncommon for adults to strike chil-

---

160. Ibid., p. 13.

161. Patricia K. Townsend, *The Situation of Children in Papua New Guinea*. Port Moresby: Papua New Guinea Institute of Applied Social and Economic Research, 1985, pp. 17, 43.

162. Margaret Mead, *Growing Up in New Guinea*. New York: William Morrow, 1930, p. 49.

163. Ann Chowning, "Child Rearing and Socialization." In Ian Hogbin, *Anthropology in Papua New Guinea*. Melbourne: Melbourne University Press, 1973, p. 65; Jane C. Goodale, *To Sing with Pigs Is Human: the Concept of Person in Papua New Guinea*. Seattle: University of Washington Press, 1995, p. 80.

164. James B. Watson and Virginia Watson, *Batanabura of New Guinea*. New Haven: HRAF, 1972, pp. 30, 534.

165. Arthur Hippler, "Culture and Personality," p. 229; Ian Hogbin, "A New Guinea Childhood from Conception to the Eighth Year." In L. L. Langness and John C. Weschler, Eds., *Melanesia: Readings on a Culture Area*. Scranton: Chandler Publishing Co., 1971, pp. 201, 212; Alome Kyakas and Polly Wiessner, *From Inside the Women's House: Enga Women's Lives and Traditions*. Buranda: Robert Brom and Associates, 1992, p. 17.

dren . . . there is no such thing as a formal spanking."[166] Since only formal disciplinary spankings as we administer them in the West count as child abuse, anthropologists have concluded that "child abuse . . . is virtually unknown" in New Guinea.[167]

Primates parallel human infanticidal mode parents in all these abusive child-rearing practices. They frequently give away their infants—a practice called "alloparenting,"[168] which often results in the infant being abused, abandoned, or killed.[169] Primates are also infanticidal, cannibalistic, and incestuous.[170] Indeed, there appears to be only a relatively small degree of child-rearing evolution between our nearest primate ancestors and infanticidal mode parenting such as that in New Guinea. Lovejoy[171] cites the high infant mortality of primates during weaning (he places it at around 40 percent) as evidence that early hominids (estimated at over 50 percent infant mortality)[172] had difficulty feeding their children once off the breast, just as New Guinea mothers still do today.

RAPE OF BOYS AS A RESTAGING OF MATERNAL INCEST

When New Guinea boys begin to want to individuate at around 7 years of age, adult men restage upon the boys their own maternal incest traumas. Mainly in the less evolved South and Eastern Lowlands, this restaging takes the form of oral and anal rape of the boys, as men force their penises into the boys' mouths or anuses the same way the mothers earlier used them both in incest and in forced feeding. The boys become sexual objects de-

---

166. L. L. Langness, "Child Abuse and Cultural Values: The Case of New Guinea." In Jill E. Korbin, Ed., *Child Abuse and Neglect: Cross-Cultural Perspectives*. Berkeley: University of California Press, 1981, pp. 26–27.

167. Ibid., p. 23.

168. James J. McKenna, "Parental Supplements and Surrogates Among Primates: Cross-Species and Cross-Cultural Comparisons." In Jane B. Lancaster, et al., Eds., *Parenting Across the Life Span: Biosocial Dimensions*. New York: Aldine DeGruyter, 1987, pp. 143–181.

169. Sarah Blaffer Hrdy, *The Woman That Never Evolved*. Cambridge: Harvard University Press, 1981, p. 98.

170. See evidence in Chapter 8.

171. C. Owen Lovejoy, "The Origin of Man." *Science* 211(1981): 341–350.

172. Anthony Walsh, *Biosociology: An Emerging Paradigm*. Westport, CT: Praeger, 1995, p. 203.

void of the mother's frightening configurations. Both the boys and the men recognize the rape as being like breast-feeding, rationalizing it as necessary for growth, telling the little boys: "You all won't grow by yourselves; if you sleep with the men you'll become a STRONG man. . . . When you hold a man's penis, you must put it inside your mouth—he can give you semen. . . . It's the same as your mother's breast milk."[173] Among many groups, the fellatio of men by young boys occurs daily and continues until puberty, when he then can begin raping younger boys himself.

The notion that boys must be given semen to stop them from growing into females has a certain logic for New Guinea men. Like all maternally incested children, they feel that being used sexually by their mothers "pollutes their blood" and—since the boys consider themselves responsible for their rape—they feel "full of women's pollution" and need semen to "get mother's poison" out of them. Since as infants they were used erotically by always being rubbed against the mothers' bodies, they were intimately familiar with her menstrual fluids, remaining with her in the menstrual hut,[174] and so an explicit association is made between menstrual fluids and poison. Everyone therefore agrees that women's blood is so poisonous that sexual intercourse at the wrong time can kill men and that wives can and do kill their husbands and children by giving them food polluted by their menstrual blood.[175] Since attacks by witches and spirits "follow the path of menstrual blood,"[176] boys who remain "polluted" by mother's blood are open to death by witchcraft, so during their whole lives this incestuous "maternal pollution" must be constantly countered through semen ingestion and blood-letting rituals where men make incisions in the boys' bodies and rub sperm into the cuts.[177]

173. Gilbert H. Herdt, "Fetish and Fantasy in Sambia Initiation." In Gilbert H. Herdt, Ed., *Rituals of Manhood: Male Initiation in Papua New Guinea.* Berkeley: University of California Press, 1982, p. 71.

174. Marilyn Strathern, *Women in Between: Female Roles in a Male World: Mount Hagen, New Guinea.* London: Seminar Press, 1972, p. 173.

175. Ibid., p. 172.

176. Fitz John Porter Poole, "Coming into Social Being: Cultural Images of Infants in Bimin-Kuskusmin Folk Psychology." In Geoffrey M. White and John Kirkpatrick, Ed., *Person, Self, and Experience: Exploring Pacific Ethnopsychologies.* Berkeley: University of California Press, 1985, p. 195.

177. J. Patrick Gray, "Growing Yams and Men: An Interpretation of Kimam Male Ritualized Homosexual Behavior." In Evelyn Blackwood, Ed., *Anthropology and Homosexual Behavior.* New York: Hayworth Press, 1986, p. 61.

TORTURE AND MUTILATION AS PUNISHMENT FOR GROWTH

Even in those Highland areas that do not have ritualized pederasty, growth is psychologically felt to be dangerous to adults, and so older children are everywhere tortured and mutilated as punishment for their individuation and independence. Although these tortures are called initiation rituals by anthropologists, they are less initiations into anything than punishments for growing up. They dramatize a cleansing of maternal poisons so boys can now be used by men for their projections. Most of them restage maternal traumas in one way or another. One ritual begins by blaming the mothers as "evil defilers" of the boys who "have polluted and weakened their sons" with their bad menstrual blood.[178] Another describes how "bad polluted maternal blood" is purged from prepubertal Gahuka-Gama boys:

> The boys, placed in the front ranks of the vast crowd, see a score of naked men standing in the river exhibiting their erect penises and masturbating. Then, several of the men stride into the river where one takes two rolls of razor-sharp leaves and pushes them up and down his nostrils until blood gushes into the water. . . . Each initiate . . . is held firmly by his sponsor, while another man thrusts the leaves back and forth in his nostrils until the boy bleeds profusely into the river. After all of the initiates have been bled, [a man] doubles a length of cane and thrusts it down his esophagus like a sword swallower and draws it back and forth until he vomits into the water.[179]

The ritual both demonstrates "we are all bleeding, polluted mothers here" and tries to undo the feeling of being polluted by cutting the boys with the razor-sharp leaves in their nostrils and the cane-sword down their throats. The boys understandably "tremble, urinating and defecating in fear" during their torture.[180] It is a purity crusade of a simple society, and, like purity

---

178. Fitz John Porter Poole, "The Ritual Forging of Identity: Aspects of Person and Self in Bimin-Kuskusmin Male Initiation." In Gilbert H. Herdt, Ed., *Rituals of Manhood: Male Initiation in Papua New Guinea*. Berkeley: University of California Press, 1982, pp. 120–121.

179. Theodore Lidz and Ruth Silmanns Lidz, *Oedipus in the Stone Age: A Psychoanalytic Study of Masculinization in Papua New Guinea*. Madison, CT: International Universities Press, 1989, pp. 52, 91.

180. Ronald M. Berndt, *Excess and Restraint: Social Control Among a New Guinea Mountain People*. Chicago: University of Chicago Press, 1962, p. 94.

crusades in developed nations, is usually followed by a purifying war designed to reverse the shame of childhood by merging with the perpetrator. Yet the feeling of still being incested, polluted maternal sex objects remains with the boys, and many continue to bleed their noses, tongues, or penises periodically the rest of their lives.[181]

Genital mutilation, which is always punishment for growing up, also occurs in New Guinea. It is not, as Reik contends, "a punishment for incestuous wishes,"[182] but rather a self-punishment for real maternal incest for which children blame themselves. Genital mutilation rituals are cross-culturally correlated with exclusive mother–infant skin-to-skin sleeping arrangements, where the father sleeps separate and the mother is more likely to use the child incestuously.[183] In the New Guinea area, they are sometimes as brutal as the infamous Australian subincision, where the penis is cut the length of its underside until it "splits open like a boiled frankfurter."[184] The long wound on the penis is then called a boy's "vagina,"[185] and the men have intercourse in it.[186]

Other punishments during initiations for growing children include brutal beating with sticks and stinging nettles, sometimes for months or years, being burned over a fire, being starved and tortured, being made to swallow lime, which severely blisters the boys' mouths and throats, shooting a miniature sharp-pointed arrow up girls' urethras until blood is drawn, pushing barbed grass up the urethra, cutting the glans penis with a crab claw, etc.[187] Although one anthropologist mentioned that "undoubtedly these rituals are exceedingly painful,"[188] they are not usually considered as traumatic to the children. Since empathy with children's

---

181. Ibid., p. 58.

182. Theodor Reik, *Ritual: Psycho-Analytic Studies.* New York: International Universities Press, 1946, p. 106.

183. Michio Kitahara, "A Cross-Cultural Test of the Freudian Theory of Circumcision." *International Journal of Psychoanalytic Psychotherapy* 5(1976): 535–546.

184. Rosalind Miles, *The Women's History of the World.* Topsfield, MA: Salem House, 1988, p. 38.

185. Géza Róheim, *Psychoanalysis and Anthropology: Culture, Personality and the Unconscious.* New York: International Universities Press, 1950, p. 117.

186. Gisela Bleibtreu-Ehrenberg, "Pederasty Among Primitives: Institutionalized Initiation and Cultic Prostitution." *Journal of Homosexuality* 20(1990): 19.

187. Ibid., p. 18.

188. Ibid.

feelings is nearly absent, gratuitous mutilation of the children is common, such as tightly binding newborn infants heads for months to elongate the skull, or chopping off or biting off infants' fingers while mourning.[189] These kinds of brutal daily abuses, added to the various types of ritual pederasty, torture, and mutilation, are so widespread that the conclusion in the standard anthropological work on cross-cultural child abuse that there is a "virtual absence of child abuse in New Guinea"[190] appears thoroughly inexplicable.

THE RESTORATION OF DISINTEGRATED SELVES IN CANNIBALISM

When switched into their violent alters resulting from all this child abuse, New Guinea men regularly join in a social trance that acts out their need to kill. Harrison writes of violence in New Guinea tribes:

> Headhunting raids required special magic, which placed the fighters in a trance-like state of dissociation and relieved them of accountability for their actions; it was supposed to make them capable of killing even their own wives and children. . . . So long as the magic was in effect, the capacity to kill was quite indiscriminate and turned the fighters into a dangerous menace to all other people, including their own families.[191]

That war among New Guinea natives is not about anger but about the restoration of disintegrated selves caused by growth panic is most obvious in cannibalism, where the penis, tongue, and muscles of the enemy were often eaten "to absorb the victim's strength."[192] It is good to have powerful enemies, they say, because they are good to kill and eat.[193] At the

---

189. L. L. Langness, "Child Abuse and Cultural Values: The Case of New Guinea." In Jill Korbin, Ed., *Child Abuse and Neglect: Cross-Cultural Perspectives.* Berkeley: University of California Press, 1981, pp. 16–17.

190. Ibid., p. 29.

191. Simon Harrison, *Violence, Ritual and the Self in Melanesia.* Manchester: Manchester University Press, 1993, p. 27.

192. Ibid., p. 88.

193. Ibid., p. 131.

same time, all war restages early traumas, including infanticide—as the Sambia myth says, "Numboolyu's wife, Chenchi, killed her first male child. . . . Because she killed the first male child, we now fight—war."[194] Like contemporary cults that kill and eat babies,[195] training for killing children in New Guinea begins early. Mead reports: "It was considered necessary that every Tchambuli should in childhood kill a victim, and for this purpose live victims, usually infants or young children, were purchased from other tribes. . . . The small boy's spearhand was held by his father, and the child, repelled and horrified, was initiated into the cult of head-hunting."[196] The genitals were choice morsels of cannibals, the victim's penis being eaten by the women and the vagina by the men; the children are reported to have had horrible nightmares after witnessing the feast.[197] The perverse ritual was so sexualized that Berndt reports that during the cannibalistic feast men sometimes copulate with the dead women's bodies they are about to eat and women pretend to copulate with the dead man's penis before eating it.[198] So powerful is this notion of internalization through cannibalism that Meigs says among the Hua "it is feared that if a person fails to eat the corpse of his or her same-sex parent, that person . . . will become stunted and weak."[199] Obviously, eating the body of one's parent or of a friend is an extremely primitive form of repairing emotional loss: "When a good man died our bodies ached with hunger. We ate him and the pain cooled."[200]

---

194. Gilbert H. Herdt, *Guardians of the Flutes: Idioms of Masculinity*. New York: McGraw-Hill Book Company, 1981, p. 351.

195. Jeanne Hill, "Believing Rachel." *The Journal of Psychohistory* 24(1996): 131–146; Michael Newton, "Written in Blood: A History of Human Sacrifice." *The Journal of Psychohistory* 24(1996): 104–131.

196. Margaret Mead, *Sex and Temperament in Three Primitive Societies*. New York: William Morrow, 1963, p. 242.

197. Fitz John Porter Poole, "Cannibals, Tricksters, and Witches: Anthropophagic Images Among Bimin-Kuskusmin," and Gillian Gillison, "Cannibalism Among Women in the Eastern Highlands of Papua New Guinea." In Paula Brown and Donald Tuzin, Eds., *The Ethnography of Cannibalism*. Washington, DC: Society for Psychological Anthropology, 1983, pp. 1–50.

198. Ronald M. Berndt, *Excess and Restraint: Social Control Among a New Guinea Mountain People*. Chicago: University of Chicago Press, 1962, p. 283.

199. Ana S. Meigs, *Food, Sex, and Pollution*, p. 110.

200. Gillian Gillison, *Between Culture and Fantasy: A New Guinea Highlands Mythology*. Chicago: University of Chicago Press, 1993, p. 72.

THE PSYCHOGENIC PUMP AND EVOLUTIONARY STAGES IN NEW GUINEA

The over 700 distinct cultures in New Guinea show a definite if complex range of evolutionary stages of child rearing, psyche, and society. The evolutionary ladder—ranging from early to middle infanticidal mode—generally runs from the more south and east "semen belt" of maternal incest and pederasty to the more evolved north and west highlands "Big Man" areas.[201] Over the millennia, the more advanced parents migrated north and west, and those who did not evolve and who preferred the more violent, pederastic, less organized southern and eastern areas either remained there or drifted back from more advanced groups. Child-rearing patterns show a definite areal distribution, centering on how much the mothers cling to their children: "In eastern highlands societies, where initiation is longest and most elaborate, boys appear to remain with their mothers and sleep in women's houses for a longer time than do boys in the western highlands where initiation is absent. . . . [Often in the east] men had little contact with their sons until the boys were ten years old or older [but] in some western highlands societies, boys left their mothers earlier and much more gradually. . . . Boys moved to men's houses at about five years of age."[202] This pattern follows Richman's cross-cultural findings that "as cultures evolve, the mother holds and makes physical contact against their infants less and talks more to them."[203] Mothers in the western highlands are somewhat less afraid of their babies' independence, so infants are allowed to crawl about more often and are trapped in slings and cradles less.

The cultures of these two areas are described as follows: "The production of 'men' [through pederasty and training as warriors] is seen to be the focus of cultural attention among Lowland groups, as is the produc-

---

201. D. K. Feil, *The Evolution of Highland Papua New Guinea Societies*. Cambridge: Cambridge University Press, 1987; Shirley Lindenbaum, "Variations on a Sociosexual Theme in Melanesia." In Gilbert H. Herdt, Ed., *Ritualized Homosexuality in Melanesia*. Berkeley: University of California Press, 1984, pp. 337–360; Bruce M. Knauft, *South Coast New Guinea Cultures: History, Comparison, Dialectic*. Cambridge: Cambridge University Press, 1993 exempts some coastal southern groups from "Big Men" classifications.

202. D. K. Feil, *The Evolution of Highland Papua New Guinea Societies*, p. 210.

203. Amy L. Richman, et al., "Maternal Behavior to Infants in Five Cultures." In Robert L. LeVine, Patricia M. Miller, Mary Maxwell West, Eds., *Parental Behavior in Diverse Societies*. San Francisco: Jossey-Bass, 1988, p. 86.

tion of 'bigmen' [leaders of status] in the Highlands."[204] The former are stuck on the evolutionary ladder between foraging and primitive horticulture, while the latter have enough innovation to develop better ways of irrigating crops and fencing pigs. Feil describes how there is an "archetypal social structure, economic pattern and social environment in which male initiations and sexual hostility flourish . . . at the eastern end and are all but absent or attenuated in the western highlands."[205] Since mothers are less engulfing in western highlands, fears of their pollution and hatred of women are less and therefore women are less exploited than in the east and south.[206] It is also not surprising that "in the eastern highlands, women were targets in hostile [warfare] encounters; in the western highlands, they were not."[207] These more evolved northwestern Big Man groups are able to construct more organized political and economic structures that are far more hierarchical than in the east and south, since they can stand more innovation without triggering growth panic, and thus can accumulate the surpluses of pigs and other exchange goods that their more complex societies revolve around. To actually *trust* a Big Man in economic exchange or in ritual feasts is possible because of reducing the incestuous and pederastic use of children and replacing abandonment with the beginnings of tolerance for individuation. Warfare is also more organized and therefore more restricted in the Big Man societies,[208] sometimes occurring as infrequently as every decade,[209] compared to the continuous headhunting, cannibalistic, and other raids of the less evolved groups.

---

204. Shirley Lindenbaum, "Variations on a Sociosexual Theme in Melanesia." In Gilbert H. Herdt, Ed., *Ritualized Homosexuality in Melanesia*. Berkeley: University of California Press, 1984, p. 340.

205. D. K. Feil, *The Evolution of Highland Papua New Guinea Societies*, p. 175.

206. Ibid., p. 231.

207. Ibid., p. 72.

208. Bruce M. Knauft, *South Coast New Guinea Cultures: History, Comparison, Dialectic*. Cambridge: Cambridge University Press, 1993, p. 120 tries unsuccessfully to "dethrone" the big-man concept, though the number of groups actually having full-fledged big men is reduced by his work.

209. Andrew P. Vayda, *War in Ecological Perspective: Persistence, Change, and Adaptive Processes in Three Oceanian Societies*. New York: Plenum Press, 1976, p. 14; Bruce M. Knauft, "Melanesian Warfare: A Theoretical History," *Oceania* 60(1990) 250–311 attempts to disprove Feil's claims that warfare is more "restrained" in Western highlands, but only disproves it necessarily is less violent everywhere in the West.

PSYCHOGENIC ARREST IN NEW GUINEA

Although New Guinea natives have evolved somewhat in the past ten millennia, they are certainly closer to the foraging and early horticultural cultures of our ancestors than the "peaceful" (actually pacified) groups in Africa that are so often used as models for early human groups. Yet the unanswered question about New Guinea remains: why have they evolved so little in the past ten millennia? They didn't get a late start, since agriculture began in New Guinea over 6,000 years ago, earlier than most other areas of the world that have since surpassed them in psychological and cultural evolution.[210] Indeed, the first foragers were in New Guinea 40,000 years ago,[211] and agriculture is considered to have developed independently there, so they actually had ecological conditions reasonably conducive to farming. It is true that they had no cereal crops nor domesticable large mammals (though they did have pigs and kangaroos),[212] but they shared this lack with other Pacific areas such as Hawaii and other Polynesian islands that evolved far higher levels of civilization than New Guinea. Diamond asks the crucial question: "Why did New Guineans continue to use stone tools instead of metal tools, remain non-literate, and fail to organize themselves into chiefdoms and states?"

Diamond's answers are (1) too few people (1,000,000), (2) too difficult terrain (swamps and jungles), and (3) too much warfare (because of fragmented groups).[213] Yet these are all conditions that cultural evolution conquers, since innovative natives elsewhere cleared jungle areas, introduced irrigation, and created larger populations through more advanced political institutions. If New Guinea never reached the complex chiefdom level of the Hawaiian or Mayan civilizations—both with similar ecologies—it was because their child rearing did not evolve enough to produce psychoclasses that were innovative enough to invent new cultural forms.

Diamond a priori rules out any variation in people's capacity for innovation, saying "all human societies contain inventive people."[214] But if,

---

210. D. K. Feil, *The Evolution of Highland Papua New Guinea Societies*. Cambridge: Cambridge University Press, 1987, p. 16.

211. Jared Diamond, *Guns, Germs, and Steel: The Fates of Human Societies*. New York: W. W. Norton & Co., 1997, p. 147.

212. Ibid., p. 148.

213. Ibid., pp. 306–307.

214. Ibid., p. 408.

as we have been insisting here, child rearing evolution is the clue to cultural evolution and innovation, the crux of New Guinea's problems lie in their inability to evolve better mothers and hopeful daughters who could raise more inventive people. Certainly their early infanticidal mode parenting and the resulting depth of their hatred and fear of women confirms this condition currently. But how have they been able to suppress psychogenesis for so long and why have they had so few innovative, evolving mothers and hopeful daughters?

Unfortunately, the study of the history of childhood in New Guinea is totally lacking. Archeology and ethnohistory never mention children,[215] so the basic materials needed to answer the question are simply missing. A few informed guesses is the best one can manage at the moment.

First, New Guinea was part of Australia when humans emigrated into it, so the original ancestors developed in one of the most arid regions in the world,[216] subject to periodic droughts that must have had some effect in devolving parenting. Droughts result in poor maternal nutrition, reducing an enzyme in the placenta that deactivates cortisol, so that fetuses get more coritsol in their brains, increasing susceptibility to stress in adulthood and passing the stress on to the next generation.[217] Droughts may even have been severe enough to alter the genetic makeup of parents, thus passing parenting down both genetically and epigenetically through the generations. Additional confirming evidence for the effects of famine on the brain wiring of fetuses is shown in the finding that babies who had prenatal exposure to famine during the Dutch Hunger Winter at the end of 1944 had higher rates of schizoid personality disorders,[218] because migration of brain cells through the neuronal subplate was disrupted, causing the faulty connections that are usually found in schizophrenics.[219]

Second, the small size of island New Guinea may have inhibited the psychogenic pump effect, limiting migration enough so that early infanti-

215. Ward H. Goodenough, Ed., *Prehistoric Settlement of the Pacific*. Philadelphia: American Philosophical Society, 1996; J. Peter White and James F. O'Connell, *A Prehistory of Australia, New Guinea and Sahul*. New York: Academic Press, 1982.

216. James Woodburn, "Hunters and Gatherers Today and Reconstruction of the Past." In Ernest Gellner, Ed., *Soviet and Western Anthropology*. London: Duckworth, 1980, p. 109.

217. *Newsweek*, September 27, 1999, p. 54.

218. Hans W. Hoek, et al., "Schizoid Personality Disorder After Prenatal Exposure to Famine." *American Journal of Psychiatry* 153(1996): 1637–1639.

219. *The New York Times*, May 28, 1996, p. C1.

cidal mothering swamped the emergence of innovating mothers (biologists sometimes call small islands "evolutionary traps")—though admittedly other even smaller islands in the Pacific have managed to climb much further up the evolutionary scale.

Third and perhaps most important, the least evolved parenting in New Guinea is to the south, while the most evolved is in the north, where the Trobrianders managed to approach the level of a chiefdom. Anthropologists admit they are puzzled as to "why the Trobriand Islanders have chiefs. They have neither exceptional population density nor agricultural productivity."[220] What is relevant to this question is that while most of New Guinea's population came from the Australian continent to the south and speak non-Austronesian languages, the Trobrianders and some other nearby groups came later mainly from Taiwan and speak Austronesian languages. Taiwan was more advanced culturally—and one can assume also in parenting—when people migrated from there to New Guinea 4,000 years ago, having grain crops, true weaving, metals, the bow and arrow, and even water buffaloes.[221] Presumably their descendants began with a head start in child rearing compared to the natives further south of them.

Yet these evolutionary speculations rest mainly on inferences that have yet to generate real archaeological field studies, so in order to answer questions of relative rates of evolution of childhood and culture we must turn to the only area of the world in which the history of childhood has been more adequately studied: Europe. The evidence that I have found for the evolution of childhood and culture in Europe from its earliest days until today is presented in Chapters 8 and 9.

220. Roy Brunton, "Why Do Trobriands Have Chiefs?" *Man* 10(1975): 144.
221. Robert Blust, "Austronesian Culture History: The Window of Language." In Ernest Gellner, Ed., *Soviet and Western Anthropology*. London: Duckworth, 1980, pp. 28–35.

8

The Evolution of Child Rearing

> *"Who would not shudder if he were given the choice of eternal death or life again as a child? Who would not choose to die?"*
>
> —*St. Augustine*

Children throughout history have arguably been more vital, more gentle, more joyous, more trustful, more curious, more courageous, and more innovative than adults. Yet adults throughout history have routinely called little children "beasts," "sinful," "greedy," "arrogant," "lumps of flesh," "vile," "polluted," "enemies," "vipers," and "infant fiends."[1] Although it is difficult to believe, parents until relatively recently have been so frightened of and have so hated their newborn infants that they have killed them by the billions; routinely sent them out to extremely neglectful wet nurses, tied them up tightly in swaddling bandages lest they be overpowered by them; starved, mutilated, raped, neglected, and beat them so badly that prior to modern times I have not been able to find evidence of a single parent who would not today be put in jail for child abuse or

---

1. Aeschylus, *Libation Bearers*, 753; Augustine, *Confessions*, I, 7.11; Michael Goodich, "Encyclopaedic Literature: Child-Rearing in the Middle Ages." *History of Education* 12(1983): 7; Jean Delumeau, *Sin and Fear*. New York: St. Martin's Press, 1990, p. 266; Lawrence Stone, *The Family, Sex and Marriage in England 1500–1800*. New York: Harper & Row, 1977, p. 408; David Cressy, *Birth, Marriage, and Death: Ritual, Religion and the Life-Cycle in Tudor and Stuart England*. New York: Oxford University Press, 1997, p. 19; Arthur P. Wolf, "The Women of Hai-shan: A Demographic Portrait. In Margery Wolf and Roxane Witke, Eds., *Women in Chinese Society*. Stanford: Stanford University Press, 1975, p. 202; George Savile Halifax, *The Lady's New-Years Gift: or, Advice to a Daughter*. London, Matt. Gillyflower, 1688, p. 80; Catherine M. Scholten, *Childbearing in American Society: 1650–1850*. New York: New York University Press, 1985, p. 60; Philip Greven, *The Protestant Temperament*. New York: New American Library, 1977, p. 28.

neglect. Historians have assumed that my evidence for routinely abusive parenting must be exaggerated, since if it were true it "would mean parents acted in direct opposition to their biological inheritance," and surely evolution "wouldn't be so careless . . . as to leave us too immature to care properly for our offspring."[2]

It is not surprising that the existence of widespread child abuse and neglect throughout history has been viewed with disbelief.[3] In this chapter, the extensive historical evidence for each abusive child-rearing practice will be presented, focusing on the actual statements made by caregivers and children so that the intrapsychic processes behind the abuse and neglect can be better understood.

THE MISSING FATHER: CHILDHOOD IN THE GYNARCHY

The problem with the conception of a patriarchy, wherein men always dominate women, both in society and in the family, is that while no purely matriarchal society has been found,[4] there is little evidence that until modern times fathers have been very much present in families. In our promiscuous chimpanzee ancestors, fathers were quite absent in child rearing, so there are no "families,"[5] only females moving about with their children.[6] It is also likely that "there were no Neanderthal families to begin with,"[7] since women and children lived in separate areas from the males in caves. Families in preliterate cultures today are always run by women, who often live in separate spaces from their husbands. In some, they have a "visiting

2. Linda Pollock, *Forgotten Children: Parent–Child Relations from 1500 to 1900*. Cambridge: Cambridge University Press, 1983, p. 51; Andrew Bard Schmookler, *Out of Weakness: Healing the Wounds That Drive Us to War*. New York: Bantam Books, 1988, p. 106.

3. See Lloyd deMause, "On Writing Childhood History." *The Journal of Psychohistory* 16(1988): 135–171.

4. Cynthia Eller, *The Myth of Matriarchal Prehistory: Why an Invented Past Will Not Give Women a Future*. New York: Beacon Press, 2000.

5. Peter J. Wilson, *Man, The Promising Primate: The Conditions of Human Evolution*. New Haven: Yale University Press, 1980, p. 63.

6. Adrienne L. Zihlman, "Sex Differences and Gender Hierarchies Among Primates: An Evolutionary Perspective." In Barbara Diane Miller, Ed., *Sex and Gender Hierarchies*. Cambridge: Cambridge University Press, 1993, p. 36.

7. James Shreeve, *The Neanderthal Enigma: Solving the Mystery of Modern Human Origins*. New York: William Morrow and Co., 1995, p. 163.

husband . . . in which the husband and wife live with their respective mothers [and] at night the man 'visits' his wife in her house."[8] In others, men spend much of their time in their own cult houses, and women in separate family or menstrual huts, "segregating themselves of their own accord."[9] Even when men live with their wives, females in simple societies are always in charge of the children and matrifocal families predominate. Although in a few very simple hunting tribes fathers are said sometimes to hold their infants, it turns out they are only hallucinating being fused with their mothers, "fondling the child as its mother does. He takes it to his breast and holds it there,"[10] or "sucks its face" in the traditional "full-lipped manner,"[11] using the infant as a breast substitute but not really caregiving. Even when the children grow up, fathers are generally not the ones who teach them skills: "Among the Hadza, as a typical example, boys learn their bow-and-arrow hunting knowledge and techniques and their tracking skills mainly informally from other boys,"[12] not from their fathers.

The historical family, it turns out, cannot remotely be termed a patriarchy until modern times. It is in fact a *gynarchy*, composed of the grandmother, mother, aunts, unmarried daughters, wet nurses, female servants, midwives, neighbors called "gossips" who acted as substitute mothers, plus the children.[13] Fathers in traditional families may sometimes eat and sleep within the gynarchy, but they do not determine its emotional atmosphere, nor do they in any way attempt to raise the children. To avoid experiencing their own domination, abuse, and neglect during childhood by females,

---

8. Francoise Zonabend, "An Anthropological Perspective on Kinship and the Family." In André Burguière, et al., Eds., *A History of the Family: Vol. One.* Cambridge: Harvard University Press, 1996, p. 41.

9. Judy Grahn, *Blood, Bread, and Roses: How Menstruation Created the World.* Boston: Beacon Press, 1993, p. 3.

10. Scott Coltrane, "Father-Child Relationships and the Status of Women: A Cross-Cultural Study." *American Journal of Sociology* 93(1988): 1073.

11. L. L. Langness, "Child Abuse and Cultural Values: The Case of New Guinea." In Jill E. Korbin, *Child Abuse and Neglect: Cross-Cultural Perspectives.* Berkeley: University of California Press, 1981, p. 24.

12. James Woodburn, "Hunters and Gatherers Today and Reconstruction of the Past." In Ernest Gellner, Ed., *Soviet and Western Anthropology.* London: Duckworth, 1980, p. 107.

13. Deborah Willis, *Malevolent Nurture: Witch-Hunting and Maternal Power in Early Modern England.* Ithaca: Cornell University Press, 1995, p. 35; Katherine Usher Henderson and Barbara F. McManus, *Half Humankind: Contexts and Texts of the Controversy About Women in England, 1540–1640.* Urbana: University of Illinois Press, 1985.

men throughout most of history have instead set up androcentric political and religious spheres for male-only activities, contributing to the family gynarchy only some sustenance, periodic temper tantrums, and occasional sexual service.

Evidence of fathers playing any real role in children's upbringing is simply missing until early modern times. I have been unable to find a single classical scholar of antiquity who has been able to cite any instance of a father saying one word to his child prior to the age of 7.[14] Little children were occasionally shown as used by fathers as sensuous objects—as when in Aristophanes' *The Wasps* the father says he "routinely enjoys letting his daughter fish small coins from his mouth with her tongue"[15]—but otherwise, scholars conclude: "In antiquity, women lived shut away [from men]. They rarely showed themselves in public [but] stayed in apartments men did not enter; they rarely ate with their husbands. . . . They never spent their days together."[16] In Greece, women had a special place. Larger houses had a room or suite of rooms in which women worked and otherwise spent much of their day, the women's apartments, the *gynaikonitis*, which Xenophon says was "separated from the men's quarters by a bolted door."[17] In two-story houses, the *gynaikonitis* would usually be upstairs.[18] The men's dining room, the *andron*, was located downstairs near the entrance, guarding the women's quarters. "Here men in the family dined and entertained male guests. . . . Vase-paintings do not depict Greek couples eating together."[19] This mainly vertical organization of most homes lasted well into the eighteenth century, when a new "structure of intimacy" began to be built, with family rooms connected to each other on the same level.[20]

---

14. Barry S. Strauss, *Fathers and Sons in Athens: Ideology and Society in the Era of the Peloponnesian War*. Princeton: Princeton University Press, 1993; Mark Golden, *Children and Childhood in Classical Athens*. Baltimore: Johns Hopkins University Press, 1990; Beryl Rawson, Ed., *Marriage, Divorce, and Children in Ancient Rome*. Oxford: Clarendon Press, 1991.

15. Aristophenes, *The Wasps*. Ann Arbor, MI: University of Michigan Press, 1962, p. 92.

16. Madelyn Gutwirth, *The Twilight of the Goddesses: Women and Representation in the French Revolutionary Era*. New Brunswick: Rutgers University Press, 1992, p. 125.

17. Sarah B. Pomeroy, *Families in Classical and Hellenistic Greece*. New York: Oxford University Press, 1997, p. 29.

18. Mark Golden, *Children and Childhood in Classical Athens*, p. 122.

19. Sarah B. Pomeroy, *Families in Classical and Hellenistic Greece*, p. 30.

20. Annik Pardailhé, *The Birth of Intimacy: Privacy and Domestic Life in Early Modern Paris*. Philadelphia: University of Pennsylvania Press, 1991, pp. 53–59.

The women's area held the grandmother, the mother, the concubines, the mistresses, the slave nurses, the aunts, and the children. Thus Herodotus could assume his reader would easily recognize families where "a boy is not seen by his father before he is five years old, but lives with the women,"[21] and Aristotle could assume his readers' agreement that "no male creatures take trouble over their young."[22] Ancient Greek, Roman, and Jewish men had all-male eating clubs where women and children were not welcome.[23] Plato suggests a utopian home arrangement with "dinners at which citizens will feast in the company of their children. . . . In general, however, children ate with their mothers, not their fathers. . . . Eating and drinking, far from offering the whole family an opportunity for communal activity, tended to express and reinforce cleavages within it."[24] Boys tended to remain in the gynarchy of their own or others' homes until their teens.[25]

The husband is usually missing from the homes of most early societies, and not just during their frequent military service. Evelyn Reed describes the typical early "matrifamily" as everywhere being ruled by mothers: "The family in Egypt . . . was matriarchal. . . . The most important person in the family was not the father, but the mother. The Egyptian wife was called the 'Ruler of the House.' . . . There is no corresponding term for the husband."[26] In rural Greek villages even today the mother owns the house, passes it on to her daughter as dowry, and continues to rule the house when her daughter has children.[27] Indeed, the husband was rarely with his family in antiquity. Legislators sometimes suggest that to prevent population decline, it would be a good idea for husbands to visit their wives occasionally, as in Solon's law "that a man should consort with his wife not less than three times a month—not for pleasure surely, but as cities renew their

21. Herodotus, *The Persian Wars*. Books I–II. Cambridge, MA: Harvard University Press, 1926, p. 177.

22. Aristotle, The *Complete Works of Aristotle*. Princeton, NJ: Princeton University Press, 1984, p. 87.

23. Lawrence A. Hoffman, *Covenant of Blood: Circumcision and Gender in Rabbinic Judaism*. Chicago: University of Chicago Press, 1996, p. 138.

24. Mark Golden, *Children and Childhood in Classical Athens*, p. 38.

25. Ibid., p. 125.

26. Evelyn Reed, *Woman's Evolution: From Matriarchal Clan to Patriarchal Family*. New York: Pathfinder, 1974, p. 438.

27. Charles Stewart, *Demons and the Devil: Moral Imagination in Modern Greek Culture*. Princeton: Princeton University Press, 1991, p. 50.

agreements from time to time."[28] In antiquity, love had nothing to do with men's wives; it is reserved for pederastic relations with boys. As Scroggs summarized Greco-Roman practice: "To enter the 'women's quarters' in search of love is to enter the world of the feminine and therefore is effeminate for a male."[29] Plutarch wrote: "Genuine love has no connections whatsoever with the women's quarters."[30] When Socrates asks, "Are there any people you talk to less than you do to your wife?" the answer was, "Possibly. But if so, very few indeed."[31] Men stayed in the *thiasos*, the men's club, with other men, and had little to do with their children. Greek boys stayed in the gynarchy of their own home until at the age of about 10 they were forced to be *eromenos*, sexual objects, in the *andron* of a much older man's home.[32] Greek girls stayed in the gynarchy until they were about 12, when they too were raped by a much older man, a stranger chosen for them by their family to be their husband. Brides went into marriages with large dowries, which remained their property for life.[33] The husband might try to enforce an occasional dominance in the gynarchy by beating the women and children, but normally it was the women of the household who wielded the family whip on the children.

The gynarchy ruled supreme in early homes. In Byzantium, women had separate spheres with strict exclusion of men from the family, where "men live in light and brightness, the *palaestra*; women live in the *gynaecaeum*, enclosed, secluded."[34] This was even true of supposedly patriarchal Chinese families. The Chinese gynarchy was described by visitors as living in separate "women's apartments behind the high walls of their husbands' compounds," dominated by women who "are reputed to terrorize the men of their households and their neighbors with their fierce tempers, searing tongues, and indomitable wills. . . . When father and son do work together,

---

28. Plutarch, *Dialogue on Love*, 768.

29. Robin Scroggs, *The New Testament and Homosexuality*. Philadelphia: Fortress Press, 1983, p. 48.

30. Ibid., p. 47.

31. Robert Flaceliere, *Love in Ancient Greece*. London: Frederick Muller, 1962, p. 103.

32. S. C. Humphreys, *The Family, Women and Death: Comparative Studies*. London: Routledge & Kegan Paul, 1983, p. 17.

33. Jack Goody, *The Oriental, the Ancient and the Primitive*. New York: Cambridge University Press, 1990, p. 390.

34. Kathryn M. Ringrose, "Living in the Shadows: Eunuchs and Gender in Byzantium." In Gilbert Herdt, Ed., *Third Sex, Third Gender*. New York: Zone Books, 1994, p. 94.

they have nothing to say, and even at home they speak only when there is business to discuss. [Otherwise] they mutually avoid each other."[35] Similarly, in Indonesian families, "fathers are simply not present very much. . . . The woman has more authority, influence and responsibility than her husband."[36] The examples can easily be extended around the world and well into the Middle Ages:

> The female world was highly structured, like a little monarchy—that monarchy wielded by the master's wife, the "lady" who dominated the other women in the house. This monarchy was often tyrannical. The chronicles of French families at the end of the twelfth and the beginning of the thirteenth century paint a picture of shrews reigning brutally over servants whom they terrorized, and over their sons' wives whom they tormented. . . . Indeed, a female power existed which rivaled that of men. . . . Men were afraid of women, especially their own wives.[37]

Feminist historians have pioneered in uncovering the evidence revealing families as gynarchies, saying "the need to keep women in line revealed permanent high tension in men around a being with disquieting power."[38] Men are shown as being excluded from the traditional *gynaecaeum*,[39] the nursery, the kitchen, even the laundry: "No man would dare approach the laundry, so feared is this group of women."[40] Even in the knightly class, "we see the male and female sections of the household staring at one another in fascination and fright, occasionally joining together or furtively communicating and interpenetrating."[41] Women are depicted as ruling both

35. Margery Wolf, "Chinese Women: Old Skills in a New Context." In M. Z. Rosaldo and L. Lamphere, Eds., *Woman, Culture, and Society*. Stanford, CA: Stanford University Press, 1974, pp. 157, 169.

36. Nancy Tanner, "Matrifocality in Indonesia and Africa and Among Black Americans." In M. Z. Rosaldo and L. Lamphere, Eds., *Woman, Culture, and Society*, pp. 135, 139.

37. Georges Duby, *Love and Marriage in the Middle Ages*. Chicago: University of Chicago Press, 1994, p. 96.

38. Madelyn Gutwirth, *The Twilight of the Goddesses*, p. 110.

39. Danielle Régnier-Bohler, "Imagining the Self." In Georges Duby, Ed., *A History of Private Life. II. Revelations of the Medieval World*. Cambridge: Harvard University Press, 1988, p. 141.

40. Edward Shorter, *A History of Women's Bodies*. New York: Basic Books, 1982, p. 292.

41. David Levine, *At the Dawn of Modernity*. Berkeley: University of California Press, 2001, p. 53.

their husbands and their children, who are often shown as fearing them,[42] and while husbands are hopefully told in moralist's instruction manuals about the duties of a husband to instruct their wives, the sections on the duties of a father on how to relate to their children are nowhere to be found until modern times.[43] Most fathers agreed with Abelard, who, after he got Heloise pregnant, sent her away, admitting, "Who can bear the screams of children. . . . Who can tolerate the unclean and continuous soilings of babies?"[44] As Buchan wrote, "Men generally keep at such a distance from even the smallest acquaintance with the affairs of the nursery [and] is not ashamed to give directions concerning the management of his dogs or horses, yet would blush were he surprised in performing the same office for [his] heir."[45] Since children of the upper classes were sent out to a wet nurse and then to school, many adults could agree with Talleyrand when he stated that he "had never slept under the same roof with his father and mother."[46] Fathers were so distant that most could agree with the 18th-century French essayist, Alexis Vandermonde, who said, "One blushes to think of loving one's children."[47] When their children died, most fathers, like William Byrd, revealed no signs of grief, writing in their diaries the night of the death only that they had "good thoughts and good humor."[48] Should a father try to play with his child, he was unable to summon the empathy needed to understand the child's capacities, as seen in the following typical interaction:

> A gentleman was playing with his child of a year old, who began to cry. He ordered silence; the child did not obey; the father then began to whip it, but this terrified the child and increased its cries. . . . The father

---

42. Joy Wiltenburg, *Disorderly Women and Female Power in the Street Literature of Early Modern England and Germany.* Charlottesville: University Press of Virginia, 1992, pp. 86–92.

43. Joan Larsen Klein, Ed., *Daughters, Wives, and Widows: Writings by Men About Women and Marriage in England, 1500–1640.* Urbana: University of Illinois Press, 1992.

44. Peter Abelard, *History of My Misfortunes.* In David Herlihy, Ed., *Medieval Culture and Society.* New York: Harper & Row, 1968, p. 199.

45. Judith Schneid Lewis, *In the Family Way: Childbearing in the British Aristocracy, 1760–1860.* New Brunswick: Rutgers University Press, 1986, p. 26.

46. Hippolyte Taine, *The Ancient Regime.* New York: Peter Smith, 1931, p. 136.

47. Bogna W. Lorence, "Parents and Children in Eighteenth-Century Europe." *History of Childhood Quarterly* 2(1974): 1.

48. Michael Zuckerman, "William Byrd's Family." *Perspectives in American History* 12(1979): 256.

thought the child would be ruined unless it was made to yield, and renewed his chastisement with increased severity. . . . On undressing it, a pin was discovered sticking into its back.[49]

As early as the colonial period, American fathers were in the forefront of the new movement to pay some attention to their young children, even though the attention was punitive.[50] By the nineteenth century, some fathers actually began to relate to their children with empathy, yet even they were seen as rare, as when Grigorii Belinskii was described as "the only father in the city who understood that in raising children it is not necessary to treat them like cattle."[51] Even those who began at this time to criticize "paternal neglect" said it was the father's sole task "to teach his children to obey their mother."[52] It wasn't actually until late socializing-mode fathers came along that they actually began some caregiving, pushing prams and otherwise trying to live up to the New Fatherhood proclamations of the twentieth century.[53] In fact, even though there are some fathers today who are helping-mode parents and who spend equal time with their wives caring for their children,[54] various time surveys in America still show that working fathers on the average spend only about 12 to 18 minutes per day with their young children.[55] The gynarchy, it appears, still reigns supreme, and fathers around the world have yet to seriously embrace the tasks and joys of fatherhood.

49. Albertine Adrienne Necker, *Progressive Education, Commencing with the Infant.* Boston: W. D. Ticknor, 1835, p. 180.

50. Lisa Wilson, "'Ye Heart of a Father' Male Parenting in Colonial New England." *Journal of Family History* 24(1999): 255–274.

51. Patrick P. Dunn, "Fathers and Sons Revisited: The Childhood of Vissarion Belinskii." *History of Childhood Quarterly* 1(1974): 389.

52. Stephen M. Frank, *Life with Father: Parenthood and Masculinity in the Nineteenth-Century American North.* Baltimore and London: Johns Hopkins University Press, 1998, p. 37.

53. Ralph LaRossa, *The Modernization of Fatherhood: A Social and Political History.* Chicago: University of Chicago Press, 1997.

54. Suzanne Braun Levine, *Father Courage: What Happens When Men Put Family First.* New York: Harcourt, 2000.

55. John P. Robinson and Geoffrey Godbey, *Time For Life: The Surprising Ways Americans Use Their Time.* University Park: Pennsylvania State University Press, 1997; Michael E. Lamb et al., "A Biosocial Perspective on Paternal Behavior and Involvement." In Jane B. Lancaster, et al., Eds., *Parenting Across the Life Span: Biosocial Dimensions.* New York: Aldine de Gruyter, 1987, p. 126.

GIRLS HAD WORSE CHILDHOODS THAN BOYS

The problem with having only women raising children is that parenting is an emotionally demanding task, requiring considerable maturity, and throughout history girls have grown up universally despised and abused. When a girl was born, said the Hebrews, "the walls wept."[56] Japanese lullabies sang, "If it's a girl, stamp on her."[57] In medieval Muslim cultures "a grave used to be prepared, even before delivery, beside the woman's resting place [and] if the new-born was a female she was immediately thrown by her mother into the grave."[58] "Blessed is the door out of which goes a dead daughter" was a popular Italian proverb that was meant quite literally.[59] Fathers in particular hated having daughters: "If a girl was born, the father feels cruel disappointment. He is almost humiliated."[60] Girls from birth have everywhere been considered full of dangerous pollution—the projected hatred toward mothers of adults—and were therefore more often killed, exposed, abandoned, malnourished, raped, and neglected than boys. Everyone agreed girls should be fed less; as Jerome put it, "Let her meals always leave her hungry."[61] Girls usually spent much of their childhood trying to avoid being raped by their neighbors or employers and thereby being forced into lives of prostitution. To expect horribly abused girls to magically become mature, loving caregivers when as teenagers they are forced to go to live as virtual slaves in a strange family simply goes against the conclusions of every clinical study we have showing the disastrous effects of trauma upon the ability to mother.[62]

---

56. Barbara Kaye Greenleaf, *Children Through the Ages: A History of Childhood*. New York: McGraw-Hill, 1978, p. 7.

57. Muriel Jolivet, *Japan: The Childless Society?* London: Routledge, 1997, p. 27.

58. Avner Gil'adi, *Children of Islam: Concepts of Childhood in Medieval Muslim Society*. Houndsmells: Macmillan Academic, 1992, p. 108.

59. Charlotte Gower Chapman, *Molocca: A Sicilian Village*. Cambridge: Schenkman Publishing Co., 1971, p. 30.

60. Wally Seccombe, *A Millennium of Family Change: Feudalism to Capitalism in Northwestern Europe*. London: Verson, 1992, p. 108.

61. F. A. Wright, *Select Letters of St. Jerome*. Cambridge, MA: Harvard University Press, 1933, p. 357.

62. David DiLillo et al., "Linking Childhood Sexual Abuse and Abusive Parenting: The Mediating Role of Maternal Anger." *Child Abuse & Neglect* 24(2000): 767–779; Kathleen M. Fox and Brenda Gilbert, "The Interpersonal and Psychological Functioning of Women Who Experienced Childhood Physical Abuse, Incest, and Parental Alcoholism." *Child Abuse & Neglect* 18(1994): 849–858.

Mothers earlier in history often saw their children as their own screaming, needy, dominating mothers—forming what Nancy Chodorow terms a "hypersymbiotic relationship,"[63] wherein the child is expected to make up for all the love missing in the mother's own life, cure her depression, and restore her vitality. Like acutely disturbed destructive mothers in current clinical studies who "indifferently admit the desire to abuse, rape, mutilate, or kill a child, any child,"[64] mothers in the past feared their infants' crying so much they were determined, they said, to "never let a child have anything it cries for. . . . I think it right to withhold it steadily, however much the little creature may cry . . . and the habit of crying would be broken."[65] The need to shut up the mother's angry voice in babies led to their being tied up, neglected and beaten. Tiny infants were experienced as being so destructive that, according to Augustine, "If left to do what he wants, there is no crime he will not plunge into."[66] In fact, infants were felt to be so full of badness that when they died they were often buried under rain gutters so the water would wash off their sinful pollution.[67] An average mother in the past was like the extremely disturbed mother of today, whose "death wishes she harboured unconsciously towards her [own] mother are now experienced in relation to the child [so that] death pervades the relationship between mother and child [with the mother often reporting,] 'I can remember hurling the baby down on the pillows once, and just screaming, and not caring. I wanted to kill him really. . . . I hated the baby for constantly being there.'"[68] Many mothers today admit that they must struggle against feeling "dominated, exploited, humiliated, drained, and criticized by their babies," saying they sometimes "want to hurt them, get rid of them, squash them like a pancake, or beat them into silence."[69]

---

63. Nancy Chodorow, *Family Structure and Feminine Personality*. Stanford: Stanford University Press, 1974, p. 48.

64. Joseph C. Rheingold, *The Mother, Anxiety: and Death: The Catastrophic Death Complex*. Boston: Little, Brown and Co., 1967, p. 129.

65. Linda Pollock, *A Lasting Relationship: Parents and Children Over Three Centuries*. Hanover: University Press of New England, 1987, p. 68.

66. Elisabeth Badinter, *Mother Love: Myth and Reality*. New York: Macmillan, 1981, p. 30.

67. Danièle Alexandre-Bidon and Didier Lett, *Children in the Middle Ages: Fifth-Fifteenth Centuries*. Notre Dame: University of Notre Dame Press, 1999, p. 30.

68. Rozsika Parker, *Mother Love/Mother Hate: The Power of Maternal Ambivalence*. New York: Basic Books, 1995, p. 18.

69. Ibid., pp. 61, 118.

Mothers in the past, unfortunately, less often won the maternal love/hate struggle because their own formative years were so abusive. The baby in the past must not *need* anything, but must just give love solely to the emotionally deprived mother:

> Augustus Hare's account of his childhood provides an insight into such relationships. . . . He could never express a wish to his mother, as she would have thought it her duty to refuse it. "The will is the thing that needs to be brought into subjection," she said. . . . [Once] his mother, finding him much attached to a household cat, ceremoniously hanged the cat in the garden, so that he should have no object but her to love.[70]

Mothers hallucinated their children as maternal breasts with such intensity that they were constantly licking and sucking their faces, lips, breasts, and genitals,[71] feeling so needy from their own loveless childhoods that they expected their children to feed and care for them emotionally. Instead, mothers confessed: "Children eat you up. . . . You are sucked dry by them. . . . My children sucked me dry; all my vitality is gone."[72] Even when mothers nursed, they rarely looked at or talked to their babies, because they felt they could not afford to invest their emotions in them: "[The mother] has been able to avoid developing a close personal bond. . . . If it should die, she would lose a part of herself—which can always be replaced by another child—and not a being whom she loves."[73] It is only when one recognizes mothers' own severe neglect and abuse and the extent to which their babies are poison containers for their feelings that one can begin to understand why mothers in the past routinely killed, neglected, and abused their children. What is miraculous—and what is the source of most social progress—is that mothers throughout history have slowly and successfully struggled with their fear and hatred with little help from others and have managed to evolve the loving, empathic child rearing one can find in many families around the world today.

---

70. Gordon Rattray Taylor, *The Angel Makers: A Study in the Psychological Origins of Historical Change 1750–1850*. New York: E. P. Dutton & Co., 1974, p. 318.

71. Lloyd deMause, *Foundations of Psychohistory*, p. 19; Alenka Puhar, "Childhood In Nineteenth-Century Slovenia." *The Journal of Psychohistory* 21 (1985): 309.

72. Elisabeth Badinter, *Mother Love: Myth and Reality*, pp. 314–315.

73. Paul Parin et al., *Fear Thy Neighbor as Thyself*. Chicago: University of Chicago Press, 1980, p. 151.

CHILD SACRIFICE AS PUNISHMENT FOR SUCCESS

The act of having a child, says Rheingold, is "the most forbidden act of self-realization, the ultimate and least pardonable offense," and brings with it inevitable fears of maternal retribution for one's success and individuation.[74] Mothers in antiquity hallucinated female demons—Lamia, Gorgo, Striga, Empusa—who were actually grandmother alters in the mothers' heads, so jealous of their having babies that they sucked out their blood and otherwise murdered them.[75] So fearful were they of the avenging spirits (alters) of their mothers, that women in antiquity would wear amulets to protect them in childbirth from Lilith, the child killer, and would write on the wall of the birthroom: "Out Lilith!"[76] Even today, peasant villages often fear the outbreak of "angry, malevolent, dangerous" hallucinations that surround the newborn and threaten the mother and keep the nursery room boarded up with the door barred to prevent the intrusion of dangerous grandmother-spirits.[77] All early societies invented sacrificial rituals wherein babies were tortured and killed to honor maternal goddesses, from Anit to Kali, vowing that, as one contemporary mother felt: "Although Mommy wants to kill me for having sex and making a baby, if I kill the baby instead [usually the first-born was sacrificed], I can then go on having sex and other babies with less fear of retribution."

The severely immature parents of the past felt under such constant threat by malevolent forces—maternal alters—that their own children were constantly being used as poison containers for their disowned feelings. As one informant in a contemporary rural Greek community said, "When you're angry, a demon gets inside of you. Only if a pure individual passes by, like a child for instance, will the bad leave you, for it will fall on the

74. Joseph C. Rheingold, *The Fear of Being a Woman*, p. 227.

75. Ovid, *Fasti*, 329; S. Vernon McCasland, *By the Finger of God; Demon Possession and Exorcism in Early Christianity in the Light of Modern Views of Mental Illness.* New York: Macmillan, 1951, p. 97.

76. Raphael Patai, *The Hebrew Goddess.* New York: Ktav Publishing House, 1967, pp. 227–228.

77. Alenka Puhar, "Childhood In Nineteenth-Century Slovenia," *The Journal of Psychohistory* 12(1985): 294; J. K. Campbell, *Honour, Family and Patronage.* Oxford: Oxford University Press, 1964, p. 154.

unpolluted."[78] The dynamics are clear: the "demon . . . inside you" is the alter; the "unpolluted child" is the poison container. A typical child sacrifice for parental success can be seen in Carthage, where archaeologists have found a child cemetery called the Tophet that is filled with over 20,000 urns containing bones of children sacrificed by the parents, who would make a vow to kill their next child if the gods would grant them a favor— for instance, if their shipment of goods were to arrive safely in a foreign port.[79] They placed their children alive in the arms of a bronze statue of "the lady Tanit. . . . The hands of the statue extended over a brazier into which the child fell once the flames had caused its limbs to contract and its mouth to open. . . . The child was alive and conscious when burned. . . . Philo specified that the sacrificed child was best-loved."[80]

Child sacrifice was the foundation of all great religions, depicted in myths as absolutely necessary to save the world from "chaos," that is, from terrible inner annihilation anxiety as punishment for success. Despite the denunciations of child sacrifice by Hebrew prophets, ancient Jews continued to "pass their children through the fire."[81] Maccoby's book, *The Sacred Executioner: Human Sacrifice and the Legacy of Guilt*, portrays the entire history of religion as dramas featuring a vengeful, bloodthirsty sacred executioner, demonstrating that the role of children, from Isaac to Christ, was to act as a sacrifice for the sins of the parents.[82] Behind even male gods demanding sacrifice are avenging terrible mothers of death, says Lederer—Belili, Inanna, Tiamat, Ishtar, Astarte, Lilith, Hathor-Sekhmet, Izanami, Chicomecoatl—all dangerous mother alters in the brains of the new parents, demanding revenge for the hubris of daring to be a parent.[83] The wealthier and more successful the family, the more

---

78. Richard and Eva Blum, *The Dangerous Hour: The Lore of Crisis and Mystery in Rural Greece*. London: Chatto & Windus, 1970, p. 55.

79. Lawrence E. Stager and Samuel R. Wolff, "Child Sacrifice at Carthage: Religious Rite or Population Control?" *Biblical Archeological Review*, January 1984, pp. 31–46.

80. Shelby Brown, *Late Carthaginian Child Sacrifice and Sacrificial Monuments in their Mediterranean Context*. Sheffield: Sheffield Academic Press, 1991, pp. 22–23.

81. H. Abt-Garrison, *The History of Pediatrics*. Philadelphia: W. B. Saunders Co., 1965, p. 29.

82. Hyam Maccoby, *The Sacred Executioner: Human Sacrifice and the Legacy of Guilt*. New York: Thames and Hudson, 1982.

83. Wolfgang Lederer, *The Fear of Women*. New York: Grune & Stratton, 1968, p. 126; John Day, *Molech: A God of Human Sacrifice in the Old Testament*. Cambridge: Cambridge University Press, 1989; Lloyd deMause, "The History of Child Assault." *The Journal of Psychohistory* 18(1990): 3–29.

children had to be sacrificed to the goddess, representing the infant's furious grandmother.[84]

Child sacrifices have been found from the beginning of human history: decapitated skeletons of early hominid children have been found, with evidence of cannibalism, as their parents ate them on behalf of the spirits of their life-devouring grandmothers[85]; young children were buried with their skulls split by an ax at Woodhenge/Stonehenge[86]; decapitated infant sacrifices to the Great Goddess were found at Jericho[87]; the bones of sacrificed children have been discovered in most of the Stone Circles of Britain[88]; early Arabians sacrificed their daughters to "the mothers"[89]; the serpent goddess of the Aztecs demanded skull and heart sacrifice of children, including the eating of the children's bodies and covering themselves with their blood[90]; Mayan and Incan sacrificed children are still being discovered in the South American mountains, along with children who have been killed by drug dealers to ward off revenge for their successful cocaine runs.[91] In India, child sacrifice was widespread, and children were still being thrown to the sharks as a sacrificial offering to the Goddess into the nineteenth century.[92] The need to sacrifice children to ward off fears of success was so powerful that right through medieval times, when people built new buildings, walls, or bridges, little children were sealed in them alive as "foundation sacrifices" to ward off the angry, avenging spirits.[93]

84. Lawrence E. Stager, "The Rite of Child Sacrifice at Carthage." In John G. Pedley, *New Light on Ancient Carthage*. Ann Arbor: University of Michigan Press, 1980, pp. 6–7.

85. E. L. Simons, "Human Origins." *Science* 245(1989): 1344.

86. Timothy Taylor, *The Prehistory of Sex*. New York: Bantam Books, 1996, p. 189.

87. Sibylle von Cles-Reden, *The Realm of the Great Goddess: The Story of the Megalith Builders*. Englewood Cliffs: Prentice-Hall, 1962, p. 21.

88. Aubrey Burl, *The Stone Circles of Britain, Ireland, and Brittany*. New Haven: Yale University Press, 2000, p. 192.

89. Evelyn Reed, *Woman's Evolution from Matriarchal Clan to Patriarchal Family*. New York: Pathfinder Press, 1975, p. 408.

90. Max Shein, *The Precolumbian Child*. Culver City: Labyrinthos, 1992, p. 97.

91. Celia Carey, "Secrets: The Incas Appeased Mountain Gods with Their Children's Lives." *Discovering Archeology* July/August 1999: 44–53.

92. Ibid., p. 77.

93. H. S. Darlington, "Ceremonial Behaviorism: Sacrifices for the Foundation of Houses." *The Psychoanalytic Review* 18(1931): 309–327.

Often when children died in the past from natural causes, the sources often reveal a deep satisfaction by the parents. Sometimes adults recalled their mother's death wishes in their memoirs—a typical passage occurs when Leopardi remembers clearly of his mother that

> when she saw the death of one of her infants approaching, she experienced a deep happiness, which she attempted to conceal only from those who were likely to blame her. . . . When, as several times happened, she seemed likely to lose an infant child, she did not pray God that it should die, since religion forbids it, but she did in fact rejoice.[94]

Over and over again death wishes are revealed in the historical sources, breaking out when adults interact with children. Epictetus admitted, "What harm is there if you whisper to yourself, at the very moment you are kissing your child, and say, 'Tomorrow you will die'?"[95] Another recalled his mother tucking him into bed nightly with the words: "Soon my son you will exchange the bed for the grave, and your clothes for a winding sheet."[96] Mothers were genuinely convinced that their children were born irredeemably evil, as the mother who, Winthrop says, "drowned her child that it might escape damnation."[97]

The deaths of children were rarely mourned: mothers were commonly reported to have "regarded the death of various daughters at school with great equanimity," and father(s) to "cheerfully remark when two of his fifteen children died that he still had left a baker's dozen."[98] Often adults recorded in their diaries a vow to have "the Lord" (the parent's parental alter) kill the child, as Cotton Mather did as one of his children died:

> I resigned the Child unto the Lord; my Will was extinguished. I could say, *My Father, Kill my Child, if it be thy Pleasure to do so.* . . . I had rather have him dy in his Infancy, than live in cursed and lothsome Wickedness. . . . [my dead child is] a *Family-Sacrifice.* . . . I would en-

---

94. Iris Origo, *Leopari: A Study in Solitude.* London: Hamish Hamilton, 1953, p. 16.
95. Epictetus, *Discourses,* 2, 213.
96. Bertram Wyatt-Brown, *Yankee Saints and Southern Sinners.* Baton Rouge: Louisiana State University Press, 1985, p. 14.
97. Perry Miller, *The New England Mind: The Seventeenth Century.* Boston: Beacon Press, 1954, p. 56.
98. Ferdinand Mount, *The Subversive Family.* London: Jonathan Cape, 1982, p. 109.

deavour exceedingly to glorify God, by making a Sacrifice of the lovely Child.[99]

INFANTICIDE AS CHILD SACRIFICE TO THE GRANDMOTHER

Mothers who feel like killing their newborn children today are found to be deeply depressed and lonely, because, according to Rheingold's study of 350 filicidal mothers,

> It is only the fear of being a woman that can create the infanticidal impulse. . . . Having a child is the most forbidden act of self-realization. . . . Punishment is inescapable and punishment means annihilation. . . . To appease the mother she must destroy the child, but the child is a love object too. To preserve the child she must renounce mother. . . . She is trapped in a desperate conflict: kill mother and preserve the baby or kill the baby and preserve the mother.[100]

Mothers in the past routinely chose killing the baby, by the billions.

In my study "The Demography of Filicide," I have shown that boy/girl sex ratios from census and other sources in European history ranged from as high as 400/100 to 140/100 in the Middle Ages.[101] With Indian and Chinese boy/girl ratios in the nineteenth century running at 300/100 and higher,[102] and with current Asian statistics still showing over 200 million girls "missing" in the census figures,[103] I have determined that it is likely that overall infanticide rates of both sexes exceeded 30 percent in antiquity and only slowly declined to the small rate of advanced societies

---

99. Cotton Mather, *Diary of Cotton Mather. Vol. 1*. New York: Frederick Ungar, n.d., pp. 7, 187, 374.

100. Joseph Rheingold, *The Fear of Being a Woman*, pp. 143, 157.

101. Lloyd deMause, *Foundations of Psychohistory*, pp. 26–31, 109–131; William Tarn and G. T. Griffith, *Helenistic Civilizations*, 3rd ed. London: Edward Arnold, 1952, p. 28; David Herlihy, *Medieval and Renaissance Pistoia: The Social History of an Italian Town, 1200–1430*. New Haven: Yale University Press, 1967, p. 38; David Herlihy, *Medieval Households*. Cambridge: Harvard University Press, 1985, p. 66.

102. Kanti B. Pakrasi, *Female Infanticide in India*. Calcutta, 1971, p. 88; Mildred Dickemann, "Female Infanticide . . ." In Napoleon A. Chagnon and William Irons, *Evolutionary Biology and Human Social Behavior*. North Scituate: Duxbury Press, 1972, p. 341.

103. *The New York Times*, November 5, 1991, p. C1; Karin Evans, *The Lost Daughters of China*. New York: Putnam, 2000, p. 118.

Fig. 8–1. Mother commits infanticide with help of her devil alter

today.[104] Multiplying these infanticide rates by the 80 billion human births in the past 100,000 years[105]—80 percent of them occurring before 1750, and even more of them occurring in areas with high Asian-style infanticide rates—a weighted average infanticide rate likely been at least 15 percent, or billions of newborn babies killed.

Even this astonishing figure is not the whole story of infanticide, however. Every study of infant death rates among children sent out to wet nurses and abandoned in foundling homes shows much higher death rates, running to over 70 percent, even in modern times.[106] Doctors throughout history agreed that "the most profound cause of the terrific waste of infant life [is] neglect . . . neglected by their own mothers and neglected by the nurses to whom they were abandoned."[107] Since parents who sent their

---

104. Lloyd deMause, *Foundations of Psychohistory*, p. 122; see chart in Chapter 6 of this book.

105. Massimo Livi Bacci, *A Concise History of World Population*. Malden: Blackwell, 1997, p. 32. Larry S. Milner, *Hardness of Heart/Hardness of Life. The Stain of Human Infanticide*. Lanham: University Press of America, 2000, p. 11, estimates 7 billion children killed.

106. George Frederic Still, *The History of Paediatrics*. London: Oxford University Press, 1931, p. 385.

107. Bogna W. Lorence, "Parents and Children in Eighteenth-Century Europe." *History of Childhood Quarterly* 2(1974): 11.

children to wet nurses and foundling homes knew quite well they would likely not see them again—indeed, often they were sent to so-called killing wet nurses with a small sum of money under the tacit assumption that they would not be returned[108]—these delayed-infanticide acts must be added to the estimated rate of child killing, increasing it by at the very least a third. No wonder people in the past so often said that everywhere in their areas "you could hear coming out of the bottom of latrines and ponds and rivers the groanings of the children that one had thrown there."[109]

Although poverty played some part in this holocaust of children, it is doubtful if it was the main cause of child deaths. When, for instance, Arabs dug a grave next to the birthing place of every new mother so "if the newborn child was a female she could be immediately thrown by her mother into the grave,"[110] it was hatred of girls, not poverty, that was the motive. Second, if scarce resources were the main cause, then wealthy parents should kill less than poor parents. But the historical record shows exactly the opposite: historical boy/girl ratios are *higher* among wealthy parents,[111] where economic necessity is not a problem. Even in early modern England, the infant mortality rates for wealthy children were higher than the same rates for ordinary farmers, day laborers, and craftsman.[112] Third, many wealthy high civilizations such as Greece, Rome, China, India, Hawaii, and Tahiti are very infanticidal, especially among their elite classes. As one visitor to Hawaii reported, there probably wasn't a single mother who didn't throw one or more of her children to the sharks.[113] There were even societies where virtually *all* newborns were killed to satisfy their overwhelming infanti-

---

108. Lloyd deMause, *Foundations of Psychohistory*, p. 32.

109. Jacques Léauté, "L'infanticide a la fin du Moyen Age . . ." *Revue historique de droit francais et étranger* 50(1972): 232.

110. Avner Gil'adi, *Children of Islam: Concepts of Childhood in Medieval Muslim Society*. Hampshire: Macmillan, 1992, p. 108.

111. See my summary of evidence in Lloyd deMause, "On Writing Childhood History." *The Journal of Psychohistory* 16(1988): 150; Richard Trexler, "Infanticide in Florence." *History of Childhood Quarterly* 1(1974): 353–365; Emily Coleman, "L'infanticide dans le Haut Moyen Age," *Annales: Economies, Societes, Civilisations* (1974): 315–335; Henri Bresc, "Europe: Town and Country (Thirteenth-Fifteenth Century)." In André Burguière et al., *A History of the Family. Vol. One*. Cambridge: Harvard University Press, 1996, p. 457.

112. S. Ryan Johansson, "Centuries of Childhood/Centuries of Parenting." *Journal of Family History* 12(1987): 358.

113. Nigel Davies, *Human Sacrifice in History and Today*. New York: William Morrow, p. 192.

cidal needs, and children had to be imported from adjoining groups to continue the society.[114] Finally, many nations—like Japan until recently—kill
their children selectively in order to balance out an equal number of boys
and girls, a practice called *mabiki*, or "thinning out" the less promising
ones,[115] again revealing a quite different motive other than the economic.
It is most certainly not economics that causes so many depressed women
on the delivery tables even today to cry out and implore their mothers not
to kill them after they have given birth.[116] Women since the beginning of
time have felt that their children really belonged to God—a symbol of the
grandmother—and that "the child was a gift that God had every right to
reclaim."[117] When killing her child, therefore, the mother was simply acting as her own mother's avenger.

We are left, unfortunately, with what one psychoanalyst calls our
"universal resistance to acknowledging the mother's filicidal drives, undoubtedly the most dreaded and uncanny truth for us to face."[118] Our only
defenses are denial and dissociation, like people in the past, who regularly
dissociated from the emotional impact of their murder of their innocent
little children with sayings such as: "Do we not cast away from us our spittle,
lice and such which are engendered out of our own selves," or "Mad dogs
we knock on the head [and] we drown even children at birth," or "When
children die there is no need to get excited. . . . One is born every year. . . .
Live and let die."[119] Both mothers and fathers knew their own parents
demanded a death; both struggled against the grandparents' dire threat to
kill them if they dared to became parents themselves. What helped the
dissociation were such beliefs as denying that the babies were human; so
during most of history, East and West, if the mother would kill the new-

114. Larry S. Milner, *Hardness of Heart*, p. 143.
115. Lloyd deMause, "The History of Childhood in Japan." *The Journal of Psychohistory* 15(1987): 149.
116. Joseph Rheingold, *The Fear of Being a Woman,* p. 38.
117. Deborah Willis, *Malevolent Nurture*, p. 60.
118. Arnold Rascovsky, "On the Genesis of Acting Out and Psychopathic Behavior
in Sophocles' *Oedipus.*" *International Journal of Psycho-Analysis* 49(1968): 390.
119. Bartholomey Batty, *The Christian Man's Closet*. 1581, p. 28; Seneca, *Moral Essays*,
145; Regina Schulte, "Infanticide in Rural Bavaria in the Nineteenth Century." In Hans
Medick and David Warren Sabean, *Interest and Emotion: Essays on the Study of Family and
Kinship*. Cambridge: Cambridge University Press, 1984, p. 91.

born before it took any nourishment, it wasn't considered "really born"; it just wasn't thought to be human yet.[120]

Usually it was the mother or one of the other women of the gynarchy who did the killing, in the past as in the present,[121] usually violently, smashing in the baby's head, crushing it between her knees, asphyxiating it against her breasts, sitting on it, or throwing it alive into the privy, with the mother sometimes earning the nickname of "child-stabber" or "child-crusher."[122] It helped to have gynecological writings like Soranus's on "How to Recognize the Newborn that Is Worth Rearing" to rationalize the infanticide.[123] It helped to share the blame for the murder with your children, who were often forced to help the mother kill their newborn siblings.[124] It helped to have demonic beliefs like those still held in rural Greece that Evil Spirits had turned the newborn into a changeling, a demon baby, a *Striga*, which must be strangled.[125] The mother's struggle against the urge to kill her children was (and is) usually a conscious one, and the role of the dissociated parental alter is often evident—as when mothers today tell therapists that "someone keeps talking to me in my mind telling me to choke my daughter" or as when Medea struggled against killing her children, saying, "I know what wickedness I am about to do; but the *thumos* is stronger than my purposes."[126]

Opposition by society to infanticide was negligible until modern times. Jews considered any child who died within thirty days after birth, even by violence, to have been a miscarriage.[127] Most ancient societies openly ap-

---

120. David Herlihy, *Medieval Households*, p. 54; Hiroshi Wagatsuma, "Child Abandonment and Infanticide: A Japanese Case." In Jill E. Korbin, Ed., *Child Abuse and Neglect: Cross-Cultural Perspectives*. Berkeley: University of California Press, 1981, p. 131.

121. Maria W. Piers, *Infanticide*. New York: W. W. Norton, 1978, p. 41; Larry S. Milner, *Hardness of Heart*, p. 126; Georges Duby, *The Knight, the Lady and the Priest: The Making of Modern Marriage in Medieval France*. New York: Pantheon Books, 1983, p. 66.

122. Muriel Jolivet, *Japan: The Childless Society?*, p. 120.

123. Soranus, *Gynecology*, 79.

124. Marjorie Shostak, *Nisa: The Life and Words of a !Kung Woman*. Cambridge: Harvard University Press, 1981, p. 54.

125. Lyndal Roper, *Oedipus and the Devil*, p. 1; Richard and Eva Blum, *Health and Healing in Rural Greece: A Study of Three Communities*. Stanford: Stanford University Press, 1965, p. 73.

126. Joseph Rheingold, *The Fear of being a Woman*, p. 65; E. R. Dodds, *The Greeks and the Irrational*. Berkeley: University of California Press, 1964, p. 61, 186.

127. Immanuel Jakobovits, "Jewish Views on Infanticide." In Marvin Kohl, Ed., *Infanticide and the Value of Life*. Buffalo: Prometheus Books, 1978, p. 24.

proved of infanticide, more for girls, saying, "If it is a girl, cast it out."[128] In Sparta, the city kept a special pit called the Apothetai into which newborn were thrown when they were deemed not worthy of living.[129] As has been previously mentioned, Christians were spoken of as odd because "they do not practice the exposure of new-born babes."[130] Although Roman law, in response to Christianity, made infanticide a capital offense in 374 C.E., no cases have been found punishing it.[131] Anglo-Saxons actually considered infanticide a virtue, not a crime, saying, "A child cries when he comes into the world, for he anticipates its wretchedness. It is well for him that he should die. . . . He was placed on a slanting roof [and] if he laughed, he was reared, but if he was frightened and cried, he was thrust out to perish."[132] Philo describes what everyone in antiquity was familiar with—places where exposed children were eaten by "all the beasts that feed in human flesh [who] visit the spot and feast unhindered on the infants [thrown away] by their fathers and mothers."[133] Prosecutions for infanticide before the modern period were rare.[134] Even medieval penitentials excused mothers who killed their newborn if they did so before feeding them.[135] By Puritan times, a few mothers began being hanged for infanticide.[136] But even in the nineteenth century it was still "not an uncommon spectacle to see the corpses of infants lying in the streets or on the dunghills of London and other large cities.[137] The English at the end of the century had over 7 mil-

---

128. Robert Rousselle, "'If it is a Girl, Cast it Out:' Infanticide/Exposure in Ancient Greece." *The Journal of Psychohistory* 28(2001): 302–333.

129. Cynthia B. Patterson, *The Family in Greek History*. Cambridge: Harvard University Press, 1998, p. 74.

130. Arnold Toynbee, *The Crucible of Christianity*. New York: World Publishing Co., p. 296.

131. Valerie French, "Children in Antiquity." In Joseph Hawes, Ed., *Children in Historical and Comparative Perspective*. New York: Greenwood Press, 1991, p. 21.

132. John Thrupp, *The Anglo-Saxon Home: A History of the Domestic Institutions and Customs of England*. London: Longman, Green, 1862, p. 78.

133. Philo, *Works. Vol. VII*. Cambridge: Harvard University Press, 1929, p. 549.

134. R. Po-Chia Hsia, *The Myth of Ritual Murder: Jews and Magic in Reformation Germany*. New Haven: Yale University Press, 1988, p. 153.

135. Rob Meens, "Children and Confession in the Early Middle Ages." In Diana Wood, Ed., *The Church and Childhood*. London: Blackwell Publishers, 1994, p. 57.

136. Lyle Koehler, *A Search for Power: The 'Weaker Sex' in Seventeenth-Century New England*. Urbana: University of Illinois Press, 1980, p. 200.

137. Daniel Beekman, *The Mechanical Baby: A Popular History of the Theory and Practice of Child Raising*. Westport: Lawrence Hill, 1977, p. 47.

lion children enrolled in burial insurance societies; since infant mortality rates were around 50 percent, parents could easily collect the insurance by killing their child. As one doctor said, "Sudden death in infants is too common a circumstance to be brought before the attention of the coroner. . . . Free medical care for children was refused. . . . 'No, thank you, he is in two burial clubs' was a frequent reply to offers of medical assistance for a sick child. Arsenic was a favorite poison."[138]

Century after century, the children in traditional societies who survived remembered the cries of their murdered brothers and sisters, feared their murderous parents, believed themselves unworthy of living and irredeemably bad, and grew up to inflict the killings on their own children.

MUTILATING CHILDREN'S BODIES

The propensity of preliterate tribes to cut, burn, and otherwise mutilate the bodies of their children has often been documented, particularly the role of genital mutilation, where during initiation rites boys' penises are sliced open under the conviction that it was necessary to expel the "mothers blood and bad words" that had lodged in them. Both circumcision of boys and mutilation of girls' genitals are found in many tribal groups, so the ritual probably was practiced as far back as the Paleolithic era. In fact, the need to mutilate children's bodies is found in nearly all cultures in some form, and may be seen in the Paleolithic caves where handprints on the walls[139] show that children's fingers were cut off in the widespread belief by many cultures that animal spirits demanded a child's finger to appease their wrath.[140] These finger sacrifice rituals have been found in many cultures, and sanctuaries have been found as far back as the Neolithic era containing finger bones, right up through antiquity, when finger sacrifice rituals were performed to pacify pursuing demons.[141]

138. George K. Behlmer, *Child Abuse and Moral Reform in England, 1870–1908.* Stanford: Stanford University Press, 1982, p. 131; Joseph C. Rheingold, *The Fear of Being a Woman*, p. 72.

139. Armando R. Favazza, *Bodies Under Siege*. Baltimore: Johns Hopkins University Press, 1987, p. 106.

140. Evelyn Reed, *Woman's Evolution: From Matriarchal Clan to Patriarchal Family*. New York: Pathfinder, 1974, p. 250.

141. Walter Burkert, *Creation of the Sacred: Tracks of Biology in Early Religions*. Cambridge: Harvard University Press, 1996, pp. 37–39.

But more often it is the genitals, head, or feet of children that are assaulted. Few mothers even today are free of dreams in which their babies are badly hurt, though most are able to laugh off the impulses and perhaps only be overprotective toward their infants. But Rheingold's clinical studies reveal many mothers ward off maternal retribution for having the baby by what he terms a "mutilation impulse," which he finds mainly directed toward the genitals of the boy and girl and toward the "insides" of the girl's body, producing in boys severe castration anxieties and "a fear of femaleness" in girls.[142]

Cutting off parts or all of the girl's genitals has been a widespread practice in many cultures,[143] possibly reaching back to Paleolithic times since a stone knife was often used. It is still practiced in tribes from Africa to Australia, where the girl's vagina is torn open with a stone knife and the child is then gang raped.[144] Historical evidence dates from ancient Egypt, where mummies have been found with clitoral excision and labial fusions,[145] and Greek physicians like Soranos and Aetius regularly advocated the removal of a girl's clitoris if it was "overly large" so she would not be overly lustful.[146]

There are over 100 million Arab females today who have had their genitals chopped off, having been told that "if the clitoris is left alone, it will grow and drag on the ground, and if left uncircumcised, they will be wild and . . . grow up horny."[147] Often the girl's labia are cut off in addition to the clitoris, and the remaining flesh is sewn together, leaving only a small opening for urination. The vagina must therefore be cut open again before intercourse, and the women have great difficulty giving birth and often must be further cut to allow the baby to pass through.

During the mutilations—usually done at around the age of 6 with rusty knives by the women of the gynarchy—the girls undergo excruciating pain,

---

142. Joseph C. Rheingold, *The Fear of Being a Woman*, pp. 85–88.

143. James DeMeo, *Saharasia*. Greensprings: Orgone Biophysical Research Lab, 1998, p. 125.

144. Nigel Davies, *The Rampant God: Eros Throughout the World*. New York: William Morrow, 1984, p. 46.

145. Sarah Blaffer Hrdy, *The Woman That Never Evolved*. Cambridge: Harvard University Press, 1983, p. 183.

146. Bernadette J. Brooten, *Love Between Women*. Chicago: University of Chicago Press, 1996, p. 170; Marilyn French, *The War Against Women*. New York: Summit Books, 1992, p. 109.

147. Linda Burstyn, "Female Circumcision Comes to America." *Atlantic Monthly*, October 1995, p. 30.

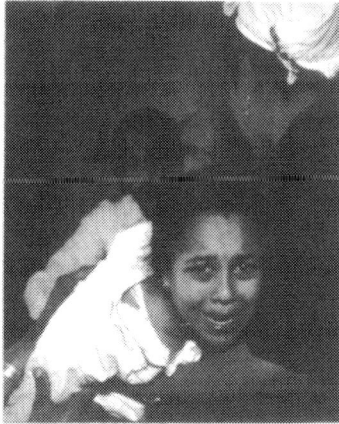

Fig. 8–2. A girl in Cairo is mutilated by her mother

sometimes die of complications, usually hemorrhage, and often pass out from the shock since no anesthetic is used.[148] The ritual—which is not a religious rite and is nowhere mentioned in the Koran—is accompanied by the joyful chanting of the women, who shout: "Now you are a woman"; "Bring her the groom now"; "Bring her a penis, she is ready for intercourse."[149] They act out in manic ritual Rheingold's observation that destructive mothers "seem to have the urge to destroy [their] daughter's femaleness: her external genitals, her 'insides' . . . her total sexuality."[150] It is not surprising that the overwhelming majority of circumcised girls grow up to be frigid. Female circumcision was practiced historically in various groups from Russia to Latin America[151] and was even inflicted on girls "who

148. Olayinka Koso-Thomas, *The Circumcision of Women: A Strategy for Eradication.* London: Zed Books, 1987; Cathy Joseph, "Compassionate Accountability: An Embodied Consideration of Female Genital Mutilation." *The Journal of Psychohistory* 24(1996): 1–17; Lloyd deMause, "The Universality of Incest," *The Journal of Psychohistory* 19(1991): 161; Hanny Lightfoot-Klein, *Prisoners of Ritual: An Odyssey into Female Genital Circumcision in Africa.* New York: Harrington Park Press, 1989.

149. John G. Kennedy, "Circumcision and Excision in Egyptian Nubia." *Man* 5(1970): 180.

150. Joseph C. Rheingold, *The Fear of Being a Woman*, p. 227.

151. Marielouise Janssen-Jurreit, *Sexism: The Male Monopoly on History and Thought.* New York: Farrar Straus & Giroux, 1982, p. 247.

masturbated too much" in Europe and America in the nineteenth century, using a red hot iron to burn away the little girl's clitoris.[152] Strabo stated that female genital mutilation was performed by the Jews, and early Christian folklore even assumed that the Virgin Mary was circumcised like other Jewish girls of the time.[153]

Circumcision for boys might be thought of as less traumatic since it involves only removal of the foreskin, a less serious mutilation. Yet in many cultures circumcision of boys is quite painful, as when Moslem boys are circumcised between the ages of 3 and 7 in a bloody ceremony, after which "he is placed on his mother's naked back [so] that his bleeding penis presses against her."[154] That this ceremony is connected with the incestuous feelings of the mother is apparent from the fact that genital mutilation is far more likely found in societies where the little boy sleeps with his mother while the father sleeps elsewhere.[155] Circumcision of boys—practiced from Egypt and Africa to Peru and Polynesia[156]—makes them into "little mothers," with the peeling away of the foreskin uncovering the glans so that it can act as a maternal nipple. That circumcision of boys is still practiced so often in America is a testimony to the continuing ubiquity of parental assault on the sexuality of children.[157]

But the more serious genital mutilation of boys that occurred throughout history, East and West, was castration. Eunuchs were found in most cultures, beginning as a sacrificial rite to early goddesses: "Piles of freshly severed genitals lay beneath the altars in Egyptian temples, where hundreds

152. Andrew Scull and Diane Favreau, "The Clitoridectomy Craze." *Social Research* 53(1986): 243–260; Uta Ranke-Heinemann, *Eunuchs for the Kingdom of Heaven,* New York: Doubleday, 1990, p. 318.

153. Strabo, *Geography* 16.2.37 and 16.4.9; Allen Edwards, *Erotica Judaica: A Sexual History of the Jews.* New York: Julian Press, 1967, p. 28.

154. Vincent Crapanzano, "Rite of Return: Circumcision in Morocco." In Werner Muensterberger and L. Bryce Boyer, Eds., *The Psychoanalytic Study of Society 9.* New York: Psychohistory Press, 1981, p. 29.

155. Michio Kitahara. "A Cross-Cultural Test of the Freudian Theory of Circumcision." *International Journal of Psychoanalytic Psychotherapy* 5(1976): 535–546.

156. Reay Tannahill, *Flesh and Blood: A History of the Cannibal Complex.* Boston: Little, Brown and Co., 1996, p. 41.

157. David L. Gollaher, "From Ritual to Science: The Medical Transformation of Circumcision in America." *Journal of Social History* 28(1994): 5–35.

of virile youths were initiated daily into male prostitution."[158] In addition, castration was necessary to satisfy the men who preferred hairless castrated boys to rape, plus all those used as harem keepers, palace officials, boy singers, actors, and many other roles thought to require castrates.[159] Nero was said to enjoy the use of eunuchs in his orgies, even marrying one of them.[160] When parents sent their boys to aristocratic households for sexual use, they were said to sometimes cut off their genitals and keep them in a jar.[161] Eunuchs were especially popular in Byzantium, while in the West Verdun was widely known as "the great eunuch factory." Infants were castrated "in the cradle" to be used in brothels by men who liked raping small castrated boys.[162] In some Italian towns, boys who were destined for the clergy were castrated at an early age; in Naples, signs hung above stores, "Boys castrated here."[163] Peter Brown concludes that among early Christians "castration was a routine operation."[164] Many cultures around the world have castrated boys when they were just infants, claiming they "really wanted" to be girls. They were then used as women, sexually and otherwise, when they grew up, as in the *hijras* of India or the *berdaches* of American Indian tribes.[165] The testicles of these boys were either torn from them, crushed, or seared off them with red-hot irons, usually between the ages of 3 and 7; in China, "both the penis and scrotum were removed with one cut."[166] Castration of boys continued until recently in areas of the Middle

158. Allen Edwards, *The Jewel in the Lotus: A Historical Survey of the Sexual Culture of the East.* New York: Julian Press, 1959, p. 187.

159. Charles Humana, *The Keeper of the Bed: The Story of the Eunuch.* London: Arlington Books, 1973; Anon., *Praeputii Incisio.* New York: The Panurge Press, 1931, p. 129.

160. Peter Tompkins, *The Eunuch and the Virgin.* New York: Clarkson N. Potter, Inc., 1962, p. 25.

161. Taisuke Mitamura, *Chinese Eunuchs: The Structure of Intimate Politics.* Rutland: Charles Tuttle, 1970, p. 36.

162. Lloyd deMause, *Foundations of Psychohistory*, p. 54.

163. Patricia A. Quinn, *Better Than the Sons of Kings: Boys and Monks in the Early Middle Ages.* New York: Peter Lang, 1989, p. 55; Richard C. Trexler, *Sex and Conquest.* Ithaca: Cornell University Press, 1995, p. 39; Albrecht Peiper, *Chronik der Kinderheilkunde.* Leipzig, 1966, p. 148.

164. Peter Brown, *The Body and Society: Men, Women and Sexual Renunciation in Early Christianity.* New York: Columbia University Press, 1988, p. 168.

165. Gilbert Herdt, Ed., *Third Sex, Third Gender: Beyond Sexual Dimorphism in Culture and History.* New York: Zone Books, 1994.

166. Vern L. Bullough, *Sexual Variance in Society and History.* Chicago: University of Chicago Press, 1976, p. 306.

East, followed by burial of the mutilated boy in hot sand for several days to reduce hemorrhage—only one in five surviving the bloody operation.[167] Some societies had variations of circumcision that approached castration, as in some Arab tribes where they performed *salkh*, which "consisted of flaying and removing all of the skin of the penis."[168]

The ancients' more usual assault on boys' genitals, however—called infibulation—was less painful. Since they were so deprived of maternal love, ancients saw the boy's glans as an exciting nipple ("It strikes terror and wonder in the heart of man") and felt they needed to hide it in little boys, so they drew the prepuce forward, drilled two holes in it, and closed it up with a ring, pin, or clamp.[169] Infibulated penises are regularly shown in drawings of Greek and Roman athletes and were popular until modern times.[170] The same practice in the East is called *mohree*, sewing or cauterizing the prepuce over the glans, preventing erection. To this day some Japanese athletes use infibulation to prevent the loss of their strength, which they think could evaporate through the glans.[171] Aztec parents used to cut both boys' and girls' genitals regularly throughout their childhood, the blood being used in a sacrifice to their goddess, a ritual that was said to "cleanse one's heart of the guilt that could drive a person crazy."[172] Indeed, one is tempted to give the Aztecs the prize for the most sadistic parenting, since their children were routinely sacrificed, cut, tied to cradle boards, had holes drilled in their lips, drugged, burned over fires, starved, stuck with spines, thrown naked into icewater, tortured, and battered.[173] But imagining they were unusual would be a mistake. Aztec childhood was simply more fully described by visitors from Europe. Equally graphic were those who described the ancient Chinese habit of beheading or strangling children who were "guilty of addressing abusive language to his or her father or mother,"[174] the common Euro-

---

167. Peter Tompkins, *The Eunuch and the Virgin*, p. 12.

168. Armando R. Favazza, *Bodies Under Siege*, p. 155.

169. Eric John Dingwall, *Male Infibulation*. London: John Bale, 1925, pp. 54, 78.

170. Uta Ranke-Heinemann, *Eunuchs for the Kingdom of Heaven*, p. 316.

171. Allen Edwards, *The Jewel in the Lotus*, p. 95.

172. David Carrasco, *City of Sacrifice: The Aztec Empire and the Role of Violence in Civilization*. Boston: Beacon Press, 1999, pp. 184–185.

173. Inga Clendinnen, *Aztecs: An Interpretation*. Cambridge: Cambridge University Press, 1991.

174. T'ung-Tsu Ch'u, *Law and Society in Traditional China*. Paris: Mouton & Co, 1965, p. 432; George Thomas Staunton, *Ta Tsing Leu Lee; Being The Fundamental Laws . . . of the Penal Code of China*. Taipei: Ch'eng-wen Publishing, 1966, p. 357.

pean practice of smearing infants with excrement and holding them over the fire or pushing them into a bread oven to cure "bewitchment," or the usual practice of hanging a baby over the fire to see if it was a "changeling."[175]

Parents in traditional societies couldn't keep their hands off their little babies; they simply were compelled to hurt and torture them all the time. The first thing most Western societies did to the newborn until recently was to cut the ligament under their tongue with their thumbnail, assaulting them in advance for what they experienced as maternal tongue-lashing.[176] Then their heads and genitals would be forcibly shaped: "All babies' heads would be reshaped to make them conform to the desired shape. The nose would [also] be corrected. . . . The nurse would gently stretch the end of the foreskin every day."[177] The painful molding of the head continued during the infant's first year of life and was sometimes fatal. As one English mother wrote in 1596 of her 9-month-old infant: "The child died. . . . The nurse had overput the mould of the head with striking it up too hard."[178] Severe cranial deformation can be seen in the drawings of Egyptian, Mayan, Aztec, Hun, Native American, and other children, as their heads were routinely put between two boards, one at the back of the head and the other on the forehead, so as to squash the head into the angle formed by the boards—a practice found as far back as the Neanderthals and continuing "throughout much of Europe, especially in Holland and France, until the middle of the nineteenth century."[179]

175. Alenka Puhar, "Childhood in Nineteenth-Century Slovenia." *The Journal of Psychohistory* 12(1985): 295–296; Barbara A. Kellum, "Infanticide in England in the Later Middle Ages." *History of Childhood Quarterly* 1(1974): 379.

176. David Hunt, *Parents and Children in History: The Psychology of Family Life in Early Modern France.* New York: Basic Books, 1970, p. 114; Alenka Puhar, "Childhood in Nineteenth-Century Slovenia," p. 296; John Theobald, *The Young Wife's Guide in the Management of Her Children.* London: W. Griffen, 1764, p. 4.

177. Aline Rousselle, *Porneia: On Desire and the Body in Antiquity.* Oxford: Basil Blackwell, 1983, p. 54.

178. A. L. Rowse, *Sex and Society in Shakespeare's Age: Simon Forman the Astrologer.* New York: Charles Scribner's Sons, 1974, p. 58.

179. Max Shein, *The PreColumbian Child.* Culver City: Labyrinthos, 1992, pp. 48–53; Timothy Taylor, *The Prehistory of Sex.* New York: Bantam Books, 1996, p. 253; John E. Pfeiffer, *The Creative Explosion: An Inquiry into the Origins of Art and Religion.* New York: Harper & Row, 1982, p. 100; E. J. Dingwall, *Artificial Cranial Deformation.* London: J. Bale, Sons, 1931; Armando R. Favazza, *Bodies Under Siege*, pp. 62–65; James DeMeo, *Saharasia*. Greensprings: Orgone Biophysical Research Lab, 1998, pp. 11–115.

Particularly widespread was the impulse to burn children. Traditional Arab children had burn marks all over their bodies from being burned by their parents with red-hot irons or pins.[180] English newspapers reported examples such as a woman "stirring up the fire with [her children's] feet so that their toes rotted off. . . . But we don't hear that there are any proceedings against her on this score."[181] The regular use of applying burning *moxa* to the child's body is still common in Japan.[182] Pouring scalding hot water ("iron water") over children was supposed to be curative in Eastern Europe.[183] Similar results are ascribed to an Italian medieval practice in which "as soon as children be born, they cauterize or burn them in the neck with a hot iron, or else drop a burning wax candle upon the place. . . . They think the brain is dried, and by pain the humour which doth flow is drawn to the hinder part of the head."[184] Every kind of excuse was given for this torture of children. Parents of every period have forced children who soiled their bed to consume their own excrement.[185] Far more crippling were mutilations like Chinese foot binding, which breaks the bones of little girls so their flesh deteriorates, so men could masturbate against it.[186]

THE LACK OF EMPATHY TOWARD CHILDREN AND MALNUTRITION IN HISTORY

Every child-rearing practice in traditional societies betrays a profound lack of empathy toward one's children. This should not, however, be simply seen as a result of poverty or even of the brutality of human nature. These parents are in thrall to their mother alters, demanding the torture of their

180. Samual M. Swemer, *Childhood in the Moslem World*. New York: Fleming H. Revell Co., 1915, p. 104.

181. Ivy Pinchbeck and Margaret Hewitt, *Children in English Society*. I. London: Routledge and Kegan Paul, 1969, p. 303.

182. Michio Kitahara, "Childhood in Japanese Culture." *The Journal of Psychohistory* 17(1989): 49.

183. Alenka Puhar, "Childhood in Slovenia," p. 301.

184. Robert Pemell, *De Morbis Puerorum, or, A Treatise of the Diseases of Children . . .* London: J. Legatt, 1653, p. 8.

185. Jules Renard, *Poil de Carotte*. Paris, 1894, p. 15.

186. Howard S. Levy, *Chinese Footbinding: The History of a Curious Erotic Custom*. London: Nevill Spearman, n.d.; Lloyd deMause, "The Universality of Incest," p. 151.

grandchildren. A typical example of this thralldom can be seen in the following observation of a visitor to Italy who described a popular religious festival:

> The most striking object of the solemnities is a procession [in which] a colossal car is dragged by a long team of buffaloes through the streets. Upon this are erected a great variety of objects, such as the sun, moon, and principal planets, set in rotary motion. . . . The heart sickens at sight of it [for] bound to the rays of sun and moon, to the circles forming the spheres of the various planets, are infants yet unweaned, whose mothers, for the gain of a few ducats, thus expose their offspring, to represent the cherub escort which is supposed to accompany the Virgin [Mary] to heaven.
>
> When this huge machine has made its jolting round, these helpless creatures . . . having been whirled round and round for a period of seven hours, are taken down from this fatal machine, already dead or dying. Then ensues a scene impossible to describe—the mothers struggling with each other, screaming, and trampling each other down. It not being possible, on account of the number, for each mother to recognize her own child among the survivors, one disputes with the other the identity of her infant. . . . The less fortunate mothers, as they receive the dead bodies of their infants, often already cold, rend the air with their fictitious lamentations, but consoled with the certainty that Maria, enamoured of her child, has taken it with her into Paradise.[187]

Thus the Mother Mary—symbol of the grandmother—is shown as demanding possession of the child even unto death.

This destructive grandmother alter in every mother's head is the missing factor in historians' accounts of the ubiquitous cruelty toward children in the past. Edward Shorter, for instance, effectively counters the poverty argument for "the manifest callousness" with which children were treated in the past by showing how upper- and middle-class mothers "got the money for large weddings, dowries, and militia uniforms . . . yet omitted just as much as did the laborers to breast-feed infants while alive."[188] Indeed, almost every mother who could afford to send their newborn out to

---

187. Richard Bentley, Ed., *Memoirs of Henrietta Caracciolo*. London: Richard Bentley, 1865, p. 15.

188. Edward Shorter, *The Making of the Modern Family*. New York: Basic Books, 1977, p. xvii.

wet nurses did so, even when the wet nurses fed them pap, not breast milk, and even though they knew their children were more than likely to die from the wet nurse's callous treatment. In fact, mothers in the past seemed unable to empathize enough with their infants to notice when they were hungry. Doctors throughout the centuries in all parts of the world routinely reported that "babies should only be fed two to three times in twenty-four hours."[189] Héroard's diary of little Louis XIII showed that despite over a dozen nurses and caregivers being assigned to provide for his needs, he was regularly malnourished, even close to death.[190] Even little princesses as late as the eighteenth century were regularly reported to be "naked and dying of hunger."[191] Mothers and nurses in the past were closer than one wishes to admit to the mother chimpanzees whom we discussed in the previous chapter, who cannot empathize with their weaned babies enough to give them food or water or show them how to get it, so that one-third starve to death during the weaning crisis.[192] Human mothers, however, have gone far beyond this lack of empathy, and purposely starved their children in fasting or punishment rituals so beloved by many societies in the past.[193] Buchan's conclusion that "almost one half of the human species perish in infancy by improper management or neglect"[194] was quite accurate, and by no means restricted to the poor. When babies cried and mothers heard their own mothers' demanding voices, they only wanted to quiet them, so they would as likely feed them beer, wine, or opium—available in every store as Godfrey's Cordial, Dalby's Carminative, or Syrup of

189. Magdelena King-Hall, *The Story of the Nursery*. London: Routledge & Kegan Paul, 1958, p. 126; William Perkins, *Christian Economy . . .* In Joan Larsen Klein, Ed., *Daughters, Wives, and Widows*, p. 199; Max Shein, *The PreColumbian Child*. Culver City: Labyrinthos, 1992, p. 56.

190. E. Soulie and E. de Barthelemy, Eds., *Journal de Jean Héroard sur l'Enfance et la Jeunesse de Louis XIII, Vol. 1*. Paris: Firmin Didot Frères, 1868, p. 35.

191. Hippolyte Adolphe Taine, *The Ancient Regime*. Gloucester: Peter Smith, 1962, p. 130; Avner Gil'adi, *Children of Islam*, p. 25.

192. Jane Beckman Lancaster, *Primate Behavior and the Emergence of Human Culture*. New York: Holt, Rinehard and Winston, 1975, p. 37.

193. William G. McLoughlin, "Evangelical Child Rearing in the Age of Jackson: Francis Wayland's Views on When and How to Subdue the Willfulness of Children." In N. Ray Hiner and Joseph M. Hawes, Eds., *Growing Up in America: Children in Historical Perspective*. Urbana: University of Illinois Press, 1985, pp. 87–89.

194. William Buchan, *Domestic Medicine*. Philadelphia: Thomas Dobson, 1809, p. 9.

Poppies,[195] which would either narcotize them enough to quiet them or would kill them.[196] The use of opium on infants goes back to ancient Egypt, where the Ebers papyrus tells parents: "It acts at once!"[197] Physicians complained of the thousands of infants killed every year by nurses "forever pouring Godfrey's Cordial down their little throats, which is a strong opiate and in the end as fatal as arsenic."[198] At all costs the baby must be quieted. Rheingold describes mothers in treatment who "stop producing milk every time their mothers appear" because they "fear their own vengeful mothers and fear that she may destroy her child."[199]

There is no conscious guilt on the part of mothers who allow their children to starve to death, since they regularly blame the children "for wanting to die."[200] Many mothers and wet nurses didn't breast-feed at all, but just gave infants pap, "gruel" (*bouillie*), made of water or sour milk mixed with flour,[201] which has very little nourishment and was so thick that "soon the whole belly is clogged, convulsions set in, and the little ones die."[202] In Bavaria, for instance, mothers considered nursing their children "disgusting," while the fathers were totally lacking in empathy, telling their wives "those breasts are mine" and threatening to go on a hunger strike if the mothers nursed their baby.[203] In Russia, mothers who didn't feel like breast-feeding normally fed them from a cow's teat, leading to infant death

195. Stephanie de Genlis, *Memoirs of the Countess de Genlis. Vol. 1.* New York: Wilder & Campbell, 1825, p. 10; John B. Beck, "The Effects of Opium on the Infant Subject." *New York Journal of Medicine*, January, 1844: 6; Thomas E. Jordan, *Victorian Childhood: Themes and Variations.* Albany: State University of New York Press, 1987, p. 99; James Walvin, *A Child's World: A Social History of English Childhood 1800–1914.* New York: Penguin Books, 1982, p. 26.

196. George Frederic Still, *The History of Paediatrics.* London: Oxford University Press, 1931, p. 466.

197. A. Hymanson, "A Short Review of the History of Infant Feeding." *Archives of Pediatrics* 51(1934): 4.

198. Ivy Pinchbeck and Margaret Hewitt, *Children in English Society, Vol. 1.* London: Routledge & Kegan Paul, 1969, p. 301.

199. Joseph Rheingold, *The Fear of Being a Woman*, p. 568.

200. Nancy Scheper-Hughes, "Culture, Scarcity and Maternal Thinking: Maternal Detachment and Infant Survival in a Brazilian Shantytown." *Ethos* 13(1985): 291–317.

201. David Hunt, *Parents and Children in History*, p. 115.

202. Elisabeth Badinter, *Mother Love: Myth and Reality*, p. 95.

203. John Knodel and Etienne Van de Walle, "Breast Feeding, Fertility and Infant Mortality: An Analysis of Some Early German Data." *Population Studies* 21(1967): 119.

rates of 70 percent.[204] After giving birth, Russian peasants often went back to field work all day, leaving their babies to starve with nothing but a *soska* in their mouth (a rag containing moldy bread).[205] All sorts of past child-rearing practices contributed to the starvation or malnutrition of infants. Newborn babies were usually not fed at all for the first week or more, since the mother's natural colostrum was believed to be poisonous to the baby. Swaddled babies were hung on a peg or put in a cradle in another room, where their hunger cries could not be heard. In addition, tight swaddling makes infants withdraw into themselves so they refrain from crying when hungry. Infants sent out to a wet nurse, after not being fed during the journey, were given to women who often attempted to nurse up to five or more babies at a time as they worked in the fields, while "the child is left to himself, drowning in his own excrement, bound like a criminal."[206] Particularly malnourished were those babies fed on pap by nurses, sometimes taking on as many as forty children at a time, most dying, while mothers continued to send them their subsequent babies.[207] These and other starvation practices made malnutrition for most babies a near certainty until modern times.

SENDING TO A WET NURSE AS A DELEGATE
OF THE DESTRUCTIVE GRANDMOTHER

Most historians have been as little able to feel empathy for infants sent to wet nurses as the mothers themselves were, claiming wet nursing "reflected not so much a lack of love for them as a deep fear of loving them,"[208] or maintaining that it was just "a harmless convention not a rejection of the child."[209] Most mothers who could afford to send their babies out did so; for instance, from the eighteenth to the early twentieth century, less than

204. David L. Ransel, *Village Mothers: Three Generations of Change in Russia and Tataria*. Bloomington, IN: Indiana University Press, 2001, pp. 21–22.

205. Ibid., pp. 29–30.

206. Elisabeth Badinter, *Mother Love: Myth and Reality*, p. 95.

207. Valerie Fildes, *Wet Nursing: A History from Antiquity to the Present*. Oxford: Basil Blackwell, 1988, p. 97.

208. Philip Gavitt, *Charity and Children in Renaissance Florence: The Ospedale degli Innocenti, 1410–1536*. Ann Arbor: University of Michigan Press, 1990, p. 19.

209. Shari L. Thurer, *The Myths of Motherhood: How Culture Reinvents the Good Mother*. Boston: Houghton Mifflin Co., 1994, p. 93.

5 percent of the babies born in Paris were nursed by their own mothers, rich or poor alike.[210] Six percent of eighteenth-century Parisian parents that wet-nursed their babies were noble, 44 percent were master artisans and tradesmen, and 24 percent were journeymen or other workers. Over a third of the children died during their time at the wet nurse, a mortality rate at least double that of maternal nursing, with the mortality rate of foundlings placed at a wet nurse being a deadly 92 percent.[211] Parents, of course, knew these enormous infant mortality figures when they condemned their innocent babies to the wet nurse. At least it was not as bad as the outright sale by parents of their children as slaves, which was often found in antiquity.[212]

Mothers knew their own mothers would be jealous if they cared about the newborn rather than devoting themselves to the grandmother, so they rarely inquired about the baby at the wet nurse. One unusual mother who actually visited her baby at the wet nurse was warned by a relative that "such exaggerated love was a crime against God, and he would surely punish it."[213] "Many young mothers say: 'If I turn nurse, I should destroy my husband's life, and my own too.'"[214] Upper-class mothers almost never nursed their babies, saying, "Nourish an infant! Indeed, Indeed! . . . I must have my sleep o'nights. . . . And a new gown to wear at the Opera. . . . What! Must the brat have my paps too?"[215] Defoe called suckling babies by ladies of quality "a thing as unnatural as if God had never intended it."[216] Newborn babies were often experienced as demons—dragon-snakes (*drákoi*)—until they were exorcized at baptism.[217] Breast milk was supposed to have been made from the mother's blood, and mothers imagined that "every time the baby sucks on her breasts, she feeleth the blood come from her heart

210. George D. Sussman, *Selling Mothers' Milk: The Wet-Nursing Business in France, 1718–1914*. Urbana, IL: University of Illinois Press, 1982.

211. Ibid., pp. 24, 67.

212. C. R. Whittaker, "Circe's Pigs: From Slavery to Serfdom in the Later Roman World." In M. I. Finly, Ed., *Classical Slavery*. London: F. Cass, 1987, p. 109.

213. Patrick P. Dunn, "Fathers and Sons Revisited: The Childhood of Vissarion Belinskii." *History of Childhood Quarterly* 1(1974): 133.

214. Mrs. Frank Malleson, *Notes on the Early Training of Children*, 3rd ed. Boston: D. C. Heath, 1887, p. 22.

215. Edmond and Jules de Goncourt, *The Woman of the Eighteenth Century*. Freeport: Books for Libraries Press, 1928, p. 145.

216. Daniel Defoe, *The Compleat English Gentleman*. London: E. Harris, 1890 (1729), p. 72.

217. Charles Stewart, *Demons and the Devil*, p. 55.

to nourish it,"[218] making her feel like the baby depleted her of her very life's blood. Doctors beginning with Soranus agreed that mothers who nursed their babies would "grow prematurely old, having spent herself through the daily suckling."[219] In addition, since it was believed that "sperm would spoil the milk and turn it sour,"[220] for most of history maternal breast-feeding meant no sex for the mother while nursing.

Physicians have complained since antiquity about parents who routinely gave their newborn over to negligent and abusive wet nurses. "At birth our children are handed over to some silly little Greek serving girl," says Tacitus.[221] Soranus warns about "wet-nurses so lacking in sympathy towards the nursling that they not only pay no heed when it cries for a long time, but [are] angry women like maniacs and sometimes when the newborn cries from fear and they are unable to restrain it, they let it drop from their hands or overturn it dangerously."[222] Aulus Gellius says wet nurses are chosen at random from the most useless slaves: "They take the first woman who has milk."[223] Throughout history, parents were quite casual about entrusting their babies for from two to seven years with wet nurses. An agent would "stop the first peasant woman he might come across, without examining her health or her milk [or use] a placement office [who would] get rid of him cheap or hand him over to the first person who comes along."[224] The child peddlers who hawked their services in the streets or by newspaper ads were not expected to know anything about the wet nurse, only to take the infant off the mother's hands. Badinter describes the process as follows:

> Out of 21,000 infants born in Paris in the sample year 1780 . . . 19,000 were deported to distant parts of the countryside in appalling conditions, having been handed, often randomly, to the illiterate child-peddlers who thronged the capital's street corners and market places. Once settled in their foster homes . . . over half of them died before

---

218. Joan Larsen Klein, Ed., *Daughters, Wives, and Widows.* Urbana: University of Illinois Press, 1992, p. 293.

219. Soranus of Ephesus, *Gynaecology*, 90.

220. Elisabeth Badinter, *Mother Love: Myth and Reality,* p. 70.

221. Tacitus, *Dialogus de Oratoribus* 29.

222. Soranus, *Gynaecology* 2.18.

223. Aulus Gellius, *Noctes atticae*, XII, I; Sandra R. Joshel, "Nurturing the Master's Child: Slavery and the Roman Child-Nurse." In Jean F. O'Barr et al., Eds., *Ties that Bind: Essays on Mothering and Patriarchy.* Chicago: University of Chicago Press, 1990, pp. 109–128.

224. Elisabeth Badinter, *Mother Love: Myth and Reality*, p. 93.

the age of two. And they died to the apparent indifference of their parents. . . .[225]

Because the wet nurse was always poor and had other babies to feed, those few parents who tried to find a good wet nurse were usually disappointed; one diarist wrote of his own life: "Four different wet-nurses were alternately turn'd out of doors on my account. . . . The first . . . nearly suffocated me in bed. . . . The second let me fall from her arms on the stones till my head was almost fractured. . . . The third carried me under an old brick wall which fell [on me] . . . while the fourth proved to be a thief, and deprived me even of my very baby clothes."[226]

The trip to the wet nurse began the infant's traumatic life experiences. "The infants were bundled upright in groups of four or five in pannier baskets strapped to the backs of donkeys. Those who died on the journey were just thrown out *en route*."[227] Once there, their parents "seldom inquired about the survival of their infants and were often uninformed as to their whereabouts."[228] Mothers sent each newborn to a wet nurse "despite the killing off, one by one, of their children. . . . Neither poverty nor ignorance explains such infanticide—only indifference. . . . Mothers on learning of their child's death at the nurse's console themselves, without wondering about the cause, by saying, 'Ah well, another angel in heaven!'"[229]

The wet nurse herself was usually an infanticidal mother. The common practice was to require that she kill her own baby in order to nurse the stranger—termed "a life for a life" by parents in the past.[230] Montaigne lamented: "Every day we snatch children from the arms of their mothers and put our own in their charge for a very small payment."[231] Society thought this system fair, since "by the sacrifice of the infant of the poor woman, the offspring of the wealthy will be preserved."[232]

---

225. Ibid., p. xi.
226. Linda A. Pollock, *Forgotten Children: Parent-Child Relations from 1500 to 1900.* Cambridge: Cambridge University Press, 1983.
227. Olwin H. Hufton, *The Poor of Eighteenth-Century France 1750–1789.* Oxford: Clarenden Press, 1974, p. 345.
228. Elisabeth Badinter, *Mother Love: Myth and Reality,* p. x.
229. Ibid., pp. 62, 113.
230. Janet Golden, *A Social History of Wet Nursing in America: From Breast to Bottle.* Cambridge: Cambridge University Press, 1996, p. 126.
231. Elisabeth Badinter, *Mother Love: Myth and Reality,* p. 41.
232. Charles West, *Lectures on the Diseases of Infancy and Childhood,* 5th ed. Philadelphia: Henry C. Lea, 1874, p. 45.

Wet nurses were universally described as "vicious, slothful and inclined to drunkenness,"[233] "debauched, indolent, superstitious,"[234] guilty
of "gross negligence . . . leaving babies . . . unattended when helping with
the harvest . . . crawling or falling into the fire and being attacked by animals, especially pigs,"[235] "hung from a nail like a bundle of old clothes . . .
the unfortunate one remains thus crucified [with] a purple face and violently compressed chest."[236] The wet nurses' superstitions included a belief "in favor of cradle cap and of human wastes, which were thought to
have therapeutic value,"[237] so infants were rarely washed and lived in their
own feces and urine for their entire time at nurse: "Infants sat in animal
and human filth, were suspended on a hook in unchanged swaddling bands
or were slung from the rafters in an improvised hammock . . . their mouths
crammed with rotting rags."[238] Even live-in wet nurses were described as
unfeeling: "When he cried she used to shake him—when she washed him
she used to stuff the sponge in his little mouth—push her finger (beast!)
in his little throat—say she hated the child, wished he were dead—used to
let him lie on the floor screaming while she sat quietly by and said screams
did not annoy her."[239]

Complaints by physicians that wet nurses let infants die of simple
neglect were legion: "While the women attend to the vineyards, the infant
remains alone . . . swaddled to a board and suspended from a hook on the
wall . . . crying and hungry in putrid diapers. Often the child cries so hard
it ends up with a hernia. . . . Turkeys peck out the eyes of a child . . . or
they fall into a fire, or drown in pails left carelessly on doorsteps."[240] Children were described as being "kept ragged and bare, sickly and starved
. . . in terror of their nurse, who handed out blows and vituperation freely"

---

233. David Hunt, *Parents and Children in History: The Psychology of Family Life in Early Modern France.* New York: Basic Books, 1970, p. 101.
234. Mary Lindemann, "Love for Hire: The Regulation of the Wet-Nursing Business in Eighteenth-Century Hamburg." *Journal of Family History* 16(1981): 379.
235. George D. Sussman, *Selling Mothers' Milk,* p. 55.
236. Lawrence Stone, *The Family, Sex and Marriage in England,* p. 425.
237. George Sussman, *Selling Mothers' Milk,* p. 54.
238. Simon Schama, *Citizens: A Chronicle of the French Revolution.* New York: Alfred A. Knopf, 1989, p. 146.
239. Linda Pollock, *A Lasting Relationship,* p 71.
240. Joan Sherwood, *Poverty in Eighteenth-Century Spain: The Women and Children of the Inclusa.* Toronto: University of Toronto Press, 1988, p. 80.

or who "tied them up by the shoulders and wrists with ragged ends of sheets . . . face down on the floor. . . . to protect them from injuring themselves while she was away. . . . Never played with or cuddled. . . . It is a holiday when they are taken for a walk around the room by the nurses."[241] Infants who are sent to "killing nurses" are described as being fed while the nurse croons, "Cry no more! Soon you will go, *deté drago*, soon. 'Tis truly better that you go, dear infant . . . onto the lap of Virgin Mary, Mother of Jesus."[242] It is no wonder that well into the nineteenth century many areas had a two-thirds mortality rate of infants sent to a wet nurse.[243]

Since their parents seldom visited them, the children were total strangers when they were returned to them years later. "If they returned home alive, they often came back in a pitiable state: thin, tiny, deformed, consumed by fevers, prone to convulsions."[244] The mother has by then nearly forgotten her baby, since, as physicians complained since antiquity: "When a child is given to another and removed from its mother's sight, the strength of maternal ardor is gradually and little by little extinguished and it is almost as completely forgotten as if it had been lost by death."[245] One typical report came from a woman who described her mother saying when she was returned at 2 from the wet nurse: "My God! What have you brought me here! This goggle-eyed, splatter-faced, gabbart-mouthed wretch is not my child! Take her away!"[246] Another is praised by Locke for beating her child when she first saw her, saying she was "forced to whip her little *Daughter*, at her first coming home from Nurse, eight times successively the same Morning, before she could master her *Stubbornness* and obtain a compliance in a very easie and indifferent matter."[247]

---

241. Ibid., pp. 81, 132.

242. Louis Adamic, *Cradle of Life: The Story of One Man's Beginnings*. New York: Harper & Bros., 1936, p. 48.

243. Jean-Louis Flandrin, *Families in Former Times: Kinship, Household and Sexuality*. Cambridge: Cambridge University Press, 1979, p. 204.

244. Elisabeth Badinter, *Mother Love: Myth and Reality*, p. 163.

245. Anna Ferraris Oliverio, "Infanticide in Western Cultures: A Historical Overview." In Stefano Parmigiani and Frederick S. vom Saal, *Infanticide and Parental Care*. Zurich: Harwood Academic Publishers, 1994, p. 113.

246. George Anne Bellamy, *An Apology for the Life of George Anne Bellamy* . . . London: London Press, 1785, p. 26.

247. Edmund Leites, *The Puritan Conscience and Modern Sexuality*. New Haven: Yale University Press, 1986, p. 45.

Wet nursing was practiced by societies all over the world, from Europe to Asia, as far back as records exist.[248] The Code of Hammurabi even allowed the wet nurse to sell the baby if the parents couldn't pay her the contracted amount.[249] The first real improvement did not come until the seventeenth century, when wet nurses began more often to be brought into the parents' homes, especially in England, Holland, and America.[250] The next step was for the mother to nurse herself. The decision to forgo wet nursing was made purely for psychogenic reasons—no new invention nor social condition caused the change. Nor was it due to a change in the opinions of experts—the pro-nursing tracts of Rousseau and others had little affect on the near-universal wet-nursing practice in France, for instance, while in America, even in the South where slave nurses were available, mothers usually themselves nursed by the eighteenth century.[251] Advanced mothers began by telling each other they would find new delights in nursing their own infant. Rather than a draining of vital blood, nursing could actually be a pleasure to the mother! The new middle class took the lead in maternal nursing. All of these changes took place before the advent of sterilized bottle feeding in the twentieth century. Infant mortality in these areas immediately plunged,[252] and mothers began to work out how to face the new emotional challenges of actually relating to their babies.

---

248. Valerie Fildes, *Wet Nursing; Pei-Yi Wu*, "Childhood Remembered: Parents and Children in China, 800–1700." In Anne Behnke Kinney, Ed., *Chinese Views of Childhood*. Honolulu: University of Hawai'i Press, 1995, p. 130; Avner Giladi, *Infants, Parents and Wet Nurses: Medieval Islamic Views on Breastfeeding and Their Social Implications*. Leiden: Brill, 1999, p. 3.

249. Valerie Fildes, *Wet Nursing*, p. 24.

250. Fiona Newall, "Wet Nursing and Child Care in Aldenham, Hertfordshire, 1595–1726: Some Evidence on the Circumstances and Effects of Seventeenth-Century Child Rearing Practices." In Valerie Fildes, Ed., *Women As Mothers in Pre-Industrial England*. London: Routledge, 1990, p. 125; Patricia Crawford, "'The Sucking Child': Adult Attitudes to Child Care in the First year of Life in Seventeenth-Century England." *Continuity and Change* 1(1986): 31; Rudolf Dekker, *Childhood, Memory and Autobiography in Holland: From the Golden Age to Romanticism*. New York: St. Martin's Press, 2000, p. 27; Janet Golden, *A Social History of Wet Nursing in America*, pp. 35, 44, 56.

251. Sally McMillen, "Mothers' Sacred Duty: Breast-feeding Patterns Among Middle- and Upper-Class Women in the Antebellum South." *Journal of Southern History* 51(1985): 333–356; Catherine M. Scholten, *Childbearing in American Society*, p. 62.

252. R. E. Jones, "Further Evidence on the Decline in Infant Mortality in Pre-industrial England: North Shropshire, 1561–1810." *Population Studies* 34(1980): 247.

SWADDLING THE EVIL INFANT

Since "infant humans are inclined in their hearts to adultery, fornication, impure desires, lewdness . . . anger, strife, gluttony, hatred and more,"[253] they had to be tightly tied up so they "be not crooked nor evil shapen."[254] It was feared that otherwise a child would "tear its ears off, scratch its eyes out, break its legs, or touch its genitals,"[255] would undoubtedly "fall to pieces,"[256] and would certainly "go upon all four, as most other animals do."[257] Worse, infants were always on the verge of turning into your own angry mother; there was so much "viciousness in all children [if you] pamper them the least little bit, at once they will rule their parents."[258] Infants were thought to be so violent that even their heads must be "firmly tied down, that they might not throw off their heads from their shoulders."[259] Physicians complained that "mothers and nurses bind and tie their children so hard [they] made me weep [as they] lie the children behind the hot oven, whereby the child may soon be stiffled or choked."[260] The swaddling process was much the same for millennia:

> [The mother] stretches the baby out on a board or straw mattress and dresses it in a little gown or a coarse, crumpled diaper, on top of which she begins to apply the swaddling bands. She pins the infant's arms against its chest, then passes the band under the armpits, which presses the arms firmly into place. Around and around she winds the band down to the buttocks, tighter and tighter . . . clear down to the feet, and . . .

253. Hugh Cunningham, *Children and Childhood in Western Society Since 1500.* London: Longman, 1995, p. 49.

254. G. G. Coulton, *Social Life in Britain: From the Conquest to the Reformation.* Cambridge: Cambridge University Press, 1918, p. 46.

255. Ruth Benedict, "Child Rearing in Certain European Countries." *American Journal of Orthopsychiatry* 19(1949): 345.

256. Rhoda E. White, *From Infancy to Womanhood. A Book of Instruction for Young Mothers.* London: Marston, Searle & Rivington, 1882, p. 19.

257. Francois Mauriceau, *The Diseases of Women with Child.* London: T. Cox, 1736, p. 309.

258. Gerald Strauss, *Luther's House of Learning: Introduction of the Young in the German Reformation.* Baltimore: Johns Hopkins University Press, 1978, p. 97.

259. John Jones, *Medical, Philosophical and Vulgar Errors of Various Kinds . . .* London: T. Cadell, 1797, p. 73.

260. Felix Würtz, *The Children's Book.* Frankfurt, 1563, pp. 202, 205.

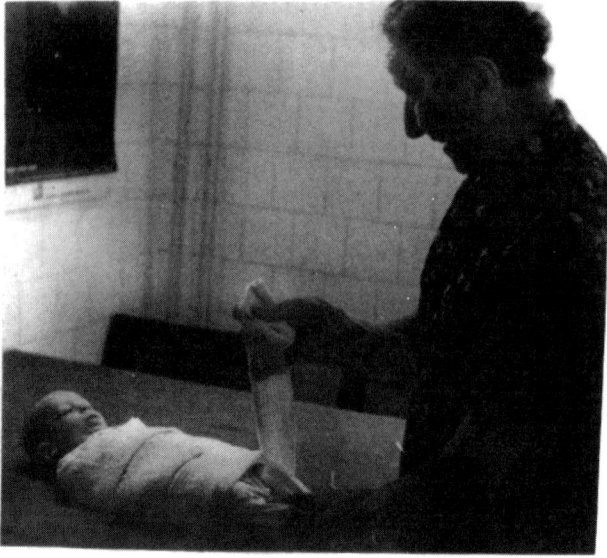

Fig. 8–3. Mother swaddling a baby

covers the baby's head with a bonnet [all of which] is fastened with pins.[261]

Swaddling in antiquity and the Middle Ages was done by tying the infant tightly to an actual board so he or she cannot move. Physicians complained that the infant "is lucky if he is not squeezed so hard that he is unable to breathe, and if he has been placed on his side, so that the water which he has to pass through his mouth can run out," or he will choke to death.[262] Swaddled Albanian infants were described as follows in a 1934 study:

> The child began immediately to passionately scream and tried to free himself. . . . This seemed to be a signal for the mother to rock the cradle violently; at the same time she covered the head of the baby with a white sheet. While the baby's miserable screaming made a strong impression

---

261. Edward Shorter, *The Making of the Modern Family*, p. 197.
262. David Hunt, *Parents and Children in History*, p. 131; Count de Buffon, *A Natural History. Vol. I*. London: Thomas Kelly, 1781, p. 211.

to us, it seemed to be an everyday thing to the mother, to which she did not react except by rocking the cradle as strongly as possible.[263]

The traditional "benumbing shaking" of the baby and "violent rocking" of the cradle—described over and over again by our sources[264]—"puts the babe into a dazed condition in order that he may not trouble those that have the care of him,"[265] and is sometimes supplemented by "a piece of linen rag stuffed into its mouth"[266] to stop the screaming. Because straight pins were used to keep the swaddling bands in place,[267] "nurses, blinded by passion and prejudice, do not hesitate to beat the helpless babe, without examining whether its cries are not occasioned by a pin."[268] Because every visitor to the home represents the jealous grandmother, infants are usually kept in dark rooms and their faces are covered by blankets to ward off the "world full of angry, malevolent, burning, glaring looks, a world dominated by evil and fear . . . usually represented by an older woman. . . . Sharp objects are placed into the cradle or stuck between the swaddling bands—knives, needles, forks, nails—to protect against incubi."[269] Salt was rubbed into the baby's skin, irritating it terribly[270]; excrement was sometimes smeared on its nipples; infants were made to drink their own urine; and neighbors would often spit on it, saying: "Ugh, aren't you just ugly," all to ward off jealous "evil eye" spirits.[271] Since the infants were nursed while swaddled, they stewed in their own excrement for days at a time, the mothers leaving their babies "crying with all their might" in the cradle or "tossed in a corner" or "hung from a nail on the wall" while they "spend hours away from their cot-

---

263. Lotte Danzinger and Liselotte Frankl, "Zum Problem der Funktionsreifung." *Zeitschrift für Kinderforschung* 43(1934): 229.

264. Edward Shorter, *The Making of the Modern Family*, p. 170.

265. W. Preyer, *Mental Development in the Child*. New York: D. Appleton and Co., 1907, p. 41.

266. Alenka Puhar, "Childhood In Nineteenth-Century Slovenia," p. 308.

267. Karin Calvert, *Children in the House*. Boston: Northeastern University Press, 1992, p. 22.

268. Christian Augustus Struve, *A Familiar Treatise on the Physical Education of Children . . .* London: J. Murray, 1801, p. 382.

269. Ibid., pp. 294–295.

270. Diana Dick, *Yesterday's Babies: A History of Babycare*. London: The Bodley Head, 1987, p. 8.

271. Alenka Puhar, "Childhood In Nineteenth-Century Slovenia," p. 295.

Fig. 8–4. Baby hanging on a nail on the wall

tages" during the day.[272] Few traditional mothers or nurses heeded doctors' pleas "not to let them lie in their filth,"[273] so that during their first year of life[274] they were usually "covered with excrement, reeking of a pestilential stench [their] skin completely inflamed [and] covered with filthy ulcerations [so that] if touched . . . they let out piercing cries."[275]

Swaddling was a worldwide practice, undoubtedly reaching back to tribal cultures, since so many of them featured tying up infants to cradle boards for as long as three years as their way of controlling their supposedly aggressive

---

272. Edward Shorter, *The Making of the Modern Family*, pp. 170–171; David Hunt, *Parents and Children in History*, p. 126.

273. Jacques Guillemeau, *A Treatise of the Diseases of Infants and Young Children.* London: A. Hatfield, 1612, p. 26.

274. Plato, *Laws* VII. 7; David Hunt, *Parents and Children in History*, p. 127; Lotte Danzinger, "Zum Problem der Funktionsreifung," p. 232; Anne Buck, *Clothes and the Child.* Carlton: Ruth Bean, 1996, p. 24; John Peckey, *A General Treatise of the Diseases of Infants and Children.* London: R. Wellington, 1697, p. 6; Nicholas Culpepper, *A Directory for Midwives . . .* London: J. Streater, 1671, p. 229.

275. Elisabeth Badinter, *Mother Love: Myth and Reality*, pp. 96–97.

tendencies.[276] Asian parents favored techniques like wrapping the child in a blanket and tying it into a basket made of straw or bamboo (*ejiko*) until it was 3 or 4 years old.[277] Eighteenth-century Anglo-Saxon physicians began to suggest doing away with swaddling entirely, at least during the day, stressing what mothers had been unable so far to notice: "that particular happiness, which a child shows by all its powers of expression, when it is newly undressed. How pleased! How delightful! it is with this new liberty."[278] Soon, more and more mothers discovered "the extreme pleasure that all children discover when stript of their incumbrances, the content and satisfaction with which they stretch themselves, enjoying the freedom of voluntary motion";[279] and by the nineteenth century swaddling was "unheard of" in France, England, and America, though continuing in Germany into the twentieth century and in various parts of Eastern Europe even today.[280]

The effects of swaddling upon every human born during the past ten millennia were catastrophic. Besides having "the pressure force blood to their heads and make their little faces purple," besides "crushing his breast and ribs" and "compressing the flesh almost to gangrene, the circulation nearly arrested,"[281] swaddled infants were severely withdrawn, listless, and

276. Stanley Walens, *Feasting with Cannibals: An Essay on Kwakiutl Cosmology.* Princeton: Princeton University Press, 1981, p. 15; John W. M. Whiting, "Adolescent Rituals and Identity Conflicts." In James W. Stigler, et al., Eds, *Cultural Psychology: Essays on Comparative Human Development.* Cambridge: Cambridge University Press, 1990, p. 358; Gwen J. Broude, *Growing Up: A Cross-Cultural Encyclopedia.* Santa Barbara: ABC-Clio, 1995, p. 172.

277. E. Lipton et al., "Swaddling, A Child Care Practice: Historical, Cultural and Experimental Observations." *Paediatrics, Supplement*, 35 (1965), pp. 519–567; Michio Kitahara, "Childhood in Japanese Culture," p. 44.

278. William Smellie, *Of the Management of New-Born Children . . .* London: D. Wilson, 1762; Catherine M. Scholten, *Childbearing in American Society*, p. 74.

279. Hester Chapone, *Chapone on the Improvement of the Mind.* Philadelphia: L. Johnson, 1830, p. 203.

280. Edward Shorter, *The Making of the Modern Family*, p. 197; Th. Bentzon, "About French Children." *Century Magazine* 52(1896): 805; Elisabeth Badinter, *Mother Love: Myth and Reality*, p. 172; An American Matron, *The Maternal Physician . . .* New York: Isaac Riley, 1811, p. 136; Alenka Puhar, "Childhood Origins of the War in Yugoslavia." *The Journal of Psychohistory* 20(1993): 374.

281. Priscilla Robertson, "Home As a Nest: Middle Class Childhood in Nineteenth-Century Europe." In deMause, Ed., *The History of Childhood*, p. 412; Daniel Beekman, *The Mechanical Baby: A Popular History of the Theory and Practice of Child Raising.* Westport: Lawrence Hill & Co., 1977, p. 31; William P. Dewees, *A Treatise on the Physical and Medical Treatment of Children.* Philadelphia: H. C. Carey, 1826, p. 4.

physically retarded in the onset of walking, which often didn't begin until from 2 to 5 years of age.[282] The effects of swaddling on all adults' emotional lives was even more profound. Because of the lack of warmth and holding, there is a lifelong deficit in oxytocin and oversupply of cortisol, the stress hormone, resulting in a lifetime of rage and anxiety states.[283] Even rats lose neurons in the hippocampus and orbital frontal lobes when tied up like human infants were, developing depletions in serotonin, norepinephrine, and dopamine, exacerbated aggressive behavior, and a severe decrease in social capabilities.[284] Chapter 9 discusses the enormous transformations produced in Western science, politics, and culture by the ending of wet nursing and swaddling and the evolution of parental love during the modern period.

THE HISTORY OF CHILD BEATING

Despite belief to the contrary, mothers beat their children today "at a rate approaching twice that of fathers,"[285] and mothers in the past were far more likely to be the child beaters than today. The typical mother was described as constantly beating her children:

---

282. D. M. Levy, "On the Problems of Movement Restraint." *American Journal of Orthopsychiatry* 14(1944): 644–671; Sylvia Brody, *Patterns of Mothering: Maternal Influence During Infancy.* New York: International Universities Press, 1956, p. 104; Michio Kitahara, "Childrearing in Japanese Culture," p. 44; Lotte Danzinger, "Zum Problem der Funktionsreifung," pp. 249–253; Scientific American, *Mind and Brain.* New York: W. H. Freeman and Co., 1993, p. 16; Lloyd deMause, "The Evolution of Childhood," p. 60.

283. Arthur Janov, *The Biology of Love.* Amherst: Prometheus Books, 2000, pp. 35, 303.

284. Bruce D. Perry, "Neurobiological Sequelae of Childhood Trauma: PTSD in Children." In M. Michele Murburg, *Catecholamine Function in Posttraumatic Stress Disorder: Emerging Concepts.* Washington, DC: American Psychiatric Press, 1994, pp. 223–254; Jean Carper, *Your Miracle Brain.* New York: HarperCollins, 2000, p. 31; Debra Hiehoff, *The Biology of Violence.* New York: The Free Press, 1999, p. 126; F. Lamprecht et al., "Rat Fighting Behavior." *Brain Research* 525(1990): 285–293.

285. Judith Sherven and James Sniechowski, "Women Are Responsible, Too." *Survivors of Female Incest Emerge* 3(1995): 5; Ross D. Parke and Armin A. Brott, *Throwaway Dads: The Myths and Barriers That Keep Men from Being the Fathers They Want to Be.* Boston: Houghton Mifflin Co., 1999, p. 50; Murray Strauss and Richard Gelles, *Physical Violence in American Families.* New Brunswick: Transaction Press, 1990, p. 4.

She was a curious woman, my mother. Children seemed to inspire her with a vindictive animosity, with a fury for beating and banging them, against walls, against chairs, upon the ground.[286]

My mother . . . strictly followed Solomon's advice, in never sparing the rod; insomuch that I have frequently been whipped for looking blue on a frosty morning; and, whether I deserved it or not, I was sure of correction every day of my life.[287]

Mama whipped us for the least thing. . . . Sometimes the chastisement could better be called a flogging. . . . We kept the marks for many many days.[288]

I was often whipped. My mother said that one mustn't spoil children, and she whipped me every morning; if she didn't have time in the morning, she would do so at noon, rarely later than four o'clock.[289]

If the mother could not spare the time to beat her child, or if she complained "I have a little pain in my back with whipping Susan today, who struggled so that I have got a wrench,"[290] she could always hire a "professional flagellant" who advertised their child-beating services in newspaper ads[291]; or, like one mother, she could hire a "garde-de-ville to whip her three children once a week, naughty or not."[292] All experts advised that mothers should "let the child from a year old be taught to fear the rod, and cry softly. . . . Make him do as he is bid, if you whip him ten times running to do it."[293] Since "God has given every mother the power [and] placed

---

286. Hannah Lynch, *Autobiography of a Child*. New York: Dodd, Mead & Co., 1899, p. 3.

287. Letitia Pilkington, *Memoirs of Mrs. Letitia Pilkington. 1712–1750*. New York, Dodd, Mead & Co., 1928, p. 31.

288. Lisi Cipriani, *A Tuscan Childhood*. New York: The Century Co., 1907, p. 40.

289. Elisabeth Badinter, *Mother Love: Myth and Reality*, p. 240.

290. Rosalind K. Marshall, *Childhood in Seventeenth Century Scotland*. Edinburgh: The Trustees of the National Galleries of Scotland, 1976, p. 20.

291. Lionel Rose, *The Erosion of Childhood: Child Oppression in Britain 1860–1918*. London: Routledge, 1991, p. 231.

292. Richard Heath, *Edgar Quinet: His Early Life and Writings*. London: Tribner & Co., 1881, p. 3.

293. John Hersey, *Advice to Christian Parents*. Baltimore: Armstrong & Berry, 1839, p. 83.

Fig. 8–5. Mother beating her child

in your hands a helpless babe. . . . If it disobeys you, all you have to do is to . . . inflict bodily pain so steadily and so invariably that disobedience and suffering shall be indissolubly connected in the mind of the child."[294] And since your child needs you so much, "he does not bear a grudge against those who have hurt him. . . . However much his mother whips him, he looks for her and values her above all others."[295]

Children throughout history began being beaten in the womb. Pregnant mothers in the past were usually beaten by their husbands, who had a legal right to do so until the twentieth century,[296] and even today over a third of pregnant women are in physically abusive relationships—physical assault escalating during pregnancy.[297] After birth, a half or more—depending on the area—of American mothers today begin hitting their infants during their first year of life.[298] Susanna Wesley's children were typical of past practices:

---

294. John S. C. Abbott, *The Mother At Home*. Boston: Crocker and Brewster, 1834, p. 39.

295. John Chrysostom, *Homily on Matthew* 62.4.

296. Terry Davidson, "Wifebeating: A Recurring Phenomenon Throughout History." In Maria Roy, Ed., *Battered Women: A Psychosociological Study of Domestic Violence.* New York: Van Nostrand Reinhold Co., 1977, p. 19.

297. Amy L. Gilliland and Thomas R. Verny, "The Effects of Domestic Abuse on the Unborn Child." *Journal of Prenatal and Perinatal Psychology and Health* 13(1999): 236.

298. R. Parke and C. Collmer, "Child Abuse: An Interdisciplinary Analysis." In M. Hetherington, Ed., *Review of Child Development*, Vol. 5. Chicago: University of Chicago Press, 1975, p. 509.

[I would] break their wills . . . before they can speak. . . . [Before they] turned a year old they were taught to fear the rod. . . . That most odious noise of the crying of children was rarely heard in the house, but the family usually lived in as much quietness as if there had not been a child among them.[299]

Even when the infant didn't cry and began to obey the mother's merest glance, the early beatings had to begin in earnest, as with this mother and her 4-month-old infant: "I whipped him till he was actually black and blue, and until I *could not* whip him any more, and he never gave up one single inch."[300] Even if the crying was because the child was sick, the rod must be applied, since the mother still hears the child's cries as critical of her: "Our little daughter . . . before she was quite a year old, we began to correct her for crying. . . . It has taught her a command over her feelings. . . . Even when she is unwell, and blurts into a loud cry, we generally correct her until she suppresses it [using] a rod."[301]

Children, says Locke, must always show total "submission and ready obedience. . . . It must be early, or else it will cost pains and blows to recover it."[302] An Irish mother puts it more succinctly: "You've got to slash them while they're still too young to remember it and hold it against you."[303]

In ancient times, children could be stoned to death if they were "uncontrollable." Philo wrote: "It is right that parents should rebuke their children . . . beat them, disgrace them, and imprison them. . . . If they still rebel . . . the law permits that they even be punished with death."[304]

Seneca described the public floggings of children in Sparta, where boys were often beaten to death by their elders. Brutal floggings continued throughout the lives of most children in history, so that diaries well into recent times are filled with entries of "the dog-whip over the door," "the razor-strap hanging on a nail on the kitchen shelf," and "the carpet-beater

299. Robert Southey, *The Life of Wesley*. London: Oxford University Press, 1925, Vol. 2, p. 304.

300. Logan Pearsall Smith, *Unforgotten Years*. Boston: Little, Brown, 1939, p. 36.

301. "Extract From a Mother's Journal." *Mother's Magazine*, 1934: 43.

302. John Locke, *Some Thoughts Concerning Education*. Indianapolis: Hackett Publishing Co., 1996, p. 23.

303. Nancy Scheper-Hughes, *Saints, Scholars, and Schizophrenics: Mental Illness in Rural Ireland*. Berkeley: University of California Press, 1983, p. 154.

304. Graeme Newman, *The Punishment Response*. Philadelphia: Lippincott, 1978, p. 61.

in the corner. Mother didn't have to use it. If we were being naughty, we just followed her eyes to the corner."[305]

The beating process was ritualized, to relieve the parents' guilt and to sexualize the process. Children often would be forced to "ask for God's blessing on the flogging"; "The wife then bares the child's bottom with delight for the flogging"; "The child must ask to be beaten . . . (theologian Bartholomew Batty rhapsodizes on God's wisdom in providing children with bottoms so they can be beaten repeatedly without permanent damage)."[306] After the beatings, the child would often be made to kiss or thank the beating instrument or the beater for the beating, as when English writer Roger North recalled "being made to stop crying and thank 'the good rail which [mother] said was to break our spirits.'"[307] Parents usually are described as being out of control, "fierce and eager upon the child, striking, flinging, kicking it, as the usual manner is."[308] Even mothers who wrote about being nice to their children stressed the need to flog until "the plough of correction makes long furrows on their back."[309] Professional floggers hired by parents used more openly sexually sadistic equipment:

> Preparations consist in having ready a strong narrow table, straps (waist-band with sliding straps, anklets and wristlets), cushions, and a good, long, pliable birch rod, telling her to prepare by removing her dress. . . . For screams increased strokes must be given. If a girl tries very hard indeed to bear it bravely, then, perhaps, I give ten instead of twelve.[310]

Children of wealthy parents were, if anything, more severely beaten than others, by both their caregivers and parents. Louis XIII was routinely "beaten mercilessly. . . . On waking in the morning . . . he was beaten on

---

305. Jeremy Seabrook, *Working-Class Childhood*. London: Gollancz, 1982, p. 22.

306. Gordon Rattray Taylor, *The Angel Makers: A Study in the Psychological Origins of Historical Change 1750–1850*. New York: E. P. Dutton & Co., 1974, p. 305–306.

307. Anthony Fletcher, *Gender, Sex and Subordination in England 1500–1800*. New Haven, CT: Yale University Press, 1995, p. 208.

308. Ezekias Woodward, *A Childes Patrimony*. London: I. Legatt, 1640, p. 30.

309. Stephanie Coontz, *The Social Origins of Private Life: A History of American Families, 1600–1900*. London: Verso, 1988, p. 87.

310. Ian Gibson, *The English Vice: Beating, Sex and Shame in Victorian England and After*. London: Duckworth, 1978, p. 55.

the buttocks by his nurse with a birch or a switch. . . . His father whipped him himself when in a rage."[311] On the day of his coronation at age 8, after being whipped, he said he "would rather do without so much obeisance and honor if they wouldn't have me whipped."[312] Noble parents demanded nurses whip their children; Henri IV wrote: "I have a complaint to make: you do not send word that you have whipped my son. . . . When I was his age I was often whipped. That is why I want you to whip him."[313] The beatings were usually bloody: "Katharine by a blow on th'ear given by her mother did bleed at the nose very much. . . . Coming home an hour, she bled again, very sore, by gushes and pulses, very fresh good blood, where-upon I perceived it to be the blood of the artery."[314]

Laws did not protect children against cruelty until the modern pe-riod unless they were beaten to death; as one thirteenth-century law put it: "If one beats a child until it bleeds, then it will remember, but if one beats it to death, the law applies."[315] Since children were beaten with the same instruments as criminals and slaves, floggings could be accomplished with whips, shovels, canes, iron rods, cat-o'-nine tails, bundles of sticks, shovels, whatever came to hand.[316] Parents could avoid killing them, said Bartholomew Batty, if they would not "strike and buffet their children about the face and head, and lace upon them like malt sacks with cudgels, staves, fork or fire shovel . . . [but instead] hit him upon the sides with the rod, he shall not die thereof."[317]

When children went to school, the beatings continued with increased ferocity. Beatings were considered the basis for learning, since, as one edu-cator said, "fear is good for putting the child in the mood to hear and to understand. A child cannot quickly forget what he has learned in fear."[318] Augustine recalled the regular beatings he received at school and described

311. Shari L. Thurer, *The Myths of Motherhood*, p. 104.

312. E. Soulie and E. de Barthelemy, Eds., *Journal de Jean Héroard sur l'Enfance et la Jeunesse de Louis XIII, Vol. 1*. Paris: Firmin Didot Frères, 1868, p. 436.

313. David Hunt, *Parents and Children in History*, p. 135.

314. Ralph Houlbrooke, Ed., *English Family Life, 1576–1716: An Anthology from Dia-ries*. Oxford: Basil Blackwell, 1988, p. 138.

315. Albrecht Peiper, *Chronik der Kinderheilkunde*, p. 309.

316. Lloyd deMause, "The Evolution of Childhood," p. 49.

317. Bartholomey Batty, *The Christian Man's Closet*, pp. 14, 26.

318. James A. Schultz, *The Knowledge of Childhood in the German Middle Ages, 1100–1350*. Philadelphia: University of Pennsylvania Press, 1995, p. 94.

the use of "racks and hooks and other torments."[319] Children were beaten for every error, such as "being flogged for not marking the ablative case,"[320] and since sexual sadism was rampant among teachers throughout the centuries, the floggings were often described as being administered to children "stripped in front of the whole community and beaten until they bled,"[321] and beatings were often described as being made by teachers "with a gloating glance of sensual cruelty."[322] Schoolmasters were often described as taking "the most pretty and amorous boys . . . into his lodgings and after a jerke or two [a blow with a rod or a whip] to meddle with their privities."[323] Many books and articles have been written detailing the "erotic flagellation" of British schools,[324] but the erotic content of school beatings was well-known everywhere since early times.[325] Children wondered why: "We are taught during our first five or six years to hide our buttocks and shameful parts; then . . . along comes a teacher who forces us to unbutton our trousers, push them down, lift our shirt, show everything and receive the whip in the middle of the class."[326] Girls were equally flogged. Hannah Lynch's beatings in the nineteenth century were typical: "The superioress took my head tightly under her arm, and the brawny red-cheeked lay-sister scourged my back with a three-pointed whip till the blood gushed from the long strips and I fainted."[327]

No child in antiquity and the Middle Ages can be found who escaped severe physical abuse—at home, at school, in apprenticeship, all suffered from "battered child syndrome" from infancy until adolescence. The Old Testament not only demands the beating of children; it says children who

319. Gerald Strauss, *Luther's House of Learning: Introduction of the Young in the German Reformation*. Baltimore: Johns Hopkins University Press, 1978, p. 13.

320. Jame Walvin, *A Child's World*, p. 48.

321. Graeme Newman, *The Punishment Response*. Philadelphia: J. P. Lippincott, 1978, p. 63.

322. William Russell, *An Autobiography of William Russell*. Baltimore: Gobright, Thorne, 1852, p. 17.

323. Guildhall Library, London, document 11588/3/295.

324. Jonathan Benthall, "Invisible Wounds: Corporal Punishment in British Schools as a Form of Ritual." *Child Abuse and Neglect* 15(1991): 377–388.

325. Carl A. Mounteer, "Roman Childhood, 200 B.C. to A.D. 600." *The Journal of Psychohistory* 14(1987): 239.

326. Ian Gibson, *The English Vice*, p. 24.

327. Hannah Lynch, *Autobiography of a Child*. New York: Dodd, Mead & Co., 1899, p. 142.

curse their mother or father "shall surely be put to death."[328] Chinese parents punished children by "a hundred blows with a bamboo . . . strangulation [or] having his flesh torn from his body with red-hot pincers."[329] St. Ambrose praised tutors for being "unsparing with the whip"[330]; Augustine "lived in dread of the whip of his teacher"; and martial "jokes about the complaints of neighbours living next to a schoolroom: the sounds of students being beaten awakens them annoyingly early in the morning."[331] Mounteer described Roman education as routinely brutal: "Canes, whips, dried eel's skin, or bundles of dried reeds were used with such ferocity on children's hands that they became so swollen the children had trouble holding their books."[332] Mothers are depicted as bringing their children to school and demanding they be beaten, and descriptions of beatings by the *ferula*, a cane with knots in it, tell how "children's hands were so swollen by this instrument that they could barely hold their books."[333]

By the Middle Ages, a few reformers, like Saint Anselm, began questioning whether whipping children "day and night" was wise,[334] saying that "casting them on the ground [and] kicking them like dogs [is a] manner of correcting I judge to be detested."[335] Still, little changed for most children, except that by the seventeenth century sometimes if they were whipped to death during apprenticeship, the master could sometimes be convicted of manslaughter.[336] Small infants were the first to be exempted from whippings: "A babe at six months cries when its mother gives it into the arms of another person. . . . the child ought not to be whipped for this."[337] By the eighteenth century's socializing-mode parenting, I have found the first

328. Deut. 21:21.

329. Larry S. Milner, *Hardness of Heart/Hardness of Life*, p. 51.

330. Saint Ambrose. *Hexameron*. New York: Fathers of the Church, 1961, p. 251.

331. Richard Saller, "Corporal Punishment, Authority, and Obedience in the Roman Household." In Beryl Rawson, Ed., *Marriage, Divorce, and Children in Ancient Rome*. Oxford: Clarendon Press, 1991, p. 163.

332. Carl A. Mounteer, "God the Father and Gregory the Great: The Discovery of a Late Roman Childhood." *The Journal of Psychohistory* 25(1998): 437.

333. Herondas, *The Schoolmaster* 1; Carl A. Mounteer, "Roman Childhood," p. 239.

334. Danièle Alexandre-Bidon, *Children in the Middle Ages: Fifth-Fifteenth Centuries*, p. 40.

335. Bartholemew Batty, *The Christian Man's Closet*, p. 25.

336. Geraldine Youda, *Minding the Children*. New York: Scribners, 1998, p. 36.

337. Albertine Adrienne Necker, *Progressive Education, Commencing with the Infant*. Boston: W. D. Ticknor, 1935, p. 336.

children in history who could be said not to have been beaten at all[338]—particularly in America, where European visitors agreed "one and all that American children were badly spoiled."[339] Although Pleck's massive study of American family violence found all eighteenth-century children she studied "were hit with an object . . . ranging from a belt to a horsewhip,"[340] she found some in the nineteenth century who were not hit at all. Mothers discovered for the first time in history that they could have "a deep, unquenchable love for their offspring,"[341] and would abjure all "whipping, caning, slapping, ear-pulling, or hair-dragging,"[342] favoring chastising words or locking up in a room instead. By the early twentieth century, 12 percent of white Americans in one study claimed never to have been spanked.[343] In schools, however, most Americans agreed with the teacher who said that "moral suasion's my belief but lickin's my practice,"[344] and Boston schools in 1850 found that it took "sixty-five beatings a day to operate a school of four hundred."[345] Even though twenty-three states approve of school beatings, and three million children are still paddled in American schools yearly,[346] corporal punishment in the United States is nothing like the infamous British school floggings that continued unabated throughout the twentieth century, where the beatings were often inflicted by flagellomaniacal teachers in public displays of cruelty.[347]

---

338. Lloyd deMause, *Foundations of Psychohistory*, p. 49.

339. Charles H. Sherrill, *French Memories of Eighteenth-Century America*. New York: C. Scribner's Sons, 1915, p. 72.

340. Elizabeth Pleck, *Domestic Tyranny: The Making of Social Policy Against Family Violence from Colonial Times to the Present*. Oxford: Oxford University Press, 1987, p. 46.

341. Jan Lewis, "Mother's Love: The Construction of an Emotion in Nineteenth-Century America." Rima D. Apple and Janet Golden, Eds., *Mothers and Motherhood: Readings in American History*. Columbus: Ohio State University Press, 1997, p. 52.

342. Melesina French, *Thoughts on Education By a Parent*. Southampton: Not Published, 1810.

343. David I. Macleod, *The Age of the Child: Children in America, 1890–1920*. New York: Twayne Publishers, 1998, p. 59.

344. LeRoy Ashby, *Endangered Children: Dependency, Neglect, and Abuse in American History*. New York: Twayne Publishers, 1997, p. 20.

345. Irwin A. Hyman, *Reading, Writing, and the Hickory Stick: The Appalling Story of Physical and Psychological Abuse in American Schools*. Lexington: Lexington Books, 1990, p. 35.

346. *The New York Times*, July 9, 1987, p. A1.

347. Ian Gibson, *The English Vice*, 1978.

Fig. 8–6. Child being beaten by teacher

Polls of American parents' spanking practices show about a quarter still hit their children with some hard object, mothers beating more than fathers, and toddlers being the ones most often beaten.[348] In 1992, over 90 percent of American parents hit their young children; this rate dropped to 57 percent by 1999.[349] No relationship has been found between amount of wealth and the use of corporal punishment.[350] In 1979 Sweden became the first country in the world to ban all corporal punishment of children, so that even though there is no penalty for parents who hit their children, the disapproval alone, plus the training of high school children in alternatives to hitting, has reduced the number of children hit to under 30 percent.[351] There are, at this writing, eight more European nations that have introduced antispanking statutes, and even Germany and England are considering them—though the practice itself has not yet been affected by

---

348. *The New York Times*, December 7, 1995, p. B16; Murray A. Straus and Anita K. Mathur, "Social Change and Trends in Approval of Corporal Punishment by Parents from 1968 to 1994." In D. Frehsee et al., Eds., *Violence Against Children*. New York: Walter de Gruyter, p. 100; Murray A. Straus, *Beating the Devil Out of Them: Corporal Punishment in American Families*. New York: Lexington Books, 1994, p. 23.

349. Tracy L. Dietz, "Disciplining Children: Characteristics Associated With The Use of Corporal Punishment." *Child Abuse & Neglect* 24(2000): 1529, 1536.

350. Ibid., p. 1531.

351. Susan H. Bitensky, "Spare the Rod, Embrace Our Humanity: Toward a New Legal Regime Prohibiting Corporal Punishment of Children." *University of Michigan Journal of Law Reform* 31(1998): 367; Joan E. Durrant, "Evaluating the Success of Sweden's Corporal Punishment Ban." *Child Abuse and Neglect* 23(1999): 435–447.

the statutes.[352] Most of the nations of Western Europe currently have hitting rates somewhat higher than those of America, while outside of Western Europe most rates are considerably higher.[353]

FREEZING, TOSSING, AND TORTURING CHILDREN

The number of daily tortures routinely inflicted upon children in the past
seem beyond comprehension. From birth, children had to endure constant
freezing practices, including ice-water bathing and baptism:

> Children were baptized by being plunged into a large hole which had
> been made in the ice [on the river] Neva, then covered with five feet of
> ice. . . . The priest happened to let one of the children slip through his
> hands. "Give me another," he cried. . . . I saw that the father and mother
> of the child were in an ecstasy of joy. . . . The babe had been carried
> straight to heaven.[354]

> The mother took the naked baby and a pot of hot water into the back-
> yard . . . poured the water on the snow, melting it and creating a pool
> which could serve as a washing basin for several days; all she had to do
> the next day was to break the ice.[355]

Ice-water bathing was a widespread historical practice from antiquity
to modern times, "the colder the Bath the better . . . use every Day,"[356] so
that "the shock was dreadful, the poor child's horror of it, every morning,

352. See Web site of EPOCH-USA at *www.stophitting.com*.

353. Detlev Frehsee, "Einige Daten zur endlosen Geschichte des Züchtigungsrechts."
Bielefeld: Deutscher Kinderschutzbund, 1997; Harry Hendrick, *Children, Childhood and
English Society, 1880–1990*. Cambridge: Cambridge University Press, 1997; Ken Schooland,
Shogun's Ghost: The Dark Side of Japanese Education. New York: Bergin & Garvey, 1990;
Michio Kitahara, "Childhood in Japanese Culture." p. 49; Catherine So-kum Tang, "The
Rate of Physical Child Abuse in Chinese Families: A Community Survey in Hong Kong."
Child Abuse & Neglect 22(1998): 381–391; Igor S. Kon, *The Sexual Revolution in Russia*. New
York: The Free Press, 1995, p. 215.

354. Arthur Machen, Trans., *The Memoirs of Jacques Casanova de Seingalt*. New York:
G. P. Putnam's Sons, n.d., Vol. V, p. 512.

355. Alenka Puhar, "On Childhood Origins of Violence in Yugoslavia: II. The
Zadruga." *The Journal of Psychohistory* 21(1993): 186.

356. Bogna Lorence, "Parents and Children in Eighteenth-Century Europe," p. 17.

when taken out of bed, still more so."[357] The excuse given was that it was necessary for "hardening" the child, "to toughen their bodies by dipping them into cold water like white-hot iron,"[358] so that when the "little infant [is washed] in cold water . . . itself in one continuous scream [the] mother covering her ears under the bed-clothes that she may not be distressed by its cries"[359] it can be hardened to life's cruelties. John Locke not only recommended parents wash the feet of their children every day in cold water, but also make them wear "shoes so thin that they might leak and let in water" and clothes and sleeping quarters that allow them to be cold all the time.[360] Most societies used these Spartan hardening practices. Russians complained about traditional hardening such as being put to bed wrapped in wet cold towels,[361] and Colonial New England children were made to sit with wet feet "more than half the time."[362] Alternatively, mothers were so unable to empathize with their children that they often "take no notice what pains they cause and make baths for children so hot" they were badly burned.[363]

Many people over the centuries complained of parents who customarily tossed infants, as when the brother of Henri IV, while being passed for amusement from one window to another, was dropped and killed.[364] Children were often put to bed tied up by the hands; made to wear corsets with bone stays, iron bodices, and steel collars; and forced to sit many hours a day in stocks, strapped to a backboard, supposedly to teach them restraint.[365]

357. Charles Southey, *The Life and Correspondence of Robert Southey*. New York: Harper, 1855, p. 24.

358. Galen, *De Sanitate Tuenda*. 33.

359. Scevole de St. Marthe, *Paedotrophia: or, The Art of Nursing and Rearing Children*. London: John Nichols, 1797, p. 63.

360. John J. Waters, "James Otis, Jr.: An Ambivalent Revolutionary." *History of Childhood Quarterly* 1(1973): 144.

361. Isaac Deutscher, *Lenin's Childhood*. London: Oxford University Press, 1970, p. 10;

362. James Bossard, *The Sociology of Child Development*. New York: Harper, 1948, p. 630.

363. Felix Wurtz, *The Surgeons Guide: or Military and Domestique Surgery with a Guide for Women in the Nursing of Their New-born Children*. London: n.p., 1658, p. 346.

364. Lloyd deMause, "The Evolution of Childhood," p. 34.

365. Alice Morse Earle, *Two Centuries of Costume in America. Vol. I.* New York: Macmillan, 1903, p. 317.

Reports of shutting up little children in closets for hours were legion.[366] Painful daily enemas were often given, since "it was thought that children should be purged especially before eating 'for fear that the milk will be mixed with some ordure.'"[367] Children were often put to bed and told to think about their death and the misery they will feel in Hell.[368] Children were religiously taken to witness public executions, then "on returning home, whipped . . . to make them remember the example."[369] Children from antiquity were endlessly frightened that they would be eaten up, abducted, or cut up by ghosts, such as Lamia, "the black man who comes for naughty children," "the goblin in the basement," "the tailor with the huge sizzors," and "Striga that attack children, defile their bodies and rend the flesh of sucklings with their beaks."[370] To make the terror more real, their caregivers would actually dress up dummies in order to terrorize them, or would paint themselves as the werewolf or bloody monster and "roar and scream at the child [and] make as if it would swallow the infant up."[371]

THE ABANDONMENT OF CHILDREN

Abandonment of children may seem less traumatic than tying up, beating, and terrorizing them, but adult autobiographers rarely fail to mention the deep hurt they felt as children when they were given away by their parents. Newborn infants who were abandoned on the side of the road almost always died,[372] but even the babies born who were abandoned to found-

366. Jack Lindsay, *1764: The Hurlyburly of Daily Life* . . . London: Frederick Muller, 1959, p. 42; Elizabeth Grant Smith, *Memoirs of a Highland Lady*. London: John Murray, 1898, p. 49.

367. David Hunt, *Parents and Children in History*, p. 144.

368. Lawrence Stone, *The Family, Sex and Marriage*, p. 173; Sanford Fleming, *Children and Puritanism*. New Haven: Yale University Press, 1933, p. 100.

369. Gordon Rattray Taylor, *The Angel Makers*, p. 313.

370. John Cuthbert Lawson, *Modern Greek Folklore and Ancient Greek Religion*. Cambridge: Cambridge University Press, 1910, p. 174–184; Ovid, *Fasti*. London: William Heinemann, 1931, p. 329; George K. Behlmer, *Child Abuse and Moral Reform in England, 1870–1908*. Stanford: Stanford University Press, 1982, p. 5; Mrs. Hoare, *Hints for the Improvement of Early Education*. Salem: James Buffum, 1826, p. 69.

371. Anon., *Dialogues on the Passions, Habits and Affections Peculiar to Children*. London: R. Griffiths, 1748, p. 31.

372. Boswell's assumption that they were picked up by other parents is wholly

ling homes, beginning in the modern period, usually died from maltreatment in the institutions.[373] Visitors to these foundling homes described the children there as

> stunted creatures, neither childlike nor human. . . . They sit close-packed against the wall or gathered into knots, dull and stupefied. . . . Never played with or cuddled. . . . It is a holiday when they are taken for a walk around the room. . . . It is a room of filth, filled with ceaseless crying, where their lack of decent covering, their misery and consequent infirmities combine to bring about their death within a few days.[374]

Most of the children abandoned in foundling homes were legitimate[375]— more girls than boys[376]—and up to 90 percent of foundlings died either in the hospital or when sent to a wet nurse. It is no wonder that it was proposed that a motto be carved over the gate of one foundling home: "Here children are killed at public expense."[377] It is unlikely that historians are correct in concluding that this mass abandonment of babies "reflected not so much a lack of love for them as a deep fear of loving them."[378]

Babies not abandoned to foundling homes could be sold by their parents as slaves during most of history; indeed, there are still hundreds of thousands of chattel slaves around the world today, even more in debt bondage.[379] Public auctions of children were common throughout Eu-

---

undocumented; see John Boswell, *The Kindness of Strangers: The Abandonment of Children in Western Europe from Late Antiquity to the Renaissance.* New York: Pantheon Books, 1988.

373. David I. Kertzer, *Sacrificed for Honor: Italian Infant Abandonment and the Politics of Reproductive Control.* Boston: Beacon Press, 1993, pp. 73.

374. Joan Sherwood, *Poverty in Eighteenth-Century Spain: The Women and Children of the Inclusa.* Toronto: University of Toronto Press, 1988, pp. 132, 148.

375. Hugh Cunningham, *Children and Childhood in Western Society Since 1500,* p. 94.

376. David I. Kertzer, *Sacrificed for Honor,* p. 111.

377. Beatrice, *The Family in the Western World from the Black Death to the Industrial Age.* New York: Oxford University Press, 1993, p. 146; Volker Hunecke, *Die Findelkider von Mailand.* Stuttgart: Klett-Cotta, 1987; Jules Michelet, *Woman.* New York: Carleton, 1867, p. 67; Janet Golden, *A Social History of Wet Nursing in America,* p. 14; Sarah Blaffer Hrdy, *Mother Nature: A History of Mothers, Infants, and Natural Selection.* New York: Pantheon Books, 1999, p. 304; Louise A. Tilly et al., "Child Abandonment in European History: A Symposium." *Journal of Family History* 17(1992): 1–23.

378. Philip Gavitt, *Charity and Children in Renaissance Florence.* Ann Arbor: University of Michigan Press, 1990, p. 19.

379. Roger Sawyer, *Children Enslaved.* London: Routledge, 1988, pp. 22, 45; LeRoy

rope and Asia well into modern times.[380] One American colonist described
the sale of children in debt bondage that took place as ships arrived in
Philadelphia: "Many parents must sell and trade away their children like
so many head of cattle; for if their children take the debt upon themselves, the parents can leave the ship free and unrestrained."[381]

The one institution to which parents could abandon their children
and know they were more likely to live was the religious order. Parents
knew monasteries and nunneries were abusive—"There is an inscription
over the gate of hell: 'Abandon all hope, you who enter'; on the gate of
monasteries, the same should appear"[382]—but they nevertheless paid good
money to dump their children in them permanently.[383] Oblates were not
usually children of the poor, so there is no argument for economic necessity—parents usually gave large gifts to the religious orders to take their
children.[384] The child became a holocaust, a sacrifice, to God, and the clois-
ter "became a cruel life of hard labor, boring routine, beatings, and fear of
sexual sin and assault.[385] In return, the parents could expect "clerical prayer
and, ultimately, salvation"[386]—i.e., some peace in their heads from their
punitive maternal alter. The children held the legal status of slaves at the
monastery, and they were endlessly whipped, stripped naked, starved in
severe fasts, only allowed to sleep for five hours a night, and used sexually
by clerics and older boys.[387] Oblation began to decline in the late twelfth
century, as wealthy parents decided they preferred to hire servants to whip,
starve, torture, and sexually abuse their children in their own home.[388]

Ashby, *Endangered Children: Dependency, Neglect, and Abuse in American History*. New York:
Twayne Publishers, 1997, p. 14; Lloyd deMause, "The Evolution of Childhood,"
p. 35.

380. James Bossard, *The Sociology of Child Development*, p. 607–608.

381. Alden T. Vaughan, *America Before the Revolution 1725–1775*. Englewood Cliffs:
Prentice-Hall, 1967, p. 43.

382. Elizabeth Abbott, *A History of Celibacy*. New York: Scribner, 2000, p. 141.

383. Danièle Alexandre-Bidon and Didier Lett, *Children in the Middle Ages*, p. 49.

384. Mayke de Jong, *In Samuel's Image: Child Oblation in the Early Medieval West*.
Leiden: E. J. Brill, 1996, pp. 5, 158.

385. Steven Ozment, *When Fathers Ruled: Family Life in Reformation Europe*. Cambridge: Harvard University Press, 1983, p. 14.

386. Mayke de Jong, *In Samuel's Image*, p. 57.

387. Patricia A. Quinn, *Better Than the Sons of Kings: Boys and Monks in the Early Middle
Ages*, pp. 26, 115, 130.

388. Joseph H. Lynch, *Simoniacal Entry into Religious Life from 1000 to 1260: A Social, Economic, and Legal Study*. Columbus: Ohio State University Press, 1976.

SENDING OUT CHILDREN TO FOSTERAGE, APPRENTICESHIP, AND SERVICE

Another widespread abandonment practice throughout history was fosterage:

> Fosterage was found mainly among royalty and other well-to-do parents [and] was so common that the remark that "all the children grew up at home" was offered as an unusual occurrence. . . . Sons obtained new networks of kin relations, but bonding with the mother was most often precluded, and—most surprising to the modern reader—she did not seem to have desired her son's company.[389]

Children might be sent to fosterage "for affection or for payment" as soon as they returned from the wet nurse, usually to other family members, and not returned until adolescence.[390] Since so many families simply traded children with each other, the custom appears puzzling unless one realizes that adults emotionally were able to treat foster children more abusively— working them like slaves, beating them, using them sexually—than if they had kept their own children and not traded them with others.[391] Parents who foster their children today usually explain that they "cannot effectively discipline their own offspring" if they keep them themselves.[392] Fostering in archaic civilizations was so common the mother's brother was often called the "upbringer" or "fostering brother," and "among Hittites, Greeks, Romans, Celts, and Germans, mother's brothers [would] supervise initiation and . . . ritually sodomize his ward."[393] Fosterage was practiced in all complex civilizations well into modern times.[394] Parents would simply ask the

389. Jenny Jochens, "Old Norse Motherhood." In John Carmi Parsons and Bonnie Wheeler, Eds., *Medieval Mothering*. New York: Garland Publishing, 1996, p. 204.

390. P. W. Joyce, *A Social History of Ancient Ireland . . .* , 3rd ed. London: Longmans, Green & Co., 1920, Vol. 2, pp. 15–19.

391. Catherine M. Scholten, *Childbearing in American Society*, p. 64.

392. Joan B. Silk, "Adoption and Fosterage in Human Societies: Adaptation or Enigmas?" *Cultural Anthropology* 2(1987): 44.

393. David F. Greenberg, *The Construction of Homosexuality*. Chicago: University of Chicago Press, 1988, p. 109; Mark Golden, *Children and Childhood in Classical Athens*, p. 145.

394. Grant McCracken, "The Exchange of Children in Tudor England: An Anthropological Phenomenon in Historical Context." *The Journal of Family History* 8(1983): 303–313.

uncles or grandparents if they "needed a child"[395] and shipped one off to them. If one sent one's child to royalty and it was killed by abuse, one was expected to thank the foster parent and bring another.[396]

There was little difference between fosterage, adoption, apprenticeship, and service. All involved virtual slavery without rights for the children. The opinion of the Italian at the end of the fifteenth century in often quoted: "The want of affection in the English is strongly manifested towards their children. . . . They put them out, both males and females, to hard service in the houses of other people. . . . Few are born who are exempted from this fate, for every one, however rich he may be, sends away his children into the houses of others; whilst he, in return, receives those of strangers into his own." But the truth is that Italians of the time equally fostered out and apprenticed their children.[397] Everyone agreed that "it is good to remove children from the sight of their father and mother and give them to friends so that they do not become quarrelsome; also, when they are in a strange house, they are more timid and do not dare to enjoy themselves and fear being scolded."[398] Half of all persons who came to the colonies in the American South were indentured children.[399] England continued to send hundreds of thousands of children to Canada and Australia for fosterage well into the twentieth century; a Canadian minister complained about England's practice of using Canada as "a dumping ground for the refuse of the highways . . . waifs, strays, and the children of vicious and criminal tendencies."[400] The practice continues in many areas of the world for millions of children today.[401]

---

395. A. I. Richards, "Authority Patterns in Traditional Buganda." In L. A. Fallers, Ed., *The King's Men: Leadership and States in Buganda* . . . Oxford: Oxford University Press, 1964, p. 260.

396. Ibid., p. 263.

397. Anon., *A Relation or Rather a True Account of the Island of England . . . About the Year 1500*, Vol. 37. London: Camden Society, 1847, p. 24.

398. Philippe Ariès, "An Interpretation to be Used for a History of Mentalities." In Patricia Ranum, Ed., *Popular Attitudes Toward Birth Control in Pre-Industrial France and England.* New York: Harper, 1972, p. 117.

399. Mary Ann Mason, *From Father's Property to Children's Rights.* New York: Columbia University Press, 1994, p. 32.

400. Patricia T. Rooke and R. L. Schnell, "The 'King's Children' in English Canada: A Psychohistorical Study of Abandonment, Rejection and Colonial Response (1869–1930)." *The Journal of Psychohistory* 8(1981): 387.

401. Esther Goody, "Parental Strategies: Calculation or Sentiment?: Fostering Practices Among West Africans." In Hans Medick and David Warren Sabean, Eds., *Interest and*

Fig. 8–7. Mother beating servant

Apprenticeship and service were the fate of virtually all children, rich or poor alike.[402] A master "may be a tiger in cruelty, he may beat, abuse, strip naked, starve or do what he will to the poor innocent lad, few people take much notice."[403] Mothers also beat the girls apprenticed to them. A typical eighteenth-century description read: "Elizabeth began to beat and kick them about, and would drag them up and down stairs making use of the most horrible expressions. She always kept a rod soaking in brine, with which she used to beat them on their bare skin when they were undressed to go to bed. . . . She frequently tied the girl up naked and beat her with a hearth broom, a horsewhip or a cane, till the child was absolutely speechless."[404] Rape of these children was widespread—since they felt so lonely and rejected, they more easily allowed themselves to be used sexually in return for the illusion of some attention. In antiquity, raping servants was routine, since it was thought fidelity only meant "to the walls around the house, not to tie it down to the marriage bed itself."[405] Entries in diaries

---

Emotion: Essays on the Study of Family and Kinship. Cambridge: Cambridge University Press, 1984, pp. 265–277.

402. Michael Mitterauer, "Servants and Youth." *Continuity and Change* 5(1990): 11–38.

403. M. Dorothy George, *London Life in the Eighteenth Century.* New York: Harper, 1964, p. 227.

404. Mary Hopkirk, *Nobody Wanted Sam: The Story of the Unwelcomed Child, 1530–1948.* London: John Murray, 1949, p. 62.

405. Peter Brown, *The Body and Society: Men, Omen and Sexual Renunciation in Early Christianity.* New York: Columbia University Press, 1988, p. 23.

throughout history like "my master came to my bed at 2 o'clock in the morning and violated my person"[406] were common, and relatives who sent children to be servants would assure the new master that "[she] will match your cock."[407] Masters frequently slept at night with both their boy and girl servants and raped them.[408]

The work done by even small children sent out to others was often the heaviest and most dangerous that needed to be done.[409] Whether it was 12 hours a day of heavy labor in the fields[410] or the risky work of "climbing boys" who were constantly "pinned, beaten, cold, pinched and abused,"[411] even small children could not count on simple empathy during their time with others:

> Little boys had to go on sweeping chimneys and getting stuck in them or suffocated with soot, or even roasted. . . . Their terror of the dark, and often suffocating, flues had somehow to be overcome by the pressure of a greater terror below. . . . Masters would threaten to beat them [or] would set straw on fire below or thrust pins into their feet. . . . No wonder nursemaids threatened to give naughty children to the sweep, and children shrieked at sight of him.[412]

Even when schools began to be more widespread in the eighteenth century, the children would only go for a few years, then be sent to apprenticeship. One English girl remembered: "On the day that I was eight years of age, I left school, and began to work fourteen hours a day in the fields, with from forty to fifty other children. . . . We were followed all day

406. Francoise Barret-Ducroca, *Love in the Time of Victoria*. New York: Penguin Books, 1989, p. 48.

407. Anthony Fletcher, *Gender, Sex and Subordination in England 1500–1800*, p. 160.

408. Jonathan Goldber, *Queering the Renaissance*. Durham: Duke University Press, 1994, pp. 236–244.

409. Colin Heywood, *Childhood in Nineteenth-Century France: Work, Health, and Education Among the Classes Populaires*. Cambridge: Cambridge University Press, 1988.

410. Ruth Inglis, *Sins of the Fathers: A Study of the Physical and Emotional Abuse of Children*. New York: St. Martin's Press, 1978, p. 19.

411. Peter G. Clamp, "Climbing Boys, Childhood, and Society in Nineteenth-Century England." *The Journal of Psychohistory* 12(1984): 194.

412. Mrs. C. S. Peel, *The Stream of Time: Social and Domestic Life in England 1805–1861*. London: John Lane, 1931, p. 56.

long by an old man carrying a long whip in his hand which he did not forget to use.[413]

Beyond formal abandonment like fosterage and apprenticeship, mothers throughout history were constantly giving away their children for all kinds of rationalizations: "Because the mother was expecting another child" (Juhannes Butzbach), "to learn to speak" (Disraeli), "to cure timidness" (Clara Barton), for "health" (Edmund Burke), "as pledge for a debt" (Madame d'Aubigné), or simply because they were not wanted (Richard Baxter, Richard Savage, Augustus Hare, Swift). Hare's mother expresses the casualness of these abandonments: "Yes, certainly, the baby shall be sent as soon as it is weaned; and, if anyone else would like one, would you kindly recollect that we have others."[414] If no one wanted the child, it would most often be assigned to older children or nurses or others to care for (autobiographers regularly recalled that "I never saw my father and mother but for an instant in the morning"),[415] and they very often wandered off into the fire or fell down into the well.[416] Even in the modern period, when mothers began to show some interest in their infants, they soon grew tired of caregiving and sent their children elsewhere. On June 7, 1748, Madame d'Epinay got her 20-month-old son back from the wet nurse, begins by writing in her diary:

> My son is back with me. . . . He cries when I leave him. He is already afraid of me, and I am not sorry for it, for I do not want to spoil him. I sometimes think, when he smiles as he looks at me, and shows his delight at seeing me by clapping his little hands, that there is no satisfaction equal to that of making one's fellow-creatures happy.[417]

But she soon finds caregiving depressing, writes about the "apathy and indifference" she feels because her children "are only an occupation, a duty for

---

413. Martin Hoyles, *Changing Childhood*. London: Writers and Readers Publishing Cooperative, 1979, p. 3.

414. Augustus J. C. Hare, *The Story of My Life*. Vol. 1. London: G. Hare, 1896, p. 51.

415. Stephanie de Genlis, *Memoirs*, p. 20.

416. Barbara A. Hanawalt, "Childrearing Among the Lower Classes of Late Medieval England." *Journal of Interdisciplinary History* 8(1977): 17; Barbara A. Hanawalt, *The Ties That Bound*, p. 158; Carl Holliday, *Woman's Life in Colonial Days*. Boston: Cornhill Publishing Co., 1922, p. 25.

417. Louise Florence P. d'Epinay, *Memoirs of Madame d'Epinay*. Vol. I. Paris: Sociétés Bibliophiles, 1903, p. 106.

me, and do not fill my heart at all," and turns them over to the nurse, taking a lover for herself. This abandonment to others has continued until recently in Eastern European nations like the Soviet Union, where authorities often complained about "the cuckoo mother [who] by no means necessarily suffering financial hardship, selfishly decided it was easier to hand over her child to be brought up in state care rather than caring for the baby herself."[418]

MATERNAL INCEST: THE CHILD AS BREAST

In the previous chapter, widespread maternal incest—with the mother using the child as an erotic breast substitute by masturbating it or sucking on its genitals—was documented for many contemporary preliterate tribes. Although equally clear evidence is hard to come by in history because of the lack of detailed observations of early mothering in the past, it is likely that sexual abuse by mothers and wet nurses continued until modern times.

Maternal incest was likely the first form of attachment behavior for humans. Primate mothers are widely reported as copulating with their children; indeed, many cannot learn to reproduce unless they have had sex with adults when they were children.[419] Many immature primates "copulate with their mothers . . . explore adult genitalia and experience manipulation of their own."[420] Our closest ancestors, the bonobo chimps—termed "the erotic champions" of primates—spend much of their time in sucking and masturbating the genitals and "genitogenital rubbing" of both male and female juveniles, "to reduce tensions."[421] Primate young are regularly observed being taught to thrust against their mothers' genitals.[422]

---

418. Judith Harwin, *Children of the Russian State, 1917–95*. Aldershot: Avebury, 1996, p. 70.

419. Jay R. Reierman, "A Biosocial Overview of Adult Human Sexual Behavior with Children and Adolescents." In Jay R. Feierman, Ed., *Pedophilia: Biosocial Dimensions*. New York: Springer-Verlag, 1990, p. 30.

420. Ray H. Bixler, "Do We/Should We Behave Like Animals?" In William O'Donohue, Ed., *The Sexual Abuse of Children*, Vol. 1. Hillsdale, NJ: Lawrence Erlbaum Associates, 1992, p. 94.

421. Frans de Waal, *Bonobo: The Forgotten Ape*. Berkeley: University of California Press, 1997, pp. 100–105; Alexandra Maryanski and Jonathan H. Turner, *The Social Cage: Human Nature and the Evolution of Society*. Stanford: Stanford University Press, 1992, pp. 22–23.

422. Clara Mears Harlow, *From Learning to Love: The Selected Papers of H. F. Harlow*. New York: Praeger, 1986, p. 228; Gregory C. Leavitt, "Sociobiological Explanations of Incest

This "sexualization of the infant" was likely extended when human infants grew much larger heads, since it meant in order to get through the narrow birth canal before the head grew too large, human infants had to be "born fetal," extremely immature and increasingly helpless, so that in early humans "maternal attention was not sufficient to care for more helpless infants."[423] This in turn meant a selection for those babies who could most satisfy the mother's erotic needs—for instance through the extension of nonhairy, erotic skin areas—for they would be best nursed and cared for as an erotic, tension-reducing object. Likewise, those human mothers were selected who had evolved the largest and most erotic breasts to reach their children[424] and who had genitals shifted around to the front, where they could rub them against their children.[425]

The psychogenic evolution of the central motivation for mothering from incest to empathy took many millennia, and incest is still far more prevalent than is realized. Since both the perpetrators and the victims of maternal incest also collude in denying its occurrence, current figures for sexual abuse by females—13 percent of girls and 24 percent of boys—are considered likely to be underestimates.[426] (Some studies actually find girls twice as likely to be abused by women as by men.[427]) This denial is possible because women sexually abuse children at a much younger age than men do, so the incidents are more likely to be repressed by victims.[428] Maternal sexual abuse is widely acknowledged to "remain undetected"[429]

Avoidance: A Critical Review of Evidential Claims." *American Anthropologist* 92(1990): 981; R. Dale Guthrie, *Body Hot Spots: The Anatomy of Human Social Organs and Behavior*. New York: Van Nostrand Reinhold Co., 1976, p. 96.

423. Wenda R. Trevathan, *Human Birth: An Evolutionary Perspective*. New York: Aldine de Gruyter, 1987, p. 33.

424. Helen E. Fisher, *Anatomy of Love: The Natural History of Monogamy, Adultery, and Divorce*. New York: W. W. Norton and Co., 1992, p. 180.

425. Lloyd deMause, "The Role of Adaptation and Selection in Psychohistorical Evolution." *The Journal of Psychohistory* 16(1989): 362.

426. Anne Banning, "Mother-Son Incest: Confronting a Prejudice." *Child Abuse & Neglect* 13(1989): 564.

427. Michele Elliott, "What Survivors Tell Us—An Overview." In Michele Elliott, Ed., *Female Sexual Abuse of Children: The Ultimate Taboo*. Harlow: Longman, 1993, p. 9.

428. Margaret M. Rudin, et al., "Characteristics of Child Sexual Abuse Victims According to Perpetrator Gender." *Child Abuse & Neglect* 19(1995): 963.

429. Adele Mayer, *Women Sex Offenders*. Holmes Beach: Learning Publications, 1992, p. 5.

and therefore to be badly "underreported . . . unless coercion was involved . . . [because] sexual abuse of children by adult females is usually non-violent and at times quite subtle [involving] intercourse, cunnilingus, analingus, fellatio, genital fondling, digital penetration . . . and direct exposure to adult sexual activity."[430] Genital contact with the mother is even more prevalent; in America, "more than fifty percent of eight- to ten-year-old daughters touched their mother's . . . genitals [and] more than forty percent of eight- to ten-year-old sons touched their mother's genitals."[431] Clinical studies reveal widespread masturbation by mothers of their little children "to counter her feelings of lethargy, depression and deadness," "the only way she could make herself go to sleep," or "painful manipulation of the genitals by mother [with] the wish to destroy the sexuality of the child."[432]

The sexual use of children by mothers has been widely reported by outside observers in nations outside the West. Childhood in much of India earlier in the century was said to begin with masturbation by the mother, "high caste or low caste, the girl 'to make her sleep well,' the boy 'to make him manly.'"[433] Like most traditional families, children rotated around the extended family as sleeping partners rather like a comfort blanket. One sociologist who did interviews reported "there is a lot of incest. . . . It is hidden along with other secrets of families and rarely gets a chance to come out, like seduction at the hands of trusted friends of the family. . . . To arrive at even a passable estimate of incest cases would be to touch the hornet's nest."[434] Throughout Indian history, says Spencer, "mothers stimulated the penises of their infants and gave a 'deep massage' to their daughters as a

---

430. Christine Lawson, "Mother-Son Sexual Abuse: Rare or Underreported? A Critique of the Research." *Child Abuse & Neglect* 17(1993): 261, 266; Ira J. Chasnoff, et al., "Maternal-Neonatal Incest." *American Journal of Orthopsychiatry* 56(1986): 577–580.

431. A. A. Rosenfeld, et al., "Determining Contact Between Parent and Child: Frequency of Children Touching Parents' Genitals in a Non-Clinical Population." *Journal of the American Academy of Child Psychiatry* 25(1986): 229.

432. Estela V. Welldon, *Mother, Madonna, Whore: The Idealization and Denigration of Motherhood.* New York: Guilford Press, 1988, p. 96; Stanley J. Coen, "Sexualization as a Predominant Mode of Defense." *Journal of the American Psychoanalytic Association* 29(1981): 905; Joseph C. Rheingold, *The Fear of Being a Woman*, p. 108. Also see Mike Lew, *Victims No Longer: Men Recovering From Incest.* New York: Harper & Row, 1988.

433. Katherine Mayo, *Mother India.* New York: Harcourt Brace and Co., 1927, p. 25.

434. S. N. Rampal, *Indian Women and Sex.* New Delhi: Printoy, 1978, p. 69.

form of affectionate consolation."[435] Arab mothers are said to "rub the penis long and energetically to increase its size"; "in China, Manchu mothers tickle the genitals of their little daughters and suck the penis of a small son"; "in Thailand, mothers habitually stroke their son's genitals."[436]

Western observers even today often notice that Japanese mothers masturbate their young children during the day in public and at night in the family bed—in order, they say, "to put them to sleep."[437] The average Japanese mother sleeps with her children until they are 10 or 15 years old, traditionally sleeping "skin-to-skin" (*dakine*) while embracing her child because the father—as in the traditional gynarchy—is usually absent, over two-thirds of Japanese husbands being involved in extramarital intercourse.[438] Japanese mothers often teach their sons how to masturbate, helping them achieve first ejaculation in much the same manner as with toilet training.[439] As Kitahara writes, boys will typically report that "when he was 14 and was bathing with his mother, he inadvertently experienced an erection. The mother said, 'It is better to discharge it,' and she petted him to ejaculate. . . . Mothers teach their sons how to masturbate when they are 10 to 14 years old and tell them how often they may masturbate, helping their sons ejaculate."[440] A mental health hotline in Tokyo recently reported being flooded with calls about incest, 29 percent of them with complaints such as that the mother would offer her body for sex while telling the son: "You cannot study if you cannot have sex. You may use my body," or "I don't want you to get into trouble with a girl. Have sex with me instead."[441]

435. Colin Spencer, *Homosexuality in History*. New York: Harcourt Brace & Co., 1996, p. 79.

436. Allen Edwardes, *The Cradle of Erotica*. New York: Julian Press, 1963, p. 40; Raphael Patai, *The Arab Mind*. New York: Charles Scribner's Sons, 1983, p. 38; Given J. Broude, *Growing Up*, p. 303.

437. Robert J. Smith and Ella Lury Wiswell, *The Women of Suye Mura*. Chicago: University of Chicago Press, 1982, pp. 68–72; Douglas G. Harig, "Aspects of Personal Character in Japan." In Douglas G. Haring, Ed., *Personal Character and Cultural Milieu*. Syracuse: Syracuse University Press, 1956, p. 416; Nicolas Bornoff, *Pink Sairai: Love, Marriage and Sex in Contemporary Japan*. New York: Pocket Books, 1991, p. 76.

438. Edgar Gregersen, *Sexual Practices: The Story of Human Sexuality*. New York: Franklin Watts, 1983, p. 246.

439. Machio Kitahara, "Childhood in Japanese Culture," p. 56.

440. Ibid., pp. 55–56.

441. Michio Kitahara, "Incest—Japanese Style." *The Journal of Psychohistory* 17(1989): 446.

Japanese gynecologist Takeshi Wagatsuma reports "Japanese mothers often exhibit an obsession with their sons' penises. . . . [They are] usually brought in by their mothers who fear that their sons' penises are abnormally small,"[442] with the result that Japanese marriage clinics find "60 percent of their patients are afflicted with the 'no-touch syndrome,' that is, they will have no physical contact with their wives for fear that it will lead to sex . . . [termed] the 'I love mommy' complex."[443] Adams and Hill and Rosenman have thoroughly documented the castration anxieties commonly resulting from Japanese maternal incest.[444]

Maternal incest in history is difficult to document. Doctors often told mothers and nurses to "gently stretch the end of the foreskin every day" and to "massage the scrotum" as well as to infibulate the foreskin later.[445] Rabbinic sources deemed "a woman 'rubbing' with her minor son" common enough to have a law concerning it.[446] Myths and drama endlessly depicted maternal incest,[447] and dream books like Artemidorus' mostly interpreted dreams of maternal incest as indicating good luck.[448] Maternal incest in antiquity was not illegal,[449] nor was it spoken of as a *miasma*, an impurity,[450] and early civilizations from Egypt and Iran to Peru and Hawaii had brother-sister incestuous marriages where the parents played out their

442. Kenneth Alan Adams and Lester Hill, Jr., "The Phallic Planet." *The Journal of Psychohistory* 28(2000): 33.

443. Ibid., p. 31.

444. Kenneth Alan Adams and Lester Hill, Jr., "Castration Anxiety in Japanese Group-Fantasies." *The Journal of Psychohistory* 26(1999): 779–809; Kenneth Alan Adams and Lester Hill, Jr., "The Phallic Planet," pp. 24–52; Stanley Rosenman, "The Spawning Grounds of the Japanese Rapists of Nanking." *The Journal of Psychohistory* 28(2000): 2–23.

445. Aline Rousselle, *Porneia,* p. 54.

446. Michael L. Satlow, "'They Abused Him Like a Woman': Homoeroticism, Gender Blurring, and the Rabbis in Late Antiquity," *Journal of the History of Sexuality* 5(1994): 15.

447. Franz Borkenau, *End and Beginning: On the Generations of Cultures and the Origins of the West.* New York: Columbia University Press, 1981, pp. 116–117; Wolfgang Lederer, *The Fear of Women.* New York: Grune & Stratton, 1968, p. 121.

448. Artemidorus, *Oneirocritica* 1, 79–80; John J. Winkler, *The Constraints of Desire: The Anthropology of Sex and Gender in Ancient Greece.* New York: Routledge, pp. 34, 211–215.

449. Luciano P. R. Santiago, *The Children of Oedipus: Brother-Sister Incest in Psychiatry, Literature, History and Mythology.* Roslyn Heights: Libra Publications, 1973, p. 23.

450. Robert Parker, *Miasma: Pollution and Purification in Early Greek Religion.* Oxford: Clarendon Press, 1983, p. 97.

incestuous needs by forcing their children to marry each other—a third or more of marriages being incestuous in the case of Roman Egypt.[451]

Still, direct evidence of widespread maternal sexual use of children in history can hardly be expected if even today it is everywhere denied. True, doctors from Soranus to Fallopius counsel mothers "to take every pain in infancy to enlarge the penis of boys" by massage and the application of stimulants.[452] But usually the only reference to maternal incest is in the penitentials, where the Canons of Theodore mention that "a mother simulating sexual intercourse with her small son is to abstain from meat for three years,"[453] or, as in Dominici and Gerson, the child is told not to allow the mother to touch him.[454] One could also cite various clerics' reports of maternal incest, the many illustrations of mothers and grandmothers being shown with their hands on or near their children's genitals; or one could detail the nearly endless accounts in autobiographies and other direct reports of the sexual use of children by nurses and other female servants who masturbated and had intercourse with their charges "to keep them quiet," "for fun," or "to put them to sleep."[455] Freud's patients reported that "nursemaids, governesses, and domestic servants [were] guilty of [grave sexual abuses]"[456] and that "seduction is common [by] nurses who

451. Keith Hopkins, "Brother-Sister Marriage in Roman Egypt." *Comparative Studies in Society and History* 22(1980): 303–354; R. H. Bixler, "Sibling Incest in the Royal Families of Egypt, Peru and Hawaii." *Journal of Sex Research* 18(1983): 264–281; Russell Middleton, "Brother-Sister and Father-Daughter Marriage in Ancient Egypt." *American Sociological Review* 27(1988): 603–611.

452. Soranus, *Gynecology*, 107; Gabriel Falloppius, "De decoraturie trachtaties," cap. 9, *Opera Omnia*, Vol. 2. Frankfurt, 1600, p. 336.

453. Pierre J. Payer, *Sex and the Penitentials: The Development of a Sexual Code: 550–1150*. Toronto: University of Toronto Press, 1984, p. 31.

454. Giovanni Dominici, *On the Education of Children*. Washington, DC: Catholic University of America, 1927, p. 41; Jean Gerson, *Oevres Complètes. Vol. IX*. Paris: Desclée & Cie, 1973, p. 43.

455. Uta Ranke-Heinemann, *Eunuchs for the Kingdom of Heaven*, p. 123; Leo Steinberg, *The Sexuality of Christ in Renaissance Art and in Modern Oblivion*, 2nd ed. Chicago: University of Chicago Press, 1996, pp. 9, 40, 73; Jean-Jacques Bouchard, *Les Confessions de Jean-Jacques Bouchard*. Paris: Librairie Gallimard, 1930, pp. 28–36; Wilhelm Reich, *Passion of Youth: An Autobiography, 1897–1922*. New York: Farrar, Straus, Giroux, 1988, pp. 6–25; Joseph W. Howe, *Excessive Venery, Masturbation and Continence*. New York: E. B. Treat, 1893, p. 63; Bernard Grebanier, *The Uninhibited Byron: An Account of His Sexual Confusion*. New York: Crown Publishers, 1970, p. 24; C. Gasquoine Hartley, *Motherhood and the Relationships of the Sexes*. New York: Dodd, Mead & Co., 1917, p. 312.

456. Freud, *Standard Edition*. Vol. III, p. 164.

Fig. 8–8. Christ's genitals are stroked by his grandmother

put crying children to sleep by stroking their genitals."[457] Alternatively, one could document various other routine practices of mothers that indicated they used their children erotically, such as the habit of grandmothers and mothers to "lick it with 'the basting tongue'" all day long, sucking their lips, faces and breasts as though the child was itself a breast[458]; or one could describe the incestuous behavior in the public baths—many of them doubling as brothels—in which mothers and children co-bathed.[459]

There is one indirect measure of maternal incestuous practice that could indicate that mothers were acting out their erotic need to violate their daughters' genitals. Mothers in China and India have been observed to

---

457. Ibid., Vol. XXI, p. 232; Vol. VII, p. 180.

458. Daphne duMaurier, *The Young George duMaurier: A Selection of His Letters 1860–67*. London: Peter Davies, 1951, p. 223; David Herlihy and Christiane Klapisch-Zuber, *Tuscans and Their Families*. New Haven: Yale University Press, 1978, p. 255; Christian Augustus Struve, *A Familiar Treatise on the Physical Education of Children . . .* London: Murray & Highley, 1801, p. 273.

459. Abeelwahab Bouhdiba, *Sexuality in Islam*. London: Routledge and Kegan Paul, 1985, pp. 119, 165–173; Norbert Elias, *The Civilizing Process*. Oxford: Blackwell, 1994, p. 135; Fernando Henriques, *Prostitution in Europe and the Americas*. New York: Citadel Press, 1965, p. 57.

Fig. 8–9. Mothers with their children in bathhouse

"clean the sexual organs of the little children during daily washings . . . so scrupulously" that the girls have no trace of a hymen. . . . Even Chinese doctors do not know anything about the existence of the hymen."[460] Arab mothers also have been reported to "practice 'deep cleansing' on their very young daughters, purposely tearing the girls' hymen."[461] A careful survey of physicians from antiquity to early modern times reveals that none of them were able to discover a hymen on any of the little girls they examined.[462] Obviously the mothers and wet nurses of little girls during this period were routinely rupturing the hymen during some assault on their vaginas. Even French physician Ambroise Paré in the sixteenth century found, when he dissected innumerable little girls as young as 3 years old: "I was never able to perceive it."[463] Occasionally a doctor like Soranus would find a hymen with his probe, but considered it an aberration.[464] If one

460. Heinrich Ploss, *Das weib in der Natur- und Völkerkunde. Anthropologische Stdien.2. Band 1.* Leipzig, 1887, p. 300.

461. Edgar Gregersen, *Sexual Practices*, p. 228.

462. Giulia Sissa, *Greek Virginity.* Cambridge: Harvard University Press, 1990.

463. Ibid., p. 176.

464. Ibid., p. 113.

wanted to determine if a girl was a virgin in Greece, one resorted to magical virginity tests, like sending her to a cave where a poisonous snake lived, and "if they were bitten, it was a sign that they were no longer chaste."[465] By the fifteenth century, the existence of the hymen and the act of deflowering by breaking it was finally recognized,[466] indicating that the practice of assaulting girls' genitals had become less than universal.[467]

By the sixteenth century, giant communal family beds, "with people packed like sardines between the blankets,"[468] including "grandparents, parents, children, servants, and visitors,"[469] began to diminish, so that over the next three centuries more and more people asked each other nostalgically, "Do you not remember those big beds in which everyone slept together without difficulty? . . . In those days men did not become aroused at the sight of naked women [but now] each one has his own separate bed."[470] The change was completely psychogenic, as it occurred in rich and poor families alike. Those too poor to afford separate beds simply turned the children around, so their heads were opposite to their parents, and nightclothes were used rather than "skin-to-skin" sleeping of previous times, so that even "working-class children seldom saw a naked body because most of their parents slept with their clothes on."[471] By 1908, incest was finally made a criminal offense; it is today a minor felony, rarely prosecuted, in most nations.[472]

---

465. Bradley A. Te Paske, *Rape and Ritual: A Psychological Study*. Toronto: Inner City Books, 1982, p. 117.

466. Danielle Jacquart and Claude Thomasset, *Sexuality and Medicine in the Middle Ages*. Princeton: Princeton University Press, 1988, p. 44.

467. Esther Lastique and Helen Rodnite Lemay, "A Medieval Physician's Guide to Virginity." In Joyce E. Salisbury, Ed., *Sex in the Middle Ages*. New York: Garland Publishing, 1991, p. 56.

468. Reginald Reynolds, *Beds: With Many Noteworthy Instances of Lying On, Under, or About Them*. Garden City: Doubleday & Co., 1951, p. 20.

469. William Manchester, *The World Lit Only by Fire: The Medieval Mind and the Renaissance*. Boston: Little, Brown and Co., 1992, p. 53.

470. Jean-Louis Flandrin, *Families in Former Times: Kinship, Household and Sexuality*. Cambridge: Cambridge University Press, 1979, p. 100.

471. J. Robert Wegs, *Growing Up Working Class: Continuity and Change Among Viennese Youth, 1890–1938*. University Park: Pennsylvania State University Press, 1989, p. 126.

472. Louise A. Jackson, *Child Sexual Abuse in Victorian England*. London: Routledge, 2000, p. 3; Andrew Vachss, "Comment on 'The Universality of Incest." *The Journal of Psychohistory* 19(1991): 219.

THE UBIQUITY OF CHILD SEXUAL MOLESTATION

The best studies of incidence of sexual molestation of children are those of American adults conducted by Wyatt and Russell,[473] both based on face-to-face interviews lasting from one to eight hours, so that time is allowed for the trust necessary for accurate recall. Russell found 38 percent and Wyatt 45 percent of women interviewed reported memories of sexual abuse during their childhood. In my article "The Universality of Incest,"[474] I corrected these figures to reflect the major biases in their studies, since their population does not include groups who have far higher than average sexual molestation experiences, such as criminals, prostitutes, and the mentally ill. The average age of the child molested was only 7 years old,[475] the average duration of abuse was 5 years,[476] and boys were more often molested by females while girls were more often molested by males.[477] The only comparable studies from interviews in other nations were a Canadian Gallup study, a York University study, and two British surveys, all four of which conclude with incidence rates the same or higher than the U.S. studies.[478]

With so many of the children today still being subjected to sexual abuse, even more children in the past were likely to have been routinely used as sexual objects by the adults around them. Although intimate historical records of past sexual abuse within the family are obviously selec-

---

473. Gail Elizabeth Wyatt, "The Sexual Abuse of Afro-American and White Women in Childhood." *Child Abuse & Neglect* 9(1985): 507–519; Diana E. H. Russell, *The Secret Trauma: Incest in the Lives of Girls and Women.* New York: Basic Books, 1986.

474. Lloyd de Mause, "The Universality of Incest." *The Journal of Psychohistory* 19(1991): 123–164.

475. Kathleen A. Kendall-Tackett and Arthur F. Simon, "Molestation and the Onset of Puberty: Data from 365 Adults Molested as Children." *Child Abuse and Neglect* 12(1988): 73.

476. Henry B. Bill and Richard S. Solomon, *Child Maltreatment and Paternal Deprivation.* Lexington: Lexington Books, 1986, p. 59.

477. M. Fromuth, "Childhood Sexual Victimization Among College Men." *Violence and Victim* 2(1987): 241–253; G. Fritz et al., "A Comparison of Males and Females Who Were Sexually Molested as Children." *Journal of Sex and Marital Therapy* 7(1981): 54–59.

478. R. F. Badgley, *Sexual Offenses Against Children. 2 Vols.* Ottawa: Canadian Government Publishing Centre, 1984; D. J. West, Ed., *Sexual Victimisation: Two Recent Researches into Sex Problems and Their Social Effects.* Aldershot: Hants, 1985; Judy Steed, *Our Little Secret: Confronting Child Sexual Abuse in Canada.* Toronto: Random House of Canada, 1994, p. xii.

tive, a few glimpses of the widespread frequency of this molestation can be recovered. For instance, when Beatrice Webb and others reported in the nineteenth century that they had found that the sexual abuse of young girls by their fathers and brothers was so common in the families they visited that the girls often joked about their babies being products of incest,[479] or when anthropologists report incest between fathers and daughters was quite common in rural villages from Greece to Japan,[480] one can reject the reports as being perhaps unrepresentative of whole nations. But when Karen Taylor studied 381 cases of venereal disease in nineteenth-century children and found that doctors in nineteenth-century Europe and America routinely treated children with venereal disease, mainly on their genitals, anuses, and mouths, she found she agreed with most of them, who reported that "there is no doubt in my mind that the father of this family was the source whence all the others received infections."[481] Since the diseases cannot spread except by sexual contact with open wounds, when doctors found fathers with ulcerations of the penis in the same families with children who had ulcerations on the genitals, anus, or mouth, incest had to be the cause. Reports from European hospitals showed similar patterns of venereal disease derived from incest in children.[482]

One method of revealing the routine nature of sexual abuse of children is to examine a child's life that is adequately recorded and see how everyone around him casually uses him sexually. The best-documented life of a child in past times was that of Louis XIII (born 1601), through the daily diary of Jean Héroard, his physician.[483] The assault on little Louis's erotic zones began at birth, with daily enemas and suppositories. These had nothing to do with toilet training or cleanliness—he was left filthy, and was nearly 7 years old before he had his first bath. As doctors regu-

---

479. Beatrice Webb, *My Apprenticeship.* London: Longmans, Green & Co., 1926, p. 321.

480. Richard and Eva Blum, *Health and Healing in Rural Greece: A Study of Three Communities.* Stanford: Stanford University Press, 1965; Shunichi Kubo, "Researches on Incest in Japan." *Hiroshima Journal of Medical Science* 8(1959): 99–159.

481. Karen J. Taylor, "Venereal Disease in Nineteenth-Century Children." *The Journal of Psychohistory* 12(1985): 441.

482. J. Robert Wegs, *Growing Up Working Class: Continuity and Change among Viennese Youth, 1890–1938,* p. 125.

483. Jean Héroard, *Journal de Jean Héroard sur l'enfance et la jeunesse de Louix XIII . . .* Ed. Soulié et Barthélemy. Paris: Firmin Didot Frères, 1868.

larly recommended for all infants,[484] frequent enemas or even fingers routinely put deep into the anus were for the purpose of removing the evil inside contents of the child, contents projected into them by the adults around them as a poison container.

Fondling, sucking, and kissing little Louis's penis and nipples were common practices by everyone around him—his parents, his nurses, his servants—beginning in his infancy and continuing throughout his childhood. This was done openly and without guilt. Sexual play with others became Louis's main topic of conversation, recorded in detail by Héroard. When he was an infant, all the women around him could hardly refrain from putting their hands up under his clothes. When he was 1 year old, still unable to walk, the entire court lined up to "kiss his cock."[485] At the same time, he was made to feel guilty for his own assault, being told, "Monsieur, never let anybody touch your nipples or your cock or they will cut it off." His parents often undressed him in the middle of the day and took him to bed with them and "gambled about freely" while they had intercourse.[486] After his father stretches out his penis and says, "Behold what made you what you are," Louis reports that "papa's penis is much longer than his, that it is this long, indicating half the length of his arm." "The Queen, touching his cock, tells him: 'Son, I am holding your spout.' . . . He was undressed and [his sister] too and they were placed naked in bed with the King, where they kissed and twittered and gave great amusement to the King. The King asked him: 'Son, where is the Infanta's bundle?' He showed it to him, saying: 'There is no bone in it, Papa.' Then, as it was slightly distended, he added: 'There is now, there is sometimes.'"[487] By the time he was 4, he was also routinely taken to bed by his ladies-in-waiting and nurses and encouraged to explore their genitals and play sexual games like whipping their buttocks, later commenting publicly, "'Mercier has a cunt as big as that,' showing his two fists, and saying that 'there's a lot of water inside. . . . The cunt of Saint-Georges is big as this box [and] the cunt

484. Seymour Byman, "Psychohistory Attacked." *The Journal of Psychohistory* 5(1978): 578; Friedrich von Zglinicki, *Geschichte des Klistiers*. Frankfurt: Viola Press, n.d.

485. Elizabeth W. Marvick, "Childhood History and Decisions of State: The Case of Louis XIII." *History of Childhood Quarterly* 2(1974): 150.

486. Lucy Crump, *Nursery Life 300 Years Ago*. London: George Routledge & Sons, 1929, p. 64.

487. Philippe Ariès, *Centuries of Childhood: A Social History of Family Life*. New York: Alfred A. Knopf, 1962, p. 101.

of Dubois is big as my belly."[488] His nurse, Mercier, usually slept with him and used him sexually. When asked "What have you seen of Mercier?" he answered, "I've seen her hole." "Is it pretty then?" "No, it's pretty fat."

THE RAPE OF GIRLS IN HISTORY

The attitude of most adults until the twentieth century toward raping girls is summed up in the comments of a British journalist in 1924 who wrote, "Cases of incest are terribly common in all classes. [Usually] the criminal goes unpunished. . . . Two men coming out from [a rape] trial were overheard saying to a woman who deplored there had been no conviction, 'What nonsense! Men should not be punished for a thing like that. It doesn't harm the child."[489] The conviction that girls always "forget" about being raped after they grow up reaches back to Maimonides, who assures us that the rape of a girl under 3 was no cause for alarm for, once past 3, "she will recover her virginity and be like other virgins."[490] Historians continue today to idealize the rape of girls in early societies who were forced to serve as "sacred prostitutes."[491] Guilt about rape was missing in the past because men recognized only two sexual categories: rapists and raped, dominators or dominated. Socarides' pedophile patient tells him why he rapes little girls:

> "Women are filthy. They have menstruation, blood. . . . Kids are cleaner. . . . I have sex with kids so I won't die. It keeps me young, keeps me youthful. Having sex with women means that you are grown up already. Kids don't have sex with women, only grownups have sex with women. If I don't grow up, I don't die."[492]

Child rapists are so afraid of individuating that grown-up sex with women means leaving their neglectful/destructive mothers, which means death to

---

488. David Hunt, *Parents and Children in History*, pp. 163, 167.

489. Maria Adelaide Lowndes, "Child Assault in England." In Sheila Jeffreys, *The Sexuality Debates*. New York: Routledge & Kegan Paul, 1987, p. 278.

490. Florence Rush, *The Best Kept Secret: Sexual Abuse of Children*. Englewood Cliffs: Prentice-Hall, 1980, p. 27.

491. Nancy Qualls-Corbett, *The Sacred Prostitute: Eternal Aspects of the Feminine*. Toronto: Inner City Books, 1988.

492. Charles W. Socarides, *The Preoedipal Origin and Psychoanalytic Therapy of Sexual Perversions*. Madison, CT: International Universities Press, 1988, p. 455.

them. Raping a child means having possession of a good breast devoid of frightening configurations and overcoming an overpowering sense of emptiness, abandonment, and death. Rapists in history over and over again tell how rejuvenating raping children can be. Epictetus gives this advice to those who want to help others overcome their fear of death· "What if you offer him a little girl? And if it is in darkness?"[493] The traditional world was full of children—slaves, servants, sisters, street urchins, child prostitutes—all available to stave off death and loneliness and to revenge oneself upon the unloving mother.

Empathy for raped girls was missing in traditional societies. Even when the rapist was punished—and this was rare—it was only because "rape or seduction without paternal consent undermined the father's sovereign authority over his daughter."[494] A girl was quite unprotected if she did not live under the actual supervision of her father. Moreover, this protection did not extend to lower class girls, and if the guilty person was of high rank he was never prosecuted.[495] It was the general practice to brutally punish the girl if she was raped, so few ever told anyone about it.[496] Vives says, "I know that many fathers have cut the throats of their daughters [if raped]. . . . Hippomenes, a great man of Athens, when he knew his daughter was debauched, shut her up in a stable with a wild horse, kept meatless, [who] tore the young woman [apart] to feed himself."[497] Girls in the past—as in many Arab countries still today—would often be killed if they had been raped.[498] Even today in rural Greek communities, anthropologists report that "incest may sometimes be practiced, with the father, or both the fathers and the brothers, exploiting the growing girl. . . . If the girl should become pregnant . . . her brothers or her father will kill her [in] an

---

493. Aline Rousselle, "The Family Under the Roman Empire: Signs and Gestures." In André Burguiére, et al., Eds., *A History of the Family: Vol. One*, p. 280.

494. Giulia Sissa, *Greek Virginity*, p. 88.

495. Martin Killias, "The Historic Origins of Penal Statutes Concerning Sexual Activities Involving Children and Adolescents." *Journal of Homosexuality* 20(1990): 43.

496. Anna Clark, *Women's Silence, Men's Violence: Sexual Assault in England 1770–1845*. London: Pandora, 1987, p. 30.

497. Juan Luis Vives, "A Very Fruitful and Pleasant Book Called the Instruction of a Christian Woman." In Joan Larsen Klein, Ed., *Daughters, Wives, and Widows*, p. 105.

498. WCBS-TV, "60 Minutes," October 19, 2000.

'honor' killing."[499] Or, in antiquity, "the father could exercise his power by putting the raped girl up for sale."[500]

Men began raping girls when they were extremely young. Even today, the average age of rape is 7 years, with 81 percent of sexual abuse occurring before puberty.[501] Incestuous rape was ubiquitous in traditional societies; as the Indian proverb put it, "For a girl to be a virgin at ten years old/ She must have neither brothers nor cousin nor father."[502] In the Babylonian Talmud, a celebrated rabbi is told by a woman that she was raped when she was under 3 years of age, and he tells her it didn't matter because she "ultimately enjoyed the experience."[503] Little girls were routinely sexually used throughout history. Well into the modern period, many people thought raping little girls was actually a good idea because it was instructive for them; a woman physician wrote in 1878:

> Infants but two and three years of age are often raped, by men of all ages, not only for present gratification, but to familiarize girls of immature ages with carnal matters and to excite, so that seduction may be easy in the future. . . . We cannot too strongly impress upon the fathers of daughters their duty in seeing that their little girls are instructed in regard to the certainty of protecting themselves against rapes, by grabbing the testicles.[504]

Although only 3 percent of women report incest with fathers in America today,[505] Gordon found far more widespread incest in nineteenth-century American families, with biological fathers accounting for nearly

---

499. Richard and Eva Blum, *Healthy and Healing in Rural Greece: A Study of Three Communities*. Stanford: Stanford University Press, 1965, p. 49.

500. Giulia Sissa, *Greek Virginity*, p. 88.

501. Kathleen A. Kendall-Tackett, "Molestation and the Onset of Puberty." *Child Abuse & Neglect* 12(1988): 76; David Finkelhor, *Child Sexual Abuse: New Theory and Research*. New York: Free Press, 1984; J. Michael Cupoli, "One Thousand Fifty-Nine Children With a Chief Complaint of Sexual Abuse." *Child Abuse & Neglect* 12(1988): 158.

502. Paul G. Brewster, *The Incest Theme in Folksong*. Helsinki: Academia Scientiarum Fennica, 1972, p. 27.

503. R. E. L. Masters and Edward Lea, *Sex Crimes in History*. New York: Julian Press, 1963, p. 195.

504. A Woman Physician and Surgeon, *Unmasked, or, The Science of Immorality*. Philadelphia: William H. Boyd, 1878, pp. 88, 91.

505. Diana E. H. Russell, *The Secret Trauma*, p. 234.

half of the cases that reached Boston courts.[506] Lowndes reported that the only reason British courts were not swamped by paternal incest cases was that they simply didn't believe the victims. The Society for Prevention of Cruelty to Children was precluded from touching incest cases.[507] "Cases were hushed up; the rapist bribed parents not to report them; and wives might refuse to believe that the husbands were capable of such monstrosity, turning on their daughters if they complained."[508] Records of mothers colluding with the fathers' rape were legion, as in the colonial American family where the mother "forced her daughter to go to bed with her stepfather, and, as the girl told the court, 'my mother held me by the hand whilst my father did abuse me and had his will of me.'"[509] Many if not most "delinquent" girls in the past were simply victims of incest:

> A Chicago study of delinquent girls in 1917 included many anecdotal cases of [sexual] abuse by relatives or neighbors, including "one girl raped by her own father when she was ten years of age, one by an uncle, two by boarders." In such accounts, phrases like "incest with a father" and "raped by a lodger" recur in a bleak litany. Jane Addams noted in 1913 that "a surprising number of little girls have first become involved in wrongdoing through the men of their own households," often as a result of assaults that occurred before the victims were eight years old.[510]

The entire gynarchy often colluded in the rapes. One of Madame Du Barry's main duties was "to search the land for the most beautiful girls who could be bought or kidnapped [as] 'baby-mistresses'" for Louis XV: "And with each of them, it was his custom before violating them to have them kneel with him in prayer at the edge of the bed which was to be the place of their defloration."[511] Even Queen Elizabeth was made to play sexual games in

506. Linda Gordon, *Heroes of Their Own Lives: The Politics and History of Family Violence—Boston 1880–1960*. New York: Viking, 1988, p. 211.

507. Maria Adelaide Lowndes, "Child Assault in England," pp. 271–278.

508. Lionel Rose, *The Erosion of Childhood: Child Oppression in Britain 1860–1918*. London: Routledge, 1991, p. 22.

509. David H. Flaherty, *Privacy in Colonial New England*. Charlottesville: University Press of Virginia, 1972, p. 80.

510. Philip Jenkins, *Moral Panic: Changing Concepts of the Child Molester in Modern America*. New Haven: Yale University Press, 1998, p. 33.

511. Russell Trainer, *The Lolita Complex*. New York: Citadel Press, 1966, p. 22.

bed with her foster father in the home where she was sent as a teenager[512]—
which could be the reason why she never married.

If the father had no daughter, he could use his son's child bride:

> Fathers marry their sons to some blooming girl in the village at a very
> early age, and then send the young men either to Moscow or St. Peters-
> burg to seek employment. . . . When the son returns to his cottage, he
> finds himself nominal father of several children, the off-spring of his
> own parent. . . . This is done all over Russia.[513]

It is not surprising that Duby reports of medieval families that they
were

> a hotbed of sexual adventure . . . penitentials forbid a man to know his
> wife's sister or daughter, his brother's wife. . . . Maidservants, female
> relatives, women still "vacant," or not yet disposed of [were] an open
> invitation to male licentiousness. In this small enclosed Paradise every
> man was an Adam: the young, the not so young, and first and foremost
> the head of the family, all were constantly exposed to temptation.[514]

Grandfathers in particular had to be warned by early psychoanalysts not
to insert their fingers into their granddaughters' vaginas.[515] The traditional
family of the past was similar to families in less advanced areas today. For
instance, a recent report of Middle Eastern women found four out of five
recalled having been forced into fellatio between the ages of 3 and 6 by
older brothers and other relatives.[516] The molestation begins with masturbation or fellatio and proceeds to intercourse: "In most cases the girl sur-
renders and is afraid to complain since, if there is any punishment to be
meted out, it will always end up by being inflicted on her."[517] Consent of

---

512. Alison Plowden, *The Young Elizabeth.* New York: Macmillan & Co., 1971,
pp. 87–88.
513. Robert Ker Porter, "Traveling Sketches in Russia and Sweden, 1805–08." In
Peter Putnam, Ed., *Seven Britons in Imperial Russia, 1698–1812.* Princeton: Princeton University Press, 1952, p. 327.
514. Georges Duby, *The Knight, the Lady and the Priest: The Making of Modern Marriage in Medieval France.* New York: Pantheon Books, 1983, p. 70.
515. Florence Rush, *The Best Kept Secret*, p. 57.
516. Allen Edwardes, *The Cradle of Erotica*, p. 300.
517. Nawal El Saadawi, *The Hidden Face of Eve: Women in the Arab World.* Boston:
Beacon Press, 1980, p. 14.

the girl to intercourse is such a foreign notion that Old French doesn't even have a word for "rape, although medieval French literature is full of comic portrayals of violent sexual assaults on young girls."[518] Rape of girls was little noticed and rarely punished well into the eighteenth century, because, as Anna Clark puts it, "men seemed to regard rape as a trivial issue."[519]

Sexual slavery—whether of actual slaves or of foster children, servants, or apprentices—was very widespread in the past. Even today there are over 100 million sexual slaves around the world, most of them starting their sexual services as children.[520] Nor is the sale always forced by poverty: "A recent survey in Thailand found that of the families who sold their daughters, two-thirds could afford not to do so but instead preferred to buy color televisions and video equipment."[521] Rape of girl servants in the past was nearly universal:

> Masters seemed to believe that they had a right to their servants' or apprentices' sexual favours, a right they would claim by force if servants did not acquiesce. . . . In 1772, when Sarah Bishop, aged sixteen, claimed to her mistress that her master had raped her, the mistress told her "he always served all his servants so the night they came into the house." . . . Rape seems to have been almost a ritual assertion of the master's authority. . . . He believed that he had committed no crime.[522]

The majority of girls raped were done so with some sort of collusion of their parents. Mothers commonly rented out rooms to boarders and forced their daughters to sleep with them.[523] Throughout medieval Europe "daughters were loaned to guests as an act of hospitality."[524] In Victorian London, "children went out onto the streets 'with the connivance of the mother,' returned home at night, and made their contribution to 'the profit

---

518. Kathryn Gravdal, *Ravishing Maidens: Writing Rape in Medieval French Literature and Law*. Philadelphia: University of Pennsylvania Press, 1991, pp. 2, 128.

519. Anna Clark, *Women's Silence, Men's Violence: Sexual Assault in England, 1770–1845*. London: Pandora Press, 1987, p. 44.

520. Gordon Thomas, *Enslaved*. New York: Pharos Books, 1991, p. 3.

521. Kevin Bales, *Disposable People*. Berkeley: University of California Press, p. 220.

522. Anna Clark, *Women's Silence, Men's Violence*, p. 41.

523. Louise A. Jackson, *Child Sexual Abuse in Victorian England*. London: Routledge, 2000, p. 111.

524. Samuel X. Radbill, "Children in a World of Violence: A History of Child Abuse." In Ray E. Helfer and Ruth S. Kampe, *The Battered Child*, 4th ed. Chicago: University of Chicago Press, 1987, p. 9.

of the household.'"[525] Children as young as 6 were openly offered for sale and sexual use by public advertisements in most cities of Europe.[526] One British chaplain declared that trying to stop child prostitution was like "taking a spoon to empty the Mersey."[527] It was estimated in Victorian London that one house in sixty was a brothel (6,000 in all) and one female in sixteen a prostitute.[528] Virtually all prostitutes began their trade either after rape in homes as children, or because they were sold by their parents into prostitution.[529] In antiquity, either "sacred" prostitution—with as many as 6,000 prostitutes available in many temples—or sex slavery was the lot of the majority of little girls born.[530] Fathers sold and rented out their daughters for sexual use without the least guilt.[531] If Genesis is to be believed, Lot handed over his two daughters for sexual use without even a payment.[532] Chinese chiefs would provide harem girls for guests to rape.[533] Greek plays portray the sexual use of slave girls as routine.[534] Greek wives were often not allowed to do farming chores lest they be raped.[535] Byzantine author John Chrysostom tells parents to frighten their children not to go out into the streets because they "ran the risk of sexual attack by pedophiles offering sweets and nuts."[536] Christianity changed little in the use of young girls for raping. Convents were open brothels where "monks

---

525. Michael Pearson, *The Five-Pound Virgins*. New York: Saturday Review Press, 1972, p. 29.

526. Russell Trainer, *The Lolita Complex*, p. 23; Charles Terrot, *The Maiden Tribute: A Study of the White Slave Traffic of the Nineteenth Century*. London: Frederick Mulley, 1959, p. 17.

527. Ronald Pearsall, *Night's Black Angels: The Forms and Faces of Victorian Cruelty*. London: Hodder and Stoughton, 1975, p. 244.

528. Florence Rush, *The Best Kept Secret*, p. 61.

529. Franz Seraphim Hügel, *Zur Geschichte, Statistik und Regelung der Prostitution*. Wien: A. Hartleben, 1865, p. 207.

530. Nancy Qualls Corbett, *The Sacred Prostitute: Eternal Aspects of the Feminine*. Toronto: Inner City Books, 1988, p. 37; Cathy Joseph, "Scarlet Wounding: Issues of Child Prostitution." *The Journal of Psychohistory* 23(1995): 14.

531. Ellen Bass, *I Never Told Anyone: Writings by Women Survivors of Child Sexual Abuse*. New York: Harper & Row, 1983, p. 34.

532. Genesis 19.8.

533. Reay Tannahill, *Flesh and Blood*, p. 49.

534. Roger Just, *Women in Athenian Law and Life*. London: Routledge, 1989, p. 142.

535. Sarah B. Pomeroy, *Families in Classical and Hellenistic Greece*, p. 21.

536. John Lascaratos and Effie Poulakou-Rebelakou, "Child Sexual Abuse: Historical Cases in the Byzantine Empire (324–1453 A.D.)" *Child Abuse & Neglect* 24(2000): 1088.

and confessors alike treated nuns and young novitiates as wives, but their victims' mouths were sealed by the dread of excommunication threatened by their spiritual fathers.'"[537] In many cities, "nunneries were often little more than whorehouses [providing] fornication between nuns and their gentlemen callers."[538] The clergy—in the past as in the present—was often reported as preferring little children to rape: "At Pope Alexander VI's celebration of Catholic Spain's victory over the Moors, children were passed amongst the clergy in a veritable 'sexual bacchanalia.'"[539]

Girls who went into the streets alone sometimes carried knives for protection against rape.[540] Since rape was thought to be "a mere trifle (*paulum quiddam*)," rapists until very recently were rarely prosecuted and even more rarely found guilty (since there had to be others who witnessed the rape),[541] and even if found guilty, most were let off with a mild fine.[542] One of the most-used excuses for raping girls was the widespread belief that rape of a virgin cures one of venereal disease; if you said this was your reason for rape, you were usually let go.[543] The belief was the typical "poison container" theory, that sexual intercourse with the pure was an antidote to the impure. Even the bubonic plague was thought to be cured by raping pure girls.[544] Many brothels in the past and in the present specialized in providing "virgins" to men suffering from venereal disease for supposed "treatment" for the disease.[545]

---

537. Florence Rush, *The Best Kept Secret*, p. 37.

538. Elizabeth Abbott, *A History of Celibacy*, p. 143.

539. Elinor Burkett and Frank Bruni, *A Gospel of Shame: Children, Sexual Abuse and the Catholic Church*. New York: Viking, 1993, p. 27.

540. David Nicholas, *The Domestic Life of a Medieval City: Women, Children, and the Family in Fourteenth-Century Ghent*. Lincoln: University of Nebraska Press, 1985, p. 64.

541. John Marshall Carter. *Rape in Medieval England: An Historical and Sociological Study*. New York: University Press of America, 1985, p. 148.

542. Ibid., p. 126; Guido Ruggiero, *The Boundaries of Eros: Sex Crimes and Sexuality in Renaissance Venice*. New York: Oxford University Press, 1985, p. 93;

543. Antony E. Simpson, "Vulnerability and the Age of Female Consent: Legal Innovation and Its Effect on Prosecutions for Rape in Eighteenth-Century London." In G. S. Rousseau and Roy Porter, Eds., *Sexual Underworlds of the Enlightenment*. Chapel Hill: University of North Carolina Press, 1988, p. 193.

544. B. W. Brewster, "The Incest Theme in Folksong." *Folklore Fellows Communications* 90(212): 3.

545. V. R. Bhalerao, "Profile of Sexually Transmitted Diseases in Child Prostitutes in the Red Light Areas of Bombay." In Usha S. Naidu and Kamini R. Kapadia, Eds., *Child Labour and Health: Problems and Prospects*. Bombay: Tata Institute of Social Sciences, 1985, p. 203.

Perhaps the most popular way to rape girls in the past was in the raping gangs that existed in nearly every country from antiquity to modern times. Roving gangs of youths—who practiced homosexual submission to the older among them[546]—practiced nightly collective raping attacks on unprotected women, "forcing the doors of a woman's house and, without concealing their identity and mixing brutality with blandishments, threats, and insults, would rape their prey on the spot [and] drag the victim through the streets, eventually pulling her into a house whose keepers were accessories to the plot, where they would do as they pleased, all night long."[547] Gang rapes made up to 80 percent of all sexual assaults in many areas,[548] and violent gang rape "constituted a veritable rite of initiation" for youth in the past.[549] Neighbors did not intervene; indeed, the rapes were considered "public performances" and the gang rapes were considered just normal, youthful "sporting" activities by their fathers and other city officials.[550] Over half of the youth of the cities participated in the gang rapes, and over the years a large minority of the young girls of the city would end up being raped, giving credence to the conclusion that gang rape was a rite of initiation for youth in traditional societies, a preparation for the violence of knightly society.[551]

Finally, even when the girl got married, the marriage was usually at a very young age and to a man who was chosen by the parents, so in fact it would be considered child rape today. Girls were usually married off in antiquity between 12 and 14, to men in their 30s[552]; "it was not uncommon," says noted Greek historian Hugo Blümner, "since Greek girls married very early, for them to play with their dolls up to the time of their marriage, and just before their wedding to take these to some temple . . .

---

546. David F. Greenberg, *The Construction of Homosexuality*, p. 259.

547. Jacques Rossiaud, "Prostitution, Youth and Society in the Towns of Southeastern France in the Fifteenth Century." In Robert Forster and Orest Ranum, Eds., *Deviants and the Abandoned in French Society*. Baltimore: Johns Hopkins Press, 1978, p. 6.

548. Jean-Louis Flandrin, *Sex in the Western World: The Development of Attitudes and Behaviour*. Chur, Switzerland: Harwood Academic Publishers, 1991, p. 272.

549. William Manchester, *A World Lit Only by Fire*, Boston: Little, Brown and Co., 1992, p. 41; John Marshall Carter, *Rape in Medieval England*, p. 57.

550. Jacques Rossiaud, *Medieval Prostitution*. New York: Basil Blackwell, 1988, p. 39.

551. Ibid., p. 21.

552. Jean-Louis Flandrin, *Sex in the Western World*, p. 269.

and there dedicate them as a pious offering."[553] Christian canon law ostensibly forbade child marriage, but the legal age for girls was 12, and for most of medieval times "it was not at all uncommon for a girl to be a bride at ten [since] one of tender years [could] be married to a septuagenarian while 'church laws did not rescind the nuptials.'"[554] Marriage thus was simply the final rape for most girls throughout history until modern times.

THE UNIVERSALITY OF HISTORICAL PEDERASTY

Pederasts past and present use boys for sexual purposes to make up for the traumas of their own childhood, "the male child representing his ideal self, whose youthfulness protects him from annihilation (death anxiety)."[555] The boy is the smooth, maternal breast, the penis is the nipple, and raping the boy is an act of revenge toward the mother, showing that the pederast is in total control, dominating the boy to overcome his sense of emptiness and abandonment. As one pederast put it, "I want to hold him in my arms, control him, dominate him, make him do my bidding, that I'm all-powerful."[556] The pederast's sexual targets are so interchangeable that he often seduces hundreds of boys in his lifetime. The sexual use of boys is not to be thought of as "a lack of impulse controls" or even as "only a different object choice" as most historians claim; pederasts are driven not by their sexual instincts but by their overwhelming anxieties.

Domination rather than tenderness was the central aim of most male sexuality until modern times. Raping boys was by far the preferred sexual activity of men; it was considered more "according to nature" than heterosexuality; it was "an ordinance enacted by divine laws."[557] Pythagoras, when asked when one should have sex with women rather than boys, replied: "When you want to lose what strength you have."[558] As one historian of

553. Philip E. Slater, *The Glory of Hera: Greek Mythology and the Greek Family.* Princeton: Princeton University Press, 1968, p. 24.

554. Florence Rush, *The Best Kept Secret*, p. 31.

555. Charles Socarides, *The Preoedipal Origin and Psychoanalytic Therapy of Sexual Perversions*, p. 463.

556. Ibid., p. 462.

557. Robin Scroggs, *The New Testament and Homosexuality: Contextual Background for Contemporary Debate*. Philadelphia: Fortress Press, 1983, p. 48.

558. Elizabeth Abbott, *A History of Celibacy*, p. 49.

Fig. 8–10. Greek pederast with boy

sexuality put it, "The world was divided into the screwers—all male—and the screwed—both male and female."[559] Because the boy represented the ideal self with whom the rapist merged, he must be without hair: "I like the smooth surface of the young boy's body, I don't like hair on it, I can't stand it."[560] So as soon as boys reached puberty, they were felt to be useless for sexual purposes, and pederastic poetry often mentions that the first hairs terminate the boy's attractiveness.

According to graffiti and poetry, the boy is most often raped anally.[561] Lucilius compares sexual relations with boys and women: "She bloodies you, but he on the other hand beshits you."[562] While the vagina is "castigated in invective as smelly, dirty, wet, loose, noisy, hairy, and so on . . . no such feeling seems to have been applied to the anuses of *pueri*."[563] Boys'

---

559. Daniel Boyarin, "Are There Any Jews in 'The History of Sexuality'?" *Journal of the History of Sexuality* 5(1995): 333.

560. Charles Socarides, *The Preoedipal Origin and Psychoanalytic Therapy of Sexual Perversions*, p. 463.

561. William Armstrong Percy III, *Pederasty and Pedagogy in Archaic Greece*. Urbana: University of Illinois Press, 1996, p. 31; Craig A. Williams, *Roman Homosexuality*, p. 20.

562. Craig A. Williams, *Roman Homosexuality*, p. 24.

563. Amy Richlin, *The Garden of Priapus: Sexuality and Aggression in Roman Humor*. New Haven: Yale University Press, 1983, p. 68.

anuses were called "rosebud, sometimes compared to the sweetest of fruits, the fig, other times again equated with gold."[564] The only precaution taken was to depilate boys' anuses, say Martial and Suetonius.[565] Indeed, as Martial put it, men must only penetrate the anus of boys, warning a man who was stimulating a boy's penis: "Nature has divided the male into two parts: one was made for girls, the other for men. Use *your* part."[566] Boys were far preferred over women; Propertius vowed, "May my enemies all fall in love with women and my friends with boys."[567] It was important that the boy not experience pleasure, only "pain and tears. . . . Of pleasure he has none at all."[568] The assault on the boy's anus also restaged the painful routine insertion by mothers and nurses of fingers, enemas, and suppositories into the rectums of children. In particular, initiatory pederasty was always anal, involving a fantasy of "the intrinsic spiritual value of sperm" that—as we have seen in the previous chapter—was needed to ejaculate into the boy's anus in order to "make him a man."[569] Parents taught boys in antiquity to "put up with it: not as a pleasure, but as a duty."[570] Parents were advised that "all those who have acquitted themselves nobly" should have the right to use any boys they want sexually.[571] Physicians were regularly expected to provide ointments and other lubricants for anal penetration of boys, and they were asked to repair the rectal tears and other injuries that were the usual results of the rapes.[572]

564. Eva Centarella, *Bisexuality in the Ancient World*. New Haven: Yale University Press, 1992, p. 26.

565. Frederick Charles Forberg, *Manual of Classical Erotology*. New York: Grove Press, 1966, p. 101–103.

566. D. R. Shakleton Bailey, Ed., *Martial: Epigrams*. Vol. III. Cambridge: Harvard University Press, 1993, p.23.

567. Paul Veyne, "Homosexuality in Ancient Rome." In Philippe Ariès and André Béjin, *Western Sexuality: Practice and Precept in Past and Present Times*. Oxford: Basil Blackwell, 1985, p. 33.

568. David M. Halperin, *One Hundred Years of Homosexuality and Other Essays on Greek Love*. New York: Routledge, 1990, p. 135.

569. Bernard Sergent, *Homosexuality in Greek Myth*. Boston: Beacon Press, 1984, p. 39.

570. Evan Cantarella, *Bisexuality in the Ancient World*, p. 213.

571. Plutarch, *The Education of Children*, 11.

572. Guido Ruggiero, *Boundaries of Eros*, p. 117; Gregory M. Pflugfelder, *Cartographies of Desire: Male-Male Sexuality in Japanese Discourse, 1600–1950*. Berkeley: University of California Press, 1999, pp. 238–239.

All early civilizations practiced boy rape and even had boys serve as temple prostitutes, including the ancient Hebrews, Sumerians, Persians, Mesopotamians, Celts, Egyptians, Etruscans, Carthaginians, Chinese, Japanese, Indians, etc.[573] Pederasty, concludes Spencer, "was almost universal among the Aztecs, involving children as young as six."[574] Boy rape was expected to be violent; men were expected to take along with them when going out in the streets "scissors, to make a hole in the trousers of the boy [and] a small pillow to put in the boy's mouth if he should scream."[575] Tutors and teachers often raped their pupils along with beating them; as Quintilian warned: "I blush to mention the shameful abuse which scoundrels sometimes make of their right to administer corporal punishment." A father in Greece chose the penetrator of his boy, often obtaining gifts or favors in return.[576] Aristophanes shows one father in *The Birds* complaining to another, "Well, this is a fine state of affairs. . . . You meet my son just as he comes out of the gymnasium, all fresh from the bath, and you don't kiss him, you don't say a word to him, you don't hug him, you don't feel his balls! And yet you're supposed to be a friend of ours!"[577] Pedagogues were hired to guard boys against rape by unapproved men, but the pedagogue might assault the boy himself.[578] Boys in Greece were blamed if they failed to find a pederast for themselves; every boy was expected to have one.[579] Greek and Roman soldiers brought boys along with them on campaigns to use sexually.[580] Slave boys were often furnished to guests for

---

573. Wainwright Churchill, *Homosexual Behavior Among Males: A Cross-Cultural and Cross-Species Investigation*. New York: Hawthorn Books, 1967, pp. 75–83; Barry D. Adam, "Age, Structure, and Sexuality: Reflections on the Anthropological Evidence on Homosexual Relations." *Journal of Homosexuality* 11(1985): 19–33; David F. Greenberg, *The Construction of Homosexuality*, p. 164.

574. Colin Spencer, *Homosexuality in History*. New York: Harcourt Brace & Co., 1995, p. 142.

575. Maarten Schild, "The Irresistible Beauty of Boys." In Joseph Geraci, Ed., *Dares To Speak: Historical and Contemporary Perspectives on Boy-Love*. Norfolk: The Gay Men's Press, 1997, p. 87.

576. Mark Golden, *Children and Childhood in Classical Athens*, p. 59.

577. Reay Tannahill, *Sex in History*. New York: Stein and Day, 1980, p. 89.

578. Keith R. Bradley, *Discovering the Roman Family: Studies in Roman Social History*. New York: Oxford University Press, 1991, p. 53.

579. John R. Ungaretti, "Pederasty, Heroism, and the Family in Classical Greece." *Journal of Homosexuality* 3(1978): 292.

580. Ibid., p. 295; Richard C. Trexler, *Sex and Conquest*, p. 23.

sexual use.[581] Doctors prescribed sex with boys as therapy.[582] Boy brothels and rent-a-boy services were widespread, and a pederast chosen by the father could even sell his rights to rape a particular boy to another man.[583] Raping boys, even when violence was obvious, was never seen as a crime against the child—only against the parents—and no concern was shown as to any harm that might be done to the boy.[584]

With the number of boy prostitutes worldwide still in the millions,[585] it is not surprising that every city in antiquity had its boy brothels. In Rome, boys could be picked up at the barbershop or at the exit of any of the games.[586] All men, even when married, were expected to have sex with boys. "Almost all of the great democratic leaders of Archaic Athens were . . . pederastic."[587] Wives found it hard to compete with their husbands' boys. Juvenal says wives were "always hot with quarrels . . . bitching away . . . about his boy-friends,"[588] and Martial describes a wife yelling, "Bumming a boy again! Don't I have a rump as well?"[589]

A few early Christians began to object to using boys sexually. John Chrysostom complained about fathers taking their boys to banquets where they were made to perform fellatio on men under the blankets, recommending that boys be placed in the care of monks at the age of 10 to avoid seduction.[590] But most medieval authors gave the pro-pederast advice of antiq-

---

581. Richard C. Trexler, *Sex and Conquest*, p. 195; Allen Edwardes, *The Cradle of Erotica*, p. 222.

582. Helen E. Elsom, "Callirhoe: Displaying the Phallic Woman." In Amy Richlin, Ed., *Pornography and Representation in Greece and Rome*. New York: Oxford University Press, 1992, p. 215.

583. Bernard Sergent, *Homosexuality in Greek Myth*, p. 41.

584. David Cohen, "Consent and Sexual Relations in Classical Athens." In Angeliki E. Laiou, Ed., *Consent and Coercion to Sex and Marriage in Ancient and Medieval Societies*. Washington, DC: Dumbarton Oaks Research Library and Collection, 1993, p. 8.

585. Cathy Joseph, "Scarlet Wounding: Issues of Child Prostitution." *The Journal of Psychohistory* 23(1995): 8.

586. Richie J. McMullen, *Male Rape: Breaking the Silence on the Last Taboo*. London: GMP Publications, 1990, p. 42; Dennis Drew and Jonathan Drake, *Boys for Sale: A Sociological Study of Boy Prostitution*. New York: Brown Book Co., 1969, pp. 22–27.

587. William Armstrong Percy III, *Pederasty and Pedagogy in Archaic Greece*, p. 183.

588. Julia O'Faolain, Ed., *Not in God's Image*. New York: Harper & Row, 1973, p. 59.

589. Martial, *Epigrams* XI.45.

590. Alline Rousselle, *Porneia*, p. 135.

uity, with medical books recommending sex with boys as "less harmful [than] sexual union with women [which] leads more quickly to old age."[591] The reason men in medieval times waited until their 30s to get married was because they routinely used young boys for sex until then; in Florence, for instance, only a quarter of the men in the fifteenth century were married by the age of 32.[592] Since over a third of most households had servants or apprentices, sexual relations between masters and male servants were even more common and acceptable than between masters and female servants.[593] Tutors and teachers in schools were expected to use their students sexually, and those who protested that it was a "vice so inveterate [and] so strong a custom" that it was "hardly likely to be discouraged" were thought odd.[594]

But placing boys as oblates into monasteries only made them available for rape by monks, who could not keep their hands off them. One abbott wrote about an infant boy brought to the monastery by his father:

> The man turned the child over to me altogether, and I received the baby with pleasure and joy and a clean heart. [But] when the boy got older and had reached the age of about ten . . . I was tortured and overwhelmed by an obscene desire, and the beast of impure lust and a desire for pleasure burned in my soul. . . . I wanted to have sex with the boy.[595]

Sex with boys was the central obsession of monks beginning with the early anchorites who went to the desert; Macarius saw so many monks having sex with boys in the desert that he strongly advised monks not to take them in.[596] But the need was too strong, and even rules such as those requiring boys to have escorts when going to the lavatory did not prevent monks from routinely using their oblates sexually.[597] So many monks raped their

---

591. Danielle Jacquat and Claude Thomasset, *Sexuality and Medicine in the Middle Ages.* Cambridge: Polity Press, 1985, p. 124.

592. Michael Rocke, *Forbidden Friendships: Homosexuality and Male Culture in Renaissance Florence.* New York: Oxford University Press, 1996, p. 14.

593. Alan Bray, *Homosexuality in Renaissance England.* London: Gay Men's Press, 1982, p. 51.

594. Ibid.

595. John Boswell, *Same-Sex Unions in Premodern Europe.* New York: Villard Books, 1994, p. 247.

596. Aline Rousselle, *Porneia,* p. 148.

597. Patricia A. Quinn, *Better than the Sons of Kings: Boys and Monks in the Early Middle Ages.* New York: Peter Lang, 1988, p. 165.

novices that there was a common saying: "With wine and boys around, the monks have no need of the Devil to tempt them."[598] Priests also commonly used confessions to solicit sex with boys, but early Christian penitentials assessed penances only for the boys, since they were blamed for their own rape. Peter Damian said in the eleventh century that sex with boys in monasteries "rages like a bloodthirsty beast in the midst of the sheepfold of Christ with bold freedom," and suggested both the man and boy be punished as accomplices for a "sin against nature."[599]

So acceptable was pederasty in medieval times that parents continued handing over their boys for sexual use to friends and others from whom they expected favors.[600] Bernardino of Sienna condemned parents as "pimps" of their own sons, saying the fathers, pederasts themselves, were the ones most responsible, taking money or gifts from their sons' rapists.[601] Boys were so likely to be raped in the streets—"a boy can't even pass nearby without having a sodomite on his tail"—that Bernardino urged mothers, "Send your girls out instead, who aren't in any danger at all if you let them out among such people. . . . This is less evil."[602] Mothers, too, colluded in the seduction of their sons. "When a boy started to mature sexually . . . his mother gave him a bedroom to himself on the ground floor, 'with a separate entrance and every convenience, so that he can do whatever he pleases and bring home whomever he likes.'"[603]

When, beginning in the fifteenth century, some of the more violent pederasty disputes began being handled by courts, the huge number of cases prosecuted revealed that every place where boys gathered—from schools and monasteries to taverns and pastry shops—were "schools of sodomy" where pederasts came to violate boys.[604] In Florence, according to the thorough analysis of court records by Michael Rocke, "In the later

---

598. Elizabeth Abbott, *A History of Celibacy*, p. 101.

599. Peter Damian, *Book of Gomorrah*. Waterloo: Wilfred Laurier University Press, 1982, pp. 27, 42.

600. Jerrold Atlas, "Pederasty, Blood Shedding and Blood Smearing: Men in Search of Mommy's Feared Powers." *The Journal of Psychohistory* 28(2000): 116–149.

601. Michael J. Rocke, "Sodomites in Fifteenth-Century Tuscany: The Views of Bernardino of Siena." In Kent Gerard and Gert Hekman, Eds., *The Pursuit of Sodomy: Male Homosexuality in Renaissance and Enlightenment Europe*. New York: Harrington Park Press, 1989, pp. 9, 13.

602. Ibid., pp. 12, 15.

603. Michael Rocke, *Forbidden Friendships*, p. 156.

604. Guido Ruggiero, *The Boundaries of Eros*, p. 138.

fifteenth century, the majority of local males at least once during their life-times were officially incriminated for engaging in homosexual relations" with boys.[605] Since many pederasts were never brought to court, because courts were reluctant to try any but the most violent cases of boy rape, and since pederasts past and present usually rape dozens of boys each, these early court statistics reveal as nothing else does the universality of pederasty in history. If the majority of men were hauled into court for cases in connection with their pederasty, the number of boys actually being raped must have been nearly universal.

As more parents evolved into the intrusive and socializing modes of modern times, they were more and more reluctant to hand over their boys to pederasts for sexual abuse. Tutors began being monitored to see that they were not pederasts, and reformers began to warn that servants too often "take liberties with a child which they would not risk with a young man."[606] Some suggested that public female brothels should be encouraged as "the best chance of keeping men away from boys."[607] The rape of boys in British public schools, "with the full knowledge and collusion, even the approval, of their elders,"[608] nevertheless continued into the twentieth century, where older boys and even teachers had younger boys as their "bitches" to use sexually.[609] Only slowly in recent decades has it become acceptable to defend children against sexual attack, and only in the most psychogenically advanced nations has the rate of sexual abuse of children dropped to around half of the children born.

Despite the achievement of empathic child rearing among some parents today, most of humankind still has a long way to evolve to get beyond severe abuse of all sorts and give their children the love and respect they

---

605. Michael Rocke, *Forbidden Friendships*, p. 7.

606. Richard Davenport-Hines, *Sex, Death and Punishment: Attitudes to Sex and Sexuality in Britain Since the Renaissance*. London: Collins, 1990, p. 61; Philippe Ariès, *Centuries of Childhood: A Social History of Family Life*. New York: Alfred A. Knopf, 1962, p. 117.

607. Richard C. Trexler, *Dependence in Context in Renaissance Florence*. Binghamton: Medieval and Renaissance Texts and Studies, 1994, p. 375.

608. Louise DeSalvo, *Virginia Woolf: The Impact of Childhood Sexual Abuse on Her Life and Work*. Boston: Beacon Press, 1989, p. 31.

609. Alisdare Hickson, *The Poisoned Bowl: Sex Repression and the Public School System*. London: Constable, 1995; Phyllis Grosskurth, Ed., *The Memoirs of John Addington Symonds*. London: Hutchinson & Co., 1984, p. 94.

deserve. The ubiquity of child abuse and neglect in historical sources makes even the most horrific descriptions found in contemporary clinical and child advocacy reports seem limited in comparison. It is no wonder that historians have chosen to hide, deny, and whitewash the record here uncovered, in order to avoid confronting the parental abuse of children that has been the central cause of violence and misery throughout history.

9

The Evolution of the Psyche and Society

"The search for meaning is the search
for expression of one's real self."
—*James F. Masterson*

Since the further back in history one goes the lower the level of child rearing, it follows that children in the past grew up in houses of horrors that were like those of dissociated personalities of today. Psychiatric studies have shown that there is a direct correlation between elevated levels of dissociative symptoms—separate alters, depersonalization, derealization—and the amount of early physical, sexual, and emotional abuse.[1] That the average person before the modern period walked streets full of spirits, demons, gods, and other alters is evidence of the dissociation that resulted from their routine abuse and neglect as children. Historical evolution of the psyche, therefore, is the slow, uneven process of integrating fragmented selves into the unified self that is the goal of modern upbringing.[2]

Biological evolution stores traits in genes that are passed down to subsequent generations with their modifications intact; a chimp has all the genes necessary to make another chimp. But the self of the human psyche must evolve anew each generation. Contemporary newborns begin with the same psyche as prehistoric newborns; it is only better child rearing that allows them to achieve a more unified self. That dissociated selves were an everyday part of life in antiquity and the Middle Ages is a much-denied fact of historians, just as anthropologists deny that their subjects are dis-

---

1. J. A. Chu et al., "Memories of Childhood Abuse: Dissociation, Amnesia and Corroboration." *American Journal of Psychiatry* 156(1999): 749–755.

2. James F. Masterson, *The Search for the Real Self: Unmasking the Personality Disorders of Our Age.* New York: Free Press, 1990.

sociated personalities who live in an animistic world full of alters inhabiting animals, objects, and dead ancestors. Thus both personal history and human history are products of a search for a real self, a search for meaning in life, an integration of separate brain networks, a development of more adaptive real selves, with the unified self being a late historical achievement of only a few.

HISTORY AS THE INTEGRATION OF THE SELF

Most people even today have only achieved a partial integration of the "relatively independent subselves" that recent studies show they begin constructing as infants.[3] The most thorough recent study of dissociation using a sophisticated interview technique finds that "14 percent of the general public experience 'substantial' dissociative symptoms"[4] and most of the rest of us experience lesser dissociative symptoms when triggered by situations similar to the original abuse. This may seem excessive, until one remembers that perhaps half of the adults today were sexually abused as children, that most of us were physically and emotionally abused to some extent, and that helping-mode parenting that respects the growth and individuation of children is everywhere still rare. We may be surprised to discover that people in the past had their demon alters exorcised or had conversations with their various inner souls, but even today religious spirit possessions are not uncommon—a third of Americans say they have experienced other spirits in themselves and over 90 percent of us believe in and at times converse with (pray to) god alters of one sort or another.[5] Even in our day-to-day personal reactions, we more often switch into alters than we like to admit: "'Mom, don't we have any cornflakes?' Shawn asked. . . . Immediately the Mean alter sprang into action. '*Screw you, Shawn! Why are you so helpless? Find something else if we don't have any goddamn cornflakes. I'm not your fucking slave!*'"[6]

---

3. Nicholas Humphrey, "One-Self: A Meditation on the Unity of Consciousness." *Social Research* 67(2000): 1060–1062.

4. Marlene Steinberg, Maxine Schnall, *The Stranger in the Mirror: Dissociation, The Hidden Epidemic.* New York: Cliff Street Books, 2001, p. xvii.

5. Michael Argyle, *Psychology and Religion.* London: Routledge, 2000, pp. 57, 78.

6. Marlene Steinberg, Maxine Schnall, *The Stranger in the Mirror*, p. 148.

Contemporary societies with overall lower-level child rearing regularly switch into their alters in possession states. Bourguignon found 90 percent of 488 societies reported institutionalized altered states of consciousness and spirit possessions,[7] with the remaining 10 percent reporting other forms of overt dissociation. One of the best studied is Bali, where people live in "a world filled with gods and spirits . . . at the core of many activities of daily life, including ceremonies, rituals, dances, plays, and possession [by] demons, witchcraft or black magic, and *leak* (spirits). Evil spirits are often present."[8] The journal *Transcultural Psychiatry* regularly reports on possession and other dissociative states in other cultures, from the "belief in spirit possession fundamental to Chinese religious systems" to the possession rituals in Indonesia.[9] Simpler cultures report more hallucinations, soul journeys, and possessions by animal spirits, while the more complex cultures report a greater variety of possession trance roles.[10] Like multiple personalities in our society, altered states in other societies follow periodic cycles,[11] as people experience growth panic due to individuation, then, as memories of early traumas threaten to surface, they switch into alters and restage their anger, guilt, and punishment in religious rituals. Even today people in most societies individuate for six days and spend the seventh worshiping a punishing spirit and asking for forgiveness for the hubris/*chutzpah* of the previous week.

The psychology of alter formation and the acting out of alter rituals has been well studied recently by clinicians. Whether experienced as inside or outside oneself, alters are actually inner voices or hallucinations that are subnetworks of the brain, centering more in the amygdalan network than the hippocampal,[12] with their own organized personalities and even unique brain-scan configurations as the person switches personali-

---

7. Erika Bourguignon, *Possession*. San Francisco: Chandler & Sharp, 1976.

8. Luh Ketut Suryani, *Trance and Possession in Bali: A Window on Western Multiple Personality, Possession Disorder and Suicide*. Oxford: Oxford University Press, 1993, p. 40.

9. Beng-Yeong Ng, "Phenomenology of Trance States Seen at a Psychiatric Hospital in Singapore." *Transcultural Psychiatry* 37(2000): 561; Douglas Hollan, "Culture and Dissociation in Toraja." *Transcultural Psychiatry* 37(2000): 545.

10. Erika Bourguignon, "Introduction." In Bourguignon, Ed., *Religion, Altered States of Consciousness, and Social Change*. Columbus: Ohio State University Press, 1973, p. 23.

11. Doris Bryant et al., *The Family Inside: Working with the Multiple*. New York: W. W. Norton & Co., 1992, pp. 169–171.

12. Martha Stout, *The Myth of Sanity: Divided Consciousness and the Promise of Awareness*. New York: Viking, 2001, p. 17.

ties.[13] All spirits, gods, demons, shamans, priests, and political leaders are *alter containers,* projections of these inner alters; they derive their traits from the early traumas, not merely from cultural transmission of beliefs. Dissociative personalities usually sense at some level that their spirits derive from their parents. As Donne put it, a separate part of ourselves—what he terms an "invisible corner" of us—derives from our past (Father Adam and Mother Eve) and contains the "poison that corrupts us."[14] People in the past used to switch into their alters regularly, hearing voices, having waking nightmares and flashbacks, experiencing loss of time, periods of unreality and deadness, hallucinating persecutors, feeling unalterably dirty, sinful, and hopeless, and acting out self-injurious episodes. All of these are evidence of dissociative identity disorders that resulted from the routine abusive child-rearing practices of the past. One can view daily encounters with alters in such studies as those of the anthropologists Richard and Eva Blum on rural Greek communities, where people today—as in ancient Greece— regularly switch into alternate states and either are possessed by or encounter outside themselves devouring demons and bloodthirsty maternal monsters as they go about their daily business.[15]

INFANTILE SOURCES OF ALTERS IN HISTORY

Alters always contain traces of the early abusive situation, so if one knows the typical kinds of traumatic child-rearing practices of an age, one can use these to decode the shared alters of that age. Goodwin's studies of demon possessions in the sixteenth century are particularly revealing, demonstrating how the demons of Jeanne Fery were both "internalized abusers" and "keepers of the secret" of her early sexual and physical abuse.[16] Whether the

---

13. Adam Crabtree, *Multiple Man: Explorations in Possession and Multiple Personality.* New York: Praeger, 1985, p. 56.

14. Jean Delumeau, *Sin and Fear: The Emergence of a Western Guilt Culture 13th–18th Centuries.* New York: St. Martin's Press, 1990, p. 245.

15. Richard and Eva Blum, *Health and Healing in Rural Greece: A Study of Three Communities.* Stanford: Stanford University Press, 1965; Richard and Eva Blum, *The Dangerous Hour: The Lore of Crisis and Mystery in Rural Greece.* London: Chatto & Windus, 1970, p. 55.

16. Onno van der Hart, Ruth Lierens, and Jean Goodwin, "Jeanne Fery: A Sixteenth-Century Case of Dissociative Identity Disorder." *The Journal of Psychohistory* 24(1996): 28; Sally Hill and Jean Goodwin, "Demonic Possession as a Consequence of Childhood Trauma." *The Journal of Psychohistory* 20(1993): 408.

dissociated personalities are perpetrator or victim alters, the original family situation is usually decipherable. Demons particularly get into you, say religious authorities, when mothers are mad at you for enjoying yourself: "Say a child is taking a nice hot shower, he is relaxed, enjoying himself. Suppose his mother yells at him to hurry up and get out, that's forbidden. . . . The child can get scared and the demon will get hold of him."[17] In Mesopotamia, each person was said to have a "personal god . . . the image of the parent— divine father or mother" inside them, with a relationship "of master and slave," and these contributed to making their worlds filled with "demons, evil gods and evil spirits."[18] The gods of every land were recognized as acting just like parents, often punishing people like noisy children, as when Enlil sent the Babylonian flood to wipe out mankind because they were "making too much noise down there so she could not sleep"[19] or as when the Aztec lords of the underworld sacrificed the Aztec ball players because they were "too noisy."[20] Hell in Christian literature was often compared to living with "an angry and furious woman."[21] Possession began early in life; in the *Acts of Thomas*, God himself advised Christians "to avoid having children [since] the majority of children [are] possessed by demons."[22] Witches were often transparently grandmothers or other women of the gynarchy (riding the grandmother's broomstick) or prone to murder children (like real mothers killing their newborn) or "dance stark naked in the night" and seduce children (like mothers who slept with their children while both were naked and while the mother masturbated them).[23] Every witch, ghost, and religious figure carried their family origin in each of their features.

God, says Julian of Eclanum, is "the persecutor of newborn children; he it is who sends tiny babies to eternal flames."[24] The pictures of Hell

17. Eli Somer, "Stambali: Dissociative Possession and Trance in a Tunisian Healing Dance." *Transcultural Psychiatry* 37(2000): 590.

18. Thorkild Jacobsen, *The Treasures of Darkness: A History of Mesopotamian Religion.* New Haven: Yale University Press, 1976, pp. 12, 160.

19. Neil Forsyth, *The Old Enemy: Satan and the Combat Myth.* Princeton: Princeton University Press, 1987, p. 151.

20. Linda Schele and Mary Ellen Mill, *The Blood of Kings: Dynasty and Ritual in Maya Art.* New York: George Braziller, 1986, p. 243.

21. Piero Camporesi, *The Fear of Hell.* Cambridge: Polity Press, 1991, p. 89.

22. Ibid., p. 344.

23. Jeffrey B. Russell, *A History of Witchcraft.* London: Thames and Hudson, 1980, p. 22.

24. Alice K. Turner, *The History of Hell.* New York: Harcourt Brace & Co., 1993, p. 80.

regularly depict tormented souls as child-sized, and their tortures are the routine tortures infants endured in the past; being in Hell meant "unbearable thirst, the punishment of hunger, of stench, of horror, of fear, of want, of darkness, the cruelty of tortures, punishment without end."[25] The tight swaddling bands were represented in Hell as "cruel fetters" with "their arms stretched down to the feet," and the feces that the infants were left in was shown in Hell as "being in a sewer" and as being "covered in the feces of their own obscenity," with Hell having "a stench worse than anything in this world."[26]

One can find Terrifying Mommy alters behind every Devil; even the Greek word for devil, *diabolos*, means "accuser." God, says Gregory, is the "Avenger," and he compares God's treatment of humans with that of a mother who "beats her child one moment as if she never loved him and the next moment loves him as if she had never beaten him."[27] Although gods are often male, this usually only represents a defensive clinging to a father to avoid worse fears of maternal abandonment and torture.[28] A cross-cultural study, *The Parental Figures and the Representation of God*, found that religious people cling to their mothers far more and actually see God with more maternal attributes than paternal.[29] Demons in the past were even portrayed as wet nurses; the Dragon of Delphi, for instance, was the wet nurse of Typhaon, Hera's child.[30] The victims of gods and demons alike are regularly depicted as "innocent," "like an innocent child." When Job complains to Yahweh, "I am innocent," he admits this makes no difference because Yahweh "destroys innocent and guilty alike." Sinners were born sinful and deserved punishment simply because they tried to be independent. The Devil, said Gerson, "sends happy thoughts" to you of "undertaking mighty works," you forget about God's [Mommy's] needs, you

---

25. Piero Camporesi, *The Fear of Hell,* p. 6.

26. Dyan Elliott, *Fallen Bodies: Pollution, Sexuality, and Demonology in the Middle Ages.* Philadelphia: University of Pennsylvania Press, 1999, p. 93; Alice K. Turner, *The History of Hell,* p. 103.

27. Carl A. Mounteer, "God the Father and Gregory the Great: The Discovery of a Late Roman Childhood." *The Journal of Psychohistory* 25(1998): 442.

28. Ana-Maria Rizzuto, *The Birth of the Living God: A Psychoanalytic Study.* Chicago: University of Chicago Press, 1979, p. 163.

29. Antoine Vergote, *The Parental Figures and the Representation of God: A Psychological and Cross-Cultural Study.* The Hague: Leuven University Press, 1980, p. 142.

30. Joseph Fontenrose, *Python: A Study of Delphic Myth and Its Origins.* Berkeley: University of California Press, 1959, p. 14.

"relax," and you become a sinner.[31] You must love God [Mommy], said Meister Eckart, "for nothing." You live, said Thomas à Kempis, only "to make yourself a more fit vessel for God's [Mommy's] purposes."[32] All religions agreed on one thing: "To assert one's self, to succeed, to enjoy, even to exist, is to dispossess the Father [Mother], to kill Him [Her]."[33]

Switching into alters began in early childhood. Children were often pictured as possessed, and historians of witchcraft often comment on "the sudden emergence, in a docile and amenable child, of a personality which raves, screams, roars with laughter, utters dreadful blasphemies [which] seems like the invasion of an alien being."[34] Children, so close in time to their traumas, could remember what it felt like to be a fetus suffering because their poisonous placenta didn't provide it with fresh, oxygenated blood, so they could identify with a suffering Christ on a placental cross and could understand priests when they said they deserved to be thrown into the "suffocations" of Hell [womb] and be tortured by "fire coursing swiftly through their veins, bubbling through their arteries, boiling like liquid lead."[35] Common child-rearing practices—like "roasting" infants in an oven to cure them of evil eye—were remembered in the many burning visions of Hell:

> Let us always keep before our mind's eye an overheated and glowing stove and inside a naked man supine, who will never be released from such pain. How lost he appears to us! Just imagine how he is writhing in the stove, how he screams, cries, lives, what dread he suffers, what sufferings pierce him, particularly when he realizes his unbearable pain will never end![36]

Demons were sometimes experienced as "creeping things," like children, who "dance, laugh, whistle, caper, fart, and prance." More often demons were like parents, "leaping on his back, beating him and whipping him and leav-

---

31. Jean Delumeau, *Sin and Fear*, p. 203.

32. Donald H. Bishop, Ed., *Mysticism and the Mystical Experience: East and West*. Selinsgrove: Susquehanna University Press, 1995, pp. 81, 102.

33. Jean Delumeau, *Sin and Fear*, p. 299.

34. Barbara Rosen, Ed., *Witchcraft in England, 1558–1618*. Amherst: University of Massachusetts Press, 1991, p. 33.

35. Piero Camporesi, *The Fear of Hell*, p. 66.

36. Johan Huizinga, *The Autumn of the Middle Ages*. Chicago: University of Chicago Press, 1996, p. 253.

ing him unconscious on the ground."[37] Demons and devils almost always contain traces of childhood rape, the Devil being, as one Colonial American woman who had intercourse with the Devil confessed, "a thing all over hairy, all the face hairy [pubic hair], and a long nose [penis]."[38] As one study of medieval rape puts it: "The main thing medieval demons and monsters do is rape virgins."[39] When hundreds of children at a time report being forced to copulate with the Devil,[40] one need not believe in demons to see the earlier reality of the rape reports. Witnesses to rape confessions often report that the girls speak in "two voices, one her normal voice, the other 'strange, coarse, unnatural, heavy, masculine.'"[41] Obviously the deeper alter voice carries the memory of the original rapist, as it so often does in contemporary rape victims. Demons during the Middle Ages were always assaulting people as incubi and succubi that sexually assault people in their beds, restaging childhood family bed rapes.[42] Some female mystics even hallucinated that Christ appeared before them and had intercourse with them.[43] Even the Holy Ghost contains a trace of rape, since the Virgin Mary was impregnated by God with it (*Yahweh* in Hebrew deriving from the Sumerian word for "sperm").[44] Religious ritual often restages the rape scene openly:

> The temple in the Near East was the womb. It was divided into three parts: the Porch, representing the lower end of the vagina up to the hymen, or Veil; the Hall, or vagina itself; and the inner sanctum, or Holy of Holies, the uterus. The priest, dressed as a penis, anointed with various saps and resins as representing the divine semen, enters through the doors of the Porch, the "labia" of the womb, past the Veil or "hymen" and so into the Hall.[45]

---

37. Jeffrey B. Russell, *Satan: The Early Christian Tradition*. Ithaca: Cornell University Press, 1981, p. 174.

38. Jeffrey B. Russell, *A History of Witchcraft*, p. 105.

39. Kathryn Gravdal, *Ravishing Maidens: Writing Rape in Medieval French Literature and Law*. Philadelphia: University of Pennsylvania Press, 1991, p. 23.

40. Joseph Klaits, *Servants of Satan: The Age of the Witch Hunts*. Bloomington, IN: Indiana University Press, 1985, p. 103.

41. Lyndal Roper, *Oedipus and the Devil: Witchcraft, Sexuality and Religion in Early Modern Europe*. London: Routledge, 1994, p. 176.

42. Dyan Elliott, *Fallen Bodies*, p. 33.

43. Ibid., p. 54.

44. John M. Allegro, *The Sacred Mushroom and the Cross*. Garden City, NY: Doubleday & Co., 1970, p. 20.

45. Ibid., p. 25.

RELIGIONS AS RITUALS USING SHARED ALTER FETISHES

In religions and politics, people turn to idealized authorities to avoid the risk of depending on themselves and to restage the painful feelings of abandonment by parents that they had when they tried to individuate as children. Religions restage traumatic events encapsulated in dangerous alters. This is why the word "sacred" (*sacer*) everywhere designates "poison," "dangerous," "taboo,"[46] because the sacred is where we store our most poisonous, dangerous early memories. Gods, demons, and spirits are not just containers for haphazard projections; they are highly organized and endurable, and so must first exist as durable, organized subselves in individual brains. It is through religious questions about God that people in the past asked their most important questions about Mommy: Why did she hate me? Why did she tie me up, leave me abandoned in my feces, let me starve? Why did she beat me? Why did she strangle my baby sister? What does she want from me? What did I do wrong to deserve such torture?

Because preverbal infants imagine they store their painful memories in various body parts, alters that carry early traumas are often pictured as inhabiting internal organs: hearts, brains, the gallbladder, even intestines. Jeffrey Dahmer used to dismember bodies, he said, because he "wanted to see what someone looked like inside," searching for alters in the organs of the corpses he decapitated, draped on altars and then—like Osiris—tried to reassemble, as though he were reassembling his own dissociated body part alters.[47] He then ate some of the body parts, like Aztecs eating the heart of their sacrificed victims, reinternalizing the projected alters that were "full of vital force." Christian saints hallucinated both Christ and devils inhabiting their hearts, and even talked to them regularly.[48] Egyptians said their double, their *ka*, inhabited their hearts, and had spells entreating the heart to "rise not up as a witness against me."[49] Aztecs believed there were three animistic souls, one in the head, one in the liver, and one in the heart, and they cut each of these organs out of victims in their sacrificial rituals.[50]

---

46. Roger Caillois, *Man and the Sacred*. Glencoe: Free Press of Glencoe, 1959, p. 35.

47. Brian Masters, *The Shrine of Jeffrey Dahmer*. London: Hodder & Stoughton, 1993, p. 130.

48. Onno van der Hart, et al., "Jeanne Fery," p. 26.

49. Alan E. Bernstein, *The Formation of Hell*. Ithaca: Cornell University Press, 1993, p. 13.

50. David Carrasco, *City of Sacrifice: The Aztec Empire and the Role of Violence in Civilization*. Boston: Beacon Press, 1999, p. 180.

To this day, children's hearts are reported cut out and thrown into the sea in Chile as sacrifices to spirits, as the child begs, "Just let me live, Grandfather."[51]

Tribal people had such primitive child rearing that they were constantly involved with the alters inhabiting their organs. "The first thing a shaman has to do when he has called up his helping spirits is to withdraw the soul from his pupil's eyes, brain, and entrails," purifying and liberating them.[52] Shamans "cured" others of "soul loss" by sucking out their poisonous organ alters through their skin.[53] Early religions are mainly concerned with purifying and acting out the feelings of organ alters, usually in rituals that use animal spirit alters, attacking, dismembering, and rebirthing initiates. Animal alters reveal their infantile origins in that they are projected into beings that crawl and are not verbal, like infants. Thus all animal sacrifices are infantile alter sacrifices, even when we today go hunting. The infantile origin of animal alters is clearly revealed in the Ainu bear sacrifice, where a black bear cub is actually suckled by the mothers before being sacrificed.[54] Shamans around the world hallucinate that they remove all their internal organs and replace them with "incorruptible" organs, often pressing quartz crystals into their body to accomplish this.[55] Egyptians not only separately mummified their internal organs, addressing their *ka* as "my heart, my mother,"[56] they also mummified animals, reptiles, birds, and fishes that were their animal alters.[57] As we saw in Chapter 4, they even mummified the royal placenta and worshiped it, like the Baganda did until recently, placing it on an actual throne and addressing it as "King."[58] Christians, too, used to col-

51. Patrick Tierney, *The Highest Altar: The Story of Human Sacrifice.* New York: Viking, 1989, p. 177.

52. Daniel Merkur, *Becoming Half Hidden: Shaminism and Initiation Among the Inuit.* New York: Garland Publishing, 1992, p. 172.

53. Colin A. Ross, *Multiple Personality Disorder: Diagnosis, Clinical Features and Treatment.* New York: John Wiley & Sons, 1989, p. 13.

54. Joseph Campbell, *The Way of the Animal Powers, Vol. 1.* San Francisco: Harper & Row, 1983, p. 170.

55. Ibid., p. 152.

56. Lloyd deMause, *Foundations of Psychohistory.* New York: Creative Roots, 1982, p. 288.

57. E. A. Wallis Budge, *The Mummy.* New York: Wings Books, 1989, p. 355.

58. Lloyd deMause, *Foundations of Psychohistory*, pp. 282–289.

lect body parts as relics, worshiping the heart, pieces of skull, limb bones, or fingers of saints dug up from their graves.[59]

Animal perpetrator alters were frequently the central gods of early religions, such as when Yahweh was represented with serpent legs or when Egyptian gods were shown as various devouring animals.[60] That gods are usually perpetrators restaging early physical abuse is the answer to Freud's question: "Why does religion seem to need violence?"[61] When violence against children disappears, religious and political violence will disappear. Religions and politics as we know them will no doubt disappear also. Religions work by constructing sacred spaces that contain triggers for switching into trances in order to access people's alters and obtain some relief from their tortures. Looking out a rose window of a cathedral triggers nothing so much as fetal memories of seeing light through your mother's abdomen. The entrainment of personal alters into a shared personal experience can be seen today most clearly in groups like the Shakers, where adherents experience dissociation states; get together in churches full of pictures of Christ as a victim alter to trigger their childhood memories of being victimized; profess their total obedience to Elders in order to trigger the obedience demanded by their parents; and have a "mother matron" wash their hands or face, also to parallel the early childhood state. Then the church leader, the "Pointer," carries out the perpetrator alter role by punishing one of the Shakers: "With a temper that flares suddenly, he takes a wide leather strap and pounds the table, altar, or Bible with the edge of it . . . then wields it against a woman [who] became dissociated as he held her hands and swung her arms from side to side . . . remarking, 'Satan, he wait for you!' He proceeded to strike the woman's open palms with his strap." The Pointer becomes the instrument of the Holy Ghost, saying, "It is the Holy Spirit who gives punishment to you," and, while the culprit is still in a possession trance, lashes her as she was lashed as a child, telling her she was now forgiven for being sinful.[62]

---

59. Ann Woodward, "The Cult of Relics in Prehistoric Britain." In Martin Carver, Ed., *In Search of Cult.* Woodbridge: Boydell, 1993, pp. 1–7.

60. Patrick Tierney, *The Highest Altar*, p. 393.

61. Mark Juergensmeyer, *Terror in the Mind of God.* Berkeley: University of California Press, 2000, p. 6.

62. Felicitas D. Goodman et al., *Trance, Healing, and Hallucination: Three Field Studies in Religious Experience.* New York: Wiley, 1974, pp. 32–35.

The neurobiology of "God experiences" is well understood. They are actually temporal lobe seizures, similar to the seizures of epileptics, explaining why so many mystics experienced clear epileptic seizures. These kindling seizures—which have been correlated with previous serious child abuse—begin in the hippocampus and spread to the amygdalan network, transforming previous painful anoxic depressive rage feelings into what Mandell calls "ecstatic joyful rage," with a disappearance of self boundaries so that the person is suddenly overcome with feelings of unity and love.[63] The neurobiology of "God in the brain" is similar to the effects of drugs like cocaine and the hallucinogens, "inducing an acute loss of serotonergic regulation of temporal lobe limbic structures and releasing the affectual and cognitive processes characteristic of religious ecstasy and conversion."[64] Persinger describes "the release of the brain's own opiates that can cause a narcotic high" during these God-merger experiences, producing "with a single burst in the temporal lobe, a personal conviction of truth and a sense of self-selection [that] shames any known therapy."[65] As Otto puts it, the *mysterium tremendum* of religious ecstasy "bursts in sudden eruption up from the depths of the soul with spasms and convulsions and leads to the strangest excitements, to intoxicated frenzy, to transport and to ecstasy . . . wild and demonic . . . and can sink to an almost grisly horror and shuddering."[66] Saint Theresa tells how it felt to experience this painful ecstasy in her organ alters: "An angel pierced its spear several times through my heart, so that it penetrated to my bowels, which were extracted when the spear was withdrawn, leaving me all aflame with an immense love for God. The pain was so great that I had to groan, but the sweetness that came with this violent pain was such that I could not wish to be free of it."[67]

Religions devise rituals to exteriorize alters and collude with others in the delusion that internal alters really exist outside oneself, providing some

---

63. Arnold J. Mandell, "Toward a Psychobiology of Transcendence: God in the Brain." In J. Davidson, Ed., *The Psychobiology of Consciousness*. New York: Plenum, 1980, pp. 379–464.

64. Ibid., p. 393.

65. Michael A. Persinger, *Neuropsychological Bases of God Beliefs*. New York: Praeger, 1987, p. 17.

66. Rudolf Otto, *The Idea of the Holy*. London: Oxford University Press, 1958, p. 12.

67. Holger Kalweit, *Dreamtime & Inner Space*. Boston: Shambhala, 1988, p. 94.

group relief from feeling unlovable by sharing myths like "Christ died for your sins" and asking for forgiveness in hopes that God, the omnipotent mommy alter, will finally love them. Each step of the shaman's or priest's ritual can be decoded to reveal its infantile origin: "In every ritual, we must do what the gods [parents] did in the beginning,"[68] The most severely abused children today who become multiple personalities (dissociated identity disorders) frequently join one of the many fundamentalist religious cults in order to decrease the pains of their dissociation.[69] Religions provide alter fetishes— shaman's rattles, Dionysian phallic replicas, suffering Christ statues—that contain the traumas of the alters and allow the worshiper to act out the guilt and punishment they demand. Most gods began as fetishes, "spirits embodied in material objects,"[70] and demon fetish figurines were plentiful in antiquity, being made to be ritually destroyed or thrown into the river or buried in deserted places to punish the victim alters that were projected into them.[71] These alter fetishes were believed to have "accumulated power so intense and dangerous" that they had to be "killed" in order to release their force.[72] All the statues and standards worshiped by the Egyptian and Mesopotamians were so concretely alternate personalities that they were regularly fed and spoken to, "in order to sustain the power with which they were charged."[73] Most early Sacred Kings only remained kings as long as they had possession of their fetish alters, the royal crown—symbol of the maternal vagina—and the throne—symbol of the maternal chair.[74] As will be discussed below, the fantasy of the omnipotent terrifying mommy always lies behind even masculine gods and demons, both in religious and political group fantasies.

---

68. Mircea Eliade, *Myths, Rites, Symbols, Vol. 1.* New York: Harper & Row, 1976, p. 133.

69. David G. Benner, "The Functions of Faith: Religious Psychodynamics in Multiple Personality Disorder." In Mark Finn, Ed., *Object Relations Theory and Religion: Clinical Applications.* Westport: Praeger, 1992, p. 37.

70. E. A. Wallis Budge, *From Fetish to God in Ancient Egypt.* New York: Dover Publications, 1988, p. 57.

71. Ann E. Farkas, et al., *Monsters and Demons in the Ancient and Medieval Worlds.* Mainz on Rhine: P. von Zabern, 1987, pp. 29–35.

72. Linda Schele and Mary Ellen Miller, *The Blood of Kings*, p. 43.

73. Henri Frankfort, *Kingship and the Gods.* Chicago: University of Chicago Press, 1978, p. 304.

74. Ibid., p. 107.

THE SEVEN STAGES OF HISTORICAL PERSONALITY

According to James Masterson, personality disorders are results of "false selves" that defend against painful affects of early life and present-day experiences, designed to camouflage the real targets of emotional life—the infantile feelings and memories—and based not on reality but on organized fantasies involving part selves. Contemporary personality disorders as described in Masterson's revisions of the *Diagnostic and Statistical Manual of Mental Disorders*, 4th edition (*DSM-IV*)[75] form a series of personality types from schizoid to narcissistic, borderline, depressive, and neurotic that conform to the stages of evolution of historical personalities that result from the child-rearing modes described in the previous two chapters.

THE SCHIZOID PSYCHOCLASS OF TRIBAL SOCIETIES

The schizoid personality cluster—including paranoid and psychopathic personalities—features magical, primary process thinking; periods of depersonalization, unreality, and grandiosity; animistic fused subject/object experiences; an inability to experience intimacy; and extreme episodes of suspicion and rage. Because tribal mothering (see Chapter 7) is so primitive, so lacking in empathy for the child and so engulfing in overt maternal incest, the schizoid tribal personality has a fear of being taken over and a "profound inability to love himself."[76] Schizoids therefore cannot stand close relationships and so cannot form higher levels of social organization based on trust. Tribal personalities since the Palaeolithic era formed animal and organ alters containing dissociated perpetrator and victim alters. Animal alters were depicted in the cave paintings of early times and were sacrificially stabbed over and over again in ecstatic rebirth rituals held deep in womb caves covered with several inches of blood-red ocher. The depersonalization of schizoids—the result of severe separation stress—is so extreme that they regularly felt themselves breaking into fragmented pieces, switching into dissociated states and going into shamanistic trances to try to put themselves together. During shamanistic journeys, schizoids expe-

75. James F. Masterson, *The Personality Disorders*. Phoenix: Zeig, Tucker & Co, 2000, pp. 59–82.

76. Ralph Klein, "Intrapsychic Structures." In James F. Masterson and Ralph Klein, Eds., *Disorders of the Self*. New York: Brunner/Mazel, 1995, p. 314.

Table 9–1. Table of Historical Personalities

Child Rearing	Personality	Ideal	Mother/God	Sacrifice
Tribal: early infanticidal	Schizoid	Shaman	Devours, seduces, abandons child	To animal alter spirits
Antiquity: late infanticidal	Narcissist	Hero	Kills, punishes evil child	To human alter gods
Christian: abandoning	Masochist	Martyr	Forgives hurt child	Self-torture
Middle Ages: ambivalent	Borderline	Vassal	Dominates, beats worshipful child	Subservient clinging
Renaissance: intrusive	Depressive	Holy warrior	Disciplines obedient child	Obeying
Modern: socializing	Neurotic	Patriot	Manipulates child	Incomplete separation
Post-Modern: helping	Individuated	Activist	Trusts, loves child	No sacrifice of real self

rience themselves as sliced up, their bones removed, their flesh devoured by female monsters, and as repeating the tortures of childhood by being starved, burned, beaten, raped, and lacerated.[77] Like schizoid personalities today, much of their lives were spent in fantasy worlds that repeated the childhood isolation that resulted from their feeling that there was simply no path to a real relationship with parents or others. Since alters are formed to contain and control memories of early terrors, when defenses threaten to break down the schizoid is flooded with agony.[78] In tribal groups, there is no hope for forgiveness, there is no "sin," no chance of atonement, only "eat Mommy or be eaten by her," only sadistic master-slave fears and detachment-alienation defenses, all restaged in endless rituals and cannibalistic feasts where organ alters are eaten. Bourguignon found spirit possession rituals (where an alter totally takes over the host personality) only in simple hunter-gatherer societies, while possession-trance rituals (where various demon alters appear as spirits during brief ritual trances) were found in agricultural or animal herding societies.[79] Possession rituals

---

77. Michael Ripinsky-Naxon, *The Nature of Shamanism: Substance and Function of a Religious Metaphor*. Albany: State University of New York Press, 1993, p. 82.

78. Doris Bryant, et al., *The Family Inside*, p. 153.

79. Erika Bourguignon, *Possession*, p. 43.

today feature a "judgement of the soul by an old woman, the mother-animal, the mistress of the dead," and in the past featured "human victims offered in sacrifice to propitiate the Master of the Animals."[80] The animal masks of the shaman are familiar from the various cave paintings that have survived this early period, with the shaman's drum said to be "the voice of the primeval mother" and with Mistress of the Animal representations continuing as late as the Greek goddess Artemis.[81] Yakut shamans still hallucinate self-sacrifice to "a Bird-of-Prey-Mother, which is like a great bird with an iron beak, hooked claws, and a long tail [who] cuts its body into bits and devours it."[82]

Animistic alter fetishes surrounded early humans. As one Chukchi put it: "All that exists lives. The lamp walks around. The walls of the house have voices of their own, while the deceased get up and visit the living."[83] Every alter fetish contains traces of the original trauma from when it was formed—even the shaman's rattle betraying the routine raping of children by having a "gourd representing the womb and a penis-handle that inseminates it."[84] Indeed, it is likely that most of the misnamed "Venus figurines" found in early caves were in fact raping wands similar to those used in contemporary cults that rape virgins in rituals,[85] with faceless heads shaped like the glans of the penis, bulbous breasts looking just like testicles, a vaginal triangle carefully indicated and covered with red ocher representing the bloody results of the childhood rape.[86] It was no coincidence that the very first art in the Upper Palaeolithic era was mainly representations of the vulva.[87] "Sacred rape" is part of shamanistic beliefs today,[88] and virgins are still cut and raped as sacrificial offerings to

---

80. Michael Ripinsky-Naxon, *The Nature of Shamanism*, pp. 27, 110.

81. Ibid., p. 32.

82. Mircea Eliade, *Shamanism: Archaic Techniques of Ecstasy.* Princeton: Princeton University Press, 1972, p. 36.

83. Joseph Campbell, *The Way of the Animal Powers. Vol. 1*, p. 178.

84. Michael Ripinsky-Naxon, *The Nature of Shamanism*, p. 51.

85. Lloyd deMause, "Why Cults Terrorize and Kill Children." *The Journal of Psychohistory* 21(1994): 512.

86. Timothy Taylor, *The Prehistory of Sex.* New York: Bantam Doubleday Dell, 1996, pp. 126–129.

87. Desmond Collins and John Onians, "The Origins of Art." *Art History* March 1978, p. 4.

88. Nevill Drury, *The Elements of Shamanism.* Longmead: Element, 1989, p. 20.

gods in some areas of the world, giving as the reason: "Only blood satisfies the *tius* [avenging spirits]."[89] Girls in some African tribes are still made to sit on erect penis figurines as punishment.[90] That tunnels and caves were the locations of these raping rituals fits well with the frequent use of tunnels and caves by contemporary cults that rape schoolchildren.[91] That the caves of the Palaeolithic era are cultic sanctuaries for trance hallucinations is further confirmed by their being covered with "entoptic" images identical to those experienced by contemporary shamans engaged in trance vision quests.[92]

Plunging into the terrifying, hallucinatory world of dreamtime trances meant revisiting the terrifying world of childhood, where mommies suck infants' penises and fathers have 7-year-olds fellate them. Initiates felt so polluted by their early seductions that they submitted themselves at adolescence to initiatory group-fantasies of disemboweling and washing of their entrails and other body parts, while endlessly cutting themselves to cleanse their blood of their badness. The !Kung bushmen of the Kalahari still switch into cleansing trances once a week to experience their alter memories in convulsion-like tremors, ending in the usual temporal lobe seizures of tribal personalities, "bursting open, like a ripe pod" when "God killed my every thought. He wiped me clean."[93] Body parts containing projected alters collected by early headhunters and cannibals existed with hallucinatory reality: "The Dyaks were obsessed with the notion that severed heads continued to exist as living beings. . . . [They were] treated for months with deep reverence and flattering speech. Choice morsels from the table would be thrust into its mouth, and at the end of the meal a cigar would be placed between its lips."[94] Alters in enemy scalps collected by warriors in many tribes were so real the scalps used to be taken home, called "my child" and

---

89. Patrick Tierney, *The Highest Altar*, p. 270.

90. Hans Cory, *African Figurines: Their Ceremonial Use in Puberty Rites*. London: Faber & Faber, 1955, p. 62.

91. Ronald C. Sumit, "The Dark Tunnels of McMartin." *The Journal of Psychohistory* 21(1994): 397–416.

92. J. D. Lewis-Williams and T. A. Dowson, "The Signs of All Times: Entoptic Phenomena in Upper Palaeolithic Art." *Current Anthropology* 29(1988): 214.

93. Richard B. Lee and Irven DeVore, *Kalahari Hunter-Gatherers: Studies of the !Kung San and Their Neighbors*. Cambridge: Harvard University Press, 1976, pp. 288, 296.

94. Nigel Davies, *Human Sacrifice in History and Today*. New York: Dorset Press, 1981, p. 173.

fed regularly.[95] Since enemies were usually quite innocent of any wrong-doing until a warrior's alters were projected into them, captured enemies were often tortured—to punish the projected childhood alters—and then eaten—to return the punished alter to the original owner.[96] Thus what Sagan calls "aggressive cannibalism" and ascribes to "vengeance" is in fact a punishment of a part of the self, projected into another body, and then returned after punishment to one's own body by eating it.

Apparently the cultural explosion at the beginning of the Upper Palaeolithic era some 35,000 years ago was the result of early language abilities affording the capacity to project alters into others and into shared cultural alter fetishes.[97] Early humans were schizoid personalities who did not have unified real selves, only dozens of subselves that they projected into other people and objects. One archaeologist suggests that the spectacular explosion of cultural developments 35,000 years ago came from "the appearance of a very simple additional cognitive affective mechanism—a disposition to engage in pretend play in childhood,"[98] which in turn depends on the ability to project parts of one's self into others and into objects. Contemporary tribal children have alters they play with, far more real to them than the "imaginary playmates" children in more complex societies have. In New Guinea, small children have alternate personalities called *finiik* that "temporarily depart from the body to wander abroad . . . during trances and other forms of mystical experience."[99] Anthropologists are often startled to be introduced by a little child to his *finiik*, projected into a certain stone or bird, or be told about how witch alters regularly possess children's bodies both in dreams and waking life—all spontaneously experienced, long before being taught in ritual.

---

95. Peggy Reeves Sanday, *Female Power and Male Dominance: On the Origins of Sexual Inequality.* Cambridge: Cambridge University Press, 1981, p. 44.

96. Eli Sagan, *Cannibalish: Human Aggression and Cultural Form.* New York: Psychohistory Press, 1983, p. 5.

97. Peter Carruthers and Andrew Chamberlain, "Introduction." In Carruthers and Chamberlain, Eds., *Evolution and the Human Mind.* Cambridge: Cambridge University Press, 2000, p. 6; Gerald M. Edelman and Giulio Tononi, *A Universe of Consciousness: How Matter Becomes Imagination.* New York: Basic Books, 2000.

98. Steven Mithen, "Mind, Brain and Material Culture: An Archaeological Perspective." In Peter Carruthers and Andrew Chamberlain, Eds., *Evolution and the Human Mind,* p. 212.

99. Lloyd deMause, "Childhood and Cultural Evolution." *The Journal of Psychohistory* 26(1999): 708–710.

Wars, too, are fought to cleanse internal alters of badness, repair the fragmented self, and restore potency. Tribal warfare against alter container enemies is accomplished mainly through ambush, with warriors spearing unarmed men, women, and children for wholly imagined grievances. Tribes switch into persecutory alters mainly on occasions of extreme growth panic, when new tasks such as building houses or expanding gardens threaten too much growth and after initiations that center on adolescents growing up. Homicide rates reach the highest levels anywhere in the world—up to 60 percent—in schizoid tribal societies, since extreme distrust of others is common: "Both men and women are volatile, prone to quarreling and quick to take offense at a suspected slight,"[100] restaging the distrust and rage of their infanticidal mothers. Women are routinely viewed as secretly being witches "who can kill simply by staring at a person" and are often killed because they are believed to poison people.[101] Wife beating is nearly universal, female suicide rates from mistreatment often reaches 10 to 25 percent of women's deaths, and routine torture and execution of women suspected of poisoning men is common.[102]

Supreme gods in schizoids—unlike the more personal gods of borderlines—are totally unloving and distant, reflecting the uncaring nature of the parents. Eliade points out that even when thought of as "eternal, omniscient, and all-powerful," creator gods in tribal cultures "withdraw to the sky," too remote and uncaring to be prayed to or addressed.[103] What takes their place is merging with guardian spirits—empowerment by first torturing yourself to cleanse your alters and then hallucinating an animal alter that might protect you against being devoured by cannibalistic maternal giant alters like the Australian "old serpent woman" or the Kwakiutl giantess Tsonoqua, who roams the forest searching for children to eat.[104]

---

100. L. L. Langness, "Child Abuse and Cultural Values: The Case of New Guinea." In Jill E. Korbin, *Child Abuse and Neglect: Cross-Cultural Perspectives.* Berkeley: University of California Press, 1981, p. 28.

101. Marie Reay, "The Magico-Religious Foundations of New Guinea Highlands Warfare." In Michele Stephen, Ed., *Sorcerer and Witch in Melanesia.* New Brunswick: Rutgers University Press, 1987, p. 144.

102. Lloyd deMause, "Childhood and Cultural Evolution," p. 711.

103. Mircea Eliade, *The Sacred and the Profane: The Nature of Religion.* New York: Harcourt Brace Jovanovich, 1959, p. 121.

104. Guy E. Swanson, "The Search for a Guardian Spirit: A Process of Empowerment in Simpler Societies." *Ethnology* 12(1973): 359; Joseph Campbell, *The Way of the Animal Powers, Vol. 1*, pp. 190–194.

Even when schizoids try to incorporate paternal features to avoid being devoured, they end up giving their gods maternal features—like the rainbow serpents of Australia, described as "gods who are male but have a womb or female breasts . . . who look like snakes but also like a woman . . . the 'bad Mother' . . . who swallowed children left in her care."[105]

The main content, however, of tribal rituals is constructed from fetal fantasies, because schizoid disintegration produces deep regression to bad womb and rebirth memories. Psychotherapists like Stan Grof—who regress their patients to fetal states—reproduce their patients' drawings in their books, and these look very much like shamanistic experiences.[106] Possessed shamans often describe switching into trances during their dances in language that closely resembles the birth experience:

> The *loa* dance suggests water [amniotic fluid] . . . when the drumbeat quickens [mother experiences contractions]. . . . The whole structure crashes like a cosmic surf over one's head [breaking of the amniotic waters]. . . . The terror strikes and with a supreme effort I wrench my leg loose, I must keep moving [trapped in birth canal]. . . . My skull is a drum, my veins will burst my skin [bloodstream anoxic because placenta no longer delivers oxygenated blood]. . . . I am sucked down and exploded upward at once [birth]. . . . Finally it is as if I lay at the far distant end of an infinitely deep-down, sunken well, then suddenly: surface; suddenly: air; suddenly: dazzling white [born].[107]

Róheim describes the initiation ritual of the Australian aborigines in which initiates were forced to drink blood as "throwing the novice into the Old Woman whose womb is symbolized by a semi-circular trench. . . . The Rainbow Serpent [Poisonous Placenta] is represented engraved on the walls of the trench. A bull-roarer, called the 'Mother' and also representing her womb, her 'shade,' is buried in the trench, his spirit [alter] later leaving it to return to his spirit home."[108] Both initiation rituals and shamanistic jour-

---

105. Ira R. Buchler, "The Fecal Crone." In Ira R. Buchler and Kenneth Maddock, *The Rainbow Serpent*. The Hague: Mouton Publishers, 1978, p. 127.

106. Stanislav Grof, *Psychology of the Future*. Albany: State University of New York Press, 2000.

107. Maya Deren, *Divine Horsemen: Voodoo Gods of Haiti*. New York: Chilsea Hous, 1970, pp. 252–261.

108. Géza Róheim, *Psychoanalysis and Anthropology*. New York: International Universities Press, 1950, p. 76.

neys usually include going through long birth tunnels with umbilical ropes attaching them to visit placental World Trees, feeling body dismemberments like those that fetuses feel during birth, performing bloody birth rituals in medicine wheel circles shaped like placentas, and restaging the "poison blood" memories of birth by being covered by "the menstrual blood that can cause you to die, called 'dead womb blood.'"[109] Only after going through poison-blood rebirth restagings could tribal men hope for a time to put their devouring mommy alters at rest and go about with the daily work of living.

The result of always being subject to infanticidal, incestuous abandoning maternal memories is that schizoid tribal personalities cannot tolerate separation or rejection in their daily life. "Rejection is unendurable. . . . Families cluster together in an encampment 'often touching against their neighbors' [because] separation and loneliness are unendurable to them. [They] cannot bear the sense of rejection that even mild disapproval makes them feel."[110] What is misnamed "egalitarianism" is really mistrust and fear of being called "selfish" for owning. Hoarding and self-aggrandizement are simply not tolerated—people were often killed for trying to keep more than their share of goods—ambition was stopped by overwhelming schizoid envy, change was feared and the surpluses and savings that were necessary for future innovation were nowhere to be found. As Murphy found, in tribal societies "the mother is an eternal threat to self-individuation, a frustrater of urges, and a swallower of emergent identity" of men.[111] The early incest was particularly destructive to separation and individuation. As one Maori sage put it: "That which destroys man is the mana of the vagina." Men are forced to merge with their mothers in order to appropriate the power of their vagina: "Warriors became the symbolic equivalent of menstruating women. . . . [Both] bloody warriors and menstruating women . . . were charged with powerful destructive energy. . . . Warriors' bodies and weapons were decorated with

---

109. Holger Kalweit, *Dreamtime & Inner Space*, p. 48; Robert B. McFarland and Will Schalaben, "Placentas and Prehistoric Art." *The Journal of Psychohistory* 23(1994): 41–50; Peggy Reeves Sanday, *Divine Hunger: Cannibalism as a Cultural System.* Cambridge: Cambridge University Press, 1986, p. 59.

110. Richard Fischer, "Psychotherapy of the Narcissistic Personality Disorder." In James F. Masterson and Ralph Klein, Eds., *Psychotherapy of the Disorders of the Self.* New York: Brunner/Mazel, 1989, p. 83; Margaret Power, *The Egalitarians—Human and Chimpanzee.* Cambridge: Cambridge University Press, 1991, p. 184.

111. Yolanda Murphy and Rober F. Murphy, *Women of the Forest.* New York: Columbia University Press, 1985, p. 3.

designs marked in red hematite [and] they expropriated the destructive power of menstruating women [by] ritual nosebleeding or subincision."[112] Often the bond between men was obtained by their sharing the mommy-alter in their blood, cutting their veins, and smearing their blood on each other to form "blood brotherhoods."[113] But strong leaders are avoided because they might bring back memories of maternal domination: "Australian aborigines traditionally eliminated aggressive men who tried to dominate them [and] in New Guinea, they execute prominent individuals who overstep their prerogatives."[114] Personal loyalty to leaders is tentative because of their overwhelming schizoid mistrust and envy, so the most social organization that can be achieved is "big men" who do not threaten to subject others too much to maternal engulfment and despair—better to stick to alter fetishes and constant gift-exchange to ward off the return of childhood memories of starvation and abandonment. Every step toward personal closeness or trust brings flashbacks to maternal distancing, since "schizoid states often lead to acute paranoid regressions because the patient's aggression becomes more threatening to him as he allows himself to get closer to other individuals."[115] Thus wars in tribal societies often follow disappointments in sexual affairs—as men fail in achieving intimacy, they become paranoid and go off to kill imagined "enemies." Only when child rearing achieved the next highest mode were men able to achieve complex societies that allowed dominant male leaders and trust in others sufficient to permit ownership and complex hierarchical organizations that could permit development of higher levels of economic production and trade.

THE NARCISSISTIC PSYCHOCLASS OF ANTIQUITY

Narcissistic personalities ward off their sense of an empty, inadequate self by fusing with the harsh attacking parent alter and forming a grandiose

---

112. Raymond D. Fogelson, "On the 'Petticoat Government' of the Eighteenth-Century Cherokee." In David K. Jordan, Ed., *Personality and the Cultural Construction of Society.* Tuscaloosa: University of Alabama Press, 1990, p. 175.

113. E. E. Evans Pritchard, *Social Anthropology and Other Essays.* New York: Free Press, 1962, p. 268.

114. Christopher Boehm, "Egalitarian Society and Reverse Dominance Hierarchy." *Current Anthropology* 34(1993): 236.

115. Harold W. Koenigsberg, et al., *Borderline Patients.* New York: Basic Books, 2000, p. 134.

self that identifies with the omnipotent parent. Or they become a latent narcissist and cling to and admire a grandiose other, a narcissistic hero who can stand up to the destructive mother alter.[116] Whereas schizoid tribal personalities tried to maintain a safe distance to avoid engulfment, the narcissistic personalities of antiquity tried to maintain some sense of self by arming themselves with grandiose exhibitionism. Thus they constantly live in the state of narcissistic display, as for instance early Greeks did when they spent their days displaying their bodies at gymnasiums and at night— rather than going home to risk intimacy with their wives—engaged in male-only drinking/raping parties. The narcissistic personalities of antiquity were exploitative, distrustful, ruthless, and lacking in empathy,[117] being preoccupied with fantasies of the power and brilliance of a world filled with arrogant, distant narcissistic heroes, and gods and grandiose political leaders upon whom they depended to validate their weak sense of self. Their pedophilia was also a result of their only being able to have sex with a narcissistic double of themselves stemming from when they were beautiful youths and, like Narcissus, fell in love with themselves, avoiding women as "vultures" who were out to catch and devour them.

Early civilizations began with both gods and leaders who had maternal characteristics: devouring goddesses everywhere prevailed, and even chiefs seemed to be mommies—as the Anyi said: "When the king's breasts are full of milk, it is his people who drink."[118] Parin found the Anyi clung to their kings because "their fear of women was greater than their fear of men" and because of "their need to find a chief or master who enjoys prestige and power so that they can submit to him and introject power" and avoid maternal engulfment.[119] As Galen put it: "Each man trembled forever on the brink of becoming 'womanish'"[120]—i.e., of switching permanently into his mommy alter and losing his self. The ever-present fear of turning into a woman found throughout early civilizations explains why religions and politics were defensive arenas filled with sadistic maternal

---

116. James F. Masterson, *The Personality Disorders*, p. 72.

117. James F. Masterson, *Psychotherapy of the Borderline Adult*. New York: Brunner/ Mazel, 1976, p. 87.

118. Paul Parin et al., *Fear Thy Neighbor as Thyself: Psychoanalysis and Society Among the Anyi of West Africa*. Chicago: University of Chicago Press, 1980, p. 29.

119. Ibid., p. 348.

120. Peter Brown, *The Body and Society*. New York: Columbia University Press, 1988, p. 11.

alters and why periodic wars were desperately needed to attempt to restore men's potency.

The daily life of the narcissistic personalities of antiquity was filled with projected alters, from the evil spirits, devils, and *dybbuks* that Jews were constantly exorcising to the bloodthirsty female spirits, serpents, and demons that Sumerians, Egyptians, Greeks, and Romans tried to ward off with their various religious fetishes. "At every corner evil spirits were on the watch. . . . There was also danger from the spells of numerous witches, in whom everyone believed implicitly."[121] Even supposedly rational Greeks were, as Gouldner put it, "deeply concerned about their capacity to go murderously berserk."[122] Egyptians regularly talked to their avenging alters, as the "world-weary man" talked to his "double," his *Ba*, about suicide, making "suicide so common that the crocodiles in the Nile could no longer cope with the corpses."[123] Hippocrates confirmed that Greeks often experienced "convulsions, fears, terrors, and delusions," and physicians in every country of antiquity were expected to treat possessions, hallucinations, frenzies, lycanthropies, and other symptoms of dissociated personalities (melancholy in Greek meaning "furor").[124] The average Greek acknowledged that his emotional life was constantly controlled by his alters, which were given names like *psyche, thumos, menos, kardia, kradie, etor, noos, ate,* and so on. Dodds says that Homer describes *ate*, for instance, as "a temporary clouding or bewildering of the normal consciousness . . . a partial and temporary insanity . . . ascribed to an external 'daemonic' agency."[125] Medea says she did not kill her children, her *thumos* forced her to kill them. One's *psyche* looks and sounds like a living person, Odysseus says, but it flies off "like a shadow or a dream."[126] Sometimes they were co-conscious with these alters, but often they were not, since they completely took over the self. Adkins wrote an entire

---

121. T. K. Oesterreich, *Possession and Exorcism*. New York: Causeway Books, 1974, p. 147.

122. A. W. Gouldner, *Enter Plato*. New York: Basic Books, 1965, p. 109.

123. Barbara Hannah, *Encounters with the Soul*. Santa Monica: Sigo Press, 1981, p. 85.

124. S. Vernon McCasland, "By the Finger of God; Demon Possession and Exorcism." In *Early Christianity in the Light of Modern Views of Mental Illness*. New York: Macmillan, 1951, p. 36; Raymond Klibansky et al., *Saturn and Melancholy*. London: Thomas Nelson & Sons, 1964, p. 15.

125. E. R. Dodds, *The Greeks and the Irrational*. Berkeley: University of California Press, 1964, p. 5.

126. A. W. H. Adkins, *From the Many to the One*. London: Constable, 1970, p. 15.

book on how the Greeks of antiquity kept switching into their subpersonalities, describing their "low degree of unity and cohesion [as] one 'little man' (so to speak) within him after another addresses and prompts him."[127] Usually the spirits and demons of antiquity betrayed their maternal origin—not so surprising when one reads statements like that of Galen who said "my mother was so very prone to anger that sometimes she bit her handmaids"[128] or that of Xenophon who said he would "rather bear a wild beast's brutality than that of his mother."[129]

The earliest civilizations uniformly worshiped vampire goddesses who were devouring maternal alters. All were what Jungians term "dragon mothers"[130]—from Lilith, Nin-Tu, Hecate, and Ishtar to Moira, Shiva, Gorgon, and Erinyes. They were usually called by their worshipers "terrible mothers," usually had serpentine features, and were called by worshipers cruel, jealous, and unjust; "her glance brings death, her will is supreme."[131] Since contemporary multiple personalities also sometimes hallucinate gigantic serpents as alters,[132] one must believe the witnesses in early civilizations when they insist they really saw these serpent goddesses. The dragon mother goddesses accurately embodied the infanticidal "infinitely needy mother who cannot let her children go because she needs them for her own psychic survival . . . giving her child the impossible task of filling her limitless void [and] engulfing them to prevent them from claiming a separate life for themselves."[133] One of the earliest vulture goddesses can be seen on the shrine walls of the Neolithic town of Catal Hüyük, a bloodthirsty goddess with wings of a vulture who is shown eating headless corpses. Corpses of people were actually thrown into the fields nearby so vultures could eat them in sacrificial rebirth rituals.[134] That vultures were maternal was shown long ago in Freud's paper showing that the Egyptian hieroglyph for "mother" clearly represents a vulture and that the Egyptians worshiped a vulture-headed

127. Ibid., p. 45.

128. Peter Brown: The Body and Society, p. 12.

129. Roger Just, *Women in Athenian Law and Life.* London: Routledge, 1989, p. 21.

130. Marisa Dillon Weston, "Anorexia as a Symbol of an Empty Matrix Dominated by the Dragon Mother." *Group Analysis* 32(1999): 71–85.

131. B. C. Dietrich, *Death, Fate and the Gods.* London: Athlone Press, 1965, p. 77.

132. Dale McCulley, *Multiple Exposure.* Nevada City: First Books, 2000, p. 40.

133. Marisa Dillon Weston, "Anorexia as Symbol of an Empty Matrix Dominated by the Dragon Mother," p. 74.

134. James Mellaart, *Catal Hüyük: A Neolithic Town in Anatolia.* London: Thames & Hudson, 1967.

mother goddess.[135] Even early Hebrews worshiped a mother goddess, Asherah,[136] who, along with Lilith, the other vampire goddess mentioned in the Bible, "ceaselessly devoured the blood" of her worshipers and "roamed the world in search of children to eat, rape, and kill." Even the Sphinx (*sphinx* means "throttler") was a maternal monster who devoured youth.[137] Most of the male animal gods of early civilizations were pictured as slaves of goddesses, like "the Bull of Heaven, the ferocious monster who killed three hundred men at each snort of his breath [whom] Ishtar in her rage sent down to devastate the land."[138] But usually the mother goddesses accomplished their own slaughters: "Kali, the Black One, breasts big with milk, adorned with the blood-dripping hands and heads of her victims, devouring the entrails of a human victim or drinking blood from a human skull."[139] Statues of these bloodthirsty goddesses were set up in ziggurats and temples all over the world, daily washed, dressed, fed, talked to, and heard to speak their commands,[140] so hallucinatory was the power of the alters. The statues were such bloodthirsty maternal alter fetishes that often priests would take the blood of the sacrificial victim and anoint the face of the idol so she could drink of it.[141] Divinely induced madness—as in the Dionysian rituals of ancient Greece—would sometimes even cause women to become possessed by their terrible mother alters and act out the killing of the victim, especially when they were experiencing postpartum depressions. As Euripides describes them: "Breasts swollen with milk, new mothers who had left their babies behind at home . . . clawed calves to pieces with bare hands [and] snatched children from their homes."[142]

---

135. Noel Bradley, "The Vulture as Mother Symbol: A Note on Freud's *Leonardo*." *American Imago* 22(1965): 47.

136. Raphael Patai, *The Hebrew Goddess*. New York: Ktav Publishing House, 1967, p. 34.

137. Joseph Fontenrose, *Python: A Study of Delphic Myth and Its Origins*. Berkeley: University of California Press, 1959, p. 309.

138. Wolfgang Lederer, *The Fear of Women*. New York: Grune & Stratton, 1968, p. 76.

139. Ibid., p. 133.

140. Julian Jaynes, *The Origins of Consciousness in the Breakdown of the Bicameral Mind*. Boston: Houghton Mifflin Co., 1990, p. 179.

141. Sylvanus G. Morley, *The Ancient Maya*, 3rd ed. Stanford: Stanford University Press, 1956, p. 157.

142. Ross S. Kraemer, "Ecstasy and Possession: The Attraction of Women to the Cult of Dionysus." *Harvard Theological Review* 71(1978): 59.

The fetal origins of early religions were everywhere evident. Actual human placentas were often hung on trees, worshiped, and offered human sacrifices.[143] Goddesses like Tiamat were referred to as "poisonous womb-snakes," Sumerians and Babylonians worshiped "placenta ghosts," and even the Hebrew name for Eve (*Khawwa*) meant "the serpent lady."[144] Peruvians used to place their actual placentas into the womb of their religious statues,[145] just as most *nagual* worshiped in ancient Meso-American religions were real placentas.[146] All the "cosmic trees" found in early religions—from the Tree of Eden to Jesus's Cross—were placental in origin, and the priest was often portrayed as a fetus: "He has become a fetus. His head is veiled and he is made to clench his fists, for the embryo in its bag has its fists clenched. He walks around the hearth just as the fetus moves within the womb. . . . He unclenches his fists, he unveils himself, he is born into divine existence, he is a god."[147] Carthaginian and other child sacrifice religions used both fetuses and newborn in their rites,[148] and cults even today often kill real fetuses in rebirth rituals.[149] Even the deluge myths—from Gilgamesh to that of the Hebrew Bible—contain many elements of the rush of amniotic waters prior to birth.

Every detail of the worship of mother goddesses has its origins in actual traumatic child-rearing experiences of antiquity. Most "terrifying mothers" had divine sons who were forced to commit incest with them,[150] similar to the Japanese mothers and others described in the previous chap-

---

143. Gertrude Jobes, *Dictionary of Mythology, Folklore and Symbols.* New York: Scarecrow Press, 1961, p. 1277.

144. Balaji Mundkur, *The Cult of the Serpent.* Albany: State University of New York Press, 1983, p. 67; Aylward M. Blackman, "The Pharaoh's Placenta and the Moon-God Khons." *Journal of Egyptian Archaeology* 3(1916): 241; Clyde E. Keeler, *Secrets of the Cuna Earthmother.* New York: Exposition Press, 1960, p. 45.

145. J. R. Davidson, "The Shadow of Life: Psychosocial Explanations for Placenta Rituals." *Culture, Medicine and Psychiatry* 9(1985): 80.

146. Martin Brennan, "The Maya Mosaic," unpublished paper, 2001.

147. Henri Hubert and Marcel Mauss, *Sacrifice: Its Nature and Function.* Chicago: University of Chicago Press, 1964, p. 21.

148. Lloyd deMause, "The History of Child Assault." *The Journal of Psychohistory* 18(1990): 17.

149. Lloyd deMause, "Why Cults Terrorize and Kill Children." *The Journal of Psychohistory* 21(1994): 513.

150. Philip E. Slater, *The Glory of Hera: Greek Mythology and the Greek Family.* Boston: Beacon Press, 1968, p. 274.

ter,[151] with "every mother goddess having their son-lovers, Inanna and Tammuz, Isis and Osiris, Cybele and Attis, Aphrodite and Adonis."[152] The religious rituals restaged accurately the maternal seduction: "Not only does the Mother Goddess love her son simply for his phallus, she castrates him, taking possession of it to make herself fruitful."[153] In India until recently, "visitors to many ancient shrines used to have symbolic intercourse with stone-cut female deities by thrusting their fingers into deep touchholes, worn by generations of finger-thrusters, at the deities' sexual centers."[154] Thus it is quite mistaken to call ancient sexual seduction rituals "sacred marriages." They are in fact "sacred maternal incests." When the incest is complete and the "insatiable appetite" of the Goddess assuaged, the Mother Goddess then castrated her son[155] and even, in the case of Ishtar, "wore a necklace of testicles in depictions of her. The Great Mother was gentler to women than to men, who had great reason to fear her dark side as Devouring-Mother. [She] existed not to be loved, but to be *placated*."[156] Worshipers of the Magna Mater, called *galli*, castrated themselves for her, "wishing to be like a child, the better to serve the goddess,"[157] "running through the city with severed organs and throwing them into any house."[158]

That sacrifices of all sorts are for "wiping out evil and guilt" of the community is well established,[159] but that sacrifice was usually equated with childbirth ("man's childbearing") and sacrificers serve inner maternal alters and often pretend to be mothers ("the priests masqueraded as pregnant

151. Kenneth Alan Adams and Lester Hill, Jr., "The Phallic Female in Japanese Group-Fantasy." *The Journal of Psychohistory* 25(1997): 43.

152. Joseph L. Henderson and Maud Oakes, *The Wisdom of the Serpent: The Myths of Death, Rebirth, and Resurrection.* Princeton: Princeton University Press, 1990, p. 17.

153. Wolfgang Lederer, *The Fear of Women*, p. 121.

154. Philip Rawson, "Early History of Sexual Art." In Rawson, Ed., *Primitive Erotic Art.* New York: G. P. Putnam's Sons, 1973, p. 12.

155. Erich Neumann, *The Origins and History of Consciousness.* Princeton: Princeton University Press, 1970, p. 51.

156. Robert S. McCully, "Dualities Associated with the Ruling of the Ancient World." *The Journal of Psychohistory* 9(1986): 7, 11.

157. Edith Weigert-Vowinkel, "The Cult and Mythology of the Magna Mater from the Standpoint of Psychoanalysis." *Psychiatry* 1(1938): 361.

158. E. O. James, *The Cult of the Mother-Goddess.* London: Thames and Hudson, 1959, p. 167.

159. E. O. James, *Sacrifice and Sacrament.* New York: Barnes & Noble, 1962, p. 13.

women during the sacrifice")[160] is less well known. Astarte "massacred mankind, young and old, causing heads and hands to fly and tying heads to her back, hands to her girdle."[161] Drawings of the goddess "show her perpetual hunger for human sacrificial victims."[162] Visnu particularly favored devouring the victims' genitals.[163] The sacrificial rituals made a point of saying the victim must be innocent, like a child. Ancient religions used to blurt out alter beliefs that we today only tentatively suggest might be true.

Because these goddesses were also the "mistresses of battle," soldiers killed in battle were also seen as sacrifices to her bloodthirsty appetite. "The goddess brings destruction to enemies; she drinks the blood of the victims who were formerly her children. . . . She could not be halted in her slaughter of the human race."[164] Since these deaths originated in such memories as watching his mother strangle his little sister when she was born, war goddesses particularly needed the death of their own soldiers. As an early Ugaritic text says of the goddess Anat: "She is filled with joy as she plunges her knees in the blood of heroes."[165] Often the sacrificer was actually female, as was the chief priestess of the Celtic moon goddess, who cut off the victims' heads with her own hands, restaging the maternal infanticide.[166]

But rituals don't just repeat early trauma: they *restage* them—rearrange them to include elements of both the violence of the perpetrating alters and the rage of the victim alters. Thus the murderous goddess Tiamat is killed by her son Marduk in a tremendous battle by an "arrow that tore through her belly and inner parts."[167] Only by defeating the infanticidal

160. Nancy Jay, *Throughout Your Generations Forever: Sacrifice, Religion, and Paternity*. Chicago: University of Chicago Press, 1992, p. xxxiv.

161. William F. Albright, *From the Stone Age to Christianity*. Baltimore: Johns Hopkins Press, 1940, p. 233.

162. Ptolemy Tompkins, *This Tree Grows Out of Hell*. San Francisco: HarperCollins, 1990, p. 34.

163. Wendy Doniger O'Flaherty, *Women, Androgynes, and Other Mythical Beasts*. Chicago: University of Chicago Press, 1980, p. 34.

164. Anne Baring and Jules Cashford, *The Myth of the Goddess: Evolution of An Image*. London: Penguin Books, 1991, p. 169.

165. Cynthia Eller, *The Myth of Matriarchal Prehistory*. Boston: Beacon Press, 2000, p. 104.

166. M. Esther Harding, *Woman's Mysteries: Ancient and Modern*. New York: Harper & Row, 1976, p. 138.

167. Miriam Robbins Dexter, *Whence The Goddess: A Source Book*. New York: Pergamon Press, 1990, p. 10.

mother could sons "overcome chaos." As Halpern says: "The hero is one who slays his mother [and] institutes a new order on earth. . . . Culture is the work of the hero, the mother-killer, and represents his attempt at self-generation."[168] That the killing is the rage of the infantile victim alter against the mother is seen by the fact that the mother goddess, after being killed, is nevertheless identified with; for instance, the Aztecs beheaded women representing their mother goddesses and flayed them, donning their skins so that they can become them and acquire their dangerous powers, their *mana*.[169]

The acquisition of the powers of the terrifying mother by a male God was only slowly and partially accomplished in antiquity. Yahweh might conquer the primordial female monster, Leviathan, symbol of chaos, and He might demand complete obedience, "with all thy heart and all thy soul and all thy might." He might even take over sacrificial demands, as when He tells Abraham to sacrifice Isaac to found Israel in a blood-brotherhood convenant. But behind what Maccoby calls the "Sacred Executioner"[170] lies the sacrificial mother alter; behind every adored Adonis lies the cruel Astarte. Greeks may have tried to defend against maternal engulfment by holding annual processions where they marched with giant phalli, but the vase illustrations of the phalli show *women* holding them up in the air. Even powerful kings, like Odin or Wodan, had to be periodically sacrificed to the mother goddess, the World Ash, to assuage her blood thirst and cleanse the people.[171] Only by sacrificing together could men establish patrilineal kinship and political power. Even in Greece and Rome, patrilineal kin only knew they were kin because they sacrificed together; sacrifice was called "a remedy for having been born of woman." Even death in war strengthened the weak bonding between males—when an Aztec captured an enemy, he called him "my beloved son" and the captive answered, "my beloved father," then killed him.[172] That the sacrificial victim contained the bad-boy alter can be seen at the beginning of the ritual, when the victim is "injected with the poison" of childhood sin, rubbed with dirt if the victim was an animal, or given many sexual partners before the sacrifice if the

168. Sidney Halpern, "The Mother-Killer." *The Psychoanalytic Review* 52(1965): 73.

169. Mircea Eliade, *Myths, Dreams and Mysteries*. New York: Harper & Row, 1960, p. 188.

170. Hyam Maccoby, *The Sacred Executioner: Human Sacrifice and the Legacy of Guilt*. New York: Thames and Hudson, 1982.

171. Nigel Davies, *Human Sacrifice*, p. 43.

172. David Carrasco, *City of Sacrifice*, p. 145.

victim was a human. That it was internal alters who demanded the sacrifice was indicated by the priest saying, "The gods have done this deed; I did not do it!" or, as in Athens, by holding a trial after the sacrifice in which the full blame for the slaying was attributed to the knife, which, "having been found guilty, was punished by being destroyed."[173]

The more wealthy and successful ancient societies became, the more guilty they felt, the more their growth panic led them to defend against their avenging maternal alters by clinging to a more and more powerful male leader. As Earle observes, "Chiefdoms are states of mind [and] chiefs rule not because of their power but because of their place in a sacredly chartered world order"[174]—the world order of alters and their containers. The more kings appropriated maternal alter power—her *mana*—the more they had to go through seasonal cleansing ceremonies, including ritual abasement and even "killing of the king," in order to punish themselves for their hubris.[175] In these ceremonies, the king was ritually called "a turd [who] has come to save us,"[176] hit in the face with a sword, and only then invested with *Heil*,[177] his portion of maternal *mana*. But everyone in antiquity knew where his power really came from: the vaginal maternal crown, which was addressed by the king as "O Red Crown, Let there be fear of me like the fear of thee"; the throne, called the "mother" of the king; and the scepter, "a branch from the placental Tree of Life."[178]

THE MASOCHISTIC PSYCHOCLASS OF EARLY CHRISTIANITY

As mothers moved from infanticidal to abandoning-mode child rearing (see Chapters 7 and 8), early Christians could internalize a mommy who doesn't actually *kill* her children but only *abandons* them, both through emotional abandonment and through sending them to wet nurses, fosterage, monas-

173. A. Leo Oppenheim, *Ancient Mesopotamia.* Chicago: University of Chicago Press, 1977, p. 179; Hyman Maccoby, *The Sacred Executioner*, p. 8.

174. Timothy Earle, *Chiefdoms: Power, Economy and Ideology.* New York: Cambridge University Press, 1991, p. 130.

175. Theodore H. Gaster, *Thespis: Ritual, Myth and Drama in the Ancient Near East.* New York: Henry Schuman, 1950, p. 32.

176. Rene Girard, *Violence and the Sacred.* Baltimore: Johns Hopkins University Press, 1972, p. 107.

177. Henry A. Myers, *Medieval Kingship.* Chicago: Nelson-Hall, 1982, p. 3.

178. Henri Frankfort, *Kingship and the Gods*, p. 107.

teries, service with others, etc. Even profound neglect is less devastating than watching your baby sister be strangled, so early Christians could for the first time in history hope to get their mother's/God's love (redemption) if they show her their pain and get her pity. This display of pain to get the love of the mother is known as the masochistic personality, a lower level borderline condition,[179] which for the first time in history enables people to imagine that if they debase and torture themselves, the mother/God will feel sorry for them and might provide salvation, eventual closeness, rather than just helplessness and unbearable loneliness.

The gods of antiquity were distant, impersonal gods: "The gods might often mingle with men and women, but they did not seem to spend their time cultivating reciprocal love."[180] As Aristotle said, "When one party is removed to a great distance, as God is, the possibility of friendship ceases."[181] But the Christian God "loves and can be loved in return."[182] For abandoning-mode children, if you worship and love your mommy/God, if you take over yourself her beating and tortures of your body, if you give up all personal needs and starve yourself and avoid sex, you will through your masochistic display gain forgiveness and perhaps even be allowed eventually to merge with her.[183]

Christ is, of course, the main suffering victim alter who has been sent to earth by God to display his wounds and ask for pity on behalf of mankind. While the narcissistic personalities of antiquity generally agreed with Socrates that "no one is willfully evil,"[184] the masochistic personalities of early Christians put sin at the center of life and built up a church of expiation and confession that for the first time allowed pardon for the sins. The musings of early theologians about Christ sounded like the ruminations of the child about his or her mother's mistreatment: "God abandoned him,

179. Karla Clark, "Psychotherapy of the Borderline Personality Disorder." In James F. Masterson and Ralph Klein, *Psychotherapy of the Disorders of the Self*, p. 148.

180. Irving Singer, *The Nature of Love: The Modern World*. Chicago: University of Chicago Press, 1987, p. 25.

181. Irving Singer, *The Nature of Love: Plato to Luther*. Chicago: University of Chicago Press, 1984, p. 108.

182. Irving Singer, *The Nature of Love: The Modern World*, p. 25.

183. John Gartner, "The Capacity to Forgive: An Object Relations Perspective." In Mark Finn & John Gartner, Eds., *Object Relations Theory and Religion*. Westport: Praeger, 1992, p. 27.

184. Jean Delumeau, *Sin and Fear*, p. 189.

he treated him as the most abominable of men; and after an infinity of disgraces, of ignominies, and suffering, without any regard that he was His own Son, he caused him to die by the most shameful and cruel torture there ever was. . . . He worked his vengeance on His Son, as if He had nothing to do with him."[185] But the Christian, like the abandoning-mode child, then totally absolved the mother/God of all blame by a simple trick, saying, "I am all to blame. I deserve the torture. Mommy/God will pity me if I torture myself." The trick is one regularly used today by lower-level borderline masochists, who show extremely high occurrences of reported childhood neglect (92 percent) and physical and sexual abuse (59 to 91 percent),[186] who cut and burn and torture themselves endlessly in order to punish themselves and gain pity from their mommy alters. Earlier gods in antiquity killed and tortured children, of course, but they, like Jehovah, only "laughed at the slaughter of the damned."[187] The Christian God *loved* you for torturing and sacrificing yourself.

The masochistic display of one's wounds had already become a popular group-fantasy of antiquity by early Christian times. Gladiatorial combats "to appease the spirits of the dead" were widespread, where warriors volunteered to be killed in the arena in order to display their wounds and gain the applause of the people.[188] Wholly gratuitous wars were fought mainly for masochistic purposes; it was said that "warriors glory in their wounds; they rejoice to display their flowing blood. . . . The man who returns from battle unhurt may have fought as well, but he who returns wounded is held in higher esteem."[189] Christian masochism ritualized the absolution/penance ritual to assure adherents that when they felt unloved they could go to a church, relive Christ's agonies, confess their sins, carry out penances, and assure their mommy/God that they still worshiped her and that it was really the child's/worshiper's fault that mommy/God was so unhappy.

Confession, penance, and absolution are endless alter propitiations: "Gregory frequently expressed his fear that, because of God's unknown and

185. Ibid., p. 294.

186. M. C. Zanarini et al., "Reported Pathological Experiences Associated with the Development of Borderline Personality Disorder." *American Journal of Psychiatry* 154(1997): 1101.

187. Piero Camporesi, *The Fear of Hell*, p. 91.

188. Carlin A. Barton, *The Sorrows of the Ancient Romans: The Gladiator and the Monster.* Princeton: Princeton University Press, 1993, p. 13.

189. Carlin A. Barton, "The Scandal of the Arena." *Representations* 27(1989): 13.

unpredictable severity, man could never know if he inflicted enough suffering upon himself to propitiate God. . . . Punishment should take the form of a constant, unremitting anxiety and sorrow for one's sins . . . as teeth tearing the flesh."[190] Both Christians and Jews "engaged in a contest and reflection about the new-fangled practice of martyrdom,"[191] even unto suicide. Jesus, too, says John, really committed suicide, and Augustine spoke of "the mania for self-destruction" of early Christians.[192] Roman authorities tried hard to avoid Christians because they "goaded, chided, belittled, and insulted the crowds until they demanded their death."[193] One man shouted to the Roman officials, "I want to die! I am a Christian," leading the officials to respond, "If they wanted to kill themselves, there was plenty of cliffs they could jump off."[194] But the Christians, following Tertullian's dicta that "martyrdom is required by God," forced their own martyrdom so they could die in an ecstatic trance: "Although their tortures were gruesome, the martyrs did not suffer, enjoying their analgesic state."[195] Even today, about 10 percent of masochistic borderlines complete suicide,[196] always with a maternal "hidden executioner" alter present to feel pity.

Short of suicide, martyrdom and asceticism was built into every element of Christian ritual and practice. Monasticism was an orgy of masochistic penance for the sins of individuation, with fasts, flagellations, continence, and pilgrimages routine requirements—restaging the starvations, bindings, beatings, and expulsions to the wet nurse of childhood. Yet, unlike earlier religions, Christianity allowed their priests to forgive, console, and reconcile the sinner/child with mommy/God after the punishment. Whereas earlier religions punished animals or others as victim alters, Christianity encouraged the punishment of one's own body as a cleansing "second birth."

190. Carl A. Mounteer, "God the Father and Gregory the Great: The Discovery of a Late Roman Childhood." *The Journal of Psychohistory* 25(1998): 440.

191. Daniel Boyarin, *Dying for God: Martyrdom and the Making of Christianity and Judaism.* Stanford: Stanford University Press, 1999, p. 40.

192. Arthur J. Droge and James D. Tabor, *A Noble Death: Suicide and Martyrdom Among Christians and Jews in Antiquity.* San Francisco: HarperSanFrancisco, 1992, p. 5.

193. Arthur F. Ide, *Martyrdom of Women: A Study of Death Psychology in the Early Christian Church to 301 CE.* Garland: Tangelwuld, 1985, p. 21.

194. Ibid., p. 136.

195. Ibid., pp. 138, 146.

196. Colin A. Ross, *Satanic Ritual Abuse: Principles of Treatment.* Toronto: University of Toronto Press, 1995, p. 35.

Mommy/God could be pacified by martyrdom and one could receive her/his love at last. Octavius described the pleasure God had at seeing Christians suffering: "How fair a spectacle for God to see when a Christian stands face to face with pain."[197] As Pope Urban told the knights in order to get them to go on the First Crusade: "We hold out to you a war which contains the glorious reward of martyrdom,"[198] with its final reward, the love of God, since "only martyrs will attain to Paradise before the Second Coming."[199]

That priests were punishers leads one to wonder if they were not really concretizations of perpetrator alters, that is, remnants of abusers. Although one usually is used to identifying the "legions of demons and spirits" that made Christians gash themselves as the perpetrators, priests themselves are usually pictured as helpful figures. Yet priestly alters of masochists today often turn out to have the features of rapists,[200] while psychotherapists who treat ritual abuse survivors find that "Satan usually turns out to be a traumatized child," raging over early sexual abuse.[201] In fact, alters and religious fantasy figures usually contain remnants of both the perpetrators and victims of childhood traumas. The Devil might embody the rage of the raped child, but he also has attributes of the rapist: he is naked, he has a long nose (penis), he is red (flush of erect penis), and he is hairy (pubic hair). The precise details of the image of Christ on the cross are all from childhood. Christ is shown as an infant (naked, except for a swaddling-band loincloth), abandoned by Mommy (God), bound or nailed to a wooden cross (the wooden board all infants were bound to during swaddling), with a crown of thorns (the painful head-shaping devices used on infants before swaddling), and with a bloody hole in his side (evidence of the childhood rape—vaginal or anal). Even the details of Christ's life conform to routine childhood conditions. For instance, Christ got the bloody wound in his side, the subject of much theological

---

197. Judith Perkins, *The Suffering Self: Sin and Narrative Representation in the Early Christian Era.* London: Routledge, 1995, p. 39.

198. John R. E. Bliese, "The Motives of the First Crusaders." *The Journal of Psychohistory* 17(1990): 460.

199. Carl A. Mounteer, "Guilt, Martyrdom and Monasticism." *The Journal of Psychohistory* 9(1981): 153.

200. Ira Brenner, *Dissociation of Trauma: Theory, Phenomenology and Technique.* Madison, CT: International Universities Press, 2001, p. 113.

201. Colin A. Ross, *Satanic Ritual Abuse: Principles of Treatment.* Toronto: University of Toronto Press, 1995, p. 161.

concern, because his Father sent him down to be crucified—just as so many real fathers at the time sent their young children to their neighbors to be used as sexual objects—and the bad soldier stripped Christ and stuck his phallic lance into him—just as the bad neighbor stripped the child and stuck his erect penis into him. If sexuality meant memories of rape to most children growing up at that time, it is no wonder that Christianity preached sexuality was shameful, "a token of human bondage," and must be avoided at all costs. The ritual of the Mass, too—with "the Lord, sacrificed, and laid upon the altar, and the priest, standing, and all the people empurpled with his most precious blood" (Chrysostom)[202]—is equally a "rite of penetration," a restaging of childhood rape, as the frightening priest in his black robe circles slowly around the helpless, naked Christ. The deepest feeling behind all these Christian rites was the loneliness and hunger of the worshiper—the abandonment depression—so it is not surprising that images of real hunger often broke through during the Christian ritual. Priests and worshipers often reported that during Holy Communion they would see in the host "a very young boy; and when the priest began to break the host, they thought they saw an angel coming down out of the sky who cut the boy up with a knife." Or else they would fear that the worshiper might not want to bite into "the Communion wafer if they could see that they were actually biting off the head, hands, and feet of a little child."[203] Even Christ himself, the victim alter, was thought to be terribly hungry: "Christ's hunger is great beyond measure; he devours us. . . . His hunger is insatiable."[204] The abandoning-mode child's hunger—for love, food, care, support—is never forgotten, and it can be found at the heart of every Christian ritual throughout the Middle Ages.

THE BORDERLINE PSYCHOCLASS OF LATER CHRISTIANITY

It must be recalled that new parenting modes begin with just a few people at a time, which means that ambivalent-mode parenting and the resulting higher level borderline personalities—which begin in the twelfth century—

202. Nancy Jay, *Throughout Your Generations Forever: Sacrifice, Religion, and Paternity*. Chicago: University of Chicago Press, 1992, p. 116.

203. Piero Camporese, *The Fear of Hell*, p. 172; Hyam Maccoby, *The Sacred Executioner*, p. 155.

204. Johan Huizinga, *The Autumn of the Middle Ages*. Chicago: University of Chicago Press, 1996, p. 230.

continued for some time to be minorities in European families, coexisting with earlier masochistic, narcissistic, and schizoid personalities in their societies. By the twelfth century, when Western Europe began to move in new directions, the empires of antiquity had collapsed in a masochistic orgy of military self-destruction. The clinging needs of the new borderline psychoclass—a symptom of their feelings of isolation, emptiness, and separation anxiety—were now defended against by constructing the profound personal bonds of feudalism. "The borderline," says Hartocollis, "is an angry individual. Characterized by oral demandingness, often with a paranoid flavour [and] a sense of emptiness or depression . . . making him feel chronically lonesome, frustrated, alienated."[205] This emptiness was known to medieval psychoclasses as *acedia*, which one twelfth-century monk says is "a disgust of the heart, an enormous loathing of yourself . . . a great bitterness. . . . Your soul is torn to pieces, confused and split up, sad and embittered."[206] From the twelfth century on, *acedia* attracted much attention as a "turning away from God," again, the fault of the person/child, not of the God/mommy. When people confessed to feelings of *acedia* and reported their feelings of despair and self-hatred, they were given severe penitentials by their priests to ward off their suicidal thoughts.

The clinging of the feudal bond is paralleled to the clinging tie to God and to Mother Mary and Jesus, who for the first time takes on overt maternal traits, even allowing worshipers to suck his breasts and wounds.[207] Real ambivalent-mode mothers were now nurturing enough so that one can even find descriptions of "God as a woman nursing the soul at her breasts, drying its tears and punishing its petty mischief-making."[208] Of course, in true borderline style, the price of some closeness with God is total devotion, the medieval Christian saying, "To my beloved, I will forever be His servant, His slave, All for God, and nothing for me."[209] As contemporary borderlines say, "I know you will love and take care of me if I don't self-

205. Peter Hartocollis, "Time and Affects in Borderline Disorders." *International Journal of Psycho-Analysis* 59(1978): 158.

206. Siegfried Wenzel, *The Sin of Sloth: Acedia in Medieval Thought and Literature.* Chapel Hill: University of North Carolina Press, 1967, p. 33.

207. Caroline Walker Bynum, *Jesus as Mother: Studies in the Spirituality of the High Middle Ages.* Berkeley: University of California Press, 1982, p. 117.

208. Ibid., p. 129.

209. Jean Delumeau, *Sin and Fear*, p. 311.

activate. I'll please you by clinging and complying with your wishes, so you will take care of me, and these bad (abandonment) feelings will go away."[210]

The advances of borderline personalities beyond lower-level masochistic psychoclasses were, however, profound, and soon began to carry Western Europe beyond the accomplishments of the rest of the world. Much has been written of "the invention of the self and individuality" beginning in the twelfth century. Prior to this period, there was not even a word for "self," and the word *personality* meant a mask held before an actor, i.e., a "false self."[211] But "the practice of self-examination was deeper and more widespread in twelfth-century Europe than at any time before [and] medieval Europe changed from a 'shame culture' to a 'guilt culture'" as inner motives and not just outer behavior became the focus of confessions and of literature.[212] Autobiographies began to multiply, seals indicating personal identity began to be used more widely, and writers began to wonder if God might allow a unique self for each person, a *homo interior* that was fashioned by one—"in the image of God," of course, but nevertheless made by one's real self.[213] The results in society from the twelfth through the fifteenth centuries of these advances in self were astonishing: a vast expansion in agriculture and early industries, the beginnings of both state formation and of capitalism, an upsurge in trade and exploration, a huge population growth as infanticide dropped, and an enormous growth of cities and civil rights. Change became not only possible but preferable for the first time in history. Those people in these centuries who were still masochistic and narcissistic decompensated from all the change, became possessed by devils, imagined they might soon be thrown in Hell for their bold new aspirations, or flagellated themselves for wanting to be independent. Growth panic soon began to produce periodic fears of millenarian violence, leading directly to the apocalyptic expectations and witch-hunts of the Renaissance and Reformation.

---

210. James F. Masterson, *The Personality Disorders*, p. 93.

211. John F. Benton, "Consciousness of Self and Perceptions of Individuality." In Robert L. Benson, et al., Eds., *Renaissance and Renewal in the Twelfth Century*. Cambridge: Harvard University Press, 1982, p. 284.

212. Ibid., pp. 264, 271.

213. Caroline Walker Bynum, *Jesus as Mother*, p. 87.

THE DEPRESSIVE PSYCHOCLASS OF THE RENAISSANCE
AND REFORMATION

The new child-rearing mode beginning around the sixteenth century—the intrusive mode—was a leap forward, when mothers stopped sending their children to a wet nurse and stopped leaving them hungry in their cradles, faced the tasks of caring for them boldly if uncertainly, ended swaddling, beat them less and reduced their being sent out as servants. As it was described earlier, parents shifted from trying to stop children's growth to trying only to control it and make it "obedient." True empathy begins with intrusive-mode parents, producing a general improvement in the level of care and reduced mortality, leading to more investment in each child. The difference between borderline and depressive personalities today has been documented to be a result of far less overt sexual and physical abuse during childhood, with far less impulsivity, low self-esteem, and self-destructive acts in the depressive, despite the presence of sadness as a major emotion.[214] This is because what the depressives are doing that borderlines cannot yet do is *facing their abandonment depression.* Psychotherapists find that after treating borderlines and confronting their defenses for some time, the patients then become more depressed, having finally to face the abandonment fears of their childhood rather than running away from them into clinging, self-destructive behavior, since "depression accompanies improvement . . . the beginnings of identity integration, the development of integrated self and object representations [and] conscious guilt and remorse."[215]

Ever since Huizinga analyzed the "sombre melancholy that weighed on people's souls" after the close of the Middle Ages, the period has been well known for its deep despondency, when, says Donne, God "reserved for these times an extraordinary sadness, a predominant melancholy."[216] From sixteenth-century diaries to Burton's *Anatomy of Melancholy*, books on inner life were little more than records of the writer's depressions and how he tried to overcome them. Humanists glorified melancholy as the heightened self-awareness of the intellectual, the cost of individualism, and

214. Susan N. Ogata et al., "Childhood Sexual and Physical Abuse in Adult Patients with Borderline Personality Disorder." *American Journal of Psychiatry* 147(1990): 1008.
215. Harold W. Koenigsberg, et al., *Borderline Patients*, pp. 144, 149.
216. J. Huizinga, *The Waning of the Middle Ages.* London: Edward Arnold, 1927, p. 22.

they were right. Melancholy had to be faced for one to be what Pico called a man "restrained by no narrow bonds, according to thine own free will in thou, thine own maker and molder, fashioning thyself in whatever manner thou likest best."[217] Both Jaques (in *As You Like It*) and Hamlet were proudly presented by Shakespeare as "melancholy philosophers," wearing black with pride, "condemning abuses, but never condemning earthly existence."[218] Renaissance scholar Marcilio Ficino speculated on "Why Melancholics Are Intelligent," noting that the most bold, learned people he knew were always melancholic,[219] and philosophers gave the excellent advice that friendship was the best antidote to "melancholy, the malaise of the age."[220] Elizabethans thought melancholy "both a very wretched state and a very happy state . . . [and] melancholy was often praised and sought after as a great felicity," a mark of an intellectual who had "risen superior to the petty concerns of ordinary men and occupied with thoughts of worth and dignity,"[221] thoughts of personal meaning and self improvement.

Though mommy's/God's grace might only come after "holy desperation" for the depressive personality of the Reformation, though her forgiveness might still be "unpredictable, unknowable, and incomprehensible," if one obeys her dicta, then she might be a forgiving God who cared for you.[222] Luther could now hope that God would actually love him because He was sometimes *kind!* This hope suddenly allowed an expansion of the real self, and the world, and its activities suddenly became invested with new vigor. For the new depressive psychoclass, mommy/God didn't need you sexually, so celibacy was not necessary. She could forgive, so one could

---

217. Richard D. Logan, "Historical Change: Prevailing Sense of Self." In K. Yardley and T. Honess, Eds., *Self and Identity: Psychosocial Perspectives*, New York: John Wiley & Sons, 1987, p. 17.

218. Donald R. Howard, "Renaissance World-Alienation." In Robert S. Kinsman, Ed., *The Darker Vision of the Renaissance.* Berkeley: University of California Press, 1974, p. 61.

219. Jennifer Radden, *The Nature of Melancholy.* Oxford: Oxford University Press, 2000, p. 91.

220. William J. Bouwsma, *The Waning of the Renaissance.* New Haven: Yale University Press, 2000, p. 119.

221. Lawrence Babb, *The Elizabethan Malady: A Study of Melancholia in English Literature from 1580 to 1642.* East Lansing: Michigan State University Press, 1951, pp. 176–177.

222. Perry Miller, *The New England Mind: The Seventeenth Century.* Boston: Beacon Press, 1954, p. 10.

actually trust her and cast oneself upon her mercy. She paid attention to your need for food, so you didn't have to fast your whole life. She actually listened to you, so you could individuate your self beyond clinging to religious and political authorities. Dissociation and splitting declined for these depressives—achieving for the first time what Melanie Klein calls "the depressive position," which allows merger of the good breast/bad breast split—so women were not split into virgins and whores (Mary and Eve) but were for the first time seen as human beings with both good and bad qualities, and marriage for the first time in history became a worthy goal rather than just a way to legitimate fornication.

By the sixteenth and seventeenth centuries, the new mode of intrusive child rearing had catapulted Western Europe far beyond the earlier psychoclasses of the rest of the world, giving their minority of depressives a new sense of self-worth and the ideal of cumulative, necessary progress that led to the modern world we know today. The growth of knowledge, the invention of printing, the new questioning of authority, the exploration of new lands and ideas, all were evidence that "European people had altered in some fundamental way"[223]—a change in their psyches, not in their environment. For the first time in history, mommy/God "was relegated to a vague and impenetrable heaven, somewhere up in the skies. Man and man alone was the standard by which all things were measured."[224] Science began its spectacular leap into the unknown. Political systems without divine sanctions and economics that were based on real trust became the goals of society. Joy in life need not be something sinful, hope was allowed and freedom for self exploration did not need to be disobedience to mommy/God. These lessons—first learned in families at the feet of innovative mothers—soon produced new institutions to express these new freedoms, particularly in France and England, where child rearing was most advanced.

Unfortunately, while depressives could begin to try to live out their new freedoms, they were still a minority in these centuries, and the earlier psychoclasses experienced the new freedoms of the age as terribly dangerous and certain to call upon them the wrath of mommy/God. These centuries of progress were therefore also centuries of apocalyptic fears and wars,

223. Lyndal Roper, *Oedipus and the Devil*, p. 145.
224. Paul Hazard, *The European Mind: 1680–1715*. New York: New American Library, 1963, p. xvii.

when people were certain that so much change would unchain Satan and his swarms of demon alters and that the world was certain to end soon. Apocalyptic prophecies, cults, and religious wars proliferated in Reformation Europe, particularly in areas like Germany where child rearing had changed the least.[225] What Trevor-Roper calls "the general crisis of the seventeenth century"[226] was in fact a psychoclass conflict, and the demons, witches, and Antichrists that roamed Europe at that time were all really the persecutory alters that inhabited the schizoid, narcissistic, masochistic, and borderline psychoclasses that still represented the majority of Europe. These earlier psychoclasses responded with violence to all the progress of the period, "acting out with fierce energy a shared [millenarian] phantasy which, though delusional, yet brought them such intense emotional relief that they . . . were willing both to kill and to die for it."[227] The new religious services of the Reformation were felt to be "full of wild liberty," and "beast-like carnal liberty" was reported seen at anabaptist prayer meetings, where services were said to be conducted in the nude.[228] All the individuation would certainly bring punishment upon mankind, and pamphlets were circulated describing how clouds were raining blood and flocks of birds were holding cosmic battles in the sky "as auguries of some impending disaster."[229] A placental "Many-Headed Monster" was hallucinated as savaging Europe, carrying out the Day of Judgment because "by now seven-year-old children demonstrated more wickedness than had previously been possible by evil old men. . . . The world had become so wicked that things could hardly get worse."[230] Religious wars broke out all over Europe, as "God was unable to bear it any longer and decided to cleanse his Church with a great scourge."[231]

---

225. Eugen Weber, *Apocalypses: Prophecies, Cults, and Millennial Beliefs Through the Ages.* Cambridge: Harvard University Press, 1999.

226. H. R. Trevor-Roper, *The European Witch-Craze of the Sixteenth and Seventeenth Centuries and Other Essays.* New York: Harper & Row, 1969, p. 78.

227. Norman Cohn, "Réflexions sur le millénarisme." *Archives de sociologie religieuse,* 5(1958): 106.

228. William Saffady, "Fears of Sexual License During the English Reformation." *History of Childhood Quarterly* 1(1973): 92.

229. B. S. Capp, *The Fifth Monarchy Men: A Study in Seventeenth-Century English Millenarianism.* Totawa: Rowman and Littlefield, 1972, p. 18.

230. Andrew Cunningham and Ole Peter Grell, *The Four Horsemen of the Apocalypse.* Cambridge: Cambridge University Press, 2000, p. 47.

231. Ibid., p. 247.

Historians have long been puzzled by why the witchcraft epidemic took place in the centuries that were most progressive, but if the craze is seen as a reaction to growth panic it becomes explainable. Tens of thousands of women responded to their new freedoms by becoming possessed by their alters and falling into trances: "Observers spoke of the possessed as 'choked,' subjected to 'thousands of cruel pinches,' 'stuck [with] innumerable pins,' and 'cut with knives and struck with blows that they could not bear,"[232] as they restaged the memories of swaddling pins, parental blows, and other childhood traumas. Those who persecuted witches were obviously taking vengeance upon their mommies; indeed, most witches were either mothers or wet nurses.[233] A witch was transparently a mommy, since she rode on a maternal broom, had special teats where "imps" sucked on her body, smothered babies in their cradles and came into your bedroom uninvited and seduced you.[234] As Roper puts it, "Relations between mothers, those occupying maternal roles and children, formed the stuff of most witchcraft accusations."[235] "Over and over again in the trial records, the accused women are addressed as 'Mother.' . . . The witch is a monstrous mother."[236]

The rape of children formed a central focus for witchcraft group-fantasies. Descriptions of the sexual orgies that went on at *sabbats* clearly reveal their origins in childhood rape attacks, and young girls who had "convulsive fits" in court "as the Devil entered them"[237] restaged each detail of their earlier rapes before their startled audiences. Nuns in particular were afflicted with demonic possession, going into trances and accusing priests of seducing them, which they often had really done.[238] The extreme youth of those raped can be seen in their complaint that "the genital organs of their Demons are so huge and so excessively rigid that they cannot be ad-

---

232. Carol F. Karlsen, *The Devil in the Shape of a Woman: Witchcraft in Colonial New England.* New York: W. W. Norton & Co., 1987, p. 11.

233. Deborah Willis, *Malevolent Nurture: Witch-Hunting and Maternal Power in Early Modern England.* Ithaca: Cornell University Press, 1995, pp. 13–18.

234. Ibid., pp. 13, 136, 141.

235. Lyndal Roper, *Oedipus and the Devil*, p. 201.

236. Deborah Willis, *Malevolent Nurture*, p. 35.

237. John Putnam Demos, *Entertaining Satan: Witchcraft and the Culture of Early New England.* New York: Oxford University Press, 1982, p. 101.

238. Anne Llewellyn Barstow, *Witchcraze: A New History of the European Witch Hunts.* New York: Pandora, 1994, p. 71.

mitted without the greatest pain."[239] Entire villages would sometimes periodically go into trances together, call themselves "Benandanti," and fight
Devils together, all while fully dissociated, "as if I was both sleeping and
not sleeping."[240] By the time the witch craze had disappeared by the
beginning of the eighteenth century, a million innocent people had died
in an orgy of alter persecution caused by too much progress during the
Reformation.

THE NEUROTIC PSYCHOCLASS OF MODERN TIMES

The socializing mode of child rearing that began in the eighteenth century
and that continues to be the ideal of most nations today replaced the absolute obedience of the intrusive psychoclass with parental manipulation and
psychological punishments, in order to make the child fit into the world
as a replica of the parent.[241] Individuation was still limited, since the needs
and goals of the parent superseded those of the child as the child attempted
to separate, but empathy was now available to parents to ensure that basic
care was provided. It was the socializing psychoclass that built the modern world, with its ideal of the competent self and the quest for a real self
as a lifelong existential quest.[242] As Masterson puts it: "The psychoneurotic
personality . . . has the capacity for whole self- and whole object-relations,
and repression has replaced splitting. From the perspective of the personality disorder, to be psychoneurotic is an achievement."[243]

Rather than switching into full possession trances and demon alters,
the neurotic psychoclass of modern times switches into their social alters,
their social roles (see Chapter 4), as organized by the group-fantasies of
nations rather than by religious groups. Sacrifice for the Mommy-Nation—

---

239. Lawrence Osborne, *The Poisoned Embrace*. New York: Pantheon Books, 1993,
p. 70.

240. Carlo Ginzburg, *The Night Battles: Witchcraft & Agrarian Cults in the Sixteenth
& Seventeenth Centuries*. New York: Penguin Books, 1985, p. 13.

241. Glenn Davis, *Childhood and History in America*. New York: Psychohistory Press,
1976.

242. Richard D. Logan, "Historical Change in Prevailing Sense of Self." In K. Yardley
and T. Honess, Eds., *Self and Identity: Psychosocial Perspectives*. New York: John Wiley &
Sons, 1987, p. 19.

243. James F. Masterson, *The Personality Disorders*, p. 78.

dying for the Motherland—replaces dying for Christ: "We are to die so that the motherland may live; for while we live the motherland is dying. . . . A nation can only regenerate itself in a bath of blood."[244] It was the *nation* as a master group-fantasy that organized and contained both the new faith in progress and its sacrificial wars, acted out in periodic cycles of innovative, depressive, manic, and war stages (see Chapter 6). In each stage, nations follow a different psychoclass style. In the innovative stage, the neurotic psychoclass provides new social, political, and economic progress; in the depressive stage, the depressive psychoclass is followed into economic depression; in the manic stage, narcissists take over with their grandiose projects; and in the war stage nations follow self-destructive masochists and paranoid schizoids into violence. Choosing earlier psychoclasses— psychological fossils—as leaders has become a constant practice in modern nations, only masked by the idealization of the public switched into their social alters. To realize that we willingly delegate to a handful of men sitting in a deep trance in the Oval Office the power to blow up much of the world depending on whether they think they feel humiliated—as in the Cuban Missile Crisis—is to realize the bizarre extent of the dissociation between fantasy and reality that continues to pervade our modern psyches.

All the other aspects of modern industrial society are equally results of the new socializing psychoclass child rearing, causing a greater increase in material prosperity in the past two centuries than in all the rest of human history. The reason for this astonishing progress is that science, technology, and economic development depend more on investments in parenting than investments in equipment, since they crucially require an "exploring self" constructed from childhood. A few economists realize that the wealth of nations lies in the development of psyches more than in the investment of capital. Everett Hagan and Lawrence Harrison, for instance, have demonstrated that those nations furthest behind today in economic development suffer from a severe underinvestment in families and children, not in capital equipment.[245] The historical record is clear: early pioneers in science and technology first had to overcome their alter projec-

244. Adam Zamoyski, *Holy Madness: Romantics, Patriots and Revolutionaries 1776–1871.* New York: Viking, 2000, pp. 23, 25.

245. Everett Hagen, *The Economics of Development*, rev. ed. Homewood: R. D. Irwin, 1975; Lawrence E. Harrison, *Underdevelopment Is a State of Mind: The Latin American Case.* Lanham: Madison Books, 1985, pp. 25, 29.

tions before they could discover how the world worked. As Keith Thomas puts it: "It was the abandonment of magic which made possible the upsurge of technology, not the other way round."[246] Newton had to stop seeing falling objects "longing to return to Mother Earth" before he could posit a force of gravity. Chemists had to give up "alchemical visions of womb-battles between good and evil" inside their flasks before they could observe the real causes of chemical change.[247] Farmers had to be able to empathize with their horses in order to invent the harness collar that moved the pressure down from their throats to their flanks so they wouldn't be choked in order to increase the loads they could pull.[248] Farmers also had to stop thinking of plowing as "tearing at the breast of Mother Earth" in order to invent the deep plow and change the face of European agriculture. Men had to begin to value their families in order to build wooden floors in their homes rather than leaving them clay as was the practice for millennia.[249] Every invention had its origin in the evolution of the psyche; every exploration of nature was a dimension of the exploration of the self.

Economic life, too, only evolved as child rearing and the psyche evolved. Tribal societies both in the past and in the present could not trust, because parents were untrustworthy, so they could not allow much wealth or surplus out of which they could create economic progress. Ownership was felt to be dangerous selfishness, envy ran rampant, and ambition was feared: "The anthropologist may see people behaving with generosity, but this is the result of fear."[250] Those who acquired too much were expected to either engage in gift exchange[251] and other redistributive rituals[252] or

---

246. Keith Thomas, *Religion and the Decline of Magic*. New York: Charles Scribner's Sons, 1971, p. 657.

247. Allison Coudert, *Alchemy: The Philosopher's Stone*. London: Wildwood House, 1980, p. 26.

248. Lynn White Jr., *Medieval Technology and Social Change*. Oxford: Oxford University Press, 1962, p. 57.

249. Barbara A. Hanawalt, *The Ties That Bound: Peasant Families in Medieval England*. Oxford: Oxford University Press, 1986, p. 37.

250. Donald Symons, *The Evolution of Human Sexuality*. Oxford: Oxford University Press, 1979, p. 146.

251. Marcel Mauss, *The Gift: Forms and Functions of Exchange in Archaic Societies*. New York: W. W. Norton & Co., 1967.

252. Raymond Firth, *Primitive Polynesian Economy*. London: George Routledge & Sons, 1939, p. 214; Ian Morris, "Gift and Commodity in Archaic Greece." *Man* n.s. 21(1986): 1–17.

else to periodically destroy their surplus in cleansing sacrificial ceremonies.[253] Even the invention of money came from the sacred objects used for sacrifice to deities.[254] "Money is condensed wealth; condensed wealth is condensed guilt. . . . Money is filthy because it remains guilt."[255]

What held back economic development for so many millennia was that early civilizations were so abusively brought up that they spent most of their energies chasing "ghosts from the nursery"—religious, political, and economic domination group-fantasies—rather than joining in together to solve the real tasks of life. The appalling poverty of most people throughout history has been simply an extension of the emotional poverty of the historical family, making real cooperation in society impossible. For instance, slavery was one of the most wasteful, uneconomical systems ever invented, since denying autonomy to one's fellow workers simply wasted both the slaves' and the owners' productivity and inventiveness. Running the world like a prison, with one half occupied with guarding the other half, has always been extremely unproductive. That unfree labor is always unproductive labor has long been acknowledged by economists.[256] Slaves were kept "as expressions of their owners' status and prestige"[257] even when they could barely manage to pick grapes because of their shackles. Owning slaves may have been very dangerous to you and to your family, and they may have often run away. But everyone still wanted to have them so they could be used to restage the tortures of one's childhood: "Galen remarked how common it was for slaves to be punched with the fists, to be kicked, to have their eyes put out, and how his own mother had had the habit of biting her maidservants."[258] Equipment for torturing slaves was widespread, including special whips and racks for beatings, special knives for facial mutilation and castration, and metal plates and flaming torches

253. Lloyd deMause, "Heads and Tails: Money as a Poison Container." *The Journal of Psychohistory* 16(1988): 1–19.

254. William H. Desmonde, *Magic, Myth and Money: The Origin of Money in Religious Ritual.* New York: Free Press of Glencoe, 1962.

255. Norman O. Brown, *The Psychoanalytic Meaning of History.* Middletown: Wesleyan University Press, 1959, p. 266.

256. David S. Landes, *The Wealth and Poverty of Nations.* New York: W. W. Norton & Co., 1998, p. 241.

257. K. R. Bradley, *Slavery and Society at Rome.* Cambridge: Cambridge University Press, 1994, p. 14.

258. Ibid., p. 28.

for burnings. "There was even a torture and execution service operated by a company of undertakers. . . . Flogging and crucifixion were standard options at a flat rate to the user."[259]

With a third or more of ancient societies being slaves, an unending supply of bodies to flog was assured, even though this meant remaining mired in low-productivity economies.[260] Throughout the Roman classical period, Finley says, improvements in economic techniques were "marginal [because] patterns of land use and methods of tillage remained unchanged."[261] It was more important to restage early traumatic beatings and domination fantasies than to improve the abysmal squalor in which nearly everyone lived. Even with the disappearance of slavery during the Middle Ages—which medieval scholar Marc Bloch called "one of the most profound transformations mankind has known"[262]—the serfdom and other kinds of bondage that replaced it kept Europe for centuries in an increase in per capita product of only a tiny fraction of a percent per year.[263] It was only by the early modern period when the need to restage family slavery began to decline that *trust* began to replace domination and the takeoff phase in economics could begin. "The ultimate explanation of economic development lies not in purely economic factors, such as land, labor, and capital. . . . these will [occur] when people learn that it is good business to be just and considerate toward one's neighbors; to solve quarrels peacefully; [and] to be held accountable for the efficient use of resources."[264] Purely economic theories that cannot conceive of psychogenic causes are reduced to statements such as: "No one planned Progress as a whole. It simply erupted."[265]

In addition to a takeoff in economic progress, the modern psychoneurotic personality began to achieve levels of intimacy between men and

259. Ibid., p. 166.

260. N. R. E. Fisher, *Slavery in Classical Greece*. London: Bristol Classical, 1993, p. 35.

261. M. I. Finley, *The Ancient Economy*. Berkeley: University of California Press, 1973, p. 109.

262. Pierre Bonassie, *From Slavery to Feudalism in South Western Europe*. Cambridge: Cambridge University Press, 1991, p. 1.

263. "Harper's Index," *Harper's Magazine*, January 2000, p. 11.

264. John P. Powelson, *Centuries of Economic Endeavor*. Ann Arbor: University of Michigan Press, 1994, p. 3.

265. Tom Nairn, *Faces of Nationalism: Janus Revisited*. London: Verso, 1997, p. 3.

women that were simply unknown to previous psychoclasses. When mothers were incestuous, it was not surprising that women were feared as sexually insatiable by men, and pederasty and rape were preferred to intimate, married love. All women were in danger of turning into dominating mothers and therefore had to be beaten; Homer's word for "wife," *damar*, means "broken into submission." In addition, that women throughout so much of history were accused of being unable to restrain their sexual appetites was not just a patriarchal myth—it was more the result of the widespread rape of young girls being restaged later in life, just as so many raped girls today grow up to repeat their sexual assaults later on in prostitution or adultery. That human sexuality through antiquity was conflated with violence and domination and that Christianity was the most antisexual religion known to mankind are only understandable as normal reactions to severe childhood seductions, not as inexplicable religious teachings.

That "conjugal love between husband and wife was considered ridiculous and impossible"[266] in antiquity is better understood as a consequence of the narcissistic personality's need to have perfection in their partner, fearing to risk attaching themselves to someone who was imperfect and whom they might lose like they lost their mothers and fathers earlier. Only through effective polygamy—either formal or through having concubines and slaves as alternatives to wives—could depending on one woman be avoided. Indeed, the jealous mothers of the gynarchies of the past would often step in between their sons and their wives in order to keep them tied to themselves—as, for instance, Augustine's mother did when she made him dismiss his concubine, who had lived faithfully with him for years. Even Christian marriages were supposed to be passionless between the spouses. God stood in for the grandmother and demanded that all love and passion be reserved for Himself. It was not really until the depressive psychoclass began to face their abandonment depression in the sixteenth century that Erasmus could startle his readers with the view that marriage was superior to virginity and Puritan wives could be able to write passionate love poems to their husbands.[267] And it was only by the eighteenth

---

266. Charles Lindholm, "Love as an Experience of Transcendence." In William Jankowiak, Ed., *Romantic Passion: a Universal Experience?* New York: Columbia University Press, 1995, p. 63.

267. Page Smith, *Daughters of the Promised Land . . .* Boston: Little, Brown, 1970, p. 44.

century's socializing psychoclass that "husbands and wives who cherished each other were begun to be held in the greatest esteem [as] conjugal love attracted not sarcasm, but the most fervent admiration, thus giving rise to a sort of contest to see who could love his or her beloved spouse the most, who could best prove to the world the unshakable fidelity felt toward one's life partner."[268]

THE INDIVIDUATED PSYCHOCLASS OF POSTMODERN TIMES

It is difficult to describe what kind of world might be made by individuated personalities, as the first helping-mode parents—where both mother and father unconditionally love their children and help them achieve their own goals and own real selves from birth—have only been around for a few decades in the most advanced societies. As I watch my own children and some of their friends grow up and establish their productive lives, I see them as very different from my own socializing psychoclass peers. They are far more empathic and therefore more concerned about others than we ever were, and this has made them far more activist in their lives in trying to make a difference and change the world for the better, mostly involving themselves in local activities rather than global political changes. They lack all need for nationalism, wars, and other grandiose projects, and in the organizations they start are genuinely nonauthoritarian. There is no question that if the world could treat children with helping-mode parenting, wars and all the other self-destructive social conditions we still suffer from in the twenty-first century will be cured, simply because the world will be filled with individuated personalities who are empathic toward others and who are not self-destructive. A world that loves and trusts its children and encourages them to develop their unique selves will be a world of very different institutions, a world without wars, jails, and other domination group-fantasies.

The main problem is that the evolution of child rearing has so far been a slow, uneven historical process, depending greatly on increasing the support given innovative mothers and their hopeful daughters. Unfortunately, in a world where our destructive technology has far outrun our child-

---

268. Evelyne Sullerot, *Women on Love: Eight Centuries of Feminine Writing.* Garden City, NY: Doubleday & Co., 1979, p. 147.

rearing progress—where a single submarine can now carry a sufficient number of nuclear warheads to destroy most of the world with the push of a button—we do not have the luxury of just waiting for child rearing to evolve. If we do, we will certainly blow ourselves up long before child abuse disappears enough to make us want to disarm. What we need now is some way for the more advanced psychoclasses to teach child rearing to the less evolved parents, a way to end child abuse and neglect quickly enough to avoid the global holocaust that is awaiting us.

ENDING CHILD ABUSE BY INVESTING IN
THE REAL WEALTH OF NATIONS

Ever since the earliest psychohistorical studies were published linking child abuse to war and social violence, one physician-psychohistorian, Robert McFarland, concluded that it must be possible to end child abuse in his community by starting a new institution, Community Parenting Centers, and with every means possible teach good parenting to the parents of every new baby born in his city, Boulder, Colorado. It seemed ridiculous to McFarland that the entire world depends on good parenting, while parenting was the only subject never taught in schools or anywhere else in the world. For the past two decades, therefore, McFarland has run The Parenting Place in several counties of Boulder, reaching out to visit every baby born in the areas and giving substantial support to all mothers and fathers—holding parenting discussion groups, baby massage courses, single mothers assistance, showing them how to bring up children without hitting them, how to foster their independence, etc. The wide range of activities of The Parenting Place can be seen in two articles in The *Journal of Psychohistory*.[269] Over half the families choose to be visited weekly in their homes for parenting instructions. Since no new mother or father wants to reject and abuse the baby, what McFarland found was that providing this help and hope for parents allowed their underlying affection to replace the abuse and neglect that comes from fear and despair—so that his statistics

---

269. Kathleen Linden and Robert B. McFarland, "Community Parenting Centers in Colorado." *The Journal of Psychohistory* 21(1993): 7–19; Robert B. McFarland and John Fanton, "Moving Towards Utopia: Prevention of Child Abuse." *The Journal of Psychohistory* 24(1997): 320–331.

from local police and hospital records now show a substantial decrease in child abuse reports.

What is most astonishing is that McFarland found that parenting center costs are far lower than what is saved in the later costs of abuse to the community. That the small budget for the centers is offset many times over by the costs to the communities of later social services and criminal behavior is a not unexpected finding, given that sociologists have calculated that "the costs to society of career criminal behavior, drug use, and high-school dropouts for a single youth is $1.7 to $2.3 million."[270] With the world spending trillions of dollars a year preparing for war and additional trillions for jails, establishing parenting centers in every community on earth for just a small part of this cost would soon provide an enormous saving to mankind—an immediate saving, even before the actual savings from the huge destructiveness of wars is realized. McFarland calculates that every community on earth can be supported by a small "children's tax" of one-tenth of one percent increase in the sales tax.

Only by starting now on a vast worldwide program to end child neglect and abuse and raise all of our precious children with respect can we avoid the likely coming global holocaust. Only by reducing dissociation to a minimum through empathic parenting can we avoid inflicting the self-destructive power we now have available to us. This is the single most important finding of the new science of psychohistory. Free universal training centers for parents may be a radical new notion, but so once was the idea of free universal schools for children. Our task is clear and our resources sufficient to make our world safe for the first time in our long, violent history. All it takes now is the will to begin.

---

270. Evvie Becker, "Adversity and Its Outcomes: The Measurement of Childhood Trauma." In Kris Franey, et al., Eds., *The Cost of Child Maltreatment: Who Pays? We All Do.* New York: The Family Violence and Sexual Assault Institute, 2001, p. 98.

Index

abandonment, 127, 188, 270, 342–344. *See also* neglect
  effects of, 92, 302–303, 306
  fosterage as, 345–350
  and masochistic psychoclass, 411–416
  in modes of child rearing, 246–248
  by mother, 98–99, 124–125
  by placenta, 80
  by primates, 273
  rationalizations for, 349
abandonment depression, 95, 416, 419, 429
abandonment fears, 80, 124–125, 130, 133, 417–418
Abelard, P., 292
aborigines. *See* Australia
abortion, 253
abuse, 216, 395. *See also* sexual abuse; trauma
  causes of, 92–93, 151, 153, 272
  of child servants, 347, 347–348
  effects of, 91, 99, 142–146, 169–170, 381–382, 413
  effects of wealth on, 163, 246–247, 255, 315–316, 334–335
  ending, 240, 431–432
  extent of, 50–51, 96–97, 243–244, 312–313

  of foster children, 345–346
  in fundamentalist Muslim families, 40–42
  in German child rearing, 49–50, 184–201
  in initiation rituals, 275–277
  of leaders, 27, 49–50
  in modes of child rearing, 246–248
  by mothers, 150, 152–154
  in New Guinea, 271–273
  perpetrators of, 30–31, 322–323
  relation to alters, 100–101, 105–106, 384–385
  representations of, 385–387
  restaging in group-fantasies of witchcraft, 423–424
  of slaves, 427–428
  through history, 96–97, 244–245, 285–286, 330–340, 332
  types of, 145, 312, 314, 340–341
accidents, due to neglect, 268–269, 322, 349
achievement, 17, 241. *See also* individuation; progress
acting-out, 96, 104–105, 262
Acts of Thomas, 385
Adams, K. A., 354
addiction, 34, 93

effeminacy. *See* femininity
ego disintegration, 82, 95, 157, 173–176, 277–278
Egypt, 289, 317
  narcissistic psychoclass in, 404–406
  religion of, 389, 393
  sexual abuse in, 40, 310, 354–355
Eigen, M., 94
Eisenhower, D., 13
Eliade, M., 399
Elizabeth, Queen, 365–366
embargo, 37–38, 171–172
emotional abuse, damage done by, 145
emotions
  dissociation of, 80, 109
  effects of abuse on, 145–146
  effects of swaddling on, 330
  ignored as causes of actions, 87–89
  leaders as poison containers for, 80, 127–128
  and memory, 78, 90–91
  mother's, 68–71, 235
  and psychoclasses, 404, 419
  of self vs. social alters, 101–103, 105–106
empathy, 94, 109, 144, 426, 430
  fathers', 292–293
  influences on, 110, 145–146, 249
  lack of, 38, 270, 276–277, 314, 341, 363
  as measure of psychogenic evolution, 241–242
  social alters lacking, 102–103, 105–106, 108
emptiness, 402, 417
Ende, A., 185, 189, 193–195
enemas, 196–197, 204, 342, 360–361
enemy, 126
  as bad-child self, 155–156, 179
  castration of, 57, 170
  in cycles of war and group-fantasies, 105, 161–162
  functions of, 56–57, 170–171, 398–399
  images of, 51, 155–156
  leaders as, 133–136

and leadership phases, 130, 132
  search for, 29–30, 132, 168, 174
  as social alters, 103–104, 180
England, 208, 232, 303, 338, 346, 378
  child prostitution in, 367–368
  evolution of child rearing in, 245, 248–249, 324
  Hitler planning rape of, 210–211
  infanticide in, 306–307
entrainment, 76, 104–105, 117, 119–120, 391
environment, 230–235, 281–283
environmental determinism, 229–233
Epictetus, 300, 363
Erasmus, 429
Erickson, M., 117, 119
ethnography, on child rearing, 257, 261
Euripides, 406
Europe, 182. *See also* specific countries
  child abuse in, 50–51, 195, 312–314, 329, 339–340, 343–344, 367–368
  comparison of child rearing of, 184–185, 193, 245, 253, 350
  evolution of child rearing in, 245–251, 421–422
  group-fantasy cycles of, 175–176
  infant mortality in, 187–188, 301
  psychoclasses in, 417–418
  war cycles of, 15, 141–142
evolution. *See* child rearing, evolution of; cultures, evolution of; psychogenic evolution

fairy tales, trauma restaged as, 112
families, 97, 167, 249. *See also* fathers; mothers; sleeping arrangements
  in development of terrorists, 39–45
  in evolution of psyche, 243–244
  extended, 345–346, 366
  fathers' influence in, 150, 279, 286–293
  number of children in, 203, 249, 255
  parenting center support for, 431–432
  in psychogenic evolution, 236, 248–249
  spirits and demons representing, 385–386